YEARNINGS

YEARNINGS

EMBRACING THE
SACRED MESSINESS
OF LIFE

IRWIN KULA
WITH LINDA LOEWENTHAL

HYPERION

NEW YORK

Library of Congress Cataloging-in-Publication Data

Kula, Irwin.
Yearnings : embracing the sacred messiness of life /
by Irwin Kula with Linda Loewenthal.
p. cm.
Includes bibliographical references.
ISBN 1-4013-0192-4
1. Spiritual life—Judiasm. 2. Life—Religious aspects—Judaism.
3. Jewish way of life. 4. Desire—Religious aspects—Judaism.
I. Loewenthal, Linda. II. Title.
BM723.K83 2006
296.7'2—dc22
2006018823

Hyperion books are available for special promotions and premiums.
For details contact Michael Rentas, Assistant Director, Inventory
Operations, Hyperion, 77 West 66th Street, 12th floor, New York,
New York 10023, or call 212-456-0133.

DESIGN BY KAREN MINSTER

FIRST EDITION

10 9 8 7 6 5 4 3 2 1

TO
DANA,
GABRIELLA,
& TALIA,

*who teach me
the meaning of life
every day*

"Keep two pieces of paper in your pockets at all times.
One that says 'I am a speck of dust.'
And the other, 'The world was created for me.'"

—Rabbi Bunim of P'shiskha

"Where is the thread now?
Off again?
The old trick!
Only I discern
Infinite passion and the pain of
Finite hearts that yearn."

—Robert Browning

CONTENTS

PREFACE

YEARNING. AFTER TWENTY-THREE YEARS AS A RABBI, I can think of no more defining human experience. So many people speak to me about their longing to answer life's deepest questions. Especially in recent years, when world events seem to be more confusing and frightening, people are looking for a center that can hold in what they see as a growing wasteland of conflicts and contradictions. They yearn for peace that comes from unity. They seek enduring truths. They hope for comfort and guidance.

Great wisdom traditions are born of this desire for answers, this urge to make sense out of chaos and discover what really matters in life. What we forget in the rush of modern life—a lapse that I believe intensifies our fear—is that these yearnings are no different today than they were in the times that gave rise to such mystic visionaries as Moses, Buddha, and Jesus. In those times, too, people were challenging traditional ideas and beliefs, and asking new questions. Institutions they had always relied on were changing, and even tumbling down. Old ways of believing, behaving, and belonging that provided meaning and security were dying and new ways had not yet been born. Like us, people were at once fearful and excited, uncertain yet animated about emerging truths and understandings.

Whether it's Buddhism, Christianity, Islam, or Judaism, wisdom traditions are rich with methods and philosophies designed to support and guide us, to help us explore and deepen our understanding of ourselves and the world. These traditions are meant to be lived. Yet so much of their wisdom is buried under centuries of dogma. Often they become a means of claiming the superiority of certain religions, cultures, and ideologies. The need to be right is winning out over the search. Ideas and insights meant to illuminate the human experience, to explore conflicts and dualities, are being used to dampen, dispel, or repress exploration and conversation, sometimes erupting into culture wars or violence.

As the world around us becomes more confusing and frightening, many of us have turned inward to find some kind of solace. The quest for self is the contemporary quest for God. We want to know exactly who we are. We want to find perfect love; to feel enduring happiness and fulfillment; to know that our work will make a difference in the world. And this personal search for purpose, joy, and contentment can be just as noble as the search for grand philosophical truths and global solutions.

This is a psychological age, the era of self-improvement and personal growth, one that offers a unique opportunity to explore and reengage with wisdom traditions. All the contradictions and conflicts that we experience in the world are born deep within

Wisdom traditions are meant to be lived.

our consciousness. When we look into our selves and discover what is radiant and dull, ugly and beautiful, clear and confusing, harsh and gentle, it isn't just ourselves we're discovering; we're unfolding the mysteries of the universe. If we can become aware of these polarities; embrace them, even celebrate them, we are taking a giant step toward what the mystical tradition of Kabbalah calls repairing the world.

Americans are sometimes accused of being blindly optimistic and materialistic. We want it all. And this does have its drawbacks. We can become overly driven or consumed by our desires. But, paradoxically, if we don't want it all, we'll never find enough. We'll never come close to reaching our own potential. At the same time, if we forget that we're always wanting and always finding, meaning will continue to elude us, and so will the love and joy we seek.

Jewish wisdom teaches that our yearnings generate life. Desire animates. As the prophet Amos says, "Seek Me and live." Jewish wisdom urges us to go for it, to seek answers to our deepest questions, to search for spiritual and personal fulfillment while knowing we will never finally get there—oh, but the discoveries we'll make along the way! We are meant to live, to search with intention. When we can uncover our deepest longings for intimacy, pleasure, creativity, and self-understanding, life yields illumination and happiness. Far from being a burden, our desires themselves become a path to blessing.

Jewish wisdom offers powerful ideas and tools for living with the anxieties of contemporary life: its ambigui-ties, its contradictions, its insecurities. I hope it won't sound grandiose to say that I want to **Our yearnings generate life. Our desire animates us.** help create a new understanding of our contemporary experience by dig-ging deep into this ancient tradition.

Through both contemporary and biblical stories, I will explore meth-ods of the sages, showing how we can use this wisdom to examine our own lives. These will not be lessons about overcoming all odds, obeying some external command, or finding some ultimate truth. Rather, they will be teachings that celebrate the inevitable messiness of life, of living with grace in uncertainty. Far from keeping us in line, this wisdom tries to push us off line. Crossing boundaries is the only way to grow. No one knew this better than the biblical authors who wrote about generations of transgressors and adventurers whose yearnings and foibles pushed them beyond their familiar selves; whose journeys took them to the place be-tween meaning and meaninglessness, to the borders of promised lands.

Rather than teach absolute truths, Jewish teachings invite us to dance with dualities and contradictions: Life and Death; Hate and Love; Right and Wrong; Sorrow and Joy. There is no perfect balance nor final solutions; no end to the highs and lows, to the darkness and the light. And thank God, because there's so much richness, so much dimension, in those tensions and anxieties; so many opportunities to deepen our understanding. Building a life is an endless and glorious project.

The practices and insights in this book are based on teachings that have evolved over three thousand years. Generations of mystics and sages have wrestled with profound questions and challenges, the messiness and complexities of the human experience, and they invite us to do the same. There are no scripts to be found in their many texts, no fixed choreography to be followed in the dance of life. Rather, this wisdom is an intricate improvisation, complete with rhythms, melodies, cues, and many dancing partners to accompany us, teach us, and support us.

Jewish wisdom invites us to allow sadness into the circle of joy, to bless our carnal pleasures, to fully express our grief, to both give and receive with generosity. Our most intimate relationships or, in religious language, our covenantal relationships are often the most challenging improvisations: dances of pain and forgiveness, excitement and boredom, hunger and satisfaction.

Life is an endless and glorious project.

Our jobs and careers are the playgrounds for our yearnings for success and accomplishment; where we play out patterns of childhood and our need to make a difference in the world; where we struggle with failure and financial need; where we compete and create partnerships.

These life challenges can be informed by such religious ideas as covenant, holiness, sacrifice, commandment, idolatry, Messiah, and Sabbath. They may seem anachronistic or confining, but when turned inside out offer dynamic, adaptable, even radical methods for broadening our perspective in all areas of life. They become lenses through which to see and celebrate our unending complexity. They facilitate and enrich our infinite unfolding.

Please join me on an excursion into the depths of this ancient tradition and into seven of our most wondrous yearnings. My deepest wish is that these insights drawn from the wells of Jewish wisdom will inform and enrich your own search for meaning; that they will bring both support and delight into your daily lives.

YEARNINGS

YEARNING FOR
TRUTH

HUMBLE ABSOLUTES

"WHEN YOU'VE GOT AN ANSWER, IT'S TIME TO FIND better questions."

My mother said this countless times during my childhood, especially when I'd come home from school, passionate about an idea I'd learned from a teacher I admired. I'd be showing off to my brothers, arguing my point over dinner, and my mother would inevitably present her challenge. My resistance followed just as inevitably: She wasn't a scholar—she should learn from me. But then I would quickly sober under her fierce gaze and raised eyebrow.

"What have other teachers taught? What other questions need to be asked? Maybe there's more." And soon I'd be wandering into my father's study to find out. When I emerged, I invariably had a new insight to report to my mother, an answer that finally would floor her. But this merely led to a whole new round of heated discussions. My mother embodied a central Jewish teaching: Every answer to our important questions leads to a new important question. The truth *can* set us free, but only if we're always in the process of discovering it.

She taught this message in many other ways as well. When my five brothers and I fought, she never wanted to know what "really" happened, who was at fault, who hit first. If one of us would try to blame the other, she'd say, "And you? Are you one hundred percent blameless?" My mother had the uncanny ability to recognize that a single story should never be told as though it's the only one, that truth lived in every telling, and that there was no escape from responsibility for our own decisions. She taught me that precisely when I was sure I was right, this was a signal to look at the other person's feelings and point of view. If I didn't, there was no winning. And when I did, winning no longer seemed to be the point.

Throughout the centuries sages have tried to pry us loose from our certainties so that we can discover still deeper insights and expand our moral universe. They understood that since no two human situations are identical, every answer is by its nature a provisional one. There always will be another moral dilemma tomorrow and another the next day. There are never final answers to life's big questions; only more profound questions. There's something so liberating and expansive about this teaching. The search for truth is not about letting go; it's about going deeper. The goal is not reaching a single realization but living the process of realizing again and again.

> **The search for truth is not about letting go; it's about going deeper. The goal is not reaching a single realization, but living the process of realizing again and again.**

Jewish wisdom encourages us to be sacred skeptics. Many think skepticism is paralyzing, hopeless, cynical; but it's the opposite. Skepticism inspires us to know more. Skepticism can be revelatory. When we both hold and question our truths we become lifelong learners rather than absolute knowers—as well as more interesting and much easier people to be with. Not seduced by certainty, we can be open to the truth.

Yet in all my years as a spiritual counselor I've never met anyone who doesn't want answers, who doesn't hope that at some point in his or her life everything will fall into place. We long for a comfortable landing place, the contentment of completion: in short, the truth of who we are and what we've been. We may pride ourselves in being open-minded, accepting, and flexible but we all maintain beliefs we consider self-evident: ideas and unquestioned presumptions that surface when the going gets tough, when we feel challenged or most vulnerable.

The world at large and American society in particular are polarized by opposing, hard-held answers to controversial issues: abortion and capital punishment; who may or may not marry; even how the world was created, to name just a few. Unfortunately, the wisdom traditions designed to help us deepen our questions—from religion to science, philosophy to psychology—have become disciplines of knowing, for defending absolutes.

We've forgotten that as mere mortals we are meant to search as much as to find. After all, each of us has had only a few decades of what has been a fourteen-billion-year evolution. We are finite creatures. How could we possibly have access to what is infinite: some all-encompassing Truth about the world or even our True selves? The fact is that there is no issue, large or small, that we can understand fully. When we think we've found the final truth we're a little less alive, a little less awake, and the world itself is diminished.

There's a wonderful story that imagines an all-knowing, infinite God, one who would surely have access to the Truth but who actually sees more value in the search. In this story, the God character wakes up on the sixth day of Creation with what may be the most creative idea ever: humankind. Full of wonder and excitement, God can hardly wait to get to work. As so many of us do before we undertake a momentous task or face a risky venture, God first asks for the advice of consultants, in this case the angels. But the angels are ambivalent, undecided, caught between Truth and Love. Truth argues against the idea of humanity, fearing that human beings will lie and kill in their pursuit of Truth. But Love understands that humanity will engage in great acts of altruism and self-sacrifice, and that God's desire is born out of that most powerful of yearnings: the yearning to love.

In the end God decides to go with Love, and in that moment has a realization: Truth on earth cannot be what it is in heaven. In heaven there is Truth; on earth there are truths. Absolute truth cannot exist for any human being. And so Truth is cast out of heaven and down to the earth. There Truth is shattered into pieces, fragments of it everywhere, so many that they are impossible to count. And Adam, the very first human being, is created out of the dust of the earth, out of those very shards of Truth. From now on there will be only partial, multiple, and

In heaven there is Truth; on earth there are truths.

contradictory truths. And human beings will search forever for truths within themselves and throughout the entire world. Life will be an ongoing act of creating, revealing, and discovering. Each person, each culture, each religion has part of the truth; none has it all.

The sages who wrote this story understood, as my mother did, that we are meant to yearn for truth; to continually search. It's built into our DNA. At the same time, there are infinite ideas, feelings, and intuitions swirling around and within us, no matter how we may try to streamline our lives. We so often feel conflicted, stuck between opposing positions. This can be unnerving, even frightening. How can we contain the anxiety and confusion? The sages remind us that more expansive and profound truths lie within every conflict awaiting our discovery. When we meet a paradox, we have the hope of making progress in discovering truth.

The Talmud, the classic Jewish wisdom text, has been studied for more than fifteen hundred years. No wonder. It contains four hundred years of recorded debates about human life and is brimming with paradoxes and insights about how to enrich our lives. There are truths tumbling onto truths, echoing off each other, allowing the reader to interpret and decide. Among the most intense of the Talmud's arguments are those between two ancient philosophers and legalists named Hillel and Shammai.

Each had his own academy and different approach, much like contemporary think tanks such as the Brookings Institute and the Heritage Foundation; the Chicago School of Economics and the London School of Economics; the Freudians and the Jungians. Students would study and discuss issues that ranged from sweeping social policies to everyday life.

Periodically the academies would emerge with decisions, most of which were in direct opposition to each other: two very different truths. Then the fun would begin. Hillel and Shammai would have a grand debate. How do we create economic justice? What do couples do when love fails? How do we make time sacred? What does it mean to be vulnerable in this world? One might think clear decisions would be necessary and appropriate given the weightiness of these matters. But rather than provide answers or a simple list of rules to follow, the Talmud shows us the arguments of these great philosophical schools. It invites us into their sparring matches and reveals the contradictions for us to contemplate.

In the large majority of cases when a decision was reached, the verdict would go according to Hillel. But it wasn't because Hillel was objectively correct. The Talmud says about both teachings "These and these are the words of the living God." So why did the rulings go to Hillel's school? Because of Hillel's ethics of discovery, the spiritual practice of his search, the method of investigation. The school of Hillel always studied and wrestled with Shammai's opinions, often teaching them before its own. Hillel's school understood and valued the partial truth of the other side, and they used Shammai's insights to inform their own, to broaden their perspective, to come up with the most inclusive answer. In other words, every truth has the potential to lead to a wider reality. Every truth offers a deeper understanding of life. Hillel didn't win at the expense of Shammai; he won for the benefit of us all.

The teacher who first taught me about these great debates was a wonderful man named Rabbi Mordechai Glatzer. I was eleven and he seemed ancient to me at the time, a real grandfather type, but in fact he was only middle-aged. He was one of the most traditionally observant Jews in the Jewish day school I attended, and he is the gentlest person I've ever met. I, on the other hand, was a problematic student, to say the least. I would shout out answers, get up and walk out of class when I got bored, and talk to my friends. I got away with constant misbehavior only because I got good grades; otherwise, I have no doubt I would have been expelled, or at least regularly suspended. As punishment I spent half of my fifth grade year sitting in the back of the third grade class doing my lessons, and incredible amounts of time in the hallway or in the principal's office.

But Rabbi Glatzer had a very different approach than my other teachers had. He sat me in a chair at the front of the classroom, right next to his desk. Whenever I would fidget, shout out an answer, or turn around to motion to a friend, he would come over, still teaching, and gently stroke my face and say under his breath, "It's okay, it's okay." He had the softest hands I can remember. And I would immediately calm down. He was the first teacher who accepted me, who could see my intelligence and my lack of self-control and somehow hold them both together. And when he died suddenly from a heart attack toward the end of that year, it was my first devastating loss. I wondered if any heart could love that much for that long without breaking from the effort.

I was grateful to him on so many levels, especially for bringing those two ancient schools, Hillel and Shammai, into my life. The idea that disagreement and friction led to revelation appealed to both my intellect and my rambunctiousness. And the fact that Rabbi Glatzer was so wedded to the most conservative interpretations of the tradition in his own life made it all the more striking that he valued the openness and dissonance of these ancient scholars. Like Hillel, he embodied this thinking. Like my mother, he shaped my thinking forever.

Whenever I disagree with someone, I think of Hillel and Shammai. I try to reframe my perspective through the lens of the other person, allowing my opinion to blend with the different truths of someone else. When I explore divisive issues with my students I ask them to argue the side with which they disagree first; to write an essay from that point of view before writing one from their own. If a student has a strong feminist interpretation, I ask her to argue for the conservative and traditional interpretation, and I ask the student with a conservative position to argue from a feminist position. It's amazing how much better the final essays are from the students who actually do this exercise. When two ideas conflict, it isn't because one is necessarily true and the other false. It's that each represents a different perspective on reality. As physicist Niels Bohr taught: The opposite of a fact is a falsehood but the opposite of a profound truth is very often another profound truth.

Some students are just too afraid, and they resist. A student once said it plainly, "I don't want to be convinced that I'm wrong." He didn't want to compromise his own position because he thought it would weaken him. But there's nothing compromising about arguing for the side you disagree with. Anyone fighting fiercely about an issue can go deeper. Anyone can find a partial truth, no matter how small, in an opposing position. And a wider truth always emerges from the fray. The intrinsic worth of every human being means every idea has some sort of claim on the truth. At the very least, every person has the right to be heard.

But, as my student intuited, there's no doubt that hearing the other side can really change you. If you teach the point of view you disagree with, you will be altered. If you listen, really listen, to your spouse or your child, your boss or your perceived enemy, if you allow their point of view to sit alongside your own, it's incredible how you and the situation can be transformed. You may even see that the ideas you are willing to fight to the death for are the very ones you're most unsure about; the fierceness of your answer a mask for uncertainty. You realize that we never have any independent opinions that are wholly ours, points of view that we came to on our own. We've inherited them from our parents or rebelled against their views; we had a childhood trauma or a fear that has influenced us greatly. Never mind the television we watch or the books we read. Even the way we feel on the day we write the paper or have the argument influences the position we take. Context is everything.

The intrinsic worth of every human being means every idea has some sort of claim on the truth.

At the same time, we must be careful not to simply say that since everything is partially true, nothing really matters, as if there aren't standards of right or wrong. Yes, in every view there is a partial truth. But not every view is equally true. There are standards of right and wrong, gradations of truth. I've heard so many people use the phrase "This is my truth" or "That's your truth" as a way to defuse conflict and stifle discussion. This relativism is just lazy absolutism. It makes the claim that in effect we each have our own absolute truth, and so any-thing goes; why fight the fight? This spineless and limp relativism is as frustrating as hostile know-it-all absolutism. Both halt the search for truth.

It's not that we shouldn't have opinions and perceptions, passionate feelings and beliefs. We should argue with and criticize those views we believe to be wrong. No idea or insight should be either automatically accepted or totally dismissed. Even extreme opinions have an impor-tant role in society: They probe the middle, ensuring neither moral in-flexibility nor flabbiness. When we engage in serious dialogue, within ourselves and with each other, our worlds expand; our truths are re-fined, and we can incorporate the truths of others, finding new posi-tions and even shared ethical visions.

Martin Buber was a twentieth-century philosopher of religion who taught at a time when other philosophers were declaring that God is dead. Like Hillel, rather than declaring this false and defending his own faith, Buber integrated this new truth into his teaching. He affirmed the validity of even the most extreme doubt and in the process softened the nihilism of his peers. Buber understood that faith is so much richer, so much more meaningful and authentic, if we also can doubt. We need faith. Without it the future seems barren, and progress and innovation would be impossible. But we also need doubt if truth is to continue to unfold.

The expression "Don't lose faith" is a half-truth; sometimes you have to lose it in order to find it more deeply. Buber spoke of "moment gods." My teacher Rabbi Irving "Yitz" Greenberg spoke about "mo-ment faith" and "moment doubt." These days there seem to be the ab-solute faith people and absolute doubt people. What would the world look like if more of us were "moment faithers" and "moment doubters," if more of us wrestled with the truth? Maybe peace would visit us more often.

. . .

IF I HADN'T GROWN up with the mother I had and the texts I studied, I would never have married my wife of twenty-five years. Relationships are a constant dialectic between faith and doubt; times of great love and profound ambivalence. When we attach to an idea—an idol—of who our lover is or should be, we set ourselves up for a fall. But if we hold the truth of who *we* are and *they* are more lightly, with room to grow and change, it's amazing the arguments and crises we can weather.

Coming from a large, closely knit family, I always knew that I wanted one of my own. So you can imagine my dismay when the woman I was convinced I wanted to marry (from the moment I met her), announced to me in the middle of a romantic, dreamlike weekend on the shore, that she never wanted to have children. I gasped, repressing the urge to literally get up from our cozy beach blanket and run. Who was this woman I thought I loved more deeply than anyone? It hurt more than anything I can remember anyone had ever said to me.

Yet in the depths of my pain and anger, I could hear myself asking again in a more gentle voice, "Yes, who is this woman I love?" In a flash I recalled some of our early conversations when we were first getting to know each other. Dana had told me about her parents' fighting, how it had hurt her as a child. And I also thought of the many times Dana had spoken to me with love and admiration about how her mother, an early feminist, had taught her the value of having a career. She feared being taken off track, engulfed by the demands society places on women even in her generation.

> Relationships are a constant dialectic between faith and doubt.

I could feel myself soften. Yes, this was her truth right now. And it made sense given the context she had been in and in which she still found herself. After all, my context of being raised in a relatively harmonious, large family surely accounted for my yearning for children. Maybe we both would continue to feel the same way. Or maybe one or both of us would change our minds. Somehow I believed our relationship would create a different context in which another truth would emerge. I married her, and we now have two teenage daughters. If I hadn't listened to Dana, listened beyond her immediate words, I certainly would have left that beach. If I hadn't believed that even the most tightly embraced truths have the potential to change, I would have lost so much.

Over the years, in the new context Dana and I created together, we both began to see another, deeper truth about her upbringing. Despite their differences with each other, which Dana found painful, her parents unconditionally loved their children—they gave of themselves in a way I'd never seen before and which became a model for me. She also began to remember the good times—how her parents, both ballroom dancers, moved so beautifully together and how, no matter what, they'd stayed loyal to each other for more than fifty years.

Jewish wisdom teaches that the truth we have access to is temporary; even those truths that seem indisputable or essential. Of course, there are obvious factual truths like two plus two equals four, the sun is shining, or I'm five-foot-eleven. But fact is not synonymous with truth and confusing the two leads to an impoverishment of mind and spirit. There are other truths—our interpretations of facts or events, our stories of who we are and where we are going, our emotional and moral truths. True here means something different than true in a news account or a lab report: It is true to life at its deepest and most complex.

Precisely when you grasp these truths, say "aha," and then relax into them, they will change or shift. I call them "moment truths." It's not that they disappear and a new truth emerges out of nowhere. Rather, each realization leads to a deeper one and then a deeper one after that. It's not that Dana lost the truth she uttered that day on the beach. She really didn't want to have a family situation like the one she grew up in, and she didn't want to sacrifice her career. But both of us needed to listen closely to her pronouncement to see if there was a deeper truth underneath.

Later, a different truth emerged. It turned out Dana did decide to leave her fast-track job in favor of creating her own business so that she could spend more time with her family. She saw that climbing the corporate ladder was no longer what she wanted but that it was also possible to not give up her career. I still remember her exact words to me nine years after that initial conversation, because the phrasing struck me. "The truth is, Irwin, I want more time with the kids." Her current "truth" couldn't have been more different than the one she was so convinced of almost a decade earlier. And once her context changes further, her truth concerning work and family will likely shift again.

When we see our truths as ever-deepening, as beginnings rather than endings, we can hold even our most prized truths more loosely. Absolute truths become humble absolutes. Humility is among the most important spiritual qualities. The only word ever used by the writers of the Hebrew Bible to describe Moses, its unequivocal hero, is the word "humble." Moses confronts the all-powerful Pharaoh; leads the Israelites out of slavery to freedom; carries the Ten Commandments down from Mt. Sinai. He's the only character to experience God face to face. And he was humble about it all.

Truth without humility can easily turn into arrogance or dominance, and inevitably leads to dead ends, both literally and figuratively. The Hebrew word for "truth" is *emet*. If you remove the first letter you have the word *met*, which means "death." In other words, the mystics taught, if you only have one side of the story you've begun a death spiral. When you think about leaders in history and today who think

> Humility is among the most important spiritual qualities.

they have the only answer, that they have access to the Truth, it becomes clear how profoundly important humility is. Only by holding our truths humbly, lightly, knowing that they are not absolute, can we avoid arrogance and dead ends in our lives.

All new understandings take time to emerge and blossom. The word "Israel" means "wrestling with God." In other words, discovering again and again the truth, reality, God, whatever we choose to call it stretches and deepens our lives and enlivens and expands our moral universe. New truths may challenge us or make us uncomfortable for a while but they always bring us to the next level of understanding.

After all, there is no final arrival in life, but rather a series of arrivals.

Insights pop up unbidden, extending the horizon of our consciousness and setting us on new paths. This may sound heavy or difficult, and some may find it frustrating, even excruciating: Is there no end to the searching? But it's actually far less painful than clinging to a familiar truth despite changing circumstances and the inevitable fluidity of life. The yearning for Truth and Enlightenment is one of our defining human qualities. We can seek clarity with passion and commitment while knowing we'll never get there.

This book is a collection of humble absolutes. It is meant to help us wrestle with, deconstruct, and re-imagine the truths we hold self-evident. *Emet* is composed of the first, middle, and last letters of the Hebrew alphabet. The very construction of the word itself urges us always to seek a wider, more encompassing truth.

GOD WILL BE WHAT
GOD WILL BE

"OH MY GOD!" THIS IS A PHRASE SO MANY OF US USE, AND it's no accident. These three words capture a core human experience. I find myself saying them when I suddenly feel outside my usual self, when I am shaken out of my ordinary reality or when I feel a sense of harmony, of mystery, of gratitude. I might be watching my children play and be overcome by their beauty. I might have an epiphany about my place in the world that comes out of nowhere. Or I am overwhelmed with gratitude as I make love with my wife. And then there are those moments of horror and tragedy when I experience an overwhelming fearful awe. Watching those two towers collapsing, I found myself saying over and over, "Oh my God. Oh my God. Oh my God." The word God is really just code for an experience felt so intensely, so deeply, that there seems to be no other word to describe it.

Yet the word God so often trips us up. For many of us the notion of a personal God seems anachronistic, something that comforted our parents or grandparents but is irrelevant to us. We've rejected those patriarchal and punitive images we were taught in religious school, in church, or in temple. Others of us are holding on for dear life to a traditional image of an Almighty up in the sky who asserts His will and keeps the score. And still others have internalized the idea; God is within, not outside; God is us. Or perhaps there's no God at all. Everyone has a truth about God or no-God, and typically we're uncomfortable with any other.

"Rabbi, I am a scientist. I must tell you upfront I don't believe in God." These were the words of the Nobel Prize–winning physicist Murray

Gell-Mann when I was introduced to him at a dinner party. It certainly wasn't the first time I'd been greeted this way. And my response is always the same, "That's okay. I don't believe in the God you don't believe in either." What could have been—and is often intended to be—a conversation stopper turned into a lively debate. In order to reject something, one must have an image to reject; quite a paradox. For Gell-Mann, it was the God he was taught about as a child; the voyeuristic Peeping Tom in the heavens who judged his every move. He laughed when I told him that his rejection made him no different from a fundamentalist who's sure the all-judging God in the sky does exist. What makes them the same? They both have the same definition of God. Behind atheism is a powerful religious impulse. God is very much on Gell-Mann's mind.

To deny or affirm; both can be holy. To define God is to express a natural human need to make sense of our existence. To envision no God purges religious conceptions that may be limiting, **It's never God or no God; it's which God?** holding us back. It's never God or no God; it's which God? All descriptions of God are projections— sacred projections. The question is, what images do we use to express the yearning?

Gell-Mann, who'd spent his career working with the highly symbolic language of mathematics in an attempt to describe the very origins of the universe and who later that evening regaled us with explanations of string theory, had forgotten that just as string theory is not to be taken literally, neither are our sacred projections. Definitions of God should never be confused with God any more than the description of an orange can capture the taste of an orange.

Gell-Mann was doing what people have done for centuries. We all have an innate desire to imagine something greater than ourselves. That's why every era and culture sees God through the lens of the metaphors and images of the day. When humans lived in caves and relied on wild animals for their survival, they expressed their anxiety and awe through animal gods. During the agrarian age, people created fertility and nature gods. During the age of great city-states when kings ruled from palaces set on high, God became the king of kings in the heavens. But the modern age was inconsonant with that image. When John Glenn brought back his pictures of earth from space, the fixed God in the sky finally was made obsolete—at least for those of us who hadn't yet let go and were willing to. With advances in medical science, humans could create and manipulate life—we were the "masters of the universe." Modern science banished God. In response to this, some have held on to the traditional image of an external Almighty in part as a way to resist the chaos of modernity. And others took their yearning inside, creating a personal divinity, an inner authority.

All images, whether societal or personal, become stultifying if we don't allow them to change and grow as we do. The second of the Ten Commandments urges us not to make a graven image of God. Graven images are not only statues; our conceptions and ideas can become just as concrete. Ironically, religion has broken this commandment again and again by attempting to institutionalize the infinite, by taking what was meant to be a wide open expanse and reducing it to one landscape. Ancient Chinese scriptures say it this way: "When you have names and forms, know that they are provisional. When you have institutions, know where their functions should end. Know when to stop."

The point of the Second Commandment is that any one image is only a partial truth. And a partial truth made absolute puts God in a box of our choosing. Every image of God, even no God, is just a resting place, a moment truth. The Christian hymn "Amazing Grace" says "I once was lost but now I am found," and this is so moving, so true. But all of us know that no one is found forever. Life is a dialectic between being lost and found, found and lost. When we've lost God, it's time to look deeper. When we've found God, it's time to get lost.

As a society we haven't yet imagined the God that captures our collective, contemporary experience. We are trapped between old images and those not yet created. Sometimes I think we shouldn't use the word God for one hundred years. Maybe by then we'll have come up with new metaphors that more fully capture our experience of God and that unite us rather than divide us. Or maybe we'll return to some of the ancient ones.

In fact, many traditions have multiple names for divinity. The *Bhagavad Gita* teaches that God has a million faces. The Muslim tradition has a practice in which one recites and meditates on ninety-nine of the most beautiful names for God. In the Jewish tradition there are hundreds of names: Father, Mother, Lover, Creator, Destroyer, Nurturer, Redeemer, Forgiver, Friend, Life-giver, to name just a few. The name used most often in Jewish texts is also the most mysterious and intimate. It is YHWH, which in English is all consonants and no vowels. In Hebrew it's actually a word with no consonants and all vowels. Either way it's unpronounceable. When you try to say it, you hear the sound of breath, a simple exhale. What is the teaching? The name of God is not meant to be uttered. YHWH is not meant to be known. YHWH is meant to be breathed. In contemporary translations and liturgy, the word YHWH is translated as Lord; quite a stark contrast to the sound of a breath and a telling statement about this traditional projection of God. The name used by the mystics is *Ein Sof*, which means "There Is No End." At this level God is without name. God is a mystery. Or, as I like to say, God is everything in drag.

Maimonides put it this way: "There is nothing higher one can say about God than what God is not." Whatever word, image, or concept we choose, we always need to go beyond it. The name YHWH comes from the same root in Hebrew as the word for becoming. God is always becoming. We will never grasp reality in all its dimensions. And all this not-knowing creates tremendous anxiety, which is exactly why our projections can get the best of us.

Every image of God, even no God, is just a resting place, a moment truth.

The challenge is to remember, even in our moments of turbulence, that God is always just outside of our perception, just ahead of where we are. It is the more expansive truth. As the mystic sage Rabbi Nachman taught, YHWH is an emergent God, evolving and learning along with us. If we remain open to the everything that is God, Reality, Self, or whatever we choose to call it, there is no end to the wonder that awaits us.

Many of us have had moments when our minds and hearts open up to new visions of the world and of ourselves—we fall in love, give birth to a child, discover a groundbreaking idea, make a significant change in our lives. Or maybe we encounter a spiritual truth that was inaccessible to us before. This happened to me in an unusual context for a rabbi: in the pews of a church. For traditional Jews, entering churches is forbidden. I was forty-two years old when I went into one for the first time. I'd passed by the same beautiful old church on my way to work for many years; then early one morning some small voice within me urged me to go in. As I sat in the wooden pew I was engulfed by unfamiliar sights and smells: incense, candles burning, light streaming in through stained glass windows. And then I looked up at the crucifix, a cross with a corpus, the figure of Jesus bleeding from the heart. As I meditated on this central symbol of Christianity for the first time, I was horrified, struck by thoughts about centuries of Christian persecution of Jews. I wanted to run away. My palms were sweating, and I had to hold on to the side of the pew in order to make myself stay. I kept looking and looking, thinking there just had to be something more here than my own tradition's perspective.

It could have been fifteen minutes or forty-five minutes, but I suddenly found myself thinking, "What if my heart was that open? What if I could feel everyone's pain, so much so that my heart exploded?" I understood in a flash the meaning of sacred heart. And I heard the words from a prayer I'd said every day since I was a boy, in a whole new way: "*Karov YHWH L'nishberai Lev*," God is Close to the Brokenhearted. I didn't convert that day, but my God got an awful lot bigger. And so did I.

When tragedy or trauma interrupts ordinary life, when the fear of loss or its actuality grips us and takes us over, it's amazing how our conceptions of God come into play; and how dramatically they can change. What I've found is that God almost always gets bigger or smaller whether we're overtly spiritual or not. After the initial shock and grief recedes, our vision of reality either becomes wider and open to more and more possibility, or narrower and dominated by fear and bitterness; it rarely stays the same.

A congregant of mine named Ruth was in the midst of one of the
most excruciating crises one can imagine. She was the mother of Josh, a
sixteen-year-old boy who was dying of cancer. She'd spent every day

**God is close to
the brokenhearted.**

since the diagnosis praying for a cure, a treatment
that would work. A few days before Josh died I was
visiting him in the hospital. His father wasn't there
because he couldn't bear the pain of watching his son in this state. He
was shut down, consumed by depression and rage. But Ruth was sitting
right by the hospital bed leaning over every few minutes to moisten her
son's lips with a wet cloth.

Josh had been in this room for more than two months and he had
made the room his. There were posters of sports heroes, rock-and-roll
celebrities, and supermodels all over the walls. The contrast between
the life force of the room and the death of this child was so stark. Josh
was sleeping. After a while, Ruth turned to me and asked: "Where is
God now?" As the words left her mouth Josh stirred and whispered in
the softest yet clearest voice, "Mommy, I am going to die. I love you. No
one could have been a better mother to me." Then he went back to
sleep. Ruth and I were both speechless with tears.

At the memorial service about a month later, Ruth announced that
she was devoting herself to raising money to add a new wing to the hospital that had cared for Josh, one that would be devoted to children
with cancer, treating them and researching a cure. She was crying as she
stood before us in the midst of profound grief and loss. But there was
the same strength and determination I'd witnessed in her as she'd cared
for Josh over those many months of his illness. I found myself thinking
that Ruth had found where God is. She had found a new place within
her broken heart. She'd discovered there was no magical curer for her
son in the sky. That image had died with Josh. Now Ruth was to become
a curer, not unlike the one she had prayed so hard for. Although she
would have done anything not to have learned this truth in this way, her
tragedy was going to lead to so much more life.

Something similar happened to Moses in the famous story of the burning bush. For him it wasn't tragedy that awoke him to a new truth, but a deep voice within that seemed to come out of nowhere. Moses was in a great place; he had escaped from Egypt, and was a husband, a father, and a wealthy shepherd of a huge flock. Then one day standing alone on a mountain, his sheep grazing around him, he noticed a "bush aflame that was not consumed." Rather than looking away in fear or continuing on, as many of us would, he stood still and gazed at the bush. And he said, "Here I am." He was fully present. Only when we know where we stand can we know the next step we need to take. Then Moses heard the voice, and it said about the last thing he wanted to hear. It told him to leave everything behind and go back to Egypt to free his fellow Israelites from slavery.

Moses was overwhelmed and wondered, "When the Israelites ask who sent me, what shall I say?" The voice said, "Tell them that I shall be what I shall be. Tell them that's who sent you." Like a Zen koan, God's answer seems to say: "It makes no difference what you call me. I am everything."

Moses had what in the 1960s we called a consciousness-blowing experience. He heard a voice from deep within, and for a moment reality seemed palpable, discernable, and at the same time infinite and impossible. YHWH can also mean "I was. I am. I will be." YHWH is past, present, and future. God is every experience, every place, every person that brought Moses to that time. And now it's up to Moses to decide where he wants to be in his journey.

Unlike Moses, most people evoke a God who tells them exactly what they want to hear—whether God is our intuition, that soft, still voice within that we feel holds some magical truth, or the guy in the heavens who affirms our perception of the world. The biblical teachings tell us that God is sometimes affirming, but more often challenging, even life-changing. After all, the word prayer comes from the same Latin root as the word precarious. What if we understood that God challenges every truth? What if we understood, as Moses did, that God is often that counterintuitive voice, the one that questions, that urges us beyond or deeper than we already are? As my mother always said, "Irwin, God rarely agrees with you. That's how you know it's God."

There's a mystical tradition that at the end of every year the names of God weaken; they wear down from use. By using God's names during the year, we actually deplete the names' ability to connect us to the experience. Like all language, the words we use for God begin to hide as much as they reveal. And so we do a kind of mouth-to-mouth resuscitation for God. Over the High Holidays, Rosh Hashana and Yom Kippur, those names must be re-infused with meaning so that once again they can serve as a connection to all that is. God then can expand to incorporate the new insights revealed in the last year and the hopes for the new year.

The central Jewish meditation is the *Shema:* "Hear Israel, YHWH is our God, God is One." It is meant to be practiced three times a day both as a kind of mantra designed to pull us outside ourselves and as a means to root us where we are. We are meant to recommit to the idea of God as we understand it every single moment, because everything is in flux and everything is God.

I got into a lot of trouble when I appeared on the national television series *Frontline,* as part of a show called "Faith and Doubt at Ground Zero." I said that I experience God as "No Thing." Was this rabbi denouncing and denying the existence of the Divine? But what I asked was simply, "How can there be something outside All-there-is?" I asked if maybe it was time for a new God, a more complex, expansive perception that suits our postmodern age; a time when most of our absolutes, including the primacy of science, have been challenged, even shattered; when definitions of God and no-God lead so often to disconnection and conflict. Perhaps we've reached a time when we can live joyfully in the face of the unknowable. Perhaps we have entered the era of panentheism. Unlike pantheism, the idea that the universe and God are the same, panentheism—another koan—is the intuition that reality doesn't ex-

The more we embrace a diversity of names for God, the more our minds and hearts will open and expand.

haust God; rather all of reality is inside God. All that is, is All that is. "I will be what I will be."

Toward the end of that dinner with Murray Gell-Mann, as I listened to him describe his career, I found myself thinking that quantum reality, an idea he helped pioneer, in fact pointed toward this new God. Whereas classical physics envisioned a reality in which things were always definitely one way or another, quantum mechanics describes a reality in which things sometimes hover in a haze of being partly one way and partly another. As the physicist Brian Greene says, "It is a reality that remains ambiguous until perceived." In other words, YHWH.

By the time we finished dessert, Gell-Mann surprised me by conceding that perhaps he was in fact doing what the author of Genesis had done. Like so many philosophers before him, he was composing a creation story, in his case for the twenty-first century. One such thinker in that great line of seekers was the twelfth-century Jewish philosopher Maimonides, who re-imagined the spiritual wisdom of his day in light of Aristotelian science. He wrote that unpredictability and spontaneity, what he called miracle, were at the core of existence. The idea of string theory, a cutting-edge field within physics in part inspired by Gell-Mann's work, captures this teaching in mathematical language and expands on it.

String theory is a leap of faith. It's in the realm of the unexplainable. Just as the names for God are metaphor, so, too, is string theory. It posits that there are particles so small that it's impossible to see them. Like violin strings create notes through vibration, these particles unite quantum reality with concrete reality through unperceivable vibrations. This is the so-called unified theory Einstein could never conceive. As Einstein said when referring to ideas about space and time, "There exists a far-reaching uncertainty of interpretation." From the earliest sages to twenty-first-century physicists, there has always been and will always be a yearning to understand all that is; an overpowering desire to grasp reality; to find truth in No Thing. We can, as Greene says, "be filled with incomparable wonderment."

If God is infinite, if reality is unknowable, then who are we? One of the earliest self-definitions is that we are images of God. We are what we imagine God to be. In other words, we're those very metaphors. The more we embrace a diversity of names for God, the more our minds and hearts will open and expand. The very names broaden our self-understanding, our sense of depth and potential. Father, Mother, Lover, Creator, Forgiver, Compassionate One, Destroyer, Curer. We are all of them.

THE SILENT, THIN SELF

"WHAT MAKES YOU UNIQUE?" MY DAUGHTER GABRIELLA was asked this question on a high school entrance application. The essay was due in a couple of days, and it seemed simple enough. Yet she put it off and put it off. When I finally pushed her to complete the essay, she said she couldn't figure out what to write. "Dad, nothing about me is unique." Had Gabriella entered that notorious stage when girls lose their sense of self in the swirl of adolescence? My wife and I were mystified. Gabriella was a developing artist—designing her own clothes— and a talented writer. She was effervescent, loving, and always making new friends. Didn't she see how special she was? Her response blew me away. "Yeah, Dad, but lots of other people are those things. And besides, none of it is all of who I am. I'm everything put together, and not even that. There's always new stuff." Her essay turned out to be a critique of the question, an argument against assuming we are ever complete, entirely knowable. As Gabriella wrote, "What makes me unique is that I am always Gabriella-ing. No one else in the world does that." Each of us is always becoming.

We all share a yearning to know ourselves, to comprehend who we are in the world. We want to find our "true self " and have been taught that if we just look deeply enough we will find it. Of course, we all need a story about who we are, how we came to be, and where we are going. No one can live every moment of one's life as an open question. We need a recognizable identity to get us through the day. But we forget that what we call self is really only a moment truth. There is no single enduring identity. As my mom would caution her sometimes smug sons, "People are always more than you think they are." Shakespeare reminds us that, "We are such stuff as dreams are made on." We need a self-image, but ought not forget that it's just an image; a sense of self. Finding our permanent Self—no matter how much we search—just isn't going to happen. When we think we have this self, it's time to search again.

When we become attached to an identity of any kind—whether it's our profession, our appearance, our talents, or special qualities we take pride in—we've made a partial truth absolute. When you think about it, are any of us really the same people we were a decade ago? Are we even recognizable? It can be mind-blowing when we read an old journal, pull out a dress three sizes smaller or larger, or discover a teenage love letter. And think of all those

> There is no single enduring identity. What we call self is really only a moment truth.

plans we made that never panned out, not only because of unpredictable external events but because we ourselves are unpredictable. As Lewis Carroll's Alice says, "Dear! Dear! How strange everything is today. I wonder if I've changed in the night. Let me think: Was I the same when I got up this morning?"

Gabriella's insight was the same one Moses had while standing at the burning bush: "I will be what I will be." Like God, in that sense, we ourselves are infinite. The Self is a projection, just as God is. This is what we mean in saying we humans are created in the image of God. The images we have of ourselves are really attempts to streamline complexity, to make a neat story out of our many facets. Freud taught that we never will know fully the contents of our minds, of our selves. He called this idea "surplus life." There is a "too-muchness" to our consciousness. In other words, our own psyche eludes our grasp. No wonder the Hebrew word for life is plural: *Hayim* means lives.

When I hear that someone is leading a double life, I think "Just two?"

As cognitive scientists are now discovering, the notion of a single

enduring self is just a way to describe how we've temporarily domesti-
cated our inner world. Identity is just a provisional arrangement. Our
self is really a container for our multiplicity. It is a resting place, a
makom; yet another name for God. Nonetheless we yearn for that place
to be permanent; to feel an inner coherence and completion; to feel settled down and rooted. We want to overcome the conflicted and contradictory viewpoints that neuroscientists have discovered are always
being constructed in our brains without our even knowing it.

The yearning for self is essential to our development but it is of
course a quest that can never be fully satisfied. We can never fully grasp
the infinite—God's or our own. There's very little difference between
the secular belief that we can know who we are and the religious fundamentalists' belief that we can know who God is. Both lead to arrogance
and what Christopher Lasch called a culture of narcissism. Could it be
that all the striving, the pushing, the climbing, the acquiring, is rooted
in this yearning to know that which can never be known? Rather than
trying to define who we are, what if we sought an ever-deepening understanding of how *much* we are? Perhaps that's what deeper yearning
is really all about.

"I'VE ALWAYS HAD a mind of my own," a friend of mine said. This was
Rhea's usual refrain in response to some trouble she'd stirred up at
work. Rhea was direct to a fault; a rabble-rouser of sorts. She'd tell colleagues in no uncertain terms how misguided they were and exactly
how they should do it next time. She always wanted to run the show
and she relished rocking the boat. Needless to say, she alienated a lot of
people, especially those who reported to her. "I always fight the good
fight, even if it's just me screaming into the wind," was her favorite
response when someone complained about her style. "I don't care what
other people think," she'd insist. I became concerned that things had
gone too far when she told me there was a virtual walkout at a meeting
after one of her more extreme outbursts.

When Rhea visited me a few months later, I noticed a dramatic change in her. When I asked her how things were at work, I expected the usual litany of complaints and dramatic stories of her triumphs. Instead she told me how she'd taken a few days off and wasn't sure where her projects stood. When I asked her about an issue I knew she'd felt very strongly about, she said she'd let it go and let her deputy decide. "What happened to the lady with a mind of her own?" I teased. She replied, "You know, Irwin, I just don't have the fight in me these days." A wistful expression crossed her face. I wondered if this metamorphosis had something to do with the death of her mother, who'd died after a long illness.

"Yes, but actually, it was the report card," she said. She told me how she'd been cleaning out her mother's basement. One morning amidst crinkling collages and magic-marker decorated loose-leaf notebooks she came across her kindergarten report card. "Who the hell grades a five-year-old?" she said, and I was relieved to hear her spirit returning. Apparently, under every category on that yellowed card there was some kind of reference to her lack of initiative, her unexplained fearfulness. Her teachers even referred to her as a "follower" and a "wallflower." Her one strength was her gentleness with the younger kids in her class.

This middle-aged woman had excavated a different—and surprising, to her—facet of her identity.

The death of a parent often leaves us more exposed and vulnerable—and sometimes more open to change. And then even an old report card can shatter our self-perceptions. I had no doubt that Rhea would find her spark once again; perhaps she'd discover a gentler, more observant rabble-rouser, one who felt a little less alone. My hope was that she'd give this new self-perception a chance to develop and expand.

I told Rhea a story about one of the most fascinating Biblical personalities: the prophet Elijah. Though on a grander scale, his story wasn't so different from hers. And it has so much to teach us about our own unravellings, those times when we feel lost and alone, when we encounter a new self that might not be so welcome.

Elijah's dramatic struggle to discover a new self redefines the phrase "identity crisis." He had been on a supremely holy mission, and he, too, felt he was screaming into the wind. A passionate, uncompromising, and yet profoundly lonely man, Elijah was filled with zeal for his God. He was determined to convince the people of Israel to cease worshipping the pagan god Baal and return their devotion to their Israelite God. It's the job of prophets to wake people up from their slumbers and set them back on course. But Elijah took this to an extreme. He presented an awesome magic show for the people, even producing fire on a water-drenched altar. Emboldened and still enraged, he then slaughtered the pagan priests. But neither his impressive "miracle" nor his powerful show of force made any difference.

Rather, in response to his murderous acts, Elijah was chased from the city. And so with his life threatened, having failed completely in his mission, Elijah went out into the wilderness where mystical figures often go in search of a new truth. The Hebrew word for wilderness is *midbar*, which literally means "word place." *Midbar* is an in-between space; a wild, unpredictable place where we can encounter parts of us that we don't yet know or haven't allowed to emerge. *Midbar* is our inner landscape. And, like Rhea's mother's basement, it is where we can experience and begin to integrate new selves.

Elijah remained in the wilderness for forty days and forty nights— the period of time in which so many Biblical transformations take place. Noah was on the ark for forty days and forty nights and this was also the amount of time Moses spent on Mt. Sinai. Any significant change takes a while; all new truths need gestation time. Elijah hid in a desert cave at Mt. Horeb, the same mountain where Moses experienced the burning bush and

All new truths need gestation time.

another name for Mt. Sinai. This mountain cave, a sort of inner heights, is the place within ourselves where we can see a new vista, a place to envision our still future self, where we can hear the faint echo of the not-yet-me.

While asleep in the cave, Elijah heard the question, "Why are you here, Elijah?" Depressed and forlorn, his answer was simple: "I am the zealous one, the only one left." But Elijah misunderstood. He wasn't being asked "Who are you?" The question "Why are you here?" is a gentle, inviting question. Where are you, Elijah, in the process of your becoming?

The answer he discovered was no longer to be found in the great winds, the splitting mountains, shattering rocks, and blazing fire— metaphors for the forces that were familiar to him. Elijah the zealous, alienated prophet no longer exhausted who Elijah was. Emerging from the cave, what Elijah heard was a "silent, thin voice." This phrase is more often translated as "a soft, still voice." A whisper is quite audible; its very softness commands attention. But a "silent, thin voice"? What a paradox! How can a voice be silent? But as so many religious traditions teach, when our minds are quiet we can hear things we otherwise would have missed. We encounter ourselves in our silence.

Elijah entered that silence. His self-image softened and his perspective shifted. He chose a disciple and successor who would continue his teachings. Elijah the preacher had become Elijah the teacher.

And yet the fiery prophet didn't totally disappear, as becomes evident at his death. Unique among the Biblical characters, Elijah "does not die." Instead, a fiery chariot and horses appear and he ascends to heaven in a whirlwind. Elijah remained full of zeal; his passion had been essential to who he was in the world. The thunderous zealot and the gentle teacher were one and the same person. Elijah had integrated his different, contradictory selves. Isn't this the way all of us wish to die, with a final deep acceptance and understanding of all that we are?

The story of Moses and the burning bush is also a teaching about how new selves are born. The "bush that burned but would not be consumed" is a symbol of the self that is always transforming but is never extinguished. Maimonides saw the story as a dream in which Moses encountered long repressed aspects of who he'd always been. From the flames, Moses heard many voices: the voice of his father calling him back to Egypt; the

We can never fully grasp the infinite.

voices of the enslaved Israelites pleading for help. And then he heard a
voice that said, "I was, I am, and I will be." His different selves were coming together in a moment of realization, taking a new form. The Shepherd of sheep would become a Shepherd of his people.

Like most other Biblical characters who encounter God, Moses was
a middle-aged man, settled into a simple, satisfying life; a wife, kids, a
good job. And yet—as is familiar to most of us—he felt something was
missing, that perhaps he had a larger purpose in life. The thought both
frightened and compelled him. Opening ourselves up to the unknown,
allowing ourselves to become unmoored, and withstanding the turbulence that accompanies this realization are perhaps the greatest human
challenges. Hearing the silence can be tremendously frightening.

Perhaps this is why Moses was in the end compassionate when the
Israelites later retreated from their own encounter with God at the site
of that very same mountain. While Moses was on top of Mt. Sinai receiving the Ten Commandments, the people below experienced smoke,
fire, thunder, the blare of a horn, and they "fell back and stood at a distance." But Mendl of Rymanoff, an eighteenth-century mystic, explained that it wasn't the thunder that frightened the people. "What had
they heard at Sinai? The first letter of the first word of the Ten Commandments." The first sentence begins, "I am your God." The first letter
of the pronoun "I" is the Hebrew letter *alef*, which is silent. The people
heard the silent, still voice; a silence so vast that they simply had to back
away. "It was so quiet," another sage taught, "that one could hear the
flapping of a bird's wings miles away." What can you hear in the silence?
You can hear everything: the everything that is God; the everything that
is "I."

Another interpretation takes special note of the phrase "God spoke
in a voice . . ." The sages were puzzled. They asked, "In a voice? What
voice?" They speculated that it was the sound of six hundred thousand
voices, a voice appropriate for every single one of the people standing
there. "A maidservant heard it as a maidservant's voice. A suckling child
heard it as a suckling child's voice. A warrior heard it as a warrior's

voice." The voice of God was their own. In other words, they experienced the enormity of who they were at that moment. And it was nothing less than awesome. They glimpsed their own inexhaustible selves.

We all have our Sinai experiences. Those times—sometimes lasting a lot longer than forty days and forty nights—when there's a crisis or crossroads in our lives. This can result from the death of a loved one, a breach in a relationship, or a loss of a job. Sometimes, this ache just appears, a growing yearning for something more or something else. We become frightened and try to fill the silence and quell the troubling voices. We feel overwhelmed, destabilized and unmoored. These junctures are sacred. For it is precisely when we become strangers to ourselves, and then love the stranger as our self, that we have the greatest potential for self, or "selves," discovery.

I saw this process of self-discovery unfold dramatically in a friend who was undergoing what we commonly call a midlife crisis. Since her mid-twenties she'd been a caring wife, a devoted rabbi, driven, confident, someone with a seemingly clear sense of her role in the world. She'd been one of the first women ordained in her denomination. I often wondered how she kept up the pace, overseeing a thriving and growing congregation while traveling the country to give talks and workshops. Then again, busyness is an effective way to protect one's self, or selves, from hearing other disturbing voices.

On one of these trips, during a particularly dry spell in her marriage, she ran into an old flame. This was her Sinai experience. "As I sat across the table from him, I felt a sense of wonder and desire. I could feel myself opening up in a way I hadn't in more than a decade, as if awakening from a deep sleep." She told me how her body tingled and boundaries began to melt. She felt overwhelmed. As she spoke to me, her voice became softer and softer and there was an unmistakable longing in her eyes. "For that entire weekend, I was head over heels. It was as if I was someone else. The minute I got on the plane to return home, I would have given anything to take back those three days." She told me all this during yet another long plane ride to yet another conference several weeks later. Maybe it was my shocked expression, or the effect of her third glass of wine, but she began to cry. I barely recognized her as her makeup ran to reveal dark circles under her eyes. "I thought I knew myself," she kept saying. But clearly the self she'd thought she knew so well was crumbling.

My friend had kept her lustful self, her restless self, her needy self so tightly under wraps that they'd erupted. She's been a radical pioneer in her work, challenging gender roles, and a "good girl" at home and in her marriage. She had become the subdued, organized, self-controlled wife she believed her husband needed. Now this professional, successful, and dutiful wife was suffocating under the constraints she herself had created. Her feelings of resentment were so unexpected and so powerful that she felt she had no choice but to act on them. As we talked, my friend said something so revealing, "Where was my self-control? What possessed me to actually do it?" She looked shocked when I said, "Out came the 'bad girl.'"

Sitting across the table from her old lover, she'd entered the *midbar*. She had encountered an unfamiliar aspect of herself. My friend hadn't lost control of herself. She hadn't realized there is no essential self, no core self to lose control of. We are, in fact, the relationship between our ever-emerging selves. This is why identities are tension-filled, contradictory, and inconsistent. Sometimes we can only experience this complexity when our carefully constructed self is interrupted, even shattered. In that moment of boundarylessness my friend felt the same yearning the ancients felt for what they referred to as God. She was overwhelmed with the anxiety of not knowing that so often accompanies or follows the ecstasy of discovery, and in response she reached out for her old lover.

We are the relationship between our ever-emerging selves.

Just as we all have our Sinai experiences we all have our golden calf experiences as well. Only forty days after encountering God in the thunder and lightning and quaking of Mt. Sinai, the Israelites commit a horrifying act of idolatry. While they waited for Moses to return from the top of the mountain with the Ten Commandments and the wisdom that would guide them in the next steps of their journey, they, too, sought an object for their awe—release for the anxiety that inevitably followed their encounter with God, with All that is. And so the Israelites begged Aaron, Moses's brother, to create for them an image of God. Perhaps out of compassion, perhaps to allay his own fears, Aaron agreed and told them to give him their gold rings, from which he created a "molten calf" and an altar before it, proclaiming the next day to be a "festival of the Lord." The festival was marked by wild dancing, a kind of ecstatic devotion and gratitude, perhaps not unlike the rapture of lovemaking. So soon after committing to one God, the Israelites worshipped another. Monotheism in theology is monogamy in the bedroom. Idolatry is adultery by another name.

The story of the golden calf is one of the most powerful and instructive biblical teachings. This notorious tale is traditionally seen as an example of how people can never seem to live up to the God character's expectations; how weak and impulsive we are; how incapable of squelching or resisting our desires. But perhaps we understand these expectations too narrowly. Are we really supposed to be obedient children, denying the full range of our selves? Should we always repress the unpredictable, the unbounded, bewitching, and at times dark and anarchic parts of who we are?

The Ishbitzer Rebbe, an important mystical thinker in the nineteenth century, offers a surprising interpretation of the golden calf story. He saw the people's sin not as an impulse toward idolatry but as an expression of a holy desire, the passion to experience ecstasy and the overflow of life. The Ishbitzer understood that the Israelites' response was a natural outgrowth of their encounter with God. Having tasted the infinite, they craved an anchor for their devotion, so that they could connect even more deeply, reach even higher stages. Think of the lyrics to George Harrison's famous song, "My Sweet Lord," where he says he really wants to know God, really wants to be with God. Rather than simply being an affront to God, the golden calf was actually born out of an overpowering yearning for the Divine: to know and express every aspect of our selves.

Notice, too, that the second of the Ten Commandments Moses brings down from the mountain urges us not to "make for yourself a graven image." It tells us not to make "any likeness of what is in the heavens above, or on the earth below, or in the waters under the earth below or in the waters under the earth. You shall not bow down to them or serve them." In other words, this commandment warns against reducing "all that is" to one idea. If the Israelites had been able to dwell in the silence, they might have had no need for a golden calf.

Similarly, if my rabbi friend had heard the "silent, thin voice," she might not have felt a need to act on her feelings, no matter how urgently she experienced them. Rather she simply might have noticed them, even reveled in the mystery of her unfolding selves. She could have welcomed the new self, the moment truth that emerged from that silence. What if she could have experienced the chafing and discomfort as invitations to expand and explore this other submerged self?

My friend's emerging, erotic self was a signal for her to broaden her self understanding and her marriage, as well. She was surprised when I asked her, "Did you ever think that there might be a 'bad boy' lurking in your husband? Why don't you ask him to come out and play?" I hoped that she might find a place in her own home, in the bedroom, too, for the new self that knocked so loudly on the door. When we are driven to act out, to do what we perceive as wrong, we have an opportunity to open the door wider, invite in that unfamiliar self and hear what it has to say. Temptation is so often a wake-up call.

With this understanding, we can better appreciate Moses's realization, "I was, I am, and I will be" or Gabriella's more simple, "there's always more stuff." We might hear the same question Elijah heard in the wilderness: "Why are you here?" "Where am I?" the question at the crux of most of our crises in life. To be sure, it is difficult to shake off this desperate need to end self-doubt and know exactly who we are. Even months later my friend was still attached to her previous notions of her old, well-defined self. She was still at sea, unable to understand how she could have broken the mold she'd so carefully created. It was clear that she was beating herself up with the same drive with which she'd done everything else in her life. She spoke about her fear that her marriage would end. But I wondered how much of her pain was about this very loss of self. And I wondered how she would save her marriage if she wouldn't confront this loss. If only, like Elijah, she found her *midbar* and returned into her cave. If only she gave herself those forty days and forty nights so that she could reemerge a more integrated, more accepting and giving wife and rabbi.

Here is the central insight: The more we allow our selves to unfold, the less likely we are to unravel. When we hold our identities lightly, knowing that they are temporary constructions, humble absolutes, the crises and crossroads in our lives tend to be less shattering. We've all experienced our angry-self lashing out from nowhere; our helpless-self erupting in tears when we didn't even know we were upset; our betraying-self sabotaging a relationship; our sensual-self coming alive at a sunset; and our spiritual-self melting away our self-established boundaries. When we can embrace these "not me" moments, our more interesting "me" becomes truly alive.

It doesn't always take forty days and forty nights to shift our perspective—mini Sinai experiences await us even in the most mundane of circumstances. The silent, thin voice can be a few seconds of silence, a moment of hesitation before we act. Thich Nhat Hanh, a Buddhist sage, asks us to take an extra breath before answering the phone. I've learned to take a breath before I open the front door after a hard workday. I ask myself, "Irwin, are you home?" When we ask a question, it forces us to pause, to step outside the habitual conversation in our heads and invite in a new voice. Other selves are poised to emerge at our beckoning. Self-realization or, I should say, selves-realization, is always available to us.

• • •

MY FRIEND RHEA and I had a lot of conversations in the weeks after she told me her report card story. One morning she told me another story about being in a different kind of *midbar*, in this case the Manhattan subway. Like many pushy New Yorkers, she always stood in the same place on the platform, where the door would open to her favorite seat in the front car; she almost always got in before the others waiting beside her. When she was lucky, the seat was empty and she'd get it, and the day got off to a good start.

> The more we allow our selves to unfold, the less likely we are to unravel.

That morning a young man was standing in "her" spot on the platform. To make matters worse, he rushed in before her, making a beeline for "her" seat. She stood right in front of him, fuming for most of the forty-five minute ride; a young man acting that way; what happened to the gentleman offering an older woman a seat? "I tried to be easygoing and let it go. But I almost tripped him on his way out of the train."

Then something unusual happened. When he left and she took the seat, rather than feeling relieved, she felt uncomfortable. As she described it, she asked herself, "Who the hell do I think I am?" Rather than digging into the newspaper—her morning ritual—she looked around the car. "Was there someone else who deserved the seat more than she did?" When she saw a pregnant woman, she sprang up to offer her seat.

Rhea, the fierce, pushy lady always demanding her space, didn't disappear during that ride, just as Elijah's fiery nature didn't go anywhere. Those qualities served her in many aspects of her life. Pushy people are often agents of change in the world. But something in her wanted to explore what it would mean to not take up space for a few minutes, to make room for a different, gentler self, one that might enrich her morning rides and maybe the rest of the world as well.

YEARNING FOR
MEANING

SACRED MESSINESS

"WHAT DOES IT ALL MEAN?" LILY'S FATHER HAD ASKED her some variation of this question ever since she could remember. "It was his fault that I spent my early adulthood looking for the answer," she joked. Lily was a serious Buddhist practitioner who spent several weeks a year in silent retreat.

Usually the question came as she and her father stood in the kitchen cleaning up together after dinner, always an elaborate, meticulous task, as was everything her father did. She remembered that he had an expression on his face that was at once playful and dead serious. His yearning was palpable. And she wanted so much to come up with the answer; what did it all mean? A girl suddenly in the position of reassuring the parent; he looking for the innocent wisdom of a child for a simple, sweet truth; something to soothe his profound anxiety born of a difficult life.

Perhaps he wanted to witness Lily unfolding before his eyes, amidst the sound of running water and the soothing rhythm of dishes being sponged and then dried. Or perhaps the neatening up night after night, the endless messes being made right, awakened in him a longing to find meaning in the smallest of things, to have it fill him up. But Lily didn't feel any of those things. Instead she felt an emptiness sweep through her, a sadness at how much she didn't yet know and maybe never would. It seemed like a million answers swirled through her head, what she'd learned in school that week or read in a novel; some adage she saw in graffiti on a subway wall. But she also experienced it as a kind of invitation: to become the kind of person who wasn't afraid to look deeper, beneath the surface of things.

Usually she just said "love," but she knew she didn't really know what it meant. He'd ask her to elaborate, and they'd talk a while longer, eventually turning back toward the tasks remaining, the dishes still on the table, the grease lingering on the stove. But that was the beginning of a lifelong search for my friend. Paradoxically, her dad's yearning for the simple wisdom of a child led Lily down a winding path of continuous discovery. When she sat in silence, she said she sometimes felt a glimmer of what she'd longed for during those evenings, and she wanted to reach out to her father, now dead, touch his hand, and smile reassuringly into his searching eyes.

Don't we all want life to make sense? To find some underlying purpose to the continuous ups and downs, the fear and joy, the accomplishments and disappointments? Like Lily's dad, we want to know "what it all means," as if there were some ultimate wisdom that could ease our striving and uncertainty. The sages encourage us to study life for clues and act as if that understanding were possible. Jewish wisdom sanctions the yearning, even ennobles it, at the same time teaching that there is no meaning: only a kind of dance between meaning and ambiguity; understanding and misunderstanding; faith and doubt; essence and no-essence. And the more joyous the dance, the richer and more holy the life.

We may accept all this intellectually, even think it's obvious. But how many of us see our daily challenges—a disagreement with a loved one, a deadline, even a traffic jam—as holy? Never mind major disappointments or crises; those eruptions of chaos. We relish order, neatness, resolution. We forget that life has no straight lines or easy paths. The process of becoming is circuitous, to say the least. Yet so many of us expend endless energy

The process of becoming is circuitous. Life has no straight lines or easy paths.

wishing and trying to make it otherwise. We long for those happy times of satisfaction, even celebration, of feeling like all is well, balanced, and fulfilling. During these times we can look back on our lives, even the tough times, and see all that led us here as somehow necessary and right. Life does have a purpose after all.

And we can't help but be surprised when those happy times don't last. We believe families are supposed to get along. Jobs are not supposed to be lost. Faces are not supposed to get wrinkles. We judge people when they don't "have it together," especially ourselves. In short, most of us think life is supposed to work out the way we hope it will or even expect it to. We secretly want the kitchen to finally be clean. And yet if the kitchen was always clean, there would be no meals.

I experienced this in the simplest of ways and quite literally when my wife reached the point of despair about the state of our younger daughter's room. No matter how many times Dana had spoken to Talia, tried to convince her that this was no way to live, her room always looked the same, with some variation on how much stuff was gathered on the floor or on the unmade bed. That particular day, it seemed like all of Talia's things were everywhere but where they were supposed to be. I could feel frustration rising in me as I glanced at the hair brush on the windowsill, clothing inside out in the corner, her diary left lying open on her floor, earrings scattered on the dresser. Then I heard myself say, "It's just like Talia: always overflowing." And I realized I was smiling. "Her cup runneth over," I said to my wife, quoting the Twenty-third Psalm.

We stood there looking at the mess, our arms around each other, our anger transformed into wonder at the "muchness" that was our daughter. Suddenly, each thing had meaning—the dress she'd worn at her first dance that last weekend, the earrings I'd bought her for her thirteenth birthday. And she'd left her diary open; how trusting, I thought. When I allowed myself to relax into the teenage messiness, I could see that each thing had a special significance. Perhaps Talia didn't want these things put away neatly, but left out, exposed as if to say "Here I am." For the first time I understood why Talia always said, "It's not a mess to me."

I found myself marveling, as I often do, at what my children have to teach me. What would happen if I slowed down and relaxed into my own messes rather than always rushing to clean them up? What if I stopped trying to solve every problem the minute it came my way, to make what seems wrong right? And how much more rich and meaningful would life be if we all learned to gently sort through our tangled lives? Perhaps our messes are the treasure boxes of our souls. Or it might be more useful to envision a treasure basket not neatly ordered or closed on top, but open and overflowing, meant to be sifted through over and over again. If we lived as though this were true, imagine how much more compassionate we would be with everyone we encounter, including ourselves.

It's a rare and wonderful experience when the vicissitudes of daily life actually expand our awareness, bringing to life something we may have believed but not yet fully embodied. When we enter into the grit of life, the stuff we may resist or want to make go away, it's amazing the gold we discover. Maybe the point isn't, as the popular saying goes, "Keep it simple, stupid," but rather "Keep it complicated, stupid." Maybe we should "sweat the small stuff" as often as we can.

WHEN I ASK an audience to define the word "holy," inevitably I hear words like "pious," "serene," "complete," "untouchable," and "beyond or above the everyday." Someone who is holy has arrived and is meant to be worshipped or looked up to. The word holiday, clearly derived from holy, is used to describe a day set apart from all others. A holy place— like the Wall in Jerusalem, Plymouth Rock, or the location of Buddha's footprint—is a site where we go to seek an experience beyond the ordinary, one that is normally inaccessible to us.

But the sages taught that holiness is available to us in every moment, in every place. We often miss these moments because they can be subtle and get lost in the routine of life, or we may repress them because holy encounters sometimes can be unsettling, at times terrifying. Majestic and awesome one day, ordinary and sweet on another, only to be messy, complex, even chaotic on yet another. Holiness isn't a state to be reached; it's an ongoing act of creativity like the origins of the universe.

In Hebrew the opposite of holy is *chol*, which is translated not as "profane" but as "empty"; in other words, "not yet filled." The word for holy in Hebrew is *kedusha*. A more accurate translation of *kedusha* is "life intensity." To be holy is to be intensely dynamic, ever-changing, and ever-realizing. The Biblical command "You Shall Be Holy" is an invitation to celebrate what philosopher Mark Taylor calls "a maze of grace that is the world." Live as richly and passionately as possible; that's as close to meaning as you will get.

And the messes are the point. Joy and sorrow, good and evil, greatness and triviality, hope and anxiety, the ideal and the actual: The ability to live with these seeming contradictions and the ambivalence and tension they create is what gives rise to wisdom. Our most chaotic periods can be catalysts for understanding. Even our daily frustrations and desires, when we bring them to the surface and wrestle with them, can imbue our lives with meaning. And our moments of wonder and awe, of sheer delight can be so much greater when we've celebrated the multiplicity of life. When things work out as we hoped, when things feel orderly and right; these, too, are holy moments.

The first time I felt this in my bones was a few minutes after my younger daughter, Talia, was born. It was the evening of Rosh Hashana, the Jewish New Year celebrating the creation of the cosmos. It was a month before Dana's due date, and we had been having a festive meal with family and friends at our apartment. As everyone ate and enjoyed the meal Dana had prepared, she began to have mild contractions. She thought nothing of it until they became increasingly stronger. Her eyes grew wide with both fear and joy as they met mine across the table. In that moment the dining room pulsated with energy, excitement, and anxiety. She was going to give birth that night.

> The ability to live with seeming contradictions—and the ambivalence and tension these contradictions create—is what gives rise to wisdom. The messes are the point.

As we walked to the hospital a few blocks away, doing her Lamaze breathing, the streets of Manhattan were transformed; every street light shone more brightly; every car sweeping by seemed to move in slow motion. Five hours after dinner, Dana gave birth to our beautiful Talia. It felt like a dream as Dana held our new baby just minutes after she emerged. Tears flowed down our cheeks. We felt joy and gratitude mixed with exhaustion and the final release of Dana's pain; blood and body fluids were everywhere, and there was that perfect child.

Then I had a thought that knocked the wind out of me. Just about one year earlier Dana had suffered a miscarriage. If she hadn't, Talia would not be in this world. In that moment I was filled with both sadness and peace. I felt the terror of that memory and the gratitude of this moment at the same time. In a flash I understood the Jewish practice of saying blessings when something good *and* when something bad happens. I saw how both good and bad are intricately knitted into the fabric of life. It wasn't that the birth of Talia made the miscarriage okay or that "it happened for a reason." It was the messiness and angst of not knowing the relationship between those two events or the outcome of any event. It was the realization that chaos and coherence are indistinguishable and awe-full.

Beginnings are almost always messy, although we often wish it were otherwise. We'd rather not experience the loss of a pregnancy, the pain and anxiety of childbirth, the digressive first draft, the bumpy first day on the job, the emptiness that is the precursor to almost any creative moment. As natural and understandable as this is, the desire for order distances us from the very meaning we yearn for. The biblical authors invite us to see both the order and chaos of the most amazing creative act of all: the story of the creation of the world. They gave us two stories of creation, two versions of how the world was born. The first version acknowledges the yearning for order, stability, and simplicity. Things seem to swim along marvelously, unfolding as God hopes and expects them to. This is the Genesis creation story most of us are familiar with. Here God is filling the void in the most orderly of ways.

"When God began to create heaven and earth—the earth being unformed and void, with darkness over the surface of the deep and a wind from God sweeping over the water—God said, 'Let there be light' and there was light. . . . And there was evening and there was morning; a first day." There are six days that follow in the story, each day a new manifestation of life: from the earth and sea to the creation of humankind, "in the image of God . . . male and female God created them." Just like that. And to top it all off, the first week ends with one day of rest, of peace and relaxation for the Creator.

But there is another, very different creation story that is embedded in the Book of Job. This version reminds us in no uncertain terms of the intensity and chaos just under the surface. At the very least, the biblical writings teach, life is a dialectic between order and chaos, harmony and conflict. Life hangs in the balance.

Job is perhaps the messiest biblical story of all: a seemingly perfect life, a man blessed in every way with good fortune who is utterly ruined, it seems, for no reason at all. He suffers poverty, illness, and the death of loved ones. It all seems senseless and totally unfair, and Job understandably cries out. There are more than thirty chapters of conversation between Job and his friends, who try to justify what has happened to Job. They even accuse him of having done something worthy of this punishment. They were desperate to find a reason, to make meaning out of something which just might be meaningless. But this actually only served to keep them from the pain of the reality that, quite simply, shit happens. Satan, Mara, Shiva, Accidents, Cancer Cells, Depression— all are ways of talking about roadblocks in our path, what frustrates us and keeps us from living our dreams.

And then there's a voice from the whirlwind that reminds the bereft Job how God created all that is. Job's friends are rebuked for trying to make sense of life at Job's expense, causing him so much more pain. Don't we all do that? In our efforts to find a "reason" for the unreasonable, to justify the unjustifiable, we blame or insinuate or deflect. Unlike Genesis, which is told by an omniscient narrator, Job's story is told in the first person voice of the Creator, the voice of "I." This is how God sees it; or really how we all, at times, experience life. Creation isn't something that happened neatly in the past. Rather, it is ongoing and excruciatingly difficult.

The language here is as beautifully poetic as it is fierce: "Where were you when I laid the earth's foundations? . . . Who closed the sea behind doors when it gushed forth out of the womb . . . when I made breakers . . . and set up its bar and doors? . . . Have you ever commanded the day to break, assigned dawn to its place so that it seizes the corners of the earth and shakes the wicked out of it? Have you seen the gates of deep darkness?" Later God asks Job, "Can you draw out Leviathan by a fishhook?" Chaos is always threatening to break through: The doors are kept closed by force of will; all of Creation is incredibly, intricately fragile. The world is not safe, not stable, but always in flux. As a teacher of mine once put it, "Creation is the story of the confinement and channeling of chaos rather than its elimination."

In this second story, God, like us, has a deep desire for order. But there is also a keen awareness of and respect for chaos. The Genesis creation story represents our deepest hope, and Job reflects our most honest experience of reality. The infinite beauty of creation is inseparable from its destructiveness.

The biblical authors don't favor one version of creation over the other. They understand that creativity alternates between chaos and order. They are in fact inseparable: an ongoing process of ordering and chaos-ing. Yet so often we confuse our yearning for meaning and understanding with a desire for stability and simplicity—and as a result meaning eludes us. It can be so liberating and enlivening to embrace the very stuff we most fear, that which can disrupt, even destroy. Life isn't neat. Meaning can be found in the sacred messiness: when we can experience, even just for fleeting moments, the fragility of creation and the necessity of chaos.

The sages invite us again and again into the soup of creativity. They remind us that even when things seem to be going swimmingly, there's

no way it's going to last, not even for more than one chapter, not even for
God. Right after the beautiful, simple act of creation in Genesis, that
blissful, productive first week where hu-
mankind is created in the image of God, we
get the Garden of Eden story. Here God
forms humankind "from the dust of the
earth," already getting a little messy. Then
there's Eden—Shangri-La and Walden Pond

> When we confuse our yearning for meaning and understanding with a desire for stability and simplicity, meaning eludes us.

rolled into one—a seemingly perfect world. It's a paradise where everything is provided, and all seems well. Or not.

The biblical author doesn't seem to want it to be for long: A tree is
placed at the very center of the garden. It's the tree of knowledge of
Good and Bad, and it's strictly off limits; a daily reminder that even
in paradise we don't have it all. The garden is a metaphor for our
consciousness—we all yearn for what we think we cannot or should not
have. We all live with absence in the middle of our gardens. The mark of
humanity, what made Adam and Eve worthy of being the very first people, was their powerful yearnings for more. And yet desires and urges
have a way of "ruining everything," of interrupting paradise, of messing
up what we thought on the surface was perfect the way it was.

The first story of humankind marks a very dramatic shattering of a
very neatly ordered world. Most of us know the story, although we may
not have read it through the prism of our own lives. Just imagine you're
Eve hanging out with Adam in the Garden of Eden. You've enjoyed
every minute, tasting all the delicious fruits, frolicking in the waterfalls,
and sleeping under gentle breezes. There's not a question or concern in
your mind, only the sweetness and pleasures of the body. Then one day
you wake up ready for a new day and you realize you've wandered
everywhere you can go in the garden; you've seen and experienced its
wonders. And you feel a little restless, bored. There's a dull ache inside
you; there has to be something more.

Then you remember The Tree, and you feel a thrill run up your
spine. It's the only mystery remaining, the only fruit you haven't tasted.

And this one might be the best one of all—why else would it be forbidden? Why else would you want it so much? There's a voice growing louder inside you that tells you that if you eat you'll be wise and knowing, and the world will be new again. You wander over to the tree, and you see that there's no fence around it; the fruit in all its lusciousness is there for the taking. You're overpowered with desire; what had been a tickle now subsumes you. When you taste the fruit, you can't believe how alive you feel, how amazing it tastes, and you give some to Adam. You want him to join you, to accompany you to that new place, wherever it is, no matter what the consequences.

And we all know the consequences.

Adam and Eve must leave the garden. Their desires messed up paradise and gave birth to the world. Now freedom and yearning will define humanity for the rest of eternity. And the rest of the story unfolds in all its sacred messiness, all its holy dysfunction, all its dynamic intensity. Would we have it any other way?

Throughout the texts, the biblical authors create situation after situation in which human beings are thrust into the goop of life. The most unsettling and confusing emotions—envy, anger, and fear—drive the story forward. There's story after story of people like Eve messing up; wounded, unconscious people who nevertheless accomplish great things, at times precisely because of their mistakes and weaknesses. Not even the God character seems to be able to make sense of it all. Imagine that; God can't quite get it together. Like all of us, God is becoming—learning, deepening, and expanding.

The Bible, a text so many people over so many centuries have deemed sacred, has at the outset the story of generations of a family in all their pain and insanity. There is no Eureka moment where the grand order of the universe is finally revealed, where life becomes simple and neat. Quite the opposite. There's no novel or soap opera that even comes close to matching the drama and dysfunction of these families: betrayal, favoritism, exile, and murder. And when the Israelites finally arrive, the Promised Land, too, is a mess; the country becomes divided and the great King David, builder of Jerusalem and author of the Psalms, commits adultery and murder both.

For every moment of courage, for every time of great healing, there is a moment of weakness, of hurt or disappointment: The balance is always there. This is exactly what makes the Bible holy. It invites us to find ever-expanding meaning in both the messy and neat; the triumphs and disappointments; the weaving and the unraveling. It's up to us to see the holiness in all this drama; to bring it to life with our own reading and our own living.

The biblical authors did their best to wake us up. They understood that so much more can be learned from disarray, from upset, than from placidity and safety. There are so many unsettling events, chapter after chapter of surprises that buck the status quo at every turn. In Genesis, the theme of the younger sibling surpassing the elder is one we see again and again. At the time it was written—and even today—the eldest son was greatly favored, inheriting the property and wealth of the family and the status of the father. How provocative to have the patriarchs and matriarchs, the very founders of a great people, jockeying for position with God and within their families! How subversive to have the younger child, often as the result of deception, parental favoritism, or even murder, be the favored child.

The story of the first dysfunctional family begins with Cain and Abel. They are the children of Adam and Eve now far from the garden. The younger is Abel, the keeper of the sheep; Cain, the eldest, is the "tiller of the soil." He's trying hard to create a garden: a substitute paradise to please his parents; to fulfill their longings and ease their regrets. When Cain brings an offering from the fruit of the soil, Abel follows with an offering of the first of his flock. What a copycat. And the first of flock, no less. Cain must have thought, "Is he trying to pretend he's the first son; trying to take my place?" God "paid heed" to Abel's offering but not to Cain's; though how Cain knew this is a mystery. Hence the beginning of sibling rivalry.

At this moment of rejection by God, Cain's face fell. God's response seems to be sympathetic to Cain. God tells him if Cain does the right thing, there is uplift. In other words, when you can know your envy and your anger and still be your brother's keeper, it's a high. Then Cain is warned with the famous line, "But if you do not do right, sin crouches at the door." This is the first use of the word "sin" in the Bible. In Hebrew, sin means missing the mark, getting it wrong. What did Cain get wrong? He had imagined, as so many of us do, that reality was designed to meet his needs. And now he had a choice. How would he react to the inevitable unfairness and perceived inequities of life?

Cain may in fact have tried to follow God's advice. The next line says: "Cain said to his brother Abel . . ." We never know what Cain says. Instead Cain kills Abel, acting on, rather than examining, his rage. Cain avoids the messiness, the intensity and pain of investigating his own feelings; he chooses to see his anger as an end rather than a beginning. And in the process Cain kills his only brother. When asked where his brother is, Cain answers, "Am I my brother's keeper?" There really are only two questions we need to answer in our lives: the first two questions of the biblical story, "Where are you?" and "Am I my brother's keeper?" When we're fully conscious, the answer to the first is "Here I am." The answer to the second is always "Yes."

What if Cain could have expressed his envy to Abel? Cain might have asked him, "Did you do something different than I did?" Cain might have looked inside himself to see if his offering was all it could have been. And maybe Abel would have responded to his older brother, "What makes you think your offering wasn't accepted?" If this conversation had happened, maybe Cain would even have seen that he was the favored son. In Hebrew Cain means "acquire or gain," and Abel means "futility." Cain goes on to become the founder of cities. He makes it into the future. And Abel disappears. The paradox is we're the children of Cain.

Perhaps because I'm one of six brothers, I'm very familiar with sibling rivalry. Like Cain, I am the eldest, and often had feelings of envy at how my younger brothers, one after the other, seemed to be coddled more than me. Often along with the privileges, the oldest carries a heavier burden: more expectations, more independence, and the memory, if only faint, of what it felt like to be the only one. I was out of the house at the age of fourteen, working my way through boarding school. This is something I'm both proud of and admit I still sometimes resent. These feelings are still very much alive in me, and I marvel at how often my role as eldest plays out in both my personal and my work life.

Brad is a close colleague of mine, someone I've mentored. I've always wanted him to succeed, to grow, to take on more of the work of running the organization that I lead. In the spirit of this effort, I encouraged Brad to go to an annual conference that, typically, I would have attended. We were both thrilled: he to have the opportunity, I to have the much-needed break from traveling. Then one day he came into my office to tell me that His Holiness the Dalai Lama would be coming to the conference and that our organization had been granted the rare honor of spending some time alone with him. I felt the sting of envy. Brad would get the honor, not I. In biblical language, Brad's offering would be accepted, and I wouldn't even have the chance to give mine. Like Cain, I was the eldest here, higher in the hierarchy, and I could exert my power if I chose to.

> Messy emotions can give rise to generation after generation of wisdom.

Brad must have seen how my face fell at this news. He said, "Irwin, do you want to go?" Perhaps it was because of the generosity of Brad's offer. Perhaps it was because I recognized my envy for what it was: a momentary reaction to an opportunity lost. Or perhaps it was because I heard the same voice Cain did: If you do "right" there is "uplift." Whatever the reason, I insisted he go. In this case the uplift would be not just Brad's but mine as well; I would rise to a greater place within myself, coming closer to being the true mentor I always wanted to be.

As uncomfortable as it was, my envy ended up making our relationship more meaningful, more so than if I had effortlessly encouraged him to go. As he walked out of my office, he smiled knowingly and said, "Thanks, big brother." He knew he'd helped me get somewhere I needed to go. And I found myself thinking about the centuries-old concept called *kinaat sofrim*, translated as "a burning envy among the scribes." This idea originated from the great debates among the ancient sages. Their jealousy of each other—which could often become rather fierce—almost always led to deeper and deeper insights, to more and more wisdom. These men understood the higher purpose of envy— they coveted their fellow scholars' depth of understanding, and as a result they would reach further into the text, often coming up with something even more revelatory: sacred envy—an envy that leads to new possibilities, new truths; messy emotions that give rise to generation after generation of wisdom.

Throughout the centuries, sages have asked the same question Lily's father asked. What does it all mean? Perhaps the only difference is that they knew there is no innocent, simple answer. There's only the search itself: the meaning-making and unmaking; the mistakes and healing; the dirty dishes washed only to be used again; life intensity unfolding everywhere. Once we know this, there is nothing to fear. We are free to dive into the messes, to get nice and dirty, and to experience the transformative power of sorting it all through.

TURNING IT OVER

ALL SACRED TEXTS CONTAIN WITHIN THEM INNATE complexities and profound teachings designed to challenge and awaken us; that's what makes them holy. But this hasn't stopped many orthodoxies, whether religious conservative or liberal secular, from finding literal, safe, and comforting ways to read these holy books. These may be the tried and true teachings some of us learned in Sunday school, lessons about morality and goodness, punishment and reward. They may never have rung true, perhaps bored us to tears, but they were still somehow reassuring, mirroring our desire to have life be normal and familiar. Or maybe we were taught the dismissive read, a way of explaining away or reducing these teachings to archaic tales that have no real meaning in contemporary life. How tempting to make such provocative, sometimes disturbing, stories obsolete.

But the ancient sages understood that spiritual texts weren't meant to confirm our values or sense of the world. They were designed to shake us up and help us discover more of who we are. There's an expression, "Turn it over one hundred times, and on the one-hundred-and-first time you'll understand." It's used by Rabbinic sages to describe the experience of studying and interpreting, turning over every sacred story—reading, discussing, and reading again. When you think you understand a teaching, when you have an interpretation of a story or character that feels comfortable or right, it's time to start over at the beginning.

> **Turn it over one hundred times, and on the one-hundred-and-first time you'll understand.**

The sages and mystics celebrated the yearning to "figure it out," to discover the essence of any text, including the text called life. This is why study is one of the most important spiritual practices in many traditions, from the Jesuits to Bakti Yoga, Tibetan Buddhism to Judaism. As one of my teachers said, "When I pray, I speak to God. When I study, God speaks to me." The goal is not to prove some divinely ordained truth but to discover exquisite ambiguities and mysteries about ourselves and the world; to find as many humble absolutes as possible. Wisdom isn't about knowing; it's an understanding that meaning is inexhaustible.

As another teacher once told me, "Think of any interpretation of Torah as a road through the countryside. If you don't stray from it, you have no reason to suspect the existence of anything you can't see as you walk along it." When we push ourselves to look more deeply, we discover unexpected insights below the surface.

Our interpretations and our stories, like bad psychotherapy, can keep us on safe, well-worn, predictable paths—but if we turn them over to find new reads we can go into the forest where the richness is. The sages urge us to seek out and celebrate those places where tensions are evoked, where we feel uncomfortable, where very little seems right. The mystical biblical text called the Zohar says that each of us is a sacred scroll. The Bible, the Koran, and the Sutras are all us and we are them. Like their teachings, we are unfinished, unclear, unfolding. We are meant to engage rather than squelch our own mysteriousness. Jewish wisdom teaches us to turn over our own lives; to reach out beyond the familiar to experience awe.

Sometimes it's the most spiritual or intellectual among us, those of us who pride ourselves in being the most probing, clear, or open-minded, who actually are the most self-protective and bound in by our perceptions.

As enlivening and enriching as this is, it can also be tremendously frightening.

All of us interpret, for the most part, without even knowing. We all read reality through the lens of our fears, desires, assumptions, and judgments. Of course, we need our interpretations: They serve as filters to domesticate the uncanny and provide stability and order. But every time we settle on one perception, every time we stop turning over a story, we limit our understanding and miss a deeper insight. In other words, we stunt meaning.

I first became aware of the limitations of my own interpretations as a young rabbi. I was counseling a member of the congregation I was particularly fond of who had been diagnosed with lung cancer. He was asking the questions we all inevitably raise when we feel desperate or devastated: Why me? How will I get through this? I wanted so badly to be gentle and sensitive, to help Harvey put his illness in perspective, to better understand its widest possible meaning.

I explained that both spiritual and secular traditions in all their wonderful pluralism offer different theories about why we get sick, why tragedy strikes. There's a traditional "religious" explanation—which I downplayed because of its harshness—that illness is a kind of punishment for some sin. I talked about the scientific perception that illness is due only to biophysical factors; to genes and the environment. I described the mystical explanation that illness and suffering are inescapable parts of life that can only be transcended in a different world or level of awareness. Then I offered the one that worked the best for me: the existential explanation that illness is itself without meaning, but we give it our own meaning. We find the lesson, the truth that will most inform our spiritual growth.

I will never forget his response. "Do you see what you're doing?" he said, not without a kind of edgy anger. "I'm not an object that warrants a theory to be explained. None of this comes out of concern or sadness. You're so scared of getting cancer yourself that it's you who needs the theories—they help you, not me." Of course, he was right. All my interpreting was a way of protecting myself. Each of these explanations was profound and true—after all, they'd emerged and been transmitted through generations for a reason—but the only authentic response to Harvey's news was an expression of love and shared vulnerability: "Here I am. I care about you. It's scary." Harvey changed my life—and my feelings about illness. I would always love the interpretation game, but I would never play it the same way.

When we can look underneath our perceptions for the feeling, fear, or desire that inevitably led us there, a more profound teaching inevitably emerges. When we don't, we remain in a fantasy land of our own design, one that often has fortified boundaries keeping us from the rest of life. When we turn it over, even the most mundane encounters can become infused with meaning.

This was the case during what started as a casual conversation with a well-dressed, athletic-looking man on a bench at an ice cream shop in Cape Cod. After talking about the weather and the ice cream, he asked me what I did for a living. Usually I receive a polite nod or a smile, maybe an averted gaze. But when I told him I was a rabbi, he immediately launched into a diatribe about how he'd rejected Judaism, the religion he was raised with, how hypocritical it was, and how useless the whole concept of spirituality was for him. Part of me just wanted to walk away: Who needs that kind of anger and bitterness on vacation? Another part of me wanted to fire back a cutting response, but I controlled myself.

The fact that I was having such a visceral reaction meant something was going on within me: He clearly was hitting some of my own doubts. How often had I expressed outrage about religion today; how it's nothing but an attempt to transmit spiritual mystery to people who haven't experienced it by people who haven't experienced it, either? But, I thought, it was one thing for an expert to criticize and another thing hearing it from some arrogant guy on the beach. Whenever there's a strong emotion—anger, fear, anxiety—it's almost always a defense against an eruption of the too-muchness of life. That's when we tend to hold on to our interpretations or judgments, literally, for dear life. And, of course, the uncomfortable place is always the place to go; it's where self-realization happens. Both he and I needed to go there.

I wondered if maybe this man had something to teach me. I asked him what he did for a living. He told me he was the head of one of the leading fertility centers at a major hospital on the East Coast. I was impressed and wondered if he saw a deeper purpose to his work. He looked perplexed and annoyed by the question. But I persisted. "Just tell me what it feels like to do what you do." He surprised me by shaking his head and saying, "You'd never understand."

Now I was hearing spiritual language, a hint at the ineffable. "Try me," I said, to which he replied with a strange calmness, his eyes looking directly into mine, "A person comes into my office thinking they have death inside them, and when I'm lucky (a secular word for "blessed"), when they leave, they have life." I was floored. From death to life: He had articulated one of the orienting metaphors of every spiritual tradition.

I took a chance and asked him if he could possibly experience even a faint connection between what he was doing and an intuition about one of the deepest human yearnings, so deep that it is no less than "God's" first blessing: "Be fruitful and multiply." I was surprised to see his face soften and tears start to come to his eyes. He hadn't realized until then that his career could be seen as a spiritual practice. By turning it over, looking underneath, he heard himself for perhaps the first time express aloud the depth dimension of his work. He was engaged on a daily basis with something so immediate, so primal: the very thirst for life.

This doctor embodied what I've so often found to be true: The very people who most resist organized religion often are the most intensely alive and engaged in the complexity of life. Although they may not see themselves as holy, they are. Religion, which was originally designed to help deepen and ignite our experience, simply doesn't fulfill its promise as it is most often practiced. When we're willing to "turn it over" it's possible to see our passionate rejection as an overpowering yearning to be part of something

> When we're willing to "turn it over," it's possible to see our passionate rejection as an overpowering yearning to be part of something larger than ourselves, as a distinctly spiritual longing.

larger than ourselves, as a distinctly spiritual longing. There's no telling what the doctor will do with this insight, but for the time being he found himself in the very tradition he had rebuked.

Sometimes I encourage people to use the actual biblical stories as catalysts for investigation; rubbing their experiences up against those of the characters in order to discover new insights about themselves. These stories provide countless opportunities to see human foibles and life's twists and turns in light of the lives of some of the most memorable characters in literary history. And they help us feel less alone.

When I read and teach these stories I encounter more of who I am. It's not that I lose myself in the characters; rather it's that I find the characters in myself. The stories become mirrors. And this can be startling and disturbing at times, because I see in a flash how I have multiple selves, some not all that appealing. The murderous rage of Cain, the despair of Noah, the grandiosity of Abraham, the bitterness of Sarah, the unworthiness of Jacob, the insecurity of Moses, the lust of King David; they're all in me. I may not have known these selves, or have denied, dismissed, or ignored them, but there they are, and they await my investigation.

The practice of "turning it over" in traditional language is called *midrash. Midrash* is the name for the Jewish practice of interpretation, filling in the gaps in the text, even creating new stories in an effort to discover new truths. The word *midrash* actually means "investigation." There are many thousands of pages of *midrash* from over many centuries; an entire literature; hundreds of interpretations of the very same biblical tales. The ancient sages believed that religious texts called out, "Expand on me. Bring me to life." And the stories, dramatic as they are, are left intentionally vague so that we can find the widest possible context and ever-deepening understanding of each story. Then we can interpret *L'tov*, for "the good."

A few years ago, a wealthy and prominent couple in despair consulted me about what they saw as their only son's abandonment of the Jewish faith. This is a common concern and a very painful one, and for many parents it is a complete misunderstanding of their children. Their son was living what they called an "alternative lifestyle," traveling across the country with his band, sleeping with different women, not observing the practices he had grown up with. "He has no idea where he is going with his life," the father said. When I asked them what made them decide to come to me now, they told me that he had tattooed his body, a practice rejected by traditional Jews. I was curious, so I asked them what the tattoo was and where on his body it was. They said the tattoo was a Star of David etched on his ankle. I started to laugh and then, to my surprise, so did they.

I found myself thinking about the story of Abraham. At the very beginning, Abraham hears a call, "Go to yourself, leave your land, your father's house and go to a land that I will show you . . . and you will be a source of blessing." Most people don't know that, in Hebrew, Abraham is literally told to "go into himself," and it's a far more powerful command when read that way. But what's most striking here is the indeterminacy of the journey. The thirteenth-century sage Nachmonides, known as the Ramban, suggested that Abraham wandered from place to place until he finally discovered *his* place. As the Grateful Dead sing, it takes us all time until we can "pick a place to go, truckin . . ."

But who travels without knowing their destination? The easy answer is the fool, the blindly rebellious son. But isn't the fool just as often the innovator; the defiant child the creator? Aren't they the ones who dare to break through conventions to find a larger truth? The nineteenth-century mystic, the Sefat Emet, re-interpreted Abraham's story this way: "Go to the land that I will show you—where I shall make you visible, where your potential will be realized in unpredictable ways." Like many pioneers, Abraham departs from his parents' tradition: The sages imagine that before he left home, Abraham went to his father's store and smashed the idols—the statues of pagan gods which were sold there. Self-actualization demands destabilization.

When I reminded these parents of the readings of Abraham's story, I could see them squirm, undoubtedly with both recognition and discomfort. They were both traditional people and the children of immigrants; driven and successful, determined to live the American dream. They married early, and she stood by his side as he worked hard to climb the ranks in a prestigious accounting firm—one of the first Jews to break through, an idol-smasher in his own way. It wasn't easy to think that their accomplishments and their faith were somehow being left behind.

I wondered if maybe their son might not be breaking with their tradition after all. I asked them, "Does your son make love with his socks on?" If not, every woman he slept with would see the Star of David and know he was Jewish and cared enough about Judaism to mark his body with its sign. He was stepping away, yes. But perhaps he did so in order to find an expression of his tradition that suited him rather than the traditional one his parents lived—working just as hard, climbing different ladders, smashing different idols.

I also thought of an often overlooked detail in the first story of Abraham. His father, Terach, had actually begun the journey to Canaan with him, making it as far as the town of Haran where Terach settled and died. Perhaps Abraham's vision was linked in some inchoate way to his father's. Wherever our parents settle is the place we must set out from. Their dreams inspire us to dream anew. Continuity often comes in the guise of discontinuity, if one looks deeply enough.

I like to think these insights made an impression on this couple. When I ran into them a few years later, I jokingly asked the mother, "How's your assimilated son?" She looked at me quizzically. Then she told me proudly how he had started a music school with a bunch of his musician friends and it was flourishing. A week later I received a copy of a CD of her son's music with a note that said only, "I think he found himself." The fifth song was a mesmerizing original piece from the Sabbath morning liturgy. Sometimes it's only in retrospect that we understand "the call."

> **Look deeply enough and you'll see that continuity often comes in the guise of discontinuity.**

I always think of the biblical stories as a kind of Rorschach test; when a character's actions spark within us an emotional reaction of some kind, even just a stirring, it's time to look further. The stories that most upset or unsettle us are always the most important. They're the ones that have the potential to teach us about our self-perceptions, our relationships, and our world.

The Genesis story about Rebecca and her two sons, Jacob and Esau, is one such juicy text. I've never met a woman who didn't judge Rebecca harshly. But one student unearthed new insights into this story that informed her own situation: her husband's claim that she favored their younger daughter. My student knew she treated her kids differently: she pushed the elder daughter, who was independent and driven, to work even harder; and she spent much more time with the younger, who was painfully shy. She felt guilty and anxious about the different feelings and hopes she had for her children. Was she pushing one too hard and keeping the other back? Why did she feel more physically affectionate toward her younger and more intellectually engaged by her elder? Did she love them both the same, as she always told them? As she put it, "Please tell me I'm no Rebecca!"

In the story, Rebecca urges her younger son, Jacob, to trick his brother out of his birthright—a blessing from their father, Isaac, that would have made Esau the heir to the covenant with God. The eldest son always inherited the family estate, and this was no different—but what an estate it was! How on earth could a mother do this?

When my student read the passage describing Rebecca's pregnancy premonition that "two nations are born in your womb . . . And the older shall serve the younger" she had an unexpected insight. Rebecca knew her children better than anyone. And so did my student. "Pretending your kids are equal isn't the point. What's really true is that they're different and unique," she said.

Of course, there are times that we do favor one child, when we seem to give one more than the other. And, as painful as this can be, sometimes not doing so can be even more harmful; sometimes favoring is

actually appropriate, even necessary. Although we can hold back our favoring and try to make everything equal, we need to ask ourselves, is
this really better for our kids? Perhaps the most important role of a parent is to recognize as best we can who our children are and to love them
equally in their uniqueness.

IN MANY CASES, other people in our lives are the text we rub up
against, and they often help us discover our selves. I don't think it's an
accident that so often when something bothers us or when we feel
deeply hurt we tend to turn to other people, whether they're friends,
lovers, rabbis, or therapists. One could say that we do so in part because
we know we need to turn over our problem, to find a new perspective,
and this process is always easier and more powerful when another person is there to console us and, in some cases, confront our hard-held
truths. By talking to someone else, we are automatically broadening our
context.

I've found that the words I use to describe a given situation often
become a kind of text for the other person to read. No one writes the
script ahead of time, of course. But how we choose to phrase something
is every bit as telling as the words the ancient scribes chose to describe
the experiences of the biblical characters. I always tell people to be sure
to call the friend who won't indulge you, who won't simply confirm
what you already think and feel. The ancient scholars never studied
alone; they read the holy texts out loud and voiced their opinions to
each other. Even today, students are urged not to study alone, but to
study with a *chavruta*, a study friend. That way there's always someone
around the table to question, to urge them to turn it over again.

This may have been at some level why a bunch of buddies and I created a men's group. A woman colleague coined it jokingly "The he-
man's woman-hating club." And we do talk about the women in our
lives an awful lot. We also talk about our dreams and about the frustrations and challenges in our careers. One of the things I love about it is

that we're fearless about calling each other on things, never letting any-one feel like a victim for long. And there's lots of joking and gibing. Inevitably, I walk away feeling like I've lightened up, like I'm holding some truth, some judgment, some struggle a little more loosely.

One year the dynamic of the group changed dramatically when one of the members' children was diagnosed with a fatal genetic disease. It's unlikely that he'll be alive on his twentieth birthday. In the meantime, Ben continued to seem like any other kid, exuberant and affectionate; but Michael always knew the timer was ticking. When he said things like, "Why Ben?"; when he questioned the meaning of his life; when he raged and blamed God, there was no comforting him. We all felt pretty useless. Nothing we usually had done to help each other seemed to apply.

One evening we gathered on the boardwalk near a beach. Michael updated us on the specialists he'd seen and the research he was helping to fund. Then abruptly he pounded the sand. "I know it's pointless, pointless! Why the hell doesn't God do something?" God was clearly a metaphor for his own guilt and feelings of helplessness. No matter how much he did he felt it wasn't enough.

I told him that I didn't think it was an accident that he talked about God more than he ever had before. Michael was like we imagine God to be—aware of the joy and the pain; of how life would unfold, and how it would end. It made me realize that omniscience was not all it was cracked up to be. Unlike the rest of us, Michael knew when one of his children would die and that he'd be alive to experience the agony and loss.

As I said this, I could feel the energy shift. He shook his head yes and then no. He told us how just the other day he'd watched Ben play-ing in the yard with a child his age. We braced ourselves for the sorrow he would express. Instead he told us that he'd enjoyed every second of watching his son yell and walk and stumble and laugh. He'd realized in that moment that life felt utterly full. I'll never forget his words, "I know it's partly his mortality that makes me love him so acutely, makes me savor every one of his smiles and every one of his tears. This is the next step, I guess. I'll smile sometimes, too, even though I cry inside always."

We were all quiet for a few minutes. One of my friends broke the silence and said he imagined a crying and smiling God reaching out to embrace Michael. He turned away from us toward the waves. The five of us walked over and hugged him at the same time; now we were crying, too.

DUALITY DIVING

PICTURE A ROOM LINED WITH SHELVES UPON SHELVES of books, and a long table in the middle of the room with several books laid open, overlapping each other. A group of men is crowded around them, some old and bearded, some barely out of boyhood. They are quietly reading aloud to each other, stopping every once in a while to discuss what they've read. Then all of a sudden they are shouting, pointing their fingers at each other and the words before them. Then they settle down again.

The traditional study halls where these debates take place are called "houses of seeking." It's there that students wrestle with the meaning of sacred texts. At the Yeshiva I attended hundreds of people sat across from each other for ten or twelve hours a day, our voices ebbing and then erupting again well into the evening. We'd discuss and analyze, parsing down each teaching sometimes to individual letters to reveal insights. There was so much emotion and vitality in the room; it was far more than an intellectual exercise. At the end of the day we would be mentally and physically drained, and spiritually energized.

> **Disagreement is a gift. It alerts us to something wonderful waiting to be uncovered, telling us it's time to dive deeper.**

Anyone listening to one of these conversations might be struck by how rarely one point of view prevails over the others. Winning isn't the point, and neither are resolutions or conclusions. What every student hopes is that out of the argument, the seemingly clashing interpretations, will come a broader perspective than any one student could create on his own. Disagreement is a gift. It alerts us to something wonderful waiting to be uncovered, telling us it's time to dive deeper.

Wouldn't life be richer if we saw all of our conflicts from this standpoint? Rather than dividing us, arguments would be about finding connection. Rather than one side coming out on top, the goal would be to find the relationship between points of view. When we look closely enough, all insights are actually dependent on and inseparable from each other. Sages from all traditions teach that there actually is no such thing as a single, stand-alone idea. There's an intricate web of insights that we are always weaving. When we clash with someone else, when we become stuck in our own perceptions, it's because we've overlooked the threads. We see boundaries and obstacles instead.

Even if we believe intellectually that everything is interconnected and interdependent, most of us still see hierarchies and pendulums everywhere. We're always swinging between seemingly exclusive and obvious opposites. I'll name just a few. As you read them see whether you naturally regard each one as equivalent or related, or tend to judge one and have a preference for the other. Order-Chaos; Clarity-Confusion; Spiritual-Carnal; Master-Slave; Sanity-Madness; Meaning-Absurdity; Anxiety-Serenity; Moral-Immoral. It's amazing how often we carve up our experiences into dualities—practically every moment if we're really honest with ourselves.

At the same time, we want so badly to believe and experience the world as one. We yearn for unity and harmony; a place where polarities magically dissolve. But we'll never get there; no such place exists. The mystical understanding of Oneness is not that there are no dualities, it's that they all flow from the same source. Opposites need not be opposing nor need they disappear—but they can coexist.

One of the clearest statements of this is from Isaiah, who says, "I form the light and create darkness. I make peace and create evil. I, the Lord, do all things." In less overtly religious language, the Taoist philosopher Lao Tzu wrote, "Is there a difference between yes and no? Must I fear what others fear? What nonsense! Having and not having rise together. Difficult and easy complement each other. Long and short contrast each other. High and low rest on each other. Front and back follow each other."

For the sages, argument and debate were sacred conversations and holy practices precisely because they unearthed dualities. The sages knew that when we divide up our world, we inevitably feel separate and alienated from others and even from ourselves. But they also knew that most of us are not mystics, and that it's an innate human quality to judge and polarize. They actually encourage us to uncover our judgments; to both confront and embrace them. They teach us to hold opposing ideas together, to live inside the paradoxes. The definition of a paradox is a seeming contradiction that holds the possibility of a new truth.

I've found that when I am in the midst of an argument with a loved one, when I'm mired in some inner conflict, when I encounter an idea or emotion that makes me uncomfortable or judgmental, the wisdom of the rabbinic sages can loosen my hold and allow me to see a new possibility, a wider perspective. I remember the first time my daughter said, "I hate you!" My first impulse was to yell back, "Don't you ever say that to me again. We don't use that word in this house!" But as it was coming out of my mouth I held back and was struck with the realization that of course this little four-year-old girl didn't hate me. Her hate was one of the many emotions bound up in her love for me. Rather than demonizing her reaction, I heard "I love you so much that I really hate you sometimes." My hope was that Gabriella would gradually become more in touch with her hate and consciously integrate it into her love. Then maybe she'd be a little mellower—at least until her teenage years!

Every relationship is a paradox, especially our more passionate ones. We dance between dualities of love and hate on a regular basis. I've often wondered how many fewer divorces there would be if we could absorb this truth. I know so many people who dismiss or distance themselves from their hateful, angry feelings out of guilt or fear— and they're always the ones who love less passionately. They also tend to hate more viciously, because their hate is no longer complemented by love. Or they project their rage and wind up feeling hated themselves.

When we recognize dualities for the paradoxes they really are, our understanding of the world and ourselves knows no bounds. There is an art to this. I call it "duality diving." When I surface my thoughts and feelings—especially to someone else who can challenge me—I can begin to examine them. When I make my internal dialogue external, giving voice to the dualities of right and wrong, strong and weak, whatever it is that particular day, I begin to see a wider perspective.

Inevitably, for everyone there comes a time (or times) when the way we divvy up our life no longer makes sense. The grandest, most operative polarities through which we see ourselves, our relationships, our work, and the world back us into a corner and cause us pain. And then it's time to dive, to widen, to make room for new truths to emerge.

A friend of mine named Ellen came to me one day in great distress about what she saw as her lack of motivation: She was resisting looking for a new job after being out of work for three months. She'd been a high-powered woman—an executive and innovator in the magazine world who'd launched several thriving businesses during her fifteen-year career. When she was forced out of her job in a nasty corporate coup, her husband, friends, and colleagues all wondered why she was letting this one bad experience keep her from re-entering the ring.

> Every relationship is a paradox, especially our more passionate ones.

She was also mystified, describing herself as depressed and lost. She described how those first few weeks she'd wake up in the morning with a familiar burst of adrenaline, as she always had, ready to take on the day; the routine running through her head—shower, grab coffee and paper for the train, make it to the office in time to answer e-mails before that first meeting. Then she'd fall back on the pillow completely disoriented and deflated. There was no place to go. She used to earn almost twice what her husband made. Now she sat in her pajamas watching him march off to work every day. She felt like a failure, like she was wasting her time, letting her family down. Her anxiety was palpable. Then why, I wondered, had she turned down a major position at a new magazine just being launched?

"I don't know. I just couldn't. I've lost my spunk, my drive," she said. She told me she'd always been a risk-taker, full of purpose and ambition. Now she felt passive and lazy, confused and stuck. She certainly was stuck, caught in dualities and judgments of her own making: active-passive, productive-lazy, purposeful-purposeless, ambitious-resigned, clear-confused.

I asked her what she did with her days. She told me about a bus ride she'd taken one afternoon; how strange it felt to sit among old ladies and school kids as the bus slowly wound through her town. She described the sunlight streaming through the windows, the sound of the grumbling motor, the sights she saw as she traveled through neighborhoods she'd never even noticed before. She also spoke with a kind of wonder about hanging out with her neighbor who had just came back from the hospital with twins; walking her son to school; stopping to get a cup of coffee at a nearby café.

"But I feel like I'm just escaping, not accomplishing anything," she said. I suggested that she was actually working pretty hard, struggling with her old definition of success, trying to find a context for these languid, restful days. After being forced out of her job she was now being forced in. Far from being lazy, she was locating the dancing partner of accomplishment that she'd relegated to a corner. It was the perfect time to escape! She might have felt she was failing or withdrawing but she actually was dancing, waltzing, weaving. True, she wasn't producing in the way she was used to; rather, she was harvesting other selves. Accomplishment and escape aren't polar opposites. They go together. When you diminish one, you end up diminishing the other. Of course, she felt confused, uncomfortable; she was learning a totally new dance.

I suggested that in this materialist, capitalist, accomplishment-oriented world, perhaps she was taking the biggest risk of her life, far bigger than those she'd taken on the job. She was allowing herself to feel the range of human experience. She had the "driven" part down; now it was time to park for a while and enjoy the scenery—the scenery of her wider self. The goal wasn't necessarily to find the perfect balance between doing and being, escape and accomplishment; to become a completely integrated person. That would be impossible anyway—and it'd be pretty boring. Rather, the goal was to find a dynamic

Accomplishment and escape aren't polar opposites. They go together. When you diminish one, you end up diminishing the other.

equilibrium. It would always be a dance—sometimes a waltz, sometimes a tango, and sometimes standing by the wall, waiting for the next song.

I asked her to entertain the possibility that withdrawing was actually a courageous act, that from pausing, from escaping, can come great creativity. Sometimes it's necessary to escape when you are imprisoned. And maybe her old ethos of success had become just that: a prison. Perhaps within her duality was a whole new possibility; what she saw as an irreconcilable conflict was really a paradox, and inside was a new truth. I told her an ancient story of heroism and escape, one that determined the entire course of the Jewish tradition.

In 70 c.e. the Temple in Jerusalem, the holy center, was under siege by the Romans. The most important rabbi of the time, Rabbi Yohanan Ben Zakkai, was in Jerusalem when it was surrounded. For many months he and his compatriots had fought the Roman siege. This, they thought, was the only true demonstration of faith. Even when things looked really bad, they resisted with everything they had. Surrender would mean failure and blasphemy, the end of Judaism. They had no choice.

But at some point Rabbi Yohanan began to feel otherwise. Did faith demand fighting to the end, even when it was clear they could lose everything? Maybe there was another way to be courageous. Instead of fighting to the bitter end, he decided to try to escape. His fellow Jews—even his own uncle, one of the leaders of the Zealots—condemned him, accusing him of being a coward, committing treason, and abandoning his people.

How Rabbi Yohanan must have felt! What anguish to leave behind his friends and family, to let the Temple go. But he sensed that escape, too, was a way of fighting for what he believed in. His compatriots favored one side of the duality; but resistance is always a dance between retreat and attack, active and passive. Defending oneself and what one values sometimes demands leaving. It can be the ultimate accomplishment and an incredible demonstration of bravery. So the rabbi had his students put him in a coffin and carry him outside the walls of Jerusalem. What an incredible image! That coffin meant the death not just of one form of Judaism, but of a way of looking at the world.

The rabbi redefined courage, finding a new way to fight for one's religious and cultural survival, for one's identity. Duality diving always demands that we allow for the death of one way of organizing reality and the birth of another. This can be so wrenching. And far from being cowardly, it's incredibly risky. In this case escape was quite literally not without its risks. Before letting coffins out of Jerusalem, the Zealots would put swords through them to make sure that no one was abandoning ship. Just before he was to meet his end, Rabbi Yohanan emerged from the coffin and asked the Roman general permission to settle with his students in a small town nearby. Remarkably, his request was granted. The Temple was destroyed and Jerusalem fell to the Romans. But the rabbi started a new school that became the foundation of the next era of Judaism, rabbinic Judaism. He taught that study and prayer, words and intention, would replace the old forms of temple worship. God would no longer be in one place but exist among the people themselves whenever they engaged in acts of loving-kindness.

Of course, there was no guarantee that the rabbi's decision would bear such fruits. Even on his deathbed many years later, he questioned his actions. As he lay thrashing around, clearly in distress, his students asked him if he was afraid of dying. He told them he feared something far greater: that his decision to leave Jerusalem decades before may have been a terrible mistake, one that would forever alter the destiny of his people, maybe not for the better. When we dive into our dualities and break them open, there's always tremendous uncertainty.

The stakes were surely lower for Ellen than they were for the rabbi, but she, too, had no idea what the result would be. Would she be able to help support her family? Would she find meaningful work? Ellen needed to allow her definition of accomplishment to die. It simply wasn't sufficient to meet the challenges of that point in time. Success for Ellen demanded that she view escape, failure, and not getting ahead as a full partner with her previous self-image.

When I saw Ellen a month or so later, she had taken on some consulting work and she was making new connections in her field. She had also begun to write for herself and play with her children every evening. "When I allowed myself that escape, when I saw that it might actually be proactive, that I might be doing something after all, I started having some fun. Now I know I don't have to rush back into the same high-powered situation. Even if I did, I wouldn't do it in the same way." Out of a seemingly irreconcilable duality came new insights. Escape led to the birth of a new understanding of accomplishment.

In our culture, some of the most painful dualities seem to surround issues of success and failure. Whether it's a child's performance in school, a relationship challenge, or a career issue, we tend to see things through the lens of this duality. Success means accomplishment, progress; life is meant to be an upward arc, a seamless line to the top. We're meant to fulfill our utmost potential. When we don't, we've failed in some way. And we better get back up on our feet and do it better next time. Of course, there's great value in ambition; without it society would not continue to evolve. But when we can dive into our dualities around success and failure, ambition and contentment, accomplishment and complacency, we might broaden and enrich our understanding of what it means to achieve.

This was certainly the case for me. A few years ago after reaching the "top" of my organization, I hit bottom. I was burnt out and disillusioned after years of teaching and aggressive fundraising, and I made the abrupt decision to take a sabbatical with the knowledge that I might not return. This was a difficult move for me, although I was incredibly grateful that my organization was willing to give me these months.

During this time, I struggled with my self-image. I had always been the driven one in my family. The eldest of six in a family of modest means, I had begun earning a living when I was a teenager, and it had been nonstop since then. Now, at the age of forty-three, I found myself sitting in my underwear in an armchair in my living room for weeks at a time, doing nothing except for taking an occasional walk. I had no motivation, no desire to accomplish or produce anything, and I felt guilty. I judged myself: "I've lost my ambition. I'm not the successful person I thought I was."

One day on one of my many walks along the Hudson River, I noticed that the water was completely placid, not a ripple anywhere, a very unusual sight for this giant river. I found myself saying out loud, "Just because it's still, does it mean nothing's going on down there?" I pictured currents beneath the surface, fish swimming everywhere. And I began to wonder if that was also true for me, that in fact my dormancy was somehow dynamic, active. Passivity on the surface was connected to constant movement underneath. I was unmoored, flowing with the tide, and I wasn't sure where it would take me. This was rather unnerving, because I sensed it just might change my life. For once being ambitious wasn't about getting to the next tier, the next manifestation of success. It was about going with the flow—my internal flow—and seeing where I'd end up.

The first place that current took me was back to my childhood. I began to think about where all this mania for external success and accomplishment had come from. I wanted to understand why I felt such disdain for slowing down. I needed to examine my own dualities. I began to see that I had always judged my father for his lack of drive, for never realizing his potential. He was so brilliant, so charismatic, such a talented musician and singer. But rather than reaching for the stars, conducting an orchestra or joining the opera, he had remained a cantor serving just a couple of congregations for over forty years. I realized that, perhaps as a result of this judgment, I'd always been motivated by a desire for public success and financial reward. I was wary of ever being complacent, determined to never settle. I always had to do more, get to that next meeting, give that next lecture, get that next donation.

During this time, I was invited to speak at a temple in a town near where I'd grown up. I almost said no. I was supposed to be on sabbatical. More than that, I didn't want to go to Long Island, the place that bound my father and that I'd been so determined to leave. But out of a sense of obligation and probably guilt as well, I went. After the services were over, an elderly lady came up to me. She asked me if I was related to Cantor Kula. When I said yes, she pulled out a manila envelope from her handbag and offered it to me as a gift.

I pulled out an old black-and-white photograph of a young man in his mid-twenties standing next to what looked like a thirteen-year-old baby-faced Bar Mitzvah boy holding a Torah. The young man had pure joy on his face. Suddenly I saw that this was my father. And except for the gray hair he looked exactly the same as he did now. He had the same sparkle in his eye, the same open, gentle smile. The woman told me how more than forty-five years ago my father had taught her son his Bar Mitzvah portion with such care and sincerity. She told me how grateful she'd been. When she saw the announcement for my lecture in the newspaper, she thought maybe I was related and that she just had to come to give me this photo. This woman, now a great-grandmother in her eighties, had kept this photograph for all those years and made a special trip to give it to me.

As I gazed at the photo, I found myself contemplating the contribution my father had made to the lives of this lovely woman and her son. But what struck me the most looking into my dad's glowing young face was that he'd been happy, that he was still happy, and that this alone was enough. I realized just then that I envied and longed for that same feeling of joy, that same sense of success and accomplishment.

What I had always seen as my father's lack of ambition was actually a kind of calm, inner satisfaction with where he was and what he had—a vital and deep connection to his community and a respect for and excellence in his art. I remembered the rabbinic saying: "He who is a hero is the one who can show restraint. He who is wealthy is happy with his lot." Suddenly my father's seeming lack of ambition was so alive and colorful—and incredibly desirable. He was a restrained hero. He was wealthier and more successful than I'd ever imagined.

That night I called my father. I told him about meeting the mother of his former student and how I'd felt as I looked at that wonderful photo. I explained how I'd misjudged him all those years, how wrong I was to think he hadn't lived up to his potential. He had prepared more than two thousand children for Bar Mitzvah and sung at more than a thousand weddings. Not only that, he'd raised six sons, all of whom were friends, and all of whom were accomplished in different ways. He didn't need a concert hall stage. His success had been in the privacy of his office, on the pulpit of the synagogue, and in the intimacy of our home. This realization was both liberating and frightening. My definition of achievement was dramatically altered by one simple encounter, as was my vision of my father. Years later, I'm continuing to search for my own definition of success, but the journey is richer and more joyful than it has ever been.

There are times when duality diving can be an organic internal process, as it was for me with my father. But there are other times when the opposite is true. Our dualities often aren't so easy to locate. We may circle around and around the very same thoughts. We may get depressed. We may spend a lot of time feeling angry at the world for not conforming to our expectations and maybe even get angry at ourselves for feeling this way. When I find myself stuck in a rut, going nowhere, I've found that when I can actually give voice to my judgments and preconceptions, as those scholars did sitting around that table, the paradoxes begin to jump out at me.

Several years ago I realized the power of voicing dualities as I sat in an audience listening to Ram Dass, a wonderful spiritual teacher, who was recovering from a debilitating stroke. He told us that all his spiritual training, all his meditation and study, had not prepared him for the suffering he experienced after the stroke. He was deeply disturbed by feelings of vulnerability and humiliation, by his loss of independence. He needed people's help to move, to eat, to dress, to go to the bathroom. He said he'd gone from the person who years earlier had written a book called *How Can I Help?* to being a "helpee."

He told us of one day as he lay in his bed, disturbing thoughts and feelings swirled in and around him. Suddenly he felt a surge of violent rage, and this frightened him. He berated himself, thinking: "I am Ram Dass. I should have a sense of acceptance and peace." A few minutes later he asked himself, again full of rage, "How could you let this happen? Why can't you be okay with this?" Referring to the title of his groundbreaking book, he remembered saying out loud, "I am supposed to 'be here now!' It's all supposed to be grace. Instead I feel so fierce."

I was struck by the vulnerability he was willing to show us, and all of us in the audience were completely silent. Then he re-enacted what had happened next. He looked from one hand to another and murmured over and over again, "Fierce. Grace. Fierce. Grace." Then he yelled out, "Fierce Grace!" He told us that he'd recognized that he hadn't just had a stroke; he'd been "stroked." And this had given birth to a new kind of grace, and also a new kind of fierceness. He realized grace was not only accepting, refined, peaceful, and loving—the grace of good things. There was also a destructive and ferocious grace. Now, he said, he had "a full view of what grace is all about."

What had seemed irreconcilable to all of us a few minutes before suddenly became integrated. It seemed that as soon as Ram Dass had named the feeling and what he perceived as its opposite, he was moving to a new place. When he held the duality fierce-grace together, a new truth emerged. He had discovered a paradox, and it felt like a revelation to us all. He also told us that this realization deepened his understanding of needing help. "There's independence and dependence. They make a beautiful tapestry." He saw that helpers and helpees dance a wonderful dance; one serves the other. "After all, without helpees, what would helpers have to do?" I remember thinking that Ram Dass's vulnerability now made him incredibly powerful, a potent example for all of us.

When we can name our emotions, as Ram Dass did, they can actually become texts for us to read. This can be a challenge, because emotions often erupt; other times they slowly creep up on us. Either way, they can take over, and it's tough to stand back from them. But when we can, even the most painful eruptions and uncomfortable stirrings become wonderful tools. The more potent the conflict, the more powerful the insight. For this reason, when I work with people, I'm less concerned with why they feel what they feel; what's important to me is helping them name their emotions in order to find new truths.

> **When we name our emotions they can become texts for us to read.**

One morning a middle-aged woman named Cindy came to me for counsel about her marriage. She told me she hoped I'd help her get to the bottom of her feelings of dissatisfaction and depression and help her "make a decision already." She wondered if there was some wisdom in the Jewish tradition that might help her decide whether she could save her marriage, which had felt more and more empty over the years. Self-help books hadn't worked and neither had marriage counseling. After we'd talked for a while, it became clear that Cindy felt her marriage was over. When I asked why she was still with her husband, she told me she felt like a failure every time she thought about divorce. Failure is a strong word. And I wondered if she might be holding a duality that was keeping her from seeing her situation more clearly. Marriage-success; divorce-failure; this is a duality our culture still fosters, and Cindy had embraced it.

I told Cindy that Jewish wisdom teaches something surprising about divorce, a teaching that Islam also shares. Divorce is a holy activity, just like marriage. This is surprising because Judaism views marriage as among the most holy and important life passages. There is a sacred document called a *ketubah* that every bride and groom sign when they marry, as do the rabbi and two witnesses. It is meant to be binding. Yet there is also a sacred document called a *get*, which is handwritten by a scribe and signed by husband and wife as well as a rabbi and two witnesses; it authorizes a divorce. The *ketubah* invites us to imagine the commitment of marriage is enduring, that we will fulfill our responsibilities to each other. The *get* dissolves those very responsibilities and reminds us that nothing is permanent, which is why the words "till death do us part" are never part of any Jewish wedding ceremony.

Jewish wisdom acknowledges the paradox that the most vital of relationships can end and this, too, can be a holy, intensely alive experience. And yet a divorce is not seen as a total breach—the couple will always be connected in some way, whether consciously or not. I invited Cindy to consider that if the marriage was painful despite all her best efforts, staying married might also be seen as a "failure." And then I asked her, "If both divorce and marriage are sacred, what about your marriage is worth saving?"

Tears came to her eyes, and then she said, "Nothing." She told me how over the last year her husband had been coming home later and later and leaving at the crack of dawn virtually every day. She admired his devotion to his burgeoning law practice, but she felt she didn't know him anymore. And worse, she doubted his love for her and her own love, as well. She also wondered if he was having an affair but had never asked him if this was true.

"Isn't marriage about trust?" she asked me. "If I love him, how can I doubt him this way? It's obvious that our marriage doesn't mean anything anymore." I couldn't counter her, of course; the fabric of her relationship with her husband was something I could never know. Instead, I shared an insight from biblical wisdom, one that's helped me enormously in my own marriage: Faith simply can't exist without doubt. Yes, a marriage is about trust but it is also sometimes about not trusting; about feeling both secure and insecure. If we don't allow ourselves to question, how can we trust? Perhaps Cindy's struggle was actually a sign of her love. Her fears about her husband might actually mean she was taking her marriage seriously; that it mattered.

A teacher of mine once called the Bible the greatest love story ever told. It's the story of the deepening love between God and a people, and it's anything but smooth sailing. Generation after generation, this relationship is a continuing dialectic between doubt and trust, questioning and loyalty. More than a few times, the bond is almost broken, only to be reengaged and strengthened. But the possibility of a permanent breach is always there and this makes the relationship even more vital and real.

The dynamic between God and the people is meant to be a metaphor for what all relationships—especially one as complex and intimate as marriage—are all about. The covenant God makes with the people is in fact very much like a marriage. The *ketubah*, the rabbis say, is the equivalent of the Torah; many *ketubahs* are actually written in calligraphy to look like the ancient scrolls. And both remind us that commitment is not an answer; it's a process. My hope was that Cindy might begin to see her feelings about her marriage in a new light; that she might broaden her concept of love. Even if her husband had had an affair, the marriage might still be worth saving. She would never know if she didn't express her doubts and fears. Only then could there be the possibility that her love would be renewed, or a *get* would be sacred.

I've seen so many people try to work out their relationship problems in isolation, or with a therapist, a spiritual teacher, a friend—anyone except the person they're having difficulties with. Confronting those we love most can be frightening, and often we do so only when the pain becomes acute, or sometimes not even then. This is in part because we believe we can do it on our own, if only we try hard enough; if only we become super-self-aware; if we accept that we're from Venus and they're from Mars.

Our culture has a strong, deeply ingrained belief in the power of the individual. Appreciating each person's uniqueness and rights is so important. But the myth of the self-made man, the solitary pioneer, has taken a new form in contemporary times. It seems that the self has become the ultimate sphere, the place where everything can be worked out and worked through, independent of anyone else. Publishers report that the self-help or self-improvement genre is the fastest growing book category in America. As the comedian George Carlin asks, "If it's really self-help, what do you need the book for?" Personal "coaches" are now replacing therapists, as if life were a game we can win if we only learn the rules.

So many of us put tremendous energy into training our children to be independent, to have self-esteem, to think they can do anything if they put their minds to it. I've often thought that it was the ultimate compliment when a friend or teacher said about my daughter, "She's got a mind of her own." But what are we really teaching our kids? I asked this question of a friend of mine who seemed so upset when his daughter, now a couple of years out of college, asked if she could move back home. He told me how afraid he was that she'd never make it on her own. He saw her return as a kind of failure. He'd invested so much in her education and he'd fully expected her to throw herself into a career or some kind of adventure after she finished school. And all she wanted to do was come home again? Clearly he was quite attached to the idea that independence means strength and dependence is a sign of weakness. And he was clearly struggling with it. "I wish I could welcome her home with open arms. I really do."

Often our dualities cause us some degree of pain, and this is a sign that we need to go deeper. Emotions like guilt, envy, anxiety, and depression often are the alarm bells. In the end, my friend's guilt got the best of him, and he and his wife told their daughter to come home. Over the months, he began to talk warmly of their dinners together, her successes as a freelance journalist, her good and bad choices in boyfriends. He saw that she was creating a life for herself after all, and that the atmosphere his home provided gave her the confidence and freedom to pursue what she really loved. Plus, he had the rare privilege of really being a part of her young-adult life. As Ram Dass said, dependence and independence make such a beautiful tapestry. They make up the web of intimacy.

Sometimes in the doing, our dualities can soften and allow new possibilities to enter. We don't always have to work it all out beforehand. It's often after the fact that we realize we were caught in a duality of our own making. When my buddy told me the story months after his daughter came home, he clearly had discovered the paradox. He realized that his daughter could be both independent and dependent at the same time. He also saw her independence in a new light. He told me with a laugh, "Thank God she was independent enough from me to come home despite my resistance." He came to understand that her dependence on him and his wife allowed for a kind of independence that was much more meaningful than he could have imagined. He was able to allow a new truth to emerge: interdependence. At one point he told me how much he'd come to count on their evening talks and walks to the subway in the mornings. I sensed that he'd become pretty dependent on her. No doubt, when his daughter did decide to leave, my friend would need to dive back into this duality and find yet another new truth.

YEARNING FOR
THE WAY

DANCING WITH
UNCERTAINTY

MOST OF US DEEPLY DESIRE AND CELEBRATE THE FRUITS
of uncertainty without realizing that without the seed, the fruit would
not exist. Discovery, revelation, insight, love, surprise, joy: We would
never have these wonderful human experiences if we didn't allow ourselves to feel unsure, to embark upon journeys without needing to know
where we will end up. Yet in my two decades as a rabbi, no one has ever
come to me for counsel about ways to become less certain, to invite more
questions, to celebrate ambiguity. Not surprisingly, hundreds have
walked into my office encumbered or even paralyzed by uncertainty,
racked with the anxiety of not knowing. They yearn for guidance, a bea-
con that will shine through the messiness and confusion. Almost always
they have a major decision to make, whether about a relationship, a
child, an aging parent, or the direction of their lives. And even if they
don't admit it, they want me to assure them of the outcome they so hope
for. Although I rarely offer that, I can't help but wish for the same thing.

The yearning for certainty—to grasp our future, to shape our des-
tinies—is so powerful and so noble. We yearn to know that things will
work out. We want to be assured that what we do will make our lives
richer and the world a better place. We long for a pathway, at least for a
"road less traveled," as the famous book by M. Scott Peck offered. But
most of the time we create our own path simply by walking even when
we have no clear idea where we are going.

Of course, we all have delicious times of certainty, clarity, confidence, and purpose—more than most of us even recognize. We are

always mastering new skills and reaching goals. Every day is filled with countless easy and seamless decisions. But the uncertain times stand out because they are often so uncomfortable. They create anxiety, fear, and vulnerability. That's why certainty is so seductive. Our culture rewards knowing and makes not-knowing a liability; but about the important things in life, it may well be the opposite. Certainty isn't all it's cracked up to be—it can lead to arrogance, boredom, complacency, and dullness. We all know those

Certainty is seductive. Our culture rewards knowing and makes not-knowing a liability; but about the important things in life, the opposite may be true.

certainty gurus, whether religious, political, or those in our own lives. We may envy them their confidence, but we don't want to be in the same room with them for long.

Living the mystery means dancing with certainty and uncertainty, knowing and not-knowing. Parenting is a perfect example of this. It's an unknown journey for anyone who undertakes it; yet there are times of knowing, of mastery along the way. It all starts before the baby's even born—there's so much excitement, fear, and anxiety leading up to that big event. There have been nine months to imagine everything that can go wrong and only so many classes and tests one can take and only so many books one can read.

Then there's the relief of knowing, of that baby in our arms; a sense of clarity and purpose that this is our child and we're going to take care of her. But then we go home and the ride really begins. Just when we get the swing of the baby stuff, we have a toddler, then a school-aged child, then a teenager, and at each stage a whole other learning curve begins. My parents tell me they're still learning how to parent—and they've raised six kids! There's no more humbling experience than parenting. The times of not-knowing far outweigh the certainties. Maybe that's why so many parents I know say having a baby is what made them finally grow up.

The biblical sages understood that the anxiety of not-knowing is the beginning of wisdom. There isn't a single character in the Bible who understood beforehand the outcome of any journey he or she underwent. What makes these characters so special is not that they are somehow superhuman, wiser, or more evolved. It's that they don't scale down their dreams to the size of their fears. They are masters of the dance between uncertainty and certainty. Every one of them is reluctant to go on his or her journey; every one of them takes a risk without knowing how things will work out; every one of them has massive doubts along the way and needs reassurance that things will be okay; and none of them fully completes what he set out to do.

Abraham uprooted his family and traveled from Babylonia, the center of civilization at the time, to a place he knew nothing about. The indeterminacy of the journey is captured in the words "Go forth to the land I will show you." The certainty and comforts of Babylonia must have been pretty appealing; it wasn't until Abraham was seventy-five that he felt there might be something more. But did even he know where he was going? Years later he retells the story of his leaving in a most unusual way: "God made me *wander* from my father's house." I love his honesty; there's neither bravado nor false humility.

Perhaps out of discomfort with the insecurities and uncertainties of our own journeys, we read or hear the stories of great characters so differently: We think they hear a loud, clear call to act, to accomplish grand things—the authoritative voice of God leading every step of the way. We think they're everything we are not, when really we are all wanderers. The mystical text the Zohar tells us that God says to every human being every day "go forth," begin the journey that is yours to make. What makes us enlightened is that we are not afraid to wander. Doubt is a prerequisite for any meaningful journey. When we can acknowledge the built-in anxiety rather than maintaining the illusion of certainty, we become humble—which in turn creates a new and more authentic confidence.

Yet the yearning for certainty is part of being human. Abraham and Moses longed to know that it all would work out for the best. The voice of God in these stories at times tells them about the wonderful things that will happen along the way—Abraham will birth many nations; Moses will lead his people into the Promised Land. This voice is actually a metaphor for their yearning to know ahead of time where their journeys would take them, what the payoff would be. They were wrestling, feeling the push and pull between the realization that they couldn't remain where they were, the certainty that there was more, and the uncertainty about where they were going or how they would get there. They needed to struggle before they could take such enormous risks. In the end they were convinced that they would be headed in the right direction even if they were trailblazing a new path. They embraced the promise but weren't seduced by certainty, or surely they would have given up.

What if we understood that all decisions, even the seeming sure things, are leaps into the unknown? What if we were galvanized, rather than paralyzed, by uncertainty? It could be that our very denial about how unsure we really are in fact causes the most anxiety of all. We mistake ambivalence for weakness, indecisiveness for failing. We try to convince ourselves that the future should be ours to see and that there's actually a discernable and consistent cause and effect to our decisions and actions. Depression, obsessiveness, even paranoia have at

Doubt is a prerequisite for any meaningful journey.

their roots a profound fear of the unknown and usually a wound from the past, a trauma lodged in our unconscious that we're afraid will reoccur. These are extreme reactions to the dread that it could all work out for the worst, that if we're not on the lookout, hypervigilant, or hiding behind the veil of disassociation, disaster awaits us. Extreme anxiety short-circuits life.

Yet if we're really honest with ourselves when we look back on our lives, we can see that all our decisions, large and small, were made from a place of uncertainty and sometimes profound conflict. Rarely have any of us had any idea where our decisions would lead, and other times what we thought would happen turned out quite differently than planned. It's not that life is a crapshoot. It's that vagaries and uncertainties are a part of the human drama. Our journey presents us with catastrophes, traumas, losses, gains, wonders, and miracles. And in the end we must act on faith, not that it will all work out as we want but that our best guess is good enough, that it will somehow lead us to a place of discovery, of new perspective, of a wider self.

A friend of mine had talked for years about starting his own consulting agency after years of hard knocks in the corporate world. He'd been laid off a number of times as companies merged and bosses changed, and even though he was currently employed, he'd had it with the politics, the endless meetings, the whole scene. He'd sweated through many a sleepless night contemplating his next move. He'd created an ambitious business plan for an agency, and at one point had even scoped out office space.

But month after month there was some reason not to go forward. It seemed that whenever our families got together, my wife or I would inevitably ask "So, Adam, hung out the shingle yet?" One evening after several drinks and a fair amount of prodding from me, he confessed that he was utterly terrified. Not only would he not be earning an income right away, but he'd be investing his hard-earned savings in his own venture. And the pain of the so-called "failures" that dotted his career to this point gave him pause—major pause. "Success just isn't in my repertoire," he said.

After more than a year of planning, he still felt that if he analyzed the possibilities, going over and over the potential outcomes in his head, he somehow could ensure the outcome he so desperately hoped for: a thriving business and a renewed sense of confidence in himself. Just maybe, he would find a way to protect himself from the failure he feared, from repeating the traumas of his previous work experiences. He wanted to know ahead of time that he would be successful. As a result, he kept coming up with more questions that needed answering before he could make his decision.

> **All of us have permission to act without knowing. Whether we acknowledge it or not, we are always doing so anyway.**

I remember feeling a rush of both frustration and compassion as I listened to him that evening, watching his increasingly pained expression as he downed glass after glass of wine. "God created the world from a place of not knowing. Surely you can start a business," I blurted out. And I wasn't kidding.

I told him the Talmudic story about how God created and destroyed ten worlds before this one. Each world was so incredibly disappointing, so different than what had been envisioned; an utter failure in the eyes of its Creator. Uncertainty drove God crazy, too. And yet the Creator kept going, desperately trying to get it "right." When God breathed life into the world we know today, once again there was incredible rage about its imperfection. No matter how we try, there's no way to guarantee that things work out as we intend.

But just as this world, like all the others, was about to be destroyed, God paused, having come to a startling moment truth: Simply because one creates something does not mean one can predict or control it. If the only way we can experience success is to be certain about how our actions will play out, we are doomed to disappointment and anger. God embarked on a journey about which very little could be known in advance; one that would be filled with surprises and learning. What a concept: God wasn't sure but did it anyway. No matter how many blows; how many expectations and hopes were dashed; never knowing what would happen next—God stayed with it. Of course, this story is really about our own need to choose life and wonder over paralyzing rage at and disappointment in ourselves and others.

I encouraged my friend to embrace his own uncertainty and go forward. He didn't need to know the outcome of his venture, but he could find the part of him that wanted to do it, make the preparations knowing the risks, and act from that place. Even if his business turned out to be a "failure" it would inevitably lead him to the next place he needed to be, perhaps eventually leading him back into the corporate world with a whole new breadth of experience behind him. And he could be reassured not by the certainty of the future but by the fact that along the way he would continue to decide; every move was an opportunity to either recommit or change directions.

THE NINETEENTH-CENTURY philosopher Franz Rosenzweig taught that life is a succession of leaps into pathlessness. We take a path, follow it, and then we must leap again. There is never a final decision, a choice to end all choices. Every decision is a partial truth; there's always a road not taken. No matter how many maps we read, no matter how hard we study the roads we or others have taken in the past—although of course we must do all these things—the future is unknown. We move at the moment of decision from path to pathlessness.

Halacha, the Hebrew word for Jewish law, comes from the root "to walk." It literally means "the path," "the way," or even more accurately "pathing"; like the Sanskrit word *pratipadyate*, "one who paths." It's the opposite of a fixed or stable law. There are so many ways to path: cut, follow, climb, run, skip, stroll, circumvent. As long as the path we're on takes us where we want to go, we barely notice it. We take in the sights and smells, enjoying the ride, taking the bumps as they come until they get too big or the path disappears or takes a turn into a darker part of the forest. Or maybe it's too straight and narrow. Then we feel trapped, frightened, or bored, and we have to retrace our steps or find another path, or wander in the wilderness for a while.

The Talmud contains twenty volumes of recorded debates about how to live spiritually, ethically, and morally. It's a series of decisions and re-decisions, paths and leaps: a series of arguments and concessions, sages agreeing and disagreeing with each other for over four hundred years. Many people to whom I teach the Talmud are struck by the fact that 75 percent of all the debates and arguments are left unresolved. No final decision is ever reached. This is unique in sacred literature. By not providing definitive decisions, the sages were teaching us that we ought not to fool ourselves. Not even the most intense debate, investigation, or wrestling will allow us to make decisions with anything less than uncertainty and indeterminacy. And the discussion continues into future generations.

All of us have permission to act without knowing. Whether we acknowledge it or not, we are always doing so anyway. Rather than imprisoning us in a malaise, uncertainty can actually liberate us and make life so much more vivid. As Edmond Jabès writes in *The Book of Yukel*, "Certainty is the region of death; uncertainty is the valley of life. Once we can liberate ourselves from the tyranny of needing to be certain, it becomes possible to take, as William Blake wrote, 'eternal delight' in the undecidable." The "undecidable" is where the action is, where the invitation to play, explore, and dance happens.

Jewish wisdom teaches that nothing is more important than what we do. Being paralyzed by indecision is not an option. It's incumbent upon every human being to contribute to the world, to make a difference. That's why our decisions are so important, why as many angles or paths as possible should be considered. The rabbis compared life to a scale: Every act tips toward more life or more death. This is not just poetic or some medieval truth. All of us are an accumulation of our actions. Every moment is a karmic moment. And this gives everything we do more meaning. Decisions are in fact moments of "selving," of cumulative evolution. And not-deciding is as much a decision as changing one's course: It's just pathing by a different rhythm.

There's a wonderful passage in the Talmud describing one of the steps in the process of becoming ordained as a rabbi. Every rabbinical student **Faith can't exist** must make an argument for the purity of a specific food, **without doubt.** offering forty-nine reasons justifying his position and forty-nine reasons justifying the position he has not taken. The Talmud had already clarified what foods are pure and what foods are not, so why bother to argue the other side?

The point is that one cannot understand the reasons for a decision unless one understands the other side. Why forty-nine reasons? Forty-nine, like most numbers presented in wisdom texts, is a metaphor: Seven is a mystical and powerful number, echoing the number of days of Creation.

The implication of seven times seven is that every decision unfolds worlds of possibilities. Every decision creates as many uncertainties as certainties.

The humble absolute that I take from this ancient teaching is that in order for any of us to make a decision about anything important in our lives, it is necessary to fully consider, to take seriously, the option or options we are not inclined to take. Eventually, though, we need to make a decision. We must act in the world. And how much easier can it be to act when we understand that we don't need to strive for 100 percent certainty? Isn't it more authentic to be 51 percent sure instead? Acting from the standpoint of 51 percent can help decisions feel less burdensome, less absolute. Even as we become clearer, we are still engaged in the questions, still aware of our uncertainty. The other 49 percent remains alive in us.

I have observed that three things happen when we act from 51 percent certainty. First, we have a lot more compassion for ourselves. We know our decision could produce an outcome we don't intend, and we accept this ahead of time. Second, if things work out as we'd hoped, we understand that the win may well be temporary. We realize that our decision could end up being a mistake, and at some future point, another choice can be made. There's no need to cling rigidly to a certainty, trying to prove it true. When we don't, it's that much easier to change directions if we choose to do so. Finally, we have much more compassion for others who make different decisions in their lives. We can support them even if we don't agree, simply because we are practiced in holding our own decisions lightly. We can experience the yearning for certainty and yet not let it consume us.

Let's face it, we make thousands of decisions a day, sorting through an infinite amount of information, firing up countless neural pathways, leaping into pathlessness without even knowing it, and usually things just hum along. Until they don't. A dissonance, a disruption, a crisis, a crossroads appears. Then what is unconscious becomes conscious and we tune in to the process that's always going on under the radar. The questions rise to the surface; the stakes suddenly seem high.

My wife, Dana, and I marvel to this day about a decision we made more than a decade ago that at the time seemed so monumental. We faced a decision about whether or not to keep our daughter Talia in kindergarten for an extra year. Talia was the youngest in her class and, although the school officially said she was ready for first grade, her teacher told us that Talia might benefit from staying in kindergarten for an additional year. Our first response was disappointment. How could we "hold her back"?

Not surprisingly, our family and friends assured us that Talia would be fine in first grade. Dana worried how Talia would deal with seeing the classmates she started school with a year ahead of her. How would this affect her self-esteem? The discussing and fretting went on for quite a while until one night close to the day we needed to give the school our decision, Dana and I began laughing at the absurdity of the whole thing.

If we'd gotten pregnant a few months earlier, there wouldn't even be an issue. It all comes down to when you choose to make love! We certainly hadn't obsessed about any of this then. Uncertainty had suited us just fine. Suddenly it seemed silly to use language like "hold back" and "repeat" to describe giving a five-year-old an extra year to play and learn without pressure. What in the world was the hurry? We both began fantasizing about being held back ourselves! Talia returned to kindergarten and she never skipped a beat: To her it was just another year with new friends. She became a leader of her class, and she still is to this day.

One might say that in the end we followed our intuition about what would be right for Talia. But what is intuition really? I'm struck by how often people reverently speak of the so-called "sixth sense." In fact, my consultant friend's wife kept urging him, "For God's sake, just go with your intuition." I wondered if her urgings actually paralyzed my friend. She, too, wanted him to be certain, in another guise. Intuition, it seems, is the modern equivalent of the traditional, authoritative voice of God.

Surprisingly, intuition actually closely resembles the way of the sages rather than some New Age magic. Cognitive scientists have observed how intuition works in the brain—it's literally a creative leap, impossible to track. But a million neurons have been fired in order for that leap to occur. Many thoughts have been had. Many actions have been taken. Many decisions have been made before this one. In other words, intuition is the result of an accumulation of decisions. It is the result of a lineage of thoughts. And what makes it more powerful, still, is that intuition is also the product of those thoughts and feelings we haven't yet even made conscious. Intuition is really a culminating voice, one that speaks of thousands of previous decisions made consciously and unconsciously.

So the ancient sages and contemporary neuroscientists agree. The grand moment of decision we all yearn for may be a necessary illusion, allowing us to take a stand and act in the world. Yet that moment masks what is really an ongoing conversation. When we realize that uncertainty is our natural human state, that ambivalence is our birthright, that we are "selving" just as the biblical authors showed us even the God character was, life becomes even more awesome. We can see that our unfolding is truly remarkable and our decisions and actions are what make that process possible.

A COMMANDING PRESENCE

"DON'T YOU EVER GET TIRED OF BEING 'THE MEANING OF life guy'?" my daughter Gabriella occasionally asks me with an exasperated roll of her eyes. On a gorgeous summer day in the mountains of Colorado, the answer is most definitely yes. A room full of people sits waiting inside to hear my talk about a grandiose topic—the transformative power of the Ten Commandments—that I'm supposed to give in fifteen minutes. I haven't prepared as I usually do and should be squirreled away somewhere jotting down some notes. Instead I'm hanging out outside talking to a few acquaintances about the little things in life—the delicious dinner we had last night, my lingering jetlag, the size of the crowd.

I'm paying special attention to a well-known philanthropist. I find myself laughing a little too loudly at his jokes. I'd like nothing more than to become a "friend" of this man and for him to contribute to my organization. At the same time, I'm getting more and more annoyed with a woman we both know who keeps interrupting. He already gives money to her institution, and it's thriving as a result; why doesn't she just be quiet? As if that weren't bad enough, when an attractive, much younger woman joins us, I decide to stay outside a few minutes longer. I find myself becoming more and more drawn to her. When she laughs at some joke I make for her benefit, I notice her beautiful smile. When she pushes back her hair, I wonder what it feels like. Sexual thoughts begin to distract me to the point that I almost lose track of our conversation.

But perhaps because of the nature of my talk, and years of practice (and occasional acting out), even as I experience these thoughts and feelings in bold relief, I also am acutely aware of them, excruciatingly so. Rather than resisting, stifling, or silencing them, I am actually consciously raising them. I'm also feeling pretty anxious; there's a tension or dissonance between what I want in the moment and my conscious intention to both acknowledge and contain those same desires.

After a few minutes I feel myself soften. The feelings don't go away, but I begin to hear a more playful voice. Here I am; Irwin the irresponsible, lustful, greedy, envious rabbi supposedly about to offer wisdom about the Ten Commandments. Some meaning of life guy! Then I think, hey, maybe I'll impress the philanthropist and come back to the office with a million bucks. And finally: Look at this gray-haired man in his mid-forties getting a flirtatious laugh out of a woman half his age.

When I finally walk into the building, now ten minutes late, I'm on fire: I feel very much alive. By the time I get to the podium I hear another voice, the voice of the husband. It reminds me that after two decades of marriage, I yearn for my wife whenever I'm away. I am also keenly aware of myself as the teacher, who, for better or worse, has been paid good money to give this talk, money that will in a very real if small way benefit my organization, which needs all the help it can get. More than that, I am here to talk to a roomful of people, some of whom have traveled far to listen. Suddenly, I feel completely present. There's nowhere I'd rather be than on this stage. I like to think I gave a pretty good speech.

Jewish wisdom teaches that our actions, from large to small, are our legacy; it's what we do that counts. There's a saying: "It's not study that is central. It's our actions." Or to put it in more contemporary language, the degree of our enlightenment can be measured by

> **Our actions are our legacy.
> It's what we do that counts.**

what we do. With spiritual audacity, the sages tell us that God says, "Better that you do what I say than that you believe in me," a paradox if there ever was one.

The sages envisioned a world in which every act would be a *mitzvah*, a word that has come to mean "good deed." Amazingly, I had actually done several *mitzvot* by the time I got to the podium that sunny morning so full of temptation. *Mitzvah* is the Hebrew word for "commandment," or any act deemed to be required by God. But its mystical meaning is "intimacy." A Talmudic poet from the fifth century said there were 613 commandments in the Bible. This was a way of saying that every moment is a commanding moment; there are so many ways (an infinite number, really) to contribute to the world, to connect to ourselves and others.

Commandments are often misunderstood as being external directives, repressive limitations, or old-fashioned lessons in morality. Contemporary religions have portrayed them as instruments of social control. But the biblical commandments, even the Ten Commandments, weren't simply meant to legislate our thoughts or feelings, or even our actions. In fact the Torah never uses the word commandment when describing these ten insights; it refers to them as *devarim*, which means "utterances" or "words." They are a poetic and profound series of intuitions about human behavior.

They make conscious some of our most primal feelings and urges with the understanding that the more we can bring them to the surface, even magnify them, the more likely we are to master them and do good in the world. They are guides—sometimes gentle, sometimes not—that take us deep into our psyches to uncover the desires and yearnings that lurk there. Rather than transcend or try to overcome them, commandments invite us to enter into them fully. What would happen if we opened ourselves up to the power and urgent nature of our longings?

No wonder the Ten Commandments have gained so much prominence. They make conscious some of the most primal human desires, those we are most likely to repress and therefore act out—from the urge to make concrete that which is unknowable (God) to stealing that which is not ours. Most of the time, we act out internal drives and desires we're unaware of—forces we scarcely comprehend. By calling forth these yearnings, the commandments are actually what I call shadow busters or ignorance busters.

Of course, simply following the commandments—not killing, not committing adultery, not stealing—is all well and good. But it's only possible to fulfill a *mitzvah* if one experiences the full range of feelings that run counter to it. If you don't feel anything contrary to the commandment, then it's like an inert chemical; it has no impact or meaning. The commandments are actually catalysts for desires that are always beneath the surface.

How can we acknowledge "I should not" until we experience "I am tempted"? How can we authentically feel "I must do this" if we don't first feel "I don't want to do it"? Whether it's "Rest on the seventh day" or "Honor your father and your mother," we need to first feel the opposing urge: "I don't need to rest. I have to make that deadline no matter what" or "I can't take my mother anymore." The more tempted we are, the more desires we experience, the more meaningful the *mitzvah*. There's no greater mitzvah than to act in the face of temptation.

When we resist a commandment it's often because we experience it as an external pressure. So many people associate commandments with a punishing parent or a nagging spouse; some kind of controlling authority. But the external pressure we feel is really our disguised desire. What we see as oppressive, external rules are merely alienated longings. It's obvious when we think about it: If we didn't have the desire to observe a commandment, we wouldn't feel anxious or pressured. We'd simply go on about our business.

Recently when my wife, Dana, asked me to clean up the study in the morning after one of my late-night working sessions, the books and papers everywhere, I genuinely wanted to do it. It's a reasonable request— my family uses this space during the day for a variety of things, and I like an orderly home as much as she does. The next afternoon, Dana asked me why the room was still a mess. And I lost it—can't she leave me alone for once?! She'd pointed out the very thing I'd hoped to do, but for some reason—probably laziness or childhood baggage—hadn't. The pressure I felt was not from her. It was my own disappointment in myself. I apologized.

The sages understood that our sense of responsibility doesn't always match our actions. We rarely choose to be lustful, lethargic, conceited, greedy, or deluded. None of us wants to do what we believe is wrong. Drives, conventions, habits, and patterns urge us to follow the most familiar course, even if it's inappropriate or destructive. Desires, emotions, thoughts, and compulsions monopolize our consciousness. Sometimes we end up acting in ways we ourselves find incomprehensible. St. Paul lamented, "The good that I would do, that I do not: that which I hate, that do I." The Talmudic sages, like Buddhist teachers, insist that "a person does not do evil except out of ignorance, unless he has taken leave of his mind."

Mitzvah is an artful technology designed to help us loosen the grip of these seemingly alien forces that take us over. The sages knew that when we push them away we make them stronger and more difficult to control. Often they erupt, and then we're really in their grasp. Commandments evoke in us the very urges that we tend to suppress. When we bring them to consciousness, we discover that these tendencies we're not so proud of can sit right next to our more positive patterns, habits, and desires in a kind of harmonious balance. When we acknowledge and integrate our impulses and longings, no matter how "naughty" or destructive, they lose their evil coloring.

There were so many compelling thoughts for me that Colorado morning, so many actions I could have taken or not taken. If I hadn't felt, even enjoyed my middle-aged lust I might have come closer to making a move on that beautiful young woman. As it happened, I did a *mitzvah*; I fulfilled the seventh commandment, which urges us not to commit adultery. We can't fully understand or experience monogamy unless we live a lustful inner life. If we are loath to admit our lustfulness—if we deny, repress, or try to transcend it out of shame or self-consciousness or self-aggrandizement—we'll wind up like Jimmy Swaggart and Jim Bakker. We'll find lustfulness everywhere out there and end up breaking the commandment.

If I hadn't been aware of how much I wanted to get hold of some of that philanthropist's money, or how jealous I was of the woman who already had it, I might have gone back to my office and made the necessary calls. Instead I fulfilled the tenth commandment, do not covet, and the sixth, do not steal (as I was already beginning to strategize about how I could outdo her organization in his eyes). You can't be generous until you know what it means to covet. By surfacing my feelings and becoming fully aware of them, I was able to move on, to do the work of *mitzvah*. I heard all the desires: "I want, I want, I want, I want" and then, a little softer, "I want. Okay, now what?"

Finally I was able to get, really *get* that I was there on that gorgeous day to fulfill the very simple *mitzvah* to teach. It may have seemed obvious that I was going to give the speech in the end. But how engaged or engaging would I have been if I'd gone on automatic, suppressing my need to breathe the fresh air, laugh with friends, have sex, or help the organization I so love?

The biblical poet suggested that there are 613 commandments: 365 (the number of days in the year) plus 248 (the number of bones in the body, according to the science of the day). In other words, we bring all the parts of who we are, "the bad and the good," into every moment, and every moment is a commanding moment. This poetic intuition allowed me to be fully present, to bring my multiple, contradictory, ever-evolving selves to the podium that day.

ALL WISDOM TRADITIONS teach that freedom—from suffering, from hate, from fear, from the material trappings of life—can come only through spiritual practice, whether it's study, prayer, meditation, ritual, or acts of loving kindess. Jewish wisdom is no different. What's surprising to many is that the commandments themselves are a liberation practice.

Those Ten Commandments or "words" were given to the Israelites three months into their desert journey. As they stood at the base of Mt. Sinai soon after being released from slavery in Egypt, it was time for them to come in contact with their inner pharoahs, to begin the real work of attaining freedom. It was time to make life a conscious performance.

The Ten Commandments were "engraved in stone." In Hebrew the word for engraved is *charut,* which comes from the same root as the word for freedom. So it's actually freedom that's inscribed on those tablets! Janis Joplin sang that freedom is another way of saying "nothing left to lose." But isn't it really, "Freedom's just another word for knowing what to do"? In other words, we are free only when we break loose from the physical, emotional, intellectual, and cultural forces that drive us without our even knowing it. Philosopher Isaiah Berlin describes two kinds of freedom. First, there's "freedom from," what he calls negative freedom: breaking free from those unconscious forces that compel us. When we achieve that, we attain positive freedom, "freedom to" do exactly what we know we're supposed to do. There are no longer barriers to being the kind of person we want to be.

The commandments unveil our desires, actually encouraging us to taste hate, greed, envy, lust; to allow them to bloom inside us; to make them fully conscious. In other words, when we can act knowing first what motivates us, and when we can act with intention, then we are free. Of course, we can't always act from a place of freedom; our desires and patterns are bound to get the best of us now and again. We'll never get to the point where we always know what we're supposed to do. But the more aware we are of what drives us, the better shot we have.

When we can act knowing first what motivates us, and when we can act with intention, then we are free.

For many of us, freedom can be uncomfortable, frightening, and overwhelming. This is another reason why so many people see the commandments as a series of concrete directives. They yearn for a prescription for life, a pathway to "goodness." So they externalize the commandments, telling themselves and others that they better follow them—or else. But the commandments can't tell you what to do; no one and nothing can. We are always free to choose. What the commandments do is help us arrive where we need to be in the moment to make a conscious decision. And the more they hassle us, pressure us, and push us, the more likely we are to make the decision that will serve us well.

I often tell people who take the commandments "literally"—whether they embrace or reject them—to follow the Zen master Baslo's advice: "Do not seek to follow in the footsteps of the wise; rather, seek what they sought." One way to do so is to explore some of the actual *mitzvot* that populate the biblical teachings. When we can *observe* the feelings—the pressure, the annoyance, even the indifference—they create, we can get a taste of freedom.

There are at least two categories of commandment in all wisdom traditions. Most people are familiar with the first, the ethical and moral laws similar to the idea of *kharma* yoga. They are acts of compassion, kindness, and love. Often they seem like simple acts of decency. Within this category are "dos" and "don'ts." The "dos" include visiting the sick, giving to the poor, conducting business honestly, being hospitable to strangers, comforting mourners, and administering justice impartially. We may not really want to do any of these acts because they entail short-term sacrifice of time, money, or emotional discomfort and unease. This is precisely the point.

When we resist, we have the opportunity to observe not only the command but ourselves. And just to be sure our consciousness is raised to the fullest, many of these commandments include very specific instructions: precisely how much harvest to give to the poor; how to treat employees; when, how, and with whom you make love; the way to tend to a dead body (considered the highest *mitzvah* because it can never be repaid).

The ethical "don'ts" are perhaps even more familiar. We are not supposed to steal, lie, gossip, use people sexually, provide false information, cheat, take revenge, or commit murder. These are the "of course" commandments; "just common sense" as a student of mine said. I get lots of surprised looks when I point out that any commandment we say "of course" to is one we are in fact not observing. When we dismiss anything out of hand, we are preventing our own growth and expansion; we become less intimate with our impulses and desires.

"Do not murder" invites us to meditate on who we want to murder. Who gets under our skin; who enrages us beyond reason; who cheats us, betrays us? Who are the people about whom we have those delicious, if only fleeting fantasies of murder or revenge, or whom we wish would disappear off the face of the planet? It can be helpful to remember that murderous desires are innate, or in religious language, "God-given"—after all, look at God's track record! In this way they are no different than our most noble ethical impulses. When we open our eyes, when we reflect on the commandment, we begin to see different forms of murder all around us. As I asked my student, "Who are you kidding?" Isn't war the practice of murder? What about poor social programs and health care? On an interpersonal level, the sages taught that humiliation is a form of murder. When we cause the "blood to drain out of someone's face," we have committed soul murder.

These sages challenge us to expand and contract the categories we've created around even the most "obvious" commandments so that we can experience and more genuinely observe them. As a teacher of mine once put it when explaining what can be learned from the Noah story: "If you want to be like God, you have to feel God's murderous rage." It's a learning curve for the "Almighty," too. God has to go all the way in the Noah story—destroying everything but one boatload of all creation—before realizing how wrong it was. If we read this as an internal story, we are obliged to fully feel everything, especially the feelings that frighten us the most.

Interestingly, there are a number of exceptions, some very clear "to dos" under the category of murder in the biblical texts. Some of these commandments are incredibly shocking and disturbing when read at a surface level. But when read at a "surfacing" level, they can be even more intense. One such commandment, one that always gets a rise out of everyone in the room, is the one that tells us to stone a child if he is rebellious. How crazy, how barbaric; who would do that, never mind

make it a practice? This is why religion is not only stupid, but dangerous! But practicing or observing this commandment isn't "doing" it. It's
letting it "do" you. When we tune in, we may hear ourselves think,
"Damn, there's a part of me that really wants to kill that kid."

The rabbis say no one has ever acted on this biblical commandment—
of course, there's no way of knowing if this is true—but they don't dismiss it. One might wonder what the purpose of this commandment is if
you're not supposed to act on it. This law invites us to think about the
times we've felt a kind of uncontrollable rage at a simple infraction, so
much so that we've wanted to strike our child, or did. How about when
we squelch their spirit, coming down hard on them for some act of disobedience, something as simple as not turning off the TV or not going
to bed on time? What about when the baby wakes up for the sixth time
in the middle of the night and for a split second we imagine smothering
it? What does it even mean when a child rebels; how do we judge and
respond to these acts? Most of the time rebelling means someone is doing what we don't want him or her to do; plain and simple. The truth is,
all children are going to rebel. The challenge is what do we do when this
happens. Allowing our murderous rage to surface is a start. The commandment is meant to amplify our anger and anxiety temporarily.
When we let it, it's amazing how rarely we act out our greatest fears.

Then there are those commandments that seem silly or obsolete.
There's the one that tells us to return our enemy's ox or ass when it's
wandering down the road. But if you meditate on that, what will happen? You may remember how many things you actually do take from
perceived enemies: a colleague you feel competitive with who really de-
serves the credit; that money you owe your ex-wife but don't pay on
time.

Those of us who find meaning and guidance in the ethical dos and
don'ts are often stumped by the second form of *mitzvah*: the ritual practices. Rituals, too, are integral to every spiritual tradition, and for good
reason. They bring us deep into our psyches, beyond common sense.
They are designed to speak to the right brain, to access the realm of the

imagination. They are pre- or post-verbal; however you choose to look at it. They are nothing less than techniques to facilitate transformation.

At the same time, rituals remind us who we are (or how much we are) and where we came from. They enact, express, and renew our relationships, whether to family, community, culture, cosmos, or God. And they are always a kind of theater. Whether using unusual objects and symbols, language and physical movement, clothing and art, rituals both root us and destabilize us. They confirm the deepest parts of who we are and disrupt our surface selves, inviting us to shed our veils and pretenses, our everyday armor, to renew and deepen our identities and connection to the world. They can weld a community, creating a kind of social magic that solidifies a group. Rituals also can open up new ways of thinking and being in our individual lives.

Rituals can be songs of grace and dances of death; they can foment aggression and inspire love; calm the mind and stir things up; enchant the ordinary or transform it.

Rituals can be songs of grace and dances of death; they can foment aggression and inspire love; calm the mind and stir things up; enchant the ordinary or transform it. The Jewish practice of blowing a shofar on the New Year, the Catholic eucharist, the Hindu mala beads, the Pueblo clowning, the Islamic Great Henna marriage ritual, the Buddhist mandala, the Hopi masked dance—each of these acts invites us to enter an alternative universe. Even if we don't participate in them, witnessing them can send chills down our spine. Many people experienced this after Pope John Paul II died and Pope Benedict XVI was chosen: Catholics and non-Catholics alike sat by their television sets waiting for that white smoke to emerge from the chimney of the Sistine Chapel. When it did, tears came to their eyes even before they knew who the new pope would be.

I'm always amused when I teach about ritual practice and some intellectually sophisticated, highly rational, ethically sensitive person says something like, "This is silly and superfluous. I don't need ritual." "Okay," I ask, "What do you eat on Thanksgiving and who carves the turkey? Do you and your lover have a favorite song? Does your family have designated seats at their dining room tables? Where does the CEO sit in your boardroom?" Imagine a graduation with no pomp and circumstance, no silk cap and gown, where we receive a xeroxed copy of our final transcript in the mail rather than a calligraphied diploma made of parchment. Imagine the death of a loved one with no funeral rites. Imagine saying to your wife or husband, "You know I love you. Who needs a ring?" and then dropping the wedding band into the toilet with a shrug. Even the most cynical people usually get the idea.

What's the difference really between business attire—that dark suit, white shirt, and sober tie you wear to important meetings—and a prayer shawl? A family's favorite expression or a liturgy? The way we set our table and what we put on an altar? In the end it's not a question of ritual or no ritual: it's *what* ritual and the extent to which it defines who we are and where we belong. Of course, there are some rituals that have more meaning than others, that go deeper and wider in our consciousness. But even the seemingly trivial or irrational ones can have an effect on our psyches. There's a ritual not to wear linen and wool at the same time. That's a hard one to explain, but certainly the practice invites us to dress with a consciousness beyond vanity: What is our clothing made of; where does it come from; are we even aware of why we choose the clothing we do? Is it to signify status, or to make us look sexy, thin, or powerful? The extent to which we enter into and participate in any ritual determines the extent to which it will open our minds and hearts.

It takes time and attention to develop a practice, and all rituals are in danger of becoming rote and boring. That's why seeing and participating in another group's rituals can be so exciting and engaging; they're fresh and exotic—and we don't have to work so hard to have an enlivening experience. My experience is that rituals were designed for the spirit, not the mind, and often need only a reinvestment in order to once again become forms of enchantment.

In the fall of 2001 I was asked by the producers of PBS's *Frontline* to be part of a special called "Faith and Doubt at Ground Zero." I had no idea what I was going to do on air. How could anything I said begin to capture or heal this unspeakably tragic experience? When the camera crew arrived, I decided to chant an ancient melody used to read the Book of Lamentations on the day that remembers the destruction of the Temple in Jerusalem. But rather than chanting the traditional Hebrew words to that scripture, I chanted the last words left by people trapped inside the World Trade Center on voicemails and in e-mails to their loved ones just minutes before they died; words that were first printed in *The New York Times.* "Honey, something terrible is happening. I don't think I'm going to make it. I love you. Take care of the children." "Mommy, the building is on fire. There's smoke coming through the walls. I can't breathe. I love you, Mommy. Good-bye." I was struck by how little anger or fear was in these messages. Rather there is simply love; love in the face of death born of hate. The chant, too, evokes this experience. There are many centuries of pain and healing in that melody. The response from viewers was so moving. One woman who lost a friend in the Trade Center sent me an e-mail that said, "It was as if the chant were reaching down inside me and pulling out the pain." Reflecting afterward, I thought it must have been the combination of that ancient chant with the fears and sadness that were so acutely alive for everyone that had made such an impact. This one-thousand-eight-hundred-year-old chant had such power and beauty when imbued with contemporary meaning.

Some rituals surprise and move us, uproot and alter us. Others are meant to root us, affirm our relationships, renew our identity, and tell our story.

Some rituals surprise and move us, uproot and alter us. Others are meant to root us, affirm our relationships, renew our identity, and tell our story. Holiday celebrations are among the most powerful of these ritual practices. Forget to wish your spouse Happy Anniversary; fail to give your child a present on her birthday; neglect to send a card to your mom on Mother's Day and you will experience something far more intense than the wrath of God! More importantly, you also will miss an opportunity to affirm and celebrate who you are and what your loved ones are to you.

Then there are spiritual or traditional holidays, like Christmas, Easter, Ramadan, and Yom Kippur, that tell a story about our culture, our values, our history. But this ritualized sacred time is not simply about remembering what happened in the past: We re-enact those stories so that they happen to us. Jews have a plethora of holidays. Perhaps this is so because when one lives with the anxiety of uncertainty, there better be a lot of opportunities to pause and take stock; to connect with others that have come before us; to laugh and cry and sing and dance and eat.

Passover is probably the most brilliant ritual/technology in the Jewish wisdom tradition. On this holiday people gather for a meal called a seder and they re-enact the Exodus from Egypt. We experience in our interior life the movement from slavery to freedom. We taste the trauma of slavery in all its bitterness as well as the sweetness of liberation. And we realize how fortunate and also how enslaved we are—whether by habits and patterns, relationships that no longer suit us, or memories of the past. We feel the tension between the ritual world—how things ought to be—and our everyday world—the way things are. This both roots us and challenges us. And we yearn for our own liberation and that of others. We feel commanded to become redeemers ourselves.

Another powerful Jewish ritual is the blowing of the shofar on Rosh Hashana, the Jewish New Year. The piercing sound is a series of one hundred loud, energetic blasts of a ram's horn. Another year is about to begin; time to WAKE UP to what this last year has been and to walk with intention into the new one. Every spiritual tradition has a technology to call us to consciousness. Some people find this one anachronistic or frighteningly primal. I encourage them to hear it as a cosmic wake-up call or a spiritual alarm clock. If the only alarm we hear is the one that gets us up in time for work every day, then how awake are we really?

Yom Kippur, which comes ten days later, is a day of introspection, a time when we are meant to reflect on how we have missed the mark over the last year, where we could have done better or heard the commandments more deeply. We're meant to take our personal inventory. There's nothing logical, didactic, or intellectualized about this process. The rituals on this holiday have a cumulative, nonverbal power, one that penetrates and unnerves. It's the holiday when Jews pour into synagogues across the world. They want a taste of this power, and to enter deeper into their psyches and encounter a different part of themselves.

Many people who observe Yom Kippur don't realize that it's a practice in which we enact our death. For twenty-five hours we fast from both food and drink; refrain from sexual relations; don't wash or shower; wear nonleather shoes (leather symbolizes life); sit in silence for long periods; and recite liturgy that remembers loved ones who've died and sacrifices people have made. We contemplate, "What would I think about on the last day of my life, or even in the last minutes?" As the day unfolds and our defenses come down, we may think about the time we've wasted, who we love and cherish most and wish we'd spent more time with or cared for a little better. Toward the end of the service, the shofar is sounded again; just one long blast. Dependent only on the breath (and it takes a lot of it!) of the blower, it's almost as if that air were entering into our bodies, bringing us back to life, to a more integrated self.

These two holidays together are called, appropriately, the Days of Awe. We enter the new year with a new perspective. And it hasn't been easy. The sages knew how hard it is to take such a serious look at ourselves. It's painful to reflect on that which we think we can't change; we ache to leave it all behind and just move on; to rush into the new year with our hopes and our dreams. No wonder the American New Year's ritual involves getting drunk, singing a song about forgetting, and making resolutions about the future.

Every year as I stand before a congregation sitting patiently waiting to hear that dramatic blast, I ask them to remember something that

happened last January, last February, last March, one thing they can recall. It's amazing how many people can't do it. And it's amazing how
many tear-filled eyes I see in the pews. The sages had an intuition that
all this remembering, all this awareness of how easy it is to forget and
deny, as painful as it can be, really works; it deepens our relationship to
all that is, and expands our vision of who we are. It empties us out and
allows us to walk into the new year ready to act in the world with renewed wonder and intention.

THE NECESSITY OF TRANSGRESSION

ONE EVENING AFTER I GAVE A LECTURE, A SMALL, SOFT-spoken woman in her fifties approached me and asked me to join her for a cup of coffee. I was ready to say no; it had been a long day, and I didn't know her. But there was a look in her eye that told me this was definitely not about a friendly cup of joe. As we walked across the street to a café, I could see that her body was tense; though the night was mild, she wrapped her coat around herself as if to shield herself from a strong wind. As we sat among the young, hip elite of Seattle, pierced bellies showing, techno music pulsing, she told me her middle-aged story of grief and longing.

Anna had married an older man who was now debilitated by Alzheimer's. His decline in the last two years had been severe, and he could barely speak. Often he didn't even recognize her. She and her husband were both quite conservative and shared a deep respect for Jewish learning. The rabbi with whom she'd consulted had told her that even in considering doing what she was about to tell me, she'd crossed the line.

On the other hand, the friends she confided in, despite their discomfort, were encouraging and supportive. She wanted to have an affair.

> There are no easy answers. Every question and answer is contextual, a moment truth.

Anna had met a man whom she felt she could love. He knew her situation and understood her commitment to care for her husband. She blushed as she told me how much she wanted to be held again, to feel again the pleasure and comfort of being held in someone's arms. Yet she felt she'd be betraying her husband and took the commandment "do not commit adultery" very seriously. She was deeply worried that if she had this affair, something might change in her relationship with her husband, an expression of distance in the nuance of her touch or the tone in her voice. At one point she grabbed my hand and said, "Please tell me what to do."

All spiritual leaders are faced with complex questions of morality from time to time, and it's always tough. There are no easy answers. Like all religious traditions, Judaism has many laws and guidelines; yet every question and answer is contextual, a moment truth. Even the seemingly obvious questions invite conflicting answers, and require us to re-examine what we thought were ironclad precedents. There was no way I could tell Anna what to do, pronounce a verdict on her wrenching dilemma. Instead, I said the first thing that came into my head when she'd begun talking, her coat still wrapped tightly around her. Could she recall the first value judgment in the Bible, the premise for the creation of Eve for Adam? I could see her eyes soften as she answered, "It is not good to be alone."

A fifth-century sage taught, "More meritorious is a transgression performed with good intent than a *mitzvah* fulfilled with an ulterior motive. Could it be better to do the wrong thing with good intention than the right thing with wrongful intention?" To be sure, the commandments are meant to be observed, but the sages also understood that the commandment that overrides all others is "choose life." And sometimes fulfilling that injunction means breaking rules, crossing boundaries, hearing the unconventional commanding voice. This is the voice that launches us into pathlessness, into territory where the old rules no longer chart our way. This, after all, is the reality of our lives: a process that asks us to respect conventional boundaries but also transgress those limits when we need to create new, more inclusive borders.

There's a Talmudic story in which the rabbis pray for the end of the evil inclination, or as psychologists might call it, the libido. But God warned them: Without the evil inclination the world would not exist.

The rabbis persevered and so God banished the evil inclination. As a result, no houses were built, no children were born. Without boundary-shattering libido, creativity isn't possible.

The spark of historical development is rooted in the challenge to accepted boundaries. Discontinuity is vital to the success of continuity, for it allows ideas and societies to evolve and grow. Innovation begins with transgression. When I ask Jewish audiences to name the three most important Jews of the modern period they answer: Marx, Freud, and Einstein. Each was a radical transgressor of the status quo. And so, too, are the greatest intellectual and artistic heroes from Copernicus to Spinoza, Beethoven to Darwin, van Gogh to Simone de Beauvoir, who defied the norms of their times, as did our greatest religious leaders such as Moses, Buddha, Jesus, and Muhammad. The major pivotal movements of American history such as the American Revolution, the Abolition Movement, the Civil Rights and Feminist Movements, all defied the prevalent laws and ideologies of their day. By transgressing precedent, these movements produced new, life-affirming social conditions that changed all our lives for the better.

I might never have become a rabbi had I not broken the rules of the yeshiva, the Jewish high school I attended. By today's standards my misbehavior might seem minor, but in the traditional setting in which I was educated it was serious business worthy of expulsion. The yeshiva was a world apart, far removed from popular culture, seemingly immune to the sea changes in society of the late '60s and early '70s. At fifteen, I snuck out of my dorm room to go to a Bob Dylan concert, a benefit concert for Rubin "Hurricane" Carter, whom many felt had been wrongly imprisoned. I was passionate about the cause and of course I loved Dylan with that intense teenage adoration of a favorite rock band.

I also had an inchoate sense that the concert was connected to what I was studying in yeshiva. There's a line in the Talmud that alerts us, "There are times when in order to do God's will, you will need to undermine the Torah." Rock and roll at its best is about breaking boundaries in search of a new kind of wisdom. The concert was my version of the forbidden fruit, and I knew I had to eat. I had gone to Madison Square Garden by myself, scared and apprehensive, but by the time my roommate pulled me up through the window of my dorm I felt changed, invigorated, dangerously alive. I realized I could be a seeker in more ways than one, that Judaism was not restricted to an insider, elite, tribal philosophy but could flourish in the world and be of the world. I could break boundaries and return inside richer and wiser and ready for more.

Maybe this is in part why transgression plays such a key role in the biblical texts. Transgression, after all, underlies the most dramatic story of our beginnings. The very first human act in the Book of Genesis is a trespass of staggering proportions, an outright defiance of the second of the very first commandments, "Do not eat of the tree." The breach was not, however, some impulsive decision borne of base temptation but a conscious move to expand reality, a willful decision to take a giant step into the unknown. Eve knows exactly what she's doing, and is well aware of its consequences. She has heard the warning and knows that if they eat, they will die. She spends several verses questioning, hesitating, and wondering. But when the serpent tells Eve, "your eyes will be opened and you will be like God, who knows good and bad," she sees that across the boundary is wisdom. And she decides it's worth the risk.

The biblical texts are in part a series of teachings about a lineage of transgressors. The word Hebrew—*ivri*—actually means "one who crosses over"; the name of the very first patriarch is Abraham Haivri, Abraham "the boundary crosser." And so he was—smasher of his father's idols, who leaves his home and undermines the conventions of his day. In every generation to follow, transgression ushers in the next stage of evolution. One generation after Abraham, Rebecca lies outright to her husband, Isaac, in order to gain the birthright for her favorite son, Jacob. Jacob, the boy who stole his brother's blessing and whose name means "heel," eventually becomes Israel, "he who wrestles with God." And, in turn, his sons sell their brother Joseph into slavery, yet become the tribes that will populate the Promised Land.

The Bible isn't prescribing sin but rather describing the human journey. The Bible understands that as hurtful as transgressions can be, there can be no life journey without them. Most of us lead conventional lives. We want to avoid the discomforts that arise from complications. But the full, creative life must be open to unpredictability. Jewish wisdom urges us to open our eyes to the possibility of change, even to the need to break a rule. Sometimes the only way to grow is to take a bite of the apple.

Perhaps this is why the messianic figure King David, the builder of the holy city of Jerusalem, the writer of Psalms, and for Christians the direct ancestor of Jesus, came from a long line of serious transgressors—sinners of the first order. Both sides of his family include generations of women who consciously choose life over toeing the line. After all the men of Sodom and Gomorrah have been killed, Lot's daughters fear that there will be no one left to carry on their family life. And so the daughters intoxicate and seduce their father. David's mother is a descendent of this morally complex incestuous relationship.

Transgression plays a key role in the biblical texts, which are, in part, a series of teachings about transgressors.

David's father is a descendent of Judah, the founder of the tribe we know as today's Jews. When Judah's son dies tragically, his daughter-in-law Tamar is bereft. She desperately misses her husband and has been left childless. It pains her to think that her husband's line will not continue and she will never be a mother. But far from passively accepting her fate, Tamar's response is nothing less than shocking. After months of intense mourning, she hears that her father-in-law will be coming to town. Maybe this is my chance, she thinks, my chance to provide my husband with an heir, for me to have a child to hold and love. Tamar removes her widow's garb, dresses herself to look like a harlot, and veils herself so she won't be recognized. Upon seeing her, Judah is gripped with lust and gives her his seal and his staff as collateral in order to sleep with her on the spot.

Amazingly, the place where Tamar stands to veil herself is called "opening of the eyes," intentionally echoing the story of Eve, a phrase captured in the daily morning blessing, "Praised are you who opens the eyes of the blind." The place of deception and violation is also the place of revelation. Even Judah seems to intuit this: Later, when he learns of Tamar's pregnancy, he says, "You are a more righteous person than me." The seeds of transgression can bear fruit. David the redeemer is a descendent of this morally complex relationship as well.

But perhaps it is in the biblical account of Aaron that we see most dramatically how an act of blatant irreverence can create an even more authentic reverence. Aaron, Moses's older brother, has been appointed the High Priest of the Israelites, their spiritual leader, chief guard of the sacred laws. And yet he becomes an idolater, the architect of the golden calf. This provocative infraction nearly leads to the destruction of the community. How can Aaron be both a scandalous rebel and an upright, holy man? How can Aaron's descendents continue through the ages to be the nation's priests?

A radical suggestion: Aaron became the High Priest precisely because he'd been a defiant idolater. He had to experience one truth before he could embrace another. The Israelites could follow him because, like them, he allowed his yearning to lead him astray. Much like the former addict who becomes the most effective drug counselor, another kind of priest, Aaron, too, had been there, hit bottom, and climbed back up to new heights.

An astonishing story recounts a parent's frustration with a child's failure to transgress. I heard this Hasidic tale from Rabbi Rami Shapiro about Reb Shneur Zalman of Liadi, the mystic thinker who lived in the late 1700s and owned a majestic library of precious texts. There is a mystical belief that certain wisdom books have unique powers. One such remarkable book in his library featured a label "Do not open or risk losing the world to come." One horrible day a massive fire destroyed the library, and Reb Shneur Zalman turned to his son and asked, "Did you ever look in the book, the one with the warning on it?" The son, surprised and expecting to please his father during this difficult time, said,

"No, Father, I never opened it. I promise you." His father looked saddened and asked, "Are you sure you never read any of it? Can you recall even a single teaching that might now restore my spirit?" Much to the son's dismay, his father bowed his head and wept: "You weren't willing to sacrifice the world to come for wisdom?"

Unlike Reb Shneur Zalman, most of us respond to a child's infraction—be it drawing on the walls or taking drugs—by devising the harshest punishment we think appropriate. At our best, we might just lose it and scream our heads off. But at that moment, we squander a precious opportunity to draw our children closer and teach them something crucial about themselves and life. And we also shortchange our own learning and development, as well as our intimacy. What if, before we judged or punished, we asked ourselves and our child: What is the yearning behind the transgression? How can we help to address it? What might we all learn from their lapses?

The rush to externalize judgments is a clue that we haven't truly recognized our own yearnings. How instructive it is, for example, that nearly every one of the politicians who aggressively condemned President Clinton for his behavior in the Oval Office also had committed adultery while in office. How much more rewarding it would have been for our society if, instead, we looked at Clinton's offenses as an opportunity to dive into our own dualities and transgressive desires. Isn't this what Jesus asked of us when he stood in the public square about to witness the murder of a prostitute and declared, "Who will cast the first stone?" Before punishing others for their yearnings and indiscretions we ought to unearth our own.

Only when we bring our yearnings and desires to consciousness, can we address them before acting on them.

On a national news show, I was asked to comment on a bizarre and disturbing trend occurring just two years after 9/11. New York City firemen were leaving their wives to marry the widows of their comrades. When I first saw the *New York Post* headline, I reacted with not only discomfort but also condemnation. How dare these supposedly noble men create more pain in a sick attempt to address another's?

But just before going on the air, I remembered another aspect of that article. The firemen it quoted referred to their comrades as brothers. And I found myself talking about the ancient practice of Levirate marriage which sanctions, even requires that a man marry his brother's widow. I'd always thought of this commandment as a practical solution appropriate for its polygamist times, a rule that protected the widow and insured the continuation of the family line. But could this ancient imperative be speaking to us now as well? I reflected on how I would feel if one of my own brothers died: How I would want to protect his wife, comfort her, take her in.

I might even begin to feel sexual stirrings borne out of a new kind of intimacy and her need to be loved and held. By acknowledging this possibility I then understood the yearnings of these firemen for their "brothers' " spouses, the desire of these trained rescuers to reach out to the wives of their colleagues who, unlike themselves, had not survived the horrid tragedy of that morning. This seeming archaic commandment, in fact, addressed a deep and positive human yearning.

If we were able to recognize this longing, would society and the firemen have been able to handle this situation differently? What if we had gone to church or synagogue and heard of this ancient law? What if the firemen's longing to protect their "brothers' " spouses had been acknowledged, affirmed, and discussed? What would we have all learned?

I have been accused of rationalizing transgression, and there is always that danger. However, there is no way to avoid rationalization whether we follow the rules or break them. When we simply observe the law, the rationalization has generally been done for us by parents, teachers, leaders—our culture. The boundary has been given and we unquestioningly accept it. When we choose to transgress, hopefully with awe and trembling, we do the rationalizing ourselves and so it is inevitably more apparent.

Only when we bring our yearnings and desires to consciousness, can we address them before acting on them. No wonder, then, that our religious or legal traditions anticipate transgression and build in guidelines designed to minimize harm. The biblical text makes it clear that humans were meant to be vegetarian, in accordance with the wish to protect and cherish all living beings. But the text also recognized the human desire for meat and the inevitability of transgression. And so rules develop that accept these desires but also minimize the pain and suffering of animals. These are the practices called *Kashrut*, or Kosher laws.

Jewish wisdom says "yes" to the impulse but builds in footholds along the slippery slope of transgression. The lesson here is fundamental: It is, in fact, possible to balance our boundary crossing with thoughtfulness and care. Of course, there's no way to predict the outcome of our actions. This is why we can't expect simple answers to such edgy societal issues as stem-cell research, abortion, genetic testing, and cloning. We are justified in worrying about what may follow these advances, even if the benefits are enormous. But we also need to worry about a society that refuses to take any risks whatsoever.

There is no way to predict the outcome of our actions. Life is rarely neat and predictable despite our best efforts.

Instead of allowing our fear and anxieties to legislate against scientific innovation we can see that—like our eating from the Tree of Knowledge—it is part of our natural human curiosity and, therefore, inevitable. Instead of allowing our fear and anxiety about the new to legislate against any controversial practice, we can welcome the exploration, while also preparing ourselves for its risks. Why not put in place the safeguards that might prevent the very results we fear? That way we can embrace the noble need to push, and even transcend, our boundaries, and keep ourselves from spinning out of control. Of course, even when our intentions are good and we do our best to build in safeguards or guidelines, sometimes we cause harm. This is the risk of being fully human.

As I sat in that Seattle café I wondered for a moment if it was Anna's lot in life to be unloved and lonely. After all, the law is the law, and adultery can't just be sanctioned for convenience or just to make someone feel better. But then I came to a deeper teaching, that the very purpose of the marital boundary is to preserve love, to ensure that neither mate be left alone. It could be that Anna would in some way be observing the spirit of the commandment by consciously breaking it. Most of the time, it is far better to obey the rules of a society. There is a reason they have endured: They work. Until they don't.

As we continued our conversation, I suggested Anna explore ways that she might connect with her prospective lover while protecting her husband and preserving the commitment she'd made to him. She said she could create strict limits around the time she spent with her lover, keeping their encounters to twice a week and making sure to be home well before her husband awoke in the morning. She would be open with his sister, her fellow caregiver, so that Anna didn't feel she was sneaking around. She'd give herself a time limit of three months, during which she would check in with her sister-in-law regularly to gain another perspective on her behavior; someone who could tell Anna whether she noticed any change in her behavior or attitude toward her husband.

There was a risk here. This choice might be a mistake and might cause hurt and disappointment, but there was no way of knowing, of revealing a new truth about her life, unless she tried. Life is rarely neat and predictable despite our best efforts. Others might have advised differently, but everyone could appreciate the consciousness and mindfulness behind her efforts; the footholds she attempted to create along the slippery slope. In some ways Anna had created more boundaries, more rules than existed before she considered having the affair.

We are all familiar with a more common story: an unhappy spouse who has an affair, followed by a bitter, wrenching divorce. We rush to judgment, angry at the violation, upset with the way the children were unprepared, irate with the unnecessarily vicious divorce proceedings. But this is rarely the full story. Sometimes a new passion unlocks a creative stream that a marriage had dammed. Sometimes, unfortunately, it takes all this pain to reach a new level of self-understanding.

When my brother underwent just this sort of transgression—an affair that ended in divorce and temporary estrangement from one of his children—I too had the usual response of indignation. Why couldn't he have initiated marriage counseling; why didn't he start divorce proceedings in a deliberate, conscious way, or prepare his children as best he could? It was messy, really messy. And the cost was great for him, his wife, and especially for his children, to whom he'd been a wonderful and dedicated father. His wife made it difficult for him to see them for quite some time. He paid a price. Yet for the first time I can remember, he talked about how loved he felt, how something had been awakened in him that seemed to have been asleep for an awfully long time.

Sometimes acting out is the only way one's eyes can be opened. Although his relationship didn't end up lasting, my brother's musical career took off in a way it probably couldn't have in the marriage, and he seemed to have a zest and an openness I'd never seen in him before. He also seemed to have reached a new level of self-understanding. Eventually, he was able to connect with his children again. There was a lot of hurt there, and years later the healing is still underway.

I didn't approve of what my brother had done; I wished so much that he had found another way. And his actions gave rise to a lot of uncomfortable feelings about times in my own marriage, times I've felt tempted. He'd done the unthinkable and suddenly the unthinkable became real and possible for everyone around him. How dare he! At the same time, I so much wanted him to be happy. And then one night on the phone a few years after the divorce, he recounted the many nights he'd cried, agonizing over the terrible hurt he'd caused. He was afraid that he'd never be able to put his life back together and, most importantly, that he'd never again be the kind of father he'd been before.

But he also went on to describe a recent night he'd spent with his younger son, how they'd talked for hours, how honest and loving they'd been with each other. He said, "Irwin, I wish I'd done it differently, but it was the best thing that ever happened to me." His transgression, disturbing and hurtful as it was, dimmed with the knowledge of the growth that had come with it. I felt so much tenderness for him in that moment. I was overwhelmed by an older-brother impulse to protect him from all future hurt. He'd had so much already.

Just before Adam and Eve are banished from the Garden of Eden, God clothes them with "garments made of skins" even though they'd already made coverings for themselves. Before they are sent out into the wide world with all its harshness and uncertainty, God acts out of love, despite understandable disappointment and anger with their transgression.

There's new life after Eden.

YEARNING FOR
LOVE

COVENANT

IT ALL BEGINS WITH THE YEARNING FOR LOVE. THE observation "It is not good to be alone" is the first intuition about human beings in the Bible, in the story of Adam and Eve. In this simple statement, we're taught that love is the fundamental human longing. And this is just the beginning: the entire Torah is a commentary on loving. If it were a Buddhist torah, it might have been a *midrash* on how to transcend suffering; a Hindu torah would have reflected on the awakening of awareness; a scientific *midrash* would have insights about randomness—all incredibly expansive and profound teachings. Yet all these traditions would agree that love eases suffering, awakens us to another dimension, and makes meaning out of randomness. As the prophet Isaiah observes, "Love swallows up death."

The first teaching about yearning in the Bible is told from the point of view of the God character. It's the Creator that makes this first value judgment. And the reader can't help but wonder: How does God know it is not good to be alone? Wow—God must know what it feels like to be lonely! Maybe God created human beings out of a deep need to love and be loved. The biblical author takes us into the realm of poetry, of myth, of imagination, telling a story that invites us to wonder if maybe we are here on this planet for those very same reasons.

The love story between God and humankind is like every romantic epic. It begins in paradise. Before creating Adam, which in Hebrew means "human," God made a wonderful home for this first person to dwell in; a garden of delights. Everything is perfect. And yet life must grow and evolve. Just as plants need soil to thrive, a human being needs relationship. The next loving act is to create a companion for this very first person. The paradox is that by creating Eve for Adam, God assures God's own loneliness. After the birth of Eve, the text tells us that henceforth every human being will leave the mother and father to cling to a lover. Isn't what's true for God true for all of us? Even when we love so deeply and fully, we are also still alone. We give up so much of ourselves, and we are always yearning.

The biblical poet gives us such a beautiful scene. Adam goes to sleep and awakens having been divided into male and female. It's love at first sight, and Adam sings a love song: "This one at last is the bone of my bones and the flesh of my flesh." Like Adam, don't we all long to become one with someone else, for a kind of unity, a person who will complete us? Don't we yearn for unconditional love, a love that will last forever? And don't we all enter into relationships with the expectation that love will feel good, that it will bring happiness and fulfillment, that we will no longer be alone? The poet recognized these profound yearnings, but also understood that such a love wasn't possible, nor was it even desirable if the world were to continue to develop and expand.

Maybe this is why the poet chose such an interesting, rather unromantic phrase to describe Eve: "a fitting helper." The word for "fitting" in Hebrew—ezer—is itself a paradox: it means "different and equal," "facing and separate," "in devoted opposition." Eve will not only be one with her lover, she will also challenge him, as will he her. They will help each other to become more fully human.

Eden is really a story about intimacy. It requires that we hold in our consciousness two intuitions that seem contradictory: Our lover is both "flesh of my flesh" and "a fitting helper." The experience of each seems so different. When I am in "bone of my bone" mode, it all seems so "Edenic." When I'm feeling the pull of my fitting helper it can be uncomfortable, even painful. Intimacy is a dance of sameness and difference, a dynamic container for our growth and expansion.

Whenever I counsel a young couple as they prepare for their wedding, I tell them that far from "settling down," now it's really going to be unsettling. Even for those who've been living together for a while, I feel compelled to remind them that a committed relationship is going to feel bad almost as much as it feels good. Their fights will be as crucial as their lovemaking. What they disagree on will be as important as what they agree on. Intimacy is a place of multiple truths, differing points of view, and misunderstandings, as well as romance and oneness. Intimacy is a never-ending dance between loneliness and connection; expectation and disappointment; hot sex and boring sex. There's the greatest risk of loss and the greatest hope for gain.

It's amazing how many couples come to me on the brink of divorce having never understood or accepted the wondrous, excruciating dialectic that is intimacy. It's not just that "marriage is a lot of work," as I hear so many people say. It's that marriage, or any close relationship, is a place where you learn about your self—your shadows and your light. It's a place of commandment and transgression.

> **Intimacy is a place of multiple truths, differing points of view, and misunderstandings, as well as romance and oneness.**

It's a place where we are meant to wrestle with ourselves, as well as our loved one, in order to give birth to a new world.

We've all experienced that moment when we emerge from, or sometimes are thrust out of, paradise, that first blissful phase of romantic love. The first fight, the first time she doesn't laugh at your joke, the first shattering of the thin glass that is romance. The wine glass that is stomped on at every Jewish wedding is meant to symbolize the wish that the couple will remain whole despite inevitable conflict. The hope is that each shattering will lead to an opportunity for growth and renewal. This ritual comes at the very end of the marriage ceremony after which everyone yells, "Mazel Tov!" Congratulations on finding a place that can withstand your brokenness.

Here's a recent example from my own life. Twenty years into my marriage, after what I thought was a lively and delightful dinner party, my wife, Dana, confronted me. "Why do you always have to be the center of attention, always talking, always performing?" I was shocked. I had always been the talker, she the listener, the observer. After most parties we went to, she would recount all the innuendos and gossip I had missed as I worked the party. We were a perfect match that way. And it had always felt right. Now I felt defensive and oddly frightened by her comment.

I experienced it as a shattering of our finely balanced relationship, a kind of ending. But we sat with it, not for days but for many weeks. And there was a strain between us that whole time, frequent bickering, criticism, an all-around unpleasantness, especially at the next few parties. Almost two months after the fight, we went to a dinner gathering. I went determined to keep my mouth shut the entire evening, mostly out of resentment. Let her carry the conversation for a change. I thought she'd look at me longingly before we finished the appetizer. But she didn't. She came alive that night, talking and laughing and reaching out to people she would have previously quietly observed. My anger turned to wonder. As I watched her I could feel love well up inside me. I felt I was discovering a whole new part of my wife after two decades of thinking I knew everything. I also had a revelation about myself. I realized that I could enjoy being quiet, that I was just as much a participant when I was observing and listening as when I was talking. When we arrived home, we made love like new lovers.

On a grander scale, the same thing happens to Adam and Eve. They're cast out of Eden, having hid from God, Adam blaming Eve for everything. Yet the first thing they do after leaving is to make love. The word for lovemaking in Hebrew is the same as the word for wisdom. They now "knew" each other deeply. They've made mistakes together, disappointed each other, failed each other, and walked out of the garden with each other. After they left paradise, that first blush of love, their journey of intimacy truly begins.

So often, like Adam, we choose a lover in order to fill something inside us, to find the flesh of our flesh, and we project onto that person our greatest hopes. This is also true with our children and our friend-ships, but with romantic love, the bubble is that much bigger and likely to pop. We may choose someone who we think is like us, who affirms our values, our hopes, our dreams. Someone who, literally, turns us on, at least to those parts of ourselves we want to see. Or, like me, we may pick someone who is our opposite, who will complete us, who will be our other side. Love is indeed blind. We don't see our lovers' flaws, nor do they see ours.

This is the narcissistic stage of love ("bone of *my* bone," as Adam says). We put our best sides forward in the effort to win the person we so desire; we idealize them as well as ourselves. We feel we'd do any-thing for our loved one. This is a crucial phase in any romantic rela-tionship. It is the love that is automatically given to us by nature. It's what opens up our shell and softens us so that the yearning comes through and a deeper love becomes possible.

Soon after we met, I traveled all the way to Israel to see Dana—who was spending a year abroad—for just four days. But it was less about her than me. I wanted to win her, make her mine, somehow guarantee that she would love me. I wanted her to think I'd give her anything. I didn't show her the withholding part; that would come years later. And thank God, because both of us yearned for something more. Just as powerful as that first bloom of romance was a longing for roots, to go deeper into the soil, to the depths of my being and hers as well. Each of us wanted a fitting helper.

Of course, one cannot exist without the other. Unless we continue to experience our lover as "flesh of my flesh" we won't be an effective or authentic helper. And unless we genuinely help each other by challeng-ing and being challenged, we cannot continue to feel that oneness. Nei-ther God nor Adam understood this at the outset. Not surprisingly, God erred on the side of seeing relationship as opposition, creating a fitting helper. This is a foreshadowing of God's disappointment with Adam and Eve after they eat from the tree. God feels contradicted and op-posed, the same way we all feel when those we love don't listen to us, do what we ask, or take our advice. The God character's expectations are always out of this world: In theological language, they are infinite while we are finite. On the other hand, Adam favors "flesh of my flesh" because he is young and new to love. He's intoxicated with the fantasy of being one with another. In the end, he, too, discovers the dance of intimacy. He eats the fruit at Eve's urging; only then can he begin to "know" her and himself more deeply.

The real work of intimacy comes when automatic love ends and intentional love begins; when we leave the garden. Continuing and maintaining that newness and passion (without changing lovers, which is one way to keep things fresh!) we must reveal more and more of ourselves and unveil more and more of the other person. Monogamy is not some pious rule that we need to follow. It's a depth practice— a way to understand self and other. This can be risky, which is why some people make the unconscious decision to let the passion die out. We must feel vulnerable and exposed in order to keep love alive. We must say whatever needs to be said, and do whatever it takes to keep a relationship growing.

Monogamy is a depth practice—a way to understand self and other.

At some point in any romantic relationship there is a crossroads. "Should I stay or should I go?" as the Clash so astutely sang. This is the moment when we decide if all the disappointment and vulnerability and risks are worth it. When my sixteen-year-old told me about her first breakup, describing how the relationship had become boring, I found myself trying to explain. "At some point in your life, you'll decide it's not just about pleasure and passion; 'not being boring' is no longer the point. Give yourself a while, sweetheart," I said glibly, trying to convince myself I wasn't repeating my parents' annoying and patronizing refrain: "You're just not ready yet." She surprised me by asking, "Are you and mommy bored? Do you think about leaving each other?" Now I'd done it! She was already upset, and I wanted so much to reassure her. But knowing her, she'd see right through it. I said, "Yes, sometimes. But I'm pretty sure we're 'lifers.'" I looked forward to the day that Gabriella would experience the dance that is intimacy, when she'd be able to celebrate the dynamic range that is love: fragility and solidity; boredom and spontaneity; selfishness and empathy; acceptance and rejection.

When we can withstand those edgy times, bridge those great divides, even the most excruciating times of insecurity and vulnerability can themselves become incredible turn-ons. I like to imagine Adam and Eve in bed one night well after they left the garden. For whatever reason—maybe they've had a fight, maybe it's the anniversary of their banishment—Eve turns to Adam and asks, "Adam, I've always wondered, why did you blame me? So I gave you the fruit. You're a big boy. You could have said no." Adam, of course, immediately feels attacked and exposed. He wants to lash out. "You did it! You listened to the serpent, not me." And then, "For God's sake, aren't you over it by now?" Blame is a big part of every relationship; it's a primal protective device, a shield against vulnerability. But imagine what the postfight lovemaking would be like if Adam said, "I could have said no. I wanted to make you happy. It's amazing how weak I can be and how powerful you can be. And then I was afraid. I couldn't face what I'd done. I'm sorry."

When we hide parts of who we are from our lover, we just ensure that it is not the full me that is being loved. And so love ends up feeding our doubt about the relationship. Sometimes Dana and I do a "fitting helper" practice. It's a way to get our disappointments and frustrations out in the open where we can look at them and hopefully work them through. We ask each other whether there's anything we might have felt too uncomfortable, embarrassing, obnoxious, or scary to share about the other over the last weeks or months. Of course, the first thing to come to mind is the one thing we'd rather keep hidden. But more often than not, after much discussion and sometimes tension, we're on solid ground again, the relationship more rich and nurturing than it had been before. Intimacy means acknowledging to each other, "Okay, I'm greedy, horny, arrogant, lazy, flirtatious, jealous, angry, nerdy, insecure." And then feeling loved. Of course, it's helpful to try to keep a balance. Dana and I also reverse the game. We practice sharing what is good and beautiful and pleasant about each other, and sometimes this is just as challenging; it can feel corny and vulnerable, and we may have a sinking feeling that words just don't suffice.

All of us yearn for a person with whom we can be vulnerable, and yet be embraced. We all long for a place that can tolerate the inevitable turbulence, disruption, anxiety, and anguish. And we want to feel cherished and celebrated as well. Jewish wisdom calls this kind of relationship a covenant. A covenantal relationship is an ever-deepening love born of the grit and insecurity of everyday life. Covenant acknowledges the paradox that the more deeply we love, the more expectations we have and the harder we fall; the more intimate we are the more likely we are to get hurt. These paradoxes can be really scary. We realize that our lover will help us grow, but as we grow we risk growing apart from the very person who helped us get here. The more secure we want to feel the more vulnerable we have to make ourselves. Our lover loves us, both as we are and as we can be—we're always being pushed. Covenantal love creates both incredible safety and radical insecurity.

Covenant is really a fancy word for agreement, but what an agreement it is! It's a container for loving in all its variations. It holds the promise that the highs and lows, the brokenness and healing will all be on the inside of the relationship and that there'll be enough pleasure and celebration to hold it all together. A covenant is like the thick cloth that contains the glass stomped on by the groom.

The word covenant is first used in the story of Noah and the ark, the most frightening and destructive story in the Biblical texts. It's only the third story in Genesis: It didn't take long for God to feel betrayed and lose patience! We learn early on that God's love could be a rage-full love, as it can be for all of us. In Hebrew the word "Noah" means "comfort." Noah is God's great hope: "Noah found favor with the Lord." But humankind as a whole has proven to be a great disappointment. People have lashed out at each other with murderous violence. God in turn lashes out at them, creating a flood that obliterates all living things— with the exception of Noah, his family, and two of every kind of animal

(a way for God to hedge bets). One could certainly say this manifestation of love is nothing less than abusive; I wouldn't wish it on anyone.
And yet out of this supreme act of violence emerges a covenant, a promise to never again destroy humankind. "Never again will I doom the
earth because of humankind . . . nor will I ever again destroy every living being, as I have done." This is when God creates the famous rainbow
as a symbol of the promise, and a new kind of love is born. The disappointments continue, and God comes pretty close to once again obliter-
ating humankind. But every transgression and conflict can now be seen
in the context of this tremendous promise.

Yet even then covenant is not a guarantee. Paradoxically, covenant is
a commitment that acknowledges impermanence—which is exactly
what makes the commitment real. There's a great scene in the comedy
series *Curb Your Enthusiasm* which captures this perfectly. Larry David,
the show's star, is standing at the altar with his wife of ten years, renewing his vows when the rabbi says ". . . forever, and forever for all eternity
'til death do us part." He looks puzzled and then anxious. He hems and
haws. His wife asks him what's wrong, and he says, "Well, uh, all eternity? I don't know about eternity." It's no accident that this vow isn't
part of the traditional Jewish wedding ceremony.

Knowing that a relationship can end makes it even more precious
and intensifies the yearning to make it last. Maybe that's why Judaism
not only has a sacred practice of marriage; it has a sacred practice of divorce. There's a Talmudic story about one of the most celebrated rabbis,
Rabbi Akiva, who at the age of forty had discovered the love of his life.
His passionate love affair with Rachel is utterly transforming. He was
able to see the spiritual depth of the Song of Songs, an erotic love story;
and he argued that it should be included in the biblical canon. If it
wasn't for him, this incredible text might have been lost. One day the
sages were arguing about what could be justification for divorce. Everyone agreed that adultery was the thing that would surely drive couples
apart. Rabbi Akiva laughed. "Don't be silly. It could be over the burning
of dinner." How odd that a happily married man would say such a

thing. He knew that the more deeply you love, the more you know how truly delicate it is. He understood that there's no such thing as a great love, only great loving, a never-ending process of learning about oneself and each other. He also knew that any marriage has a better shot at lasting if we sweat the small stuff, if we keep our eyes and heart open, especially when pettiness threatens to pull us apart.

Yet in our most important relationships the stakes are so high that we convince ourselves otherwise. Jewish wisdom acknowledges that even the greatest loves may not last forever. We are always on the razor's edge. We really never can know if we love someone or they love us 100 percent. We can never be sure that the brokenness won't drive us apart. Maybe that's why we need to say "I love you" so often, and why we need to hear it. We need to remind ourselves of the longing for an enduring love even while acknowledging that it's not really possible to fulfill. The yearning itself can keep the relationship strong.

I met Dana when we were teenagers, and we've been married for twenty-four years. I'm often asked what our secret is. Of course, there is none. Dana's patience and calm enable her to tolerate an awful lot. We laugh a lot. And we're honest with each other, sometimes to a fault. If there's one aspect of my personality that might help us along the rocky road of marriage, it's that I tend to respond to many of our tense moments with a question I internalized from years of immersion in Jewish wisdom: "Where are you?"

"Where are you?" is the question the God character asked Adam in the garden after Eve and he ate the fruit. We may hear the question as a judgment and so we hide as the first couple did, pulling away in our fear of being discovered and rejected. The Hasidic Rebbe Shlomo Carlbach taught that Adam and Eve were thrown out of the garden because they thought they had to be perfect in their relationship. But this is not what paradise is all about. In paradise one day we are good; one day we are bad. One day we get things right; one day we make mistakes. We can't stay in paradise if we're afraid to mess up. So the original "sin" isn't sexual. It's not disobedience. Rather the sin is letting insecurity and distrustfulness take over. Reb Shlomo said that had Adam not blamed Eve, had he owned up to his mistake rather than exposing her, they would still be in Eden. If we trust, take those risks, expose our flaws, we, too, can stay there. Covenantal love is sharing the struggle to know: eating from the tree together, and together discovering wisdom.

When "the food is burned," when the small stuff over which most couples fight threatens to blow up, my response on a good day is to enter into a silence in which I hear some variation of that same question. "Where are we coming from? Where is she now? Where am I?" It doesn't always work, and I lose it sometimes, believe me. But when it does, it's amazing what happens.

One Sunday afternoon Dana wanted to see a movie at a time that interfered with a football game I had planned to watch—a classic husband-wife scenario. I was willing to go to the movie before or after the game, but the times didn't work. When I suggested going to a different film, the fight began. Dana stormed out of the apartment and then called me from downstairs on her cell phone. She was crying and yelling: I always chose the movies we saw; she always went along with it; why did I always have to be in the driver's seat? My first response was "always?" Come on! I almost said it, which would have sent us on another round of yelling. But luckily I heard the silence and then the question, "Where is she?" And where she was, my gut told me, was with her father. He'd been diagnosed with a tumor in his pancreas the week before. Depending on what the tests told us, it could be very serious. She had no power to change anything. Suddenly, the movie took on great importance. Our conversation ended in tears, but of a very different sort. Dana went to the movie of her choice on her own. When she came home she said the film was great. So was the game.

Covenantal love means learning to support our lovers, whether silently or in words or actions, to help them discover themselves in the emotional storm. The most committed relationship is called *kiddushin* from the word "holy." To be holy is to be intensely alive; it also means to be set apart, special. So the secret to a committed relationship is covenant; a context or container in which to do our most risky loving. It's a place for our moment truths to wrestle with each other in a perpetual dance of discovery. And, more than that, it represents our deepest hope that it will all hang together in the end, that the loving will continue, expand, and nurture us for the rest of our lives.

GIVING AND RECEIVING

IT'S AMAZING HOW WE TEACH OUR CHILDREN WHAT WE ourselves need to learn. We yearn for them to understand what we never did; to be the perfect, balanced people we always wanted to be. Yet our feelings are often contradictory. We want them to have it all, but not be greedy. We want them to be giving, but not give it all away. We want them to have everything they want but to always share. I remember the incredible tension I used to feel when I took my daughters to the sandbox in Central Park; not among the kids but among the parents. The sandbox is a kind of testing ground for our feelings about giving and taking, offering and receiving.

Parents would be sitting around the edges, presiding over sand throwing, shovel snatchings, dump truck nappings, deciding whose hole was whose, who knocked over whose sand castle. Most of the parents spoke softly, coaxingly, patiently to their kids, urging them toward the right thing to do, as the parents saw it; looking apologetically at the parent of the wronged child or beseechingly at the parent who did nothing to control theirs. I myself remember seesawing between not wanting Gabriella to take someone else's stuff and hoping Talia wouldn't too easily cede territory. I'd feel flashes of anger at the child who would take too much, and embarrassment for the ones who let the others walk all over them. I also occasionally would be really touched by the child who would give a toy away without asking for one back or the other child

> The "give and take" that we all accept as an integral part of life and love is actually pretty complicated.

who would graciously accept it. I surprised myself with the intensity of my feelings. The "give and take" that we all accept as an integral part of life and love is actually pretty complicated.

I'll never forget the afternoon in the neighborhood bookstore when Gabriella brought over a copy of Shel Silverstein's classic children's book *The Giving Tree* for me to read. I'd heard of the book but had never seen it before. As I thumbed through the pages, I began to get that same feeling I had at the sandbox, and it only got worse the more I read. Fortunately, Gabriella turned to another book, because I really didn't want to read it to her. I was horrified. How could this be such a beloved classic? How could anyone read this to their kids?

The story is deceptively simple: A little boy plays on a tree eating its apples, swinging on its branches, and the tree is happy. When the boy gets older he wants toys instead, so the tree tells him to cut his branches to make them, and the tree is once again happy. Later the boy wants a house so he can marry and settle down; the tree tells him to cut more and the tree is happy. When the boy wants a boat to take him away, the tree gives him the remainder of his trunk and—you guessed it—is happy. At the end of the story, the boy stays away for a long time; when he finally returns, the tree, now a stump, tells him that he has nothing left to give. The boy, a bent old man at this point, says he doesn't want anything, he only needs a stump to sit on. And the tree is happy.

I've spent a career teaching people to dive into the stories and texts that provoke the strongest reactions. Where there's discomfort or judgment, a kind of unease or chafing, as a psychologist friend of mine calls it, that's where learning can and needs to happen. It's time to turn it over. *The Giving Tree* really disturbed me—clearly I needed to go there. So I bought the book and looked at it over a period of days. I learned that I'm far from the first person to have a strong response; there are hundreds of pages of commentary on this children's tale: feminist perspectives, religious interpretations, philosophical deconstructions. And young or old, virtually everyone I talked to about the book had an opinion, almost always a strong one. Though a children's book, *The Giving*

Tree has informed my understanding of the most important dynamic in any relationship, especially our most intimate and loving ones: the dance of giving and receiving.

There are so many strong responses to this tale, and each has a moment truth, a powerful teaching about how we see ourselves in a relationship. Shel Silverstein has given us a wonderful tool for uncovering what we most yearn for and also what we're most afraid to face. It may seem obvious—every relationship has give and take, as the expression goes. But nothing is more stressful and unnerving than seeing our most raw and honest responses to this dance. All we need do is pause and explore, and the feelings and anxieties about how we give and receive tend to come pouring out. I've found that this process can be both healing and inspiring. I've also found that there are four most common interpretations of *The Giving Tree*, each of which has much to offer.

The first is what might be called the conventional read. It is a message many of us want to teach our children, perhaps especially because we never quite learned it ourselves. It is the Christian understanding of love. It is also a transpersonal psychological read—one that takes us beyond the ego-self. Here the tree is a selfless, unconditional giver, whole-hearted, joyful, and pure of motive. Giving doesn't diminish the tree but makes it happy. It has no expectations of getting anything back, and it's not trying to prove anything. It simply loves; and love means giving all. In wisdom language, it is abiding love; in religious language, sacrificial love or offering. This love, free of any conditions, allows the boy to live a full and independent life while always staying connected, which is all the tree desires.

Unconditional love is forever on the horizon because it is infinite and we are finite.

I've found that those who resonate with this reading yearn to be able to give unconditionally to those they love. A friend of mine told me, "I made my mother read it again and again. I remember thinking, 'Wow, the tree loves the boy so much, she only wants to make him happy.' I wanted to give that way. I still do." There is a giving self in each of us that wishes we could give all,

surrender in our love. This is Christ dying for us on the cross. It speaks
to a non-rational (not irrational) part of who we are.

Sometimes I wake up in the middle of the night and look at Dana,
and I feel so overwhelmed with love that I feel I'd do anything for her. My
daughters are teenagers now, and to this day I go into their room before
I go to sleep and give each sleeping child a kiss. I always stand there
for what seems like a flash of eternity, feeling a rush of wanting them to
know that I love them more than life itself. Not surprisingly, the words
that flow out of me are, "God, I love you so much." This is a love that
echoes the divine.

We've all had these experiences. And sometimes they are both awesome and frightening. We also feel we fall short. Unconditional love is
forever on the horizon because it is infinite and we are finite. The fact
that I don't always, or even usually, follow through on those night-
time feelings during my daytime life bespeaks my—and all of our—
limitations in giving. Some of us are afraid of being taken advantage of.
We've been disappointed and hurt and abandoned in love, and we've
learned to protect ourselves by giving only so much. And we fear we'll
empty out, with nothing left for ourselves. It takes an incredibly rooted
and secure self to love with no ulterior motives. And most of us can't be
in that self for long.

We hold back, and yet we long to love this way. That's why we create
stories, whether it's *The Giving Tree* (or really, *The Giving It All Tree*), *The
Passion of the Christ*, *The Little Mermaid*, or other "martyr"-like tales. Or
we front-page stories of self-sacrificing mothers who work five jobs,
denying themselves everything to give their child what they need, or the
fireman who runs into a burning building. Whether the story is about unconditional love for God or for another human being, each inspires us to
give a little more of ourselves, to trust that whether reciprocated or not, no
love is lost in the end. We may be scarred or even "stumped," but, like the
tree, the mark of love will be inscribed onto our very being and endure
forever. *The All-Giving Tree* interpretation requires us to ask ourselves: Am
I honestly giving enough or am I holding back out of fear or insecurity?

Then there's the more secular, modernist response that is the flip-side; the one I resonate with the most. It's a seemingly rational interpre-tation. One could also say it's a first wave feminist understanding; it's no accident that the tree is female. It's also a psychological or self-help read. Here the tree is a compulsive giver, perhaps well-meaning but foolish. She has low self-esteem and has allowed herself to be exploited: giving without getting anything back. She's also being irresponsible by allowing the boy to think all his needs and wants will be answered with-out giving anything in return. The tree is out of touch with her own needs and desires. Tragically, she is so self-loathing that she destroys herself. Clearly the tree's happiness is delusional and the book should really be called *The Victim Tree*.

Many of us respond to this reading because we feel the pain of the tree's gradual dismemberment. We are angry about not standing up for ourselves, not asking for what we need in our relationships. And yet we also feel that if we gave enough, nurtured more, we'd gain the love we so desperately lack. We can become hijackers of the giving part of a rela-tionship, leaving no room for the other person to be generous. This may be because of some old wound; a need to feel valuable and needed; even an unconscious desire to control others by keeping them indebted. Of-ten we don't feel entitled to ask for what we want and need. There's also the guilt trip that society lays on mothers: if we give unconditionally we are saintly and will be adored and loved forever. If not, we're unworthy of being loved. Some women buy into this; others resent it. After all, this kind of giving can turn us into a dead stump, with nothing left to give.

All of us need to pay attention to feelings of exploitation or of hav-ing unmet needs, and we need to work to change—or even leave—any relationship that gives rise to them. Any relationship in which no one ever says, "What am I, the giving tree?!" is one that is either abusive or a dead end. Neither person will grow if giving and receiving aren't always being probed and explored. *The Victim Tree* invites us to ask: Am I giv-ing in order to avoid grappling with my own desires? Or am I really not giving enough of myself?

The third version is *The Taking Boy*. This is a story about a boy who shamelessly exploits a weak and vulnerable and caring soul. As the six-year-old son of a friend said, "That boy is the greediest person I ever met!" In more adult language, he is pathologically selfish, incapable of gratitude, and insatiable. In short, he's spoiled rotten; expecting not only every need but every want to be completely met and fulfilled. But all this taking doesn't fill him up; it corrupts him, in the end makes him a stooped, hollow, diminished shell of a man. This interpretation holds such an important moment truth. We are all susceptible to being takers, to exploiting others. When this read speaks to us, it's likely that we're dangerously close to exploiting those around us, or at least deep down we think we are. For whatever reason we may be wounded and genuinely needier. Or it may be because our loved ones seem to have a limitless capacity to give. Whatever the reason, we become takers, and we then judge others as a way to mask our own disappointment in ourselves.

Every culture has its own particular excess and pathology. Ours is competition and getting ahead; success at all costs; the quicker the better. Baby boomers in particular, who have on the whole been given so much by our parents, tend to feel a little guilty about how much we have. When not acknowledged, these emotions easily can give rise to feelings of entitlement: not only to everything we've acquired, but to what we don't have as well. We all need to regularly ask ourselves, "Am I taking advantage?"

The interpretation that in my informal survey is the least popular is *The Receiving Boy*. Here the boy-turned-man is able to voice his vulnerability and accept the care of the tree. He is unafraid of showing his dependence. He is joyfully dependent, freely expressing his weaknesses, needs, and dreams. This in turn evokes unconditional generosity from the tree. In our society, being dependent and needy tends to make us feel diminished because we value self-sufficiency and independence so highly. We will take care of others, up to a point, but we dare not let ourselves be taken care of.

Some of us feel resentful of giving too much, when really it's that we can't, or don't, receive. If we can never really feel dependent, can never ask for help, then we shortchange ourselves and those around us. We miss a whole side of life. We may even become arrogant to mask our need to be nurtured.

This interpretation touches the part of us that longs to be cared for unconditionally; to share our neediness with our hands fully open and our hearts exposed. When we can overcome our fears, and surrender in this way, the boundaries between giving and receiving can dissolve. There is an honesty and transparency between helper and helpee. When we receive, we give. When we give, we receive.

I felt this when I hurt my back a while ago. I could barely stand up and literally couldn't put on my socks and shoes. I had never been hurt like that and always prided myself in never being sick. Even when I did get the flu I'd go to work no matter how bad I felt. My motto: I pull my weight and do not accept help. But when my back went I really needed people and there was no way around it. For the first few days, I was like my daughters when they were in their terrible twos throwing tantrums when I tried to help them with something, even if they obviously couldn't do it on their own. Needing help embarrassed me, made me feel weak and, therefore, resentful of my helpers when I should have felt grateful. And then—out of the mouths of babes—my daughters came into my room early one morning and together they said, "We want to help you get out of bed and get dressed before the school bus comes." When I resisted, they said, "We love you and you need us." I wept as they put my socks on. Being a receiving boy can be nothing short of transformative.

Different interpretations of this story—or any story—are bound to resonate with us more or less at different points in our lives. The balance of giving and receiving with my children is different at five than at fifteen and then different still when they are twenty-five. When I'm an old man the balance will shift again. For lovers, the balance also shifts dramatically—from the courting stage to the prechildren years, to the career-building years and the child-raising years, and then again when the nest is empty.

There's an insightful teaching in the Talmud: Love will always upset the balance. The energy and dynamism of love doesn't allow for anything but very temporary resting places, calms before the next storm. Just when the roles seem clear and defined—the giving and receiving going smoothly without a hitch—something will upset

**Love will always
upset the balance.**

things and throw everything into play once again. Someone loses a job or gets sick or gets that promotion or recovers from an illness. The key is not to pretend we have roles for life, and to remember that no role captures all of who we are. When we can be fluid and accepting of the imbalances, our relationships can be more nimble and lasting.

It's also important to remember that sometimes the balance is off, and that's as it should be. We've all heard others or ourselves say some variation of "Those ungrateful kids (those taking boys!). We give them everything, and they don't . . ." Fill in the blanks: clean up their rooms, do well in school, defer to us, obey the rules. Of course, our kids take too much! Yes, we want them to have a sense of responsibility and gratitude, but inequity is what parenting is about. It's what we sign on for.

Sometimes when I come home after being out of town for four or five days in a row, my kids start asking for the most insignificant things: a glass of water that they can get themselves; the phone, which is across the room; help on homework that they can do with their eyes closed. Until recently I had a refrain in my head during these times: "They take, take, take!" Or I'd act out in some resentful way. Maybe it was all those readings of *The Giving Tree,* but one day I realized that my feelings were less about them taking than about my guilt about being away; about not having given what I know they needed. The giving tree in me was sleeping, but it really wanted to give.

Yet, part of what it means to be a child is to take more than you give. Sometimes children feel a kind of burden of indebtedness and obligation that comes from so many years of taking and receiving from their parents. I know I feel this every time I hear my mother joke about how she'd go for a week at a time without as much as crossing our street when we were kids. This feeling of pressure created by our obligation can be very positive if we stand back and recalibrate, rather than feel guilty. As adults, if we can focus on all that we received as children, we may feel a deep desire to give back both to our parents and to society.

Other times children feel that their parents didn't give enough. This certainly happens, and we may feel genuinely and rightfully deprived. A lot of healing may need to happen, either with our parents or without them. This, too, can inspire us to give to others in a way we never experienced. With time we may also find that we were given to in ways we may have overlooked.

All relationships are dances of giving and receiving, taking and offering. The more intimate we are, the more dynamic the dance. And sometimes it's a real challenge to give without resentment and to receive with grace. We all yearn for a perfect balance, a love that is fluid, evenly alternating between giving and receiving. We want to think each person will get what she needs and will give only what she's comfortable giving. We believe we should be infinite givers and finite takers even when we act more like infinite takers and finite givers. Not surprisingly, we tell stories about gods who are always demanding more and more and always resentful for our ingratitude; and humans who are always taking and always feeling burdened with obligation. Jewish wisdom encourages us to reach for that place of balance while knowing that even if we get there, we won't remain there for long We all give too much or take too much, and feel resentful or greedy in our close relationships.

In the fourth-century wisdom text called *The Ethics of the Fathers*, two very different forms of love are described. The first refers to the story of Amnon and Tamar, children of King David, half-brother and half-sister. Amnon becomes lovesick over Tamar and forces himself on his beautiful sister, then turns away from her in shame. The second is the story of Jonathan, son of King Saul, and young David. The sages said, "The first depends on getting something back. And when that thing is gone, the love, too, disappears. This is the love between Amnon and Tamar. But a love that is not based on some external thing will not come to an end. This is the love between David and Jonathan." The former is conditional love (born out of lust that Amnon had for Tamar and an obvious attempt to own the other person) and the latter is unconditional. Between David and Jonathan, it would seem, there's no reciprocity expected; it's a love without expectation or self-consciousness, and at least no overt sexual expectations or desires (although this is debatable). For the sages, it's a supremely pure love.

The story goes like this: David is not yet king but a young man when he slays the mighty Philistine Goliath. As grateful as King Saul is, it becomes clear to him that David, and not his son Jonathan, will be the next king. This infuriates him, and Saul fears that David might even usurp the throne before Saul's time is up. Unlike Saul, Jonathan is not afraid. Instead Jonathan's soul becomes "bound up with the soul of David; Jonathan loves David as himself." The word love is used five times to describe the relationship between these two young men, and it's the only time in the Bible that two individual human beings make a *brit*, a sacred pact, with each other, a ritual reserved for God and man.

So clearly the sages were right: the biblical authors wanted us to pay very close attention to this particular love story. In the first scene, Jonathan, who at first reading is the obvious giver in the relationship, takes off his cloak, tunic, sword, bow, and belt and gives them to David. Then things get really interesting: King Saul orders Jonathan to kill David, and instead Jonathan warns David and protects him in several elaborate plots. Eventually both Saul and Jonathan are killed in battle, and David's eulogy—a precursor to his incredible poetry in the Psalms—is elegiac. In one verse, he finally declares his love for Jonathan, as Jonathan has done throughout the story for David. "I grieve for you, my brother Jonathan. You were most dear to me. Your love was wonderful to me. More than the love of women."

It's hard to argue with the fact that theirs was a pretty amazing love.

Yet the biblical authors set up the story in such a way that the reader might well question the motives of both men. The first time Jonathan declares his love and makes the pact with David it's just after David slays Golaith, showing his incredible prowess and worthiness to be king. Could it be that Jonathan, like Saul, was afraid that David might do him harm in order to become king himself? Might Jonathan's love have been double-edged: self-sacrifice that is also self-serving? David, too, may have had ulterior motives. It certainly was convenient to have a loyal spy in the palace, reporting Saul's every move against David. After all, without Jonathan, David might well have been killed by Saul.

David seems to be a bit like the boy in *The Giving Tree*, taking, and also receiving, but not giving anything back or showing his gratitude until after Jonathan's death. Even then, David refers to Jonathan's love for him, rather than the other way around. There's an earlier scene in which David seems to doubt Jonathan's intentions and Jonathan reassures him. Later Jonathan doubts David and is reassured. This hardly seems like undying trust.

The authors of *The Ethics of the Fathers* must have wondered about this relationship, and yet they saw this as the ultimate love story between human beings. They affirmed the supremacy of the relationship despite all the potential underlying political motives. They understood that David's and Jonathan's love was unconditional not because it was equally balanced or unsullied by self-serving motives—it was unconditional because it was transparent in its imbalance.

The rabbinic sages are teaching something quite radical. Purity of love is not about being perfectly reciprocal. It's about how honest people are to each other as to how they are giving and receiving. David, the powerful and charismatic king-to-be, could be totally vulnerable with Jonathan. He's the only person David lets his guard down with and to whom he shows his fears and doubts. Jonathan is able to give support and provide strength in a way that makes him very powerful. Their giving and receiving in its inequality creates a depth to their relationship that is unmatched in the Bible.

The message here seems to be that all loves have ulterior motives lurking somewhere, and all loves have imbalances. There are always reasons that we fall in love; it's never by accident. Even our love for our children can be conditional: As deep and enduring as it is, we expect to be loved back, and we usually expect that love to be demonstrated in particular ways. Mothering can become smothering with indebtedness, and fathering can become about expecting accomplishment, or vice versa. There really is no pure love, no pure action. As much as we give, it's impossible to know if we do so wholeheartedly; we'll never know what motivates us under the surface. Don't we tend to offer what we perceive to be ours in the first place? And don't we expect that the gift be recognized? Don't we sometimes want power over the other person? Don't we want praise?

Although the Bible has been called one of the greatest love stories ever written, the love between God and human be-

Purity of love is not about being perfectly reciprocal. It's about how honest people are to each other as to how they are giving and receiving.

ings is wrought with conflict over what is given and how it is received. We might expect the God character to be like the giving tree, an endless well of plenty, overflowing with and bestowing gifts. But the God character's gifts are always double-edged, abundant yet full of tests, conditions, and obligations.

The very first gift of life—what gift could top that?—isn't a very gracious story on either side. Like a good parent, God provides everything the first couple could possibly need or desire, and yet it isn't enough. They take more than they've been given: The one forbidden fruit just can't be resisted. At first reading, the story seems to be a parable about our greed and insatiability. But then one has to wonder why God didn't offer them that fruit; why did God hold back? It seems the giving tree had its limits; God's giving came with expectations articulated and unarticulated. Although the post-Eden God does continue to give, now human beings are going to have to share the burden, providing for themselves and caring for each other. And the dynamic quality of giving and receiving will enliven their and our ongoing story. God will never be sure about us and we will never be sure about God, ourselves, or each other. That is the exquisite insecurity of love.

The very first time the word love is used in the Bible is in the story of the Binding of Isaac, called the Akedah. This is among the most disturbing stories in the entire text. Abraham is commanded to bring his beloved son Isaac to the top of Mt. Moriah and offer him up as a sacrifice, which Abraham does. Isaac is bound to the altar, a knife at his throat, when at the last minute Abraham replaces him with a ram, and Isaac's life is spared. What kind of God would make such a demand? And what kind of father would actually be willing to give such an offering? Centuries of interpretations try to make sense of this story, from Kierkegaard declaring Abraham a Knight of Faith to Woody Allen, who declares Abraham mad.

What if the Akedah is a meditation on giving and receiving? "God put Abraham to the test." But what is the test really about? Here are some of the questions it raises. What does Abraham need to do to prove his love? Is he willing to give it all? What does it take for any of us to trust the selflessness of our love? What do we have to give to know that we can love unconditionally? And then on the other side, how much does God need in order to trust Abraham's love? How much proof do we need to feel we are loved? How much do we need to be given to by those who love us in order to feel secure? There's madness in imagining what we would be willing to give in order to finally and unambiguously prove our love. And there is madness in imagining what we would need in order to clearly and unequivocally know that we are loved. We can be driven crazy by the self-doubt and insecurity of love. All this madness is present in any passionate relationship.

In the end, Abraham and God come to their senses, saving Isaac. Maybe they've learned what they need to know about love and mystery, giving and taking. More than a thousand years later, just a short walk from Mt. Moriah, where this binding takes place, another son will be bound—and this time it will be love to the end. The power of

Christianity is this demonstration of giving all for love. It creates the ultimate indebtedness, one which can never be paid off and leaves us all yearning for grace.

In our contemporary, largely secular times, sacrifice is a bad word. It's frequently associated with the violent, seemingly senseless taking of a life; an anachronistic religious brutality from another era long behind us—or perhaps only a part of "unevolved" cultures where religious fanaticism reigns. Sacrifice in a nonreligious context is usually used to indicate a quality of selflessness: giving up something precious for the benefit of someone or something else, often a belief or an ideal. The self-sacrificing mother; the soldier killed in battle; the giving tree. But there is no word for sacrifice in the Hebrew Bible. The word used is *korban*, which means "to come closer," "to bring near"—an intimacy maker.

Korban is an act of love as well as the product of a deep longing to feel embraced, if only briefly. In the ancient days of the Temple in Jerusalem, the practice of *korban* took the form of animal offerings: sin offerings, gratitude offerings, life-cycle offerings. Whether in times of vulnerability, security, joy, sadness, or loss, these expressions of awe involved giving up what is most precious; what in agricultural times sustained life itself. After the destruction of the Temple by the Romans in 70 C.E., this form of *korban* came to an end and was replaced with acts of loving kindness. In other words, sacrificing time and money, giving from the heart to another human being became a way to create intimacy, or what I call cosmic closeness.

I'll never forget the first time I donated more than my usual $50 or so to a cause I believed in. At the time, I was earning a very modest salary. I had attended a meeting at the State Department about the possible rescue and airlift of thousands of suffering, oppressed Ethiopians. Money needed to be raised immediately to bribe public officials and pay for the flights. It cost a thousand dollars to rescue one person: This was a real stretch for me. I remember calling Dana to ask how she felt about it, half hoping she'd object, telling me I had gotten caught up in the moment. She didn't, and as I wrote the check my hand trembled and I literally felt expansiveness in my chest—my heart was opening. I understood *korban* just then better than I had in all my years of studying.

The most powerful form of *korban* in contemporary times—the only thing we can give and know we can't get back—is time. This is why volunteering and activism are such profound offerings. There have been studies that show the enormous psychological and even physical benefits of *korban*: When we give to others we feel closer to them, but also to some deeper place within ourselves. Giving is actually sustaining. This is especially true in our intimate relationships. From the small things in life like getting up night after night to tend to a crying child to caring for a sick parent who can no longer care for himself, we all make offerings in the course of our lives. They are no less powerful, maybe more so, than the *korban* at the Temple altar.

A friend of mine described how making her husband's lunch every day made her feel as close to him as lovemaking; quite a surprising statement. She told me how she'd been a feminist from a very early age. This stance was born from decades of watching her mother serve her father to the point where he seemed to do nothing for himself, not even make his own breakfast or dress himself in the morning. His clothes were laid out; and her mom would be pouring the milk in his cereal as he sat down to eat it.

My friend's marriage had always been one of "equals," tasks divided down the line so that one person wouldn't feel more burdened than the other, but mostly to protect herself from feeling the resentment she'd had as a child. Yet during a challenging financial time, she decided to make not just her own, but her husband's lunch every morning to save money. When things improved financially she found herself continuing the chore, even on the most rushed, pressured mornings when she had a deadline or an early meeting. She felt that lunch was even more important than it had been before. Now it seemed that in making that sandwich she was actually giving of herself. I'm guessing that her husband felt that same closeness.

Jewish wisdom has an ethics of giving. Even someone impover-
ished and hungry should be able to experience the intimacy and joy of
giving. There's a homeless man named Robert who usually hangs
around my building, and to me he embodies this law. He's a poet, and
he won't accept money unless he can recite a poem in return. One
morning when Talia was about six I stopped to speak with Robert and

**Our yearning to give
generously and receive
gracefully is at the heart
of our quest for intimacy.**

to give him a few dollars for coffee and a
bagel. Before I could walk away, he pulled a
dirty teddy bear out of his bag and said to
Talia in his raspy voice, "This is for you, dear."
Clearly Robert understood the necessity of
giving and the nobility it can bestow. Just as a poor person needs to
give, no matter how little, the rich are encouraged to give, but only so
much. A wealthy person is to give no more than 20 percent of what he
or she possesses. Giving can be so intoxicating, such a high that it can
do more harm than good: The giver can become depleted, and then
what would there be left to give?

In the Temple days there were three kinds of offerings; three ways
of becoming closer to God, to expanding one's consciousness of reality
and self. The first is called *olah*, which means "going up." Here the entire
animal was burned at the altar. The second is called *minha*, which
means "gift," and it entailed the same ritual at the altar, except part of
the offering was given to the High Priests of the Temple. What's interesting is that this offering was considered no less important than an
olah. The third kind, *shelamim*, means "wholeness" and is even more
amazing: The animal was killed yet the entire thing was eaten by family
and friends. Our ability to receive, to take in sustenance fully and joyfully, is actually a way to express gratitude for the gift of life, which explains why the meal is such a central part of every Jewish celebration. In
religious language, if we don't partake of the meal, if we can't take it in,
we've disappointed God.

Our yearning to give generously and receive gracefully is at the
heart of our quest for intimacy. Intimacy in turn demands that we hold

the tension of opposites: the yearning to love unconditionally and the craving to be loved for just being; the lust for control and the desire for surrender; the dread of entrapment and the longing for engulfment; the vitality of creative partnership and the deadness of status quo routine. George Orwell wrote, "The essence of being human is that we are in the end prepared to be broken up by life—which is the inevitable process of fastening our love upon other human beings." The yearning to love asks us to live with the fear that we may burn up in our giving and receiving— but it's worth it.

We are all needy. We all want to give. If we're lucky, we will work at it for a lifetime, taking and receiving from those around us and giving and offering to just as many. We'll be forever learning that in giving, we receive and in receiving, we give. May we all be able to recite whole-heartedly the 2500-year-old mantra: "Blessed is the giver and blessed is the taker. May he be blessed."

FORGIVENESS

"LOVE MEANS NEVER HAVING TO SAY YOU'RE SORRY" ARE the words spoken by Ali MacGraw in that classic '70s movie, *Love Story*. This line captures a yearning so many of us have, even if we don't want to admit it. We long for someone who understands us and accepts us so fully—despite all our faults and mistakes—that apologizing seems beside the point. The ultimate relationship, we can't help but think, is one in which forgiveness is easy, free-flowing, and immediate; where it requires little or no effort from either party, even when the hurt may be deep.

Of course, it's just the opposite. Our most loving relationships are those in which we say "sorry" continuously. Forgiveness is central to the workings of love. If we're not seeking and receiving, being asked for and granting forgiveness on a regular basis, it's most likely that our relationship is not as intimate, dynamic, or alive as we think it is. And it's likely that we're holding in plenty of bitterness, resentment, guilt, and shame. Quite simply, things aren't messy enough. One could say that forgiveness is the glue of loving relationships, holding them all together and constantly renewing and repairing them. But there is no such thing as "an act" of forgiveness. Forgiveness is a process, a way of being in the world.

Forgiveness is a process, a way of being in the world.

I hear so often about the hurts that won't go away: the person who holds a grudge, who nurtures a resentment; or the one who never admitted his wrong, who simply can't humble himself to ask for forgiveness, although it's clear he's burdened by the not asking. The yearning to forgive and be forgiven is palpable. We want to make our relationships right, to make things whole again. A recent Gallup poll reported that 94 percent of Americans say forgiveness is one of the central virtues. Yet 48 percent of those same people say they've never had a forgiving experience. How can this be?

Perhaps it's because the forgiveness so many of us yearn for is total and complete. When people talk to me about forgiveness, they want so badly to be able to start again, to have everything be okay, to wipe the slate clean. Before they open themselves up again by either granting or seeking forgiveness, they want some guarantee that it will all work out. They imagine a single conversation that will end in tears or laughter, at the end of which both parties will be able to go on as if nothing had ever happened, the hurt and disappointment having been erased or healed. When this doesn't happen, one person may become defensive, giving up too soon. Some grant forgiveness too quickly, wanting to let the other person off the hook, wanting to feel better themselves, to retreat from the pain and the uncertainty. Others tell me they want to simply let it go, to forgive someone on their own without interacting with or confronting the person at all. Or they think it's possible to forgive themselves. Anything but approach or confront another person.

This is understandable: Few things make us as vulnerable as admitting our mistakes, especially to someone we have every reason to think will be angry at us or, even worse, unreceptive or shut down. When we ask for forgiveness, there's no place for defenses, for justifications. We have to make ourselves naked. At the same time, to forgive is an act of faith and trust. There's little reason to expect that the transgression won't happen again; once someone crosses a line, what's the guarantee they won't again? We live in a culture of avoidance; few of us have had models of forgiveness or were taught that feeling vulnerable and taking risks is a necessary part of intimacy. So, instead, we seek a kind of cheap grace.

There are no guarantees, no absolutes, no lasting sense of completeness. We get hurt; we're vulnerable; doors shut in our faces. And yet we
are obliged to seek forgiveness anyway. Jewish wisdom has an expansive
understanding of the process of forgiveness and a method born of centuries of practice. The sages taught that most of the time it's not possible
to have our offenses wiped away, to have that feeling of starting over, of
being whole again with ourselves and the other person. But there's a lot
that *can* happen. We can realign our relationships, initiate some healing,
and reconnect, sometimes more deeply than we ever have before.

The twelfth-century philosopher Maimonides offered a practice of
forgiveness that I call the "four Rs" of forgiveness: Recognition; Regret;

**To forgive is an act
of faith and trust.**

Resolution; Reconciliation. The premise of this process is that forgiveness is not some pious commandment that compels obedience. It's something to be
striven for, and it must be practiced in the context of a relationship. It is
as much external as internal. We must dive into the muck together.

Love Story really had it wrong: Not only is it ridiculous to believe
that love is never having to say we're sorry, many times it's not even
enough to say we're sorry—not even close. We must recognize what we
did, how we hurt the other person; we must genuinely regret our actions, and resolve not to repeat them. Sometimes we need to do more
than just talk, actually demonstrating that we'll behave differently
when we're in the same situation again. And if we've been hurt or diminished by another person, we should communicate our needs, encouraging the other person, as a friend of mine says, "to walk the walk
and then come back and talk." Only then is real reconciliation possible.
Jewish wisdom assumes people can change, that we want to grow and
deepen our relationships, that breaches in intimacy are always opportunities.

I had the opportunity to practice the four Rs recently in the midst of
an ongoing struggle with my daughter Talia. She'd always been a night
owl, just like me. These late hours with everyone else asleep could have
been a time of closeness—daughter and father talking into the night, or

at least keeping each other company as we did our own thing. But I'd always resented her presence. At a certain point, during an especially stressful time at work, my frustration got the best of me, and I began to lash out at her, berating her for spending so much time watching TV and playing on the computer. "Go to sleep, already!" "Can't you read a book in bed?" "You won't be able to focus in school!" But, like me, she couldn't just go to bed, and one night I really lost it and she crumbled in tears. I apologized profusely. How could I make my little girl cry like that? What was my problem? As she said, she was a straight A student and never missed the bus in the mornings. I felt terrible.

Much as I hate to admit it, a few nights later I lost it again. Once again I apologized. And Talia nailed me. "Don't say you're sorry. Just don't yell at me anymore!" Clearly, sorry wasn't good enough, not when she knew nothing had really changed. This got me thinking. What was this really about? Every parent needs time to themselves, but the extent of my rage, my inability to stop myself from screaming at her, clearly was coming from someplace else.

I sat with my anger for a few days and realized that it wasn't really about Talia at all. I recognized a pattern from childhood—isn't that always the case? As the eldest of six brothers, I had never been alone. We shared a room and I spent a lot of time caring for, talking to, and studying with my siblings. It seemed every minute of the day there was someone around: You couldn't use the bathroom without someone knocking. I hated the lack of privacy. As an adult, I seemed to be bent on making up for lost time. Hadn't I earned it? Wasn't this now my house where I could finally have my own space! I finally *recognized* where my bad temper was all coming from. That was a moment of realization for me, and the first stage of forgiveness.

Blaming Talia was a defense against feeling pain. Now my *regret* took on another dimension: I was burdening my child with baggage from my own childhood. I was taking fifteen years of childhood frustration out on her. I explained this to her one night after yet another outburst, and she listened with genuine interest to stories from my youth. I could see she understood. Now it was time for *resolution*: I had to show her I could act differently, that the recognition and regret actually meant something.

There's a big difference between regret and guilt, and yet the two are often confused. Guilt more often than not keeps us from action. It is often paralyzing and self-destructive. "I feel guilty" can become an indictment. We beat ourselves up, but rarely do we do something about it. On the other hand, regret generates action; we are compelled to make things better. "I regret what I did" inspires us to do it differently next time. When we regret, it becomes possible to genuinely resolve not to do the same thing again when confronted with a similar situation. Only then is reconciliation possible.

As I write this, it's been weeks since that last fight. Talia's still at the computer, in front of the TV, or reading by my side on the couch late into the night. I still long for time alone, but the edge is gone. The other night she looked up at me, and said with that ironic smile of hers, "Now isn't that better, Dad?" We both laughed; *reconciliation* at last. Although Talia probably knows I might lose it again some day, the struggle was resolved for now, and it even seemed to have strengthened our relationship. There was a new understanding between us, a kind of expanded consciousness and renewed bond. As the Hasidic Rabbi Levi Yitzchak of Berditchev said, "When one repents out of love the previous evil acts are considered changed into good deeds."

> **Guilt keeps us from action, but regret inspires us to be different next time.**

Here's a far more powerful example of the four Rs—one of the most moving stories of brothers in the biblical texts. Once again sibling rivalry is at the center of a family conflict. This is the story of Joseph, the eleventh of Jacob's twelve sons, his first child by Rachel, his favored wife. When Rachel died, Jacob understandably turned his affections toward the eldest of Rachel's two sons. Also understandably, the hurt among Jacob's other sons was nothing short of excruciating.

Hence the Broadway musical of *Joseph and the Amazing Technicolor*

Dream Coat. It wasn't enough that Joseph was more loved; Jacob had to go and give Joseph a fancy coat on top of everything. And, of course, Jacob gave his other sons nothing. To make matters worse, Joseph was a special child who had prophetic dreams, and he told his brothers about these dreams which foretold the power he someday would have. When Joseph shared the images of his brothers' bowing down to him, their resentment and envy grew into hate.

One day while out in the fields, his brothers plotted to kill Joseph. They stripped him of his beloved coat and threw him in a pit. They surely would have murdered him had the eldest, Judah, not convinced his brothers to sell, rather than kill, Joseph. A caravan of Ishmaelites came by and the brothers sold Joseph, who was taken to Egypt. Remarkably, once again Joseph was favored, this time by his owner, and he quickly rose to a position of power in the household, a status that again gave rise to envy among the others in the house and, this time, to a false accusation. He was accused of trying to seduce his master's wife and was sent off to prison.

While there, Joseph's skill in interpreting dreams came to the attention of the Pharaoh, who invited Joseph into his court as an adviser. Yet again Joseph rose to great heights, becoming second to the Pharaoh himself. His dreams came true. Years later Joseph had the opportunity to exercise his power. At the time, he was in charge of administering food to all of Egypt. A seven-year famine struck the entire region including Canaan, where Joseph's family lived. When word got out that food could be bought in Egypt, Jacob sent his sons there. All except Benjamin—Joseph's younger brother and Rachel's other son—who Jacob favored as he had Joseph.

Imagine Joseph's surprise when his brothers showed up. Joseph had changed so much in dress, speech, and demeanor that, combined with his elevated role, his brothers didn't recognize him. But Joseph knew them, and he must have been overwhelmed with emotion as they bowed down to him. In a flash he may have remembered the years of slavery and imprisonment; that agonizing time in the pit as he waited to be murdered; his dreams; his father; his younger brother; his dead mother. All that loss and pain must have felt like a kind of eruption. In response, he decided to take revenge, calmly and methodically. He accused the brothers of being spies and threw them into prison for three days. After interrogating them and learning about Jacob and Benjamin back home, Joseph insisted that they prove their honesty in a kind of test. One of the brothers was to remain there as a hostage while the others returned home to bring Benjamin to Egypt.

Perhaps underneath his rage and bitterness, Joseph had some longing for reconciliation. He could have killed his brothers or kept them in jail. Instead he decided to create a theater of revenge to see how his brothers would respond. The brothers agreed to Joseph's demand. But before they left his court, Joseph heard his brothers whispering among themselves about the crime they had committed against Joseph years earlier. They wondered if this cruelty on the part of a stranger was some kind of payback for their betrayal. Joseph turned away from them and wept. His plot had set into motion two unexpected reactions: His brothers began to recognize and regret the terrible thing they'd done, and Joseph began to feel a longing to connect with his brothers. The theater of revenge now became a dance of both vengeance and atonement.

The brothers minus one returned home with food and told their father everything that had happened. After the food was finished, Jacob, threatened with starvation once again, with great reluctance and fear, agreed to let the brothers take Benjamin to Egypt to procure more food and redeem their older brother. As soon as Joseph saw Benjamin, he was overcome with feelings and rushed out of the room to weep again. Later, he threw a feast and sat his brothers in order from youngest to eldest. Understandably, the brothers feared he was playing with them. But that was the least of it—Joseph was far from done.

As they prepared to leave again for Canaan, Joseph had a royal silver goblet placed in Benjamin's bag. Then Joseph called his brothers before him and accused them of stealing his cup, threatening to kill the person responsible. Joseph had set a cruel trap in which they would have to decide the fate of another brother. And Judah rose to the occasion. When the cup was found in Benjamin's bag, the same brother who years earlier had argued to sell Joseph into slavery stepped forward and, in an eloquent plea, expressed his love for Benjamin and his empathy for his father, who would be broken by this loss of the second favored son. Judah offered himself in Benjamin's place. Jacob's favoritism, this time for Benjamin, was no longer a source of murderous bitterness; Judah's love for his father and brother trumped his jealousy. Put in the same situation again, he proved he was capable of acting differently. Judah would be his brother's keeper.

Upon hearing Judah's words Joseph couldn't control himself and sobbed openly. This time he cried out, "I am Joseph!" Suddenly Joseph was able to see the betrayal of him in the largest possible context, telling his brothers, "Do not be distressed or reproach yourselves because you sold me here; it was to save life that God sent me ahead of you!" If Joseph hadn't wound up in Egypt he would not have been able to save his family from starvation. There was a purpose to all that conflict and suffering.

And yet life can never be made perfect, and relationships sometimes don't completely heal. When Jacob died, the brothers feared Joseph would now take his revenge. Understandably they wanted their relationship with Joseph to be repaired, to have the whole thing behind them. So they lied to him. They told him their father's dying wish was that Joseph forgive them. The very first time the word "forgive" is used in the Bible, it is as part of a deception. Sometimes our yearning to be forgiven is so great that we may go to great lengths to attain it. We want to do it perfectly or with pure intention. But there is always something self-serving about asking for forgiveness.

> Anger is not always the enemy of forgiveness. What we do out of hurt and rage can actually sometimes lead to reconciliation.

Unaware of the lie, Joseph responded by comforting them and

speaking kindly to them; by helping and sustaining them. But he never used the word "forgive." We can only assume it wasn't granted. Reconciliation doesn't wash away all the hurt, eliminate all the fears, nor diminish all the doubts. And isn't this the way things usually are? Forgiveness is one of the most complex processes in any intimate relationship. Maybe saints and enlightened beings forgive neatly and fully, but for the rest of us, when we are seriously hurt and betrayed by jealous siblings, abusive parents, or unfaithful spouses, forgiveness is rarely achievable in some fairy tale way.

Like Joseph's story, our forgiveness stories have many faces and rhythms, different outcomes and conclusions. Each time we open to another person, no matter how small or incomplete the opening, we become more intimate with them and with ourselves. When we are asked to forgive, sparing the other's life as Joseph did—literally or figuratively—may in fact be a remarkable first step. Rage, the desire to lash out, plotting revenge, testing—all may be subtle movements on the forgiveness continuum. Our desire to hurt back is actually an expression of our love, a kind of distorted yearning to stay connected.

Contrary to some "religious" views, anger is not the enemy of forgiveness, and what we do out of hurt and rage can sometimes actually lead to reconciliation, as it did for the brothers. Joseph saw the humanity and vulnerability of the very people who had hurt him only after expressing his anger, however dramatic and painful. I have seen so many instances of people who felt wronged opening their hearts to forgive when they saw their abuser suffering emotionally or ill or on a deathbed. It may take many years to reconnect, to allow someone to apologize, to gain confidence in them again, but if we don't eventually unblock the dams, forgiveness will remain an unconscious yearning. It's always there whether we acknowledge it or not. And even if we do, sadness and hurt, resentment and regret—although lessened—may still be part of the relationship. Amazingly, that pain can coexist with healing and forgiveness, becoming softer and less central over time.

Often we ourselves emerge stronger, clearer, and wiser when we wrestle with forgiveness, no matter what the outcome. Joseph's two sons gave rise to two of the twelve tribes of Israel from whom the Jewish people emerged. And Judah became the leading tribe from whom King David descended.

The sages taught that there are three kinds of forgiveness. One of them is called *selicha*, and it is the kind Joseph granted. It's a forgiveness born of a heartfelt empathy for the transgressor, and an ability to see the widest possible context, even the positive outcome of the conflict. As Joseph said, if his brothers hadn't betrayed him, he wouldn't have been able to help his family survive a bitter famine. More often than not, *selicha* doesn't happen right away just as it did not for Joseph and Judah. It takes time, especially when the hurt is great. And it's not something we can ever expect or ask for. Quite often, unforeseen circumstances are the impetus for it. There are so many stories of family members who've been alienated for years forgiving each other and reconnecting after the death of a parent. As painful as it is, a death creates an interruption of old patterns, an opening and a perspective in the midst of the grief.

Selicha also can unfold in the course of living and growing together. Typically, it's a process rather than a moment in time. This was the case for Freddie, whose mother had been an alcoholic all through Freddie's childhood and teenage years. I was surprised when she told me the story. She and her mother seemed very close. She said her mother had been neglectful and hurtful during those drunken years, leaving Freddie to serve as a buffer between her parents as they fought and struggled in a bad marriage fueled by addiction. As a young adult, she'd gone through periods where she didn't speak to her mother, and felt enraged even years after her mother joined Alcoholics Anonymous and began the recovery process. Didn't her mother recognize what she'd done? Why hadn't she approached Freddie and her sister to ask forgiveness and begin the healing process?

But her mother never did. As the years went by, she just "showed up," as Freddie put it: During Freddie's breakups with men, her mom was on the other end of the phone. Job disappointment: Mom was there. When Freddie had children of her own, her mother proved to be an exceptional grandma, down on the floor playing through long afternoons despite a bum knee. One day Freddie was listening to a talk of mine about forgiveness, and she had the thought, "Wow, I guess I've forgiven my mom." Freddie knew that those feelings of resentment and hurt hadn't disappeared. The way she described it, every time her mother disappointed her, and each time her mother showed up, Freddie forgave at deeper and deeper levels. What mattered most was that her mom was doing her best to make up for lost time. There was no moment of tears and reconciliation between them as there was in the Joseph story. There was simply living day in and day out with the hurt and the resolve to make it right.

Forgiveness so often comes into play in bold relief when it comes to our mothers and fathers. Everyone has to come to terms with negative or conflicted feelings about their parents, no matter how loving the relationship. What makes it so difficult is that we have three sets of parents: the ones who raised us and with whom we actively struggled; those who live in our memory today; and our living parents (assuming they are still alive). The parents in our memory have larger-than-life dimensions. They are the ones who adored us and ignored us, whom we idealized and demonized. Our parents today are people like us, with fears and flaws, trials and conflicts. And they likely will never live up to our childhood expectations and hopes, which are often still with us in adulthood, whether we're aware of them or not. Our job is to separate these three manifestations and work as best we can toward reconciliation, trying not to carry too much of the baggage of the past into the present, while always engaging with it. Our first great shock is when we realize that our parents are not God, and our next shock is when we realize that God is not our parent. This realization is the beginning of forgiveness for our parents and for God.

Even when reconciliation occurs, it doesn't mean the relationship continues where it left off. Another story of brothers illustrates this in a

scene full of pathos and suspense: the reunion of the previous generation of warring siblings, Jacob and Esau. Many decades after Jacob, the
younger twin, stole his brother's birthright in a plot devised by their
mother, Rebecca, Jacob and Esau come face to face with each other in
the desert.

Both men are now well established with large camps rich with animals, servants, and children. Jacob is journeying back to Canaan, his
home, when he's told Esau is approaching. Jacob is terrified, and his
guilt is palpable. After he sends ahead gifts and promises of more to
Esau, he spends the entire night before their meeting in a torturous
wrestling match with an angel (who in his dream may have been Esau
or himself). The fight leaves him wounded and limping in the morning. What happens next is remarkable: When they finally encounter
each other, Esau weeps and then hugs and kisses his brother.

The scribes found this level of forgiveness so hard to believe that
they actually played with the Hebrew word for "kiss," hinting to the
reader that the word might also be "bite." Then Esau refuses Jacob's
gifts, saying that he has enough. He invites Jacob to travel and settle
with him in town just ahead. Jacob agrees, but he never joins Esau. His
camp moves right on past that town, and the brothers see each other
again only at the death of their father, where the Bible simply says,
"Isaac was buried by his sons." We're never told and can only imagine
how their lives might have been changed by this startling reunion in the
desert. What's clear is that both of them go on to create great nations.

The second kind of forgiveness is the only kind we can ask for and
ever expect to receive. It's called *mechila*. Although we may not recognize it as forgiveness, most of us grant and receive it regularly. *Mechila*
is a kind of pardon. In legal language *mechila* is a relinquishing of a
claim or debt: You don't owe me anything for the wrong you have done.
And, contrary to the common understanding of forgiveness, it's not
necessarily a profound or heartfelt experience for either person. Certainly it's far from having the slate wiped clean. It's not the forgiveness
most of us yearn for, but the sages taught that it was enough. Let's say a

coworker cuts you off in a meeting, or dismisses something you said. She comes into your office later to apologize, and you tell her not to worry about it. There's no need for tears, although you may have been very upset with her. You don't want to know what was going on in her head or her heart. You don't need to go there. You let her off the hook. She owned up to her mistake and that's enough. *Mechila* also happens countless times with those close to us—a spouse doesn't pay attention to us as we tell him the details of our day and when we call him on it, a simple "Sorry, honey" does the trick. A child writes on the wall and, when confronted, seems to understand what she's done. Forgiveness granted.

Not every apology need be full-hearted and transforming. Apologies can be partial and still be real. There is something to be said for an apology that is done honestly just because that's what we should do and not as some great admission of guilt and shame. I have found that the key to this kind of apology is to not make any excuses. There should be no explanations of extenuating circumstances and no "I'm sorry but . . . ," which actually undermines the apology. We all do things that are thoughtless, inconsiderate, selfish, and mean, and thus we have a debt to the other person that we need to own up to as much for ourselves as for her. Sometimes an apology comes first and our feelings follow, but much of the time, we aren't even aware of our offenses. The truth is, rarely a week or even a day goes by when we don't annoy, disappoint, or hurt someone. Jewish wisdom has a system for addressing even these relatively minor or unconscious hurts, and it's one that can inform our everyday interactions. Every year before Yom Kippur, the Day of Atonement—of forgiveness—there is a centuries-old forgiveness practice. We are to speak to those close to us and say, "If there's anything over the last year that I've done to hurt or offend you, I'm sorry." These days it's often done over the phone (I'm not sure about e-mail). And it's literally a mantra, which like any mantra can seem rote. But when we make a few of these calls it's amazing the impact it can have. Most of the time, the person grants *mechila* and asks for it in return.

When they don't, that's when things get really interesting. When we're lucky, that's when the process of *selicha* can begin.

Sometimes we hurt people more than we imagine: A joke at the expense of a coworker at a meeting, a slight of a family member at the dinner table, teasing a spouse at a party. These things may barely register on our guilt meter, but it cuts to their heart. These hurts often take more than one apology to mend. The *mechila* practice is to ask for forgiveness three times. As random as that number may seem, practices can be like that. The onus is always on the person seeking forgiveness to keep trying. And if in the end forgiveness is not granted, you can feel you've truly given it your best shot. There is no knowing what eventual effect our asking will have.

One day not long before the High Holidays, I got one of those calls. It was from the former vice principal of my old high school, who I hadn't even thought about in decades. Obviously, I remembered how much he had upset me, though, because I didn't return his call; not until my assistant, uncomfortable with his frequent calls over the course of a week, asked me why I wasn't calling this guy back. Her question embarrassed me. It wasn't like me to not return a call. I couldn't imagine what he wanted, but I reluctantly picked up the phone. As I did, I could feel old feelings of resentment and anger coming back from more than thirty years ago.

I had been fourteen at the time. It was my first year away from home at a very traditional and rigorous parochial high school. Like most of my classmates in that first year, I longed for the weekends when I went home to my family. Every Saturday I went to synagogue with my father, who was a cantor there; this weekly ritual was particularly comforting and grounding at that vulnerable time. Then, one day, the vice principal called me into his office. He was young for his position and had a friendly demeanor, but behind it he was very rigid, strict, and judgmental. He told me I should no longer pray in my father's synagogue. He insisted that it wasn't traditional enough and, therefore, I wasn't fulfilling the obligation to pray. I completely lost it. "Are you fucking crazy?"

I yelled. Cursing at the vice principal was already unthinkable, but then I pushed him, and we ended up wrestling on the floor. His secretary had to separate us. I have no idea why I wasn't expelled, or how I got the nerve to write him an angry letter after this episode. I remember making a vigorous argument challenging him ethically on the grounds that the commandment to honor one's parents trumped the obligation to pray in a traditional fashion. He dropped it, but from time to time he'd needle me about not fully observing the Sabbath.

As an adult I understood that his demand was nothing personal against me or my father. All ideologies demand that we break or weaken our blood relations, that we be willing to reexamine our loyalties and make sacrifices in order to realize new truths. But even with this adult understanding I couldn't help but hold the principal's extremism against him; he'd used his power and authority in an insensitive and uncompromising way.

Thirty-one years later, there was his voice on the other end of the phone. He explained that he'd been sorting through his belongings, preparing for a move, and had come across my letter. He told me that it was a "beautiful" letter, and that he wanted me to know who he was now, how he'd changed. He told me about his years directing a different school, about the ways he'd "loosened up" and opened the curriculum to new approaches and ideas. He apologized for how he'd treated me: He'd been immature and just plain wrong. His last words to me were, "You'd be proud of me now." I was really touched, and I told him so. Without effort or hesitation, I granted *mechila*. When I hung up the phone I felt some small part of me was healed, and I really hope he felt forgiven, that maybe he experienced *selicha*.

Sometimes, we need to be rebuked in order to understand that we need to ask for forgiveness. Without the letter in hand, it's doubtful that the vice principal would have made the call. But all those years later, he was able to hear my reproval differently. We all know the famous verse from the Book of Leviticus that says, "Love your neighbor as yourself" but few of us remember that this intuition begins with the following words: "Rebuke, rebuke! Criticize your neighbor, but do not hold a grudge in your heart." Confrontation is a practice. An essential part of loving is critiquing. This is especially important to remember when we feel we're nurturing an injury, when our resentment is keeping us from living fully, or when it's stunting the growth of a relationship. It's incumbent upon us to criticize when we feel the person could benefit from our doing so.

I had a major wake-up call born of rebuke when I was a young rabbi in St. Louis. I was especially ambitious at that time, in a promising position at a synagogue of one thousand families. I was high on my new role; it was all so intense and alive. And I had a balance problem. There was always one more thing to do before I left the office, one more call, one more letter to write, one more sentence to add to that sermon. Even when the wonder of it all wore off, I was chronically late. It was a habit, and I really didn't think much about it; I was always gracious and apologetic when I finally arrived. People knew I didn't mean anything by it—at least I thought so.

It took my leaving the synagogue for me to realize that this was anything but the case. My realization came just in time for me to begin a new chapter in my life, but it was incredibly painful, however deserved. I had arrived at my good-bye dinner close to an hour and a half late. All my friends were in the middle of eating their entrees as was my wife, sitting there next to my empty chair. I did my usual round of apologies, assuming it was no big deal: Everyone knew I had this lateness thing, and this time I really needed to get everything done before we moved; I was being a responsible rabbi. As I went up to everyone, talking them up as is my usual way, I began to realize that no one was paying any attention to me, literally. They continued their conversation, eating and drinking as if I wasn't there.

Could this really be happening? I kept trying to engage people, then finally gave up, sat down, turned to Dana, and asked her what was up. Then the fun really began. She told me how hurt she was by my continual lateness, and one by one my closest friends laid into me about how insulting it had been to them all these years; how egotistical and self-important it was for me to assume all should be forgiven no matter how late I was, no matter how important the event or meeting. Weren't my wife, my friends, more important than the speech, the filing, or whatever it was that kept me from being where I'd promised to be? They were palpably angry.

I broke down in tears. I turned to Dana and apologized through my sobs. She nodded and kissed me, but her eyes were still full of hurt. I felt incredibly humbled. Of course, they were right. My lateness was a retreat from intimacy and an arrogant control move. I had a lot of repair work to do. Not even a heartfelt apology would make it any better. I had to change. I had to be on time. And I'm happy to say that, for the most part, I am a pretty prompt person these days. Years later, whenever I'm late I see Dana's eyes and hear my friends' angry voices. Theirs was an incredibly effective rebuke; a true intervention, a sacred practice.

There is an ethics of rebuke that my wife and friends intuitively understood. It is also an art. Of course, things had gone so far on my end that it was clear more harm was being done to my loved ones and me than any rebuke could cause. But they also knew that I could handle the intensity of their criticism. In the second century, Rabbi Tarfon exclaimed, "No one knows how to give rebuke, and no one knows how to hear it!" Too often we are accusing and humiliating when we confront someone, so angry the person can't hear us, can't take it in. There's another verse in Leviticus that says, "Reprove your brother but incur no guilt because of him." We should rebuke only if we're pretty sure we won't make the situation worse, or do more harm than good.

As a student of mine noted, the phrase in Leviticus uses the word "rebuke" twice. As in our dreams, repetition is always significant in sacred texts; it indicates that there's more than one meaning to a word or more than one person or consciousness it's addressing. Perhaps we're meant to rebuke the other person only after we've rebuked ourselves. If we're thoughtful, if we take confrontation seriously, before we pick up the phone and tell someone they wronged us, we generally need to take a good look in the mirror. What we find is that often our anger has masked our complicity in the hurt. Our inner drama has colored our perceptions.

This insight helped me understand why I'd never confronted the person who damaged me professionally more than anyone I know. For typical corporate political reasons, and perhaps leftover childhood jealousies and insecurities, he had rather viciously and adeptly undermined me with a few of my institution's financial support-

> Perhaps we're meant to rebuke another only after we've rebuked ourselves.

ers. For more than two years I harbored such resentment against him that I rarely allowed myself to be in the same room with him. When I did have to greet him it was with a barely professional coolness. And then I decided I would confront him. Before calling him I reviewed exactly how I was going to rebuke or criticize him, but as I thought about him in the context of the meditation from Leviticus, I realized how instrumental I'd been in our struggle.

Unbeknownst to him, I had actually strongly recommended him for the major position he now had, the one from which he'd been so destructive. I asked myself why I had recommended him, and it came to me. I thought his toughness, even his meanness, would be an asset to a man I saw as kind and generous but not strong enough to make a difference in the world, a difference I thought he genuinely wanted to make. And I knew that if I recommended this candidate he might even be loyal and give me better access.

I never called. I saw that I had much more to gain by rebuking myself for being complicit in the very events that had hurt me. If anything, I, too, had amends to make; not to him, but to my old patron. I'd recommended this person against my "better" judgment because, ironically, I felt there was something in it for me.

The third mode of forgiveness is called *kappara*, and it's the one we all yearn for. In religious language, this kind of forgiveness can only be granted by God. In Christian language, this is grace. It can't be earned or asked for—it comes after all the asking and all the work. It can't be predicted or expected; rather, it seems to be granted from the depths or on high. When we say "To err is human, to forgive is divine," this is the kind of forgiveness we mean.

Kappara is the kind of forgiveness that wipes the slate clean. It cancels out the offense. In psychological language it's an inner experience of return, of feeling whole again. We are able to integrate our transgression into a more expanded self. And we literally have a sense of expansion, of tremendous relief and elevation. *Kappara* is a transpersonal experience in which we simultaneously understand our finitude and our infinitude. It's a vision of our widest range of selves at that point in time.

The word *kappara* comes from the same root as the word *kippur*. Hence the sacred day of Yom Kippur, the Day of Atonement. On this holiday, which comes one week after the celebration of the Jewish New Year, we're meant to reach deep down into our selves and consciously yearn for *kappara*. It's a twenty-five-hour forgiveness retreat. Only on Yom Kippur is the goal *kappara*.

It's no wonder that more people come to temple on Yom Kippur than on any other day. Millions of otherwise secular Jews who never go to the synagogue pour through its doors in order to make themselves naked, to look into their own Book of Life, as the liturgy calls it, and see themselves more clearly. I'm often asked about the symbolism of the day: why do we meditate so many times in the service on the phrase "inscribe us in the Book of Life?" I tell people to imagine their entire year on film; pretend they can look in a Godlike way, frame by frame, at themselves, their interactions with people, their mistakes, their lovemaking, their fights, their triumphs. This is their Book of Life, their record of what they did and didn't do. To be inscribed is to take note, to become conscious of ourselves, the authors.

The central metaphor of the day is a court being convened. This image may seem cold or intimidating. But don't we all have a deep desire to be judged, to be held accountable? Don't we want our actions to matter? Since we were children in school waiting for that report card, we've wanted to know where we stand. The problem is that we confuse judged and judgmental. We imagine all judgment is through harsh and severe lenses. But where did that come from? Perhaps it's a projection of how we tend to see ourselves and others. There is a paradoxical power in this metaphor of standing in court when no external authority is on the bench. The things we feel most guilty about are not the illegalities but the stuff we try at our inner court that no one knows about. And the most severe judge, whether consciously or not, is the only judge that ultimately counts, the Self, Reality, God—whatever you choose to call this higher or deeper consciousness.

The major practice on Yom Kippur is to fast for that twenty-five hours as a way to loosen our ego boundaries and make us more receptive; to open up to new truths. I have often thought that we are also reenacting our death. This is an especially important place from which to ask for forgiveness. So often we stand on ceremony with loved ones and friends waiting for them to apologize first; to humble themselves so that we can feel bigger. And then the resentments only congeal, and weeks, months, years go by without speaking—even after the cause of the fight may be forgotten and irrelevant. Every so often, it is a good exercise to ask oneself: If one of us died before we made up, would I really want to hold that grudge, not having spoken, have it all end without an attempt at reconciliation?

In my experience as a rabbi, there is nothing sadder than officiating at a funeral at which a child is burying a parent she hasn't spoken to in years. Or a brother burying his brother who he hasn't had contact with in decades. It happens all the time. Sometimes we need to apologize even if we feel we are wronged. We can be the one who has the larger context, the furthest vision, and with that the responsibility to start the process.

By the end of Yom Kippur, after fasting, meditating, chanting, studying sacred texts, and reviewing their lives over the last year, most people's boundaries are pretty thin. They are weak and tired, not quite their ordinary selves. During the last part of the service, I invite everyone, whether alone or with their families or friends, to stand before the open ark where the Torah scrolls reside; in other words, to stand before his or her open heart. In the service, I ask hundreds of people, unafraid to inhabit themselves, unafraid of what they might find inside their Holy of Holies (at least for a minute or two), to come up to make a personal prayer. Often, as someone comes forward, there is a split second in which my eye catches his or hers. I can see that for many of them it is an intensely powerful time in which all the shared memories or the past year's hard truths become palpable—whether it's the job that was lost, the parent with Alzheimer's, the marriage that ended, or the child who is ill. It's amazing and awe-fully humbling to see and hear so many people praying, or simply talking softly to each other, some of them visibly crying. One year I overheard a mother wishing healing on an addicted daughter; a husband and wife whom I knew to be on the brink of divorce holding each other, whispering. I also saw a teenager normally sullen and distant become wide-eyed and teary, holding his father's hand. Whether one has fully engaged with the practices and rituals leading up to that point of the day or not, one's perception shifts. Somehow one can enter the year with resentments diminished, bitterness eased, and a sense of possibility.

One would think that by evening, after the long blast of the shofar which marks the end of the day, we'd just be able to go home and eat. But a few minutes after that final blast, when technically the day is over, we once again pray for *selicha*. It isn't possible that we've misstepped yet; that there's anything to be forgiven. Yet the sages had an insight: We're going to walk out of that synagogue and err again. So just in case we think we're free and clear, here's a reminder that Yom Kippur is not a preventative ritual. There is no ultimate moment of forgiveness. We're always making mistakes and correcting, offending and asking for forgiveness. We're never permanently guilty, nor permanently clean. Welcome to your humanity. Welcome to the new year.

Yom Kippur is a process of re-covenanting, of reestablishing our connection to others and a deeper level of awareness. There's a story about the Israelites receiving the second set of the Ten Commandments on Yom Kippur. The story goes like this. After forty days atop Mt. Sinai, Moses came down with the tablets. What could be more holy? But contrary to popular belief, these are not the set the Israelites received. When Moses saw the people worshipping the golden calf (a blatant defiance of the first three commandments), he did the unthinkable. He smashed the tablets in rage. Then he returned to the mountain for another forty days, during which time he managed to convince an even more enraged God not to destroy the people. When Moses returned to the Israelites he brought new tablets that he himself had created. These were the commandments the people received, and this is the event Yom Kippur remembers.

There is no great moment of healing or repair in this story. Yes, of course the people show regret but, as in our own lives, the slate is not wiped clean. Something even more amazing happens. Moses places the old, smashed tablets into the Holy Ark along with the new, intact ones. The relationship continues; the covenant is renewed with the brokenness on the inside. There is no perfect reconciliation, no permanent forgiveness, no forgetting. But betrayal is not the last word. There is a larger context: Love and betrayal can merge into and out of one another in astonishing ways. There is always a more enveloping pattern—and forgiveness is the most enveloping of all.

The mistakes we make and the wrongs that are done to us needn't imprison us in some dark place. Rather we should always remember that wholeness and brokenness can be held together in a sacred place. The tradition teaches that in the days of the ancient Temple, the Ark resided in the innermost chamber called The Holy of Holies. This place was so powerful that only the High Priest could enter the room, and then, only on Yom Kippur. On this day we are meant to remember our brokenness; and this alone is healing. As the Hasidic Master Menachem Mendel of Kotzk taught, "Nothing is as whole as a broken heart."

YEARNING TO
CREATE

INSPIRATION
AND ILLUMINATION

"In the beginning God created heaven and earth—
the earth being unformed and void,
with darkness over the surface of the deep and a wind
from God sweeping over the water . . ."

THE POET WHO WROTE THIS BREATHTAKING NARRATIVE
was someone just like us, someone who wanted to understand, to imagine the origins of life itself. And what a vision: The world began with an act of supreme creativity. Something was made out of nothing, and life began its glorious unfolding. There's such a wonderful order to it all: each day yielding a new form of life; every day seeming to reach such a satisfying conclusion; then humankind, created "in the image of the Creator."

It's no wonder so many people over so many centuries have wanted to take the opening of Genesis literally. How incredible to think the world emerged from a fourteen-billion-year "week" of awesome power and sheer inspiration. How marvelous to imagine that humankind was made in the image of an artistic genius worthy of being named the Creator, God, or "all that is." St. Thomas Aquinas called God "Artist of Artists."

> The world was left unfinished so that humans could have a part in Creation.

The first chapter of Genesis is a meditation on the yearning to create; a yearning, the Biblical author intuited, that is our very birthright. It was actually a unique mythological innovation to imbue human beings with a creative spirit. In the Greek myth, Prometheus rebels against Zeus, steals fire from him, and then gives this symbol of the creative force to humans. In Genesis human beings are invited into the creative process on Day Six. After the rest of the world unfolds, human beings are created in order to tend and protect it. The world was left unfinished so that humans could have a part in Creation.

These wonderfully poetic passages invite us to imagine that we, too, can create with purpose and intention; that we, too, can craft worlds. The Creation story is so powerful in part because it awakens this yearning. It taps into a basic human desire to connect with something larger than ourselves, to feel like we contribute to the continuation and evolution of the universe.

There's a daily meditation that reminds us that Genesis happens every morning when we open our eyes to the light that marks what is always the first day. This meditation is an expression of gratitude for the continuing renewal of the act of Creation. It expresses the intuition that by simply waking up we are part of the rhythm of life. Then we really can wake up: We can consciously participate in the creative process.

The poet understood that we are all world builders. When we write a poem, give birth to a child, build a home, or help launch a company, we are acting from that same Godlike impulse. We are answering that overwhelming, wondrous yearning to be creative, to contribute something of value, to make a difference.

Whenever I teach the Creation story from this perspective, describing the wonder of the creative impulse, I get a mix of reactions. "Would it be that creativity was always that way! I'd be out of business," a therapist who counseled artists and actors for a living once said to me. Like her, I often hear people bemoan their creative output. Some people talk about those wonderful, productive times when they feel at one with their project, whether it's an art piece, a yoga class, or a strategic plan. But then they inevitably speak of the disappointment and anxiety when they don't have that experience. If creativity is our birthright, why aren't we always creative? Or, as a writer friend of mine put it, "creative on command"?

So many of us see creativity as some kind of magic spell, rare form of genius, or external energy we should be able to tap into if only we escaped the mundane demands of life, had the right space, enough money, lived in the city, the country, out of the country! Perhaps our expectations are so high in part because we live in the most creative and productive time in human history. We have become the kind of world builders the Genesis poet could never have imagined. Technological innovation, medical breakthroughs, and scientific discoveries are regular occurrences. Contemporary museums are overflowing with masterpieces. Whereas it once took hundreds of years to build a cathedral, now we plan to rebuild the World Trade Center in seven years.

It all seems so amazing, so intoxicating, so full of possibility, that we forget how complex and contradictory the process of creativity is. We want that feeling of flow, of being at one with our work, not sometimes but all the time. I noticed recently that creativity occupies its own shelf in the Personal Growth section of Barnes & Noble. We want creativity to be self-actualizing without being self-sacrificing. We want it always to feel good.

But creativity is so full of anxieties and failures, boredom and drudgery. When we resist these experiences because they are painful or frightening, we deny ourselves a rich aspect of life. We also may not realize how creative we are already—because we expect creativity to look and feel a certain way. We want creativity to only be that experience of flow, that feeling of boundarylessness and becoming one with our project. In fact, we misunderstand the experience of flow, that seamless creative moment; that feeling of mastery we so desire.

Mihaly Csikszentmihalyi, the psychologist who coined the term "flow" and researched its characteristics, showed that one of the primary impediments to this experience is our expectation that it will feel pleasant and fulfilling. Only after the fact does the champion swimmer remember those hours of laps, those times her muscles burned, and those fiercely competitive races as the best times of her life. The renowned cellist Pablo Casals spoke about his "tyrannical" twelve-hour practice sessions, his bleeding fingers. Gymnasts describe their calluses and swollen knees. Of course, there are those moments of losing oneself in the process, but most of the time the experience of flow is only in retrospect. It comes at the end of the process.

There are so many aspects of creativity and so many manifestations of the creative act, and when we really think about it creativity entails a complex array of feelings: exuberance and anxiety; fear and hope; dissonance and harmony; discomfort and determination. I've found it helpful to identify four basic stages: Inspiration, Preparation, Incubation, and Illumination. Each has its own feeling tone and none of them has a schedule: We can't control or predict how long each stage will last nor what our experience of it will be. We are always being creative—but it's not a command performance.

I've never known anyone who couldn't report at least one experience of being creatively inspired. Inspiration is commonly mistaken for being the moment of finding a solution, but actually inspiration is the moment we recognize a problem that needs solving. Inspiration is about yearning, not finding. We've all felt inspiration, that need to create order out of chaos; that experience of seeing a void and wanting to fill it. We want to find a new way that will yield different and better results. The spirit of creation arises in us: We are inspirited—inspired. Inspiration is truly a holy experience, not because it's transcendent or wonderful, but because it's an experience of the intensity of life, a reminder that there is so much more to be discovered, to be known. Suddenly we're submerged in the toomuchness of life.

Inspiration is about yearning, not finding. It is the moment we recognize a problem that needs solving, not the moment of finding a solution.

Of course we feel anxiety and fear! We've been inspired to see the problem, and that is always uncomfortable. Innovation is almost always born of a feeling that something is missing or wrong. It's the post office worker who thinks there's a better way to sort the mail. It's the writer who stays up night after night after her kids go to sleep to try to get that opening chapter right. It's the parent who sees that the old ways of disciplining his child aren't working. Or the spouse who sees the patterns in her relationship that need changing.

Creativity demands that we break from our habitual forms of thinking and acting. The conventions and rules we grew up with, the old solutions, just won't suffice. And we must divert our energy from the known to the unknown. We must turn possibility into actuality. Nothing could be more daunting; which is why there's almost always a period of resistance, of self-judgment, of fear of failure. We may just up and abandon the project at this point—often we do so without being aware of it. Maybe we're not ready. Maybe we'll come back to it. Maybe we'll move on to the next thing. Inspiration can be that scary.

But when we decide to go for it, when we step away from our preprogrammed reactions to the world, we have the opportunity to launch ourselves into a whole new landscape, a new reality, whether in our work, our relationships, or the wider world. The Hindu tradition describes this process so beautifully: When we can overcome our primal nature or libido (*rajas*) and our past conditioning and habits (*tamas*), we can be creative; we can achieve a new world (*sattawa*). Victor Havel said, "The ultimate creativity is to choose one's attitude in any set of circumstances." Creativity is not a gift or a personality bestowed upon us from on high or by our DNA; it's a conscious choice to enter the realm of the unknown. To be inspired is to enter the spirit of life in all its messiness and awesomeness.

Once we choose to follow our inspiration, to heed the call, it's time to do the work. We've opened ourselves up to the possibility of new ideas—now it's time to find them. This is the information-gathering stage, the period of preparation. We need to study the inner workings of the problem and the other solutions. We need to listen to and watch other creators who've traveled similar paths. We must research and learn. These are those hours at the library, on the internet, consulting experts, observing and absorbing.

It's also a period of practice, of skill development, a time during which we develop our craft. I remember talking to the father of a Little League champion pitcher about how she got to be so good: She'd just pitched a no-hitter, and we were all in awe. He told me she watched hours of base-ball, both live and taped games, on television and then went outside to the yard and imitated each move. She did all this for the entire off season two years in a row. It's like those thousands of jump shots Michael Jordan had to take before he made the one from that impossible angle; the hours in the lab trying different combinations; the pages and pages of notes scattered around your office.

Creativity demands that we break from our habitual forms of thinking and acting. And it demands a high tolerance for failure.

No innovative idea comes out of nowhere. There really is no such thing as a true "aha" moment, although we may experience it that way. There are always incredible amounts of preparation involved in any creative project. We may see the jump shot and hear the announcer call it magic, the most creative move ever, but we don't see the six-year-old, the twelve-year-old, the twenty-year-old standing in front of that basket day after day. As Ben Hogan, the golf champion, said, "The more I practice, the luckier I get." On a grander note, before the ancient Israelites experienced their revelation at Mt. Sinai, we're told they prepared themselves for three days. We can't encounter a new idea, have that "eureka" moment, or experience the silence that is everything until we do the work, walk the walk, step-by-step until we reach the mountainside.

Then it's time to incubate, to allow those ideas to swim in our consciousness, to rub up against each other, even bang against each other occasionally. Ideas are germinating and settling in, giving rise to new ones. We are outlining, drafting, playing, guessing, experimenting. We're uncovering contradictions, impious meanings, different combinations. We may come up against obstacles, both internally and externally: people who resist our ideas; ways we judge ourselves. We're doubting as much as we're discovering; eliminating as much as we're generating. We're struggling and wrestling with both new and old truths. We can sometimes be difficult to be with during these periods— the most creatively engaged people usually are.

For every breakthrough that we have, we have hundreds of periods of drudgery and boredom. A writer once told me that when it was time to start a new chapter after weeks of research, she'd have the overwhelming desire to take a nap. The task seemed simultaneously overwhelming and mundane; quite simply not worth it. "I'd rather be doing anything but this," she said. And then when she did take a nap, things incubated in ways she never expected. Thomas Edison would doze off in a chair with his hands draped over the armrest. In each hand he held a ball. When he drifted into a state between sleeping and waking, his hands would relax and the balls would drop. He'd be awakened by the noise the balls made and he'd immediately make notes on whatever ideas had come to him. That's the meaning of "sleep on it." Our seeming diversions are so often part of the incubation stage. We may experience these as distinctly uncreative times. We may even judge them and ourselves, thereby disrupting or preempting the creative process itself. For many of us, boredom equals disengagement and failure, especially in the context of this stimulation-driven culture.

Then there are those infamous creative blocks: the periods when we don't produce anything at all. These times of tedium, even despair, are often precursors to some great discovery: periods of dormancy that actually give birth to extraordinary output. Boredom is really an invitation to be creative. The drone of the Xerox machine, the endlessly long meeting, the moments staring at a blank screen—if we stay open and receptive, these can lead us to new plateaus.

When I was working on my first public-television series, I often felt blocked and afraid. I found taking a different walk to work made a world of difference. It allowed me to break from routine ways of thinking and feeling—to create on the inside what was happening on the outside. The night before the first show was to be filmed, my doubts and fears turned into overwhelming anxiety. I was to stand up in front of the cameras and talk about ideas I'd been developing for a lifetime;

I had no idea how I was going to do it, how to be Irwin on camera. I lay in my bed sobbing; I felt so alone, so inadequate, so frightened. I was convinced I couldn't do it, and to top it off I was ashamed of such a seemingly lame response to a creative challenge. I got up and took a shower and then went for a long walk around the harbor outside my hotel.

During my walk I remembered a scene from the movie *Broadcast News*: The producer, played by actress Holly Hunter, is a great innovator in a whole new media form—live television news. But in this scene she's sitting hunched over at her desk before what was to be an incredibly intense workday, one in which failure in front of the cameras faced her at every turn. She's weeping loudly and uncontrollably. Then she simply gets up and begins her day. I wondered if she'd have been as good as she was if she hadn't lost it on a regular basis. Creativity means being on the edge. When we can acknowledge and fully experience that, we can be all the more creative. She took her vulnerability and anxiety with her into her day—and that's in part what made her so amazingly effective. Fear and uncertainty are inside the incubation process. I realized when I came back from my walk that if I could be as honest the next morning as I was just then, the show would be great. Suddenly the possibility of failure seemed dimmer and much less important.

Creativity demands that we have a high tolerance for failure. In our celebrity-oriented culture, we tend to mistake creativity for success and fame, when creativity actually very often means failure. We all know the stories. Edison tried thousands of different light bulbs before the first one worked. Einstein once said, "I have not failed. I've just found ten thousand ways that would not work." He said he loved mistakes, because it meant there was one more thing he understood.

Making mistakes is messy, unnerving, and sometimes discouraging—especially during these times of preparation and incubation. Sometimes we have to throw out those first drafts and start from the beginning. We have to clean up the messes we've left in our path in order to start with a clean slate. As a teacher of mine used to say, "Even Leonardo da Vinci destroyed some of his canvases. Even he had to clean his brushes and start over."

At one of my talks about Creation in the Genesis story, an artist asked a great question: "Where were the mounds of dried-out clay thrown in anguish into a corner?" Creation seems so quick and effortless. Maybe da Vinci had to clean up after himself, but what about God? What kind of model for creativity did that Genesis poet create after all? It all seems so glorious, so neat, so perfect, so unrealistic, especially when seen in the context of our own creative experiences. But there's a Talmudic teaching that imagines that God created ten worlds, destroying each one, then trying again, until finally having that one wonderful, productive week. And in the Book of Job, there's that very different creation story in which chaos is always at the doorstep of creation, and God is continually keeping things from falling apart. Besides, there was plenty of dried-out clay in the first Creation story—Adam was created out of dust. Earlier failures became the stuff of innovation.

This emblematic story of Creation has a powerful underlying message. Embedded in this seemingly idyllic fairy tale is a surprising teaching: Our work is never really done; no creation is ever perfect. One would think words like "excellent," "awesome," or "complete" would describe the acts of Creation. This is the very first scene in the Bible in which all that is comes to be; what could be more awesome than that! Yet the word used to describe each day's creation is simply *tov* or "good." If there were creative highs or declarations of triumph during that first week we don't hear them. On the sixth day, we read: "And God saw all that God had made and found it very good." Creation is less than perfect, but good is good enough.

We have images of the lonely artist; the isolated writer in his garret; the scientist late at night in her lab. The Creation story turns this on its head. No worthy project can be completed alone. At the end of that first week, human beings join in the effort. The Creator makes cocreators or coevolvers. The God character is no longer the only one making it happen. God's next job is another supremely creative role: nurturing and teaching other creators. Creativity and innovation are always collaborations of some kind. We are always responding to the work that has preceded us, even if we're departing from it. Most of us have colleagues or partners who either support us or contribute directly to the goal. And we're always inspiring our successors.

So many of the tensions endemic to creativity are captured in the story of the Israelites at Mt. Sinai. There are two paradigms of creativity juxtaposed in this one scene, one coming right after the other as if to invite our comparison. The first is the story of the golden calf, followed by the building of a tabernacle in the desert. That moment at the base of the mountain was wide open with possibilities for human expression and realization. Both stories have so much to teach us about our process, the dark side of creativity and the light.

As the ancient Israelites stood at the base of Mt. Sinai, they experienced the full dimensions of the creative moment. Having been freed from slavery in Egypt, they were now free to create their lives. They were given an opportunity to experience a new sense of their own capacities, which they simply couldn't have had as slaves. They'd left their old identity behind, broken from their past, and now had to construct a new future. Meanwhile, on top of Mt. Sinai, Moses received instructions for building a tabernacle, a temporary temple in the desert, a sanctuary for the divine presence. In Hebrew the word "tabernacle" also means neighborhood, a dwelling place for a people, a community.

What kind of world do you want to create?

Below, the people had an encounter with the Creator that was dramatic and fiery, as creative inspiration can so often be. Everything seemed altered. Time stood still, and everything hung in the balance. Their senses fused: We're told they saw thunder and heard lightning. They were in a different reality. Then they heard the *aleph*, the great silence, and experienced the vast openness of life. The questions they heard in all that silence were, "What now? Who will we be?" The fear of the unknown is central to creativity. Will the Israelites be able to rise to the creative challenge? To follow the inspiration? To become a people? We, too, face similar turning points. We all have our Egypts. When we're freed from the authority of our parents, the expectations of our bosses, the limitations of a dysfunctional marriage—what now? Do we really want the power to create our own lives? When it's time for us to run the company, create our own family, construct a new relationship—are we up to the challenge? Or would we rather stay in Egypt, where the landmarks are familiar, if confining?

For the Israelites, the encounter was overwhelming. They shuddered, were knocked off their feet, and fell back from the mountain. They retreated from the questions. The problem of freedom seemed too difficult to tackle. And then they tried to fill the silence with their old script; to resurrect the past. Instead of building a tabernacle, they built the golden calf. At that moment of unprecedented freedom they engaged in what was a magnificent act of creativity and construction. But it was an old image, one that was worshipped in Egypt. Just at the moment when they were invited to create something new, they preserved a deadened form of the past. They literally recast it. They affirmed what they already knew rather than stretching into the future. Inspiration aborted.

Of course they were attracted to the golden, glittering calf: The past is compelling. Their idolatry was the creation of what had been rather than what could be. They didn't yet know that creativity dissolves the system of givens that one inherits. Instead of facing their discomfort and fear, in the confusion of the inspirational moment, they regressed. After building the calf out of their own golden jewelry, they eat, drink, and dance. The biblical author chose such a telling word to describe this dance: "circle dance." They were dancing around in circles. The Israelites had chosen to go around in circles rather than reach toward the future.

Often, after we see the challenge, our first move is to retreat. Only then can we step forward. Sometimes we need to reach backward before we can reach toward something new. The key is to not mistake our first move as our last. Just because we misstep doesn't mean we preempt illumination. We can be loyal to our past and still transcend it. When Moses came down from the mountain and saw what the people had done, he was enraged. Is this what you do when you're invited to create your own lives?! Moses destroyed the calf, and then something remarkable happened. A different kind of construction began. It was the onset of illumination.

It was as if the people heard the question once again: What kind of world do you really want to create? This time they heard it as an invitation rather than a demand; an evolution rather than an abrupt break from the past. The golden calf might not have been a failure, but part of the preparation. And the language in these passages is so markedly different than in those which precede them. The construction of the calf takes only a few lines; you don't need preparation and incubation if you're simply repeating the past. The people bring Aaron their gold rings and the calf is built. But the tabernacle takes six chapters to build.

Before that there are six chapters of instructions about how to build it and what it should contain. The people are to use gold once again, but also hundreds of other materials to be combined in many new and intricate ways. This is the information-gathering stage; now they are willing to jump in and learn. This time their response to the unknown, to the call of inspiration, has been to prepare. Rather than creating a solid idol, they construct a space, a safe place for creativity to continue, for the Creator to dwell.

Craft, design, make. These words are used eighty times in these passages describing the building of the tabernacle. They're the same three words used to describe the acts of Creation in Genesis. Now it's the people who are working hard to make a world; a house worthy of containing all that is. The people are clearly in a state of flow, which Csikszentmihalyi describes as "a sense of participation in determining the content of life."

We, too, can create with purpose and intention. We, too, can craft worlds.

The poet's language so beautifully captures our creative yearnings. Everyone "whose heart so moves him" is invited to bring gifts with which to build. The Israelites contribute their gold and silver, their yarns and linens, and their oil and spices and wood as a "freewill offering" until there's more than enough. The people are called "inspired artisans, carvers, designers, weavers." They use their expertise to address their new challenge of freedom. The women spin blue, purple, and crimson yarns as the men build the grand tent in very specific dimensions, with silver sockets and bars of acacia wood and planks of gold.

One commentary describes a tapestry with a different scene on each side. When you've been inspired, prepared, and incubated, there's an element of impossibility to the next stage—illumination. We can combine fragments of our imagination in untold ways. What a glorious world! What amazing creators! Miraculously, in the middle of the desert there's a tabernacle: illumination in the midst of a barren landscape. Creation in the shadow of idolatry now becomes creation in the shadow of God.

The head architect of this monumental and complex structure is Bezalel, whose name actually means "in the shadow of God." He's "endowed with a divine spirit of skill, ability, and knowledge." In Hebrew the word for knowledge is the same word as that for lovemaking, intimacy. Bezalel combines materials both old and new to create. The sages say he pulled himself loose of all the forms of Egypt to build something new.

Moses told Bezalel to make the tabernacle according to God's instructions, but he made it according to his vision of his own time and place. The tabernacle is an improvisation. But you can only improvise after you've been inspired and gone through all the preparation and incubation. Then you can integrate and leap into the future. The commentators say that when Bezalel was praised, he said none of it had anything to do with him. As so many artists describe it, he became a channel for creativity itself.

We are all Bezalels. We are lovers and weavers; architects and poets. The playwright George Bernard Shaw once said that life is not about finding yourself but creating yourself. Like the ancient Israelites, we always have a choice: Will we build golden calves or tabernacles? Sometimes it's hard to know the difference. The good news is, we can always start again.

THE PRACTICE OF BEING

"MOMMY, WHY DO YOU GO TO WORK?" A FRIEND OF MINE told me her son asked her this question as she rushed out the door one morning. It was what she'd always dreaded he might ask, and as she described it she had a serious pang of that all-too-familiar "working mom's guilt." She dropped her bags, took off her coat, and began to explain. She told him that her job paid her money which gave them the beautiful house they live in. "But, Mommy, why do we need a beautiful house?" To each answer, he had a question: "Why do we need so much food?" "Why do I need all these toys?" Finally, the killer: "Why is work more important than me?"

She described how in a flash she'd realized his questioning had nothing to do with her going to work every day: He'd never known her to do anything else. In fact, she'd come home from work early the previous day, as she sometimes did, to spend time with him. But had she really spent time with him? As they'd sat on the floor playing with LEGOs, she remembered feeling antsy, distracted, and worried that she'd left so many e-mails unanswered, that she might not meet next week's deadline—and she found herself thinking that work was way more fun and engaging than LEGO. To top it off, her son couldn't make the pieces fit, couldn't really make anything at all. She'd not only been disinterested, but felt unable to help him in any constructive way. After a while she told him she'd be right back and went to the kitchen to get a jump on making dinner.

I remember thinking how honest she was, how self-aware. But the obvious pain it caused her made me want to ask, "Why in the world can't you cool out? Why can't you just be?" I restrained myself only because I knew she was asking herself the same questions and that the answers were anything but simple.

I hear so many people complain that they don't know how to relax; that they just can't seem to "let it all go" so that they can enjoy the rest of life. At the same time, they talk about how much they fear falling behind at work, that it's gotten so much more intense, jobs so much less secure. They really can't afford to step away, not even on weekends. They may compromise by limiting their after-hours work to "just e-mails." I know others who are quite wealthy, who really don't need to be working so hard, but who can't seem to bring themselves to

We all yearn for a sense of completion, of accomplishment.

slow down. Their identities are so wrapped up in what they do, and they fear they won't be able to maintain their "standard of living," a turn of phrase I find ironic since their standard undermines their living. And even when people do take time off, they often don't find it all that relaxing. One mom told me guiltily, "When I go to work on Monday, I feel like I'm going to a spa!"

Of course, parents seem to struggle the most. The balance issues facing working mothers and fathers today are real; society simply isn't offering the support and services families need. But there's also a kind of addiction to doing, an epidemic of busyness that seems to plague many families, often without them even realizing it. Soccer practice, play dates, errands, home improvement, working out—you name it; there's always an activity or project that needs doing, even on the days supposedly set aside for family. The kids have to do what their friends are doing; they just can't fall behind—go to museums to become cultured, or participate in after-school activities to keep stimulated. Others compensate for their lack of relaxation by buying more stuff, trying to make their homes more beautiful and comfortable, plopping down in front of the TV with an indulgent snack in hand, or going out to a bar. On Sunday nights, so many people lament, "Where did the weekend go?" None of this is news; there've been countless articles and books about simplifying our lives, the overscheduled child, and the health benefits of relaxing with friends and family. But our drive to achieve and our inability to rest seem to get the best of us nevertheless.

Even those of us who love our work, who have found creative expression in our vocations, have a hard time stopping, even if the demands of the job itself are not that great. Because of advances in technology and education levels, more and more of us see our work as an end in itself, a creative act that connects us to something larger than ourselves. We've become intoxicated with the effort and addicted to the financial rewards (which for some levels of society have become so much greater in the last fifty years). We want a sense of completion, of accomplishment, and when we don't have it, we feel unfulfilled and even more determined to get it the next time. Work can crowd out the rest of life and become a kind of idolatry. Eventually our work, too, will suffer. We're in danger of burning out. America's work ethic is out of whack and so, of course, is our ethics of leisure. We yearn for a break but we don't know how to take one.

Although modern society has greatly exacerbated the problem, burnout is hardly new. There's a scene in Exodus which captures this syndrome perfectly. Moses has succumbed to the allure and pull of his own creative efforts and responsibilities. This might seem appropriate; after all, he is the leader of the people and teaching people to live responsibly when they've been slaves their entire lives is no easy task. Leadership positions can be especially intoxicating, as there's often the desire to be a hero, to go it alone. The best of leaders tend to be simultaneously self-important and self-sacrificing; that's, in part, what makes them great.

At one point Moses's wife Zipporah and their two sons, accompanied by Moses's father-in-law Jethro, come to visit Moses at his encampment in the desert after many months of separation. Moses had left his family behind when he returned to Egypt to free his people. In the scene, Moses embraces only Jethro. This is a painful, glaring act of neglect.

Later Jethro sees Moses standing before a line of thousands of Israelites who are waiting to hear his wisdom about their life challenges and questions; to get his judgments; to tell them what to do. And Moses speaks to them one by one well into the night. Jethro is clearly concerned. He's just seen Moses ignore Jethro's daughter and grandchildren. He says, "You're going to wither up." He sees that Moses's flow has gotten the best of him, and he's headed toward burnout. He's not even serving the people well by making them wait. Things have gone too far.

Perhaps Jethro sees an arrogance that can't possibly serve Moses or his people in the long run. He approaches Moses and asks him what he's doing taking care of so many people on his own. Moses is mystified: These are his people; he's got to attend to them. Jethro encourages Moses, practically insists that he appoint deputies and judges—a kind of graded delegation of authority—who he can train to issue judgments in his stead. Remarkably for a workaholic, Moses immediately institutes Jethro's plans. The rabbinic sages knew the price of work subsuming all else. They described Zipporah crying out to the wives of Moses's appointees, warning them that they'll never make love again.

Even the most meaningful work can become a form of slavery. It can trump the rest of life. We all need people like Jethro in our lives; people who understand that being is an essential aspect of our humanness, as important as any other. But most of us don't have Jethros, and so the yearning for rest and replenishment is ignored and buried. We may feel guilty about or dismiss this need as secondary to our productivity and our commitment to helping others and contributing to the world.

Rabbi Joseph B. Soloveitchik, one of the most important Jewish thinkers of the twentieth century, taught that there are two human typologies portrayed in the two different Creation stories at the beginning of Genesis. In the first, human beings are told to master and rule the land. This represents our drive to produce and transform, design and build, improve and control, achieve and accomplish. And it's an essential creative mindset.

In the second story the language and mood are markedly different. The story is softer, more gentle. There is nothing to do or accomplish. The garden is already planted and flourishing, and humans are there to enjoy it. Everything is provided: The rivers overflow, the fruit is ripe and ready to eat. In other words, part of being human is pausing to marvel at and partake in all that is. We are to relate to the world in all its glory. We are to breathe deeply, rest, reflect, lounge, and love. We are to *be* in the garden. This, too, is an essential creative mindset.

The Genesis poet gave life to human beings on the last day of Creation because he saw us as being at the very cutting edge of evolution. We are after all the only creatures to reflect on our own creative impulse; the only ones conscious of our need to create. But you need to be careful when you're on the cutting edge. It's easy to experience oneself as being somehow superior to the rest of the world rather than being a part of it, and also profoundly responsible for it. Making time to experience, rather than rule, over nature is so essential. It's a reminder of the broader context of creativity. When you're on the cutting edge, you'd better stand back and gain perspective or risk destroying what you are meant to protect.

Together these two Creation stories teach that we are meant both to do and to be; and both require creativity. Creativity is more expansive than we imagined, and relaxation requires as much discipline and effort as work. Just as God doesn't ask Adam and Eve to sweat over their role in Creation or work hard to improve themselves, they're also not encouraged to just lie around, let it all go, and mellow out. When we aren't busying ourselves, many of us think a day off should be effortless, fluid, simple; that we need only give ourselves permission and we'll enter a different head space, and that peace and relaxation will come flooding in. But the first two humans were encouraged to "till and tend" the land. There's creative effort, although it's of a very different kind. They move from master to tend-er.

It's no accident that Sabbath has been recovered, reappropriated, and in some cases re-envisioned in the last few years. A number of books have been published recently about the Sabbath as an antidote to hectic, modern living—and as a stopgap to the unceasing desire to create and contribute to the world. More and more people are coming to me for advice about how to make Sabbath a part of their lives. They see it as a way to alleviate or cure their workaholism. They desperately want

Even the most meaningful work can trump the rest of life.

to learn to take a genuine break, and without exception they resonate with the four qualities of Sabbath: rest, reflection, relationship, and replenishment. We all need a breather, a time to literally experience our breathing, to take it in fully and let it out. We need an opportunity to reflect on our lives, to remember other parts of who we are, to spend time with our loved ones, and to gain perspective on the week so that we can wake up on the next workday, our "doing" energy restored.

Sabbath is a time to attend to the nonwork aspects of life, but here's the other side: There's nothing more creative than rest. Being is as essential as doing. Sabbath is another way in which we can become partners in Creation. And just as there's a discipline to creative work, there's a practice of creative rest as well. In fact the same verb "make" is used to describe both the work of creating the tabernacle in the desert and the Sabbath day. As Abraham Joshua Heschel wrote, on Sabbath we are to build a sanctuary in time, a place to just be.

New skills and expertise are necessary to "make" any project. All creative acts involve entering different levels of awareness in which we can access new insights and perspectives. The art of being is no different. Yogis study for years before being able to rest still in "corpse" pose. Meditators describe the effort and skill it takes to focus on a mantra. Sabbath is a day-long "being" practice that calls on four levels of consciousness, and they, too, take time and practice to cultivate. They correspond to the four verbs used to describe the first Sabbath day in the Creation story: cease, rest, bless, and make holy.

The first level of being is to cease doing. Quite simply, we need to stop the work of the week. This can be a lot tougher than it sounds.

Sometimes I find myself sneaking in a few extra minutes at the office even when I know it's time to leave. I call it the "one more" dance: one more phone call, one more e-mail, one more paragraph, one more minute. A minute can turn into an hour before we know it. I know many people who just can't leave work behind even when they do leave—they'll pile their bags full of work to do at home; e-mail themselves additional files; if they don't actually get to the work, they feel better knowing they can.

The Genesis poet invites us to cultivate a stopping mindset. If God can stop working at the end of that first cosmic week, surely we can. The poet tells us that on the seventh day God is "finished" when obviously this isn't the case. It's the very beginning of the larger project of Creation, of humankind's unfolding. And yet the Creator was "done." Like the God character, we're encouraged to suspend disbelief; to have a fantasy of completion. Can we have that sense of being done even when we know there's always more to do, so much toil and struggle ahead of us? If we're willing to try, we enter the second level of being; we can begin to rest.

For many of us, making believe our work is done and stepping out of the rat race is really tough. The first thing people notice when they begin a Sabbath practice is how work and material desires crowd out other thoughts. What I say to them is, "Congratulations, you've reached the second level of Sabbath consciousness." Even when I physically stop working, worries, thoughts, and insights about my day or week keep popping into my mind, sometimes gnawing at me. As with any meditation practice, I try to gently observe them, to breathe through them. When work mode grips me, I start again. Eventually these thoughts soften and recede. I begin to feel clarity of mind and a fuller range of emotions. It helps when I can stop working before sunset so that twilight becomes a transition not only between day and night, but between doing and being. Other people I know take an earlier train home once a week or they walk along a more scenic route, even if it takes longer to get home.

The more we abstain from our work week activities over the next twenty-five hours, the deeper we can sink into rest consciousness. I try to abstain from anything related to business, producing, or any economic activity through the next day. I don't shop, clean the house, or answer the phone. For those beginning to think about a Sabbath practice I ask: "What activities would you need to stop in order to have one day out of the rat race?" It could be a

There's nothing more creative than rest.

day that you cease the work for which you get paid. In our culture that's already a tremendous accomplishment of being. Maybe you'll put your Daytimer away; not look at your BlackBerry; set your cell phone to silent. Some people find it meaningful to cease from being a "consumer" as well; they cook meals with the food they have, or leave the dry cleaning for another day. They allow for a one-day fantasy that they have everything they need.

For others, even imagining "not" doing anything seems stifling and oppressive, the very opposite of creative. You know how much one more day of work might further your career goals; how much easier your week would be if you could do the laundry. If you could drive to the mall and grab a burger, wouldn't that be more relaxing than having to prepare your own food beforehand? And if you love your work because it engages your mind and heart, isn't that a more sacred way to spend the day? I encourage you to try it all—doing and not doing a number of different activities to see how your consciousness shifts or how it doesn't.

Like most disciplines, a Sabbath practice can't be designed or adopted overnight. No one has an "aha" experience every time, or even most of the time: that perfect day of rest, a profound twenty-five hours of reflection, or the feeling of being totally rejuvenated. And when one first begins a Sabbath practice it can feel uncomfortable, odd, or even unnecessary. But as Ram Dass teaches, give any practice forty days before deciding whether it's working. And if you're fortunate to have an inherited practice—whether it's a Friday, Saturday, or Sunday Sabbath, or a meditation or prayer practice, I encourage you to reexplore it before trying something new. There's incredible richness to be found in rituals that have a connection to your past and your community.

Whether you decide not to work, not to shop, whether you spend the day reading a novel, socializing with friends, or playing with your kids (really playing), the most important thing is your intention; *kavanah* in Hebrew. It's important to become conscious of your actions and the meaning behind them; to slow down enough to do so. Sabbath actually is not at all about letting go, and it's not just about stopping. It's about inviting in: It's about *doing* being.

The next level of being is blessing consciousness. We expand our sense of who we are and treasure our lives. On my day of being, the first act of blessing is when my family lights candles to usher in the Sabbath before sundown. So many wisdom traditions ritualize light, whether votive candles or candles on a Buddhist altar. Candlelight casts different shadows and gives off different light. Candlelight dinners bring couples closer. Candles create a magical, romantic, separate space that evokes and awakens feelings that stay under the surface in brighter light. The psalmist says the candle of God is like the soul of the human being. Light brings the soul out of slumber.

There's a tradition of closing one's eyes and ushering the light toward you with your hands, awakening oneself to the interior light. With our eyes closed we always can see more clearly. What do I want to see more clearly? I want to see myself in a wider context, connected to something more than just my ambitious, work self. Sometimes, when the candles are lit, I imagine that brightest of lights fourteen billion years ago: the big bang that brought us all to this moment standing together at this table.

What a blessing it is to reconnect with those we love, rekindling our most cherished relationships. Some families also reach out beyond their smallest circle to offer hospitality to acquaintances and sometimes strangers. In our home, we eat a leisurely, special Friday-night meal— perhaps from a new recipe or with some new delicacy—at a beautifully set table. When I sit down in the candlelight, a home-cooked meal before me, and look across the table at the glowing faces of family and friends, I find myself thinking how little I saw of them during the week; how fast I grabbed those meals before rushing out the door; how rarely I checked in with my kids; how little I spoke with friends; wondering if I even kissed my wife all week.

We've all experienced times with those we love when we feel so grateful to have them in our lives, aware of how lucky we are. During the week we rarely have time to stop and feel thankful for even the most pleasant and wonderful things; and gratitude is such a central quality of being. There's a Friday night meditation in which each person gives thanks for one thing that happened during the week. As you go around the table you learn so much about what happened to everyone during those days. You feel you somehow know them better—and your gratitude is deepened.

Every family has a favorite saying, some maxim, some teaching, a song or expression that captures the uniqueness of the group. Singing a favorite song, telling a familiar story, or having everyone share a thought or observation from the week can be a way to create a different environment, a specialness to the evening meal. A family I know has a member who attends Twelve-Step recovery meetings. They say the Serenity Prayer together over dinner to usher in every weekend: "Grant me the serenity to accept the things I cannot change; to change the things I can; and the wisdom to know the difference." What a wonderful way to let go of the anxiety of the week.

I bless my children with words from the most ancient recorded blessing: "May God bless you and keep you. May God's light shine upon you and be gracious to you. May God's presence be lifted upon you and give you peace." My wife thinks of something during the week that she wants to emphasize about each child's goodness, some unique quality, some story that she tells them quietly. Lovers also bless each other on Sabbath eve. I sing to Dana a traditional love song. It's important to each of us, but also to our daughters, who get to see their normally busy parents stopping to offer public affection and kind words.

Some people resist these practices: Why should there be some specific time to tell my kids or my mate that I love them? Shouldn't it be natural and spontaneous? Yes and no. Our culture highly values spontaneity and tends to ignore ritual practice, but most of our lifestyles don't actually allow for much spontaneity at all. The intuition behind **Our actions change our thoughts and feelings.** the Friday night ritual is that when we practice expressing love, it becomes more natural. When we bless or intentionally express love to our partner or our children once a week, we are actually more apt to be spontaneously affectionate during the other days.

Our actions change our thoughts and feelings; this is, in fact, the purpose of ritual. There have been many times when I've fought with my wife during the week and the tension is still there on Friday nights, or when my kids have been driving me crazy to the point where I'd like nothing more than to get away for the weekend. But when blessing is a discipline, when you observe a ritual of loving, it's incredible the way feelings of resentment and anger can be softened, even transformed by the meal's end. We're reminded of the wider context of these relationships, of how blessed we are to have each other, how even the struggles and conflict can add dimension to life.

Some of the things we do on Sabbath are not all that different from what we do during the week. It's the way we do them, the shift in intention. We may go to sleep a little earlier and awaken without an alarm clock; rather than watching the news, we read that novel that we've been wanting to get to; we might walk more slowly or get up from the couch less often; we talk about the joyful things of life, tell jokes, laugh at ourselves—keeping the arguments and complaining to a minimum. And we spend time reflecting, taking long walks, studying sacred texts, or praying.

Here's my Sabbath in a nutshell: I eat, sing, take walks, nap, meditate, tell stories, read for enjoyment, listen, watch the sun set, and see the stars come up. And I make love. Traditionally, sex is a key activity of the day. We're encouraged to return to our bodies, to take full pleasure in the sensual parts of life. Making love is slow, luscious, playful. I remember my parents' Saturday "naps"; the sound of music floating down from upstairs; how they'd emerge from their bedroom so happy and relaxed. Our Saturday night dinners were some of the best times we had as a family—the many qualities of the Sabbath had sunk in, but also the joyous, satiated mood of my parents infused the evening with a kind of softness and generosity.

Actually, napping itself is considered a sacred practice. It's a way to refresh and replenish. But it's also a means of entering a different mindspace, of integrating the different parts of ourselves. Wisdom traditions always have understood that there are multiple states of awareness. In our dreams, different selves are revealed. When I wake up from a Saturday afternoon nap, my house seems aglow. I feel simultaneously languid and refreshed; settled into myself.

And then there are those rare moments of grace; those times when I experience the fourth level of consciousness; when I feel a sense of sacred stillness and release from all worry and anxiety. I'm subsumed in love and gratitude. I feel a sense of completeness, of all-encompassing holiness and joy. I call this the "flow of being," as it can only be matched by the creative flow of work at its best. There's no way to make it happen. This level of consciousness only can be reached after experiencing the other three; after practicing being and accomplishing not-accomplishing.

When we make being a practice, whether on Friday or Sunday or Tuesday, whether for twenty-five hours, twelve hours, or two hours, we come to realize that being isn't simply an antidote to the frenzy of doing. It not only counteracts our productive obsessions but actually can mitigate the fever of the week before it descends on us. And it can become the nurturing ground for all kinds of creativity.

Before the Israelites began building the tabernacle in the desert, they were reminded of the Sabbath. This seems kind of odd: Why talk about rest before the work has even begun? You'd think the Ultimate Manager, the Creator, would try to motivate the people by telling them how amazing the work will be, how incredible the result, getting them focused on the task at hand. After all, they're being asked to give up the precious possessions they painstakingly took out of Egypt; they're being invited to undertake a Herculean effort: building a structure worthy of their God in the middle of nowhere.

But would they have had that marvelous, masterful work experience if they hadn't remembered the Sabbath? Would they have built such a breathtaking sanctuary if they hadn't first experienced the blessing of being? Don't we all want to contribute more to the world when we know we can enjoy the fruits of what we've created? Just imagine how much more glorious our world would be if we all understood that Sabbath is the reverie that precedes Creation.

THE SABBATH OF WORK

THE AVERAGE AMERICAN SPENDS 65 PERCENT OF HIS OR
her adult life on the job. Work takes more time than all the other wakeful activities combined. Yet 50 percent of us claim not to be happy
with our work, according to recent studies. I hear people describe their
jobs as overwhelming, dead end, suffocating. Recent articles report
that some of the most educated women are leaving their well-paying
careers to stay home with their children in part because, as one book
title summed it up, *Work Doesn't Work Anymore*. There's more
turnover at most companies than there ever has been: People are
being laid off or quitting to find something better. The cynicism about
work has turned to bitterness for some as companies like Enron and
WorldCom have taken such brutal advantage of those who work for
them.

Sayings like "I survived the week" or "Thank God It's Friday" capture the widespread depression and anxiety about what much of work
has become. And some of us aren't surviving the week; most heart attacks occur between 8:00–9:00 on Monday mornings. Even those of us
lucky enough to be engaged in fulfilling and creative work also feel
there's too much of it. In America it's par for the course to complain
about the burdens of work; being busy and overwhelmed is a badge of
honor. For many of us, work is a four-letter word.

Yet for the first time in history, many of us have a choice about the
work we do. Most of us don't have to start at sunrise. Most of us don't have

to do backbreaking labor. Most of us have enough to eat when we don't work for a day. Many of us have the opportunity to engage our minds and hearts in creative projects. Even in our disillusionment, few of us would deny that work is an aspect of our identity and has an impact on our sense of self-worth. In many communities the first question we ask when we meet some-one is, "What do you do for a living?" And

> The yearning to produce something of value, to contribute to the unfolding of the world, is apparent in the smallest child.

there's no greater cause of depression in this country than being unemployed.

Burdensome as it can be, work is central to our sense of dignity. The yearning to produce something of value, to contribute to the unfolding of the world, is apparent in the smallest child, as Maria Montessori taught. There's the three-year-old who asks to set the table and then smiles with pride when she puts the spoon on the right side and the napkin just so—even before she's looked to you for approval. There's the teenager who earns his first five dollars mowing the lawn and who does it so much more carefully when he knows it's a real job. The young adult who proudly tells you she landed her first position. The lifelong employee who finally gets up the courage to start his own business. The retiree with a good pension and a strong golf swing who nevertheless chooses to spend every afternoon tutoring high school students. It's not just that work brings out our creativity. It's not just that we have to earn money to live. Work has intrinsic value. It is an integral part of the human journey.

Until very recently, spiritual leaders were required to have other vocations. In some traditions, many still do. Work on the material plane was considered essential and it didn't matter how holy you were considered to be. Monasteries and nunneries still produce wonderful wine, bread, and arts and crafts. Hillel was a porter; Rashi was a winemaker; Maimonides was a physician. There was an intuition that to make one's only work spiritual seeking was to try to live in Sabbath all the time, and this is not what the fourth commandment intended. Most of us forget that the first part of the fourth commandment says "you shall work."

The biblical author of those famous commandments chose to give work incredible primacy. The work and rest commandment comes before the ones that tell us to honor our parents, to not murder or steal. Work is directly connected to the acts of Creation; a way to expand the self and the world. The workweek is no less sacred than Sabbath. Perhaps what's missing is that we haven't yet made work a practice, a discipline, a spiritual art. We haven't yet developed a work consciousness, a way to bring more of who we are to the job. We need to imbue our work with as much intention and enchantment as the Sabbath day.

There's a meditation of gratitude for every weekday morning. The opening of this prayer is for some reason rarely translated into English and so is overlooked: "On this first day of the week of Sabbath . . ." "On this second day of the week of Sabbath . . ." This simple phrase invites us to take that profound appreciation for the world we cultivated on the Sabbath into the world of work. It urges us to create a Sabbath of work; in other words, to really *be* on the job.

In Hebrew the word for meaningful work, for work that is a service to Creation, is *avodah*, which is also used to mean prayer and Torah study. The Greek word for work comes from the same root as the word for energy and orgy. If we want our work to contribute to the vitality and unfolding of life, if we want our vocation to be a source of fulfillment and dignity, maybe even ecstasy, we need to develop a practice of work. We need a litmus test of the soul with which to question and probe our chosen work on a regular basis.

Whether we're an orderly or a surgeon, a clerk or a CEO, a teacher or a techie, we all can benefit from standing back from our work and asking some simple questions. When I consult with business owners and executives, I encourage them to do so at the same time as they're evaluating their quarterly earnings statements. I urge them to produce quarterly consciousness-raising statements as well. Here are four basic questions every worker should ask:

The first question is: Am I being fairly compensated or fairly compensating those who work for me? Profit is the oxygen of any work endeavor—we literally have to make a living. Salaries are the subject of so much anxiety but they are rarely seriously or openly discussed. When we reflect on compensation, when we research competitive salaries, and consult others in similar positions, we may begin to value our own and others' work differently. Money and work are inseparable; rather than denying it or resenting it, we can make salary discussions and budgeting a regular practice.

The next question to ask is: Am I proud of the product? Is what I'm working to create something of quality; does it have a purpose and benefit? If we're simply producing to produce, selling to sell, we have work without purpose; work that is disconnected from the work of Creation and evolution. It's in danger of becoming pure drudgery.

There's an exercise I encourage people to do that helps them meditate on the value of the product they make and the contribution they feel their job is making. It begins with the simple question: What is the purpose of your work? Usually money is the first answer. Then ask: What do you get from money that is even more valuable than money itself? I get to buy what I need. What do you get from buying what you need that's even more valuable than that? With every answer, the same question is asked. If within a few rounds the answer doesn't grow wider in context, entering into the emotional or spiritual realm—joy, fullness, freedom, pleasure—chances are your work is lacking.

The third question: Is my work contributing to my personal and spiritual evolution? Am I perfecting my talents and gifts? It's possible to be employed in work that makes a genuine contribution to the world but feel inwardly stalled or stifled. Even the most seemingly challenging or creative work can eventually deaden our imagination. Then we have a choice: We can reimagine the existing work, taking greater risks from where we are standing, or we can stand in a different place and find new work that will take us someplace new. No one can tell you which would be the right move, although they may try. But in the end we need to ask, "Am I being stretched?"

I think one of the reasons so many people are starting new businesses on their own today is because they are asking this question. They may make less money in the short run and have all the hassles and risks involved with self-employment and employing others, but they feel they can put their heart and soul into the process. They can bring more of their selves through that office door. Not only is the product more in their control, but the group dynamic and work environment is likely to be more aligned with their values.

Of course, our individual experience is shaped in large part by the group we work with and the relationships we have on the job. The fourth set of questions is about this very issue. What is the currency or energy of the group I work with? Do the values of the group reflect my own? Do these relationships allow me to be more honest—or cause me to be less honest? Is the energy between people alive and electric? Is there as much cooperation as competition? Does the competition motivate me or paralyze me?

Some of the first work advice I ever received was that I should keep my emotions out of the office. And it couldn't have been more wrong. A healthy work environment invites everyone to experience the full range of emotions. We should feel happy and sad, excited and afraid, angry and grateful, guilty and proud. When I became president of my organization, I felt I had to narrow my emotional range in order to be a leader. I tried to be moderate and consistent in my responses. What happened almost immediately was that my own enjoyment began to diminish—and I was far less engaging to others as well. If you want people to feel passionately committed to their jobs, there's going to need to be exuberance and disappointment in equal measure. A workplace can be largely orderly and efficient while also making room for the dialectic of emotions involved in any creative project.

I always worry when someone explains her actions at work with the often abused phrase, "It's just business." Whenever anyone says this, it means they are compromising their values. There is no such thing as a business value that is any different than it would be in the rest of life. Care and compassion, and honesty and responsibility all belong at work as much as they do at home.

When we can answer these four questions, we'll have a much clearer idea of the nature of our work. On balance, is it serving the world; is it serving me? There are four people who to me embody the Sabbath of work. They are masters of *avodah*, although they manifest their creativity and sense of purpose in different ways.

First, there's Daniel, the guru of taxi drivers, who I was lucky enough to study with for an unforgettable forty-five-minute ride. He was lively and cheerful, even at five o'clock in the morning on a rainy morning in humid, stifling Washington, D.C. When I got into his car, I was struck by the fancy-looking computer set up on the dashboard. I asked him what it did. He told me he kept an updated list of every regular customer: who expected him to come a few minutes early; who was always late; who typically asked him to stop at the ATM; what kind of bagel and coffee they liked, which he provided. I asked, "Why do you do all that?" "I get people from here to there," he said with a smile. "Whenever you take people from here to there, it's more than just a taxi ride." I thought to myself, "Wow, this guy sees taxi driving as a metaphor for the journey through life." The rest of the ride was a delight—he'd also made it his business to know everything there was to know about Washington, its highlights and history, which he shared with me as we drove.

When we got to the airport and he was taking my bags out of the trunk, it occurred to me that this bright, ambitious, affable man could have done anything he wanted with his life. I thought to say this to him, asking him if he considered going back to school, which he told me he'd never finished. Then it hit me that he was already doing everything anyone could aspire to. I got a chill as I realized I had just met a *baal agalah*, which means "wagon driver." In mystical literature, the person who takes people from town to town is almost always Elijah, who is the harbinger of the messiah. The mythical messiah ushers us into the next world, the next evolutionary moment. Daniel was doing more than I could have imagined. I told him the story as I handed him his tip. I expected him to be so grateful for my insight, to tear up, to understand his purpose more deeply. Instead he simply nodded appreciatively and knowingly and said under his breath, "*baal agalah.*"

So often we denigrate or glorify the work of others. When we find ourselves thinking, "He's not maximizing his potential" or "That's the ultimate work," it means we're masking our feelings about our own profession. I wasn't feeling much like Elijah when I took that trip; I was on my fourth consecutive week of lecturing, and I'd not yet realized that my sense of purpose was fading and burnout was on its way. I found myself feeling jealous of the vision Daniel had of his work and the clarity he had about its purpose. What if we all took the care he did in getting ourselves from here to there in life and helping others do the same? What if we could find such a broad context for our work and allow it to make the most of our gifts and capacities? He had given his work nothing short of cosmic significance.

Although his story may seem grander, Aaron Feurstein also saw his business in the context of Creation—as a lifeline for a community and a sacred collaboration. Mr. Feurstein is the owner of Malden Mills in Lawrence, Massachusetts, producers of polar fleece and Polartec. When the mill burned down in 1995 in a devastating fire, he could have walked away with $309 million in insurance payments. Lawrence was a depressed area, and the loss of the 2,500 jobs would have devastated the community. In an era of downsizing, Aaron Feurstein made the radical decision to up-size. All employees were paid full salaries while they set about rebuilding the plant. Outsiders contributed whatever they could to the building, as that, combined with the salaries, would cost more than the insurance payments. One year later, everything was rebuilt. Feurstein and the people of Lawrence had a modern plant that, within a few years, was doing $425 million in annual sales. And needless to say the group dynamic—the employees' sense of accomplishment and connection to each other and their work—was nothing less than inspiring. It's no stretch of the imagination to see that in the Enron and WorldCom era Aaron Feurstein was an Elijah.

Perhaps my most moving and surprising work encounter of all was with yet another rabbi of work: the young orderly who took care of my grandfather when he was dying of prostate cancer. I was feeling helpless and sad that morning when the orderly came into the room to empty my grandfather's bedpans and wash his body. I'd seen this orderly two or three other times, but I'd left when he entered, not bothering to engage with him at all. As I watched him this time, I saw that this muscle-bound man who looked barely twenty was handling my grandfather with incredible gentleness, singing quietly as he washed my grandfather's bottom and legs. At first, my grandfather grimaced with discomfort and humiliation, the embarrassment of being washed up by a stranger. But when he heard the singing, he looked up and smiled weakly.

As the orderly left, I quickly followed him out of the room and awkwardly and inelegantly thanked him for taking care so beautifully. I felt painfully aware of how little I was doing for my grandfather in the face of how much this orderly had done. I said I was sure it wasn't the easiest job in the world. He looked me straight in the eye and smiled, "Don't worry, my friend. Remember, your shit is my bread and butter." Suddenly, in the face of sadness there was sacred comedy. We both laughed. Here was a man who wasn't just making money at this job. Bread and butter, I couldn't help thinking, is the staff of life. His work was primal, corporeal, intimate: soothing and cleaning people as they entered the next stage of their lives, as they declined. His work wasn't all that different from a midwife's. My interpretation of his joke and his easy laugh was that cleaning this eighty-year-old man's excrement was also an affirmation of the sacred cycle of birth and death.

I realized as I left the hospital that part of my discomfort before I spoke to the orderly was about how disconnected I'd become from the labor, grit, and sweat of work. Work isn't only a calling. Work isn't always *avodah.* Work isn't only energy and orgy. Work is burdensome and dirty. It sometimes stinks. And the truth is that most of us don't make meaning of our own grit, even though it is as central to the fullness and dignity of work as service. Without labor there's no birth; there is no Elijah. For us "white collar" types there's a kind of lie of work—that we should have a higher purpose, a sense of energy and creativity all the time. White collar is a way of imagining that we are above, or immune from, the toil of labor, which in turn keeps us disconnected from the pulse and effort behind Creation.

Unlike the orderly, most of us don't make meaning out of the crap of our own jobs. Instead, we divide up the world into management and employees; faculty and administration; orderlies and doctors. We all have to get our hands dirty, either literally or metaphorically, in the intimacy and messiness of human relations. We need to fully face and enter into "bloody" office skirmishes; confront or actively filter the nonsense of corporate bureaucracy; spend time on those assembly lines, in those warehouses, or on those switchboards. If we don't, *avodah* becomes an empty illusion, a glorified narcissism.

When we take on the full dimensions of our work—the pain and the pleasure, the messiness and the order, the triumphs and the failures,

> **When we take on the full dimensions of our work—the messiness and the order, the triumphs and the failures—we can transform just about any situation into an opportunity for connection and deepening, for both ourselves and the others around us.**

the grit and the gold—we can transform just about any work situation into an opportunity for connection and deepening for both ourselves and the others around us. I read a story in the *New York Times* that described a high school teacher in the South Bronx, one of New York City's toughest neighborhoods. She was a new teacher at the school, and the kids were giving her a particularly difficult time and learning practically nothing as a result. Not surprisingly, the rate of teacher turnover at this school was incredibly high. But this young teacher did something amazing.

She asked each child to write down one good thing about another child in the class, handing out names as assignments to each student so that everyone would be covered. Then she collected the cards, shuffled them, and redistributed them. Each student had someone else's interpretation of a classmate. She asked each of them to read that card. This group of kids who were always being dumped on, called failures, and coming to school with little expectation of being taught, were now hearing about their strengths and assets. The effect was nothing short of miraculous. The energy of the classroom completely shifted; there was laughter, embarrassment, and recognition as each of them read the comments. There was palpable gratitude to this teacher for creating a moment of remembering the "being" in each of them in the middle of the school week. She had brought a Sabbath consciousness to the most stressful of work situations and transformed it in the process.

Sometimes, like the teacher, we can shift our attitude and others' as well, imbuing our work with meaning. We can answer those four questions and change our perspective. Other times we can't, and we need to be honest with ourselves and switch jobs or careers. However we choose to do it, we are all obligated, as philosopher Thomas Berry says, to "connect our work to the great project," to the work of world-making. There actually is a practice designed to have just that effect. It's called *havdalah*, and it's a mirror of the Friday night ushering in of the Sabbath day. It is both the closing practice of Sabbath and the beginning practice of the workweek.

In short, *havdalah* is a TGIM (Thank-God-it's-Monday) practice. It's designed to make sure that our work makes a difference in the world; to remind us that our work can always stretch us and connect us to people more deeply—if we make it a practice. Like any ritual, it also surfaces what we don't feel we have, enabling us to see when our work isn't allowing that connection to happen so that we're more likely to make a change.

Havdalah is a ritual for entering the workweek; a celebration of creativity in the external world. We are literally being asked to join hands with the mythic Creator to begin the job of building once again; to be a partner in the evolution of the planet. *Havdalah* also acknowledges the complexity of creativity and world-building. It ennobles the dialectical relationships between Creation and destruction, doing and being, meaningful work and drudgery.

Havdalah actually means "distinction." There's a difference between rest and work, but they do so much to inform each other. When we observe some form of Sabbath, a time of self-reflection and rest, we are far less likely to create golden calves and much more likely to use our creativity to expand and deepen, rather than reduce or narrow reality. The ancient ritual of *havdalah* encourages us to integrate the being consciousness of Sabbath into the doing consciousness of the week.

The ritual is performed one hour after sunset on a Saturday evening, and it's every bit as mystical and beautiful as the Friday-night practice. There are three practices contained in the ritual. Just as we welcome in the Sabbath, we welcome the workweek with the same kind of joy—by drinking wine. Next, a container of fragrant spices is passed around and we are meant to deeply breathe in the scent. The sweet smell of the Sabbath, the spirit of being, is inhaled deep within. This is a symbolic way of bringing that consciousness we reached on the Sabbath into the workweek. It's an invitation to take a deep breath and the intentionality that comes with it into our work. It's a breathing meditation with a fragrance; a perfume for the week.

The Sabbath is opened with candles and it's closed with candles, but there are important differences. Whereas on Sabbath, two single-wicked candles are lit, on *havdalah* there is a single candle with multiple wicks wrapped together to create one; an invitation to remember that we do not enter the workweek alone, that all of our creative work is in the end collaborative. We have collaborators in the present and from the past; people we've been inspired by, whose work we are expanding upon. Because of the size of the wick, the fire is wild and big, the effect quite dramatic. It evokes the fire of creativity—a fire that can create and destroy, consume and enliven. It's the fire of illumination.

To enhance the drama, the candle is lit in a completely dark room. It awakens the hope that our labors will bring light to darkness; a poetic way to describe the yearning for meaningful work. Rather than closing our eyes as we do on Friday nights, our eyes are wide open. We are entering the external world again. We cup our hands and bring them close to the candle, creating a shadow. Then we open them; a way of saying that our hands can be vehicles of life.

> There's a difference between rest and work, but the two do so much to inform each other.

The ecstatic flame of the candle always reminds me that the dance between being and doing is the most creative act of all. *Havdalah* awakens us to the ongoing construction of ourselves and the world. Unlike other holy days which come around once a year, we need to practice Sabbath and *havdalah* every single week. We need to recalibrate and rebalance, and in the end, even the richest rest and work consciousness won't ensure that we'll get the balance right. We're learning how to *be* better doers and *do* being better.

There's a story told about Rabbi Zusya lying on his deathbed. His adoring students surrounded him, comforting him as he wept. One student asked, "Why are you crying?" He said, "I'm scared." His students said, "Why? You were like Abraham, like Moses to us!" But instead of being soothed, he wept louder. "God won't ask me why I wasn't more like Abraham or Moses. He will ask me why I wasn't more like Zusya!" The rabbi was articulating the exquisite yearning to fully manifest who we are, to reach our creative potential—and the realization that we're always going to fall short. The study of being and doing teaches us that we can celebrate our finitude as we seek the infinite. This is in fact the very essence of creativity.

YEARNING FOR
HAPPINESS

THE BLESSING
OF PLEASURE

IN AMERICA, THE YEARNING FOR HAPPINESS MAY BE THE
most all-encompassing yearning of them all. Whether it's the Dalai
Lama's art of happiness; cognitive scientists' promises to find the "happiness set point" in the brain; or the latest iPod advertising campaign,
the messages that happiness is attainable are everywhere. Happiness is
yours if you have an open heart, a set of talents or skills, the right genes,
or even that latest product. We should be happy in our relationships, at
work, with our bodies, and if we're not, something is seriously wrong.
We'd better fix it quick—medicate it, soothe it, or drown it out with the
multiplicity of delights and "cures" available in our "advanced" culture.

The intent of the founding fathers when they wrote about the right to
pursue happiness has been much debated, but few would disagree that
this promise is unique. No other nation in history has held out the hope
of self-fulfillment and individual freedom. Most also would agree that
with this freedom, many sometimes-conflicting
ideas about how to find happiness have arisen:
versions those erudite gentlemen could never
have imagined. And they undoubtedly would

> When we seek happiness
> for its own sake, it will
> most likely elude us.

have been mystified by the fact that in the wealthiest, most privileged
country in the world, twenty-five million Americans report being depressed. Clinical depression is undeniably a syndrome that demands
treatment, but is that really all that's going on?

If the founding fathers could spend one week in contemporary America, one wonders if they might have agreed with another distinguished

gentleman, John Stuart Mill, who said the search for happiness is one of the chief sources of unhappiness. When we seek happiness for its own sake, it will most likely elude us. Perhaps unhappiness is not the problem at all, but rather our understandings of how happiness should look and feel—and our expectation that we somehow can find the golden key.

Critiques of modern materialism and its accompanying excesses are prevalent, and there are shifts in this dynamic, from the "simplify your life" movement to the widespread disillusionment with corporate greed. But on the whole it's clear that Americans want to feel good by living big at all costs: big cars, luxury goods, beautiful homes—and the accompanying credit card bills. It used to be that credit was something you earned: you were a regular customer who could be trusted to pay later. Now, credit really means debt. It's a way to satisfy desires at all cost. What Freud called the pleasure principle has become a central code. Material and sensual pleasure has become a prescription for all that ails us. Our other needs—our spiritual longings, our relational needs, our yearning to serve or contribute—have been trumped by our desire to experience immediate happiness.

I was a witness to the birth of this very syndrome at, of all places, a five-year-old boy's birthday party. His extended family had gathered to celebrate, bearing an astounding number of gifts. His face was full of light and joy as he opened the first one; an action figure he'd been wanting forever (as he put it). He carried it around for every guest to see and then began to play with it. After a couple of minutes, a relative handed him her gift, which, much to everyone's surprise, he put aside. With some urging, he opened it, and then the next and the next and the next, ripping open the paper, putting each present down, sometimes throwing it and reaching for another. At the end of what was nothing short of a gift orgy, he cried for more and then completely melted down and was given a time out. I heard one guest remark to another about how spoiled and ungrateful he was. What had really happened, of course, was that this joyful child wasn't allowed to savor his beloved toy, to enjoy it fully and express his gratitude. He was learning to be a good little consumer, to always want more.

The intensity of popular culture's celebration of happiness through consumption is matched by another cultural perspective, one that goes back centuries. This is the religious perspective, and America is among the most religiously focused countries in the world. Religions tend to be suspicious of personal happiness and judging of excess. Fulfillment and sensual pleasures will keep us from pursuing grander and more transcendent goals—and finding the ultimate happiness. Satisfying the needs and desires of the body, acting on our impulses, and following our id will subsume our yearnings to connect to something larger; we will cease to long for God. Christianity, Buddhism, and Hinduism all urge us to get in touch with our "noble" and "higher" yearnings. And with rare exception they universally diminish carnal or "lower" desires. There's an idealization of asceticism and self-denial.

The ancient Greek and Roman philosophers were in part responsible for this understanding of the potential dangers of all things sensual. They taught that the transient nature of pleasure makes it inferior to what is lasting, unchanging, or transcendent. Spirit is separate from body; mind can control desire. Christians picked up on this and took it a few steps further, pitting morality against the body. Rather than God being a metaphor for everything, God became elevated, outside this world, not to be experienced by most mortals. This God judges and condemns the sensual; what feels good is, by definition, not good. The most puritanical strain of Christianity took hold early in America's history; perhaps in part because the country's first immigrant inhabitants were struggling in a new land without material comforts.

> The lust for the spiritual can be as intoxicating and consuming as the lust for the material.

Of course there's truth to the claim that the yearning for pleasure can crowd out other experiences of life: There's an intoxicating effect of plenty. It creates a fleeting happiness that can lead to the desire for more and more. And it can be a distraction from mindful and spiritual pursuits, as we constantly seek new and ever more exhilarating and satiating experiences to get those endorphins going. We need to shop, eat, or drink too much in order to have the same experience a toddler gets from looking at a leaf.

But the lust for the spiritual can be as intoxicating and consuming as the lust for the material. The enemy of happiness is the tendency to be consumed or devoured by any one impulse. When materialists neglect the spiritual, they become narcissistic pleasure seekers and eventually create a wasteland. When the religious neglect the sensual, they can create body hunger and abusive religious leaders who take their material desires underground.

Of course, we all have both spiritual and sensual longings. Happiness is about having the full range of yearnings in dialogue. It may seem like a funny example, but there isn't a currency in the world that doesn't represent these two sides: One side of a coin or bill has a secular or national symbol, a wordly reference, and the other side has a spiritual invitation, whether it's the pyramid or "In God We Trust." There's an understanding that this world is the place where we can struggle with these two yearnings. Happiness is the ongoing process of wrestling with and integrating these sensibilities—our spiritual strivings and sensual needs. We need to embody spirituality and spiritually enliven the corporeal. Happiness is the product of the conversation among our many desires, needs, and wants; becoming more fully aware of them. As Plato said, "There is no happiness that's not somehow rooted in the task of systematic self-examination."

Critics of our over-the-top, oversexed, buy-your-happiness era actually miss the point. The American problem is that we misunderstand and diminish sensual and carnal pleasure, whether we reject it or indulge in it. We don't take the sensual and material seriously enough. The polarities created by this society's Puritan roots, combined with its modern consumer-driven economy, create a dangerous deflection from what pleasure is really about. We tend to float between indulgence and guilt, consumerism and self-restraint, bingeing and fasting, desire and shame, overdoing it on both ends of the spectrum—devouring or denying rather than savoring, and often not really feeling very good at all. Materialism is not a sin but an error of perception. Pleasure is deeper, more expansive than we imagine—and it can create genuine and profound joy.

I often surprise audiences by saying that Judaism is first and foremost a system of enjoyment. Most spiritual traditions in some way engage the senses to communicate the spiritual, whether with beautiful churches, incense, music, gardens, tea ceremonies, or art. Jewish wisdom actually embraces and celebrates the carnal for its own sake. It urges us to delight in sensual pleasure and pursue it in all its possible incarnations. The very first commandment to the first humans is, "From every tree of the garden you must eat." The Talmud, the classical Jewish text, tells us that if we don't enjoy life's pleasures, we will be disappointing God. In other words, we'll diminish reality itself.

When I ask the average audience what comes to mind when they think of the Garden of Eden story, almost everyone says it is Adam and Eve, their heads hanging low, clothed in fig leaves, being cast out of paradise. Once in a while someone will mention Eve being created out of Adam's side. But few have remarked at the gloriousness and lusciousness of Eden, at "every tree that was pleasing to the sight and good for food," at the gold and the four flowing rivers or Adam's love song to Eve just after she is created. The word "Eden" means "delight" in Hebrew. It is a world of sensuality and abundance. In this country, we are so focused on original sin that we've forgotten original pleasure and the endless opportunities for personal fulfillment it has to offer.

Most don't know that the fruit from the tree of good and evil is called "good for eating and a delight to the eyes." Rather than being referred to as a forbidden fruit, it is "desirable as a source of wisdom." Eve eats it because she wants "her eyes to be open"; she wants to "be like divine beings who know good from bad." Hers is not so much an act of defiance as much as an act born of an overpowering yearning to experience a wider reality. When you delight in the fruit, you may discover more of who you are.

Why was the fruit so desirable; why was the tree placed in the center of the garden anyway? Perhaps the biblical author decided that God wanted humans to leave paradise to learn to create pleasure on their own terms. The contemporary Christian philosopher Mathew Fox calls the Creation story a tale of "original blessing." When Adam and Eve leave Eden, the first thing they do is make love and have a child. Perhaps toiling on the soil—as Adam must now do—or perhaps pain during childbirth for Eve actually will create more pleasure in the end. It will be pleasure earned "by the sweat of their brow."

The garden metaphor entered my life in bold relief when my family moved to St. Louis and had a backyard for the first time. A city boy through and through, I was determined to grow our own tomatoes. And my first time out with the hoe, I got the worst case of poison ivy you can imagine, from head to toe. I kept at it after the cortisone did its job, and that first tomato of the season tasted just so divine. In reality, it was probably not all that different from the tomatoes in the grocery store, but it tasted different to me. On a grander scale, when Eve held the first baby for the first time, the pain was undoubtedly more than worth it, and the joy was all the greater. Rather than dwelling in Eden, Adam and Eve and their descendents would now always be "Eden-ing."

The biblical author clearly knew and appreciated the importance of the material. All the blessings God gave to the patriarchs and the covenant itself are essentially "stuff" blessings. Abraham is promised a great nation if he leaves to go to "a land I will show you." The blessing that Jacob and Esau fought over so bitterly is nothing if not sensual. It opens with the lines: "May God give you of the dew of heaven and the fat of the earth. Abundance of new grain and wine." The dream Jacob had later in the desert is not about ascending or transcending, leaving what is earthly behind: It's about going up and down the ladder, bringing earth to heaven and heaven to earth.

All the patriarchs are quite wealthy and acquisitive. It's only the descendent of the wealthy and powerful King David—Jesus—who is born into a poor family. Christianity has such important teachings about relinquishing the material to discover other aspects of our being, to find different forms of abundance and love. But there are equally important teachings about enhancing and expanding pleasure.

Material goods have an inherent goodness. We're not meant to feel guilty for having enough, or even more than enough, money, a beautiful home, great sex, lovely clothes, and delicious food. There isn't a single holiday that doesn't have a meal attached to it, not even the Day of Atonement, after which the feast is as much of a *mitzvah* as the fast of the previous hours. In Hebrew the word for such a celebration is *oneg*, which literally means "pleasure" or "enjoyment." Jewish wisdom teaches that we need a lot of sensual pleasures. When we really enjoy them, we will ongoingly feel we have enough. The hunger, the need for more, will be less. And when we feel full, we have more to give. We'll be that much more creative, joyful, gracious, and alive.

There's a practice of putting something sweet—candy or honey— on the first page of the very first Bible a child receives. You'd think the honey would be on the last page, or midway, to reward the child for hard work, but the hope is that the entire ride will be a pleasure-filled experience, that the taste at the beginning will motivate the child to read on.

Imagine if schools put something delicious on the first page of every math book. How would it change the experience of that first- grader who is nervous about the first day of school? What would the message of that candy be? So much pleasure awaits you. There's no dif- ference between the delight of a new idea and the burst of sensation that a lollipop provides. What this is teaching us is that the intellec- tual and the spiritual, the religious and the physical, are integrated. They feed and support each other. This is the very meaning of holistic.

The body is, quite literally, our temple, as the Bible tells us. There is no distinction between body **We're so focused on original sin that we've forgotten original pleasure.** and spirit. There is only holy embodiedness. In fact, there is no word for spirit or soul in biblical Hebrew. There is *nefesh*, which translates as "breathing body spirit." The medieval philosopher Maimonides warned against negating the body, and he instructed us to take care of it before attending to any other needs. There's a concept called "service through the material"; we are serving God, expanding reality, connecting to a deeper self when we experience the sensual. The more intense the pleasure, the closer we are to God. As the poet W.H. Auden wrote, "It's the pleasure haters who become unjust." By denying our bodies, our "God-given" gift, we will deny others as well.

It seems that in America, we're cut off from this wisdom about our innate sensuality, particularly when it comes to sex. We either demonize sex through religion or express our carnal desires without restraint, whether in our own lives or vicariously through the entertainment industry. The paradox is that so many of us don't enjoy sex, and so we look for more and more titillation or we hold back, dulling our senses and protecting ourselves from the stimulation all around us. There's a proliferation of taboos and an accompanying yearning to break them. The result is that we have become a voyeuristic culture with a high divorce rate.

Marriage and committed romantic relationships have suffered from what's been a domestication of sex in recent years. Sex has been watered down, tamed, dulled. All relationships struggle with the tensions created by two often conflicting needs. One is the need for steadiness, trust, reliability, security, stability, and predictability—all of which are necessary for commitment to be real. The other is the riskiness, seduction, friskiness, unpredictability, mystery, unruliness, and instability necessary to maintain desire. For so many of us, sex becomes less exciting, the range of intensity so much lower than when we were single. We all know that committed relationships can get boring, and we know that sex can get routine and that erotic pleasure can be diminished with time. In a committed relationship we're always available to each other, so why bother to seduce?

When we think we don't need to seduce our lover, we'll end up seeking seduction outside the relationship. When we don't have erotic adventure within our relationships, we'll seek it elsewhere. When our illicit fantasies are banished from our own bedroom, when we play it safe at home, we'll look for danger somewhere else. And so sex with someone new and forbidden becomes so appealing. Or if we don't dare do that, there's always the titillation of *Desperate Housewives*, or pornography.

What if we could stop dualizing and separating our need for commitment and our need for lust? What if what we really yearn for are lusty commitments and commitments to lust? In order for monogamy to work, monogamy has to be "dirty." If the forbidden is what's exciting, we have to work hard to bring the taboo into our most intimate relationships. If transgression is so titillating, we have to learn to transgress where we're most safe.

Our committed relationships can be nothing less than pleasure chambers. But we need to create situations and take risks that are out of the ordinary and push the envelope. Dana and I once took a trip to Northern California to celebrate our seventeenth wedding anniversary. We took a beautiful hike in Big Sur, climbing a winding path to the top of a cliff. It was foggy and yet still sunny, as it can be in that part of the country. There was a bench at a scenic overlook. It couldn't have been more romantic. As we sat there, I knew what I was thinking, but I didn't say anything. Instead I leaned over and took a risk. I started kissing her. And then . . . It turned out we were both thinking the same thing. The illicit, transgressive lovemaking in that public space was far more erotic and pleasurable that any first-time sex could ever be.

Of the hundreds of times happiness, *simcha*, is used in Jewish wisdom texts, the majority are in regard to committed lovers. It's really pretty simple: If we don't have great sex, we can't have a great spiritual life. Jewish wisdom has a kind of Torah of seduction; a *mitzvah* of foreplay. There's a funny story from the Talmud about a teacher, Rav, and his devoted student, Rav Kahana. One night Rav is making love to his wife, and he hears something under his bed. When he calls out, Rav Kahana answers that it is he, and he is here to learn at the feet of his master:

"This is a matter of Torah, and I must study." Rav and his wife must have had a lot to teach about sex for Rav Kahana to want to hide under the bed. Rav Kahana knew that if you want to understand the Torah of life, you have to study the Torah of sex.

There's also a text written by the famous thirteenth-century philosopher Nachmonides called the Holy Letter, which is an actual Torah of sex. Nachmonides recommends that we talk about our fantasies in order to increase our desire. Lovers are encouraged to invite new positions. Foreplay isn't fore-play; it's the play. Nachmonides suggests foods and menus to stimulate desire. Holding back one's orgasm to deepen pleasure is a sacred practice.

Committed relationships are where we are literally obligated to be vulnerable and make mistakes, to experience sexual pleasure and even pain as long as both partners are in agreement. Sex is a dance between the masculine and feminine, a way to join both dimensions, so nothing should be held back. We must be exposed and open, be willing to improvise. Nothing is off limits.

The Talmud says that when committed lovers cleave to each other, the *Shekinah*, or divine presence, is a third partner. It is a kind of cosmic *ménage à trois*. The first blessing said at every wedding, which I think of as the sex blessing, is: "Be grateful for the consciousness to make love to those with whom we are meant to make love." The last blessing of the ceremony describes the multiple forms of joy that emerge from committed lovemaking: the happiness that washes over you and circles back, a kind of luxuriating sensuality; the more subtle joy that hums through your body; the dance of exultation that makes you buoyant and energetic; and the happiness that takes over, subsuming everything.

When we see our bodies as a blessing, our sensual desires as sacred, there's no end to the pleasure that awaits us. The challenge is to raise our consciousness to the delights everywhere around us; to anticipate and celebrate every momentary pleasure with intention. One of the cornerstones of the Jewish tradition is a two-thousand-year-old method for raising our awareness, and thereby increasing our pleasure: the practice of blessing.

It's nothing short of a pleasure practice. We are to say a hundred blessings a day, which is a metaphor for as many times as possible and symbolic of each of the hundred sockets that held together the ancient tabernacle, a microcosm of the world. In other words, our experience of pleasure is integral to the ongoing creation of all-that-is. It may seem like an awful lot of work, but there's such a power to all this blessing. Quite simply, it brings the sensual world to life in all its splendor—from the marriage of two people in love to a new pair of shoes; from a delicious meal to a new home. Blessing is a gratitude practice—when we pause to recognize the gifts we've been given, it's amazing how much happier we are.

The origin of the Hebrew word for blessing says so much. If you change one vowel of the Hebrew word *bracha* you have the word for "pool of water." *Bracha* also comes from the same root as the word for "bent knee." The word "blessing" was first used by a desert people. Imagine the experience of coming across a reservoir of water in the middle of a barren wilderness and then kneeling before that pool to drink fully. The ancient Israelites saw water as a blessing, and blessing as a spring of happiness. So the word for blessing was born of a sensual yearning, out of thirst and the wonder that comes from quenching it. In other words, the pool is a symbol of life itself, and blessing connects us to the energy current that sustains us.

In Hebrew, the blessings are called "blessings of enjoyment." Pleasure is God manifested, or, as Buddhists believe, form is formlessness made material. Blessings are a way of contextualizing pleasure, a reminder of the source of everything. Abraham Joshua Heschel wrote beautifully about this: "When we drink a glass of water, we remind ourselves of the eternal mystery of creation, 'Blessed are You . . . by whose word all things came into being,' whether a trivial act or a supreme miracle. When we wish to eat bread or fruit, to enjoy a pleasant fragrance or a cup of wine . . . on noticing trees when they blossom; on meeting a sage in Torah or in secular learning, we are taught to evoke His great name and our awareness of Him. . . . This is one of the goals of the Jewish way of living; to feel the hidden love and wisdom in all things."

I feel so fortunate to have grown up in a tradition that continually raised my pleasure consciousness. The first time I remember being aware of what a gift I'd been given was as a teenager when I put on a new pair of jeans. I remember relishing the stiffness and snugness, anticipating all the mornings I would put them on, how each time they'd be a little more faded, fit a little bit better. That morning, my mother had taken my brothers and me for our semiannual shopping spree. These expeditions always took place around the seasonal festivals of

Pleasure is God manifested.

Passover in the spring and Succot in the fall. They were literally a ritual. Of course, there was the practical aspect: We needed clothes for the winter and then the summer months. But no less important was the fact that we were anticipating these two important holidays by celebrating the sensual: ushering in the spiritually new with sensual delight and pleasure. That spring afternoon before I put those jeans on I said a simple blessing, which is made with any new experience. After I put them on I remember feeling a rush of contentment as I glanced in the mirror at my jeans and did a little dance.

Blessings are said before; not after. The blessing gives us a hit of gratitude even before we indulge. We feel thankful not only after having the great experience, but as a way to enhance that experience as we're having it. We surface our desire so that we feel it fully and therefore bring intention to the act of satisfying it. The blessing I said over those jeans was, "Praised are you who clothes the naked." When we really can experience the yearning to be clothed; when we can appreciate the feeling of being protected from the elements, or covered by a soft or silky fabric; we are so much more satiated than we would be after a frenetic day shopping at the mall. Clothing ourselves can then be a metaphor for clothing the world. One practice I learned growing up is to give away one piece of clothing whenever we buy a new one. When we feel blessed, we are more likely to become a blessing to the world.

There was another time several years later that really stuck with me. I was at summer camp before the campers arrived, setting things up with the other counselors. Every week, we left the grounds to go to town to buy bread for Friday-night dinner. We'd wait outside the bakery to get the first morning's batch fresh out of the oven. When it was ready and purchased, before heading back we'd sit on the curb in front of the bakery and eat some of the steaming, fluffy, crispy bread saturated with melting butter. But before I did, I said a blessing that I'd said hundreds of times before. That morning maybe the bread was especially wonderful, or maybe I was just in a great mood or happy to be in the company of my friends. But I remember thinking, wow, the blessing over bread is so perfect, so right. Just then it named exactly what I was feeling in that moment: It allowed me to really notice my own pleasure; to have it fully sink in. The taste of the bread was prolonged somehow and my tongue seemed to tingle during the whole trip back to the grounds. I don't always have such a delightful experience when I eat bread, but I've never said that blessing the same way since.

Once again the depth of my experience was enhanced by the actual words of the blessing, which are "Praised are you who feeds the whole world." Mine was a bittersweet, complex enjoyment, because, of course, everybody isn't able to eat bread, to enjoy abundance. But rather than guilt, the blessing evokes a profound appreciation for the gift and awakens an even more powerful yearning that goes beyond the sensual self. The blessing adds texture and authenticity to the pleasure. It reminds us that whatever delight is before us, it is enough. When we bless the bread, we are invited to think about how we got the money to buy it, about the people who put it on the shelves at the grocer, the farmer who picked the wheat, the baker that baked it, the rain and the sun that enabled it to grow—all of that for me? The experience of that handful of bread is so conscious and full-filling that we're less likely to want another piece.

Jewish wisdom teaches that it's a serious mistake to refuse to taste a new kind of food. There's a law that you are not allowed to eat standing up, as you can't fully enjoy your food if you are not sitting. Our mothers' "sit down when you eat" or "take a plate" or "do not drink out of the bottle" are actually spiritual insights. It's so important to energize the eating experience with intention or *kavanah*. We are all meant to be gourmets; not gourmands. When we exclaim over the chocolate, "Oh, it's divine!" it really is. But if we immediately take another piece, the pleasure will decrease. A gourmet is enthusiastic—which means infused with God's spirit. A gourmand can never get enough. When we don't savor, we want more.

A doctor friend of mine refers to the practice of blessing as a satiation diet. He calls the epidemic of obesity in this country "malnutrition of happiness." Maybe this is why there are so many bestselling diet books and only the rare cookbook that rises to the top of the bestseller lists. Perhaps if we cooked for each other more often, we'd eat less. I find it hopeful that the latest research is showing that nutrition is not about low fat or high protein. It's about feeling full. In other words, it's about feeling blessed.

People are always surprised when I tell them that there's also a blessing for when the food comes out the other end. This, too, is a form of pleasure, something to feel thankful for. And the rabbis had no qualms about acknowledging the base corporeal sensation of going to the bathroom. We've all had that experience of holding it in; for whatever reason waiting until we can barely stand it and then having that feeling of "Oh, thank God" as we finally let it go. If we tune in, we may feel a sense of gratitude that it all works. The blessing reads: "Blessed are You, who fashions the human body with wisdom and created in him orifices . . . and completely knows that if one of these holes or orifices should open all the way or close all the way we would not be able to live or stand before You who heals all bodies in wondrous ways." As my grandmother used to say, "Eat, sleep, and eliminate." Remember that it's all blessed.

There are so many blessings for the things we normally take for granted, so that they, too, become a source of joy. There are blessings for waking up in the morning, standing up straight, and for walking. There's one for seeing a crowd of people—"Oh, my God, look how many stories there are!" Awe, wonder, and surprise are all deeply pleasurable.

Among Jews, the most commonly known blessing is called the *Shecheyanu*—"who has kept us alive." It's the blessing said over any new experience: tasting a fruit for the first time in the season, the return of an annual holiday or festival, a new purchase, opening a gift. "Blessed are You, who has kept us alive and has sustained us and has enabled us to arrive at this moment." It is literally a method for keeping things fresh; of recognizing that if we really think about it everything is always new. It's also an acknowledgment that life is a series of moments, of moment pleasures, moment happinesses, and that the most significant blessing of all is that we are here to enjoy them.

THE ETHICS OF JOY

IT WAS AN UNUSUALLY COLD FEBRUARY DAY FOR ISRAEL. I was visiting a temporary village that housed and helped Ethiopian immigrants adjust to their new land. They'd just arrived after a long journey and decades of struggle to leave their country where, for generations, they'd been an oppressed minority. They stood around makeshift caravans of prefabricated housing, shivering in the new experience of winter chill after a life near the equator.

As I walked around not quite knowing what to do to help, I spotted two boys, about ten years old. They were standing off to the side of the camp rubbing their hands together, their eyes wide as they took in the landscape and all the new faces. I walked over and offered them my gloves. They hesitated at first, glancing from one to the other until one of them took the gloves and put them on. He immediately started laughing: He'd never worn gloves before. It was a laugh of sheer delight at these second hands over his, warm and scratchy. He motioned to me to give his friend gloves, too. When it was apparent from my body language that I didn't have another pair, he took off one glove and gave it to his friend, who also started laughing in that same wonderful way, both their faces beaming with joy.

I, too, felt a rush of happiness, of warmth, even though my hands were now pretty cold. When I got back to Jerusalem I bought myself a new pair of gloves. This was back in 1984. I still wear those gloves every winter. Although they're pretty worn-out by now I continue to welcome the extra warmth that comes along with that memory of the gleeful laugh of those young boys each with a single gloved hand.

There was such a rich intersection of happiness for all three of us in that short encounter. The unexpected sensual pleasure of the gloves and the emotional joy of sharing the gloves with each other created an explosion of happiness for those boys. For me there was the joy of offering something of myself, a happiness born of giving pleasure and creating an opportunity for others to do the same.

Most of us have experienced feelings of pleasure and happiness that rise within when we care for others. For example, we all can feel the difference between cooking a tasty meal just for ourselves, cooking a meal for ourselves and a loved one, and cooking that same meal with enough to share with a friend or neighbor who is ill. The same food tastes so much better, our pleasure intensified. So too, giving charity is a joy, perhaps even more so when our donation exceeds our own expectation. The pleasure of getting a holiday bonus is often less pleasurable than giving it away to someone who desperately needs it. Or compare the enjoyment of sitting down and reading a good book with the deeper enjoyment of then passing the book on to someone else when we're done, or reading that very same book to an elderly person.

Mahatma Gandhi once observed, "Consciously or unconsciously, every one of us does render some service or other. If we cultivate the habit of doing this service deliberately, our desire for service will steadily grow stronger, and it will make not only for our own happiness, but that of the world at large." Whether through random acts of kindness, planned gifts, routine caretaking, or generous lovemaking, acting from concern for others makes us happier human beings; our lives more satisfying and meaningful. It might sound like a platitude, but it is true nonetheless: Being happy isn't only about feeling good, but also about doing good.

Being happy isn't only about feeling good; it's about doing good.

Nevertheless, despite our own experiences, so many still insist on posing morality in opposition to happiness. Pleasure is usually associated with one's own sensual and physical pleasure—whether gastronomic, aesthetic, or sexual—not with activities directed to the welfare of others. Too often, we assume that any self-serving motivation, such as our own personal happiness, automatically undermines the morality of what we do. So we tend to be reluctant to admit and even to feel embarrassed by the joy that comes from acting decently, doing the right thing, and helping others. Maybe this accounts for why so many parents, when asked what they want for their children, initially respond that they want their children to be happy and then may say they want their children to be kind or good—as if happiness and goodness were disconnected. But can our children genuinely feel happy about themselves without developing character and being ethical?

We have gotten ourselves into a strange bind. When we indulge in sensual pleasure, we often feel guilty. And when we do a good deed, we tend to ignore the accompanying sense of well-being. But ignoring the joy of being ethical can lead to a sense of self-righteousness or entitlement. Self-righteous, because if we do not genuinely feel personal joy we will wind up feeling we've acted from some purely selfless state. Entitled, because if we feel we're acting from some purely selfless state, we are superior. We may give of ourselves because we want to be profusely praised by our friends; or in wealthier circles, want our name on a building or to be honored at a gala. Or we wind up creating models of generosity that are completely selfless, as if we aren't really giving unless we are sacrificing and suffering. Think of Mother Teresa. In so many ways, she is our culture's exemplar of pure generosity. When she's our example, we can become so discouraged about ever living up to her or someone like her, that we may do nothing. And so either way, when we're really honest with ourselves we aren't as good as we would like to be. As Gandhi said, if we all brought happiness born of goodness to consciousness, our lives—and the world—might be transformed.

What accounts for this pervasive disconnection between happiness and goodness? The answer traces, I believe, to three deeply imbedded ethical presumptions in our culture and, as a consequence, in our individual unconsciousnesses as well. The first is a religious inheritance which distrusts carnal pleasure and teaches that what feels good can't be good. This reflects the old body-spirit divide bequeathed to us by the Greeks and traditional Christianity. This separation between physical pleasure and spiritual happiness often leads to our being painfully torn between wild indulgence and rigid denial of our physical and sensual desires. But is this truncated notion of happiness and morality really true to our experience?

The second is the philosophical legacy of Immanuel Kant's duty-based ethical theory. Kant wrote, "It is one thing to make a man happy, it is quite another to make him good." He drove a wedge between happiness and goodness and, in the process, made the search for happiness empty and denied the ethical life its real pleasures. In fact, he argued that if we perform a moral action because we are emotionally moved to do so, that act has no moral worth. For example, Kant thought that although love between parents and children is natural, it has no moral weight because morality has to involve a struggle against the self. (It should be of no surprise that Kant had no children.) When duty calls we must be prepared to yield our personal interest and fulfill our obligation. Doing the right thing then becomes associated with the inflexible demands of duty unspoiled by thoughts of happiness. This idea that happiness and morality are in conflict sometimes leads to an almost pathological conclusion that if something makes us happy, then that is evidence it is morally suspect.

The third legacy is the psychological theory of Sigmund Freud. A pioneer of explicating sensual urges, he also argued that acting morally requires sacrificing a degree of happiness. For Freud the only meaningful notion of happiness is the satisfaction of our instinctual desires. Because we need to live in society, we must repress our desires and can never be genuinely happy. As Freud put it, "Civilized man has exchanged a portion of his happiness for a portion of security." Discontent is the price we pay for civilization, thus his book, *Civilization and*

Its Discontents. We have a choice: We can have a good life that rules out happiness or a happy life that makes being good problematic. (It should not surprise us that throughout his life Freud suffered from bouts of depression and near the end of his life asked, "What good to us is a long life if it is difficult and barren of joys . . . ?")

These three legacies teach that if we hope to attain true, wholesome happiness we have to rise above our born inclinations. I suspect this idea is mostly a handy excuse for those who would rather critique others for their selfish behavior than face the shame of their own self-centeredness. It's also a useful tool to manipulate others into donating to a cause, be it political or religious. But are these divides true to our experience?

The truth is, I don't spend much time calibrating how much pleasure I receive from doing good deeds, and I doubt you do either. My decisions tend to be taken up with choosing between such things as getting TiVo and buying great tickets to the Rolling Stones, or spending my limited funds on a dining room table or a vacation. But I do know that when I visit a friend in the hospital rather than spend hours in front of the television watching my favorite shows, my contentment is richer and more abiding. I can say with certainty that the joy that comes with spending a Sunday morning raising money by participating in the AIDS Walk is truly more sustaining than the pleasures of sitting with a perfect cup of coffee reading the paper. We all seek this enriching, self-affirming joy that comes with caring for others. We long for the kind of happiness that will keep us warm during colder seasons, like those worn gloves.

Acting from a place of generosity and compassion creates sustaining happiness.

To be sure, the intensity and flash of happiness that flows from a sensual experience is more brilliant and enlivening than the experience of doing for others. The intensity of finer pleasures, says Freud, is mild compared with that from the satisfying of crude, primary, instinctual impulses. I recall the ecstasy and heightened perception I experienced from tripping on LSD years ago. It's no accident that drugs are called intoxicants and spirits. But with sensual pleasures, both the joy and the insights quickly evaporate. In contrast, the higher state of awareness and understanding attained through an ethical practice is always more sustaining and embracing. Such practices can give rise to perceptions that last a lifetime. Doing "good" demands intention and the delay of gratification; yet the ensuing pleasure is so much greater and so much deeper.

All spiritual traditions teach that acting from a place of generosity and compassion creates sustaining happiness; whether it's the Eightfold Path for ending suffering in Buddhism, the practice of good works in the Christian tradition, or the ethical commandments of Judaism. Abraham Joshua Heschel wrote, "The experience of bliss in doing good is the greatest moment that mortals know." Doing good is a practice and it takes discipline, but the discipline is an ingredient in the joy. When we hold together the truths of sense and heart, we realize that we need not minimize our material delights to attain the greater joy of giving. One informs the other. If we don't have pleasure in our lives, the world seems barren. If we aren't sources of happiness, our pleasure is fleeting.

There are spiritual practices designed to heighten our awareness of abiding happiness. The Jewish tradition, for example, urges us to begin our day with a contemplative practice, what Hindus call *jnana* yoga (inquiry and discrimination). We are asked to study the very first paragraph in the Talmud: "These are the deeds that yield immediate fruit and continue to yield fruit in time to come; honoring parents; deeds of kindness; providing hospitality; visiting the sick; helping the needy bride (which in ancient times meant providing dowries); making peace between people; taking care of the dead; study; and spiritual introspection." The Talmudic sage understood that lasting happiness can only come from deeper self-awareness and commitment that extends beyond one's self.

Paradoxically, when we do good deeds, when we act ethically, we tend to enjoy our material pleasures even more. When we don't, we may feel guilty or even ashamed, as if we haven't earned or merited such abundance. We feel a gnawing emptiness that precludes the happiness we seek and causes us to yearn for more and more. Then there's that unconscious feeling of indebtedness that crops up in all of us from time to time, a kind of existential angst: After all, what did we do to earn the greatest gift of all—our very lives? It is almost as if there's a switch inside that flips when we get something for nothing, which then keeps us from enjoying the world in all of its sensual beauty. These feelings can be mitigated by the simple act of giving: by offering our service, kindness, and love and transforming ourselves from receivers to givers.

There's a teaching called *simcha shel mitzvah*, which means "the joy of doing good deeds" or "the pleasure in acting as we know we should." Underlying this concept is the recognition that happiness does not depend on feeling good all the time, but on the ability to reflect on what is worthwhile in one's life. Happiness is, therefore, not just a feeling or emotion but a profound connection to the world. The wise of every generation understood this, as did Aristotle when he concluded, "A happy life is a virtuous life." The new science of happiness is now making the same discovery: Doing acts of kindness creates more happiness than just about anything else.

The Hebrew word *mitzvah* is often translated as obligation. Most of us feel constrained or burdened when we hear this word, as though freedom is now constrained and happiness compromised. But, in fact, when we heed our obligations, take responsibility for our decisions, place our duties for others before our immediate satisfactions, we actually are happier as a result.

Happiness is not just a mood or an emotion, but a profound connection to the world. It doesn't depend on feeling good all the time, but on the ability to reflect on what is worthwhile in life.

We're faced with ethical choices every day. Do I tell my husband the truth or lie to avoid conflict? Do I take the credit for what someone else did or point to whom it's due? Do I give money to the beggar or assume he's a drug addict who doesn't deserve it? Do I help my child with his homework or take a much-needed break? Do I take office supplies home from my workplace for personal use or buy my own? Do I put the unwanted product back on the right shelf, or leave it by the register and let the underpaid clerk do it for me? Whenever we face these kinds of choices—from the grand to the trivial—we hear so many voices: those of our parents, traditions, peers, wounded selves, tired selves, selfish selves, angry selves, guilty selves, generous selves, and kind selves. Our happiness depends on which voice we choose to follow.

This is why practice is so important. The sages imagined that by doing *mitzvot* regularly, eventually all acts of loving kindness and obligation would eventually become *simcha shel mitzvot*. In other words, our "shoulds" and our "wants" would become one and the same. We will want to do what we know we should. Our personal pleasure and our service to others will be aligned. On the other hand, when we know what we should do but we don't do it, we are following a recipe for unhappiness. While right and wrong may not be as absolute as fundamentalists preach, neither is right and wrong hopelessly relative either. Right and wrong may be dependent on context, contingent and open to constant change, but the distinction does exist. And although we may do a good job at denying it in the moment of decision, the ethical choice is always alive within us.

Sometimes we excuse unethical behavior because we determine no harm will come from what we do. We can think of a million good reasons—usually self-serving ones—to justify our decisions. When we hear that dialogue going on inside our head, it's time to have a different conversation, and if we're honest most of the time it's pretty hard to fool ourselves. Of course, we can choose not to have that conversation; instead, to rationalize and justify, but in the end the God inside is immeasurably more investigative, has much clearer standards, and is far more punitive than the god in the sky.

I wish I'd had that internal conversation several years ago when I took a monetary gift from someone I taught. Instead, my dialogue went like this: "I've worked hard for this man, far beyond the call of duty or the needs of my organization. He's so wealthy; the money is nothing to him. He's offering a gift of thanks; I should be gracious and receive it." And then the bottom line: "This would be one year's private school tuition for my daughter; a 20 percent increase in my salary." I was breaking no laws or overt rules. But even as I accepted the money I felt it wasn't right.

Not surprisingly, it changed the nature of my relationship with this man, who I cared about very much. Was I now his friend or his employee? Did I have to accept his invitations or requests because he was paying me? Did he see me the same way as he did before? Every quarter, I was supposed to send out a bill as a formality. Each time I filled out his bill, I had a gnawing feeling of discomfort. Once again, I'd run through my justifications, and soon found myself with a new worry: Will I still get my money next quarter? During that period I wasn't racked with guilt—obviously not, because I never did give the money back. But a chronic unhappiness hovered in the background, a bitter flavor that tainted my successes during that period. For someone else, taking the money could have been comfortable and right, but it wasn't for me. What I did was not who I wanted to be.

There will always be arguments—internal and external—about what makes for an ethical life and what generates happiness. Our unprecedented personal freedom exacerbates this confusion. For the most part, traditional, external forms of authority—parental, religious, social, and cultural—have weakened, leaving us as our own authorities to choose how we want to live. Rather than being a series of tightly knit communities with shared values—as we've been for most of human history—we've become a pluralist, fragmented, postmodern culture.

There is no agreed-upon moral position across every context and every situation. There is no moral code, no algorithm for ethics, no easily accessible precedents. As a result, the determination of what it means to lead a good life is now more complicated than ever before. But the fact that there aren't such clear answers makes it even more vital that the debate continues, and that it continues with even greater openness and honesty.

Wrestling with these central questions about the good life turns out to be the central ingredient for a flourishing, happy life. Israel means "God wrestler." Jacob is named Israel after wrestling with an angel during that agonizing night in which he grapples with having stolen his brother's blessing. There were more obviously worthy candidates to be the founder of Israel—more upstanding, more humble, more powerful—but that honor was bestowed on Jacob because he was willing to wrestle his way through his own doubts and conflicts. From the encounter, Jacob emerged limping, but also a more compassionate, always-evolving son, father, and leader.

Plato taught that happiness is rooted in an examined life and the Psalmist wrote, "Know Before Whom You Stand." In other words, happiness comes from learning to appreciate living in the gap between what we desire and what we have, who we are and who we want to be, how we act and how we ought to act. In the end, maybe a happy life is one in which we regularly reflect on what makes for a happy life.

FULL OF ENOUGH

IT WAS FOUR WEEKS BEFORE MY NIECE MELISSA'S wedding. Dana's sister, the mother of the bride, had been orchestrating a grand affair. Everyone had been buzzing about the details of the occasion for months—who would sit where, what the bridal party should wear—the usual wedding mania. Three generations of our scattered family would come together for a weekend of joyous celebration of the marriage of two beautiful people and the miracle of all being together. It made it even more special to me that my father and I would lead the ceremony. *Simcha*, the Hebrew word for "joy," also means "a happy occasion." Weddings are considered one of the greatest *simchas* of all.

Three weeks before the ceremony my father-in-law, Jules, was diagnosed with cancer of the pancreas, with a very serious prognosis. We were devastated. He is our precious Grandpa. Dana, the kids, and I are incredibly close to him. The blow hit us all very hard. Dana accompanied her parents to every appointment. In the evenings, we would lie in bed, talk, and cry. My kids couldn't concentrate on their work or sleep: This was the grandfather who ran after them when they were young; taught them to harvest the many vegetables from his garden; and coached them as they rode their boogie boards in the Atlantic. My mother-in-law, Janice, worked around the clock caring for her husband of more than fifty years. We were all racked with anxiety as he underwent a dangerous surgery, which we weren't sure he'd survive. Even if he did, the outcome was far from clear.

Dana and I found ourselves praying that somehow at least he'd make it to the wedding of his precious granddaughter. Over the course of our relationship, whenever I pictured Jules in my mind I saw him, with his full head of jet-black hair well into his eighth decade, on the dance floor—he and Janice were beautiful ballroom dancers. As I waited for the six-hour surgery to be over, I visualized him dancing at the wedding, his face radiant with health as he beamed with pride and delight.

Jules came through the surgery, although there were complications and not all the cancer could be removed. Until two days before the wedding, we weren't sure if he'd be strong enough to attend. But he did come. As we drove from New York City to Baltimore for the weekend of celebration that would culminate in a Sunday-evening wedding, the car was pulsating with life. What happened over that weekend forever changed my understanding of *simcha*. The wedding was nothing short of breathtaking. The night sparkled with candles and crystal; the wedding canopy was covered in sprays of beautiful flowers; the guests looked fabulous in their fancy attire; the bride and groom were exuberant and gracious. Every moment, every detail, was enriched by Jules's presence. I could barely keep my eyes off him as he joked with my father. After twenty-five years of being family, they were like brothers. I watched him stroke his granddaughters' hair and compliment them on how mature and beautiful they looked. Pale and visibly thin under his tux, he beamed nevertheless.

When I looked over and saw him dancing with Dana, tears streamed down my face. When they circled closer I could see Dana also had tears in her eyes and both of their faces were lit up with the biggest smiles I'd ever seen. I had watched them dance together many times but this time there was a shimmering light around them. It was a different kind of dancing than the one that I'd imagined while waiting for the surgery to be over—sadness and happiness were intertwined in every step, and no one wanted the music to stop.

The Hassidic mystic Rabbi Nachman struggled with depression his

entire life. In one of his parables he describes a person watching a traditional dance at a village wedding, with people joyfully circling the bride
and groom. Too sad to join in, he stands outside the circle of the
dancers until someone takes hold of his hand and pulls him into the

> **There is no happiness without sadness; no pleasure without pain; no fullness without loss. They are inseparable.**

dance, despite his protestations. He finds
himself dancing hesitantly at first and
then joyfully; then turning to watch his
sad self looking on with disappointment.
The task, says Rabbi Nachman, is to bring
that sadness itself into the circle; to see that it, too, is transformed into
joy. The truth of Nachman's teaching could not be any more real than it
was at Melissa's wedding. We had taken sadness by the hand and somehow transformed it into joy.

There was nothing any of us wouldn't have done to take back the
last month, to have Jules's health fully restored, and yet the joy we felt
during those two days was so life-affirming and richly layered. There
was a depth of gratitude, an appreciation for every detail, and a feeling
of preciousness. The sorrow that had overwhelmed and consumed us
in the previous days—and likely would again—somehow generated a
more profound happiness, a feeling of being in the pulse and intensity
of life. There is no happiness without sadness; no pleasure without pain;
no fullness without loss. They go together; they are inseparable. Naturally, we always want to get rid of the sadness rather than see how it
works together with joy. We forget that the point is not to cultivate one
thing as opposed to the other, but to see clearly where we are.

I realized that weekend that joy is deepened by sadness, and that
very joy can carry you through that very sadness. This is precisely the
power of the final practice at every Jewish wedding: A glass is stomped
on and shattered as a reminder of the destruction of the ancient temple
and the fragility of everything precious. At the sound of the shattering,
all those watching the ceremony applaud and yell "*Mazel tov!*" or "Good
luck"; and the marriage has begun with the brokenness brought into
the circle of joy.

Happiness is about embracing the cycle of life, about seeing everything in its widest possible context and experiencing it all to the fullest.
The Dalai Lama captures this in his definition of happiness: "Deliberately broadening one's outlook and finding meaning in suffering; a
transformation of outlook." It's not that he sees things through rose-
colored glasses; it's that he views suffering and joy along the same continuum. Our hope for Jules's recovery, for many more dances with him,
sat side-by-side with our awareness that this might in fact be his very
last *simcha*. Somehow, for that glorious weekend, it was enough.

There's a song sung at every Passover seder, although I've often
thought it should be a daily meditation. It's called "*Dayenu*," which means
"it's enough for us." The song is a remarkable and deceptively simple
teaching about embracing the present, while having a keen awareness of
the past and a yearning for the future. It's about feeling longing and gratitude; triumph and tragedy. It's about celebrating every single step along
the way and yet fiercely longing for the fulfillment of one's dream.

The song acknowledges fifteen major Biblical events, asking us to sing
dayenu after each one. If God had brought us out of Egypt but not divided the sea for us, *dayenu*; it would have been enough for us. If God
had led us to Mt. Sinai but there had been no encounter, *dayenu*; it would
have been enough for us. If we had had the encounter at Sinai but had not
made it through the desert, *dayenu*; it would have been enough for us.

As I watched Jules and Dana dance, I thought, *dayenu*. If they had
that one dance but never another, *dayenu*. I felt so full and so grateful.
Yet at the same time, I knew it wouldn't always feel like enough. I wondered if anything would. Would two more years be enough?; would
ten?; would twenty? The song can be sung multiple ways: with joy and
gusto—*dayenu* as a declarative, an affirmation that every moment in
life is a gift, that it really is enough; or slowly and mournfully—*dayenu*
as resignation that, given the cycle of life, it would have to be enough.
Or as a protest—it's not enough! *Dayenu* also can be a question; would
it ever be enough for us? There's an inherent tension and edginess in the
song—there's both comfort and challenge.

Anyone familiar with the stories mentioned in each verse of *"Dayenu"* knows that forty-eight hours after escaping Egypt, rather than celebrating their freedom and feeling it was enough, the Israelites were complaining that they were thirsty and there was no water. After going through the sea they complained about there not being enough food. A few weeks after encountering the divine at Mt. Sinai, after having a vision of the deepest dimensions of reality, the Israelites worshipped the golden calf. Nothing seemed to be enough. Isn't this true for all of us? We have a breakthrough in our lives: finally launching that new business, falling in love with the girl we've pursued, having that healthy child after years of trying, having our sick father-in-law dance at a family celebration—and whether it's the next minute, the next day, or the next year, we want something more.

The last line of the song is, "If we were brought into the Promised Land, and the Temple was not built, it would have been enough for us, *dayenu.*" The Temple is metaphor for that place where everything is as it should be—the cure is found, love wins out, life triumphs. It is pure joy and happiness; nothing short of the ultimate. Yet the song was written well over one thousand years after the destruction of the Temple. The Temple was clearly not going to be rebuilt. How can we be grateful for what we will never have? How can we sing *dayenu* while wanting so much more? How can we parse the journey into steps and be thankful for each one, even though we don't really know where we're going?

Only by becoming proficient at both gratitude and longing can our happiness become richer and more real.

We all want to rebuild our temples, to reach our Promised Land—the place in life where our dreams are fulfilled, where our father-in-law can be cured—but we need to remember that it's called the Promised Land for a reason. It is always promised, just beyond us. And so we better enjoy every dance. *"Dayenu"* urges us to go for it, to long for the ultimate and to know that regardless of what happens, every step along the way is enough. When we become proficient at gratitude and longing, when we can experience the fullness of *dayenu*—as affirmation, lament, protest, and question—our happiness will be so much richer and more real.

After all, if we're only happy when everything works out, happiness will always elude us and our experience of reality will be so much narrower. One of the many names for God is the mystical name *Shaddai*, which comes from the same root as the word *dayenu*. Why would there be a name for the infinite one that means "enough"? One master taught that after that first week of Creation, the work was far from done and never would be done, but God was able to say enough for now. In other words, one of the qualities of the divine presence is the sense of enough. Incompleteness is a quality of reality. "*Dayenu*" is not simply about being satisfied with what we have, it's about feeling the fullness of the partial. It's about experiencing the exquisiteness of two yearnings: how very much we want the Temple and how much we long to feel "enough" even if it's never built.

If we were to practice *dayenu* every morning and every night before we went to sleep, imagine how we'd reframe our goals and anxieties; how differently we'd parse our day. "If I walk into my kids' room just before they awaken and see them stir, and nothing else happens today, *dayenu*. If I have breakfast with them, but I fail to close the deal this afternoon, *dayenu*. If I close the deal but miss a date with an old friend, *dayenu*." *Dayenu* is like a marinade for our consciousness. The more time we dwell there, the richer and more delicious life becomes.

The Talmud teaches that if one eats as little as an olive-size amount of food, one should feel gratitude. To be honest, I do not think I have ever eaten only an olive-size amount of anything, and can barely imagine what it is to feel grateful for just a morsel of food. It may well be easier to feel the fullness in the partial when we actually have less to begin with, just as one can feel deeper joy when the backdrop is sadness. I remember once, when I was about ten, eating dinner with my grandfather, who visited every week. He was literally gnawing and sucking on a steak bone and enjoying it immensely. When I asked him why he didn't take another slice of steak, he told me about how he came from Russia to this country alone at sixteen. There were plenty of days in the first couple of years when he was hungry, and sucking on bones would make him full. And so even now he enjoyed the bone as much as the steak. If feeling full and grateful when one has very little was the challenge for my grandfather, the challenge for me and many of us today is how to feel full and grateful in the midst of abundance.

By dozens of measures, life has gotten better for most Americans since the 1950s. We have achieved what our grandparents or great-grandparents could barely dream of, and yet polling data shows that we are no happier than we were back then; 60 percent of Americans feel less well-off than their parents. We have greater prosperity and yet the number of people who consider themselves depressed has dramatically increased—some social scientists say by as much as twenty-fold. We suffer what some have called "abundance denial."

Abundance poses very different psychospiritual questions than scarcity. The question of scarcity is, how do I get what I need to feel happy and secure? The question of abundance is, how do I really know what I need? How do I distinguish between my real needs and my desires? What does enough, or *dayenu*, mean when I have an overwhelming number of choices and manufactured desires for things I didn't even know I wanted, let alone needed? In our culture, wants get converted so quickly into needs that feeling satisfied becomes incredibly elusive. In other words, the question is not, how can I feel grateful for an olive-size amount of food, but how can I feel satisfied when I can have as many olives as I want? That's the *dayenu* challenge for most of us.

There's a daring Hasidic teaching that says Esau was the happiest, most satisfied character in the Bible. Esau, the same guy whose blessing, whose sacred inheritance was stolen by his younger brother? Esau, whose mother betrayed him and whose father didn't stop it from happening? Esau, the hunter who sold his birthright blessing for a pot of lentils? The sages taught that despite it all, Esau still felt blessed. He was happy with his lot and appreciated his own uniqueness. The pot of lentils was enough: When you feel blessed your blessing can't be sold or stolen. When he meets Jacob decades later, Esau greets his brother warmly, saying he has plenty in response to his brother's offers of gifts. For Jacob, not even the blessing had been enough: He wanted the more beautiful sister as his wife, a larger share of the herd from his father-in-law. Jacob could never have appreciated the simple pleasure of a pot of lentils; he could only see it as a vehicle to something else—to being more and more blessed. Yet at that chance meeting in the desert, both brothers in fact seem happy and blessed. Together, the twins seem to embody *dayenu*—wanting it all and finding enough.

Friends have sometimes described me as one of the happiest people they've ever met. "Lucky in life" is a phrase I've heard a lot. "Lucky" is the secular word for "blessed." I guess I've been a little like Esau. For most of my life I've barely ever planned anything, and I had very few dreams or visions for the future. I've missed planes because I got into engaging conversations with people I'd just met in the airport. I worked hard and trusted that I'd be rewarded with success without worrying too much about it. Happiness was to be found in the moment and things would always work out.

Then one day I was unexpectedly named president of the organization I still run today. And so I ran the Center for Learning and Leadership the same way I lived my life—by the seat of my pants. I coasted from one great adventure to another. I dealt with issues as they came up and tried to be kind and encouraging to the people who worked for me.

Then, one evening, a major donor asked me with a slight edge in his voice, "So what do you want to do with your life? What's your vision for the organization?" He was a millionaire many times over and had become very accomplished at a young age. I felt defensive, to say the least. Crazy as it might seem, it was the first time I'd ever been asked those questions, and it was the first time I can remember not having an answer. I was really uncomfortable. And then I got annoyed. How could he put me on the spot that way? Besides, the organization was growing, financially secure, and programmatically interesting. I offered some deflective answer, but over the next few weeks his question haunted me.

"What was my dream? What was I really up to?" Suddenly, enough wasn't enough.

Within a few weeks, and after much thinking—and some of the most interesting conversations with friends and colleagues I had ever had—I came back to my supporter with an answer. I had a really big dream and it felt great. I decided that the mission of the organization would be to take Jewish wisdom public, to offer a philosophical, spiritual, and psychological life-approach that could benefit everyone, whether they were Jewish or not. My job was no longer just a gig, but a tremendous opportunity. I saw my Promised Land and I was hell-bent on getting there. Family and colleagues barely recognized me as I worked late into the night, pushing them and myself to come up with a strategic plan for a center that would nourish wisdom and imagination. We accomplished so much over those many months. It was such an amazing time. Until it wasn't.

I found myself running from meeting to meeting, traveling constantly, accomplishing one goal and quickly moving on to the next. Instead of talking to people for sheer pleasure and engagement, I began to think about what I needed from them, or in what possible way they could help me and my organization accomplish our goals. In other words, people in my life became means to manifest my dream—a little like Jacob. One day, a very close friend asked me, with genuine love and hurt in his voice, why I rarely returned his calls, and when I did, it was often days later. I was always apologetic, but I wasn't really there. There was a time when I could sit with a stranger for three hours and now I was barely in touch with someone I cared about so much. I remember feeling so sad after that call. I had gone from a person happy in the present to one who lived obsessed in the anticipation of the future I was working to create.

I have come to realize that when I feel this kind of sadness about being neither here nor there, it means that I have either invested too much in transitory moments or put too much stock in the future. Most of us have a predisposition one way or the other. We're either planners or moment-to-moment people. Now I'd gone full-steam both ways. Neither had worked, and it hurt.

In the end I walked away with a renewed understanding of life; sadness often enlightens. I saw that I could strive for my goals—yearn for the Promised Land—and still savor every step of the way. I could be fiercely in the present and be fiercely building for the future. If I did, I'd have a better chance of both being happy and reaching my goals. Yet I'd never get the balance just right. There'd be many more agonizing times of disappointment and always a lot more work to do. But there also could be a kind of sweet agony. *Dayenu* is a way to discipline the dream without suppressing it. It enables us to live with great visions, and love the journey. There's no great answer but a lot of little answers. If you listen they all just might add up. And even if they don't, sing "*Dayenu*."

Holidays, like songs and stories, are reframing practices—ways to contextualize our deep yearnings in the memory of a historical or mythical event, which in turn gives meaning and depth to our lives. The festival of Succot, which falls in the autumn, is also called the "The Holiday of Rejoicing." Originally a celebration of the harvest, it is an eight-day thanksgiving. It's a celebration of abundance, plentitude, and fullness. And yet it also recalls those difficult forty years the Israelites spent wandering in the desert; all the longing and the yearning; all the waiting to get in to the Promised Land. Unlike the American version of Thanksgiving, Succot celebrates the pilgrimage rather than the arrival. It's a weeklong party designed to expand our experience of happiness.

Succot is a journey practice—a retreat in the wilderness, both figuratively and literally. A structure called a Succah is built, in which family and guests eat their meals: It's a reproduction of the temporary shelters built by the Israelites in the desert. The Succah is made of canvas or thin wooden boards, strong enough to survive the basic elements but not able to withstand winds of unusual force. The roof of wooden slats is not nailed down and is open enough to allow the rain to fall in and to see the stars in the sky. There's a playfulness in building a temporary structure in the backyard that, for a week, we move into—or at least eat our meals in. It's like when you were a kid sleeping in a tent or tree house in your own yard, and you see the lights of your home, your bedroom window above, and you feel the excitement of being both safe and exposed.

The Succah teaches that we are neither as vulnerable as we fear nor as invulnerable as we fantasize. It's a way to reenvision our own messy, incomplete journeys, to celebrate the daily strain of pursuing our dreams. What does it mean to celebrate the forty-year journey—a metaphor for the journey that is our lifetime? As my teacher, Rabbi Irving "Yitz" Greenberg, offers: "It is celebrating pitching tents and taking them down over the course of 14,600 days. It honors forty-three thousand meals prepared on the desert trek; the cleanups, the washing of utensils . . . the gritty days of marching." If we can cele-

> **Our journeys are messy and incomplete, but if we can still celebrate the daily strain of pursuing our dreams we can be happy.**

brate all of that we will be happy. The question is, can we enjoy the long strange trip? to quote the Grateful Dead. Like *dayenu*, Succot is about the joy of appreciating every step of the journey, even relishing those uncertain times before our feet hit the ground. It's a celebration of how we lose and find our way over and over again.

It also teaches that we only can be as happy as we ourselves believe we can be—we can't reach a Promised Land that we're too afraid to envision. But the only Promised Land worth envisioning is the one that we can never reach. It only took the Israelites two years to get to the borders of the Promised Land, but they were too frightened to go in. "We looked like grasshoppers to ourselves, and so we must have looked to them," said the spies sent ahead to investigate the enemy inhabitants. The people saw themselves as weak and small, and so they were not able to enter for thirty-eight more years. Aren't most of us afraid to dream big? It also could be that a richer, more expansive happiness awaited the people back in the desert. If they'd entered the land they'd have lost the promise. There was so much more to be discovered in the wilderness, in the *midbar*. They knew that wandering is the source of wonder. In yearning there is so much fullness.

The first words God says to Abraham, the first biblical wanderer, are "go to yourself." Abraham lived an edgy, painful life: years of childlessness; then the loss of one son and almost the second; constant doubt in his God, and conflict with his wife; and a nagging feeling of always wanting more, of never having enough. Yet as he breathed his last breaths, we are told that he was "old, good, full, and contented." Similarly, the great philosopher Ludwig Wittgenstein is often described as being sad and isolated a good part of the time. He struggled with new interpretations and visions that changed the way we understand reality, yet he seemed never to be happy with himself. On a typical day of teaching, he could be heard mumbling to himself, "Wittgenstein, what a terrible teacher you are." Yet his last reported words as he lay dying were, "Tell them it's been wonderful!"

That kind of fullness and satisfaction, of knowing you led a good life, can only come after having lived a lifetime of questioning and yearning—after many dances of happiness and sadness; many moments of *dayenu*. Maybe that's why the Jewish tradition celebrates the anniversary of someone's death, but not their birth. The only character in the Bible to celebrate a birthday is the Pharaoh, who would never know what it means to feel full and good.

I've always marveled at how we Americans go to such great pains to fill our children's arms with presents and their stomachs with delights one day a year. Perhaps we do so because attaining that sense of authentic contentment is simply not possible, and yet we yearn for it. What if birthdays instead became practices to help us appreciate the steps along the way? What if they were days of storytelling and mythmaking; of introspection and (more than one) song? What if we sang *dayenu* about the last year and the next one? What if what we meant by wishing *happy* birthday is that all that *happens* will be cause for a deeper joy; that the person will live intensely and tap into the energy current of life; that she take chances and not be afraid to yearn? What if we made a practice of reframing and reinterpreting our own lives every year; celebrating our own personal harvest day? Then, just maybe, we'd feel contented at the end of it all. And that would be enough. *Dayenu.*

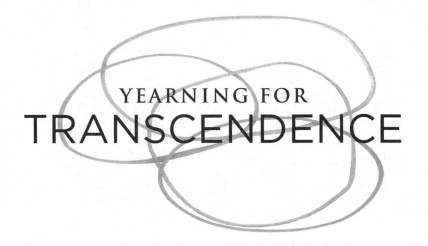

YEARNING FOR
TRANSCENDENCE

DYING FOR LIFE

ONCE, WHEN I WAS TRAVELING, I WENT INTO ONE OF those gadget stores in the airport. They had something they called a "personal life clock," and I was intrigued. I entered my age, my gender, and a few other facts, and it made some kind of statistical computation that told me how many hours, minutes, and seconds I had left to live. As the clock went to work computing the data, it made an unnerving *tick-tock*. I literally could hear my life ticking away. At some point I had to turn away, and when I came back to the clock ten minutes later, I remember there were about 300,000 hours left in my life, which seemed not only incomprehensible but really disturbing. It took me a few days to recover, and it still makes me anxious whenever I think of it.

I didn't feel so different than Rav Nachman, who the Talmud tells us showed himself to his friend Rava in a dream after Rav Nachman died. Rava asked him, "Was death painful?" Rav Nachman replied, "It was as painless as lifting a hair from a cup of milk. But were the Holy One to say to me, 'You may return to that world where you were before,' I would not wish to do it. The fear of death is too great." Or, as Woody Allen said, "I don't mind dying. I just don't want to be there when it happens."

The mystery of death is al-

> Dying, and being with those who are dying, is the ultimate challenge and the greatest spiritual opportunity.

ways there in the background, an ever-present anxiety that most of the time we effectively deny or push aside in order to live our daily lives. And then inevitably we're forced to confront the reality of our own or a loved one's death. Or perhaps we aren't even given the time to say good-bye to someone we care about. Either way, our fear and panic, along with our grief, surface in Technicolor.

Every wisdom system until the modern period has taught that dying and being with those who are dying is the ultimate challenge and the greatest spiritual opportunity. As Rabbi Jack Reimer says, "No one can claim to be wise about life whose wisdom does not include a relationship to death." Whether we are facing our own death or confronting the death of a loved one, there are a host of tensions that revolve around this mystery, and we can gain understanding by grappling with them. When we're faced with serious or terminal illness, we have the chance to decide whether to fight fiercely for life or surrender peacefully to death. We wonder when is the right time to let go, to prepare to die, to say good-bye. If we're a loved one, we agonize over whether to work toward closure and allow things to take their course or use every medical means necessary to keep the person alive, hoping a cure is possible. To paraphrase Dylan Thomas, will we rage against the dying of the light or go gently into that good night?

We always need to ask ourselves whether living as long as possible is the right option. I have come to trust the wisdom of the dying person. I have seen people fight fiercely for life and literally come back from comas; live years beyond the terminal prognosis given to them; gain time no one could have expected, while somehow maintaining quality of life. I also have seen people who, unable to let go, died with incredible anxiousness and lack of peace. Others seem to surrender to death when those around them felt they were giving up before their time. Still others let go beautifully, taking the time that might otherwise be spent resisting death to settle their relationships, make peace with their lives, and then die with such little regret that all I can do is marvel and learn.

When to fight and when to let go; how hard to resist and how easily to surrender: There are no rules about dying. When society tries to determine a "one-size-fits-all" rule we wind up with Doctor Kevorkian on the one side and Terri Schiavo–type controversies on the other. We turn what ought to be a deeply personal and familial time into a public spectacle and an ideological battle. Death trumps all ideologies, and anyone or any system that thinks it is 100 percent right has allowed their fear to reach a dangerous extreme and is therefore disrespectful to the sanctity of life and the intimacy of death.

In my own life there have been few moments more frightening, more life-affirming, and more enlightening than holding the hands of people who are about to find out what happens next. Sam Golden-hersch was my first rebbe of death. I was a new rabbi, and he was one of the first people with whom I went through the process of dying. Sam was a gruff, hard-nosed building contractor in his sixties. He had a strong personality, a loud booming voice, and he was no lover of rabbis, rebuking anything that smacked of the spiritual. But he was a friend whose challenging, confrontational personality kept me on my toes.

It was so painful to watch his diabetes slowly kill him, and to see how much severe pain he was in. Over a couple of years he lost one limb after another as he went in and out of the hospital for amputations. He told me there was no way he would give up; not until there was nothing left—no toes, no feet, no legs—no matter how much it hurt.

Every time I saw him, I felt more depressed and frightened. Of course, as a spiritual leader, "I knew better" than Sam: If he would just stop fighting and let go he would be so much happier. It was inevitable, and he needed to face it. But there was no taking him on: His strength and resolve were palpable, even when he was confined to his bed. I would visit on Friday afternoon before the Sabbath when I made my rounds in the hospital, usually making small talk and gauging his frame of both body and mind before I left for the weekend. I felt so helpless; I wanted to do something. Yet as things got worse, his gruffness and bitterness began to put me off. When I'd ask how he was doing, he'd answer with some variation of, "How would you be if they took you apart limb-by-limb?" He didn't make visiting easy.

One day he was in a particularly prickly mood, and after my ritual-istic brief visit I wished him Shabbat Shalom and got up to leave, to which he said, "Leaving so soon?" I asked him what he meant by the question. "Did you ever notice how you conveniently visit when you have to be home in time for the Sabbath?" Trying to keep it light, I joked, "Sam, you just think that because you're so tough you don't need the Sabbath." He laughed and said, "That may be, but I smell fear. I think you are more afraid of what is going on with me than I am, which means you must be pretty frightened. Why don't you sit down?"

Over the next three months, I had some of the most uncomfortable encounters of my life. Sam taught me that waves of sadness, pity, aversion, fear, and, yes, even bitterness can be healthy parts of dying. He taught me about the subtle and not-so-subtle ways many of us distance ourselves from death in order to protect ourselves; that there is no model of a "good death" which can be imposed from the outside. Sam was honest and transparent. Every time a different part of his body would be amputated he would urge me to look at the stump; and then, in what seemed to be a strange mix of courage, disgust, pride, and resistance, he'd challenge me to physically touch the area. I didn't conquer my fears but I learned to dwell in them.

Sam never became any calmer about dying—no theology or attempts to make things better were going to work for him. He taught me that fear and fighting can be as spiritual and life-affirming as serenity and acceptance. I learned that being with the dying is not about pious answers. Sam had been a tough guy all his life, and he was going to die a tough guy. His death was as enlightening as the most peaceful, calm, and gentle deaths that I have been honored to witness.

About two weeks before Sam died, I went to visit him. When I walked into his room his wife was there. The room had that acrid smell hospitals can have when death is close; it made my stomach churn. Sam was barely conscious, and now it was painful even to look at him. A few months earlier I would have mumbled a prayer, said something appropriately comforting to his wife, and then left. Instead I stood at the bedside and looked at Sam for the longest time. I don't know what came over me but I found myself putting my hands on his face, leaning over, and planting a big kiss right on his mouth. His wife started laughing and said, "Irwin, if Sam knew you'd kissed him on the mouth he'd die!" Then we both began to cry.

There is great courage in letting go and great courage in fighting. And, of course, there are often many stages people go through during the process of dying: denial, anger, bargaining, despair, and acceptance. But they are not clean or linear. They bleed into each other and double back on each other and mask each other. Our feelings about death are moment truths; they change and evolve. Coping with death is really the ultimate humility practice, and when we can hold the various truths and experiences together, there's so much insight to be gained. There are moments of acceptance and moments of resistance; moments of fighting and moments of softening.

> **Our feelings about death are moment truths that change and evolve: moments of acceptance and moments of resistance, moments of fighting and moments of softening.**

Here's an ancient story, an example of how to hold truths together even in the midst of dying. It's the story about the death of Moses. The Bible tells us that Moses died on a mountain overlooking the Promised Land as the next generation of Israelites crossed the border. He was one hundred and twenty years old at the time, and what a life! He'd freed his people from slavery and then spent forty years in the desert as their leader. How could it be that he wouldn't even get to enter the land he spent decades yearning for! The rabbinic sages describe a scene that is far from peaceful. Moses fights death fiercely. He argues with God about the injustice of it all, writhing as he lies there, lashing out and cursing. "How can you do this to me? You've got to let me live long enough to enter the land!"

In the end Moses accepts his death and, as sages imagine, dies with a kiss from God. He faces his death as all of us must, but not before he fights like crazy. There's never a perfect time to die. There's no such thing as dying when it's your time. Moses isn't over the hill; he's on top of the mountain. He knows full well that his project isn't over, and it hurts like hell. What an amazing teaching this is. Dream big but don't complete the project. If your dream comes true you've dreamed too small. It's enough to look over a mountainside and get a glimpse of what comes next, and see how you've contributed to the unfolding of the story. What vision of afterlife can beat that?

The story of Moses's death gave me a rich context for dealing with the death of my own Moses, one of the most influential teachers I'd ever had. Rabbi Hyman was truly larger than life, with wild red hair, a piercing voice, and always a playful look in his eye. And he had such a mastery over Jewish wisdom. All of us who'd experienced his teaching loved him deeply. Midway into our second year in his Talmud class, Rabbi Hyman was diagnosed with brain cancer, and he quickly declined. One day, a group of us went to visit him in his home. The scene was so unreal. His kids were playing outside, yelling and laughing as they threw a ball around: They were so young and couldn't have known or understood how sick their father was. Their voices were so full of life.

When I first saw him, I couldn't help but gasp. His head was swollen almost beyond recognition, and he lay very still in his bed. One of us began to cry and then we all did. I can't remember who said, "You have to fight this. How can it be that you'll never teach again?" He seemed so accepting and resigned—and we couldn't help it; it made us angry. Rabbi Hyman looked up at us and that twinkle was still there. "What do you mean?" he asked. "Now I'll be able to study with God; to see it all; to finally understand all that I've ever tried to teach." I said, "That's not good enough! How can we keep going without you?" And he turned to me with a raised eyebrow and said, "Leave you? Where could I go?" As we left his room, I imagined that, like Moses, he was watching the next generation continue the journey and for him there was no greater comfort.

In the Bible the word for where you go after death is *sheol*, which comes from the same root as the word for "question." When we or a loved one is dying some of us who'd never contemplated an afterlife inevitably wonder, "Could this be all there is?" "Is there a spirit that lives on?" Even if we don't have these questions, we begin to struggle at a whole other level with our own mortality and that of others we love. We may fight against the inevitability of death or seek new ways of looking at it. Either way, death begins to inform our lives. And the yearning to understand, even transcend the finality of death, to find meaning in loss, is awakened at a whole other level. This yearning is one of the most noble, defining aspects of our humanness.

Every culture and wisdom tradition offers insights in an attempt to fill the vacuum of not-knowing. None of them resolves the mystery, but each offers moment truths that can help us through the process. In America, there's a polarity between the modern, rationalist, scientific view that death is final and this life is all there is, and every single spiritual and religious tradition that claims this life is not the end, that there is something after life.

The perception that death is final has generated a full-scale assault on illness in the last century: It's doubled life spans and dramatically lowered infant mortality. The starkness of this view has created a fierce desire to push back death. If you are a grandparent or great-grandparent who is in good health and enjoys your grandchild, you have the tremendous advances in medicine to thank. This contemporary view of the finality of death allows us to feel the preciousness of life. The scarcer something is, the more valuable it becomes—and nothing is more valuable than time.

The downside of the modern, scientific view is that it can create extreme fear—even paranoia. Death becomes the enemy and so we sanitize it, and are overly youth-conscious and preoccupied with making sure people do not take dying into their own hands. More than half our national health budget goes to the last months of life when little or nothing can be done, and that diverts resources from health care that could enhance people's lives or ease them into death. As Woody Allen said, "In America, we've decided that death is optional."

On the other side are the varieties of afterlife intuitions—immortality of the soul, the next world, resurrection, reincarnation, rebirth, heaven, hell, the bardos, Kabbalistic mansions. These mystical perceptions are based on centuries of intuitions and practices that teach that there's more than just this life, and they can mitigate our fear, providing comfort and hope. Soul, Atman, Ruach—there are so many names for the part of us that lives on or that never was born and, therefore, can never die.

There's a belief in many Eastern traditions that like the self, death is an illusion, so what is there to fear? Life isn't about beginnings and endings; it's an endless cycle of unfolding and evolution. We return to the ocean of all that is. This certainly puts things in perspective: In fourteen billion years of unfolding, my individual self is either a blip or a microcosm and it shouldn't be overdramatized. The ancient Greeks taught that there is a spirit that continues after death. Christianity was greatly influenced by this idea, and took it one step further to say that resurrection is possible and that there's a heaven, a world beyond ours where we live on in an elevated state. Islam shares this teaching, as does Judaism beginning in the third century when it was heavily influenced by Christian beliefs.

In response to the stark, modern view, more traditional views of heaven and an afterlife are returning as Christian evangelical and fundamentalist communities have grown in numbers. At the same time so-called New Age beliefs have grown in popularity. There's the relocation theory—we are just going to a better place—and the reincarnation theory—we will be coming back. Both Christianity and New Age teachings share the belief that the soul is immortal. Some believe the dead remain as spirits or souls lingering in the corners of our lives.

I've seen that those who are open to the idea of an afterlife can experience new levels of intimacy, new modes of connecting, a softening of the seemingly hard boundary between life and death. But the same afterlife intuitions that can generate hope, comfort, and meaning can lead to resignation and a dismissal of this world. And even more hurtful, many believers deal with the uncertainty inherent in any afterlife teaching by turning it into a system

The yearning for forever is an essential part of being human.

of rigid reward and punishment: who is entitled to an afterlife and who isn't.

Can we really allow ourselves to believe any of it? Voltaire said, "It would be no more surprising to be born twice than born once." After all, to even be here to ask these questions is a wild result of billions of consecutive throws of the genetic dice. What are the odds that we as unique individuals even exist? The finality of death and the afterlife are both moment truths. The challenge is to know when to embrace which and how lightly.

What guidelines can we use to determine where along the continuum we ought to be? First we need to leave ourselves open to the ever-shifting quality of the truths about what happens after we die. The tensions, mysteries, and ignorance surrounding death are actually invitations to seek unfolding levels of insight and trust our own experience. If we hold on too tightly to any one view of death, we risk losing out on the intuitions of the others. The poet Rilke wrote that we should "try to love the questions themselves . . . live everything . . . live into the answers."

After close to three decades of sitting with people who are dying, as well as their families, I have become very pragmatic. Our responses to death do not have to be intellectually sound or consistent. Rather, they need to be existentially comforting and enlightening. My criteria are simple. Does your view create less terror around death? Does your view support you as you fight for life until you're ready to let go? Does it allow you and those around you to be more honest, more hopeful, calmer, more compassionate, more loving, and even more joyful? Does it allow you to grasp the truth of the Ecclesiastes poet who wrote that there's a time for birth and a time for death; to feel the intensity and beauty of the cycle of life?

It's important to remember that all perceptions of the afterlife or no-afterlife grow out of genuine interior experiences. They can be life-changing as well as life-affirming. When you remain open, they can really take you by surprise. My dead grandfather once came back to me in a waking dream; I couldn't believe it when I heard his voice, but there it was, clear as a bell. He had always been really tough on me, pushing me to follow a conventional path to success and giving me such a hard time about my long hair. He'd often ask me, "Who do you think you are, Jesus?" Before he died I'd become an assistant rabbi at a major congregation, and I'd finally made him happy. But in my vision, or waking dream, he urged me to leave that very job to take a far more risky, unconventional one I'd been contemplating and was very conflicted about. It's not important whether or not this was a projection or really happened; the experience was real and it comforted me deeply. More than that, it released me to do something I needed and wanted to do.

Another time I attended a funeral of the mother of a student of mine. She had died suddenly of a stroke, and there was so much sorrow, so much loss and hurt in the room. As the casket was carried out of the funeral home, a flower fell loose from the spray on top; it landed at the feet of the husband, who then burst into loud sobs. At the gathering afterward, it seemed like everyone was talking about that flower. I learned that the husband had brought his wife a bouquet every Friday night for decades. For the husband, that single flower was his wife's loving goodbye; her hand reaching out from beyond.

The yearning for forever is an essential part of being human. The Adam and Eve story is, in part, a teaching about keeping the questions about death alive. There are two trees that are off limits: The tree of knowledge of good and bad is one; the tree of knowledge of life and death is the other. One of God's motivations for banishing Adam and Eve is the fear that they might now eat of the other tree and therefore be immortal. To be human is to die and to know it. If they had eaten from the Tree of Life, Adam and Eve would have lost their very humanity. Of course they had to leave that temptation behind! And yet they, like us, always will long to taste that fruit, to live forever. Perhaps this is why the first thing the couple does after leaving the garden is to make love and have a child; love can transcend death.

Jewish wisdom holds together many of the tensions surrounding death. It encourages us to fight fiercely and to let go; to face the finality

of death and then to hope the person lives on. The tradition understands that death is often tougher on those who are left to live on without a loved one than it is on the dying. It teaches that for survivors,
death causes a profound collapse of meaning that no belief system in
the world can mitigate. Whatever intuition we embrace about what
happens to our loved one next, there's no escaping the immediate devastation of death. Anything we say or do that doesn't acknowledge this
reality simply isn't true to our experience. Jewish wisdom invites us to
address the death directly, to embrace the finality of loss fully. If we can
face the stark, tragic reality of death, eventually we will heal.

In the Jewish tradition there are no sayings like "passed away" or "final resting place." We are to call death by its real name—feel the blow,
sink into the loss, let it subsume us—and we're to do so when it's most
painful and intense: in the first twenty-four hours after someone dies.
We need to deepen, rather than minimize, our sorrow and express our
anger. Only then can we hope for reconciliation and return. As psychologist Joyce Slochower wrote, "Jewish wisdom provides a structure to
address death, not to control or contain it, but to express and experience it as fully as possible."

Our first job is to attend to the dead. The body is buried in a plain
pine box within those twenty-four hours. Death makes no distinction
between rich and poor. There's no embalming, no making things beautiful or lifelike; the body is to be left in its natural state. We are meant to
see death, feel it, no pretending. "From dust to dust" is considered a sacred experience. We are to be buried so that we can return to the earth,
and we're to be dressed in a simple white cloak, with no adornments. As
Job said, "Naked did I emerge from my mother's womb. And naked
shall I return there."

There's a name for the twenty-four hours just after a death and before the burial: *aninut*, which means "between." Many people are surprised when I tell them that during this time we are not supposed to
pray. This is not the time for meaning-making, rationalizing, or making
sense of the experience. One would think the opposite; that one should

call upon a larger power as a source of comfort, a way to put death in a larger context. But when we're in the grip of such utter despair, there's no use pretending there's a larger plan, a reason, or a purpose. When your life has been completely shattered, there's no way to imagine wholeness, and trying to do so can short-circuit our grief.

Before the burial we are invited to honor the dead. During the funeral someone close to the deceased is to stand before those gathered and create a narrative of the person's life. The most common word for this is "eulogy," which is Greek for "good words" or "praise." The word in Hebrew is *hesped*, which has the same root as the word for mourning. Once again, there's no glossing over the difficult feelings associated with death. You are meant to make everyone in the room cry. And there's to be no sugar-coating; rather we're to capture the person's complexity and richness. Part of honoring someone is to acknowledge their messiness. Speak of the full range of feelings around the loss; show your rawness and vulnerability. Be honest. This allows us to preserve a relationship with the dead person in all its complexity. We are reconstructing the person so that they can live on in our hearts.

I remember a *hesped* given by a woman in her twenties about her father, who'd died in his early fifties, far too young. Her grief was palpable and she spoke of how he would never meet her future children, be at her wedding, or see her succeed and grow up. She said that at every important moment in her life from then on she would feel a cold wind blow through the hole that was once him. She spoke of his love and caring, but she also spoke of his perfectionism, how he drove his children too hard; his obsessive need for everything to be right. Like his love, this drive would always be part of her. He'd always be whispering in her ear, "You can do better."

At the gravesite there are a number of practices designed to help us integrate the finality of death and begin to find comfort from community. The Hebrew word for "funeral"—*levaya*—means "accompaniment"; people surround us as we face our loss and remember our loved one. This is the moment when we can pray or begin to try to make sense of the loss. The name for God that is evoked at the gravesite is *Rachamim,* which means "compassion" and comes from the same Hebrew root as "womb." This is meant to remind us of the compassion we will eventually feel toward ourselves and the deceased, even though it is likely not accessible to us now. The anger and raw grief is still very much with us; we are still wrestling with finality. There's a wrenching and cathartic practice of ripping one's clothes at the gravesite to physically express one's broken heart and the feeling of being ripped away from a loved one.

The *Kaddish,* the mourner's prayer, also is first said at the gravesite. *Kaddish* is a powerful and complex meditation. It has a hypnotic rhythm that some have described as being a kind of rocking, like a lullaby. The entire prayer praises God: "*Yitgadal ve-yitkadash, Shmei rabbah*—May Thy Name be magnified and holy. . . ." But why would we praise God when we're memorializing the dead, and not mention death at all?

Israeli Nobel laureate S.Y. Agnon said that the prayer is not *to* God but *for* God; it's a way to reconstruct God, to rebuild reality after it's been torn asunder. God has been diminished by this death, and so needs to be magnified. It's a practice for building back a sense of meaning in the face of devastation. Ancient mystics taught that saying *Kaddish* also helps settle the dead or help them get where they next need to be. Translating the mystical into the psychological, it's a transition prayer for us to figure out how we're going to continue our relationship with the person in this new reality. Adult children of the deceased say *Kaddish* three times a day for eleven months. That's how devastating that loss is; parents are the only people who cannot be replaced. If you are the spouse or other close relative, you say *Kaddish* for thirty days. We say it so many times and for so long because reconstructing and remembering are practiced one day at a time.

At the gravesite, adult children and spouses of the deceased shovel dirt into the grave themselves. The sound of the dirt hitting the coffin is so raw and powerful: a thud that you will never forget. The finality is almost unbearable. I attended the funeral of the father of four adult daughters less than a year after the death of their mother. The eldest daughter threw the first shovel of dirt and then the four of them went into a kind of trance. They threw shovelful after shovelful into the grave; each taking a turn and then all doing it together in a kind of frenzy, crying out and sobbing. Many people had to turn away, so intimate and overwhelming was this scene.

During the week after the burial, the finality-reconstruction dance continues for the mourners. There is an intensive seven-day mourning retreat; an immersion course in the experience of loss and rebuilding life. It took God seven days to create the world, and every one of us is a world, one that never was before and never will be again. Mourning is a form of re-creation. These seven days are called *Shiva* (which literally means seven), and this ritual holds so many different truths together: The grief is profound and the remembering is sweet. During this time mourners stay home and family and friends visit them bearing both food and memories of the deceased.

It's almost as if you're a guest in your own home, because your house really isn't the same anymore. People are there to comfort you and feed you and there's no indulging in idle chatter. Visitors are not supposed to speak to the bereaved until he or she speaks to them first. After all, there's really nothing to say in the face of the void that death creates. Yet we are invited to tell stories about the dead, to help create the narrative of the person's life, to give them a life after life. These stories expand and deepen the memory of the person for the mourners as well. A friend of mine described how moving it was to hear former and current students of his mother, who'd been a professor, come up to him at the *Shiva* and tell him what an amazing teacher she'd been; how she made jokes, asked questions in a Socratic style, always kept them on their toes. He'd never seen her teach and now this, too, was one of his memories. He told me how he'd gotten to know his mother in some ways even better after she died.

Shiva is also a period in which to go inward. The external things of life fade into the background as virtually every aspect of ordinary behavior is transformed. Traditionally, mourners don't bathe or shave or change clothing every day; they don't use cosmetics or fix their hair; they don't do household tasks or any work. They're not to worry about social propriety or obligation or be held accountable for anything they say. There is a practice of covering up the mirrors in one's home. Seeing our image in this state can be distracting and upsetting. We are literally not our selves. A mourner sits on a low stool rather than chairs as an expression of how low they feel. A memorial candle burns for the whole week, a reminder that the light in each person lives on in another form, and it's up to us to find the place where it shines. The traditional parting greeting is "May you be comforted among other mourners." It is a way of saying that you are not alone—everyone on the planet is going through, has gone through, or will go through this very process.

When *Shiva* ends, we're expected to return to our regular lives, but mourning is far from over. There are two times we can die, and the second time is the most devastating: It's when we are forgotten. One way a person can be remembered is when loved ones do acts of loving kindness or service in their name. Acts of generosity and compassion literally make the memory of the person a blessing to the world. Yet remembering, like mourning, is a continuous, conscious practice, not a one-time act. We return to the gravesite every year on the anniversary of the person's death, and there's a tradition of placing rocks on the monument. Flowers are not part of the Jewish practice, as there's a feeling that they are ephemeral and themselves die. Therefore they don't speak to the memory that never goes away. Rocks speak to the weightiness of the person and the heaviness we feel when we miss them.

And there's literally a cycle of remembering. Four times a year on different holidays—Yom Kippur, Succot, Passover, and Shavuot—we say special memorial prayers called *yizkor*, which means "remember." When we summon up the memory, meditate, or visualize a person in different seasons, we see the person differently. As we grow and change, as the year unfolds, there are new memories as feelings surface and others soften. Some people try to remember their loved one in the spirit of the holiday being celebrated. At Passover we free ourselves from memories that enslave us; on Succot, the harvest festival, we focus on gratitude and the joy they brought us; at Shavuot, which celebrates the giving of the Torah, we remember the wisdom they gave us; on Yom Kippur, we think about what we'd like them to forgive us for or what we need to forgive them for. All year long we are enriching and expanding our memories, integrating the person into the rhythms of our lives, into our happy times and our sad ones.

Yom Kippur is in part a way to enact our own death in order to imbue our lives with meaning. The opening practice of Yom Kippur is freeing ourselves from all our promises and obligations: "They shall be null and void" for the next twenty-five hours. We imagine ourselves as no longer married, a parent, holding a job that we're responsible for. These parts of our selves die and we're left alone to contemplate what life would be like without its usual trappings and delights. Who are we without them? There's the sense that we are reassessing everything from our deathbed. What an opportunity! And the next evening we are, in a sense, born again. We accept our obligations back, hopefully at a higher or deeper level of appreciation and meaning. Or we recognize that we need to let go of obligations that have distorted or confined us.

It's no accident that one of the bestselling novels ever is Mitch Albom's *The Five People You Meet in Heaven*. It speaks so powerfully to our yearning for transcendence. The book imagines that heaven is about revisiting your life from a larger, more expansive perspective. Heaven means that we get to have a take on our life: It really did make sense; more sense than I knew. There's no ultimate happy ending—we can't make everything right—but the most painful events have a meaning we never could have understood at the time. There's also the message that all of us can have heaven right here. Heaven is those moments when we can hold it all together, even when it's almost too much to bear.

There is no way to know how we will be when it is time for us to die. Plato, on his deathbed, was asked by his students for one final piece of wisdom. He said, "Practice dying." A second-century mystic sage put it this way: "Repent one day before your death." Of course none of us can really know when our time will come, but when that time does come, will we be ready? It all depends on how we are living right here, right now in this very moment, which could be our last. Almost every

> To be ready to die, we have to be ready to live.

day, we have the opportunities to embrace life more fully, to be free from pretense, to do the right thing for the right reasons. But we often put things off, thinking we still have time.

Whatever your theory of death, the ultimate test is, does it help you harness death for the service of life? To be ready to die we have to be ready to live—to live with such care and passion that we redeem life from the harshness and absurdity that death imposes. The question becomes less about death than about what kind of person we want to be so we can die that much more fully alive.

MESSIAH-ING

IMAGINE THAT YOU'RE ABOUT TO BE BORN, AND YOU'RE given a choice about what kind of family you want to be part of. This is a pretty heavy decision for someone who's not even born yet, so it's boiled down to one very simple, almost trivial element. Do you want a family that allows you to believe in the tooth fairy or one that doesn't? "It all comes down to a measly tooth?" you ask. But when you think about it, it's actually not that easy to decide. There are three possible scenarios to choose from.

In the first, you're six years old and you put your first lost tooth under your pillow. When you wake up in the morning, the tooth is gone and there's a dollar there. It's delightful and magical. Wow, there's a fairy that wants my tooth so much that she comes at night and leaves me a gift. The same thing happens with every tooth until you're almost eight and one day you have a sinking feeling that it's all a charade. You go to your mother and tell her not to bother anymore. There is no tooth fairy. She looks disappointed, angry, and even a little afraid; she tells you you're wrong. It's a shame you don't believe in the tooth fairy anymore; now she won't come.

Second scenario. You have the same delightful experience until you're eight; then one day you wake up in the morning and the tooth is still there. You go to your mother and ask her why the tooth fairy didn't come. She says, "Oh, I forgot." With a knowing look and a touch of sadness she tells you you're really too old for that now; it's time to be a big boy. Then she hands you a dollar and says, "Now you get an allowance. You can keep the tooth."

Third scenario. The tooth goes under the pillow; the dollar's always there. It's really great—until one day it isn't. You're eight again, and you get that disappointed feeling of having been duped. You go to your mother and tell her you don't believe in the tooth fairy anymore. And she looks at you knowingly: A few tears are in her eyes; her little boy is growing up. She takes you to her bedroom and pulls a beautiful little box out of the back of her dresser drawer. When she opens it there's every tooth you ever lost. She smiles and touches your face and asks, "What do you think the tooth fairy does with the teeth?" A week later you lose another tooth, and there's a dollar under your pillow.

Whenever I lead people through this visualization I get the same response. Without skipping a beat, everyone chooses the third scenario. "Come on, it's so obvious," someone once said. Oh, really? We live in an age and culture in which our most educated elite sees as real only that which can be proven empirically; everything else is merely an illusion, nonsense, or an opiate for the masses. We may go along with some of that touchy-feely stuff for nostalgia's sake, but then it's time to get real. This is mom number two. At the same time there are a growing number of people in the world who fiercely defend their beliefs in the most literal way and who dismiss all doubters. You won't be included or rewarded if you don't believe. This is mom number one.

So, how many people like mom number three are there? How many of us honestly make the choice on a daily basis to hold two seemingly opposing truths together: tooth fairy and no tooth fairy; the empirical and the magical; the mystical and the pragmatic; the fantastic and the mundane; the idealistic and the realistic; the ordinary and the enchanted. More often than not we come down on one side or the other, sure that the other is hopelessly naïve, chillingly sophisticated, foolishly faithful, or smartly cynical. And yet we yearn for a more expansive view, for the beautiful little box that can contain the

vision and the reality; success and disappointment; the knowledge
and the dream.

On a far grander scale than the tooth fairy, all of us have yearnings, longings, hopes for a time in which suffering—racism, poverty,
disease, war—will be lessened or eliminated; a future in which every
individual is valued, even if we don't intellectually believe that that
time will ever come. The prophet Jeremiah
spoke of "a day when you will have a new
heart," when reason and emotion will teach
the same thing, enabling us always to know
what's right. There'll be no bad or good; no
guilt or merit. Isaiah imagined that someday
we "shall beat swords into plowshares and spears into pruning hooks.
Nation shall not take up sword against nation; they shall never again
know war." He imagined "The wolf shall lie down with the lamb. The
leopard with the kid."

> There isn't a culture or tradition in the history of the world that doesn't have a dream of a world of peace and goodness.

There isn't a culture or tradition in the history of the world that
doesn't have such a dream. There's the Jewish end of days when peace
will reign; the Christian second coming when death shall be overcome;
a Marxist utopian vision of economic equality and justice; the American dream of democratic freedom, individual rights, and prosperity;
Samadhi, a state of personal enlightenment and transcendence; and the
scientific belief that reason and technology will perfect the world.
"Messianic" is the name for our greatest hopes for what the world can
be and hasn't yet become. It's no accident that messianic hopes have
tended to arise during dark times. Buddhism emerged out of a particularly chaotic time in Indian history. The Jewish prophetic dream was a
response to the destruction of the first Temple. The Christian tradition
arose during the first century when Rome was subjugating the people of
Israel, and there was tremendous political and social unrest. Commu-
nism took hold in countries where there was abject poverty. And both
the self-help movement and religious fundamentalisms are modern responses to the devaluing of the inner life and the spirit on the one hand,

and the dashed hopes of science, reason, and technology to transform the human condition on the other.

Whatever form it takes, the messianic longing—the yearning for transcendence, salvation, redemption, and transformation—is an integral part of the human experience and can lead to so much good. But with this yearning comes a gripping fear of the inevitable disappointment, disillusionment, and even despair that comes with such profound hope. And this fear can be dangerous—just look at the first two mothers.

They want more than anything else to shield their children from the dashed hopes, injustices, harshness, insecurity, and vulnerability that we all experience—anxieties captured so poignantly in the loss of a child's tooth. They are afraid they can't, and in their fear they hurt their children, however unwittingly. These mothers have precisely the same anxieties but respond in such different ways.

The first mother is holding on for dear life to the literalness of the tooth fairy: a version of an actual messiah. She really wants to protect and love her child. Wouldn't it be great if that pure magic could last forever? Yet in her response to her child's question and doubt, by telling him that if he doesn't believe there will be no more tooth fairy, she is actually denying him that very love, even threatening him with exclusion. She simply can't see that she *is* the tooth fairy. At her most extreme, this mother embodies the sentiments Bruce Springsteen sings about in his song "Devils and Dust," in which he asks whether having God on our side can turn our hearts black and actually kill the things we love.

The upside of the fundamentalist vision can be incredible hope, optimism, and joy for those who believe; just think of the exuberant singing in a Pentecostal church or in a West Bank settlement synagogue. The downside is that one often becomes harsh and severe, demonizing and in extreme cases even destroying nonbelievers. Here's the question for believers: Can we usher in a better world with beliefs that evoke such fierce anger and hurt so many people even if we think those people are wrong?

And then there's mother number two. She wants to love and protect her child just as fiercely. She is trying to spare him years of delusion and help him grow up and mature. In the process, she breaks her child's heart. Yes, the tooth fairy is a projection, and if we forget that, we become stalled, arrested, and uncompromising. But its enchanting, mystical qualities are enlivening. Just because the tooth fairy isn't real doesn't mean she isn't *real*. In this mother's rationalization, she simply can't see that she's the tooth fairy.

One of our holiest yearnings is to probe, to question, to deconstruct. Critical thinking advances our knowledge of how the world works—penicillin does work better than exorcisms. However, the danger of critical thinking is cynicism. We wind up living in a dis-enchanted world, in T. S. Eliot's wasteland. Here are the questions for cynics: Okay, the tooth fairy and the messiah are empirically senseless, even stupid, now what? Is life richer deconstructed? Yes, we have much more knowledge, but do we have more love?

One of our holiest yearnings is to probe, to question, to deconstruct.

As a society, we are trapped between two poles. On the one hand are the true believers, the naïve idealists who in defending the literalness of their traditions undermine their traditions' insights about love, awe, and compassion. And then there are the narrow realists, who in their desire to "know" deny the reality of anything science can't prove. In the process they desacrilize the world, diminishing meaning and depth.

One of the most profound realizations of my academic life occurred during the semester I studied the postmodernist philosopher Paul Ricoeur at Columbia University. When he first explained his idea of "second naïveté," it blew my mind. First naïveté is belief without reflection. We are so enmeshed that we don't see the cultural, historical, literary, social, and psychological forces and experiences out of which our belief arises. There is only one value system, one interpretation, one way that is meaningful and right.

Then there is the stage of critical distancing. We scrutinize and analyze the beliefs we've been taught since childhood: whether it's the parting of the sea or the resurrection. We lose the immediacy of the belief and turn away in what we experience as an act of maturity. Sometimes all hell breaks loose in our families, and we need to break away completely, leaving tradition and spirituality behind.

Then, over time, other disillusionments and disappointments may invite us to a higher level. This is second naïveté. We return to our so-called naïve ideas and experiences with a new kind of openness, seeking a deeper, more intuitive understanding of life. We appreciate similar, or maybe the same, stories, myths, and insights, but sung to a different melody. We reconnect to what we no longer believe in literally, integrating these visions and understandings into our inner life where they enchant and enrich our world.

Second naïveté is naïve because it revivifies our past beliefs rather than pushing them away, and it is second because it requires a high tolerance for contradiction and uncertainty. Second naïveté is an exquisite paradox. It combines the passion of first naïveté with the humility of critical thinking. Skepticism becomes revelatory, and we live "as if." Second naïveté is postdeconstruction: After we take reality apart, we put it back together on our own terms. We recover the outlines of the original inspiration. And in an act of what Catholic theologian Hans Kung calls "sacred retrieval," we reconstruct the yearning, the hope, the dream. Second naïveté is chosen hopefulness.

After all, fiction is not the enemy of reality; fiction informs and expands reality. Even new biological species begin as a kind of fiction, "a spontaneous variation," as Darwin called it, which corresponds to nothing previously found in the world. Innovative cultural and societal ideals begin as fiction as well, and they test and stretch us in new ways. How credible and provable was "all men are created equal" at the time it was first written? How real is it today? Theologian Reinhold Niebuhr wrote, "The truest visions of religion are illusions, which may be partially realized by being believed."

When we dwell in second naïveté, we feel the ongoing yearning for a perfect world while acknowledging the reality that our ideas of perfection are not only ever-changing but unattainable. Picture kids building a sand castle on the beach knowing full well the water will wash it away. They put their all into it and when the big wave comes they run away laughing. Fully and enthusiastically nested in first naïveté, the next day they're right back at it. Second naïveté is the experience of the child grown up. We don't leave sand castle building to our kids. We're right down in the sand with them, helping to build an elaborate, intricate castle that stretches our children's imaginations. When it's washed away, we laugh, too. It's a knowing laugh; even louder and more exuberant than the squeals of thirty years ago. We've absorbed the teaching that building beautiful worlds is about dreaming and creating and being washed away—only then setting out to build something even more amazing.

Second naïveté invites us to live as if the world could be transformed. It's idealistic realism or a realistic idealism. It is what the writer Thomas Moore calls the reenchantment of the world, and what I call being an enchanted skeptic. Second naïveté is the beautiful little box within which the ideal and the real continue to expand and illuminate. Second naïveté is mother number three. She lives her imagination, understanding that there is not a tooth fairy but we can always be "tooth-fairying."

The word for "hope" in Hebrew is *tikvah*, which comes from the same root as the word for "tension." It is the bow just before the arrow is released: poised, suspended, determined, but not there yet. Hope is often seen as pure, liberating, positive, optimistic. But *tikvah* emphasizes the yearning side of hope. *Tikvah* hope is taut, dynamic, and uncertain. Will the arrow hit the target? It's anyone's guess. *Tikvah* is a kind of holy anxiety.

To experience such hope, one must pull oneself into the future but stay fully present. You have to want so much that it hurts and be conscious enough to know that you will heal. *Tikvah* is a disciplined dream; a messy messianism; an incremental revolution. *Tikvah* reminds us that hope itself is a paradox.

The experience of giving birth to a child is the very embodiment of *tikvah.* There's so much risk, so much wonder, so much pain, so much love, so much anxiety, and so many dreams. Will the child be healthy? Will we be able to meet her needs? Who will she be? Nothing can be more messianic than that. This is, in part, why Christmas is such a moving and powerful holiday: The birth of a child is an expression of hope for a new world. And maybe that's why Jewish lore invites Elijah, the mythical prophet and harbinger of the Messiah, to every birth.

There's a practice during the Passover seder of leaving a specially designated glass full of wine in the middle of the table should Elijah come during this holiday so full of hope for freedom. Just after everyone at the table has told and reenacted the story of Exodus, a foreshadowing of final redemption, a child opens the front door for Elijah to usher him in. I remember the experience of this simple ritual being both frightening and magical: He might actually walk in the door and everything would be forever changed. But if I don't open the door, there's no way for him to come in. It's up to me. Of course, the wine doesn't get drunk by a visiting Elijah, and yet we sing songs of redemption. This practice, whimsical as it may seem, infuses dreams of transformation and radical patience. We need to develop a passion for actively waiting, not because we don't have the means to make the Messiah come but because we're always ushering him in the door.

Many people are struck when I tell them that the very people who invented or named the messianic yearning never accepted a single messianic figure, and yet they believed the messianic moment would come. Life is a mobius strip—cyclical and linear at the same time. There are both the repeating patterns of nature and the unfolding of a story. We are part of the constantly evolving, expanding universe, and we are conscious of our role in the universe. We can have an attuned relationship with the cosmos and know that we'll never fully be able to understand or envision all that is. We are here on this planet to strive for completion and perfection, but not to realize them. "We believe in the coming of the Messiah, not the arrival," wrote philosopher Herman Cohen.

The paradox of wanting it all and finding enough is captured so beautifully in jokes about the messianic yearning. Jokes, like Zen koans, hold together more than one truth. They play with contradictions and offer flashes of insight. When you juxtapose hope and reality, faith and skepticism, the effect can be quite funny.

In a small Russian town, the community council decides to pay a poor Jew a ruble a week to sit at the town's entrance and be the first to greet the Messiah when he arrives. The man's brother comes to see him and is puzzled as to why he took such a low-paying job. "It's true," the poor man admits. "The pay is low. But the work is steady."

A man visits a zoo. When he gets to the lion's cage he sees the literal fulfillment of Isaiah's prophecy—a lion and a lamb inside together. Amazed, he calls over an attendant. "How long have you had a lion and a lamb in a cage together?" "Over a year already," the attendant tells him. The man is breathless with awe. "How is this possible?" "It's easy," says the attendant. "Every morning we put in a new lamb."

And then there's Woody Allen's famous prediction: "The lamb and the lion will lie down together, but the lamb won't get much sleep."

If I were to boil these jokes down to one message, it's that lions don't become vegetarians and we'll always have to keep one eye open even when we're sleeping peacefully in that cage.

It may seem contradictory to live in the present and yearn for a transformed future. But isn't this true to our experience? So many of us practice the contemplative and meditative techniques of Eastern traditions, which are so effective at grounding us in the present. And many of us spend so much time thinking about the future, in part because our culture is rooted in monotheistic religions that emphasize progress and more linear visions of the world. Living in the present prevents us from living a life deferred. And yearning for a new age keeps us from settling for less than what's possible. There is a power of now and a power of what can be. We'll never fully reconcile these leanings; but we can dance between them.

> **To experience hope, we must pull ourselves into the future, but stay fully in the present.**

The messianic longing at its best pulls us into a better future while we remain present in the imperfect moment. There won't be a new garden of Eden, but we can create—however slowly and tediously, with however many false starts and missteps—Eden in our gardens. The messianic yearning is actually a call to love this world more deeply—whether our hopes can be realized or not.

The rabbis imagined that the only holiday that would remain in the messianic age would be Purim. The word "Purim" means "lot" or "luck"—the only holiday in a perfect world is about random luck? I imagine the rabbis sitting around a table doing shots of vodka. One said to the other, "Okay, let's say the Messiah comes. What holiday will we observe—will there be any holidays at all?" One rabbi says Yom Kippur will remain, but the first rabbi says, "What's to atone for in a perfect world?" The next says Passover, and the first says, "Redemption in a redeemed world?" Another says Sabbath: "Won't it be Sabbath every day?" By now they're getting pretty drunk. Suddenly the first rabbi's eyes light up and he shouts out, "Of course! Purim."

On Purim we tell the story of Esther, a kind of comic-book tale of larger-than-life characters, incredible intrigue, and wild twists and turns. Esther is the perfect heroine: a beautiful woman who is chosen by the king to be his wife. She is a Jew, but out of fear keeps her heritage a secret: The name "Esther" means "hidden." Her cousin Mordechai, who serves in the king's court, is open about being Jewish, but his relationship to Esther is not revealed so as to protect her.

Haman, the perfect bad guy, is the king's second in command, and out of hubris demands that those below him bow down to him in deference. When Mordechai refuses to flout his tradition and bow down to Haman, Haman plots to kill him and to annihilate the Jews. Haman orders that lots be cast to decide on a day for the destruction; the word "Purim" means lots. But the intrigue has only just begun. In a series of court and harem intrigues, in which Esther saves the day, the plot is revealed; Haman is hung; good defeats evil by the thread of a hair.

The Purim rituals are playful and raucous. Everyone yells and screams whenever Haman's name is mentioned; a way to drown out evil, which, of course, can never be drowned out. We eat a sweet pastry called hamantasch; a way to make even what is most bitter, sweet. And adults are supposed to get drunk so that they won't know the difference between Haman and Mordechai: between good and evil.

The holiday, hopeful and playful as it is, also has an edge. In the end Mordechai has Haman's job. Is this comforting or frightening? After all, this seems to be a rotating position. There is no end to the cycle. Good and evil will always exist. But don't stop hoping that they won't. Get drunk if you have to, but don't stop hoping.

Purim is about holding it all together—the anxiety, uncertainty, and the yearning for peace and love to prevail; for everything to work out when, really, everything is precarious and perilous. Purim is the only holiday that commemorates a story in which God doesn't appear. There's no apparent divine plan: Life is unpredictable, and danger is everywhere. The story teaches that good and evil are intertwined; Purim is a second naïveté story about the randomness of life and how if we all act consciously, take big risks in spite of it all, we will be "messiah-ing."

I once heard a wonderful story about the Messiah. Like the Purim story it teaches that when we can hold together the messianic yearning with the reality of the present, we'll have an explosive intuition that every one of us has the power to make the Messiah manifest in every moment.

Once upon a time, there was a magnificent monastery that had fallen on hard times. Only a few aging monks remained. One day, the abbot of the monastery met the local rabbi during a walk in the woods. The abbot told the rabbi about the monastery's troubles. The monks had tried everything to attract people but nothing had worked and now the end was coming. "There is only one thing I can tell you," said the rabbi, "and even of that I am not certain. I have on good authority that one of the remaining monks in your monastery may be the Messiah." Amazed and awed, the abbot returned to the monastery to share the rabbi's message. Unclear about what it all could mean, they all continued to go about their business. But during their daily chores, sitting in prayer, walking together through the abbey, the same thought kept arising in each of them. If the Messiah may be one of us, I wonder who it is.

It must be the abbot, they each thought at first—after all, he's our leader. But then they wondered whether it was John, the scholar, because surely the Messiah would have great knowledge. Then there was Thomas, the kindest and most compassionate of the monks. And finally, being human, each of them couldn't help but imagine, "Maybe it's me." In their uncertainty and wonder, they began to look at each other differently. And then they began to treat each other and themselves with more love and respect. Every day their appreciation of and affection for each other grew deeper. Soon a new aura pervaded the monastery. It was so enchanting and loving that people were drawn to visit in great numbers, and some even stayed on. Soon the monastery was thriving beyond the abbot's and the monks' wildest dreams.

The sages teach that if the Messiah comes when we are busy planting a sapling, we should continue our planting. Ignore the Messiah in favor of a small tree? Yes, because the planting of a tree is messianic work; a supreme act of hope about the future. We likely will not see the final result of this planting, the tree in full maturity, or even know if it will survive, yet we plant it anyway. Or maybe, if we're planting the tree, we don't need a messiah.

> The planting of a tree is a supreme act of hope in the future.

Franz Kafka said, "The Messiah will come, not on the last day, but on the *very* last." What could this mean? The writer Leibel Fein, a teacher of mine, offers the following parable in explanation: Imagine that we're gathered in a performance hall, our minds hardly focused on the Messiah. Suddenly, he enters and announces himself. His presence is so compelling that all of us instantly recognize his authenticity. Incredibly, it really is the Messiah! Some of us burst into applause, cheering and giving him a standing ovation. Others weep, overcome by the wholly unexpected gift.

But very soon, a few of us begin to get uncomfortable, even angry, and we ask, "For God's sake, where have you been?" The Messiah has no answer. Where, indeed, was he during all the savagery, the tragedy, the annihilations? Ashamed, the Messiah leaves. This was the question he feared. He'd wanted to arrive unnoticed, at a time that this terrible question wouldn't be asked. How can there be such a time? Not on the last day, no. But on the day after the very last day. After the messianic era has already begun. On the day that his coming has been rendered irrelevant.

We have not yet reached that day, and it's never been more important to recognize that. We live in a time of such great possibility and such great danger. Mother number one and mother number two are at war with each other, each having become more convinced of her beliefs and convictions. Hamans are everywhere on the world stage. And tooth fairies and messiahs are being used and abused in an attempt to create a final truth. But mother number three, second naïveté, is also becoming manifest as she becomes more and more necessary. She embodies the faith that all three mothers, all of us, will be able to sit down at one table and share our yearnings, our fears, our hopes, and our plans to build a better world.

And who will be mother number four? She'll be the one who, decades ago, when she was eight years old, walked into her mother's bedroom one morning wearing a sweet and knowing smile. As she leaned over to kiss her mother and stroke her face, she said, "Thank you for the dollar, Mom. Thank you for being the tooth fairy. I love you." That will be the day after the final day.

REPAIRING THE WORLD

ISAAC LURIA WAS A SIXTEENTH-CENTURY MYSTIC WHO had a wondrous vision about how the world came to be. Mystics are always looking beneath things, uncovering and imagining hidden patterns and indiscernable realities. Their wisdom takes us to whole new realms of understanding, extending the metaphors deeper into our psyches, giving us new questions and truths; inviting us to deconstruct and reenvision our myths and imaginings. There have been countless mystical tellings of the Genesis creation story, and Luria's is among the most influential; his thinking is an essential component of the radical wisdom tradition of the Kabbalah.

As he read and reread Genesis, imagining and reimagining the world's beginnings, Luria wondered: How can an all-perfect, all-encompassing God create something less than itself? The essential paradox of creation, Luria thought, is how the unity of the Divine gave rise to the multiplicity of this world. How does Oneness make room for otherness? In other words, how did God make room for life?

Luria imagined that God contracted, became smaller, in order to allow life to unfold. This alone is an amazing image. But Luria went further. He envisioned God as a series of vessels, luminous containers of all that is. When God contracted, the vessels shattered from the incredible energy and force, and shards were scattered throughout the universe. Each of these fragments contained a spark of light, a grain of God.

Luria came up with this teaching after the devastating expulsion of

Jews from Spain. He taught that humankind could heal the Divine, restore God through contemplative practice such as study, prayer, and

We all have the potential to raise holy sparks.

meditation, and through acts of loving kindness. If humankind can gather the shards of
good and evil, love and hate, destruction and
creativity, we can release the sacred sparks within them, dissolve all dualities, and repair all that is. We can make God whole again.

This Kabbalistic call to repair the world by making it whole is called
tikkun olam. Olam, "world," comes from the same root as the word for
"hidden." Luria taught that there is a parallel world to ours—the heavenly realm, invisible to the eye. Everything we do to heal the material
plane here on earth will heal the divine realm as well. Of course, high and
low, and heavenly and earthly, are metaphors for our own consciousness.

Luria recognized our yearning for a unified world and taught that,
in each moment of existence, we have the potential to raise holy sparks.
Other traditions similarly emphasize theologies of nonduality, monistic
systems of total unity. They remind us of our failure to see the unity
that has always existed, and still does. For example, our human view of
the universe is referred to in Sanskrit as *maya* or "illusion"—we are
trapped behind a series of veils that "distort" reality. But, in fact, there is
only oneness, and multiplicity is imaginary. This world appears to be
pluralistic only because our awareness is limited. Other systems teach
that wholeness awaits us only in the afterlife; polarities don't exist in
heaven. And in contemporary America, *tikkun olam* has taken on a secular meaning as well. The phrase is used to exhort us to mend the
disharmonies of the world through the pursuit of social justice.

These can be such beautiful visions. They awaken our own yearnings for wholeness and healing. They urge us to integrate what appears
fragmented, including our broken, wounded selves, so that we finally
can feel peace and oneness with all of who we are. And we also hope for
a world that is healed and united. We see our separateness from each
other as the cause of poverty, injustice, and suffering. Broken shards are
everywhere waiting for us to retrieve them and to put them back to-

gether again. But what if, in labeling our pain and yearnings as pathological and in need of repair, we prevent our own self-actualization?
What if, in lamenting the world's brokenness and working toward Oneness, we extinguish those sparks? Suppose in our drive to love the whole
we exile the parts?

What if the shattering, itself, is the point?

After all, those sparks were part of God's dream, the original design.
The Big Bang was a divine contraction, a sacred eruption. All-that-is exploded so that the universe in all its multiplicity and unknowingness
could exist. What if God doesn't want to be made One again? What if
the fantasy of the whole actually keeps us distanced from the blessing of
diversity, from more and more life?

Throughout the centuries efforts toward wholeness and Oneness
have actually caused far more suffering than healing. Utopian revolu-
tions, crusades of conversion, manifest destiny, and redemptive jihads—
we're so scared of difference that we fight and kill for sameness and
call it the pursuit of unity. We're so frightened by our inner diversity
and unknowableness that we forget that this is in fact what makes us
human.

Our current consciousness crusaders who preach a new age of personal enlightenment and self-discovery create the thickest veil of all.
Our many selves get labeled as fragments; our complexity, confusion;
our pain, neuroses; our uniqueness, loneliness; our dissonance, cacoph-
ony; our vulnerability, weakness. And our sparks get ignored in our
quest for infinite light. This is *tikkun hanefesh*, "repair of the self," of the
inner world. But this dream of self-realization actually can sometimes
dim the magnificent kaleidoscope of our many selves. After all, we are
finite creatures who cannot perceive the infinite sparks, let alone gather
them. And rather than strive to make our selves one thing, we might do
better to recognize how we are constantly discovering new selves, new
facets of who we are.

We are strangers in a strange land, as the biblical sages remind us.
Strangers in a new land. Strangers to ourselves. D. W. Winnicott called

this the incommunicado element, a matrix of emotional experience that can never be fully communicated, a self that's impossible to breach. When we confront our own strangeness, we are less likely to project strangeness onto others. When we embrace our own lack of wholeness, our own complexities, we are less likely to be oppressors, even passively.

I remember attending my very first demonstration as a teenager. My compatriots and I chained ourselves to the fence around the Russian embassy in silent protest, letting our signs speak for us. We were protesting the treatment of Jews in the Soviet Union. I felt high on our cause, such a strong sense of belonging to something larger than myself.

We are constantly discovering new selves, new facets of who we are.

Tears filled my eyes as I imagined my fellow Jews trying to escape and being turned back, being persecuted and ostracized by other Russians. But something in me shifted as I quietly watched the groundskeepers mowing and clipping in the early morning light, and the cleaning women arriving in old, beat-up cars, greeting each other in Russian. I felt my heart sinking, my rage soften. I thought, "Are these the people to whom my anger is directed? Are they evil? Are they hurting anyone? I don't even know them."

When we feel whole, often it's because we've ejected the other. Our worldview designates them as outsiders, people who must be eliminated. When there's no tolerance for sparks—the multiplicity within every People, every Nation, every Religion—the world may be more unified, but it's also a lot smaller. Dreams of unity and oneness are so dangerous because they can feel so right. They temporarily ease our anxieties and guilt about our judgments of others. When we preach the value of uniqueness, we often deceive ourselves by making the unique less frightening than it actually is.

When I was in college—and I imagine this hasn't changed much— there was much talk about "diversity," pride in how many ethnicities were being successfully recruited, especially by the white administrators. This was followed by the inevitable disappointment: Why was everyone sitting with his or her own group in the cafeteria? Why weren't people bonding? Where was the unity? What happened to the integrative dream? Of course, it was all so patronizing. The people who considered themselves the Ones were recruiting the Others to be part of the One. We appreciate your uniqueness. Now join Us, and make us feel good about being the Unifiers. Confirm for us who we already think we are. How different would the recruiting have been if those administrators saw their own inner diversity; if the white students perceived their own otherness and we remembered that we are all strangers. Maybe then there would have been a genuine openness and curiosity, a commonality of difference.

Martin Buber, in his influential book *I and Thou*, teaches that we each have our own integrity: you in your subjectivity and me in mine. Separateness and distinctiveness are crucial to the flourishing of any relationship. When we avoid objectifying or subsuming the other, we can truly be intimate. What if we said "I love you" out of a sense of awe of our lover's uniqueness? What if we had a genuine appreciation and celebration of our lover's uncanny differences, of the sparks which we only glimpse but never wholly understand or know? "I love you" would retain its mystery, its magic: It would have so much more meaning. Even periods of conflict become opportunities for still more revelation.

Most people doubt this is possible. I've heard many people say that human beings are hardwired to resist what feels different or alien. But haven't we all had the experience of embracing the other? Perhaps there is no such hardwiring and we just need better software. Our current software with its visions of oneness and unconditional love, as beautiful as they may seem, in fact really only intensifies our alienation. It's time to realize that repairing the world is not about gathering the sparks, but about dignifying each one.

There's no surrendering our differences. There's no absorbing embrace that removes distinctions. What's enlivening is not what is similar about us but what is different. What is life-affirming is the ever-expanding uniqueness of our selves and the uniqueness of others. What's important is that we share an interest in each other's strangeness; that we're one with our diversity.

It's time for a new generation of seekers to reinterpret Luria's kabbalistic vision, to embrace a messy messianism rather than a glorified, unified one. It's time to create a more evolved mystical teaching that challenges us to celebrate rather than fear the anarchy, mystery, and multiplicity of the spark-filled cosmos.

The deeper truth is that there is no cohesive self awaiting our discovery; no world waiting to be redeemed. There is no unity behind the curtain. The mystical realization that awaits us is not a leap into Oneness but a soaring into solidarity with and empathy for all the world's multiplicities.

These radical mystical ideas are present in all spiritual systems: They are sparks themselves, lost in the blinding light and seductive unity of the bonfire. If we look more closely at our own respective cultural and religious stories, we will find the sparks of this humbling insight and no longer feel a need to preach ultimate Oneness as the only truth. We need to shatter our myopia of wholeness and contract to make room for new light. Maybe then we'll be able to feel the depth and expansiveness of our vulnerability; our yearning to be loved for all of the many things we are and have yet to be.

In this light, we can read the story of the Tower of Babel not as an allegory about punishment or curse, but a teaching about blessing. What if the scattering of people and creation of so many languages was an act of liberation? The story tells us of a time when everyone in the world spoke a single language. At some point the people got the idea that to "make a name for themselves" they would build a city with a tower that reached to the heavens. When God took notice of their project he asked, "Is this how a unified people act? Now nothing will be beyond their reach." So God confounded their language, "making babble of the whole world" so that no one would understand each other. And God dispersed the people all over the earth.

The rabbis asked, "What was so bad about Babel? When a brick fell on someone's head, no one cared because they were building toward heaven." The height meant more than life itself. The people's obsession with making a name for themselves caused them to forget about the individual human being destroyed by those very efforts. Here's the thing about reaching for the heavens: In order to be all-one, an awful lot of people get hurt.

And so it was actually an act of love and mercy to disperse the people of Babel. The hope now was that, rather than destroying each other for the sake of being one, human beings could thrive, unfold, create breathtaking poetry in thousands of tongues, and spread light all over the earth. Rather than only One, there now would be an infinite number of ways to interpret and understand life.

One of the first nursery rhymes we recite to our children isn't so different from that biblical allegory. "Humpty Dumpty sat on a wall. Humpty Dumpty had a great fall. All the king's horses and all the king's men couldn't put Humpty together again." It's an edgy tale, even for grownups. From a young age, our deepest fear is that we're Humpty Dumpty, that we'll fall and shatter into so many pieces that no one will be able to put us back together again; that we'll be dispersed across the face of the earth and be alone in our brokenness. The story makes us wonder if we haven't already fallen and become irreparably splintered. The ditty makes light of that very real fear and helps soften it.

> What's enlivening is not what is similar about us but what is different. There's no surrendering our differences.

But what if we taught this story differently? Maybe Humpty jumped. Maybe he was stuck in his own Tower of Babel on top of that wall and wanted desperately to get down. Maybe the "great fall" was actually a deepening and expansion of his consciousness—a startling vision of his many selves. What if Humpty didn't want to be what the king wanted to him to be? He didn't want to be put back together again; to be an egg so full of the promise of life but giving birth to nothing. He didn't want to reach for the heavens; he wanted to be down on earth where the action is. What if what really happened is that he hatched?

After all, isn't that what happened to God when those vessels shattered? There's an edgy mystical teaching that captures the Kabbalisitic paradox of destruction and creation. It's a story about the ancient Temple in Jerusalem, which was the seat of the Divine One. In the Temple the presence of God was like holding a bottle of perfume under your nose: intense, powerful, subsuming. When the Temple was destroyed, devastating though it was, God's presence was actually liberated. The perfume spread around the world. The fragrance was less intense in any one place but so much more accessible, widespread, and, some say, even sweeter.

After the destruction of the Temple, the study table and the kitchen table become the new altars where, with the right intention, sparks of wisdom can be revealed. The bedroom becomes a sacred chamber, where *Shekinah* can manifest. Whenever a judge delivers a just decision, whenever anyone visits the sick, God is present. Acts of loving kindness would reconstruct our temples, and blessings would reenchant the world. Blessings release the light in every spark; every food we eat, every new thing we experience, every moment we're alive. There's a beautiful blessing that's said when you encounter a large crowd of people, "Praised are You who knows all of the secrets." Praised are You who created all this strangeness and distinctiveness. Praised are You for never putting it all back together.

There's a related but rarely cited vision of the messianic day in the book of Isaiah. "In that day, there shall be a highway from Egypt to Assyria. The Assyrians will join with the Egyptians; and the Egyptians with the Assyrians, for God will bless them, saying 'Blessed be My people Egypt, My handiwork Assyria, and My very own Israel.'" Isaiah proclaimed this when Egypt and Assyria were still archenemies of Israel; when Egypt was the biblical archetype of enslavers; and Assyria the destroyer of the northern kingdom. This vision translated to today might read: "Blessed be My people of Iran, My handiwork the people North Korea, and My very own people of America." Here, each nation in its own integrity (not its leadership) becomes beloved. Unlike so many

other messianic stories, in this version, the "good guys" don't win the day
and we don't become one people. Isaiah's scene is a profound affirmation
of difference: three warring nations secure in their distinctiveness and
connected in all their diversity with the capacity for being beloved.

IT MAY SEEM like a peculiar image, but when I look at a concrete
sidewalk after it rains—all the broken pieces of glass and rock
glistening—I get a visual hit of this more radical *tikkun olam*. The ordinary suddenly becomes glorious. The cement isn't as mundane or
seamless as it might normally appear. Its luminousness shines forth
from its diversity. Like that sidewalk, suddenly alight, we are not simply
the sum of our parts. But we need to remind ourselves of that. We need
to let the rain fall on us once in a while. Sometimes, we need to jump
off that wall. We don't need to transcend, but to see as many sparks as
possible, to sink into the messiness, to fall in love with multiplicity. We
need to tune in to the conversation that is always going on among our
many selves, and the dialogue, the contradictions, the harmony, and the
dissonance that fills the world.

Sometimes it takes a tragedy to get us to this place. So it was for my
friend Isabel. She grew up in a tough neighborhood and a broken home;
she described herself as a survivor. She'd put herself through school and
created the kind of family she'd always wanted—a husband who was kind
and a daughter who would have everything Isabel didn't. She had a
fiery, formidable personality; confrontational;
no bullshit. And she also could be wild and
provocative; yelling out in meetings at work

> We are more than simply
> the sum of our parts.

when she was bored or irritated, smoking like a fiend, and when she had to
let loose, drinking until dawn. Except for those occasional binges, Isabel
seemed to know exactly where she was going, and she was going there fast.
Type A didn't even begin to describe Isabel. Her aggressive nature was
matched only by her tremendous warmth. She was a loyal, loving friend.

The year she hit fifty, Isabel was diagnosed with a virulent form of bone cancer. We feared her reaction to a challenge she couldn't easily conquer. As one might expect, she was often angry and despairing and spoke of her terror of dying. As she said, referring to her chemotherapy, "I don't need to smoke now. I'm being smoked." But something had changed about her. She seemed to have arrived at a new dynamic equilibrium: Her intensity was somehow contained. She seemed so fully alive. I found myself talking to her about problems I was facing, not because she'd give me an answer but because she seemed so comfortable with the questions.

After months of tests and chemo, the doctors still couldn't locate the source of the cancer. At some point they determined that Isabel would be able to live with the cancer, but would never be cured. It would be a chronic disease that might eventually kill her. She'd be in chemo for the rest of her life. One week I'd see her and she had her hair back; the next time it would be gone. "Now I'm really a survivor," she once said with an abrupt laugh, "except I don't know of what. I don't know when I'll need a haircut and when a wig. And I don't know if the cancer will eat me alive."

I found myself thinking, aren't we all survivors? Isn't everything chronic? Isn't there some brokenness within us that can never be healed, no matter how we "treat" it? Can't being shattered release even more of our sparks? I wondered if, like Humpty, Isabel was being hatched. The way she lived now in her uncertainty seemed so much more honest. She was so vulnerable and yet so fierce; in so much pain and yet healing in such profound ways; so terrified, yet so wise.

Isabel's prognosis is now much improved, but I still think of her as being my rabbi of brokenness, my priestess of sparks. She taught me that no one is sum-up-able. Our parts, our fragments, are so much richer than any whole. One day she said to me, "I used to think I'd take the world by storm. Now the storm has got me." I responded with a quote I remembered from the first century sage Hillel, also a lover of fragments and contradictions. I told her, "Keep two pieces of paper in your pocket at all times. One says 'I am a speck of dust.' On the other,

'The world was created for me.' " Always the one to have the last word, Isabel said she didn't need a pocket; she wore it on her shiny, naked head for everyone to see.

Isabel perfectly embodied the wisdom of comedian Gilda Radner, who died from cancer and wrote one of my favorite insights about life. "I wanted to wrap this book up in a neat little package. Now I've learned the hard way that some poems don't rhyme. Some stories don't have a clear beginning, middle and end. I've learned that life is about not-knowing and having to change and I've discovered that life is filled with ambiguity. Delicious ambiguity."

Of all the biblical characters, Moses was a master of not-knowing. He was the passionate defender of ambiguity. He was a mythic priest of brokenness with all his stuttering and questioning; his unfulfilled yearning for the Promised Land; his leadership over an unruly people; his continual wrestling with God and with death. Indeed, Moses even names his first son "Stranger in a strange land" so both he and his son Gershom won't forget their origins—and so that we won't forget ours.

Moses was a preacher of uniqueness, a lover of sparks. He chose to listen rather than run from the burning bush and then left his peaceful "whole" life to free a people who were being oppressed for being different. And he fought for them even when they recklessly strayed from "the way."

In his humility, this patriarch of freedom, this leader of a people who would be a great nation knew that wholeness was a momentary illusion. Maybe that's why he had the audacity and courage to shatter the stone tablets when he came down from Sinai and witnessed the people worshipping the golden calf. Moses saw the dangers of the yearning for oneness. He knew the tablets of insight would only become another calf.

So rather than see divinity idolatrized, Moses threw the holy tablets to the ground, breaking them into so many pieces it was impossible to count. One might think that after he calmed down that he'd try to put them back together in some act of superhuman strength, like in the miracles in Egypt. Or maybe that he'd bemoan the loss of the divine word.

But in another amazing scene, Moses creates new tablets himself. These were earthly tablets; grounded insights. And he puts them into the Ark right next to the fragments from Sinai. The Ark then becomes the guiding light on the desert journey; our guiding light as we wander through the desert in wonder always on the way to the Promised Land.

I like to imagine what would happen if the Ark were actually discovered one hundred years from now. If it were to be found, what treasure of wisdom would be waiting? First, I picture the Ark in all its beauty and mystery traveling through that desert for those forty years; residing peacefully in the heart of the ancient Temple for centuries; somehow surviving the destruction of the Temple; lying buried for millennia.

Then, I imagine that, miraculously, one day we find it.

We're afraid to touch it at first. When we do we're both relieved and disappointed that it's not too hot to handle, as legend has it. The Ark is worn and fragile and yet still very beautiful. We can't wait to hold those tablets and sort through the fragments; maybe even keep some as souvenirs. We open the Ark. Our hands are shaking in anticipation of the truths we will find. And what do we see? Dust. Wait, where are the tablets? Where are the fragments?

Our distress soon turns to laughter as we take handfuls of dust and throw them up into the air. The dust flies in the wind, illuminated and glistening; then falls to the ground in a haze of light. We wonder aloud which dust was from the fragmented tablets and which was from the whole. Then we laugh even louder: Does it even make a difference?

It's all magic dust.

ACKNOWLEDGMENTS

AUTHORSHIP IS NEVER ORIGINAL. LIKE ALL CREATIVE enterprises, it is collaborative: dependent on the support, ideas, and influence of others past and present. I am profoundly grateful to the many people in my life who have contributed to making *Yearnings* a reality.

I am indebted to Linda Loewenthal, with whom I wrote this book. Linda is my muse. We shared hours and hours of intense conversation and more sandwiches and cups of coffee than I can count. Her excitement, perseverance, dedication, clarity of vision, sensitivity, and immense talent midwifed this book. Linda has done much more than capture my voice. She's a teacher of wisdom in her own right and I have learned much from her. I also want to thank Eric, Sam, and Ben for their support of Linda and their insight throughout the writing process.

I'm deeply grateful to David Black, my extraordinary literary agent, who has been an endless source of encouragement and confidence. From the moment we met, he overwhelmed me with his faith in people, his love for books, and his unmatched integrity. He was wise enough, throughout the writing of this book, to give me the freedom to find my voice and the firm guidance that ensured the book's completion. He is a confidant and friend.

Thank you to Hyperion for the way they got behind this book from the beginning. Hyperion president Bob Miller literally changed my life. He saw the possibility of a book before there was a word on a page. His unwavering interest and support have been invaluable. In a country polarized by religious and secular fundamentalisms, Bob took a chance on a first-time author because he had faith that a spiritual, thoughtful, and pluralist exploration of our yearnings using Jewish wisdom could be taken public. I am forever grateful. Thank you to Ellen Archer and her dedicated and innovative team for helping to bring *Yearnings* out into the world; to my editor, Bill Strachan, whose sensitive editorial comments and gentle touch were invaluable as I worked to improve the text; to Brenda Copeland for stepping in with passion, joy, and skill to help bring the book to fruition.

Jay Sanderson, the tireless president of JTN Productions, planted the first seeds of this book by producing and directing my thirteen-part public-television series, *Simple Wisdom*. The success of *Simple Wisdom* directly led to *Yearnings*, and it is Jay who has directed and produced the upcoming public-television special based on this book. Jay thinks big, believes in people, and is the most loyal of friends.

I owe a huge debt of gratitude to my colleagues at CLAL—The National Jewish Center for Learning and Leadership, a unique setting of creativity and imagination, where I am privileged to serve as president. Rabbi Brad Hirschfield has been my intellectual partner for the past decade. We finish each other's sentences, challenge each other's thinking, and celebrate each other's successes. Our relationship is proof that pluralism is not an intellectual abstraction, but a method of leading.

I am deeply appreciative to Donna Rosenthal, the executive vice chairman of CLAL. Donna has made CLAL a first-class non-profit operation, freeing me to think, teach, and write. She is a talented and formidable executive who cares deeply about people and is eternally optimistic. Her unwavering commitment to this book was as responsible for it becoming a reality as any other factor.

Special thanks to Janet R. Kirchheimer, my assistant. Besides being a published poet in her own right, a source of ideas, and a wonderful editor, she is the perfect assistant, who ensures my life runs smoothly. Thank you to the faculty at CLAL—Rabbi Tsvi Blanchard, one of the smartest people I know, who is always willing to help me think more clearly; to

Dr. Michael Gottsegen, Rabbi Steve Greenberg, and Dr. David Kraemer. I have learned much from all of them. Thank you to the administrative staff—Meredith Appell, Ruth Bregman, Dale Brown, Judy Epstein, Aliza Kaplan, Theresa Perruzza, Anna Rakhlin, and Cynthia Schupf.

Thank you to the past chairs of CLAL during the time I have been president—Radine Spier for the transition; Charles Bronfman for his generosity; Barbara Friedman for the sabbatical; Tom Katz for deep friendship; Fern Hurst for commitment. Each, in their own way, has contributed to making CLAL a secure place to fearlessly explore Jewish wisdom and the human spirit, and has ensured that I had the space and support to write this book.

This book could not have been written without the inspiration and support of teachers and friends. Unending gratitude to my teacher Rabbi Irving "Yitz" Greenberg, the founder and president emeritus of CLAL. Yitz has been the single most important teacher in my life since that day we met more than two decades ago and sat overlooking the Atlantic Ocean talking for eight hours straight about the "third era" in Jewish history. Yitz is an intellectual giant, a daring theologian, and an enchanting teacher. He is among the most religiously and intellectually sophisticated pluralists in the world and, not surprisingly, a teacher who celebrates his students' accomplishments even when he disagrees.

Thank you to Professor Joshua Halberstam, who read this book with such care and concern. Joshua provided the kind of sage counsel that could only come from someone deeply steeped in Jewish sources and general philosophy. Joshua is a true renaissance man and his wide-ranging intellect, sharp wit, and warm friendship helped me in more ways than I can express.

Thank you to Rabbi Joseph Telushkin. We have been blessed to have him and his family as our upstairs neighbors. Joseph read this book with his unique ethical genius and Jewish knowledge. His very constructive comments made *Yearnings* a more sensitive and inclusive book. He is the most dependable guide I know to doing the right thing.

I am most blessed to have wonderful friends. I can't imagine what my life would be like without Richie Pearlstone, who has taught me a love for life, mountain biking, and how to run a business; Gary Davis, who has been my mentor in the classical, spiritual understanding of that word; Al Engelberg for his moral passion, sharp mind, flawless counsel, and fierce loyalty. Dr. Marc Slutsky, my chaver in the rabbinic understanding, for helping me understand my dreams of Torah. I thank them for their inspiration, instruction, friendship, and generosity.

Ongoing conversations with J. J. Goldberg and Shifra Bronznick, Benyamin Cirlin, Michael Goldberg, David Gitlitz, Miriam Ben Hayim, Carmi and Shelley Fredman, Jonathan Jacoby, Rabbis Roly Matalon and Michael Paley, John Ruskay, Ken and Debra Tuchman. Each in their own way has enriched me intellectually, emotionally, and spiritually. Thank you to Barry and Mindy Gavrin, my oldest friends, who in the early·years made sure I had dinner.

There is no *Yearnings* without my intense and loving family. My in-laws—Janice and Jules Kurzweil—break every in-law stereotype imaginable. They have been another ever-loving Mom and Dad, and I have learned much about love for children from them. They have profoundly enriched my life, and I love them dearly.

The stories in this book about my mother and father, Charlotte and Morton Kula, can only hint at their immeasurable influence on my life. They are among the most developed and evolved people I know. But their greatest contribution to my life has been my five brothers, Aaron, Mark, Barry, Elliot, and David, each of whom I love dearly. We live all around the country, and every brother speaks to every brother at least once a week. That says it all.

There is a saying—the last, the last is the most dear. Just as there are no words to adequately describe God, I have no words that can adequately express my love for my wife, Dana Kurzweil, my friend, partner, spouse, "lifer," and lover, and our beautiful and passionate children, Gabriella Leah Mirit and Talia Hadas. They have created a life of sweetness, stimulation, adventure, comfort and joy, laughter and dreams. They put up with my absences, listen to my ideas, and keep me grounded. So many of my yearnings revolve around them and it is they who have taught me I can want it all and always have enough.

I thank God for the privilege of being alive at this hour with all its conflicts and tensions and opportunities that call for courage, moral imagination, and deeper understanding of our yearnings for the infinite.

BIBLIOGRAPHY

Albacete, Lorenzo. *God at the Ritz: Attraction to Infinity.*
New York: Crossroads Publishing, 2002.

Berlin, Isaiah, and Henry Hardy, editors. *The Proper Study of Mankind.*
New York: Farrar, Straus, Giroux, 1997.

Bialik, Hayim Nahman, and Ravnitzky, Yehoshua Hana.
The Book of Legends. Translated by William Braude.
New York: Schocken Books, 1992.

Bloom, Harold. "Freud and Beyond," in *Ruin the Sacred Truths:
Poetry and Belief from the Bible to the Present.*
Cambridge: Harvard University Press, 1987.

Buber, Martin. *I and Thou.* Translated by Walter Kaufman.
New York: Free Press. 1971

Chopra, Deepak. *How to Know God.* New York: Harmony Books, 2000.

Csikszentmihalyi, Mihaly. *Flow: The Psychology of Optimal Experience.*
New York: HarperCollins, 1990.

Dalai Lama. *The Art of Happiness.* New York: Riverhead Books, 1998.

Dass, Ram. *Still Here.* New York: Riverhead Books, 2000.

During, Simon, editor. *The Cultural Studies Reader.*
New York: Routledge, 1993.

Dyer, Wayne W. *Wisdom of the Ages.* New York: HarperCollins, 1998.

Fish, Stanley. *The Trouble with Principle.*
Cambridge: Harvard University Press, 1999.

Fox, Mathew. *One River, Many Wells.* New York: Putnam Books, 2000.

Fox, Mathew. *Sins of the Spirit, Blessings of the Flesh.*
New York: Harmony Books, 1999.

Freud, Sigmund. *Civilization and Its Discontents.* Translated by James Strachey. New York: Norton, 1966 (orig. 1930).

Fromm, Erich. *You Shall Be As Gods.* New York: Holt, Rinehart and Winston, 1966.

Gallagher, Winifred. *Working on God.* New York: Random House, 1999.

Genesis Rabbah. Translated by H. Freedman. New York: Soncino Press, 1983.

Gergen, Kenneth J. *The Saturated Self.* New York: Basic Books, 1991.

Greenberg, Rabbi Irving. "Cloud of Smoke, Pillar of Fire," in *Auschwitz,* ed. Eva Fleischer. New York: Ktav, 1977.

Greenberg, Irving. *The Jewish Way.* New York: Summit Books, 1988.

Greene, Brian. *The Elegant Universe.* New York: Vintage Books, 1999.

Grimes, Ronald. *Readings in Ritual Studies.* New Jersey: Prentice Hall, 1996.

Halberstam, Joshua. *Everday Ethics.* New York: Penguin, 1993.

Hammerschlag, Carl. *The Theft of the Spirit.* New York: Fireside Publishing, 1992.

Heschel, Abraham Joshua. *Man Is Not Alone.* New York: Harper & Row, 1951.

Jabès, Edmond. *The Book of Questions.* Translated by R. Waldrop. Middletown, CT: Wesleyan University Press, 1978.

Jacobson, Simon. *60 Days: A Spiritual Guide to the High Holidays.* New York: Kiyum Press, 2003.

James, William. *The Varieties of Religious Experience.* New York: Macmillan Publishing, 1961.

Keen, Sam. *To a Dancing God.* San Francisco: HarperCollins, 1990.

Kraemer, David. *The Mind of the Talmud.* New York: Oxford University Press, 1990.

Kornfield, Jack. *A Path with Heart.* New York: Bantam Books, 1993.

Kushner, Harold. *When All You Ever Wanted Isn't Enough.* New York: Summit Books, 1986.

Lama Surya Das. *Letting Go of the Person You Used to Be.* New York: Broadway Books, 2003.

Lasch, Christopher. *The Culture of Narcissism.* New York: Norton, 1978.

Lew, Alan. *This Is Real and You Are Completely Unprepared.*
New York: Little, Brown, 2003.

Lifton, Robert Jay. *The Protean Self.* New York: Basic Books, 1993.

Loeb, Paul Rogat. *Soul of a Citizen.* New York: St. Martin's Press, 1999.

Miles, Jack. *God: A Biography.* New York: Knopf, 1995.

Needelman, Jacob. *A Little Book on Love.* New York: Dell, 1996.

Needelman, Jacob. *The Heart of Philosophy.* New York: Knopf, 1982.

Prager, Marcia. *The Path of Blessing.*
New York: Bell Tower, 1998.

Quinby, Lee. *Millennial Seduction.*
New York: Cornell University Press, 1999.

Ricoeur, Paul. *The Conflict of Interpretations.* Edited by Don Idhe.
Illinois: Northwestern University Press, 1974.

Safran, Jeremy. *Pscyhoanalysis and Buddhism.*
Boston: Wisdom Publications, 2003.

Santner, Eric. *On the Psychotheology of Everyday Life.*
Chicago: University of Chicago Press, 2001.

Santoni, Ronald, editor. *Religious Language and the Problem of Religious
Knowledge.* Bloomington: Indiana University Press, 1968.

Schacther-Shalomi, Zalman. *Hello God, It's Me.*
New York: Riverhead Books, 2001.

Schacther-Shalomi, Zalman. *Wrapped in a Holy Flame.*
San Francisco: Jossey-Bass, 2003.

Sexson, Lynda. *Ordinarily Sacred.*
Charlottesville: University of Virginia Press, 1992.

Shapiro, Rami. *Hasidic Tales.*
Woodstock: Skylight Paths Publishing, 2004.

Talmud Bavli. Translated by Maurice Simon.
London: Soncino Press, 1984.

Tanakh: The Holy Scriptures.
New York: Jewish Publication Society of America, 1985.

Taylor, Mark C. *Erring: A Post Modern A/theology.*
Chicago: University of Chicago Press, 1984.

Teilhard de Chardin, Pierre. *On Happiness.* London: Harper&Row, 1973.

Wilber, Ken. *A Theory of Everything*. Boston: Shambhala, 2000.

Williamson, Marianne. *The Gift of Change*.
San Francisco: HarperSanFrancisco, 2004.

Zornberg, Avivah Gottlieb. *Genesis: The Beginning of Desire*.
New York: Jewish Publication Society of America, 1995.

Zornberg, Avivah Gottlieb. *The Particulars of Rapture*.
New York: Doubleday, 2001.

Zweg, Connie. *The Holy Longing*. Boulder: Sentient Publications, 2004.

Orchestrated
Death

Orchestrated Death

A Mystery Introducing Inspector Bill Slider

Cynthia Harrod-Eagles

Charles Scribner's Sons
New York

Maxwell Macmillan International
New York   Oxford   Singapore   Sydney

This is a work of fiction. Names, characters, places, and incidents either are
the product of the author's imagination or are used fictitiously. Any
resemblance to events or persons, living or dead, is entirely coincidental.

First American Edition

Charles Scribner's Sons
Macmillan Publishing Company
866 Third Avenue
New York, NY 10022

Macmillan Publishing Company is part of
the Maxwell Communication Group of Companies.

Library of Congress Cataloging-in-Publication Data

Harrod-Eagles, Cynthia.
    Orchestrated death: a mystery introducing inspector Bill Slider /
Cynthia Harrod-Eagles.—1st American ed.
    p.   cm.
    ISBN: 0-684-19388-4
    I. Title.
    PR6058.A6945O73   1992   91-29042   CIP
    823'.914—dc20

10 9 8 7 6 5 4 3 2 1

Printed in the United States of America

APR. .   1993

For Peter Lavery, fellow Leo, and *rara avis* – thanks.

1

Absence of Brown Boots

Slider woke with that particular sense of doom generated by Rogan Josh and Mixed Vegetable Bhaji eaten too late at night, followed by a row with Irene. She had been asleep when he crept in, but as he slid into bed beside her, she had woken and laid into him with that capacity of hers for passing straight from sleep into altercation which he could only admire.

He and Atherton, his sergeant, had been working late. They had been out on loan to the Notting Hill Drug Squad to help stake out a house where some kind of major deal was supposed to be going down. He had called Irene to say that he wouldn't be back in time to take her to the dinner party she had been looking forward to, and then spent the evening sitting in Atherton's powder-blue Sierra in Pembridge Road, watching a dark and silent house. Nothing happened, and when the Notting Hill CID man eventually strolled over to put his head through their window and tell them they might as well push off, they were both starving.

Atherton was a tall, bony, fair-skinned, high-shouldered young man, who wore his toffee-coloured hair in the style made famous by David McCallum in *The Man From UNCLE* in the days when Atherton was still too young to stay up and watch it. He looked at his watch cheerfully and said there was just time for a pint at The Dog and Scrotum before Hilda put the towels up.

It wasn't really called The Dog and Scrotum, of course. It was The Dog and Sportsman in Wood Lane, one of those

1

gigantic arterial road pubs built in the fifties, all dingy tiled corridors and ginger-varnished doors, short on comfort, echoing like a swimming-pool, smelling of Jeyes and old smoke and piss and sour beer. The inn sign showed a man in tweeds and a trilby cradling a gun in his arm, while a black labrador jumped up at him – presumably in an excess of high spirits, but Atherton insisted it was depicted in the act of sinking its teeth into its master's hairy Harris crutch.

It was a sodawful pub really, Slider reflected, as he did every time they went there. He didn't like drinking on his patch, but since he lived in Ruislip and Atherton lived in the Hampstead-overspill bit of Kilburn, it was the only pub reasonably on both their ways. Atherton, whom nothing ever depressed, said that Hilda, the ancient barmaid, had hidden depths, and the beer was all right. There was at least a kind of reassuring anonymity about it. Anyone willing to be a regular of such a dismal place must be introspective to the point of coma.

So they had two pints while Atherton chatted up Hilda. Ever since he had bought the Sierra, Atherton had been weaving a fiction that he was a software rep, but Slider was sure that Hilda, who looked as though the inside of a magistrates' court would hold no surprises for her, knew perfectly well that they were coppers. Rozzers, she might even call them; or Busies? No, that was a bit too Dickensian: Hilda couldn't be more than about sixty-eight or seventy. She had the black, empty eyes of an old snake, and her hands trembled all the time except, miraculously, when she pulled a pint. It was hard to tell whether she knew everything that went on, or nothing. Certainly she looked as though she had never believed in Father Christmas or George Dixon.

After the beer, they decided to go for a curry; or rather, since the only place still open at that time of night would be an Indian restaurant, they decided which curry-house to patronise – the horrendously named Anglabangla, or The New Delhi, which smelled relentlessly of damp basements. And then home, to the row with Irene, and indigestion. Both were so much a part of any evening that began with working late, that nowadays when he ate in an Indian restaurant it was with an anticipatory sense of unease.

After a bit of preliminary squaring up. Irene pitched into the usual tirade, all too familiar to Slider for him to need to listen or reply. When she got to the bit about What Did He Think It Was Like To Sit By The Phone Hour After Hour Wondering Whether He Was Alive Or Dead? Slider unwisely muttered that he had often wondered the same thing himself, which didn't help at all. Irene had in any case little sense of humour, and none at all where the sorrows of being a policeman's wife were concerned.

Slider had ceased to argue, even to himself, that she had known what she was letting herself in for when she married him. People, he had discovered, married each other for reasons which ranged from the insufficient to the ludicrous, and no-one ever paid any attention to warnings of that sort. He himself had married Irene knowing what she was like, and despite a very serious warning from his friend-and-mentor O'Flaherty, the desk sergeant at Shepherd's Bush.

'For God's sake, Billy darlin',' the outsize son of Erin had said anxiously, thrusting forward his veined face to emphasise the point, 'you can't marry a woman with no sense-a-humour.'

But he had gone and done it all the same, though in retrospect he could see that even then there had been things about her that irritated him. Now he lay in bed beside her and listened to her breathing, and when he turned his head carefully to look at her, he felt the rise inside him of the vast pity which had replaced love and desire. *Tout comprendre c'est tout embêter* Atherton said once, and translated it roughly as 'once you know everything it's boring'. Slider pitied Irene because he understood her, and it was that fatal ability of his to see both sides of every question which most irritated her, and made even their quarrels inconclusive.

He could sense the puzzlement under her anger, because she wanted to be a good wife and love him, but how could she respect anyone so ineffectual? Other people's husbands Got On, got promoted and earned more money. Slider believed his work was important and that he did it well, but Irene could not value an achievement so static, and sometimes he had to struggle not to absorb her values. If once he

began to judge himself by her criteria, it would be All Up
With Slider.

His intestines seethed and groaned like an old steam
clamp as the curry and beer resolved themselves into acid
and wind. He longed to ease his position, but knew that any
shift of weight on his part would disturb Irene. The Slumber-
well Dreamland Deluxe was sprung like a young trampoline,
and overreaction was as much in its nature as in a Cadillac's
suspension.

He thought of the evening he had spent, apparently result-
less as was so much of his police work. Then he thought of
the one he might have spent, of disguised food and tinkly
talk at the Harpers', who always had matching candles and
napkins on their dinner-table, but served Le Piat d'Or with
everything.

The Harpers had good taste, according to Irene. You
could tell they had good taste, because everything in their
house resembled the advertising pages of the Sundry Trends
Colour Supplement. Well, it was comforting to know you
were right, he supposed; to be sure of your friends' approval
of your stripped pine, your Sanderson soft furnishings, your
oatmeal Berber, your Pampas bathroom suite, your
numbered limited-edition prints of bare trees on a skyline in
Norfolk, the varnished cork tiles on your kitchen floor, and
the excitingly chunky stonewear from Peter Jones. And when
you lived on an estate in Ruislip where they still thought
plastic onions hanging in the kitchen were a pretty cute idea,
it must all seem a world of sophistication apart.

Slider had a sudden, familiar spasm of hating it all; and
especially this horrible Ranch-style Executive Home, with its
picture windows and no chimneys, its open-plan front garden
in which all the dogs of the neighbourhood could crap at will,
with its carefully designed rocky outcrop containing two
poncey little dwarf conifers and three clumps of heather; this
utterly undesirable residence on a new and sought-after
estate, at the still centre of the fat and neutered universe of
the lower middle classes. Here struggle and passion had been
ousted by Terence Conran, and the old, dark and insanitary
religions had been replaced by the single lustral rite of
washing the car. A Homage to Catatonia. This was it, mate,

authentic, guaranteed, nice-work-if-you-can-get-it style. This was Eden.

The spasm passed. It was silly really, because he was one of the self-appointed guardians of Catatonia; and because, in the end, he had to prefer vacuity to vice. He had seen enough of the other side, of the appalling waste and sheer stupidity of crime, to know that the most thoughtless and smug of his neighbours was still marginally better worth protecting than the greedy and self-pitying thugs who preyed on him. You're a bastion, bhoy, he told himself in O'Flaherty's voice. A right little bastion.

The phone rang.

Slider plunged and caught it before its second shriek, and Irene moaned and stirred but didn't wake. She had been hankering after a Trimphone, using as an excuse the theory that it would disturb her less when it rang at unseasonable hours. There were so many Trimphones down their street now that the starlings had started imitating them, and Slider had made one of his rare firm stands. He didn't mind being woken up in the middle of the night, but he was damned if he'd be warbled at in his own home.

'Hullo Bill. Sorry to wake you up, mate.' It was Nicholls, the sergeant on night duty.

'You didn't actually. I was already awake. What's up?'

'I've got a corpus for you.' Nicholls' residual Scottish accent made his consonants so deliberate it always sounded like corpus. 'It's at Barry House, New Zealand Road, on the White City Estate.'

Slider glanced across at the clock. It was a quarter past five. 'Just been found?'

'It came in on a 999 call – anonymous tip-off, but it took a while to get on to it, because it was a kid who phoned, and naturally they thought it was a hoax. But Uniform's there now, and Atherton's on his way. Nice start to your day.'

'Could be worse,' Slider said automatically, and then seeing Irene beginning to wake, realised that if he didn't get on his way quickly before she woke properly, it most certainly would be.

* * *

The White City Estate was built on the site of the Commonwealth Exhibition, for whose sake not only a gigantic athletics stadium, but a whole new underground station had been built. The vast area of low-rise flats was bordered on one side by the Western Avenue, the embryo motorway of the A40. On another side lay the stadium itself, and the BBC's Television Centre, which kept its back firmly turned on the flats and faced Wood Lane instead. On the other two sides were the teeming back streets of Shepherd's Bush and Acton. In the Thirties, the estate had been a showpiece, but it had become rather dirty and depressing. Now they were even pulling down the stadium, where dogs had been racing every Thursday and Saturday night since Time began.

Slider had had business on the estate on many an occasion, usually just the daily grind of car theft and housebreaking; though sometimes an escaped inmate of the nearby Wormwood Scrubs prison would brighten up everyone's day by going to earth in the rabbit warren of flats. It was a good place to hide: Slider always got lost. The local council had once put up boards displaying maps with an alphabetical index of the blocks, but they had been eagerly defaced by the waiting local kids as soon as they were erected. Slider was of the opinion that either you were born there, or you never learnt your way about.

In memory of the original exhibition, the roads were named after outposts of the Empire – Australia Road, India Way and so on – and the blocks of flats after its heroes – Lawrence, Rhodes, Nightingale. They all looked the same to Slider, as he drove in a dazed way about the identical streets. Barry House, New Zealand Road. Who the hell was Barry anyway?

At last he caught sight of the familiar shapes of panda and jam sandwich, parked in a yard framed by two small blocks, five storeys high, three flats to a floor, each a mirror image of the other. Many of the flats were boarded up, and the yard was half blocked by building equipment, but the balconies were lined with leaning, chattering, thrilled onlookers, and despite the early hour the yard was thronged with small black children.

A tall, heavy, bearded constable was holding the bottom

of the stairway, chatting genially with the front members of the crowd as he kept them effortlessly at bay. It was Andy Cosgrove who, under the new regime of community policing, had this labyrinth as his beat, and apparently not only knew but also liked it.

'It's on the top floor I'm afraid, sir,' he told Slider as he parted the bodies for him, 'and no lift. This is one of the older blocks. As you can see, they're just starting to modernise it.'

Slider cocked an eye upwards. 'Know who it is?'

'No sir. I don't think it's a local, though. Sergeant Atherton's up there already, and the surgeon's just arrived.'

Slider grimaced. 'I'm always last at the party.'

'Penalties of living in the country, sir,' Cosgrove said, and Slider couldn't tell if he were joking or not.

He started up the stairs. They were built to last, of solid granite, with cast-iron banisters and glazed tiles on the walls, all calculated to reject any trace of those passing up them. Ah, they don't make 'em like that any more. On the top-floor landing, almost breathless, he found Atherton, obscenely cheerful.

'One more flight,' he said encouragingly. Slider glared at him and tramped, grey building rubble gritting under his soles. The stairs divided the flats two to one side and one to the other. 'It's the middle flat. They're all empty on this floor.' A uniformed constable, Willans, stood guard at the door. 'It's been empty about six weeks, apparently. Cosgrove says there's been some trouble with tramps sleeping in there, and kids breaking in for a smoke, the usual things. Here's how they got in.'

The glass panel of the front door had been boarded over. Atherton demonstrated the loosened nails in one corner, wiggled his fingers under to show how the knob of the Yale lock could be reached.

'No broken glass?' Slider frowned.

'Someone's cleaned up the whole place,' Atherton admitted sadly. 'Swept it clean as a whistle.'

'Who found the body?'

'Some kid phoned emergency around three this morning. Nicholls thought it was a hoax – the kid was very young, and wouldn't give his name – but he passed it on to the night patrol anyway, only the panda took its time getting here. She was found about a quarter to five.'

'She?' Funny how you always expect it to be male.

'Female, middle-twenties. Naked,' Atherton said economically.

Slider felt a familiar sinking of heart. 'Oh no.'

'I don't think so,' Atherton said quickly, answering the thought behind the words. 'She doesn't seem to have been touched at all. But the doc's in there now.'

'Oh well, let's have a look,' Slider said wearily.

Apart from the foul taste in his mouth and the ferment in his bowels, he had a small but gripping pain in the socket behind his right eye, and he longed inexpressibly for untroubled sleep. Atherton on the other hand, who had shared his debauch and presumably been up before him, looked not only fresh and healthy, but happy, with the intent and eager expression of a sheepdog on its way up into the hills. Slider could only trust that age and marriage would catch up with him, too, one day.

He found the flat gloomy and depressing in the unnatural glare from the spotlight on the roof opposite – installed to deter vandals, he supposed. 'The electricity's off, of course,' Atherton said, producing his torch. Boy scout, thought Slider savagely. In the room itself DC Hunt was holding another torch, illuminating the scene for the police surgeon, Freddie Cameron, who nodded a greeting and silently gave Slider place beside the victim.

She was lying on her left side with her back to the wall, her legs drawn up, her left arm folded with its hand under her head. Her dark hair, cut in a long pageboy bob, fell over her face and neck. Slider could see why Cosgrove thought she wasn't a resident. She was what pathologists describe as 'well-nourished': her flesh was sleek and unblemished, her hair and skin had the indefinable sheen of affluence that comes from a well-balanced protein-based diet. She also had an expensive tan, which left a white bikini-mark over her hips.

Slider picked up her right hand. It was icy cold, but still flexible: a strong, long-fingered, but curiously ugly hand, the fingernails cut so short that the flesh of the fingertips bulged a little round them. The cuticles were well-kept and there were no marks or scratches. He put the hand down and drew the hair back from the face. She looked about twenty-five – perhaps younger, for her cheek still had the full and blooming curve of extreme youth. Small straight nose, full mouth, with a short upper lip which showed the white edge of her teeth. Strongly marked dark brows, and below them a semicircle of black eyelashes brushing the curve of her cheekbone. Her eyes were closed reposefully. Death, though untimely, had come to her quietly, like sleep.

He lifted her shoulder carefully to raise her a little against the hideously papered wall. Her small, unripe breasts were no paler than her shoulders – wherever she had sunbathed last year, it had been topless. Her body had the slender taut-ness of unuse; below her flat golden belly, the stripe of white flesh looked like velvet. He had a sudden vision of her, strutting along a foreign beach under an expensive sun, care-lessly self-conscious as a young foal, all her life before her, and pleasure still something that did not surprise her. An enormous, unwanted pity shook him; the dark raspberry nipples seemed to reproach him like eyes, and he let her subside into her former position, and abruptly walked away to let Cameron take his place.

He walked around the rest of the flat. There were three bedrooms, living-room, kitchen, bathroom and WC. The whole place was stripped bare, and had been swept clean. No litter of tramps and children, hardly even any dust. He remembered the grittiness of the stairs outside and sighed. There would be nothing here for them, no footprints, no fingerprints, no material evidence. What had become of her clothes and handbag? He felt already a sense of unpleasant anxiety about this business. It was too well organised, too professional. And the wallpaper in each room was more depressing than the last.

Atherton appeared at the door, startling him. 'Dr Cameron wants you, guv.'

Freddie Cameron looked up as Slider came in. 'No sign of a struggle. No visible wounds. No apparent marks or bruises.'

'A fine upstanding body of negatives,' Slider said. 'What does that leave? Heart? Drugs?'

'Give me a chance,' Cameron grumbled. 'I can't see anything in this bloody awful light. I can't find a puncture, but it's probably narcotics – look at the pupils.' He let the eyelids roll back, and picked up the arms one by one, peering at the soft crook of the elbow. 'No sign of usage or abusage. Of course you can see from the general condition that she wasn't an addict. Could have taken something by mouth, I suppose, but where's the container?'

'Where are her clothes, for the matter of that,' said Slider. 'Unless she walked up here in the nude, I think we can rule out suicide. *Someone* was obviously here.'

'Obviously,' Cameron said drily. 'I can't help you much, Bill, until I can examine her by a good light. My guess is an overdose, probably by mouth, though I may find a puncture wound. No marks on her anywhere at all, except for the cuts, and they were inflicted post mortem.'

'Cuts?'

'On the foot.' Cameron gestured. Slider hunkered down and stared. He had not noticed before, but the softly curled palm of her foot had been marked with two deep cuts, roughly in the shape of a T. They had not bled, only oozed a little, and the blood had set darkly. Left foot only – the right was unmarked. The pads of the small toes rimmed the foot like fat pink pearls. Slider began to feel very bad indeed.

'Time of death?' he managed to say.

'Eight hours, very roughly. Rigor's just starting. I'll have a better idea when it starts to pass off.'

'About ten last night, then?' Slider stared at the body with deep perplexity. Her glossy skin was so out of place against the background of that disgusting wallpaper. 'I don't like it,' he said aloud.

Cameron put his hand on Slider's shoulder comfortingly. 'There is no sign of forcible sexual penetration,' he said.

Slider managed to smile. 'Anyone else would simply have said rape.'

'Language, my dear Bill, is a tool – not a blunt instrument. Anyway, I'll be able to confirm it after the post. She'll be as stiff as a board by this afternoon. Let me see – I can do it

Friday afternoon, about four-ish, if it's passed off by then. I'll let you know, in case you want to come. Nice-looking kid. I wonder who she is? Someone must be missing her. Ah, here's the photographer. Oh, it's you, Sid. No lights. I hope you've got yours with you, dear boy, because it's as dark as a mole's entry in here.'

Sid got to work, complaining uniformly about the conditions as a bee buzzes about its work. Cameron turned the body over so that he could get some mugshots, and as the brown hair slid away from the face, Slider leaned forward with sudden interest.

'Hullo, what's that mark on her neck?'

It was large and roughly round, about the size of a half-crown, an area of darkened and roughened skin about halfway down the left side of the neck; ugly against the otherwise flawless whiteness.

'It looks like a bloody great lovebite,' Sid said boisterously. 'I wouldn't mind giving her one meself.' He had captured for police posterity some gruesome objects in his time, including a suicide-by-hanging so long undiscovered that only its clothes were holding it together. Decomposing corpses held no horrors for him, but Slider was interested to note that something about this one's nude composure had unnerved the photographer too, making him overcompensate.

'Is it a bruise? Or a burn – a chloroform burn or something like that?'

'Oh no, it isn't a new mark,' Cameron said. 'It's more like a callus – see the pigmentation, where something's rubbed there – and some abnormal hair growth, too, look, here. Whatever it is, it's chronic.'

'Chronic? I'd call it bloody ugly,' Sid said.

'I mean it's been there a long time,' Cameron explained kindly. 'Can you get a good shot of it? Good. All right, then, Bill – seen all you want? Let's get her out of here, then. I'm bloody cold.'

A short while later, having seen the body lifted onto a stretcher, covered and removed, Cameron paused on his way out to say to Slider, 'I suppose you'll want to have the prints and dental records *toot sweet*? Not that her teeth'll tell you much – a near perfect set. Fluoride has a lot to answer for.'

'Thanks Freddie,' Slider said absently. *Someone must be missing her.* Parents, flatmates, boyfriend – certainly, surely, a boyfriend? He stared at the bare and dirty room: *Why here, for heaven's sake?*

'The fingerprint boys are here, guv,' Atherton said in his ear, jerking him back from the darkness.

'Right. Start Hunt and Hope on taking statements,' Slider said. 'Not that anyone will have seen anything, of course – not here.'

The long grind begins, he thought. Questions and statements, hundreds of statements, and nearly all of them would boil down to the Three Wise Monkeys, or another fine regiment of negatives.

In detective novels, he thought sadly, there was always someone who, having just checked his watch against the Greenwich Time Signal, glanced out of the window and saw the car with the memorable numberplate being driven off by a tall one-legged red-headed man with a black eyepatch and a zigzag scar down the left cheek. *I could tell 'e wasn't a gentleman, Hinspector, 'cause 'e was wearing brown boots.*

'Might be a good idea to get Cosgrove onto taking statements,' Atherton was saying. 'At least he speaks the lingo.'

2
All Quiet on the Western Avenue

A grey sky, which Slider had thought was simply pre-dawn greyness, settled in for the day, and resolved itself into a steady, cold and sordid rain.

'All life is at its lowest ebb in January,' Atherton said. 'Except, of course, in Tierra del Fuego, where they're miserable all year round. Cheese salad or ham salad?' He held up a roll in each hand and wiggled them a little, like a conjurer demonstrating his bona fides.

Slider looked at them doubtfully. 'Is that the ham I can see hanging out of the side?'

Atherton tilted the roll to inspect it, and the pink extrusion flapped dismally, like a ragged white vest which had accidentally been washed in company with a red teeshirt. 'Well, yes,' he admitted. 'All right, then,' he conceded, 'cheese salad or rubber salad?'

'Cheese salad.'

'I was afraid you'd say that. I never thought you were the sort to pull rank, guv,' Atherton grumbled, passing it across. 'Funny how the act of making sandwiches brings out the Calvinist in us. If you enjoy it, it must be sinful.' He looked for a moment at the bent head and sad face of his superior. 'I could make you feel good about the rolls,' he offered gently. 'I could tell you about the pork pies.'

The corner of Slider's mouth twitched in response, but only briefly. Atherton let him be, and went on with his lunch

13

and his newspaper. They had made a para in the lunchtime *Standard*:

The body of a naked woman has been discovered in an empty flat on the White City Estate in West London. The police are investigating.

Short and nutty, he thought. He was going to pass it over to Slider, and then decided against disturbing his brown study. He knew Slider well, and knew Irene as well as he imagined anyone would ever want to, and guessed that she had been giving him a hard time last night. Irene, he thought, was an excellent deterrent to his getting married.

Atherton led a happy bachelor life in a dear little terraced artisan's cottage in what Yuppies nowadays called West Hampstead – the same kind of logic as referring to Battersea as South Chelsea. It had two rooms up and two down, with the kitchen extended into the tiny, high-walled garden, and the whole thing had been modernised and upmarketised to the point where its original owners entering it through a time warp would have apologised hastily and backed out tugging their forelocks.

Here he lived with a ruggedly handsome black ex-tomcat called, unimaginatively, Oedipus; and used the lack of space as an excuse not to get seriously involved with any of his succession of girlfriends. He fell in love frequently, but never for very long, which he realised was a reprehensible trait in him. But the conquest was all – once he had them, he lost interest.

Apart from Oedipus, the person in life he loved best was probably Slider. It was certainly the most important and permanent relationship he'd had in adult life, and in some ways it was like a marriage. They spent a lot of time in each other's company, were forced to get on together and work together for a common end. Atherton knew himself to be a bit of a misfit in the force – a whizz kid without the whizz. He thought of himself as a career man, a go-getter, keen on advancement, but he knew his intellectual curiosity was against him. He was too well read, too interested in the truth for its own sake, too little inclined to tailor his efforts to the results that were either possible or required. He would never be groomed for stardom – he left unlicked those things which he ought to have licked, and there was no grace in him.

In that respect he resembled Slider, but for different reasons. Slider was dogged, thorough, painstaking, because it was in his nature to be: he was no intellectual gazelle. But Atherton not only admired Slider as a good policeman and a good man, he also liked him, was even fond of him; and he felt that Slider, who was reserved and didn't make friends easily, depended on him, both on his judgement and his affection. It was a good relationship, and it worked well, and if it weren't for Irene, he thought they would have been even closer.

Irene disliked Atherton for taking up her husband's time which she felt ought to be spent with her. He thought she probably suspected him vaguely of leading Bill astray and keeping him out late deliberately on wild debauches. God knew he would have done given the chance! The fact that Slider could have married someone like Irene was a fundamental mark against him which Atherton sometimes had difficulty in dismissing. It also meant that their relationship was restricted mainly to work, which might or might not have been a good thing.

Slider looked up, feeling Atherton's eyes on him. Slider was a smallish man, with a mild, fair face, blue eyes, and thick, soft, rather untidy brown hair. Jane Austen – of whom amongst others Atherton was a devotee – might have said Slider had a sweetness of expression. Atherton thought that was because his face was a clear window on his character, which was one of the things Atherton liked about him. In a dark and tangled world, it was good to know one person who was exactly what he seemed to be: a decent, kindly, honest, hard-working man, perhaps a little overconscientious. Slider's faint, worried frown was the outward sign of his inner desire to compensate personally for all the short-comings of the world. Atherton felt sometimes protective towards him, sometimes irritable: he felt that a man who was so little surprised at the wickedness of others ought surely to be less puzzled by it.

'What's up, guv?' he asked. 'You look hounded.'

'I can't stop thinking about the girl. Seeing her in my mind's eye.'

'You've seen corpses before. At least this one wasn't mangled.'

'It's the incongruity,' Slider said reluctantly, knowing that he didn't really know what it was that was bothering him. 'A girl like her, in a place like that. Why would anyone want to murder her *there* of all places?'

'We don't know it was murder,' Atherton said.

'She could hardly have walked up there stark naked and let herself in without someone seeing her,' Slider pointed out. Atherton gestured with his head towards the pile of statements Slider had been sifting through.

'She walked up there at some point without being seen. Unless all those residents are lying. Which is entirely possible. Most people seem to lie to us automatically. Like shouting at foreigners.'

Slider sighed and pushed the pile with his hands. 'I don't see how any of them could have had anything to do with it. Unless it was robbery from the person – and who takes all the clothes, right down to the underwear?'

'A second-hand clothes dealer?'

Slider ignored him. 'Anyway, the whole thing's too thorough. Everything that might have identified her removed. The whole place swept clean, the door knobs wiped. The only prints in the whole place are the kid's on the front-door knob. Someone went to a lot of trouble.'

Atherton grunted. 'There are no signs of a struggle, and no sounds of one according to the neighbours. Couldn't it have been an accident? Maybe she went there with a boyfriend for a bit of sex-and-drugs naughtiness, and something went wrong. Boom – she's dead! Boyfriend's left with a very difficult corpse to explain. So he strips her, cleans the place up, takes her clothes and handbag, and bunks.'

'And cuts her foot?'

'She might have done that any time – stepped on the broken glass from the front door for instance.'

'In the shape of the letter T? Anyway, they were post-mortem cuts.'

'Oh – yeah, I'd forgotten. Well, she might have been killed

somewhere else, and taken up there naked in a black plastic sack.'

'Well, she might,' Slider said, but only because he was essentially fair-minded.

Atherton grinned. 'Thanks. She's not very big, you know. A well-built man could have carried her. Everyone indoors watching telly – he could just pick his moment to walk up the stairs. Dump her, walk down again.'

'He'd have to arrive in a car of some sort.'

'Who looks at cars?' Atherton shrugged. 'In a place like that – ideal, really, for your average murderer. In an ordinary street, people know each other's cars, they look out of the window, they know what their neighbours look like at least. But with a common yard, people are coming and going all the time. It's a thoroughfare. And all the living-room windows are at the back, remember. It would be easy not to be noticed.'

Slider shook his head. 'I know all that. I just don't see why anyone would go to all that trouble. No, it's got a bad smell to it, this one. A setup. She was enticed there by the killer, murdered, and then all traces were removed to prevent her from being identified.'

'But why cut her foot?'

'That's the part I hate most of all,' Slider grimaced.

'"I don't know nothin' I hate so much as a cut toe,"' Atherton said absently.

'Uh?'

'Quotation. Steinbeck. *The Grapes of Wrath.*'

The duty officer stuck his head round the door, registered Slider, and said, 'Records just phoned, sir. I've been ringing your phone – didn't know you were in here. It's negative on those fingerprints, sir. No previous.'

'I didn't think there would be,' Slider said, his gloom intensifying a millimetre.

The disembodied face softened: everybody liked Slider.

'I'm just going to make some tea, sir. Would you like a cup?'

Nicholls came into Slider's room in the afternoon holding a

large brown envelope. Slider looked up in surprise.
'You're early, aren't you? Or has my watch stopped?'
'Doing Fergus a favour. He's tortured with the toothache,'
Nicholls said. He and O'Flaherty were old friends, having
gone through police college together. He called O'Flaherty
'Flatulent Fergus', and O'Flaherty called him 'Nutty
Nicholls'. They sometimes dropped into a well-polished
routine about having been in the trenches together. Nicholls
was a ripely handsome Highlander with a surprising range of
musical talents. At a police concert in aid of charity he had
once brought the house down by singing 'The Queen of the
Night' aria from *The Magic Flute* in a true and powerful
soprano, hitting the cruel F in alt fair and square on the
button. Not so much the school of Bel Canto, he had claimed
afterwards, as the school of Can Belto.

'So much tortured,' Nicholls went on, rolling his Rs
impressively, 'that he forgot to give you these. I found them
lying on his desk. I expect you've been waiting for them.'

He held out the envelope and Slider took and opened it.

'Yes, I was wondering where they'd got to,' he said,
drawing out the sheaf of photographs and spreading them on
his desk. Nicholls leaned on his fists and whistled soundlessly.

'Is that your corpus? A bit of a stunner, isn't she? You'd
best not let the wife see any of these, or bang goes your overtime for the next ten years.' He pushed the top ones back
with a forefinger. 'Poor wee lassie,' he said. 'No luck ID-ing
her yet?'

'We've got nothing to go on,' Slider said. 'Not so much as
a signet ring, or an appendix scar. Nothing but this mark on
her neck, and I don't know that that's going to get us
anywhere.'

Nicholls picked up one of the close-ups of the neck, and
grinned at Slider. 'Oh Mrs Stein – or may I call you Phyllis?'

'You know something?'

Nicholls tapped the photograph with a forefinger. 'You
and Freddie Cameron I can understand, but I'm a wee bit
surprised young Atherton hasn't picked up on this.'

'Perhaps he didn't see it at the flat. And we've been
waiting for the photographs,' Slider said patiently.

'Tell me, Bill, did you notice anything about her fingers?'

'Nothing in particular. Except that she had very short fingernails. I suppose she bit them.'

'Ah-huh. Nothing of the sort, man. She was a fiddle-player. A vi-o-linist. This is the mark they get from gripping the violin between the neck and the shoulder.'

'You're sure?'

'Well, I couldn't swear it wasnae a viola,' Nicholls said gravely. 'And the fingernails have to be short, you see, for pressing down on the strings.'

Slider thought. 'They were short on both hands.'

'I expect she'd want them symmetrical,' Nicholls said kindly. 'Well, this gives you a way of tracing her, anyway. Narrows the field. It's a closed kind of world – everyone knows everyone.'

'I suppose I'd start with the musicians' union,' Slider hazarded. Like most people, he had no idea how the musical world was arranged internally. He'd never been to a live symphony concert, though he had a few classical records, and could tell Beethoven from Bach. Just.

'I doubt that'd be much use to you,' Nicholls said. 'Not without the name. They don't have photographs in their central records. No, if I were you, I'd ask around the orchestras.'

'We don't know that she was a member of an orchestra.'

'No, but if she played the fiddle, it's likely she was on the classical side of the business rather than the pop. And if she wasn't a member of an orchestra, she'd still likely be known to someone. As I said, it's a closed world.'

'Well, it's a lead, anyway,' Slider said, getting up with renewed energy and shuffling the photographs together. 'Thanks, Nutty.'

Nicholls grinned. 'N't'all. Get yon Atherton onto it, I should. I heard a rumour he was havin' social intercourse with a flute-player at last year's Proms. That's why I was surprised he didn't recognise the mark.'

'If it was a mark on the navel, he'd have spotted it straight off,' Slider said.

* * *

It was a mistake to try to go home at half past five, as anyone more in the habit of doing so than Slider would have known. The A40 – the Western Avenue – was jammed solid with Rovers and BMWs heading out for Gerrard's Crawse. Slider was locked in his car for an hour with a disc jockey called Chas or Mike or Dave – they always seemed to have names like the bark of a dog – who burbled on about a major tailback on the A40 due to roadworks at Perivale. So he was further hindered in his desire to forget his work for a while by finding himself stationary for a long period on the section of the road which ran beside the White City Estate.

Sometime this afternoon Freddie Cameron would have done the post. Slider had been to one or two out of interest, in order to know what happened, and he had not wished to attend this one. It was a particularly human horror, this minute and dispassionate mutilation of a dead body. No other species practised it on its own kind. He felt inexplicably unnerved at the thought. For some reason this particular young woman refused to take on the status of a corpse but remained a person in his mind, her white body floating there like the memory of someone he had known. She was in the back of his head, like the horrors seen out of the corner of the eye in childhood: like the man with no face behind the bedroom door after Mum had put the light out. He knew he mustn't look at it, or it would get him; and yet the half-admitted shape called the eye irresistibly.

He tried to concentrate on the radio programme. A listener had just called in, apparently – to judge by the background noise – from some place a long way off that was suffering from a hailstorm, or possibly an earthquake. A distorted voice said, 'Hullo Dive, this is Eric from Hendon. I am a first-time caller. I jussliketsay, I lissnayour programme every day, iss reelly grite.' Slider remembered being told that soundwaves never die, simply stream off into space for ever and ever. What would they make of that, out on Alpha Centauri Beta?

He was going home early in the hope of scoring some Brownie points after the storms of the last few days. It struck him as a dismal sort of reason for going home, and he thought enviously of Atherton heading back to his bijou little cottage, a few delectable things to eat, and a stimulating evening with a new young woman to be conquered. Not that Slider wanted stimulation or a new young woman – he was too tired these days for the thought of illicit sex to do other than appal him; but peace and comfort would have been nice to look forward to.

But the house, which he hated, was Irene's, decorated and furnished to her requirements, not his. Wasn't it the same for all married men? Probably. Probably. All the same, the three-piece suite seemed to have been designed for looking at, not sitting on. All the furniture was like that: it rejected human advances like a chilly woman. It was like living in one of those display houses at the Ideal Home Exhibition.

And Irene cooked like someone meting out punishment. No, that wasn't strictly fair. The food was probably perfectly wholesome and well-balanced nutritionally, but it never seemed to taste of anything. It was joyless food, imbued with the salt water of tears. The subconscious knowledge that she hated cooking would have made him feel guilty about evincing any pleasure in eating it, even if there had been any.

When they were first married, Slider had done a lot of the cooking in their little bedsit in Holland Park. He liked trying out new dishes, and they had often laughed together over the results. He examined the memory doubtfully. It didn't seem possible that the Irene he was going home to was the same Irene who had sat cross-legged on the floor and eaten chilli con carne out of a pot with a tablespoon. She didn't like him to cook now – she thought it was unmanly. In fact, she didn't like him going into the kitchen at all. If he so much as made a cup of tea, she followed him round with a J cloth and a tight-lipped expression, wiping up imaginary spillings.

When he got home at last, it was all effort wasted, because Irene was not there. She had gone out to play bridge with the Harpers and Ernie Newman, which, had he thought hard enough, he should have known, because she had told him last week about it. Slider had said sooner her than him, and she'd asked why in a dangerous sort of way, and he'd said because Newman was an intolerable, stuffed-shirted, patronising, constipated prick. Irene primmed her lips and said there was no need for him to bring bowels into it, he wasn't talking to one of his low Met friends now, and if he spent less time with them and more with decent people he'd be able to hold a civilised conversation once in a while.

Then they had had a row, which ended with Irene complaining that they never went anywhere together any more, and that was more or less true, not only because of his job, but because they no longer liked doing the same kind of things. He liked eating out, which she thought was just a waste of money. And she liked playing bridge, for God's sake!

Actually, he was pretty sure she didn't like bridge, that she had only learned it as the entrée to the sort of society to which she thought they ought to belong. The Commissioner and his wife played bridge. He didn't say that to her of course, when she badgered him to learn. He just said he didn't like card games and she said he didn't like anything, and he had found that hard to refute just for the moment. His concerns seemed to have been whittled down to work, and slumping in front of the telly for ten minutes before passing out. It was years since he had stayed awake all the way through a film. He was becoming a boring old fart.

Of course, that wasn't congenital. He had lots of interests really: good food and wine and vintage cars and gardening and walking in the country and visiting old houses – architecture had always been a passion of his, and he used to sketch rather well in a painstaking way – but there just didn't seem to be room in his life any more. Not time, somehow, but room, as if his wife and his children and his mortgage and his job swelled like wet rice year by year – bland, damp and weighty – and squeezed everything else out of him.

No Brownie points tonight, then. No peace either – the living-room was occupied by the babysitter, who was watching a gameshow on television. A ten-second glance at the screen suggested that the rules of the game comprised the contestants having to guess which of the Christian names on the illuminated board was their own in order to win a microwave oven or a cut-glass decanter and glasses. The applause following a right answer was as impassioned as an ovation for a Nobel-prize winner.

The babysitter was fifteen and, for some reason Slider had

never discovered, her name was Chantal. Slider regarded her as marginally less competent to deal with an emergency than a goldfish, and this was not only because, short of actual self-mutilation, she had done everything possible to make herself appear as ugly and degenerate as possible. Her clothes hung sadly on her in uneven layers of conflictingly ugly colours, her shoes looked like surgical boots, and her hair was died coke-black, while the roots were growing out blonde: a mind-numbing reversal of the normal order of things which made Slider feel as if he were seeing in negative.

To add to this, her eyelids were painted red and her fingernails black, she chewed constantly like a ruminant, and she wore both earrings in the same ear, though Slider assumed that this was fashion and not absent-mindedness. She was actually quite harmless, apart from her villainous appearance, and her parents were decent, pleasant people with a comfortable income.

She looked up at him now with the intensely unreliable expression of an Old English sheepdog.

'Oh, hullo, Mr Slider. I wasn't expecting you,' she said, and a surprising hot blush ran up from under her collar. She fingered her Phurnacite hair nervously. She was in fact desperately in love with him, though Slider hadn't twigged it. He had replaced Dennis Waterman in her heart the instant she discovered that Dennis Waterman was married to Rula Lenska. 'Shall I turn this off?'

'No, it's all right. I won't disturb you. Where are the children?'

'Matthew's round his friend Simon's, and Kate's in her room reading.' They eyed each other for a moment, trapped by politeness. 'Shall I fix you a drink?' Chantal asked suddenly. It was like a scene from *Dynasty*. Slider glanced around nervously for the television cameras.

'Oh – er – no, thanks. You watch your programme. Don't mind me. I've got things to do.'

He backed out into the hall and closed the door. Fix him a drink, indeed! He looked round, wondering what to do next. No comfort, he thought. He really hadn't anything to do. He was so unused to having time on his hands that he felt hobbled by it. He decided to go upstairs and see Kate, who hadn't been awake when he left that morning, and whom he hardly ever saw at night because she usually went to bed before he got home. The door of her room was closed, and through it he heard the muted tones of what must surely be the same radio programme.

'Hullo Mike. This is Sharon from Tooting. I jussliketersay, I lissnayour programme all the time, iss reelly grite ...'

Or perhaps there was only ever one, an endless loop of tape run by a computer from a basement somewhere behind Ludgate Circus.

He stopped on the dim landing, and suddenly the dead girl was there with him, ambushing him from the back of his mind: the childlike fall of her hair and the curve of her cheek, the innocence of her nakedness. He put his fingers to his temples and pressed and drew his breath long and hard. He felt on the brink of some unknown crisis; he felt suddenly out of control.

Kate must have heard something – she called out 'Is that you Daddy?' from inside her room. Slider let out his breath shudderingly, drew another more normal. He reached for the door handle.

'Hullo, my sweetheart,' he said cheerfully, going in.

3

Drowsy Syrups

It was an old-fashioned morgue, cold and high-ceilinged, with marble floors that echoed hollowly when you walked across them, and a sink in the corner with a tap that dripped. There was a strong smell of disinfectant and formalin, which did not quite mask a different smell underneath – warmer, sweetish and dirty.

Cameron, fresh from the path unit at one of the newer hospitals, contrasted this chilly old tomb with the low-ceilinged, strip-lighted, air-conditioned, rubber-tile-floored place he had just left. He felt a vague fondness, all the same, for the old morgues like this which were fast disappearing. Not only had he done his training in such places, but the architecture reminded him cosily of his primary school in Edinburgh. All the same, he decided to leave his waistcoat on.

His dapper form enveloped in protective apron and gloves, he bent forward over the pale cadaver on the herringbone-gullied table, his breath just faintly visible on the cold air as, whistling, he made the first sweeping incision from the point of the chin to the top of the pubic bone.

'Right then, here we go,' he said, reaching under the table with his foot for the pedal which turned on the audio recorder. Out of sheer force of habit he reached up and tapped the microphone with a knuckle to see if it was working, and it clunked hollowly. The assistant watched him phlegmatically. He had tested the machinery himself as a matter of course, as he always did, as Cameron knew he always did; but Cameron had no faith in machines. He had done his training in the days of handwritten notes, and even then he had known fountain pens to go wrong.

Now, like a cheerful gardener pruning roses, Cameron snipped through the cartilages which joined the ribs, freed them from the breastbone, separated the breastbone from the collarbones, and then with the economical force of long practice, opened out the two sides of the chest like cabinet doors. Inside, neatly disposed in their ordained order, were the internal organs, displayed like an anatomical drawing in a medical textbook before his enquiring eyes.

Slider was not present. Cameron had phoned him earlier to say that he would not be posting the girl until six-thirty, in case he wanted to come, but Slider had refused. Cameron thought his old friend sounded distinctly odd. He hoped old Bill wasn't going to crack up. Many a good man had gone that way: Cameron had seen it in the army as well as in the force, time and time again, and it was always the quiet, conscientious ones you had to watch. When a man had worry at work and worry at home – well, pressure started to build up. And poor old Bill's Madam was not exactly the Pal of the Period.

The words *male menopause* floated through his mind and he dismissed them irritably. He disliked jargon, particularly inaccurate jargon. When a man of forty-odd started fancying young girls, it was either because things were not right at home, or he was trying to prove something to himself – in either case, it was nothing to do with hormones. Not that Bill was chasing skirts, of course – he simply wasn't that sort – but it came to the same thing. He was jumpy, distinctly jumpy.

'I'd like to come, Freddie, but I've got a heap of reports I've been putting off,' Slider had said. 'It's quiet now, and I daren't put them off again.' Now this was transparently an excuse. Cameron knew how much there was to do when a division handled a murder case – the Incident Room to be set up, thousands of statements to go over – no need to go dragging in reports. Then Slider had given a nervous laugh and added unnecessarily, 'You know what paperwork is.' When a close friend starts talking to you like an idiot,

Cameron considered, you knew there was something seriously on his mind.

Still whistling, and wielding his large knife with a flourish, more the jolly family butcher now than the cheerful gardener, he removed the internal organs in turn, weighed, sliced and examined them, and took sections for analysis, which the assistant sealed in sterile jars and labelled while Cameron watched sternly. He had a natural horror of unlabelled specimens. When the body was completely eviscerated, he made a lateral cut across the scalp from ear to ear, freed the tissues from the bone, and drew the front half of the scalp down over the face like a mask, and the rear half down over the neck like a coalman's flap. Then with an electric bone-saw he cut through the cranium and lifted the top off the skull, much as he had taken the top off his boiled egg that morning, and with very little more effort. With a little more cutting and snipping, he was able to slide his hands in under the brain and lift it out whole. He laid it on the slab and sliced it like a rather pallid country loaf.

'All normal,' he said. As he worked, he had spoken his commentary aloud for the machine, and between comments he whistled. Sometimes he forgot to touch the foot pedal, so the whistle got recorded too. This was particularly trying for the audio-typist who transcribed his reports, for the machinery played the whistle back at a pitch which was quite painful through an earpiece. She had spoken to him again and again about it, and he always apologised profusely, but it made no difference. He had always whistled. He had begun it as a student thirty years ago, an assumption of insouciance which was designed to deceive himself more than other people, and to stop him thinking of the cadavers as human beings; and the habit was so ingrained by now he wasn't even aware he was doing it.

'Right, I think that will do,' he said at last, switching off the machine and nodding to the assistant. 'I'll be off then. I've got two more to do at Charing Cross before I've finished, and I promised Martha I wouldn't be late tonight. She's got some ghastly people coming in for drinks.' He looked at his watch. 'Not much chance of making it before they leave, thank God, but I'll have missed the traffic, anyway.'

'Goodnight, then, sir,' said the assistant. When the doctor had gone, he had his own tasks to perform. The body would have to be stuffed and sewn up, the skull packed and the scalp drawn back into place and stitched, and the viscera disposed of in the incinerator. When this was done, he returned the body to the trolley and, because he was a bit of a perfectionist in his own way, he fetched a damp cloth and cleaned it up. Dead bodies don't bleed, but they leak a bit.

With a gentle hand he wiped the pink-tinged bone-dust from the face. Poor kid, he thought. It was tragic when they caught it as young as that. And pretty too. From her label he could see she was unidentified, which struck him as odd, because she didn't look like the kind of girl no-one would miss. Still, sooner or later, someone would want her, so she ought to be made a bit decent. Kindly he smoothed the hair back to hide the stitches, and then wheeled her back to her waiting numbered drawer in the mortuary.

When you're born, and when you die, a stranger washes you, he thought, as he had thought a hundred times before. It was a funny old life.

It was silly weather for January, warm and sunny as April never was, and all down Kingsway there were window boxes crammed with yellow daffodils. Pedestrians were either looking sheepish in spring clothes, or self-righteous and hot in boots and overcoats, and the bus queues were suddenly chatty.

Only the paperseller outside Holborn Station looked unchanged and unchangeable in his multifoliate sweaters, greasy cap, and overcoat tied in the middle with baling-string. His fingers were as black and shiny as anthracite from the newsprint, as was the end of his nose where he had wiped it with his hand. He scowled in disproportionate rage when Slider asked him where the Orchestra's office was.

'Why don't you buy yourself an *A ter Z*?' he enquired uncharitably. 'I'm not Leslie Fuckin' Welch, the fuckin' Memory Man, am I? I'm here to sell papers. Right? *Noos*-papers,' he added fiercely, as if Slider had queried the word. Slider meekly bought the noon edition of the *Standard,* asked again, and was given very precise directions.

'Next time ask a bleedin' policeman,' the paper-seller suggested helpfully. Am I that obvious? Slider thought uneasily as he walked away.

The office turned out to be on the third floor of a building that had known better days, one of those late-Victorian monsters of red brick and white-stone coping, a cross between a ship and a gigantic birthday cake. Inside were marble-chip floors and dark-panelled walls, and a creaking, protesting lift caged like a sullen beast in the centre of the entrance hall, with the stairs winding round it.

There was a legend on the wall inside the door, and Slider looked up the Orchestra office's location, considered the lift, and took the stairs, flinching when the lift clanged and lurched into action a moment later, and loomed past him, summoned from above. He didn't like its being above him, and hurried upwards while coils of cable like entrails descended mysteriously inside the shaft.

On the third floor he found the half-frosted door, tapped on it, and entered an office empty of humanity, but otherwise breathtakingly untidy, crammed with desks, filing cabinets, hat stands, dying pot plants, and files and papers everywhere in tottering piles. On the windowsill amongst the plants was a tin tray on which reposed a teapot, a caddy, a jar of Gold Blend, an opened carton of milk, and a sticky teaspoon. The empty but unwashed mugs were disposed about the desks, evidence to the trained mind that coffee-break was over. A navy-blue cardigan hung inside-out over the back of a chair which stood askew from a desk on which the telephone rang monotonously and disregarded.

Soon there were brisk footsteps outside in the hallway, the door was flung open, and the cardigan's owner hurried in, bringing with her the evocative scent of Palmolive soap, and reached for the telephone just as it stopped ringing.

She laughed. 'Isn't it maddening how they always do that? I've been waiting for a call from New York all day, and just when I dash out to the loo for a second ... Now I suppose I'll have to ring them. Can I do something for you?'

She was a small, slight, handsome woman in her forties; shiny black hair cut very short, large-nosed face carefully made-up, a string of very good pearls around her neck. Slider would have known even without looking that she was wearing a white blouse, a plain navy skirt with an inverse pleat at the front, navy stockings, and black patent-leather court shoes with a small gold bar round the heel. He felt he knew her well: he had met her a hundred times in the service flats round the back of Harrods or the Albert Hall; in Kensington High Street; in Chalfont and Datchet and Taplow. Her husband would be a publisher or an agent, something on the administrative side of The Arts, and their son would be at Cambridge.

Slider smiled and introduced himself and proffered his ID, which she declined gracefully with a wave of the hand, like someone refusing a cigarette.

'How can I help you, Inspector?'

Slider was impressed. Few people nowadays, he found, could call a policeman 'Inspector' or 'Officer' without sounding either self-conscious or rude. He produced the mugshot.

'I'm hoping you may be able to identify this young woman. We have reason to believe she may be a violinist.'

The woman took the picture and looked at it, and said at once, 'Yes, she's one of ours. Oh dear, how awful! She's dead, isn't she? How very dreadful. Poor child.'

That was quick of her, he thought. 'What's her name?'

'Anne-Marie Austen. Second fiddle. She hasn't long been with us. What was it, Inspector – a traffic accident?'

'We don't yet know how she died, Mrs –'

'Bernstein. Like the composer,' she said absently, looking at the photo again. 'It's so awful to think this was taken after she – I'm sorry. Silly of me. I suppose you must get used to this sort of thing.'

She looked up at Slider, demanding an answer to what ought to have been a rhetorical question, and he said, 'Yes and no,' and she looked suitably abashed. He took the photo back from her. 'As I said, Mrs Bernstein, we don't yet know the cause of death. Do you know if she had any chronic condition, heart or anything, that might have been a factor?'

'None that I know of. She seemed healthy enough – not that I saw much of her. And she hadn't been with us long –

she came from the Birmingham about six months ago.'

'I was wondering,' Slider said musingly, running his fingers along the edge of the desk, 'why she hadn't been missed? If one of your members doesn't turn up, don't you make any enquiries?'

'Well, yes, normally we would, but this is one of our quiet periods. We're often slack just after Christmas, and in fact we haven't any dates for the Orchestra until the middle of next week.'

'I see. And you wouldn't contact your members in the mean time?'

'Not unless some work came in. There'd be no need.'

'When did the Orchestra last work together?'

'On Monday, a recording session for the BBC, at the Television Centre, Wood Lane. Two sessions, actually – two-thirty to five-thirty, and six-thirty to nine-thirty.'

'Was Anne-Marie there?'

'She was booked. As far as I know she was there. I don't attend the sessions myself, you know, but at any rate, nobody has told me she was absent.'

'I see.' Another little piece had slipped into place in Slider's mind – well, quite a big piece really. It explained why the girl was in that area in the first place. She finished work at nine-thirty at the TVC, and half an hour or so later she was killed less than half a mile away. Probably she had met her murderer as soon as she came out of the Centre. Someone might have seen her walk off with him, or get into his car. 'Did she have any particular friends in the Orchestra?'

Mrs Bernstein shrugged charmingly. 'Really, I'm not the person to answer that. I work mostly here in the office – I don't often get to see the Orchestra working. The personnel manager, John Brown, would be able to tell you more about her. He's with the players all the time. And she shared a desk with Joanna Marshall – she might be able to help you.'

'Shared a desk?'

'Oh – the string players sit in pairs, you know, with one music stand and one piece of music between them. We call each pair a desk – don't ask me why.' Slider gave her an obedient smile in response to hers. 'Desk partners, particularly at the back of the section, are quite often close friends.'

'I see. Well, perhaps you could put me in touch with Miss Marshall, and Mr Brown. And would you give me Miss Austen's address, too?'

'Of course, I'll write them down for you.' She went to a filing cabinet and brought out a thick file containing a computer print-out of names and addresses. Flicking through it she found the right place, and copied the information onto a piece of headed paper in a quick, neat hand.

'The phone number of the office is here at the top of the sheet, in case you want to ask me anything else. And I'll put my home number too. Don't hesitate to contact me if you think I can help.'

'Thank you. You're very kind,' Slider said, pocketing the paper. 'By the way, do you know who was her next of kin?'

'I'm afraid I don't. The members are all self-employed people, you see, and it's up to them to worry about that sort of thing.' The quick dark eyes searched his face. 'I suppose she was murdered?'

'Why do you suppose that?' Slider asked impassively.

'Well, if it was all above board, if she'd tumbled downstairs or been run over or something, you'd have said, wouldn't you?'

'We don't yet know how she met her death,' he said again, and she gave him a quick-knit smile.

'I suppose you have to be discreet. But really, I can't imagine anyone wanting to kill a child of her age, unless –' She looked suddenly distressed. 'She wasn't – it wasn't –?'

'No,' said Slider.

'Thank God!' She seemed genuinely relieved. 'Well, I should think Joanna Marshall would be your best bet. She's a nice, friendly creature. If anyone knows anything about Anne-Marie's private life, it'll be her.'

Out in the street again, Slider tried the name out on his tongue. Anne-Marie Austen. Anne-Marie. Yes, it suited her. Now he knew it, he felt as though he had always known it.

John Brown's telephone number produced an answering machine inviting him tersely to leave a message. He declined. Joanna Marshall's number produced an answering machine giving the number of a diary service, which Slider wasn't quick enough to catch the first time round. He had to dial again, pencil at the ready, and took down a Hertfordshire number. The Hertfordshire number rang a long time and then produced a breathless woman with a dog barking monotonously in the background.

'I'm so sorry, I was down the garden and the girl seems to have disappeared. Shut up Kaiser! I'm sorry, who? Oh yes, Joanna Marshall, yes, just a minute, yes. Today? And what time? Oh, I see, you want to know where she is? Shut *up* Kaiser! Well I'm afraid I can't tell you, because she's not working this afternoon. Have you tried her home number? Oh I see. She's not in trouble, is she? Well all I can tell you is that she's on tonight at the Barbican. Yes, that's right. Seven-thirty. Kaiser get *down*, you foul dog! I'm sorry? Yes. No. Of course. Not at all. Goodbye.'

Slider left the telephone box and walked back into Kingsway. The sunshine and warmth had persuaded the proprietor of an Italian café to put tables outside on the pavement, and two early lunchers were sitting there, remarkably unselfconscious, eating pizza and drinking bottled lager, blinking in the sunshine like cats. A mad impulse came over Slider. Well, why not? His morning cornflakes were a distant memory now, and a man must eat. He hadn't been in an Italian restaurant in years. He lingered, looking longingly at the tables on the pavement, and then went regretfully inside. He'd feel a fool. He hadn't their sureness of youth and beauty and each other.

He plunged into the dark interior, into the smell of hot oil and garlic, and felt suddenly ravenous and cheerful. He ordered spaghetti with *pesto* and *escalope alla rustica*, and half a carafe of red, and it came and was excellent. The frank, pungent tastes worked strangely on his palate, accustomed as it was to sandwich lunches and grilled chops and boiled vegetables at night: he began to feel almost drunk, and it was nothing to do with the wine. Anne-Marie, he thought. Anne-Marie. His mind turned and fondled the name. Was she French? Did she like Italian food? He imagined her sitting opposite him now: garlic bread and gutsy wine, talk and laughter, everything new and easy. She would tell him about music, and he would regale her with the stories of his trade which would all be new to her, and she would marvel and be amused and admire. Everything was interesting and wonderful when you were twenty-five. Until someone murdered you, of course.

'You only just caught me. I was just going out for something to eat,' said Atherton.

'I've had mine. And I've found out who the girl is.'

'I deduced both those facts – you smell of garlic and you're looking smug.'

'I also know why she was where she was: she was working at the TVC that evening.'

'Lunch can wait. Tell me all,' Atherton said. He sat down on the edge of a desk, raising a cloud of dust into the streams of sunlight that were fighting their way through the grime on the windows of the CID room, which no-one had ever washed in the history of Time. Everyone else was out, the telephones dozed, and the room had that unnatural midday hush.

Slider told him what he had learned that morning. 'It's possible that whoever killed her knew that the Orchestra wouldn't be working again for ten days, and that therefore she wouldn't be missed. Stripping the body, too – they'd have expected it to delay us for weeks. After all, if it hadn't been for Nicholls identifying that mark on her neck –'

'Unlike Nicholls, I didn't have the benefit of seeing it. And unlike you, by the way.'

'All right, sonny – how would you like to go back to tracing stolen videos?'

It was a familiar joking exchange of sass and threat, but suddenly there was a harsher note in it that surprised both of them, and they eyed each other with some embarrassment. Atherton opened his mouth to say something placatory, but Slider forestalled him. 'You'd better go and get your lunch, hadn't you? Who's minding the shop, anyway?'

'Fletcher. He's in the bog.'

Slider shrugged and went away to his own room, angry with himself, and a little puzzled. Everyone needed help in this job – why was he suddenly so defensive?

Freddie Cameron phoned.

'I've got the forensic reports from Lambeth, Bill. I've just sent off a full copy of the post-mortem report to you, but I thought you'd like to know straight away, as it's your case.'

'Yes, thanks, Freddie. What was it?'

'As I thought – an overdose of barbiturate.'

'Self-administered?'

'I think it very unlikely. The puncture was in the back of the right hand, damned awkward place to do it to yourself. The veins slide about if you don't pull the skin taut. Anyway, I found the puncture as soon as I got her into a good light, and it was the only one, so there's no doubt about that. But there was some very slight subcutaneous bruising of the left upper arm and right wrist. I'd say she was handled by an expert – someone who knew how to subdue with the minimum force, and without damaging the goods. Professional.'

'Left upper arm and right wrist?'

'Yes. It seems to me that if she was sitting down, for instance, someone could pass their arm right round her body from behind and grip the wrist to hold it still while administering the injection with the other hand.'

'Or there might have been two of them. She'd probably struggle. No other marks? No ligatures?'

'Nothing. But they wouldn't have to hold her for long. She'd have been unconscious within seconds, and dead within minutes.'

'What was it, then?'

'Pentathol.'

'Pentathol?'

'Short-acting anaesthetic. It's what they give you in the anteroom of an operating theatre to put you under, before they give you the gas.'

'Yes, I know that. But it seems an odd choice.'

'It produces deep anaesthesia very quickly. Of course, it also wears off very quickly – except that this poor child was given enough to fell a horse. Wasteful chaps, murderers.'

'And you're sure that's what it was? No other drugs?'

'Of course I'm sure. As I said, this stuff normally wears off very quickly, but if you administer enough of it, it paralyses the victim's respiratory system. They stop breathing, and death follows without a struggle.'

'Presumably only a doctor would have access to it?'

'Yes, but even then, not every doctor. It would have to be an anaesthetist at a hospital, or someone with access to hospital theatre drugs. An ordinary GP who wrote out a prescription for it wouldn't get it. Not what I'd call the murderer's usual choice. It's eminently detectable, and so difficult to come by that I should have thought the source would be easily traceable. Now if it were me, I'd have –'

'I think they wanted it to be detected,' Slider said abruptly.

'What's that?'

'Well, look – there was no attempt to hide the body, or to make it look like suicide. They must have known she'd be found before long. And then there were the cuts on her foot.'

'Ah yes, the cuts. Inflicted after death, of course.'

'Yes.'

'With a very sharp blade. They were deep, but quite clean – no haggling. A strong hand and something like an old-fashioned cutthroat razor, but with a shorter blade.'

'A scalpel, perhaps,' Slider said quietly.

'Yes, I'm afraid so. Exactly like that.' There was a silence, filled only with the hollow, subaural thrumming of an open line. 'Bill, I'm not liking this. Are you thinking what I'm thinking?'

'It looks,' Slider said slowly, 'like an execution.'

'*Pour encourager les autres*,' Cameron said in his appalling Scottish French. 'The letter T – Traitor? Or Talker perhaps? But put pentathol, scalpel and a strong, steady hand together, and it comes out Surgeon. That's what I don't like.'

'I don't like any part of it,' Slider said. An execution? What could she have been into, that young girl with her unused body?

'Well, you should have your copy of the report this afternoon, with any luck. When's the inquest?'

'As soon as possible. At least we don't have any distraught parents clamouring for release of her body.'

'You've not ID'd her then?'

'Yes, but we've no next of kin yet, and no-one's asked after her. No-one at all.'

He must have sounded a little how he felt, for Cameron said kindly, 'She wouldn't have felt a thing, you know. It would have been very quick and easy, like a mercy killing. They just put her to sleep, like an old dog.'

4
Digging for Buttered Rolls

Anne-Marie Austen had lived in a shabby, three-storeyed Edwardian house off the Chiswick High Road. There were three bells on the front door, with paper labels: Gostyn, Barclay and Austen. A prolonged ringing at the lowest bell eventually produced Mrs Gostyn, the erstwhile owner of the house, who now lived as a protected tenant in the ground-floor accommodation with use of garden.

She was very old, and had presumably once been fat, for her thick, white, ginger-freckled skin was now much too big for her and hung around her sadly like borrowed clothes. She gripped Atherton's forearm with surprising strength to keep him still while she told him her tale of the glories from which she had fallen; passing on, when he showed signs of restless-ness, to the iniquities of the Barclays on the first floor, who left their baby with a child minder so that they could both go out to work, and who hoovered at all hours of the evening which interfered with Mrs Gostyn's television, and who made the whole ceiling shake with their washing machine, she gave him her word, so it was a wonder the house didn't come down around her ears.

Miss Austen? Yes, Miss Austen lived on the top floor. She played the violin in an orchestra, which was very nice in its way, but there was the coming and going at all hours, and then practising, practising, up and down scales until you thought you'd go mad. It wasn't even as if it was a nice tune you could tap your feet to. You mightn't think it to look at her, but Mrs Gostyn had been a great dancer in her time, when Mr Gostyn was alive.

Atherton recoiled slightly from the arch look, and tried to withdraw his arm, but though the flesh of her hand slid about, the bones inside still gripped him fiercely. He murmured as little encouragingly as he could.

'Oh yes, a great dancer. Max Jaffa, Victor Sylvester – we used to roll the carpet back, you know, whenever there was anything like that on the wireless. Of course,' with a moist sigh, 'we had the whole house then. Lodgers were not thought of. But you can't get servants these days, dear, not even if you could afford them, and I can't climb those stairs any more.'

'Did Miss Austen have many visitors?' Slider asked quickly, before she could tack off again.

'Well, no, not so many. She was away a lot, of course, for her work – sometimes for days at a time, but even when she was home she didn't seem to be much of a one for entertaining. There's her friend – a young lady – the one she worked with, who came sometimes –'

'Boyfriends?' Atherton asked.

Mrs Gostyn sniffed. 'There have been men going up there, once or twice. It's not my business to ask questions. But when a young woman lives alone in a flat like that, she's bound to get into trouble sooner or later. Far be it from me to speak ill of the dead, but –'

Atherton felt Slider's surprise. There had been no official identification given out, no photograph in the press.

'How did you know she was dead, Mrs Gostyn?'

The old woman looked merely surprised. 'The other policeman told me, of course. The one who came before.'

'Before?'

'Tuesday afternoon. Or was it Wednesday? Inspector Petrie he said his name was. A very nice man. I offered him a cup of tea, but he couldn't stop.'

'He came in a police car?'

'Oh no, an ordinary car, like yours. Not a panda car or anything.'

'Did he show you his identification?' Slider tried.

'Of course he did,' she said indignantly. 'Otherwise I

wouldn't have given him the key.'

Atherton made a sound like a moan, and she glanced at him disapprovingly. Slider went on, 'Did he say why he wanted the key?'

'To collect Miss Austen's things. He took them away with him in a bag. I offered him a cup of tea but he said he hadn't time. Thank you very much for asking, though, he said. A very nice, polite man, he was.'

'Shit fire,' Atherton muttered, and Slider quelled him with a glance.

'I'm afraid I don't know this Inspector Petrie,' he said patiently. 'Did he happen to mention to you, Mrs Gostyn, where he came from? Which police station? Or did you see it on his identity card?'

'No, dear, I couldn't see it properly because of not having my reading glasses on, but he very kindly read it out to me, his name, I mean – Inspector Petrie, CID, it said. Such a nice voice – what I'd call a cultured voice, like Alvar Liddell. Unusual these days. Are you telling me there's something wrong with him?'

Atherton intercepted a glance from Slider and headed back to the car radio.

'I'm afraid there may have been some little confusion,' Slider said gently. 'I don't think I know Inspector Petrie. Could you describe him to me?'

'He was a tall man,' she said after some thought. 'Very nicely spoken.'

'Clean-shaven?'

She thought again. 'I think he was wearing a hat. Yes, of course, because he lifted it to me – a trilby. I remember thinking you don't see many men wearing hats these days. I always think a person looks unfinished without a hat on, out of doors.'

Slider changed direction. 'He arrived yesterday – at what time?'

'About two o'clock, I should think it was.'

'And you gave him the key to Miss Austen's flat? Did you go upstairs with him?'

'I did not. It's not my business to be doing that sort of thing, and so I've told Mrs Barclay many a time when she

wanted delivery men letting in. I only keep the keys for the
meter man and emergencies, that's what I've told her,
besides going up and down those stairs, which is too much
for me now, with my leg. Not that I'd give anyone the key,
dear, but I've known the meter man for fifteen years, and if
you can't trust the police, who can you trust?'

'Who indeed,' Slider agreed. 'And did you see him come
down again?'

'I came out when I heard him on the stairs. He was very
quick, only five or ten minutes. He had one of those black
plastic sacks, which he said he'd got Miss Austen's things in.
"To give to her next of kin, Mrs Gostyn," he said, and I
asked him if he'd like a cup of tea, because it's not a nice job
to have to do, is it, even for strangers, but he said no, he had
to go. He said he had everything he needed and touched his
hat to me. Such a nice man.'

'Has anyone else been up there since? Have you been up
there?'

'I have not,' she said firmly. 'And besides, Inspector Petrie
has the key, so I couldn't get in if I wanted to.'

Atherton came back, and spoke to Slider aside through
wooden lips. 'Petrie my arse.'

'I'll go up,' Slider said quietly. 'See if you can get a
description out of her. Don't bully her, or she'll clam up.
And a description of the car.'

'You wouldn't like the registration number, I suppose?'
Atherton enquired ironically, and turned without relish to his
task while Slider went upstairs to lock the stable door.

Mrs Gostyn proved extremely helpful. From her Atherton
learnt that the bogus inspector was a tall, short, fat, thin
man; a fair, dark-haired red-headed bald man in a hat, clean-
shaven with a beard and moustache, wore glasses, didn't
wear glasses, and had a nice speaking voice – she was quite
sure about that much. The car he drove was a car, had four
wheels, and was painted a colour, but she didn't know which
one.

Atherton sighed and turned a page. On the day of the
murder, he learnt, Miss Austen had driven off in her little car
at about nine-thirty in the morning and hadn't returned,
unless it was while Mrs Gostyn was at the chiropodist

between two and four in the afternoon. But her car wasn't there when Mrs Gostyn returned, and she hadn't heard her come in that night.

Atherton put his notebook away again. 'Thank you very much for your help. If you remember anything else, anything at all, you'll let us know, won't you?'

'Anything about what?' Mrs Gostyn asked with apparently genuine puzzlement.

'About Miss Austen or Inspector Petrie – anything that happened on that day. I'll give you this card, look – it has a telephone number where you can reach us, all right?'

He disentangled himself with diminishing patience and went upstairs after Slider, to find that his superior had already opened the flat door and gone in.

'Who needs keys,' he said aloud. 'What was it this time – Barclaycard or Our Flexible Friend?' He examined the lock. It was a very old Yale, and the door had shrunk in its frame, leaving it loose, so that the tongue of the lock was barely retained by the keeper. He shook his head. *Morceau de gateau*, opening that.

The door opened directly into a large attic room furnished both as living-room and bedroom. It was indecently tidy, the bed neatly made. Slider was sitting on it playing back the answering machine, which stood with the telephone on a bedside table.

He looked up as Atherton came in. 'Three clicks, and a female called Only Me saying she'd call back. Get anything from the old lady?'

'Nothing, again nothing. The girl went out in the morning and didn't come back. The rest is silence.'

Slider shook his head. 'She must have come back at some point – there's her violin in the corner.'

Atherton looked. 'Unless she had a spare.'

'Oh. Yes.'

The violin case was propped on its end in the corner of the room nearest the window. In front of it there was a music stand adjusted to standing height, on which stood open a book of practice studies. From a distance the music looked like an army of caterpillars crawling over the page. On the floor was other music scattered as if it had been dropped, and on a low table under the window was yet more, together with a metronome, a box containing a block of resin, two yellow dusters and a large silk handkerchief patterned in shades of brown and purple, three pencils of varying length, a glass ashtray containing an India rubber, six paper clips and a pencil-sharpener, and an octavo-sized manuscript book with nothing written in it at all. It was the only untidy, living, lived-in corner of the flat.

Apart from the bedsitting room there was a kitchen and a bathroom. Together they went over every inch and found nothing. There were clothes in the wardrobe and in drawers, including three black, full-length evening dresses – her working clothes, Atherton explained. There were a few books and a lot of records, and even more audio-tapes, some commercial, some home-made. There were odds and ends and ornaments, a cheap quartz carriage clock, a plaster model of the leaning tower of Pisa, some interesting sea-shells, a nightdress case in the shape of a rabbit, a sugar bowl full of potpourri – but there were no papers. Diary, address book, letters, bills, personal documents, old cheque books – anything that might have given any clue to Anne-Marie's life had been taken.

'He got the lot,' Atherton said, slamming an empty drawer shut. 'Bastard.'

'He was very thorough,' Slider said, 'and yet Mrs Gostyn said he was only here five or ten minutes. I wonder if he knew his way around?'

The bathroom revealed soap, face cloth, towels, spare toilet rolls, bath essence – she seemed to have had a prefer-ence for The Body Shop – and no secrets. The medicine cabinet at first appeared cheeringly full, but it turned out to contain only aspirin, insect repellent, Diocalm, a very large bottle of kaolin and morphia, travel-sickness pills, half a packet of Coldrex, a packet of ten Tampax with one missing, a bottle of Optrex, four different sorts of suntan lotion, and three opened packets of Elastoplast. On the top of the cupboard stood a bottle of TCP, another of Listerine, a spare tube of Mentadent toothpaste, unopened, and right at the back and rather dusty, another packet of Elastoplast.

'No mysterious packages of white powder,' Slider said

sadly. 'No syringe. Not even a tell-tale packet of cigarette papers.'

'But at least we have established some facts,' Atherton said, dusting off his hands. 'We know now that she was female, below menopausal age, travelled abroad, and cut herself a lot.'

'Don't be misled by appearances,' Slider said darkly.

The kitchen was long and narrow, with the usual sort of built-in units along one wall, sink under the window, fridge and gas stove. 'No washing machine,' Atherton said. 'I suppose she used the launderette.'

'Look in the cupboards.'

'I'm looking. Sometimes I dig for buttered rolls. Does it occur to you that we've nothing to go on in this case, nothing at all?'

'It occurs to me.'

There was a good stock of dry goods, herbs and spices, tea and coffee, rice and sugar, but little in the way of fresh food. A bottle of milk in the fridge was open and part-used but still fresh. There were five eggs, two packs of unsalted butter, a wrapped sliced loaf, and a piece of hard cheese wrapped in tin foil.

'She wasn't intending to eat at home that night, at any rate,' said Slider.

As he straightened up the word VIRGIN caught his eye, and he turned towards it. Behind the bread bin in the far corner of the work surface were two tins of olive oil, like diminutive petrol cans. They were brightly, not to say gaudily, decorated in primary colours depicting a rustic scene: goitrous peasants with manic grins were gathering improbable olives the size of avocados, from trees which, if trees could smile, would have been positively hilarious with good health and good will towards the gatherers.

Atherton, following his gaze, read the words on the face of the front tin. 'VIRGIN GREEN – Premium Olive Oil – First Pressing – Produce of Italy.' He pushed the bread bin out of the way. 'Two tins? She must have been fond of Italian food.'

The words set up echoes in Slider's mind of his lunchtime fantasy about her. Coincidence.

'She was,' he said. 'Packets of dried pasta and tubes of tomato purée in the cupboard.'

Atherton gave an admiring look. 'What a detective you'd have made, sir.'

Slider smiled kindly. 'And a lump of Parmesan cheese in the fridge.'

Atherton lifted the second tin and hefted it; unscrewed the lid and peered in, tilting it this way and that, and then applied a nostril to the opening and sniffed. 'Empty. Looks as though it's been washed out, too, or never used. I wonder why she kept it?'

'Perhaps she thought it was pretty.'

'You jest, of course.' He turned it round. 'Virgin Green, indeed. It sounds like a film title. Science fiction, maybe. Or pornography – but we know she wasn't interested in pornography.'

'Do we?' Slider said incautiously.

'Of course. She didn't have a pornograph.'

Slider wandered back into the living-room and stared about him, his usual anxious frown deepening between his brows. Atherton stood in the doorway and watched him. 'I don't think we're going to find anything. It all looks very professional.'

'Somebody went to a lot of trouble,' Slider said. 'There must have been something very important they didn't want us to know about. But what?'

'Drugs,' said Atherton, and when Slider looked at him, he shrugged. 'Well, it always is these days, isn't it?'

'Yes. But I don't think so. This doesn't smell that way to me.'

Atherton waited for enlightenment and didn't get it. 'Have you got a hunch, guv?' he asked. No answer. 'Or is it just the way you stand?'

But Slider merely grunted. He walked across to the music corner, the only place with any trace of Anne-Marie's personality about it, and picked up the violin case, sat down on the bed with it across his knees, opened it. The violin glowed darkly against the electric-blue plush of the lining with the unmistakable patina of age. It looked warm and somehow alive, inviting to the touch, like the rump of a well-groomed bay horse. In the rests of the lid were slung two violin bows, and behind them was tucked a snapshot. Slider pulled it out and turned it to the light to examine it.

It was taken on a beach in some place where the sun was hot enough to make the shadows very short and underfoot. A typical amateur holiday snapshot, featuring the shoulder and flank of a lean young man in bathing-trunks disappearing out of the edge of the picture, and Anne-Marie in the centre in a red bikini, one hand resting on the anonymous shoulder. She was laughing, her eyes screwed up with amusement and sea-dazzle, her head tilted back so that her dark bob of hair fell back from her throat. Her other hand was flung out – to balance her, perhaps – and was silhouetted sharply against the dark-blue sea in the background like a small, white starfish. She looked as though she hadn't a care in the world; her youthful innocence seemed the epitome of what being young ought to be like, and so seldom was.

Slider stared at it hungrily, trying to blot out the memory of her small abandoned body lying dead in that grim and dingy, empty flat. *Murdered.* But why? The white starfish hand, pinned for ever against time in that casual snapshot, had rested finally against the old and splintered wood of those dusty floorboards. She was so young and pretty. What could she possibly have known or done to warrant her death? Not fair, not fair. She laughed at him out of the photograph, and he had only ever known her dead.

One thing he was sure about – there was an organisation behind her death. That was bad news for him: if they were good, they'd have second-guessed him all the way along the line. But however good they were, they would have made one mistake. A benign God saw to that – one mistake, to give the good guys a chance, that was the rule. There was a good sensible reason for it, of course – that the criminals were working to a finite time-scale, and the investigators had for ever more to investigate – but Slider believed in a benign God anyway. He had to, to make sense of his world at all.

Atherton had evinced no interest in the photograph, but was staring intently at the violin. He took it from the case and turned it over carefully, and then said hesitantly, 'Guv?'

Slider looked up. 'I think this violin might be something rather special.'

'What do you mean?'

'I'm no expert, but it's got A. Stradivarius written on it.'

Slider stared. 'You mean it's a Stradivarius?'

Atherton shrugged. 'I said I'm no expert.'

'It might be a fake.'

'It might. But if it were genuine –'

Slider noticed, as he had noticed before, how even under stress Atherton's grammar did not desert him. 'Yes, if it were,' he agreed.

One mistake. Could this be it?

'Take it. Find out,' he said. 'Find out what it's worth. But for God's sake be careful with it.'

'Tell your grandmother,' Atherton said, replacing it with awed hands. 'What now?'

'I'm going to see her best friend. You realise we still don't have a next of kin, thanks to Inspector Petrie? So it's the Barbican for me.'

'Wouldn't you like me to go for you? Concert halls are more my province than yours.'

'It'll be good for me to widen my experience,' Slider said. 'Rôle reversal.'

'That's dangerous,' said Atherton. 'The filling might fall out.'

5

Utterly Barbicanned

Slider left his car in the Barbican car park and immediately got lost. He had heard tales of how impossible it was to find your way around in there, and had assumed they were exaggerated. He found a security guard and asked directions, was sent through some swing doors and got lost again. He entered a lift which had been designed, disconcertingly, only to stop at alternate floors, and eventually, with a sense of profound relief, emerged into the car park where he had begun. At least now I know where I am, he thought, even if I don't know where I've just been.

He was contemplating his next move when the sound of footsteps made him turn, and he saw a woman coming towards him carrying a violin case. His heart lifted, and he went towards her like an American tourist in London who has just spotted the Savoy Hotel.

'Are you a member of the Orchestra? Can you tell me how to get to the backstage area from here?'

She stopped and looked at him – looked up at him in fact, for she was about six inches shorter than him, which made Slider, who was not a tall man, feel agreeably large and powerful.

'I can't tell you, but I can take you,' she said pleasantly. 'It is a rabbit warren, isn't it? Did you know it's even given rise to a new verb – to be Barbicanned?'

'I'm not surprised,' Slider said, falling in beside her as she set off with brisk steps.

'They ought to issue us with balls of thread really. I only

know one route, and I stick to it. One diversion, and I'd never be found again.' She glanced sideways at him. 'I'm not actually a member of the Orchestra, but I'm playing with them today. You're not a musician, are you.'

It was plainly a statement, not a question. Slider merely said no, without elaborating, and continued to examine her covertly. Though small she had a real figure, proper womanly curves which he knew were not fashionable but which, being married to a thin and uncommodious woman, he liked the look of. She was dressed in white trousers, pale blue plimsolls, a blue velvet bomber jacket, and a teeshirt horizontally striped in pale- and dark-blue. Her clothes were attractive on her, but seemed somehow eccentric, though he couldn't quite decide why. It made it difficult to deduce anything about her.

She led him through a steel door in the concrete wall and down a flight of stairs of streaked and dimly lit desolation. On the landing she suddenly stopped and looked up at him.

'I say, I've just realised – I bet you're looking for me anyway. Are you Inspector Slider?'

She regarded him with bright-eyed and unaffected friendliness, something he had rarely come across since becoming a policeman. Her face was framed with heavy, rough-cut gold hair which looked as though it might have been trimmed with hedge-cutters, and he suddenly realised what it was about her that made her seem eccentric. Her clothes were youthful, her face innocent of make-up, her whole appearance casual and easy and confident, and yet she was not young. He had never seen a woman of her age less disguised or protected against the critical eyes of the world. And framed by a background of as much squalor as modern building techniques could devise, she gazed at him without hostility or even reserve, with the calm candour of a child, as if she simply wanted to know what he was like.

'You're Joanna Marshall,' he heard himself say.

'Of course,' she said, as if it were very much of course, and held out her hand with such an air of being ready to give him all possible credit that he took it and held it as though this were a social meeting. Warmth came back to him along the line of contact, and pleasure; their eyes met with that particular meeting which is never arrived at by design, and which changes everything that comes afterwards.

As simple as that? he thought with a distant but profound sense of shock. The moment seemed scaffolded with the awareness of possibility – or, well, to be honest, of probability, which was infinitely more disturbing. Like the blind stirring of something under the earth at the first approach of the change of season, he felt all sorts of sensations in him turning towards her, and he let go of her hand hastily. At once the staircase seemed more dank and dreary than ever.

She resumed the downward trot and he hurried after her. 'How did you know who I was?' he asked.

'Sue Bernstein phoned me. She said you'd probably want to talk to me. I knew you weren't a musician of course. Come to think of it, I suppose you do look like a detective.'

'What does a detective look like?' he asked, amused.

She flicked a glance at him over her shoulder, smiling. 'Oh, I hadn't any preconceived ideas about it. It's just that now I see you, I know.'

She shouldered through another pair of steel doors, and then another, and suddenly they were back in civilization: lights, sounds, and the smell of indoors.

She stopped and rounded on him again. 'It's so terrible about Anne-Marie. I suppose there's no doubt that it is her? I simply can't believe she's dead.'

'There's no doubt,' he said, and showed her one of the mugshots. She took it flinchingly, fearing God-knew-what sketch of carnage. Her first glance registered relief, her second a deeper distress. Few people in this modern, organised world ever see a corpse, or even the picture of a corpse. After a moment she drew a sigh.

'I see,' she said. 'Sue said it was murder. Is that true?'

'I'm afraid so.'

She frowned. 'Look, I want to help you, of course, but I've got to get changed and warm up, and I've only just got time. But I'm only on in the first piece – can you wait? Or come back a bit later? I should be finished by a quarter past eight – then I'll be free and I can talk to you for as long as you like.'

As long as you like. She looked up at him again, straight into the eyes. This directness of hers, he thought, was very disturbing. It was childlike, though there was nothing childish about her. It was something outside the range of his normal experience, and made him feel both exposed and off-balance – as if she were of a different species, or from a parallel universe where, despite appearance, the laws of physics were unnervingly different.

'I'll wait,' he said. 'Perhaps I could take you to supper afterwards,' he heard himself add. What in God's name was he doing?

'Oh, that would be lovely,' she said warmly. 'Look, I must dash. Why don't you go in and listen? The auditorium's through that door there.'

'Won't I need a ticket?'

'No, it won't be full, and no-one ever checks. Just slip through and sit somewhere near the side, and then at the end of the first piece come back through here, and I'll meet you here when I've changed again.'

She was a quick changer; and at half past eight they were sitting down in an Italian restaurant nearby. The tablecloths and napkins were pale pink, and there were huge parlour palms everywhere, one of which shielded them nicely from the other diners as they sat opposite each other at a corner table. She moved the little lamp to one side to leave the space clear between them, put her elbows on the table, and waited for his questions.

Close to her, he wondered again about her age. Clearly she was quite a bit older than Anne-Marie: there were lines about her eyes, and the moulding of experience in her face. Yet because she wore no make-up and no disguise, she seemed younger; or, well, perhaps not really younger, but without age – ageless. It troubled him, and he took a moment to ask himself why, but he could only think it was because if she asked him a question about himself, he would feel obliged to tell her the truth – the real truth, as opposed to the social truth. And then, this immediacy of hers made him feel as though there were no barrier between them and that touching her, which he was beginning to want very much to do, was not only possible, but inevitable.

He had better not follow that train of thought. He got a grip on himself.

'I suppose we must make a start somewhere. Do you know of anyone who would have reason to want to kill your friend Anne-Marie?'

'I've been thinking about that, of course, and I honestly don't. Actually, I can't imagine why anyone would ever want to kill anyone. Death is so surprising, isn't it? And murder doubly so.'

'Would you have found suicide less surprising?'

'Oh yes,' she said at once. 'Not because I had any reason to think she was contemplating it, but one can always find reasons to hate oneself. And one's own life is so much more accessible. Murder, though –' she paused. 'It's such an affront, isn't it?'

'I'd never really thought of it like that.'

'It must be awful for you,' she said suddenly, and he was surprised.

'Worse for you, surely?'

'I don't think so. I have no responsibility about it, as you have. And then, because I only knew her alive, I'll remember her that way. You only ever saw her dead – no comfort there.'

Why in the world did she think he needed comforting? he thought; and then, more honestly, amended it to how did she know he needed comforting?

'Who were her friends?' he asked.

'Well, I suppose I was her closest friend, though really, I can't say I knew her very intimately. We shared a desk, so we used to hang about together while we were working. I went to her flat once or twice, and we went to the pictures a couple of times. She hadn't been with the Orchestra long, and she was a private sort of person. She didn't make friends easily.'

'What about friends outside the Orchestra?'

'I don't know. She never mentioned any.'

'Boyfriends?'

She smiled. 'I can tell you don't know about orchestra life. Female players can't have boyfriends. The hours of work prevent us from mixing with ordinary mortals, and getting together with someone in the Orchestra is fatal.'

'Why?'

'Because of the talk. You can't get away from each other, and everyone bitches and gossips, and it's horribly incestuous. Men are much more spiteful than women, you know – and censorious. If a woman goes out with someone in the Orchestra, everyone knows all about it at once, and then she gets called filthy names, and all the other men think she's easy meat – just as if women never discriminate at all.'

'But Anne-Marie was very attractive. Surely some of the men must have made passes at her?'

'Yes, of course. They do that with any new woman joining.'

'And she rejected them?'

'She had a thing going with Simon Thompson on tour last year, but tours are a different matter: the normal rules are suspended, and what happens there doesn't count as real life. And I think she may have gone out with Martin Cutts once or twice, but that doesn't count either. He's just something everyone has to go through at some point, like chickenpox.'

Slider suppressed a smile and wrote the names down. 'I see.'

'Do you?'

He looked into her face, wondering how she had coped with the situation. She had said those things about being a female player without bitterness, merely matter-of-fact, as though it were something like the weather than could not be altered. But did she know those things from first-hand experience?

She smiled as though she had read his thoughts and said, 'I have my own way of dealing with things. I'll tell you one day.'

The waiter came with their first course, and they waited in silence until he had gone away. Then Slider said, 'So you were Anne-Marie's only friend?'

'Mmm.' She made an equivocal sound through her mouthful, chewed, swallowed, and said, 'She didn't confide in me particularly, but I suppose I was the person in the Orchestra who was closest to her.'

'Did you like her?'

She hesitated. 'I didn't dislike her. She was a hard person

to get to know. She was quite good company, but of course we talked a lot about work, and that was mostly what we had in common. I felt rather sorry for her, really. She didn't strike me as a happy person.'

'What were her interests?'

'I don't know that she had any really, outside of music. Except that she liked to cook. She was a good cook –'

'Italian food?'

'How did you know?'

'I was at her flat today. There were packets of pasta, and two enormous tins of olive oil.'

'Oh yes, the dear old green virgins. That was one of her fads – she said you had to have exactly the right kind of olive oil for things to taste right, and she wouldn't use any other sort. The stuff was lethally expensive, too. I don't suppose anyone else could've told the difference, but she was very knowledgeable about Italian cooking. I think she was part Italian herself,' she added vaguely.

'Was she? Did you ever meet her parents?'

'Both dead,' she said succinctly. 'I think she said they died when she was a baby, and an aunt brought her up. I never met the aunt. I don't think they got on. Anne-Marie used to go and visit her once in a while, but I gathered it was a chore rather than a pleasure.'

'Brothers and sisters? Any other relatives?'

'She never mentioned any. I gather she had rather a lonely childhood. She went to boarding school, I think because the aunt didn't want her around the house. I remember she told me once that she hated school holidays because her aunt would never let her have friends home to play in case they made a mess. Wouldn't let her have a pet, either. One of those intensely houseproud women, I suppose – hell to live with, especially for a child. Have you spoken to her yet?'

'I didn't know until this moment that she existed. We asked your Mrs Bernstein, but she didn't know who the next of kin was.'

'No, I suppose she wouldn't,' she said thoughtfully. 'I suppose if it was me instead of Anne-Marie, it would be just the same. So the aunt won't know yet, even that Anne-Marie's dead?'

Slider shook his head. 'I suppose you don't know her name and address?'

'Oh dear! Did she ever tell me her aunt's name? I know she lived in a village called Stourton-on-Fosse, somewhere in the Cotswolds. The house was called something like The Grange or The Manor, I can't remember exactly. But Anne-Marie said it was a large house, and the village is tiny, so you ought to be able to find it easily enough. Wait a minute,' she frowned, 'I think I saw the name on an envelope once. Now what was it? I was going to the post box and she asked me to post it along with mine.' She thought for a moment, screwing up her eyes. 'Ringwood. Yes, that was it – Mrs Ringwood.'

She looked at him delightedly, as though waiting for praise or applause, but their main course arrived and distracted her.

'Mm,' she said, sniffing delightedly. 'Lovely garlic! You could give me matchboxes to eat as long as you fried them in garlic. I hope you like it?'

'I love it,' he said.

Long, long ago in his youth, before Real Life had happened to him, he had cooked for Irene on a grease-encrusted, ancient and popping gas stove in their little flat; and he had used garlic – and onions and herbs and wine and spices and ginger – and food had been an immediate and sensuous pleasure. So it still was, he could see, for Joanna. She seemed very close to him, and warm, and what he felt towards her was so basic it seemed earth-movingly profound. He wanted to take hold of her, to have her, to make good, wholesome, tiring love to her, and then to sleep with her all night with their bodies slotted down together like spoons. But did anything so simple and good happen in Real Life? To anyone?

Under the table he had a truly amazing erection, and it couldn't be entirely because of the garlic. He saw with an agony of disappointment what life could be like with the right person. He imagined waking up beside her, and having her again, warm and sleepy in the early morning quiet; eating with her and sleeping with her and filling her up night after night with himself. Just being together in that uncluttered way, like two animals, no questions to answer and none to ask. He wanted to walk with her hand in hand along some bloody beach in the sunset, with or without the soaring music.

The erection didn't go down, but the pressure seemed to even itself out, so that he could adjust to it, like adjusting to travelling at speed, all reactions sharpened. He watched her eating not only with desire, but also, surprisingly, with affection. He could see how the rough, heavy locks of her hair were like those sculpted on the bronze head of a Greek hero, soft and dense, pulling straight of their own weight. She ate with simple attention, and when she looked up at him she smiled, as if that were something obvious and easy, and then all her attention was on him.

She put out her hand for her wine glass, and almost before he knew what he had done, he intercepted it across the table. To his astonished relief, her warm fingers curled happily round his and returned his pressure, and the situation resolved itself simply and gracefully, like crystals forming at crystallising point. Nothing to worry about. He released her and they both went on eating, and Slider felt as though he were flying, and was utterly astonished at himself, that he could have done such a thing.

In the interval between the main course and dessert he went to the telephone to ring the station, and spoke to Hunt, who was Duty Officer.

'I've got a next of kin in the Austen case,' he said, and relayed the information about Mrs Ringwood. 'Can you put a trace on that, and get one of the local blokes to go round and inform her. She'll have to formally ID the body. And then we can have the inquest. Would you tell Atherton to get onto it first thing in the morning?'

'Righto, guv,' said Hunt.

'Also I want him to get Mrs Gostyn in to make a statement and see if she can help us put together a photofit of this Inspector Petrie.'

'Okay, sir. Anything else?'

There was, but not for his ears. 'Is Nicholls on the desk? Put me through to him will you?'

To Nicholls he said, 'Listen, Nutty – will you ring Irene for me, and tell her not to wait up. I've got a lot of interviews to do, and I won't be back until very late.'

'Sure I'll tell her,' he said, but with the end of the sentence clearly open for the unspoken words *but she'll not believe it.*

'Thanks, mate.'

'Okay Bill. Cheeroh. Be careful, won't you?'

That, thought Slider, was like telling a man about to go over Niagara Falls in a barrel not to get his feet wet.

'Tell me about that last evening,' he said over the profiteroles.

'We were on until nine-thirty at the Television Centre. We packed up –'

'Did you finish on time?'

She smiled. 'You bet. Otherwise they have to pay us overtime. We're fierce about that. We packed up – that would take five minutes or so – and then I'd arranged with a couple of the others – Phil Redcliffe and John Delaney and Anne-Marie – to go for a drink.'

'Which pub did you use?' he asked, having a sudden dread that it would be The Dog and Scrotum, which after all was the nearest pub to the TVC.

'We always go to The Crown and Sceptre – it's Fullers, you see,' she said simply, and he nodded. For a beer-drinker, it was that simple. 'As I was going out, Simon Thompson asked me if I was going for a drink, and I said yes but Anne-Marie was coming, and he said in that case he didn't want to come, and that delayed me a bit –'

'Why didn't he want to come if she was going?' Slider interrupted.

'They'd been having a bit of trouble.' She grimaced. 'Look, I don't want you to make too much of this, but I'll tell you about it, because *someone* will, so it had better be me. I told you Anne-Marie and Simon had been together on tour?'

'Yes, you did. Do you mean they were having an affair?'

'Oh, it didn't really amount to that. Being on tour is sort of like fainlights –' She demonstrated the crossed fingers of childhood games. 'It doesn't really count. People sleep together, go round together, and when they get back to England, it's all forgotten. Anne-Marie and Simon were like that, except that after the last tour in October, to Italy, Anne-Marie tried to carry it on. Simon didn't like that because he's got a permanent girlfriend, and Anne-Marie –' She paused. 'Well, she got a bit funny about it. She insisted that Simon had been serious about her, that they had decided to get married, and that now he was trying to get out of it.'

'Did you believe her?'

'I don't know. There must have been something in it, surely? Simon said she was just making it up, of course, but then he would, wouldn't he? He started saying all sorts of nasty things about her, that she was unbalanced and so on, but I don't know what the truth of it was. Anne-Marie just gave it up after a while and left him alone, but he made a great performance out of not having anything to do with her – changing tables in the coffee-bar if she sat down near him, not going for a drink with a group of us if she was included – that sort of thing.'

'I see,' Slider said encouragingly, hoping that he would. 'How did she seem to you that last day? Did she seem in her normal spirits?'

'I didn't notice really, one way or the other. She'd been a bit quiet since that trouble with Simon – a bit low, you know, withdrawn. As I said, I never thought she was a particularly happy person, and that could only make it worse.'

Slider nodded. 'So you spoke to Simon Thompson, and then what? You went out to your car?'

'Yes. We were all in separate cars, of course. Phil and John had already gone, and with Simon stopping me – oh, and I talked to John Brown as well about something, the fixer, so I was the last one out. Anne-Marie had rushed off when she saw Simon coming. She left her car outside, you know in that narrow bit to the side of the main gate where the Minis and small cars are parked.'

'Yes, I know. Did she drive a Mini?'

'No, she had a red MG – just about the one thing in her life she really loved, that car. Anyway, as I came out, she was just running back across the yard towards me. She said she was glad she'd caught me, and why didn't we go to The Dog and Sportsman instead. That's another pub, along the –'

'I know,' Slider said. I knew it, he thought flatly. I should never have drunk on my own manor.

Joanna eyed him curiously. 'Well, it's a horrible pub, and in any case Phil and John had already gone. I said so, and she seemed quite put out, and tried to persuade me to go to The Dog, just the two of us, but I didn't want to, and in the end she just left me and went back to her car. I went to The Crown and Sceptre, and of course she never showed up. I don't know if eventually she did go to the other pub, or if she – if they –' She stopped.

'Did she say why she wanted to go to the other pub?' Slider asked, not without sympathy.

'No. She didn't give any reason. I've wondered since whether, if we'd gone with her, she might not have been killed. Do you think she could have known something was going to happen to her?'

Slider was thinking. 'At what stage did she change her mind? She was going to The Crown with you? She knew that's where you planned to go?'

'Oh yes, we always went there. And when she left the first time, when she went out to her car, she knew that's where we were going. In fact I think when she went past me as I was talking to John Brown she said something like "See you in there".'

'So something happened to make her change her mind when she was outside, going to her car. Did she speak to someone in the car park?'

'I don't know. When I came out she was already running back towards me. The men in the gatehouse might have seen something. There are always two of them on duty, and they'd have been able to see her car from their windows.'

'Yes,' Slider said, and made a note: *Gatekeepers*? and *Ask Hilda*. He looked up. Joanna was staring at him unhappily. 'What is it?'

'Maybe she was afraid, and wanted us to come with her for protection. Maybe if we'd gone with her –'

Slider felt compelled to offer her some comfort. 'I don't think it would have made any difference. I think it would just have happened some other time.'

Her eyes widened as she considered the implications of this. 'I don't think that helps very much,' she said.

The eating and drinking were over. He paid, and they walked out into the street. 'It was a good meal,' he said. 'I like Italian food.' He remembered Anne-Marie like touching a mouth ulcer he'd forgotten.

'You mind, don't you,' Joanna said. 'About Anne-Marie. Why do you? I mean, all murder is dreadful, but you must have seen some horrible cases in your time, worse than this. Why is it different?'

He wanted to ask how she knew, but was afraid of the answer. Instead he said, 'I don't know,' which was unoriginal, but true, and she accepted it at face value.

'I can't feel it much – not continuously. She still doesn't feel dead to me. She was so young, and I always thought her rather silly – not a particularly capable person. Vulnerable. It seems almost like cheating to kill someone so easy to kill.'

They stood looking at each other on the pavement. Now the moment had come, he didn't know how he could possibly ask her. He had no right to. He had nothing to offer – he could only take. But how, otherwise, were they ever to move from this spot? He looked at her helplessly.

'Can you be struck off, like doctors, for fraternising with witnesses?' she asked lightly. She had seen his trouble, and was doing the job for him, making it easy for him either to go on or to go away. He knew how generous that was of her, and yet still he blundered.

'I'm married,' he said – blurted – and he actually saw it hurt her.

'I know that,' she said quietly.

'How do you know?' Now he was simply delaying, evading.

She shrugged. 'You have the look – hungry. Like a man with worms, you eat but it doesn't satisfy you.' She looked at him consideringly, and he was aware painfully that he had put this distance between them, that it was all his fault. 'I even know what she looks like,' she went on. 'Pretty, very slim, smart. Keeps the house spotless, and hasn't much sense of humour.'

'How can you know that?' he said uneasily.

He saw her suddenly tire of it. She had placed everything at his service, and he had been too weak and cowardly to do the right thing, one way or the other. She hitched her bag onto her shoulder and said, 'I'd better be going. Thank you very much for supper.'

Leave it be, let it go. Don't ask for trouble. Life is complicated enough as it is.

'Where do you live?' he gasped. One last breath before going under, one last grasp at the straw. She would say north or south, anything, not west, and that would be that. Let God decide. Yet if she said west, what then? She turned back the little she had turned away, and it seemed an effort, and she looked at him doubtfully, as if she were not sure whether to answer him or not.

'Turnham Green,' she said at last, with no inflection at all.

He licked his lips. 'That's on my way,' he said in a voice like fishbones. 'I live in Ruislip.'

'You can follow me,' she said, 'if you promise not to book me for speeding.'

His stomach went away from him like an express lift and he nodded, and they walked towards their cars, parked nose-to-tail down the side street. Even in his extremity he told himself he was not committed yet, that it would be perfectly easy for him to lose her on the cross-town drive. But of course she knew that too, and it was too late, by several hours at least.

The drive back to Chiswick was long enough for Slider to think of everything and fear everything several times over. It was close to twenty years since he had made love to anyone but Irene, and it was a long time – he paused – good God, was it really over a year? – since he had made love even to her. Large-scale social and moral considerations jostled for space in his cringing mind with mute and ignoble worries about custom, expectation, performance, and even underwear, to the point where desire was suppressed and he could no longer think of any good and sufficient reason to be doing what he was doing at all.

And yet still he followed her, almost automatically, keeping the taillights of her Alfa GTV just two lengths ahead of him, copying her lefts and rights like a colt following its dam, because doing anything else would have involved him in a decision he was no longer capable of making.

They stopped at last, parked, got out of their cars. Hollow excuses formed themselves inside his head, and if she had spoken to him or even looked back at him, he would probably have babbled them and fled. But she had her door key ready in her hand, opened her front door and went in, leaving it open for him, without once looking round, and so he simply followed, as if the moment for making the absolutely definitely final decision had not yet arrived.

Afterwards he wondered how much of his state of mind she had guessed and was making allowance for. Inside the hallway of her flat she was waiting for him. She had not put on the lights or taken off her coat. She had simply put down her bags on the floor, and as he entered the half dark of the passage she put her arms round him inside his coat and lifted her mouth to be kissed.

Slider went tremblingly to pieces. No questions to ask and none to answer. He pulled the female softness against him and was kissing her ravenously, and her mouth and tongue led him with the rightness of a familiar dancing-partner. She moved her pelvis, and he could feel his erection like a rock between them, and he felt distantly, ridiculously proud. She broke off from kissing him at last, but it was only to lead the way into her bedroom beyond, which was lit dimly by the glow from a streetlamp outside – just light enough, and not too much.

There was the bed, a big double, covered by a counterpane. She went round to the far side and sat on the edge with her back to him and began to take off her clothes with neat, economical movements. So they were really going to do it, part of his mind said in amazement. He was glad she was letting him undress himself. His state of mind was so far gone he was no longer sure what he'd got on, or whether he could get it off without fumbling stupidly. By the time he was down to his underpants she had finished, and slid gracefully in under the sheets and looked at him calmly from the pillows.

He pulled in his stomach and took off his pants. The air felt cold on his skin, but his erection felt so huge and hot he half thought it would warm up the room, like an immersion heater. What a ridiculous thing to think, he rebuked himself; but he must have smiled, for she smiled in response and pulled back the covers for him.

After all his fears, it was all so beautifully simple. He lay down beside her, feeling the whole length of her against his body warm and delicious; and before he could start wondering what she would expect of him by way of preliminaries, she drew him onto and into her so easily that he sighed in enormous relief, as if he were coming home. Being in her was both exotic and familiar in such piercing, blissful combination that he knew it could not last long. But it didn't matter – there would be time for everything later. He turned his mouth, nuzzling for hers, and as they connected he felt her lift and close on him, and that was it. He let go gratefully and flooded her as though all of his life he had been saving up for this moment.

Close and far away he heard her sigh 'Ah!' And then they were drifting out together into dark water, clean and complete as if newborn. A long time later she kissed his cheek and lay her face against his neck, and he slid over onto his back and took her in his arms, with her head on his shoulder, and it felt very good. He wanted to tell her he loved her, but he couldn't speak: everything was too vivid, as though all his nerve endings were exposed, and the difference between pleasure and pain was slight. He needed to be silent for a while, to discover whether this new and perilous existence could be sustained.

6

Moth and Behemoth

He woke gently, with that Christmas-Day feeling of something delicious having happened that he had forgotten about while asleep. He moved slightly and felt a responding movement beside him, and knew he was not in his own bed and not alone, and everything came back to him all-of-a-piece. He opened his eyes. In the light from the window he looked at her, curled on her side, sleeping quietly. The covers had slipped off her, and she seemed all made of curves, strongly indented at the waist, richly rounded at breast and hip. Her hair looked soft and heavy as if it were moulded from bullion, too dense to curl, each lock lying separately like the petals of a bronze chrysanthemum.

He reached out a hand to push it from her face and she smiled and moved her face to his hand. He smoothed her eyebrows and the smiling dents at the corners of her mouth, and her face felt pliant and flowing under his fingers as if he could shape her. He felt powerful. The world outside was dark and damp like something newborn, and it was all his. She shivered suddenly, and he drew her to him and pulled the covers over her. She stretched gratefully in the restored warmth, and her hand contacted his penis, and it rose to meet her.

'Hmm?' she enquired gently, her eyes still closed.

'Hmm,' he replied, running his hands over her shoulders and sides. She uncurled like a flower, and he seemed to flow into her effortlessly. This time they took time over it, seeking out pleasure softly, kissing and touching a great deal, and it was unbelievably good, unlike anything he had ever experi-

64

enced before. He was happy and amazed.

'I love you,' he said afterwards, and then got up on his elbows and looked at her to see her reaction.

'Don't you think it's a little early to be saying that?' she asked, amused.

'Is it? I don't know. I've nothing to compare it with. I've never done this before, you know.'

'In that case, I'm very flattered.'

'I wish I'd met you years ago,' he said, as people will at such a moment.

'You wouldn't have liked me,' she said consolingly.

'Of course I would. You must have –' The green, luminous read-out of her bedside clock-radio caught his eye. He turned his head slightly and went cold with shock. 'Christ, it's twenty to seven!'

'Is it?' She didn't seem perturbed by the news.

'It can't be! We can't have slept the whole night through!'

'Not so much of a whole night,' she murmured, and then, seeing he really was upset, 'What's the matter?' But he was off her, rolling to the side of the bed, swinging his legs out, groping on the floor for clothes. She knew what was wrong, and her mouth turned down sourly.

'Christ,' he was muttering, 'that's done it. What the hell do I do now? Jesus.'

She propped herself up to look at him. 'You can't go home now,' she said reasonably. 'You've been out all night, and that's that. Come back to bed for a bit. Seven o'clock is early enough to start making excuses.'

But it was no good: the world had rolled onto him like a stone. All the clean simplicity had been delusion, his omnipotence had fled. There was going to be a row at home, and he was going to have to think of lies to tell. Probably Irene would not believe him, and he was going to feel bad about it whether she did or she didn't.

'Christ,' he muttered. 'Jesus.'

'Take it easy,' she said protestingly.

He shook his head, hunching his shoulders away from her. 'I'll have to make some phone calls,' he said miserably. 'I'm sorry.'

She looked at him a moment longer, and then got quietly

out of bed on the other side, and drew a cotton wrap over her glowing nakedness. 'Phone's beside you. I'll go and make some tea.'

She padded away, and he understood that she didn't want to hear him lying, and that was nearly the worst thing of all. He reached for the phone.

Atherton was a long time answering. 'I was in the shower. What's up? You're up early.'

'Actually, I haven't been to bed yet.'

'What?'

'Not my own bed. I've been out all night.'

There was a short and horrible silence. Then, 'I'm not hearing straight. Please tell me you don't mean what I think you mean.'

Slider could tell from his tone of voice that he really didn't think that's what it was, and the knowledge depressed him even further.

'I've been with Joanna Marshall. I'm at her place now.'

Another, slightly worse silence. 'Christ, guv, you don't mean –'

'I took her out for supper last night, and then –' No possible way of ending that sentence. Slider grew irritable with guilt. 'Oh, for God's sake, I don't have to draw you pictures, do I? You can use your imagination. You've done it yourself often enough.'

'Yes, but I –'

'The thing is, I've got to tell Irene something. Can I tell her I was with you?'

'Oh great.' Atherton's voice hardened. 'She'll love me after that.'

'I don't think she likes you much anyway. It can't make any difference. Please. I'll ring her up and say we were working late at your house, and we had a few drinks, and it got too late to come home.'

'Why didn't you phone her from my place?'

'Oh God – it got too late, I thought she'd have gone to bed and I didn't want to wake her.'

'Jesus, is that the best you can do?'

'What the hell else can I say? Come on, for God's sake, back me up.'

'All right,' Atherton said shortly. 'But I don't like it. It's not like you, either. What's got into you?'

'Every dog has its day,' Slider said weakly. 'I mean, messing around with a witness –'

'She's not a material witness. For God's sake, what does it matter? It's going to be bad enough facing Irene – don't you give me a hard time as well.'

'All right, all right, don't bite me! I'll say whatever you want. I'm just worried for you, that's all.'

'Thanks. I'm sorry.'

'Take it easy.' The concern was naked in his voice. 'You going to phone Irene now? You going home?'

The idea made Slider shudder. 'I think it's best not to. I'll go down and talk to the next of kin – the aunt in the Cotswolds. Will you do the paperwork for me? You got my messages last night?'

'Yeah. Okay. I'll get old Mother Gostyn in this morning, and check out John Brown. And I thought I'd take the violin down to Sotheby's.'

'Good. And you might see if you can get hold of Anne-Marie's ex-boyfriend, this Simon Thompson type.'

'Okay. Will I see you later?'

'Depends what comes up. I'll phone you, anyway.'

'Right.' A pause. 'Are you taking her with you?'

The idea flooded Slider's brain with its bright originality. 'Well, I – yes, I thought I might.'

He heard Atherton sigh. 'Well – be careful, won't you, guv?'

'Of course,' he said stiffly, and put the phone down. Joanna came in with a mug of tea.

'Finished?'

'That was Atherton, my sergeant. He said he'll – back me up. You know.'

'Oh.' She turned her head away.

'But now I've got to –'

'I'll go and run my bath,' she said abruptly and left him again, her face expressionless. And that was the easy part, he thought, dialling his own number.

Irene picked it up at the second ring. 'Bill?'

'Hullo. Did I wake you up?'

'Where are you? What's happened? I've been worried sick!'

'I've been with Atherton, at his flat. Didn't Nicholls phone you?'

'He phoned yesterday evening to say you'd be late, that's all. He didn't say you wouldn't be home at all. How late can you be, interviewing witnesses? What were they, night workers?'

Her anger was at least easier to deal with than hurt or worry. He felt guiltily grateful.

'They were musicians and they were giving a concert and we had to wait until they'd finished. Then Atherton and I went over some of the statements. We had a couple of drinks and – well, I didn't think I'd better drive.'

'Why the hell didn't you *phone*? I didn't know what had happened to you. You might have been dead.'

'Oh, darling – it got late, and we hadn't noticed the time. I thought you'd have gone to bed. I didn't want to wake you up –'

'I wasn't asleep. How do you think I could sleep, not knowing where you were? I don't care what time it was, you should have phoned!'

'I'm sorry. I just didn't want to disturb you. I'll know another time,' Slider said unhappily.

'You're a selfish bastard, you know that? Anything might have happened to you, with your job. I just sit at home wondering if I'm ever going to see you again, if some madman hasn't gone for you with a knife –'

'They'd have got in touch with you if anything had happened to me.'

'Don't joke about it, you bastard!' He said nothing. After a moment she went on in a lower voice, 'I know what it was – you and that bloody Atherton got drunk, didn't you?'

'We just had a couple of scotches –' He tried not to let the relief show in his voice as the danger disappeared up a side track. Let her go on thinking that was it!

'Don't tell me! I hate that man – he's always trying to set you against me. I know how you two go on when you're together – telling smutty stories and giggling like stupid little boys. You don't realise how he's holding you back. If it wasn't for him, you'd have been promoted long ago.'

'Oh come on, darling –'

'Don't darling me,' she said, but he could hear that the heat was going out of her voice. The new, sharp-edged grievance had been put aside for the old, dulled one. 'You should be a chief inspector by now – everyone knows that. Your precious bloody Atherton knows that. He's jealous of you – that's why he tries to hold you back.'

Slider ignored that. He made his voice as sensible and man-to-man as he could. 'Look, darling, I'm sorry you were worried, and I promise I'll phone if it ever happens again. But I'll have to go now – I've got a hell of a lot to do today.'

'Aren't you coming home to change?'

'I'll make do as I am. The shirt I've got on isn't too bad, and I'll get a shave at the station.'

The domestic details seemed to soothe her. 'I suppose it's no use asking you what time you'll be home tonight?'

'I'll try not to be late, but I can't promise. You know what it's like.'

'Yes, I know what it's like,' she said ironically, but she had accepted it. She had accepted it all. The boat had righted itself again. He rang off, and found himself sweating, despite the cold air of January.

He felt rather sick. So this was what it was like. He thought of the thousands of men there must be to whom such lying and dissembling were part of normal, everyday life, and wondered how they ever got used to it. And yet he had just coped, hadn't he? Coped well. Lied like an expert, and got away with it, and felt relief when she'd swallowed it. Self-disgust reached its peak. Perhaps all men were born with the ability, he thought. Well, he knew what they knew now.

The peak passed. He listened and heard water splashing somewhere, and thought of Joanna, and at once the distress of the phone calls dropped off him cleanly, leaving no mark. He thought of making love to her, and heat ran under his skin. We can spend the whole day together, if she's not working. Oh pray she's not working! A whole day with her –!

That was the other half of it, wasn't it? And it was the fact that they could exist in complete isolation from each other that made the whole thing possible. What absolute shits we are, he thought, but it was without any real conviction. Oh pray she's not working today! And that she's got a razor in her bathroom with a half-way decent blade. He got up and padded in the direction of the splashing.

The man from Sotheby's, Andrew Watson, apart from being tall, slim, blond, and impeccably suited, was also possessed of that unmistakably upper-class beauty that stems from generations of protein diet and modern sanitation. It gave him the air of possessing youth and wisdom in equal, incompatible proportions. Actually, he couldn't possibly be as young as he looked, and be as senior as he was. Atherton's upbringing in Weybridge and his grammar-school education were weighing heavily on him. He felt, by comparison, as huge and ungainly as a behemoth. He saw himself looming dangerously over the other man as if he might crush him underfoot like a butterfly. And Andrew Watson's aftershave was so expensively subtle that for some time Atherton put it down to imagination.

All that apart, however, he was quite endearingly excited by the violin, the more endearingly because Atherton guessed he wanted to display only a calm, professional interest. After a long and careful examination, prolonged conference with a colleague, and reference to a book as thick as an eighteenth-century Bible, Watson seemed prepared to go over every inch of the fiddle again with a magnifying glass, and Atherton stirred restively. He had other things to do. And he wanted to be around when Mrs Gostyn was brought in. There had been no reply from her telephone that morning, so Atherton had arranged for one of the uniformed men to go round and fetch her.

At last Watson came back to him. 'May I ask where you obtained this instrument, sir?'

'You may ask, but I'm not at liberty to tell you,' Atherton replied. It was catching, that sort of thing. 'Is it, in fact, a Stradivarius?'

'It is indeed, and a valuable one – a very valuable one. My colleague agrees with me that this is a piece made by Antonio Stradivari in Cremona in 1707, which has always been known by the name of La Donna – The Lady,' he translated kindly. Atherton nodded gravely.

'There is, as you see, a particular grain to the wood forming the back of the instrument, which is very unusual and distinctive,' Watson went on, turning it over to demonstrate. Atherton looked, saw nothing very distinguishable, and nodded again. Watson resumed. 'The piece was very well known, and its history is well documented right up to the Second World War, when it disappeared, as so many treasures did, during the Nazi occupation of Italy. Since then there's been a great deal of speculation as to its fate, naturally. It would be of great interest –' his voice took on an urgency '– not just to me personally, but to the world, to know how it has come to light again.'

Atherton shook his head. 'If I could tell you, I would. You're quite sure this is the genuine thing?'

'Oh, quite! There are many features which make it unique. For instance, if you look at the scroll, here –'

'I'm happy to take your word for it,' Atherton said hastily.

Watson looked hurt. 'You can, of course, ask for a second opinion. I could recommend –'

'I'm sure that isn't necessary,' Atherton smiled politely, trying not to overshadow him with his colossal, Viking bulk. 'Can you give me an estimate of its value?'

'With a piece of this importance, it's always hard to say. It would depend entirely on who was at the auction, and there are often great surprises when rarities like this come to be sold. Prices can go far beyond expectations. But if you were to ask me to place it at auction for you, I should recommend that you put it in with a reserve price of at least seven or eight hundred thousand.'

'*Pounds?*'

'Oh yes. We don't deal in guineas any more.' Watson regained his composure as Atherton lost his. 'You must understand that this is a very rare and important instrument. And it's in beautiful condition, I'm glad to say.' He ran a hand over it with the affection of a true connoisseur, and then raised his speedwell eyes to Atherton's face. 'In fact it could easily fetch over a million. If you ever do come to sell it, I should feel privileged to handle the sale for you. And if you ever feel able to divulge its history, I should be extremely grateful.' Atherton said nothing, and Watson sighed and placed the violin gently in its case. 'It's a shock to see such a beautiful instrument lying in this horrible case – and with these horrible bows. I hope no-one ever tried to play it with one of them.'

Atherton was interested. 'You think the bows – incongruous?' He chose the word with care.

'I can't believe any true musician would ever touch this violin with either of them,' Watson said with simple faith.

'I didn't know there were good bows and bad ones.'

'Oh yes. And good bows are becoming quite an investment these days. I'm not as well up on them as I ought to be, I'm afraid – they're a study in themselves. If you wanted to know about bows, you should go and see Mr Saloman of Vincey's – Vincey's the antiquarian's, a few doors down in Bond Street. Mr Saloman is probably the leading authority in the country on bows. I'm sure he'd love to see this violin, too.'

'Thank you, Mr Watson,' Atherton said, restraining the urge to press his hand lovingly, and took his massive bulk and the Stradivarius out of Mr Watson's life.

First he went to find a phone and call the station. Mackay answered from the CID room to say that there was still no reply from Mrs Gostyn's telephone or door. Atherton felt a stirring of anxiety.

'Tell them to keep trying, will you? An old bird like her can't have gone far. She's bound to be back some time soon. I'll ring in from time to time and see if you've got her.'

He was then free to keep his appointment with John Brown, the Orchestra's personnel manager – a rosy, chubby man in his forties, with the flat and hostile eyes of the ageing homosexual. He received Atherton impassively, but with a faint air of affront, like a cat at the vet's, as of one on whom life heaps ever more undeserved burdens.

'She hadn't long been with us. She came from the Birmingham,' he said, as though thus dissociating himself from the business.

'Where in Birmingham?' Atherton asked ingenuously.

Brown looked scornful. 'It's an orchestra – the

Birmingham Municipal Orchestra. She'd been there about three years. They could tell you more about her personal life than I could,' he added with a sniff.

'Had she any particular friends in the Orchestra?'

Brown shrugged. 'She hung around with Joanna Marshall and her lot, but then they shared a desk, so what would you expect? Most of them stay with their own sections in coffee-breaks and so on. I don't think she was particularly chummy with anyone. Not the chummy sort. Out of hours, I couldn't tell you *what* she got up to.'

'Did she drink a lot? Take drugs – pot or anything like that? Was she ever in any kind of trouble?'

'How should I know?' Brown said, turning his head away.

'You didn't like her, did you?' Atherton asked, woman to woman.

'I neither liked her nor disliked her,' Brown said with dignity, refusing the overture. 'She was a good player, and no less reliable than the rest of them. That was the only way in which her personality could interest me in the slightest. I'm not paid to like them, you know.'

'What do you mean, no less reliable? Less reliable than whom?'

'Oh, they're always wanting releases to do outside work. With her it was wanting to go back and play for her old orchestra. They're all like that these days – greedy. No loyalty. Never think about how much work it makes for everyone else. She used to go up there at least once a month, and frankly I'm surprised they wanted her. I mean there must have been plenty of other extras they could have used, locally. She wasn't so wonderful no-one else would do.'

Atherton let this sink in, unable yet to make anything of it. 'Did she have a boyfriend? Someone in the Orchestra, perhaps?' he asked next.

Brown shrugged again. 'I imagine so. They all have the morals of alley cats.'

'What, musicians?'

'Women,' he spat, his face darkening. 'I don't like females in the Orchestra, I'll tell you that for nothing. They're troublemakers. They go round making factions and setting one against the other, whispering behind people's backs.

And if you say anything to them, they start crying, and you have to lay off them. Discipline goes to pieces. We never had any of that kind of trouble before we started taking in females. But of course,' he sneered, 'it's the *law* now. We're not allowed to keep them out.'

Atherton's expression was schooled to impassivity. 'But wasn't there someone in particular?' he insisted. 'Some man in her section?'

The eyes slid away sideways. 'I suppose you mean Simon Thompson? They were together on tour, once. You should ask him about that, not me. It's not my business.'

'Thanks, I will.' Doesn't like women, Atherton thought. What else? 'When did you last see Miss Austen?'

'At the Centre on Monday of course. You know that.'

'Yes, but exactly when? Did you see her leave, for instance?'

'I didn't see her leave the building, if that's what you mean. I was standing at the door of the studio handing out payslips. I gave her hers, and that's the last I saw of her. By the time I'd left the building they'd all gone.'

'How are they paid? Direct into the bank?'

'Yes – I just give out the notifications.'

'How much did she earn? I suppose you'd know that, wouldn't you?'

'I have the computer read-out, if you want to look at it. I wouldn't know offhand. They're all self-employed, and paid by the session, so it varies in any case from month to month, depending on how much work there is.'

'So if it was a quiet month, they'd all be a bit short?'

'Not necessarily. They all do work outside, for other orchestras. They might get other dates if we have no work.'

Brown brought forth the green striped paper, put it down on the table and flicked through it rapidly and efficiently.

'Here you are – Austen, A. Last month she grossed £812.33.'

'Was that about average?'

'I couldn't say. We were fairly busy last month, but it wasn't the best month of the year. There are always gaps around Christmas.'

Atherton calculated. So she was earning between ten and

twelve thousand a year – not enough to have bought a Stradivarius, anyway, not even on the lay-away plan. It looked as though she must have been into some pretty big shit to have come by it. Over Brown's shoulder he took down the details of Anne-Marie's bank account and, watching his face from the corner of his eye, asked casually, 'Do you know what sort of violin she played?'

The reaction was one of simple, mild surprise. 'I've no idea. Joanna Marshall would probably know, if it's important to you.'

Well, if the Strad was the key to all this, Brown didn't know about it. 'Okay – so you gave Miss Austen her pay-slip, and that's the last time you ever saw her?'

The sulkiness returned. 'I've told you so.'

'And what did you do afterwards, as a matter of routine?'

'I went home and went to bed.'

'Is there anyone who can confirm that? Do you live here alone?'

The sulkiness was replaced by a dull anger – or was it apprehension? 'I share the flat, as it happens. My flatmate can tell you what time I got in.'

'Your flatmate?'

'Yes.' He spat the word. 'Trevor Byers is his name. You might have heard of him – he's the consultant orthopaedic surgeon at St Mary's. Is that respectable enough for you?'

Oho, thought Atherton, writing it down, is that how the milk got into the coconut? 'Eminently so,' he said, trying to goad him a little more. He decided to try the old by-the-way ploy. 'By the way, wasn't there some sort of trouble between you and Miss Austen? A quarrel, or something?'

Brown shoved his fists down onto the table and leaned on them, his red and angry face thrust forward.

'What are you trying to suggest? I didn't like her, I make no bones about it. She was a troublemaker. They're all troublemakers. There's no place for women in orchestras – I've said that. They're all trollops, and their minds are never on their jobs.'

'You disapproved of her relationship with Thompson.'

He controlled himself, straightening up and breathing hard. 'I've told you, that was none of my business. It was she who caused the trouble, talking about people behind their backs – telling lies –'

'About you?'

'No!' He took a breath. 'I couldn't care less about anything she said. And if you think I murdered her you're barking up the wrong tree – I wouldn't soil my hands. As far as her being a troublemaker's concerned, ask Simon Thompson about it. He'll tell you.'

'This is all purely routine, sir,' Atherton said soothingly. 'We have to ask about everything, however unlikely, and check up on everyone – all simply routine, you know.'

Back in his car he wondered about it. Brown a homosexual – Austen with too much money? Was she blackmailing him, perhaps? It's not illegal to be bent, but an eminent surgeon might perhaps not like it to come out. On the other hand.... He sighed. Check everybody, he'd said, and there were a hell of a lot of them to check. Why couldn't the damned woman be a lighthouse keeper or something agreeably solitary, instead of a member of a hundred-piece orchestra of irregular habits?

And Bill's pure and perfect woman was beginning to sound a little tarnished. Making all possible allowance for Brown's prejudice, there must have been something unlikeable about Anne-Marie Austen. A faint frown drew down his fair brows. What was going on with old Bill? First he got a thing about the Austen girl, and now he had stepped right out of character and screwed a witness – a man who had never been unfaithful to his wife in however many years it was of marriage. It was all very worrying.

7

The Last Furnished Flat in the World

Slider drove at first as though he and the car were made of glass, breathing with enormous, drunken care, sometimes even holding his breath, as if to see whether anything would change, whether Joanna would disappear and he would find himself alone in his car in a traffic jam in Perivale again. His mind felt hugely, spuriously expanded, like candyfloss, blown out of its normal dimensions with the effort of encompassing the impossible along with the familiar. The new knowledge of Joanna was laid alongside his ingrained experience of Irene and the children, both occupying the space one had occupied before – an affront to physics, as he had learned at school.

He had never felt like this before. The trite words of every love song – but it was literally true. This was not just the intensification of a previously charted emotion, it was something entirely new, and he hardly knew what to do with it. In his life there had been one or two tentative teenage fumblings, and then there had been Irene, and he had never felt like this with Irene.

He didn't remember ever having felt anything intense about Irene. He had proposed to her as the next, the correct thing to do: you left school, you got a job, then you got married. He had admired her for his mother's reasons, as the goal to attain, and had naturally assumed, since he was going to marry her, that he must love her.

Once married to her, he had behaved well by her because it was the right thing to do, and also, perhaps, because it was in his nature to sympathise. You've made your bed, his mother might have said if she'd ever known about his disappointment, and now you must lie on it. Well, so he had thought. But now he had to grapple with the possibility, wounding to the self-esteem, that he had dealt justly with Irene only because he had experienced no temptation to do otherwise.

But no, that was not the whole story. He had been married to Irene for fifteen years, and he had never known her, except in the sense that he recognised her and could predict pretty well what she would say or do in any situation. Joanna he had only just met, and he could not in the least predict her, and yet he felt as though he knew her absolutely, right to the bones. He felt that while anything she might do or say would probably astonish, it would never really surprise him.

The threatened crisis was here. He had deceived his wife. He had been unfaithful to her, slept with another woman, and told lies to cover up for it. Worse than that, he intended to go on doing it, as long and as often as possible. Broken things might be mended, but they could never be quite right again, he knew that: thus he had begun something that would change his whole life. There was peril implicit in it, and unhappiness for Irene and the children, and that peril was minutely perceived and understood. What he couldn't understand was why it entirely failed to alarm him; why, knowing that what he was doing was both wrong and dangerous to all concerned, he could feel only this huge and expanding joy, as though his life were at last unrolling before him.

Joanna, looking sideways at him, saw only a faint smile. 'What are you thinking about, dear Inspector?'

Happiness bubbled over into laughter. 'You really can't go on calling me Inspector!'

'Well, what then? Ridiculous though it seems, I don't know your first name.'

'It was on my identity card.'

'I didn't notice it at the time.'

'George William Slider. But I've always been called Bill,

because my father's a George as well.' Saying his own name aloud made him feel ridiculously shy, as though he were sixteen and on his first date.

'Oh yes,' she said. 'Now I know, I can see it suits you. Do you like to be called Bill?'

'Well, hardly anyone does these days. There's still a lot of surname-calling in the force. The quasi-military setup, you see. I suppose it makes it seem a bit like public school. I always called Atherton by his surname, for instance. I simply can't think of him as Jim, though the younger ones do.'

'Did you go to public school?'

He laughed at the thought. 'Good Lord, no! Timberlog Lane Secondary Modern, that was me.'

'What a pretty name,' she teased. 'Where's Timberlog Lane?'

'In Essex, Upper Hawksey. It was a brand new school in those days, one of those Prides of the Fifties, knocked up to cope with the post-war bulge.'

'Where's Upper Hawksey?'

'Near Colchester. It used to be just a little village, and then they built a housing estate onto it – hence the school – and now it's practically an urban overspill. You know the sort of thing.'

'Yes, I know – there's the village green and the old blacksmith's forge, carefully preserved, and backed up against it streets and streets of modern open-plan houses with a Volvo parked in front of each.'

'Sort of. And further back there's an older council estate – that was there when I was a child.'

'The rot had set in even then?'

'Mmm. It's funny – we lived in the old village, so we thought ourselves a cut above the estate people, the newcomers. But they thought themselves above us, because we had no bathrooms and only outside privies. But my father had nearly an acre of garden, and grew all our own vegetables. And he kept rabbits. And a donkey.'

'A donkey?'

'For the manure.'

'Ah. Messy, but practical. So you're a real country boy, then?'

'Original hayseed. Dad used to take me out into the woods and fields and sit me down somewhere and say, "Now, lad, keep your mouth shut and your eyes open, and you'll learn what there is to be learnt". I've always thought that was a very good training for a detective.'

'So you always meant to be a detective?'

'I suppose so. Once I'd got past the engine-driver stage. Reading all those Sherlock Holmes and Sexton Blake stories must have turned my brain.'

She smiled. 'I bet they're proud of you. Do they still live in Upper Whatsit, your parents?'

'Hawksey. Dad does – in the same cottage, still with the outside lavvy. Mum's – Mum died.' He still hated to say she was dead. The verb seemed somehow less destructive. 'What about your parents?'

'They're both alive. They live in Eastbourne.'

'Is that where you come from?'

'No, they retired there. I was brought up in London – Willesden, in fact. You see I've never strayed very far.'

'And are they proud of you?'

'I suppose so,' she shrugged, and then caught his eye and smiled. 'Oh, I don't mean they don't care about me or anything like that, but there were an awful lot of us – I was seventh of ten. I don't think you can care so intensely about each when you've got so many. And I left home so long ago I don't think of myself in relation to them any more. I expect they're glad I earn an honest crust and haven't ended up in Holloway or Shepherds' Market, but beyond that –' She let the sentence go. 'Are you an only child?'

'Yes.'

'Well, there you are then. Do you still visit your father?'

'Sometimes. Not so much now. There never seems to be time, and he never got on with –' He checked himself, and she glanced at him.

'With your wife? Well, I suppose you'll have to mention her sometime. What's her name?'

'Irene,' he said reluctantly. He didn't want to talk about her to Joanna. On the other hand, when he said no more the silence seemed to grow ominous and unnatural, and at last he said in a sort of desperation, 'Mum liked her very much. She was always glad we got married. But Dad couldn't get on with her, and after Mum died it got to be a bit of a strain going down there with Irene, and it looked rather pointed to go without her.'

'I suppose it is rather a long way,' Joanna said neutrally.

Another silence fell. Slider drove on, and the whole ugly, familiar, unnecessary edifice of in-law trouble crowded into his mind; cluttering the view, like those wartime prefabs that somehow never got taken down. Mum had been so proud when he'd married Irene. She saw it as a step-up – for her only son to marry a girl from the Estate, a girl who came from a house with a bathroom. Irene was 'superior'. She came from a 'superior' family, people who had a car and a television and went abroad for their holidays. Irene's mother didn't go to work, and had a washing-machine. Irene's father worked in an office, not with his hands.

Mum's perceptions and her ambitions were equally uncomplicated. Her Bill had got a good education and a good job, and now he was marrying a superior girl, and might one day own his own house. He thought with a familiar spasm of hatred of Catatonia, and how Mum would have loved it. Well, they said men always married women like their mothers.

Dad, on the other hand, had somehow managed to avoid the standardisation of state education. He could read and write and his general knowledge was extensive, but his approach to life had not been moulded. He lived close to the earth, and on his own terms, clear-sighted and sharp-witted as wild animals were. Stubborn, too, like his donkey. He had said Irene wouldn't do, and he had stuck by that. To be fair, he had never really given her a chance, or made allowances for her youth and inexperience. What had been nervousness on her side, Dad saw as 'being stuck up'. Slider, seeing both sides, as was his wont, had been unable to reconcile them.

But they had gone on putting up with each other as people will, rather than risk open breach. Slider remembered with muted horror those Sunday visits. Oh the High Tea, complete with tinned salmon and salad and a fruit cake and trifle with hundreds-and-thousands on the top! The polite, monotonous conversation; the photograph album and the walk round the garden and the glass of sweet sherry 'for the road'. It was a pattern which might have endured to this day, had Mum not died and ended the necessity for dissembling.

'What did he do, your father?' Joanna asked suddenly. 'Are you from a long line of policemen?'

'God, no, I'm the first. Dad was a farm-worker.' Even after all these years he still said it with a touch of defiant pride, legacy of the days when Irene, ashamed, would tell people her father-in-law was a farmer, or sometimes an estate-manager. 'The cottage we lived in was a tied cottage, but by the time Dad retired things had changed, and the new generation of estate workers wouldn't have wanted to live there, so they let him stay on. He'll die there, and then I suppose they'll gut it and modernise it and put in central heating, and let it to some account executive as a weekend cottage.'

He knew he sounded bitter, and tried to lighten his tone. 'You wouldn't recognise the farm Dad worked on now. When I was a kid, it used to have a bit of everything – a few dairy cows, some pigs, a bit of arable, chickens and ducks and geese wandering about everywhere. Now it's all down to fruit. Acres and acres of little stunted fruit trees, all in straight rows. They grubbed up all the hedges and filled in all the ditches and planted thousands of those dwarf trees, in regiments, right up to the road. It's like a desert.'

How could fruit trees be like a desert? his logic challenged him as he lapsed into silence. But they gave the impression of desolation, all the same. Joanna laid a hand on his knee for an instant and said as if to comfort him, 'Things are changing now. They're beginning to realise their mistake and replant the hedgerows –'

'But it's too late for the hedgerows I knew,' he said. He turned his head for an instant to look at her. Her eyes, which he had thought were plain brown, he now saw were richly tapestried in gold and tawny and russet, glowing in the sunlight. 'That's the terrible thing about my job,' he added. 'By its very nature, almost everything I do is done too late.'

'If it makes you so unhappy, why do you do it?' she asked, as people had asked before, as he had asked himself.

'Because it would be worse if I didn't,' he said.

* * *

Simon Thompson lived in a flat in the Newington Green Road, where people lived who couldn't yet quite afford Islington. It was above a butcher's shop and must, Atherton thought, be one of the last furnished flats in the world. He walked up the dark and dirty stairs to the first floor and stopped before the gimcrack, cardboard door with the sticky-paper label. The stairs went on upward, more sordidly than ever, and a smell of nappies and burnt fat slid down them towards him.

Thompson opened the door violently at the first knock as though he had been crouched behind it listening to the foot-falls. On the phone he had sounded nervous, protesting and consenting almost simultaneously. Presumably he was well aware that he was the person, after Joanna Marshall, who would be presumed to have been closest to Anne-Marie Austen.

'Sergeant Atherton.' He stated rather than asked. 'Come in. I don't know why you want to speak to me. I don't know anything about it.'

'Don't you, sir?' Atherton said peacefully, following Thompson into a flat so perilously untidy that it would have taken a properties-buyer a month at least to recreate it for a television serial.

'In here,' Thompson said, and they entered what was evidently the sitting-room. There was a massive and ancient sofa, around which the flat had probably been built in the first place, and a set of mutually intolerant chairs and tables. A hi-fi system occupied one wall, incongruously new and expensive, and at least answering the question as to what Thompson spent his income on. It seemed to have every-thing, including a compact-disc player, and was ranked with a huge collection of records, tapes and discs, and a pair of speakers like black refrigerators.

Everything else in the room was swamped with a making tide of clothes, newspapers, sheet music, empty bottles, dirty crockery, books, correspondence, empty record sleeves, apple cores, crumpled towels, and overflowing ashtrays. The windows were swathed in net so dirty it was at first glance invisible. Curtains lay folded, and evidently laundered, on the windowsill waiting to be rehung, but even from where he stood Atherton could see the thick film of dust on them.

'I hardly knew her, you know,' Thompson said defensively as soon as they were inside. He turned to face Atherton. He was a small and slender young man of ripe and theatrical good looks. His hair was dark and glossy and a little too carefully styled, his skin expensively tanned, his eyes large and blue with long curly lashes. His features were delicately pretty, his mouth full and petulant, his teeth white as only capping or cosmetic toothpaste could make them. He wore a ring on each hand and a heavy gold bracelet on his right wrist. His left wrist was weighed down with the sort of watch usually called a chronometer, which was designed to do everything except make toast, and would operate under water to a depth of three nautical miles.

He was the sort of man who would infallibly appeal to a certain kind of woman, who would equally infallibly be exploited by him. 'Spoilt', Atherton's mother would have put it more simply. A mummy's boy: all his life women had made a pet of him, and would continue to do so. Probably had elder sisters who'd liked dressing him up when he was a toddler and taking him out to show off to friends. He was also, Atherton noted, extremely nervous. His hands, held before him defensively, were never still, and there was a film of moisture on his deeply indented upper lip. His eyes flickered to Atherton's and away again, like those of a man who knows that the corpse under the sofa is imperfectly concealed, and fears that a foot may be sticking out at one end.

'May I sit down?' Atherton said, digging himself out a space at the end of the sofa and sitting in it quickly before the tide of junk could flow back in. 'It's purely a matter of routine, sir, nothing to worry about. We have to talk to everyone who might be able to help us.'

'But I hardly knew her,' Thompson said again, perching himself on the arm of the chair opposite, with the air of being ready to run.

Atherton smiled. 'No-one seems to have known her well, from what we're told, but you must have known her better than the rest. After all, you did have an affair with her, didn't you?'

He licked his lips. 'Someone told you that, did they?' He leaned forward confidentially. 'Look here, I've got nothing to hide. I went to bed with her a couple of times, that's all. It happens all the time on tour. It doesn't mean anything. Anyone will tell you that.'

'Will they, sir?' Atherton was writing notes, and Thompson took the bait like a lamb. Lamb-bait?

'Yes, of course. It wasn't serious. She and I had a bit of fun, just while we were on tour. So did lots of people. It ends when we get back on the plane to come home. That's the way it's played. But then when we got home she started to pretend it had been serious, and saying I'd promised to marry her.'

'And had you?'

'Of course not,' he cried in frustration. 'I never said anything like that. And she kept hanging around me and it was really embarrassing. Then when I told her to get lost, she said she'd make me sorry, and tried to make trouble with my girlfriend –'

'Oh, you have a girlfriend, then, have you sir?'

Thompson looked sulky. 'She knew about that from the beginning, Anne-Marie I mean. So she knew it wasn't serious. Helen and I have been together for six years now. We've been living together for two years. Anne-Marie knew that. She threatened to tell Helen about – well, about the tour.' His indignation had driven out his nervousness now. 'It would've really killed Helen, and she knew it, the bitch. And when she first joined, I thought she was such a nice girl. But underneath all that baby-face business, she was a nasty piece of work.'

Atherton listened sympathetically, while his mind whirled at Thompson's double standards. 'And did she in fact tell your girlfriend?'

'Well, no, fortunately she never did. She phoned a couple of times, and then put the phone down when Helen answered. And she kept hanging around me in the bar during concerts and saying things in front of Helen, sugges-tive things, you know. Well, Helen's very understanding, but there are some things a girl can't stand. But she gave it up in the end, thank God.'

Atherton turned a page. 'Can I have some dates from you, sir? You first met Anne-Marie when?'

'In July, when she joined.'

'You hadn't known her before? I believe she was at the Royal College?'

'I went to the Guildhall. No, I hadn't come across her before. I think she worked out of London.'

'And then you went on tour together – when?'

'In August, to Athens, and then to Italy in October.'

'Did you – sleep together on both tours?'

'Well, yes. I mean – yes, we did.' He looked embarrassed for once, perhaps realising that the return engagement might be construed as having aroused expectations.

'And it was when you came back from Italy that she started "making trouble for you"?'

Thompson frowned. 'Well, no, not immediately. At first it was all right, but after a week or so she suddenly started this business about marrying me.'

'What made her change, do you think?'

He began to sweat again. 'I don't know. She just – *changed.*'

'Is there anything you said or did that might have made her think you wanted to go on seeing her?'

'No! No, nothing I swear it! I'm happy with Helen. I didn't want anyone else. It was just meant to be while we were on tour, and I never said anything about marrying her.' He lifted anxious eyes to Atherton's face, passive victim looking at his torturer.

'After that session at the Television Centre on the fifteenth of January – what did you do?'

'I came home.'

'You didn't go for a drink with any of your friends?'

'No, I – I was going to go with Phil Redcliffe, but he was going with Joanna and Anne-Marie, and I wanted to avoid her. So I just went home.'

'Straight home?'

There was a faint hesitation. 'Well, I just went for a drink first at a local pub, round here.'

'Which one?'

'Steptoes. It's my regular.'

'They know you there, do they? They'd remember you coming in that night?'

He looked hunted. 'I don't know. It was pretty crowded. I don't know if they'd remember.'

'Did you speak to anyone?'

'No.'

'You're sure of that, are you? You went to a pub for a drink and didn't speak to anyone?'

'I – no, I didn't. I just had a drink and came home.'

'What time did you get home?'

Again the slight hesitation. 'I don't know exactly. About half past ten or eleven o'clock, I think.'

'Your girlfriend will be able to confirm that, I suppose.'

Thompson looked wretched. 'She wasn't here. She was at work. She's on nights.'

'She's a shift-worker?'

'She's a theatre nurse at St Thomas's.'

Atherton's heart sang, but he betrayed no emotion. He wrote it down and said without pausing, 'So no-one saw you at the pub, and no-one saw you come home?'

Thompson burst out, 'I didn't kill her! I wouldn't. I'm not that type. I wouldn't have the courage, for God's sake! Ask anyone. I had nothing to do with it. You must believe me.'

Atherton only smiled. 'It isn't my business to believe or not believe, sir.' He had found that calling young men 'sir' a lot unsettled them. 'I just have to ask these questions, as a matter of routine. What sort of car do you drive, sir?'

He looked startled. 'Car? It's a maroon Alfa Spyder. Why d'you want to know about my car?'

'Just routine. Downstairs, is it?'

'No, Helen's borrowed it – hers is being serviced.'

'And your young lady's full name, sir.'

'Helen Morris. Look, she won't have to know about – you won't tell her about – on tour and all that, will you?'

Atherton looked stern. 'Not if I don't have to, sir. But this is a murder enquiry.'

Thompson subsided unhappily, and did not think to ask what that meant. A few moments later Atherton was in his own Sierra and driving away, mentally rubbing his hands. He's lying, he thought, and he's scared shitless – now we only have to find out what about. And best of all, the girlfriend is a theatre nurse. A much more promising lead, he thought, even than the Brown one.

The Lodge, Stourton-on-Fosse, had evidently never been anyone's lodge, and from the look of it Slider deduced that if Anne-Marie had been poor, it was not hereditary. It was an elegant, expensive, neo-classical villa, built in the Thirties of handsome red brick, with white pillars and porticoes and green shutters. Its grounds were extensive and immaculate, with a gravelled drive leading from the white five-barred gate which looked as though it had been raked with a fine-toothed comb and weeded with tweezers.

'Crikey,' said Joanna weakly as they drove slowly past the gate to have a look.

'Is that all you can say about it?'

'It's the smell of money making me feel faint. I never knew she came from this sort of background.'

'You said it was a large house in the village.'

'Yes, but I was thinking of a four-bed, double-fronted Edwardian villa, the sort of thing that goes for a hundred and fifty thousand in North Acton. You need practice to imagine anything as rich as this.'

'Did she never give any hint that there was money in the family?'

'Nary a one. She lived in a crummy sort of bedsit – oh, you've seen it, of course – and as far as I know, she lived off what she earned in the Orchestra. She never mentioned private income or rich relatives. Perhaps she was proud.'

'You said she didn't get on with her aunt.'

'I said I got that impression. She didn't say so in so many words.' Slider stopped the car and turned it in a farm gateway. 'Are you going to drive in?'

'On that gravel? I wouldn't dare. No, I'll park out in the lane.'

'Then I can wait for you in the car.'

'I thought of that too.'

'I bet you did.' She leaned over and kissed him, short and full, on the mouth. He felt dizzy.

'Don't,' he said unconvincingly. She kissed him again, more slowly, and when she stopped he said, 'Now I'm going to have to walk up the drive with my coat held closed.'

'I thought it would give you the courage to face people above your station,' she said gravely.

He pushed her hand away and wriggled out, leaning back in for one last kiss. 'Be good,' he said. 'Bark if anyone comes.'

An elderly maid or housekeeper opened the door to him and showed him into a drawing-room handsomely furnished with antiques, a thick, washed-Chinese carpet on the polished parquet, and heavy velvet curtains at the French windows. Just what he would have expected it to look like, judging from the outside. Left alone, he walked round the room a little, looking at the pictures. He didn't know much about paintings, but judging by the frames these were expensive and old, and some of them were of horses. Everything was spotless and well polished, and the air smelled of lavender wax.

He made a second circuit, examining the ornaments this time, and noting that there were no photographs, not even on the top of the piano, which he thought unusual for a house of this sort, and particularly for an aunt of her generation. It was a remarkably impersonal room, revealing nothing but that there had been, at some point in the family's history, a lot of money.

He perched on the edge of a slippery, brocade sofa, and then the door opened and two Cairn terriers shot in yapping hysterically, closely followed by a white toy poodle, its coat stained disagreeably brown around eyes and anus. Slider drew back his feet as the terriers darted alternately at them, while the poodle stood and glared, its muzzle drawn back to show its yellow teeth in a continuous rattling snarl.

Mrs Ringwood followed them in. 'Boys, boys,' she admonished them, without conviction. 'They'll be quite all right if you just ignore them.'

Slider, doubting it, regarded Anne-Marie's aunt with astonishment. He had been expecting a stout and ample aunt, a tightly-coiffeured termagant; but Mrs Ringwood, though in her late fifties, was small and very slim, with bright golden hair cut in an Audrey Hepburn urchin. Her jewellery was expensively chunky, her clothes so fashionable that Slider had seen nothing remotely like them in the high street. She sat opposite him angularly, her thin legs crossed high up, her heavy bracelets rattling down her arms like shackles. The whole impression was so girlish that unless one saw her face, one would have thought her in her twenties.

Slider began by offering his condolences, though Mrs Ringwood showed no sign of needing or welcoming them.

'It must have been a terrible shock to you,' he persisted, 'and I'm sorry to have to intrude on you at such a moment.'

'You must do your job, of course,' she conceded reluctantly. 'Though I may as well tell you at once that Anne-Marie and I were not close. We had no great affection for one another.'

Didn't anyone like the poor creature? Slider thought, while saying aloud, 'It's very frank of you to tell me so, ma'am.'

'I would not like anything to hamper your investigation. I think it better to be open with you from the beginning. You believe she was murdered, I understand?'

'Yes, ma'am.'

'It seems very unlikely. How could a girl like that have enemies? However, you know best I suppose.'

'You brought Miss Austen up from childhood, I believe?'

'I was made responsible for her when my sister died,' Mrs Ringwood said, making it clear that there was a world of difference. 'I was the child's only close relative, so it was expected that I should become responsible for her, and I accepted that. But I did not think myself qualified – or obliged – to become a second mother to her. I sent her to a good boarding school, and in the holidays she lived here under the charge of a governess. I did my duty by her.'

'It must have been something of a financial burden to you,' Slider tried. 'School fees and so on.'

She looked at him shrewdly. 'Anne-Marie's school fees and living expenses were paid for out of the trust. Her grandfather – my father – was a very wealthy man. It was he who built this house. Rachel – Anne-Marie's mother – and I were brought up here, and of course we expected to share his estate when he died. But Rachel married without his approval, and he disowned her and left everything to me, except for the amount left in trust for Anne-Marie's upbringing. So you see I suffered no personal expense in the matter.'

'Anne-Marie was the only child of the marriage?'

Mrs Ringwood assented.

'And when she finished school, what happened then?'

'She went to the Royal College of Music in London to study the violin. It was the only thing she had ever shown any interest in, and for that reason I encouraged her. I insisted that she could not remain here doing nothing, which I'm afraid was what she wanted to do. She was always a lazy child, giving to mooning about and daydreaming. I told her she must earn her own living and not look to me to keep her. So she did three years at the College, and then went to the Birmingham Municipal Orchestra, and took a flat in Birmingham. The rest I'm sure you know.'

'How much did you know about her life in London?'

'Nothing at all. I rarely go to London, and when I do I shop and take lunch with an old friend. I never visited her there.'

'But she came to see you here?'

'From time to time.'

'How often did she come?'

'Three or four times a year, perhaps.'

'And when was the last time?'

'Last year – October, I think, or November. Yes, early November. She had just been on a tour with her Orchestra.'

'Did she mention any particular reason for visiting you at that time?'

'No. But she never discussed her personal life. She came from time to time, on a formal basis, that's all.'

'Did you pay her an allowance?'

She looked slightly disconcerted at the question. 'While she was at the College, I was obliged to. Once she had her own establishment and was capable of earning her own living, I considered my obligations as having ceased.'

'Did you ever give or lend her money?'

She looked pinker. 'Certainly not. It would have been very bad for her to think that she could come to me for money whenever she wanted to.'

'She had no other income? Nothing except her salary from the Orchestra?'

'Not that I was aware of.'

'Did you know that she owned a very rare and valuable violin, a Stradivarius?'

Mrs Ringwood displayed neither surprise nor interest. 'I knew nothing about her private life, her London life. I am not interested in music, and I know nothing about violins.'

Slider did not press this, though surely everyone must know what a Stradivarius was, and anyone would be surprised if a penniless relative turned out to own one. He felt Mrs Ringwood was departing somewhat from her self-imposed duty of complete openness.

'On that last visit, in November, did she talk about any of her friends?'

'I really cannot remember at this distance what she talked about.'

'But you said she had just been on tour – presumably then she must have mentioned it to you?'

'She must have spoken about it, I suppose. The places she'd been to, and the concerts she'd done. But as to friends –' Mrs Ringwood looked irritable. 'As far as I knew she never had any. When I was her age I was always up and doing – parties, tennis, dances – scores of friends – and admirers. But Anne-Marie never seemed to have any interest in anything, except drooping about the house and reading. She seemed to have no *go* in her at all!'

Slider was beginning to form a much clearer picture of Anne-Marie's childhood, and the clash of personalities that was inevitable between this former Bright Young Thing and an introverted orphan who cared only for music. Mrs Ringwood's perceptions about her niece would not be likely to be helpful to him. Instead he tried a shot in the dark. 'Can you tell me who her solicitor was?'

Was there a very slight hesitation before she answered?

'The family solicitor, Mr Battershaw, attended to her business.'

'Mr Battershaw of –?'

'Riggs and Felper, in Woodstock,' she completed, faintly unwillingly. Slider appeared not to notice, and wrote the name down in his careful secondary-modern-taught hand. He looked up to ask the next question and his attention was drawn to the French windows behind Mrs Ringwood, just a fraction of a second before the dogs also noticed the man standing there, and rushed at him, barking shrilly.

'Boys, boys!' Mrs Ringwood turned with the automatic admonition, but the newcomer was in no danger. The yappings were welcoming, and the attenuated tails were wagging. 'Ah, Bernard,' Mrs Ringwood said.

He stepped forward into the room, a tall, thin man a year or two older than her, dressed in a suit of expensive and extremely disagreeable tweed, and a yellow waistcoat. His face was long, mobile and yellowish, much freckled. He had a ginger moustache, grey eyebrows sparked with red, and thin, despairing, gingery hair, combined into careful strands across the top of his freckled, balding skull.

As he stooped in, he put up a hand in what was obviously an automatic gesture to smooth the strands down, and Slider noticed that the hand, too, was yellow with freckles, and that the nails were rather too long. The man smiled ingratiatingly behind his moustache, but his eyes were everywhere, quick and penetrating under the undisciplined eyebrows.

Slider, freed of the dogs' vigilance, stood politely, and Mrs Ringwood performed the introduction. 'Inspector Slider – Captain Hildyard, our local vet, and a great personal friend of mine. He looks after my boys, of course, and he often pops in on his way past. I hope he didn't startle you.'

Slider shook the strong, bony yellow hand, and the vet bent over him charmingly and said, 'How do you do, Inspector? What brings you here? Nothing serious, I hope. Has Esther been parking on double yellow lines?'

Slider merely gave a tight smile and left it to Mrs Ringwood to elucidate if she wanted.

'I suppose you've come to look at Elgar's foot?' she said. 'It was kind of you to drop by, but I'm sure it's nothing serious. Tomorrow would have done just as well.'

'No trouble at all, my dear Esther,' Hildyard said promptly. Slider watched them, unimpressed. Something about them struck a false note with him. Had she warned him off, provided him with the excuse? Was there some kind of collusion between them, and if so, why?

'I'll look at it while I'm here,' Hildyard went on. 'Don't want the little chap suffering. By the way, Inspector, is that your car out in the lane?'

'Yes,' said Slider. He met the vet's eyes and discovered that they were grey with yellow flecks, and curiously shiny, as if they were made of glass, like the eyes of a stuffed animal. 'Is it in your way?'

'Oh no, not at all. I was merely wondering. As a matter of fact, that was partly why I called in. We keep an eye on each other in a neighbourly way in this village, and a strange car parked near a house like this is always cause for concern.'

He paused. With five pairs of eyes on him, watchful and waiting, Slider felt pressed to take his leave. He moved, and the dogs rushed upon him, yapping.

'I'd better be on my way,' he said. 'Thank you for your help, Mrs Ringwood. Nice to have met you, Captain Hildyard.'

Hildyard bowed slightly, and Mrs Ringwood smiled graciously, but they were waiting side by side for him to leave with a palpable air of having things to say as soon as he was out of earshot. There was more between them than vet and client. Old friend? Or something closer?

'Who was that utterly bogus character in the hairy tweeds?' Joanna asked as he got in and started the engine. 'He looked like a refugee from a Noël Coward play.'

'He purported to be one Captain Hildyard, the local vet.' Slider drove off, feeling relief at the putting of some distance between him and the house.

'He gave me a fairly savage once-over as he passed. Why only purported to be?'

'Oh, I suppose he's a vet all right,' Slider said tautly.

'He seems to have ruffled you.'

'He had long fingernails. I absolutely abominate long fingernails on men. And I don't like people who use military rank when they're not in the army.'

'I said he looked bogus. What was he doing there, anyway?'

'It did seem rather opportune, the way he suddenly appeared. But on the other hand, the dogs of the house evidently knew him all right, and he said he'd called because he was worried by a strange car being parked near the house, which is not only reasonable, but even laudable.'

'You do like to be fair, don't you?' she said. 'I bet you're Libra.'

'Close,' he admitted. 'I'm told I'm on the cusp. But listen, he had long fingernails, which is not only disgusting, but I would have thought a distinct handicap for a vet.'

'Perhaps he's such an eminent vet he only does diagnoses from X-rays, and never has to shove his hands up things like Mr Herriot.'

'Maybe. Still, I found out a couple of things, despite the aunt's unwillingness.'

'Why was she unwilling?'

'That's what I hope to find out. She told me, you see, that Anne-Marie had nothing but her income from the Orchestra. But when I asked casually who her solicitor was, she gave me the name.'

'Anne-Marie's solicitor, you mean?'

'Of course.'

'I'm not with you. What's significant about that?'

'Well, look, ordinary people don't have a solicitor. Do you have one?'

'I've consulted one on a couple of occasions. I couldn't exactly say I "have" one.'

'Precisely. If you talk about "having" a solicitor, it suggests a continuing need for one. And the only continuing need I can think of is the management of property, real or otherwise.'

'Aha,' Joanna said.

'Exactly,' Slider agreed. 'So what we do now is have some lunch, and then go in search of the Man of Business. Shall we find a pub, or would you prefer a restaurant?'

'Silly question – pub of course. You forget I'm a musician.'

8
Where There's a Will There's a Relative

'Has it occurred to you,' said Joanna as they strolled into The Blacksmiths Arms a few villages further on, 'that the pub is the only modern example of the old rule of supply and demand?'

'No,' said Slider obligingly. They had chosen the pub because it had a Pub Grub sign and sold Wethereds, and when they got inside they found it smelled agreeably of chips and furniture polish.

'It's true,' she said. 'In every other field of commerce the rule has broken down. The customer bloody well has to take what the supplier feels like supplying. Complaining gets you nowhere. You can look dignified and say "I shall take my custom elsewhere" and the least offensive thing they'll say is "Suit yourself".'

'I suppose so. Well?'

'Remember what pubs used to be like in the Sixties and Seventies? Keg beer, lino on the floor, no ice except Sunday lunchtimes, never any food. Now look! They've actually changed in response to public demand, which is a total denial of the Keynes theory.'

'What, Maynard?' he hazarded.

'No, Milton.'

They reached the bar. 'What will you have?'

'A pint please.'

'Two pints, then,' Slider nodded. It was lovely to be in a

96

pub with someone other than Irene, who never entered into the spirit of the thing. The most she would ever have was a vodka and tonic, which Slider always felt was a pointless drink. More often she would ask, with a pinching of her lips, for an orange juice, than which there was nothing more frustrating for a beer-drinker. It makes it quite clear that the asker really doesn't want a drink at all and would sooner be anywhere but here, thus at a stroke putting the askee firmly in the wrong and destroying any possibility of enjoyment for either.

They ordered ham, egg and chips as well, and went to sit down in the window seat, where the pale sunshine was puddling on a round, polished table. Joanna drank off a quarter of her pint with fluid ease and sighed happily.

'Oh, this is nice,' she said, smiling at him, and then an expression of remorse crossed her face so obviously that Slider wanted to laugh.

'You were thinking that if Anne-Marie hadn't died we wouldn't be sitting here at all.'

'How did you know?'

'Your face. It's like watching a cartoon character – everything larger than life.'

'Gee, thanks!'

'No, it's nice. Most people are so world-weary.'

'Even when they've nothing to be weary about. Poor things, I think it's a habit they get into. It must be terrible never being able to admit to enjoying anything.'

'So why are you different?' he asked, really wanting to know.

She gave the question her serious consideration. 'I think because I never have time to watch television.' He laughed protestingly, but she said, 'No, I mean it. Television's so depressing – the universal assumption of vice. I don't think it can be good for people to be told so continuously that mankind is low, evil, petty, vicious and disgusting.'

'Even if it is?'

She contemplated his face. 'But you don't think so. That's much more remarkable, considering the job you do. How do you manage to keep your illusions? Especially as –' She broke off, looking confused.

'Especially as what?'

'Oh dear, I was going to say something impertinent. I was going to say, especially as you aren't happily married, either. Sorry.'

Considering they had just spent the night making torrid love together, considering he was being unfaithful to his wife with her, 'impertinent' was a deliciously inappropriate word, besides being pretty well obsolete in this modern age, and he laughed.

He had never in his life before felt so at ease in someone's company. More even than making love with her, he wanted to spend the rest of his life talking to her, to put an end to the years – his whole life, really – of having conversations inside his head and never aloud, because there had never been anyone who would not be bored, or contemptuous, or simply not understand, not see the point, or pretend not to in order to manipulate the situation. He knew that he could talk to her about absolutely anything, and she would listen and respond, and a vast hunger filled him for conversation – not necessarily important or intellectual, but simply absorbing, unimportant, supremely comfortable chat.

'Talking of your job,' she said, following Humpty Dumpty's principle of going back to the last remark but one, 'shouldn't you be asking me questions to justify bringing me along with you? I shouldn't like you to get into trouble. Come to think of it, you've been pretty indiscreet, haven't you, Inspector? I mean, suppose I did it?'

'Did you?'

'No, of course not.'

'Well there you are, then.' Slider said comfortably.

'I'm worried about you,' she said. 'You seem to have no instinct for self-preservation.'

Where she was concerned, he thought, that was painfully true. The number of things he ought to be worried about was multiplying by the minute, but he was completely comfortable, and her left leg was pressed against his right from hip to knee. He roused himself with an effort. 'Tell me about your friend Simon Thompson, then.'

'No friend of mine, the slimy little snake,' she said promptly. 'However, I don't suppose he could have been the murderer. He's like a kipper – two-faced, and no guts.'

'Never mind supposing. You've been reading too many books.'

'True,' she admitted, and then tacked off again. 'On the other hand, and come to think of it, he might just have been capable of it. These self-regarding people can be surprisingly ruthless, and he had convinced himself that she was the Phantom Wife-Phoner.'

'Come again?'

'Oh – well – you know I told you that people often do things on tour that they wouldn't do at home? Of course everybody knows about it, but everybody keeps quiet about it. Except that once or twice people's wives have received anonymous phone calls spilling the beans, and of course that makes terrible trouble all round. Well, after Anne-Marie and Simon had split up, he put it about that she was the Phantom, and that made things very nasty for her, because of course there will always be people who says things like "there's no smoke without fire".'

'Do you think she was the Phantom?'

'No, of course not. What possible reason could she have for wanting to do that?'

'What reason could anyone have?'

She thought, and sighed. 'Well, I don't think it was her. Poor Anne-Marie, she never made it to the top of the popularity stakes.'

Slider drank a little beer, thoughtfully. 'When she and Simon were having their affair – did they get on well? Were they friendly?'

'Oh yes. They were all over each other. Martin Cutts said it made him feel horny just to look at them.' She frowned as a thought crossed her mind. 'They did have a quarrel on the last day in Florence, come to think of it. But they must have made it up, because they sat together on the plane coming home.'

'What was the quarrel about?'

'I don't know.' She grinned. 'I had my own fish to fry, so I wasn't particularly interested.'

He felt a brief surge of jealousy. Other fish? 'Tell me about Martin Cutts,' he said evenly.

She leaned her elbows on the table and cupped her face. 'Oh, Martin's all right as long as you don't take him seriously, and hardly anyone does. He simply never grew up. He got fossilised at the randy adolescent stage, and feels he has to have a crack at every new female that crosses his path, but he doesn't mean anything by it. He's quite childlike, really – rather endearing.'

Slider thought he knew the type, and anything less endearing was hard to imagine. Dangerous, selfish, self-regarding – and what had been his relationship with Joanna? But he didn't want to wonder about that. Fortunately the food arrived at that moment and prevented his asking any really stupid questions. The food was good: the ham was thick and cut off the bone, moist and fragrant and as unlike as possible the slippery pink plastic of the sandwich bar; the chips were golden, crisp on the outside and fluffy on the inside; and the eggs were as spotlessly beautiful as daisies. They ate, and the simple pleasure of good food and good company was almost painful. O'Flaherty's voice came to him from somewhere in memory, saying 'A lonely man is dangerous, Billy-boy'.'

'Thank heaven for pub grub,' Joanna sighed, echoing his pleasure.

'I suppose you must eat out a lot,' Slider said.

'It's the curry syndrome,' she said cheerfully. 'One of the hazards of the job. When you're on an out-of-town date, you have to get a meal between the rehearsal and the concert, which is usually between five-thirty and seven, and nothing is open that early except Indian restaurants. And when you're playing in town, you want to eat after the show, and you have a couple of pints first to wind down, and by that time the only thing *left* open is the curry-house.'

'It all sounds horribly familiar,' Slider said. 'You could be describing my life.' Then he told her about his late meals with Atherton and The Anglabangla and his lone indigestion, and that brought him back to Irene and he stopped abruptly and ate the last of his chips in silence. Joanna eyed him sympathetically as though she knew exactly what he was thinking, and he thought that she probably did. But married life is different he told himself fiercely. If he and Joanna were married, they wouldn't go on having cheerful, chatty, comfortable lunches together like this. Of course they wouldn't. It would all change. A lonely man is a dangerous man, Billy-boy. He gets to believing what it suits him to believe.

Atherton decided, as he was in the area, to check out Thompson's story as far as the pub, Steptoes, was concerned. He found it moderately busy, filled with suited young men in run-down shoes and smart women with tired faces under hard make-up – the office crowd, and how, he wondered, could they get away with it? He ordered a pint of Marston's and a toasted cheese sandwich and got chatting to the governor, a short and muscle-bound ex-boxer, who in turn introduced him to the Australian barmaid who had been on duty on Monday night.

To Atherton's surprise they both said they knew Simon Thompson and his girlfriend, the nurse. They came in a lot, usually with a crowd of other musicians and nurses. The two professions seemed to go together for some reason. But neither barmaid nor governor remembered seeing Simon on the Monday night.

'But we were busy,' the barmaid pointed out in fairness. 'The fact that I didn't see him doesn't mean to say that he wasn't here.'

Which was true, Atherton thought, and just about what you could expect with this job.

Slider left Joanna to wander about Woodstock while he went in to see the solicitor.

Mr Battershaw was at first reluctant to believe that Anne-Marie was dead at all. 'I shall have to see a death certificate,' he said more than once; and, 'Why wasn't I informed before this?'

Patiently Slider explained about the difficulty of identifying the body and tracing the next of kin. 'I've just been to see Mrs Ringwood, and she gave me your name and address. I understand that you were Miss Austen's solicitor?'

Once properly convinced that Anne-Marie was no more, Battershaw became co-operative. He was a big, gaunt man in his late fifties, with surprised, pale eyes and a long jaw, which made him look like a bloodless horse. He offered Slider tea, which Slider refused, and under steady questioning settled down to tell the family story.

'Anne-Marie's grandfather, Mr Bindman, was the client of my predecessor here, the younger Mr Riggs. He's retired now, but he told me all about Mr Bindman. He was a self-made man, who started off as the son of a penniless refugee who came over during the First World War. Our Mr Bindman set himself up in business and made his fortune, built himself that lovely house, and was altogether a pillar of society.'

'What sort of business?'

'Boots and shoes. Nothing exciting, I'm afraid. Well now, he was married twice – his first wife died in 1929 or '30 – and he had a son, David, by his first marriage, and two daughters, Rachel and Esther, by his second wife. David was killed in 1942 – a great tragedy. He was only eighteen, poor boy – just joined up. He'd only served a few weeks. And the second Mrs Bindman was killed in the Blitz, so there were just the two little girls left.

'Mr Bindman doted on them both, but the younger girl, Rachel, was his pet. Esther married in 1957, and Gregory Ringwood was a very solid young man, steady and reliable, just the sort a careful father would approve of. But later the same year Rachel fell in love with a violin player called Austen, and that was a different matter altogether.'

'How old was she?'

'Oh, let me see – she'd be eighteen or nineteen. Very young. Well, Mr Bindman was very definite in his ideas. He loved music, and it was he who encouraged Rachel to go to concerts, and even bought her gramophone records and her own radiogram. But when it came to marrying a fiddle-player – that wasn't good enough for his pet. He told her there was no future in it, and that Austen would never be able to earn enough to keep her, and forbade her to marry him, or even see him again. Rachel, I'm afraid, was a very strong-willed young woman, very like her father, in fact, and they spent two years or so quarrelling fiercely about it. Then in the end, as soon as she was twenty-one and the old man could no longer prevent her, she married Austen, and broke her father's heart.' Battershaw sighed. 'Mr Bindman reacted in the only way he knew: he cut her out of his will, and vowed never to speak to her again.'

'Pretty drastic,' Slider said mildly.

'Oh, positively Victorian! Mind you, I'm sure he would have changed his mind in the end, given time, because he adored Rachel, and she'd have found a way to get round him. I think he probably just wanted to register his disapproval in the time-honoured way. But unfortunately time wasn't on his side. The following year, 1960, Anne-Marie was born, and Rachel attempted a reconciliation, and there were signs that the old fellow was softening; but then when Anne-Marie was a year old, Rachel and her husband were both killed in a car crash.'

'How dreadful.'

Battershaw nodded. 'That was the year I joined the firm, and in a short time I saw old Mr Bindman age ten years. He blamed himself, as people will after the event, and poured out all the love he should have given to Rachel onto the little girl. And he changed his will, leaving half the estate to his daughter Esther, and the other half in trust for Anne-Marie.'

The words fell into Slider's mind like pieces of a jigsaw slotting into place. Mrs Ringwood's hesitations aside, there was so often money at the bottom of things. When there's a way, there's a will, he thought.

'What were the terms of the trust?' he asked.

Battershaw looked disapproving. 'I'm afraid they were very ill-advised, and I argued strenuously with Mr Bindman about them, but he was a stubborn old man, and wouldn't budge an inch. Money was to be released from the income to pay for Anne-Marie's upbringing and education, but the capital and any accrued interest were not to be handed over to her until she married.' He shook his head. 'He didn't trust women to handle money, you see – he thought they needed a man to guide them. Of course, I'm sure he didn't anticipate the way things fell out. He must have expected that Anne-Marie would marry straight from school, and that he would still be around to approve or even arrange the marriage.'

'And then, presumably, he would have changed the terms?'

'Indeed. Oh, I did my best to persuade him anyway. I begged him at least to put a date to the winding-up of the trust, so that she would inherit either when she married or when she reached the age of, say twenty-five, but he wouldn't have it. I dare say that given time I could have brought him round to it, but there again time was not on our side. Rachel's death had broken his health, and he died within a year of her, leaving Anne-Marie in a most invidious position, without a penny she could touch until and unless she married.'

Slider mused. 'Did Mrs Ringwood know the terms of the trust?'

'Indeed. She is the other trustee, you see, along with myself.'

'And Anne-Marie? Did she know?'

Battershaw looked a little disconcerted. 'Now, it's a strange thing, if you had asked me that question a year ago I would have had to say I didn't know. I had never discussed the matter with her, and I have strong doubts as to how much Mrs Ringwood would have thought wise to tell her. The terms of the trust, you see, are certainly an encouragement to improvident marriage, and –' He paused, embarrassed.

'She might have married just anyone, simply to get away from home?' Slider offered.

'Yes,' Battershaw said gratefully. He cleared his throat and continued. 'But then last autumn Anne-Marie made an appointment to see me.'

'Can you tell me the exact date?'

'Oh, certainly. I don't remember offhand – I think it was towards the end of October – but Mrs Kaplan, my secretary, will be able to tell you. It will be in my diary.'

'Thank you. So Anne-Marie came to see you – here? In this office?'

'Yes.'

'And how did she seem?'

'Seem? She was very well – quite sun-tanned, in fact. I remember I commented on the fact, and she said she had just come back from Italy. She had been on a tour with her Orchestra, I think, but she'd always been fond of Italy.'

'Was she happy?'

Battershaw seemed puzzled. 'Really, Inspector, I don't quite know. I had had very little personal contact with Anne-Marie, not enough to know how she was feeling. All I can say is I didn't notice that she seemed *un*happy.'

'Of course. Please go on.' Slider rescued him from these uncharted seas. 'What did she want to see you about?'

'She wanted to know the exact terms of her grandfather's bequest to her. I told her –'

'Just a moment, please – did she ask you what were the terms, or did she already know the terms, and ask you to confirm them?'

Battershaw looked intelligent. 'I understand you. As I remember, she said that she understood she had no money of her own until she married, and asked me if that were true. Of course, I told her that it was.'

'And what was her reaction?'

'She didn't say anything at once, although she looked rather thoughtful, and not entirely pleased, which was under-standable. Then she asked if there were any way round it, any way of changing the provision of the will. I told her there was not. And then she said, "You are quite sure that the only way I can lay my hands on my money is to get married?" Or words to that effect. I said yes, and then she got up to go.'

'That was all?'

'That was all. I asked if there were anything else I could do for her, and she said no.' The anaemic horse smiled almost roguishly. 'I think she said "Not a thing", to be precise.' The smile disappeared like a rabbit down a hole. 'That was the last time I saw her. It's hard to believe the poor child is dead. Are you quite sure it was murder?'

'Quite sure.'

'Because I hate to think that she might have – laid hands on herself, for the want of money. That would not at all have been her grandfather's intention.'

'We're confident it wasn't suicide,' Slider said. His mind was elsewhere. 'Did Miss Austen have any relatives on her father's side?'

'None that I know of. Her father was an only child, I know, so there would not have been aunts and uncles, or cousins. There may have been second cousins, but I never heard of any.'

Slider tried a long shot. 'Did she have any relatives in Italy? Was Austen perhaps part-Italian?'

Battershaw looked merely bewildered. 'I never heard that he was. But really, I had nothing to do with him at all. Mrs Ringwood would be the person to ask.'

'Of course. Thank you.' Slider got up to go. 'Your secretary will give me the date of that meeting?'

'Yes, indeed.' Battershaw accompanied him to the door, and Slider checked him before he could open it.

'By the way,' he said, 'the estate was a large one, was it?'

'Quite large. The capital was soundly invested.' He named a sum which made Slider's eyebrows rise.

'And who does it all go to, now that Miss Austen is dead?'

Battershaw looked unhappy now, a pale horse with colic. 'Mrs Ringwood is the residuary legatee,' he said.

'I see. Thank you,' said Slider.

Slider walked out into the smeary, intemperate sunshine and stood there for a moment, blinking. The tangle of the case, he felt, was beginning to resolve. He could see ends of string that he could begin to wind in. The favoured sister; the dead favoured sister's child – helpless, hapless infant; the dutiful daughter who had never been properly appreciated, forced to take care of the rival for her father's love; the money that should have been hers, and was now hers again. No wonder she hadn't wanted to talk about it, he thought. But motive doesn't make a case. All the same –

Suddenly he remembered Joanna. While he had been engrossed with Battershaw he had entirely forgotten her. It was one of the reasons he loved his job: it had the power to absorb him completely, so that it became his refuge, the one place where he could escape from wearying self-consciousness.

But coming back to the thought of Joanna was refreshment and renewal. She was sitting in the window of the tearoom they had appointed as meeting-place, and she didn't see him for a moment, so that he was able to look at her unobserved. Her face was already familiar to him, but now he saw it in the unmerciful sunlight in all its planes and textures, its shapes and inconsistencies, its simple uniqueness. There was all the evidence of a lifetime of experience entirely separate from him. She had lived, and living had marked her. She had spent perhaps half her allotted span, without him – he more than half of his, without her. Of all the thousands of days and nights, they had spent only one together. But still, looking at her, he had the extraordinary feeling of belonging. This was how it was, then, he thought. His righteous place was on her side of the glass, ranged with her against the incoming tide of the rest of the world, and it didn't matter a damn that he knew nothing she knew: he knew *her*.

She saw him. The focus of her eyes changed and she smiled and he went in.

Sunshine or not, it was only January, and the gathering darkness as they drove back to London affected their mood, dampening their lightness with the realisation of their problems. Slider voiced it unwillingly as he drew up outside her house.

'I mustn't be too late back tonight.' She made a small turning-away movement of her head, and he recognised it as hurt, which hurt him. 'We could go out for a quick bite to eat, if you like,' he said tentatively.

She turned back to look at him clearly. 'No, that would waste time. Let's have a drink here, and a snack if you like. I'll light the fire.'

'I'll have to make some phone calls,' he said, and then added hastily, 'to Atherton, and the station. I haven't called in all day.'

'It's all right,' she said. 'You must do what you have to.'

But when they went in the phone began instantly to ring, and she sprinted for it and picked it up before the answering-machine could intercept. Slider felt a chill of foreboding even before she made polite responses into the receiver and then turned to offer it to him.

'For you,' she said. It was too dark in the hall to see the expression of her face, but her voice said clearly enough that she knew the day was over for them.

It was O'Flaherty. 'Izzat you Billy? Christ, we been trying to get yez all day. Atherton said y' might be there. Jaysus, are you at that owl caper, now?'

'What is it, Pat?' Slider forbore to rise to the bait.

'Ah, the world's a wheel o' fortune, so it is,' O'Flaherty remarked cryptically. 'Well, I'm sorry to spoil your shenanigans, but you'd better come in here straight away, me fine Billy, and thank God and Little Boy Blue that we never phoned your owl lady to ask where y' were.' Little Boy Blue was what O'Flaherty called Atherton. They had a robust but not unfriendly contempt for each other.

A complex blend of relief, disappointment and apprehension was having its effect on Slider's bowels, and he said impatiently, 'For Christ's sake, Pat, what's happened?'

'The owl woman, Mrs Gostyn. They been trying to raise her all day, and getting anxious as time went on and she never showed up. So Boy Blue goes in troo the winder and finds her dead on the floor.'

The receiver suddenly felt slippery and cold in his grasp. In the darkness of the unlit hall he sought Joanna's eyes, and her face seemed to swim unattached in the shadows. Then she reached out and switched on the light, and everything was ordinary again, and he only felt very tired.

'How did it happen?' he asked.

'Well, she might've slipped and banged her head on the fender,' O'Flaherty said with an emphasis on the word 'might' that told Slider all he needed to know.

'I'm on my way,' he said. Joanna turned away and went into the kitchen, which he recognised as her way of relieving him of responsibility for her. Their day was over; but under the surface of churning reactions there was still a peacefulness, because she was there, and they felt what they felt about each other, which meant that they couldn't *not* go on being together in some way or another, and so everything was all right really, wasn't it?

9
Other Fish?

Atherton had set his alarm to get him up with the birds, but what he was in fact up with was a disgusting crunching and slurping noise from under the bed, where Oedipus had retired to eat a mouse. Atherton got out of bed with a curse, and on his hands and knees cautiously lifted the corner of the counterpane. In the fluffy twilight the cat looked at him over its shoulder with yellow headlamp eyes and a tail hanging out of the corner of its mouth.

'Just be sure you eat it all,' Atherton said, remembering the time he had found four abandoned feet on his pillow, and headed for the bathroom. He had a hot shower, shaved under it, washed his hair, and then stood under the streaming, steaming water and thought about Slider.

It was really the most extraordinary thing to have happened. He hadn't met the Marshall woman, of course, but even if she combined all the feminine charms, it was hard to see how she could have got Slider off the rails of a lifetime in a matter of hours. To have slept with her – and really slept – the first evening of their acquaintance, and then to have taken her with him when he went out on police business, was so far out of character for his superior that Atherton, who believed in Love only as a theoretical possibility – as something that hadn't been definitely disproved – could only think that Slider was heading for some kind of a breakdown.

There was no fool like an unpractised fool, he thought, turning off the water and stepping into a very large, thick bath sheet – Atherton took washing very seriously – and to his knowledge Slider had never been unfaithful to Irene before, probably not even in thought. He was one of those rarities, a truly virtuous man, and Atherton, who was all for Slider's getting out from under Irene's thumb on principle, didn't know whether the poor sap could handle it. If he was going to go off the rails, he'd probably do it in a spectacular way, and to be heading for that kind of crisis in the middle of a murder investigation was catastrophic.

There were plenty of people in the department, he thought as he wielded the hairdryer, who would be happy to clamber a step higher up the ladder by treading on the head of anyone else, however much they liked them, who seemed not to have his entire mind on his job. And Slider, as Atherton was aware, had been passed over for promotion before because of department politics. All in all, it behoved Atherton to get his head down and produce something to show up at the next meeting, because so far they seemed to have got precisely nowhere.

He dressed, checked quickly under the bed – Oedipus had departed, leaving only a forlorn scrap of grey fur – and went off to St Thomas's to try to intercept Helen Morris as she came off duty.

Slider was woken by Kate spilling tea onto his chest as she climbed onto the bed balancing a mug.

'Time to get up, Daddy,' she said, her bubblegum-sweet breath stertorous with the effort of retaining at least some of the tea within the mug. Slider elbowed himself sufficiently upright to field it before she scalded him again.

'Thank you, sweetheart,' he said dopily, and tried for the sake of her feelings to sip. It had been one hell of a session last night. He felt as though he had only just gone to sleep. He felt as though he had been beaten all over, and he had a smoke-headache and a dire feeling of oppression in his sinuses. He abandoned the attempt at creative parenthood, put the mug on the bedside table and flopped back onto the pillows with a groan.

'You mustn't go back to sleep, Daddy – you've got to get *up*,' Kate said severely. She eyed him curiously like a bird

eyeing a wormhole. 'Were you drunk last night?'
'Of course not,' Slider mumbled. 'Why d'you say that?'
'Mummy thought you were.'
He opened one eye. 'She didn't say that,' he said with
some assurance. Kate shrugged her birdlike shoulders.
'She didn't say so, but I bet that's what she thought
anyway. She's cross about something, and she said you were
very late coming home, and when Chantal's Dad comes
home late *he's* usually drunk.'
'You think too much,' Slider said. 'Anyway, I was
working, not drinking. You know, don't you, that I have to
work funny hours sometimes?' She shrugged, unconvinced,
and opened her mouth to deliver more opinions. Desperate
to deflect her, Slider said unguardedly, 'What are you going
to do today?'
The already opened mouth dropped still further in amazement at his stupidity. 'But it's the school *fair* today,' she said
with huge and patient emphasis, like a nurse in a home for
the senile. 'I'm going to be on a *stall.* I'm going to be a *Mister
Man.* Mummy's made me a costume and *everything!*'
'Oh, is that today?' Slider said feebly.
Kate sighed heavily, blowing a strand of sticky, light-
brown hair across her face. 'Of course it's today. You *know*
it is,' she said inexorably.
'I thought it was next week,' Slider said with a growing
sense of doom.
'Well it isn't.' She eyes him suspiciously. 'You are coming,
aren't you?'
'Darling, I can't. I've got to go to work.'
Violent despair contorted her features. 'But Daddy, you
promised!' she wailed.
'I'm sorry, sweetheart, but I can't help it. I've got an
important case on at the moment, and I just have to go in to
work. It's a murder case – you know what that is, don't you?'
'Of course I do. I'm not stupid,' she said crossly. 'But you
don't really have to go, do you? Not all day?'
'I'm afraid so.'
'Is that why Mummy's cross?'
'I don't think she knows yet,' Slider said weakly. 'Get off
the bed, darling, I have to go to the bathroom.'

'I *bet* she doesn't know,' Kate said with relish, bounced off the bed and hared off downstairs, a delighted harbinger of doom. Blast the child, Slider thought as he plodded what felt like uphill to the bathroom. He urinated, stood for a pleasurable moment or two scratching himself, and then started to run a bath. The running water made so much noise he didn't hear Irene behind him until she spoke.

'Is it true?'

'Is what true?' he temporised.

'Kate says you've got to work today.' Her voice was icy, and he turned to see how bad it was. It was bad. Her lips were thin and white, which made her look five years older than her true age. It was an unlovely expression, he thought, on any woman. He felt around in his mind for a moment for guilt, and could find nothing new there, only the familiar old sorts with which he was almost comfortable. Joanna was there, but as a loosely woven, shining net of pleasure, and the glow coming off the thoughts of her seemed to be protecting him from feeling anything bad about it.

'I'm afraid so,' he said, and drew breath to add some extenuating detail, but she was in first.

'I'm surprised you bothered to come home at all,' she said bitterly. 'It hardly seems worth it. Why don't you move in with Atherton? At least you won't disturb him coming in all hours of the night – especially if it's him you're sitting up drinking with.'

Slider allowed himself a touch of impatience. 'Oh come on! I wasn't drinking last night, as you know perfectly well. I was working. I told you the old lady, the only witness in this blasted case, was found dead. You know how much work that means. And,' he added, managing to work up a bit of momentum. 'I think it's a bit much for you to go telling Kate I came in drunk.'

He thought the false accusation would sidetrack her, but she only said with deep irony, 'And now I suppose you've got to go in again?'

'Yes, I've got to,' he returned her words defiantly.

'And you couldn't possibly have told me earlier, of course?'

'No, of course I couldn't. I didn't know earlier, did I?'

'You realise that it's Kate's fair today. Of course, she's only been looking forward to it for weeks.'

'Well, I can't see that that –'

'And that Matthew's playing in the match today. His first chance in the school team. Which you said you were so proud of.'

'Oh God, is that today as well? I'd forgotten –'

'Yes, you're good at forgetting things like that, aren't you? Things to do with your home and family. Unimportant things – like the fact that you were supposed to take Kate and me to the fair and then take Matthew on to the match. You forgot that you were supposed to be *here* for a change.'

'Well I can't help it, can I?' he defended himself automatically. 'What do you want me to do, tell Division I'm busy?'

Irene never answered inconvenient questions. 'One day,' she said bitterly. 'Just one day. Is that so much to ask? Of course I wouldn't expect you to do anything for me, but I would have thought you could spare a few hours for your children, when they've been looking forward to it so much. But you're much too busy. I should have expected it.'

'It's my job, for God's sake!' he cried, goaded.

'Your job,' she said in tones of withering scorn.

'It's an important case –'

'So you say. But I'll bet you one thing – it won't get you anywhere. It won't get you promoted. And shall I tell you why? Because you run around like their little dog, working all the hours God sends, at their beck and call, and they don't respect you for it, oh no! They're going to keep you down because you're too useful for them to promote you!'

'Oh for God's sake, Irene, do you think I'd do it if it wasn't necessary? Do you think I like going to work on a Saturday?'

Suddenly things changed. Her face, taut with anger, seemed to loosen. She was no longer playing a part in her own personal soap opera: she looked at him for once as though she really saw him; she looked at him with a sadness of disillusion which hurt him unbearably.

'Yes,' she said. 'I think you do. I think you prefer working at any time to being with us.'

It was too close to the truth. He stared at her helplessly, wanting to reach out his hands to her, but it was too long since they had touched habitually for the gesture to be possible without intolerable exposure. If he reached out and she rejected him, it would hurt both of them too much. The distance they had established between them was the optimum for being able to continue living together, and this was not the moment to change the parameters.

'Oh Irene,' was all he managed to say from the depths of his pity.

'Don't,' she said abruptly, and went away.

Slider sat down on the rim of the bath and stared at his hands, and longed suddenly and fiercely for Joanna, for someone not filled to the brim with obscure and irremediable hurt. He remembered Atherton once saying that the best thing you could give to someone you loved was the ability to please you. He didn't know where Atherton got it from, but it was true. He loved Joanna not least because he could so easily give her pleasure; but he was not so naïve that he didn't know that might easily be true of the beginning of any affair.

Sighing, he rose and got on with his shaving and bathing and dressing, thinking about the Irene problem and the Joanna not-problem in uncoordinated bursts, while the back of his mind leafed endlessly through the documents of the case. His mind was like Snow White's apple, one half sweet, one half poisoned.

'Miss Morris?'

'You must be Sergeant Atherton. They rang me from downstairs to say you wanted to see me.'

Helen Morris was plump and pretty with friendly dark eyes and neat, short brown hair. She had the deliciously scrubbed-clean look of all nurses, and dark shadows under her eyes which could be the result of night-duty, Atherton supposed. On the other hand, he had already made enquiries downstairs before he came up to this floor, which put him at an advantage over the weary nurse.

'I'm sorry to make your working day longer, but I wanted

to talk to you alone,' he said, giving her a disarming, non-alarming smile.

She didn't respond. 'I don't like doing things behind Simon's back,' she said.

Atherton smiled ever more genially. 'It's purely a matter of routine – independent confirmation, that's all.'

She put her head up a little. 'I've complete confidence in Simon. He had nothing whatever to do with – with what happened to Anne-Marie.'

'Well that's all right then, isn't it?' Atherton said blandly, turning as if to walk with her along the corridor.

Finding she seemed to have agreed to it, she shrugged and went along. 'I must have a cup of coffee,' she stipulated.

'Fine. We can talk in the canteen.'

They walked along the wakening corridors and into the canteen, which was filled with the hollow, swimming-bath sounds of a half-empty public place early in the morning. There was a pleasant smell of frying bacon, and the bad-breath smell of instant coffee. A number of nurses were breakfasting, but there were plenty of empty tables to enable them to sit out of earshot of anyone else. Atherton bought two coffees, and sat down opposite her across the smeared melamine.

'I suppose you know why I'm here,' he began, working on the principle of letting people put their own feet in it first.

She shrugged, stirring her coffee with an appearance of calm indifference. He admired her nerve; though he supposed that after a night in the operating theatre, anything that happened out here might seem tame. On the other hand, she had a full and sexy mouth which just now was set in lines of discontent, and the attitude of her body as she leaned on one elbow seemed expressive not only of tiredness but also unhappiness.

'How well did you know Anne-Marie Austen?' he began.

'Hardly at all. I saw her backstage a few times, and once or twice she was in a group of us that went for a drink after a concert – that sort of thing. I knew her to speak to, that's all.'

'She wasn't a particular friend of your boyfriend's?'

She had lifted her cup two-handed to her lips, and now made a small face of distaste and put the cup down without drinking. Now was that the coffee, or his question?

'I knew about her and Simon in Italy, if that's what you're getting at.'

'Someone told you?'

'These things have a way of getting about in an orchestra.'

'Did you mind about it?'

She looked at him with a flash of anger. 'Of course I *minded.* What do you think? But there was nothing I could do about it, was there?' He kept his silence, and after a moment she went on, 'You may as well know – she wasn't the first.' She smiled unconvincingly. 'Musicians are like that. It's the stress of the job. They do things on tour that they wouldn't do at home, and it would be stupid to make a big thing about it. As long as it ended at the airport, that's what I always said – and it did.'

'Always?'

'Simon and I have been together a long time, and I know him pretty well. With all his faults, he's always been fair to me. He would never have carried on with her after the tour. That was all on *her* side.'

She met Atherton's eyes as she said these noble lines, as people do who are bent on convincing you of something they don't really believe. She keeps up a good shop-front, he thought, but she's too intelligent not to know what he is.

'So Anne-Marie wasn't willing to let things go?'

Her lips hardened. 'Because they'd been to bed together, I suppose she – fell in love with him, or something. She started chasing him, and Simon felt sorry for her, and I suppose she took it for encouragement.'

'How do you mean, chasing him?'

She took it for a criticism, and looked at him defiantly. 'It wasn't just my imagination, you know – ask anyone. She was pretty blatant about it. She hung around him, kept asking him out for drinks, even phoned the flat a couple of times.'

'It upset you,' he suggested.

She shrugged. 'I just pretended nothing was happening. I wouldn't give her the satisfaction.'

'You didn't like her much, I gather?'

'I despise women like that. They've got to have a man – any man. They don't care who. It's pathetic.'

'But I would have thought a girl as pretty as her wouldn't have any trouble finding a boyfriend,' he said as though thoughtfully.

She looked a little disconcerted. 'People didn't like her. *Men* didn't like her. Look, I know you think I was jealous –'

'Not at all,' Atherton murmured.

'But it wasn't that. I had nothing to be jealous of. I just thought she was – weak.'

Atherton absorbed all this, and tried a new tack. 'Tell me about that day – the Monday.'

'The day she died?' She frowned in thought. 'Well, I'd been on duty Sunday night. I got home on Monday morning about half past eight. Simon was in bed. I got in with him and we went to sleep. He got up about half past twelve and made some lunch – scrambled eggs, if you want to be particular – and brought them in, and then he got dressed and went off to work.'

'At what time?'

'Well, he had a session at half past two, so it would be about half past one, I suppose. I didn't particularly notice, but he'd leave about an hour to get there.'

'And you were on duty again that night?'

'Yes.'

'When did you next see Mr Thompson?'

'Well, it would be the next morning, when I got home.'

'So you didn't see him between the time he left home on Monday – about half past one in the afternoon – and Tuesday morning at – what? – half past eight?'

'I've said so.' He said nothing, and she went on as if compelled. 'We were both working. I was here all night, and Simon was working until half past nine.'

'And then he went home?'

'He had a drink, and went home.'

'That's what he told you?' She was looking at him warily now. 'But you see, I happen to know that he came here to the hospital when he left the TVC that Monday evening. And why would he come here, if not to see you?'

She whitened so rapidly that he was afraid she might actually faint, and for a long moment she said nothing, though her dark eyes were intelligent, thinking through things at great speed, not focused on him. At last she said faintly, 'He wasn't here. He didn't –'

'You didn't see him? You didn't, by any chance, arrange to meet him and hand over a certain package?'

'No!' she protested, though it came out as hardly more than a whisper. She was evidently badly shaken, but Atherton knew that there would not have been time for Thompson to come here to the hospital, collect the drug, and still be back in time to murder Anne-Marie by the established time. If he were the murderer, his purpose in coming here must surely have been to establish his alibi, and Helen Morris ought therefore to be claiming to have seen him, not the reverse. It looked as though, if he did it, she was not in on it.

Her mind had been speeding along on a different track, however. She said, 'Look, I can guess what you're thinking, but there's no way in the world I could have got hold of any drugs. It's checked and double-checked every night. If anything was missing, it would be discovered at once. And Simon couldn't have got hold of anything, either. They're incredibly security-minded at this hospital.'

'Yes, I know. That's how I know he came here on that Monday night. And you're quite sure he didn't come here to see you?'

She hesitated, and Atherton watched with interest the struggle between her loyalty to Thompson, which wanted to bail him out of possible trouble, and her intelligence, which told her that if she changed her story now, it would look suspicious. In the end she said, 'I didn't see him. But he might have come to see me, and not been able to find me.'

Clever, thought Atherton.

'Look,' she went on with a touch of irritation. 'I'm very tired. Can I go home now? You know where to find me if you want to ask me any more questions. I'm not going to leave the country.'

Atherton rose and smiled graciously at the irony. He was not displeased with the interview. Someone intelligent and determined – and she was both – could overcome the problem of falsifying the drugs record; and he had established to his own satisfaction that she was not as sure of Thompson as she claimed to be. She knew he was a shit; she was also nervous and worried. She had by no means told Atherton everything. Perhaps she knew where Thompson had been that evening. Or perhaps she didn't know, and wondered.

Out in the clear air of the morning, Slider found himself ravenously hungry. He had declined breakfast at home in the company of his grieving son, his self-righteous daughter and his tight-lipped wife. Consequently he had a little time in hand; enough to drive to a coffee-stall he knew in Hammersmith Grove where they made bacon sandwiches with thick, white crusty bread of the sort he remembered from his childhood, before everyone went wholemeal. The other early workers made room for him in companionable silence, and they all sipped their dark-brown tea out of thick white mugs like shaving-pots and blinked at nothing through the comforting steam.

Restored, he drove to Joanna's house. She opened the door as he was parking the car and stood watching him until he came up the path. Discovering her again was a series of delightful shocks which registered all over his body. She had on a pair of soft and faded grey cord trousers, tucked into ankle-boots, and a buttercup yellow vyella shirt which seemed to glow in the colourlessness of a winter morning. She looked wonderful, but best of all, so approachable, so accessible. He put his arms round her and she turned her face up to him, smiling, and she seemed both familiar and dear. He caught the scent of her skin, and it seemed so surprising and exciting that he already knew the smell of her so well, that it gave him an erection.

'Hullo,' she said. 'How did you sleep?'

'Like the dead. And you?' It didn't matter what they said. He felt suddenly safe and optimistic.

They went into the house and she shut the door behind them with a practised flick of one foot. In his arms again, she pressed against him and felt his condition. 'Have we time?' she asked simply.

His stomach tightened. He was not yet used to such directness. 'What time is he coming?'

She cocked his watch towards her. 'Twenty minutes.'

'Then we've time,' he said, taking her face in his hands and kissing her. With one hand on the wall to guide her, she backed with him down the passage to the bedroom.

Martin Cutts turned out to be about forty-five, a small, almost delicate man with the very black hair and very white skin of the Far North, and the carefully upright gait of the back-sufferer. He had an alert face and an engaging smile, and was as jewel-bright as a bluetit – in a sapphire suede jacket over a canary-yellow roll-neck sweater. Slider was regarding with some suspicion and even contempt a man of that age who would dress so brightly, until it occurred to him depressingly that he was merely jealous of a man who he suspected might once have been Joanna's lover, and then he laid himself out to be affable.

Joanna had arranged the interview for Slider at her house, since there were things Cutts would not be able to say at home in front of his wife, as Slider, newly sensitive on that score, had appreciated. Joanna now left them tactfully alone and went and had her bath, and the thought of her naked and soapy in the steam beckoned distractingly from the corner of Slider's mind.

He cleared his throat determinedly and said, 'It was good of you to give me your time like this.'

'Not at all,' Cutts said, seating himself carefully on the arm of the chesterfield. 'It was good of you to let me answer your questions here rather than at home.' He crinkled his eyes in what Slider realised with a start was a conspiratorial grin. It brought home to him all over again his new status as a Man of the World, a Man with a Bit on the Side, and he wasn't sure he liked it.

'Perhaps you'd tell me how you got to know Miss Austen,' he asked, poising his pen above his pad in the manner which laid obligation on the interviewee to give one something to write down.

Cutts was not unwilling. 'Well of course I knew her in Birmingham,' he began, and Slider hid his surprise and nodded safely instead.

'You were in the same orchestra?'

'For a short time. She joined just before I left to come to London.'

'Did you have an affair with her while you were both in Birmingham?'

Martin Cutts did not seem at all put out by the question. He answered as if it were as natural a thing as having his hair cut. 'I went to bed with her, yes, but it wasn't really what you'd call an affair. I had to be more careful up there, of course, because I was between wives.'

Slider was puzzled. 'I don't follow.'

'I'd just divorced my first wife, and hadn't yet married my second,' he explained obligingly.

'Yes, but why did that mean you had to be more careful? Surely –'

'Well, obviously,' Cutts said as if it were, indeed, obvious, 'if you're not married and you go about with a single girl, she's bound to take you more seriously and try to pin you down. If you've got a current wife, you're safe. She knows she can't have you. That's the beauty of it.'

Slider nodded unemphatically at this remarkable philosophy. 'Do you think Miss Austen was on the look-out for a husband?'

'Well they all are underneath, aren't they? Mind you, she didn't particularly show it in those days, not like later. She was pretty chipper, and it was all quite light-hearted. We had a lot of fun, and no hard feelings on either side when we parted.'

'She struck you as being happy – contented with life?'

'Oh yes. She'd got her own place, and she'd just bought a car, and I think she was enjoying being away from home and having her freedom. I don't think she'd been happy as a child.'

'Did she talk to you about her childhood?'

'Not in detail, but I gathered she was an orphan, and she'd been brought up by an aunt who hated her and wanted her out of the way. Am I telling you things you already know?'

'I'd like to have your impressions,' Slider said. 'It all helps to build up the picture. Did she tell you why the aunt hated her?'

'Personality clash, I think,' he said vaguely. 'She was always being shoved out of the way, sent to boarding school and so on. And apparently the aunt kept her short of money while she was at college, even though she was pretty well-off – the aunt, I mean.'

'Did Miss Austen ever intimate to you that she might have expectations? A legacy or something of that sort?'

He watched Cutts under his eyebrows for some reaction, but the other man only smiled to himself.

'Expectations. Nice old-fashioned expression. No, she never said anything of that sort. But she did live in a pretty swanky flat, so perhaps she had come into some money. Or it might have belonged to the aunt, I suppose. It wasn't like a young person's flat, now I come to think of it.'

'How do you mean?'

'It was one of those luxury service flats, you know, with a porter in the hall and everything laid on. More the kind of place you'd expect to find rich old ladies with Pekineses. And it struck me –'

He stopped, as if it had only just struck him. Slider made a helpfully interrogative sound.

'Well,' Martin Cutts went on, 'it never struck me as being very cosy or homelike. There was never anything lying around. It didn't look as though anyone lived there – it was more like one of those company flats, where all the furniture and decorations have been done by a firm. Everything co-ordinated, like a luxury hotel. Awful, really.'

Slider thought of the shabby bedsitter and then, involuntarily, of the bare council flat, and the anomaly threatened to overload the circuits. He needed to move on, to let the subconscious get to work on it.

'After you left Birmingham, did you keep in touch with each other?'

'Oh no,' said Cutts, and the words 'of course not' hung on the air.

'As far as you were concerned, you never expected to see her again?'

He shrugged. 'I'd married my present wife, you see, and Anne-Marie and I were only ever a bit of fun. She understood that all right.'

But did she, Slider thought. He considered her childhood, the impersonal luxury flat, the desperate attempt to persuade Simon Thompson to marry her, the number of people who had said 'I didn't really know her'. No-one, he thought, had ever wanted her. She had never been more than used and rejected, and Joanna, casual and incurious, was the nearest that poor child had ever had to a friend. The loneliness of her life and death appalled him. He wanted to shake this self-satisfied rat by the neck, and hoped for a whole new set of reasons that he had never been in Joanna's bed.

'But when she joined your present orchestra, you took up with her again?' he managed to say evenly.

'Oh, it wasn't really like that. We were friendly, of course, and I think we may have gone to bed a couple of times, but there was nothing between us. She was perfectly all right until she had this bust-up with Simon Thompson.'

'And what happened then?'

He looked away. 'She – approached me.'

'Why do you think she did that?'

'Shoulder to cry on, I suppose.' The eyes returned. 'She really was cut up about it, poor kid. She said Simon had proposed marriage to her, and then backed out. I didn't believe that – I mean Simon may be a prize pratt, but he isn't stupid – but she evidently believed it, so it was all the same as far as she was concerned.'

'What form did this "approach" take?'

'She asked me to go for a drink with her after a concert one night, and when we'd had a couple, she asked me back to her flat.'

'And you went to bed with her?' Slider concealed his fury, he thought, very well.

'Yes. But I don't think it was me she really wanted. Her heart didn't really seem in it. I suppose she was still hankering after Simon.'

'Was it just the one occasion?'

'No, a few times. I can't remember – four or five perhaps.'

'And when was the last time?'

'Just before Christmas. After our last date – the Orchestra's last date, I mean – before the Christmas break.'

Slider nodded. 'Tell me what happened.'

Martin Cutts looked helpless, as if he didn't know what he was being asked. 'We had a few drinks, and went back to her flat. Like before.'

'And went to bed together?'

'Yes.'

'And how did she seem to you? Happy? Sad? Worried?'

'Depressed, I'd say. Well, she was worried, for a start, because she'd lost her diary. That may sound silly to you, but it's a major disaster for a musician. And she was worried that Simon was going to make trouble for her in the Orchestra – that phone-call business. Do you know about that? Oh, right. But there was more than that.' He paused, evidently marshalling his thoughts. His eyes were a very bright blue, but small and rather round, which made him look more than ever like a bird with its head on one side. 'After we'd made love, she started to cry, and went on about how nobody cared about her, and that she hadn't got a boyfriend and so on. I was a bit pissed off about that – I mean, nobody likes being wept over – so I tried to jolly her up a bit, and then I thought I'd slope off. But when I tried to get up, she clung to me, and started really crying, and saying she was frightened.'

'Frightened? Of what?'

'She didn't say. She just kept saying "I'm so afraid. I'm so afraid" over and over, just like that. And sobbing fit to choke. Got herself really worked up.'

'And what did you do?'

'Well, what could I do? I held her and patted her a bit, and when she quietened down, I made love to her again, just to cheer her up.'

'I see,' Slider said remotely.

Martin Cutts eyed him unhappily. 'What could I do?' he said again. 'People on their own do get depressed around Christmas. It's not nice being on your own when everyone else is with their families, but I couldn't take her home with me, could I? And she wouldn't go back to her aunt. I felt rotten leaving her, but I had to get home.'

'How was she when you left her?'

'Quiet. She wasn't crying any more, but she seemed very depressed. She said something like "I can't go on any longer". I said of course you can, don't be silly, and she said,

"No, it's all over for me".'
'Were those her actual words?'
'I think so. Yes. Well, you can imagine how I felt, leaving her like that. But then, when we met again in January, she seemed to be all right again – quiet, you know, as if she'd resigned herself. Then when I heard she was dead, I naturally thought she must have killed herself, and I felt terrible all over again. But she didn't, did she?'
'It wasn't suicide,' Slider acknowledged.
'So there was nothing I could have done, was there?' he appealed.

Slider had no wish to let him off the hook of responsibility, since what he had done must have added to Anne-Marie's overall misery, but he could hardly blame Cutts for her murder. *Quiet*, he thought, *as if she'd resigned herself*. But to what? Had she foreseen her death? What had she done to bring it upon herself? Perhaps, lonely and unwanted as she was, she had really ceased to care if she lived or died – until, of course, that last moment in the car park when the realisation had come upon her (how?) that it was going to happen, and she made the one last futile effort to escape, one last pathetic flutter of a bird in a trap.

Joanna came in cautiously, pink and scented, and looked from one to the other. 'The voices had stopped, so I thought you'd finished.'

Slider roused himself. 'Yes, we've finished. For the moment, anyway. Thank you, Mr Cutts.'

'Mr Cutts?' Joanna said in ribald derision. '*Mr Cutts*?'

And Cutts reached out a hand and grabbed her by the neck, pulling her against his chest in an affectionate death-lock. It was not a lover's gesture, but it was the more disturbing for that, for Slider could easily imagine what depths of intimacy might have preceded such casual manhandling.

'Don't chance your arm, woman,' Cutts said, grinning, and when he released her she slipped an arm round his waist and gave him a brief, hard hug.

Catching Slider's eye she said, almost apologetically, 'Martin and I are old friends, you know.'

Cutts smiled at Slider disarmingly. 'Yeah, Jo and I go back

a long way. I hope you're taking good care of her – she's a remarkable woman.'

This, Slider knew, was where he was supposed to smirk and say something complacent along the lines of *she certainly is* or *I'm a lucky man*, thus accepting gracefully the implied compliment that Cutts knew that he was Joanna's lover and was assuring him that he had no rival here. But Slider's feelings were too new and unfamiliar to him, and above all too large and too overwhelmingly important for such social backgammon. He could do no more than mutter something stiff and graceless, and feel a fool, and angry. Joanna gave him a thoughtful look, and led Martin Cutts away to show him out, leaving Slider alone to regain his composure.

Accustomed to marital warfare, he expected her to re-enter the room with a rebuke, and made sure he got his blow in first. 'You certainly know some really lovely people. Are they all like him in your business, or is he better than most?'

She stood before him, looking at him without hostility. In fact, there was even a smile lurking under the surface.

'Oh, Martin's not too bad a bloke, if you don't take him seriously. He's like a greedy child let loose in a sweetshop, except that his lollies are women's bodies. He has to prove himself all the time.' She put her arms round Slider's unyielding neck, and her breasts nudged him like two fat, friendly puppies. 'And you know, about fifty per cent of all men would behave exactly like him, given his opportunities. Why do so few men ever grow up? It's depressing.'

She laid her mouth against his, waiting for him to react, but he struggled with his resentment and would not kiss her back. She drew her head back to look at him enquiringly. 'What are you so mad about?'

It was hovering on his lips to demand whether that man had been her lover, but he saw in time the amusement lurking in her dark eyes and knew that she was just waiting for him to ask. He thrust the thought away. It was of no interest to him, he told himself sternly.

She followed his struggles, recorded minutely in his expression, 'You're quite right,' she said. 'It's impossible to be jealous of someone like Martin. He isn't real. He's a sort of sexual Yogi Bear, always snitching picnic baskets, and being chased by Mister Ranger.'

Slider began to laugh, his resentment dissolving. 'I don't deserve you,' he said.

'Of course you don't,' she assured him. 'I'm a remarkable woman.'

10
Through the Dark Glassily

'Are you sure Atherton won't mind?' Joanna said as they
sped northwards through the blissfully empty streets. It was
another clear, sunny day, but there was a small and bitter
wind much more in keeping with the bare trees. Joanna was
wearing an overlarge and densely woolly white jacket, so that
with her dark eyes and pale face she looked like a small,
stout polar bear. Slider glanced sideways at her with affection, thinking how natural it seemed already to have her
beside him in the car.

'Of course he won't. Why should he?'

'I can think of lots of reasons. For a start, he may not have
enough food for three if he was expecting to feed two. And
for another, he might want to have you to himself.'

'He's my sergeant, not my wife. Anyway, if we're going to
go over the case, we need you there. You were the person
closest to Anne-Marie.'

'That sounds perilously thin to me, and I'm not even a
detective. He's bound to see through it.'

'He's my friend as well as my partner. And I need you.'

'Ah well, there's no answer to that, is there? Do I call him
Atherton as well? Or should I make an attempt at Jim?'

Atherton's face, when he opened the door, was carefully
schooled to show nothing of his feelings either of annoyance
or surprise, and he invited them in politely. Joanna eyed him,
unconvinced.

'I hope you don't mind too much having me here? It was
terribly short notice, I know, with no shops open. You don't

128

have to feed me, if there isn't enough.'

'There's enough,' he said economically. 'Go on in, take your coats off.'

Slider glanced at him defensively, and followed Joanna in under Atherton's door-holding arm. The front door opened directly onto the living-room, a haven of deep armchairs, crammed bookshelves, and a real fire leaping energetically in the grate and reflecting cheerfully in the brass scuttle.

'Oh, what a gorgeous room!' Joanna said at once. She turned to Atherton an innocent face, 'I had an elderly aunt once who lived in an artesian cottage, and it wasn't a bit like this.'

Atherton walked into it. 'You mean artisan cottage,' he said, his eyebrows alone deploring her ignorance.

'Oh no,' she said gravely, 'it was very damp.'

There was a brief silence during which Slider watched Atherton anxiously, knowing he was proud, and more accustomed to using Slider as his straight man than being one himself. But an uncontrollable smirk began to tug at his lips, and after a moment he gave in to it and grinned along with Joanna.

'You should have told me she was silly,' he said to Slider. 'Have a drink and enjoy the fire. What will you have?'

Oedipus, who had been stretched out belly to the flames, got up politely and came across to wipe some of his loose hair onto Joanna's pink velvet dungarees. She bent and offered him a hand, and he arched himself and walked under it lingeringly, by inches.

'Gin and tonic if there is, please. What's his name?'

'Oedipus. Bill?'

'Same please. Thanks.'

'Why Oedipus?'

'Because Oedipus that lives here, of course. Really, you are very dull.'

Slider was surprised at the rudeness, but Joanna grinned and said, 'There are two sorts of people in the world, those who quote from *Alice* –'

'And those who don't.'

'Alice?' Slider said blankly.

'*In Wonderland,*' Atherton elucidated, and smiled at

Joanna on his way to the kitchen. Slider sat down, acknowledging, while not necessarily understanding, that the simple fact of sharing a quotation with Joanna had changed Atherton from not-very-well-concealed hostility to open partisanship. There was nowt queerer than intellectuals, he told himself resignedly; unless it was cows.

Joanna had taken the armchair by the fire, and Oedipus now jumped up onto her lap, sniffed it delicately, turned round once, and settled himself majestically with one massive, Landseer paw on each of her knees. Atherton brought all three glasses at once in his large, long hands, distributed them, and settled himself.

'Well, what first?' he said. 'You've seen the preliminary report on Mrs Gostyn?'

'Yes, and there's no doubt, except that there's every doubt,' Slider sighed. 'Beevers went round there, didn't he?'

'Yes. The carpet was rucked up, as if she'd put her foot on it and it slid away from her. He tested it, and it was slippery enough to have done that. She would have fallen backwards and struck her head on the corner of the fender. There was a smear of blood there, and the wound was consistent, according to Freddie Cameron, in shape, kind and force needed, with such a fall. Sufficient in a woman of her age and general condition to have proved fatal. No sign of a struggle, or of forcible entry –'

'But there wouldn't have been.' Slider interrupted, staring into his glass darkly. 'She knew him, didn't she? That nice Inspector Petrie – why shouldn't she let him in? I should have warned her –'

'Come on, Bill, it's not your fault. We don't even know it was him. Why should he come back? He'd got what he came for the first time.'

'Maybe he came back to silence her. She was the only one who could identify him.'

'We don't know that it wasn't an accident. She might have got nervous and stepped back from him, for instance, and just slipped.'

Slider smiled. 'I thought he wasn't even there?'

Atherton looked a little put out. 'Someone was there all right. Beevers interviewed the couple upstairs, the Barclays, and they think they heard someone moving about in Anne-Marie's flat, about the time we reckon it happened.'

'He went back for something. Something he'd forgotten the first time. What?'

'The violin?'

'Got to be. And then went downstairs to stop Mrs Gostyn's mouth. One out of two, better than nothing.'

'Well, it's possible ,' Atherton conceded. He gave a grim sort of smile. 'The Barclays are moving out, going to stay with her mother in Milton Keynes. That's a sign of desperation if ever I heard one.'

'Scared?'

The grin widened. 'They wouldn't let Beevers in. Even after he put his ID through the letterbox. He persuaded them to phone the station and Nicholls gave them a description and the number of his car. Even then, when they let him in, Mrs B was standing well back with the baby clutched in her arms, while Mr B tried to look menacing with a large spanner.'

'It's all very well, but they must have been terrified,' Joanna said indignantly. 'Two of their neighbours murdered ...'

'You haven't seen Beevers,' Atherton said. 'He's all of five-foot-five, completely spherical, with a chubby little phizog like a teddy bear. He looks about as dangerous as a scatter cushion.'

Joanna, unconvinced, turned to Slider. 'What was that about a violin? Surely it would have been in her car? She had it with her at the session.'

'That's what we would have assumed. We haven't found her car yet, of course, but we certainly found a violin in her flat, so either someone took it back there, or she had two.'

'Not that I know of,' Joanna said. 'I only ever saw the one. But in any case, why would anyone want to risk going back there to collect it?'

'Because it's extremely valuable, of course,' said Atherton.

'But it was nothing special,' she said, puzzled.

'You call a Stradivarius nothing special?'

Now Joanna laughed. 'She didn't have a Strad! She had a perfectly ordinary German fiddle, nineteenth-century, nice enough, but not spectacular.'

'Are you sure?' Slider asked.

'Of course I'm sure!' She looked from one to the other. 'I sat next to her, remember, I saw it hundreds of times. She bought it for nine thousand. She had to take out a bank loan to buy it.'

'Nevertheless,' Slider said, 'we found a Stradivarius in her flat, in an old, cheap case with two cheap bows.'

'I took it to Sotheby's to have it valued,' said Atherton. 'They think it might be worth as much as a million pounds.'

Joanna's lips rehearsed the price silently, as if she didn't understand what the figures meant. Then she shook her head. 'I don't understand. Where would she get a fiddle like that? How could she possibly afford it? And why didn't she use it? How could anyone who owned a Strad like that not play it?'

'Maybe she thought it was too valuable to use,' Slider hazarded.

Joanna shook her head again. 'It isn't like that. A fiddle's not like a diamond ring. You have to play them, use them. Even the insurance companies understand that.'

'Then the only other explanation is that she didn't want anyone to know she had it.'

'Stolen?' Joanna said, but Slider could see she didn't believe that, either. 'Look, fiddles like that are like – like famous paintings. You know, "Sunflowers" or the "Mona Lisa". They don't just appear and disappear. People know them, and they know who has them. If one had been stolen, everyone would know about it. *You'd* have the details somewhere.'

'Are you quite sure she didn't play it? Would you really know what violin she was playing, if you had no particular reason to notice?'

'It's one of the first things you discuss when you get a new desk partner,' she said without emphasis. 'What sort of fiddle do you play? How much was it? Where did you get it? That sort of thing. And you get used to the sound of it. There are all sorts of little peculiarities you have to adapt to. Even if you never look at the thing, you'd know instantly if your partner played on a different instrument, especially if it was one of Stradivarius quality. It just wouldn't sound the same.'

Atherton, at least, understood; Slider accepted without understanding because it was her. Their drinks were finished, and Atherton said, 'Let's eat, shall we? Feed the beast. Would you two like to lay the table while I do things in the kitchen? You'll find everything in that drawer, there.'

A little while later they were seated round the gate-leg table eating smoked mackerel pâté and hot toast, and drinking Chablis. Oedipus also had a chair drawn up to the table, where he sat very upright with his eyes half closed, as if he could hardly bear the sight of such unattainable delicacies.

'He's better if he sits where he can see,' Atherton said without apology. 'Otherwise his curiosity sometimes gets the better of his manners.'

'This is delicious,' Joanna said. 'Did you make the pâté yourself?'

Atherton looked gratified at the compliment. 'Marks and Sparks. Purveyors of comestibles to the rich and single. One of the truly great things about not being married and having children is that you never have to eat boring food. You can have what you like, when you like.'

'Oh, I agree,' Joanna said. 'I'd sooner not bother to eat if there's nothing interesting around. I like small amounts of really exotic things.'

Slider looked at them grimly. 'All right for you youngsters. You wait until you grow up. Bird's Eye Beefburgers and Findus Crispy Pancakes will catch up with you in the end.'

'I shall never be that old,' Atherton said with a delicate shudder. 'I'll go and get the next course.'

'Can I help?' Joanna said dutifully, but he was already gone. He returned very soon with a recipe-dish pheasant, re-heated. 'Marks and Spencer?' Joanna said.

'Wainwright and Daughter,' Atherton corrected. 'I always thought Daughter was the other bloke's name – you know, Mr Daughter.'

He added Egyptian new potatoes, Spanish broccoli, and Guatemalan petits pois.

'Harrods?' Joanna tried.

'Marks and Spencer,' he said triumphantly. 'Air travel and greenhouse forcing have effectively eliminated the seasons.'

'And freezing,' Joanna added.

'Nothing can eliminate freezing, unless you go and live on the equator. Have some more Chablis.'

While they ate, Slider told them about his interview with Martin Cutts, and Anne-Marie's fear. Atherton listened attentively, and then said, 'I know you think she was mixed up in something really heavy, and that this was a gang murder of some kind, but you know there's nothing to go on. The boys from Lambeth went over her flat with a fine-tooth comb and found absolutely zilch.'

'The boys from Lambeth?' Joanna asked.

'The Metropolitan Police Forensic Science Laboratories, at Lambeth.'

'But they wouldn't,' Slider said patiently. 'That's what really convinces me, that the whole thing was so carefully organised. They haven't made a single mistake, except for the violin.'

'It's circular thinking to say that because there's no evidence it means that they were too good to leave any. Why flog a dead horse? The Thompson lead is much better. It only wants working up a bit to look presentable.'

'All right, tell me the way you see it,' Slider sighed.

'Point one: Thompson had a good reason for wanting to get rid of her. She was being a bloody nuisance.'

'That's not much of a motive.'

'Better than no motive at all. Anyway, point two: his girl-friend is a theatre nurse and has access to the drug used to kill Anne-Marie.'

'Except that none was missing. You know we checked with all the hospitals first thing.'

Atherton shrugged. 'If she was smart enough to steal it she'd be smart enough to forge the records, or cover up the theft in some way. Whoever got the stuff would have to do that.'

'Well, go on.'

'Point three: Thompson lied about where he was that evening. He says he went for a drink at a certain pub – where no-one remembers seeing him – and then went straight home. But the hall porter at the hospital saw him there that night – he's seen him often enough picking up his girlfriend to recognise him.'

'Well, maybe he was picking her up that night, too.'

'But she says she didn't see him. Why would he go there, unless to see his girlfriend? Or, if he did go there to see her, why is she lying?'

'It's not much,' Slider said, shaking his head.

'Oh come on,' Joanna interrupted, having restrained herself long enough, 'you can't believe that weed Simon Thompson murdered Anne-Marie? He's a complete rabbit.'

Atherton looked at her. 'Well, as it happens, I agree with you, but that isn't evidence, is it? And Bill will tell you that there are plenty of murderers – particularly domestic murderers – who don't look as if they could or would hurt a fly. Now, I've got a Polish cheesecake to finish off with, delicious enough to make a strong man weep, and the coffee's made. If you'd like to go and sit by the fire, I'll bring it all over on a tray and we can be comfortable.'

Slider settled in the armchair by the fire and Joanna sat on the floor by his feet. Atherton shut the remains of the pheasant in the fridge, and Oedipus pretty soon came mooching back in to enjoy the second-best pleasures of the fire and Slider's trousers, which being light grey showed up either black or white hair most satisfactorily. When everyone had plate, fork, cup and glass disposed about them, Atherton settled himself on the sofa and said, 'All right, Bill. Let's hear what you think.'

'There are several things about this case that bother me,' he began slowly. 'I haven't yet begun to put them together. But look – her body was stripped naked, surely to prevent her from being identified? But then her foot was marked after death in a way that looked like a signal or warning to someone. She lived in a modest way in a poky little bedsitter, but she had in her possession a violin worth almost a million pounds. Her aunt says she had no money but what she earned as a musician, but in Birmingham she lived in an expensive luxury flat. She had a large inheritance that she couldn't get her hands on until she married, and suddenly after the trip to Italy she made a desperate attempt to persuade Simon Thompson to marry her. When the attempt failed, she seemed depressed, and told Martin Cutts she was afraid. Just before Christmas her diary goes missing, and she's murdered at a time when it's most likely she won't be missed for a considerable time. On the night of her murder she goes out to her car, and then comes running back to try to persuade Joanna and the others to go with her to a different pub.'

He stopped, and there was silence, except for the crackling of the fire and the suddenly audible purring of Oedipus, now seated in Atherton's lap.

'So what does it all add up to,' Atherton said. It wasn't a question.

'One thing is obvious – the Birmingham connection's got to be followed up. John Brown said that she still went up there on a regular basis, to play for her old orchestra.' He turned to Joanna. 'Is that likely?'

She frowned. 'We all do outside work when we can get it, and Ruth Chisholm – their fixer – is much nicer than our horrible old Queen John, who wouldn't put a woman on the call list to save his life. But she was very lucky they wanted her. There must have been plenty of other people – local people – after the work.'

'So it's quite possible that she wasn't really working for her old orchestra, but simply putting that forward as a reason for going up there.'

'But why did she want to go up there?'

'Why would anyone want to go to Birmingham?' Atherton agreed. 'But on the other hand, why put forward a reason at all? Why not just go and tell no-one.'

'Presumably,' Slider said slowly, 'on instructions.'

Atherton looked at him sidelong. 'You still believe there's a big organisation behind all this?'

He shrugged. 'Otherwise, as you say, why give a reason at all?'

'You don't know yet that she didn't go there to work,' Joanna said.

'Easy enough to find out,' Atherton said. 'I suppose that means you'll be putting in another 728, Bill?'

What's a 728?' Joanna asked obediently.

'Permission to leave the Metropolitan Area,' Slider supplied. 'We have to apply for it if we go out on police business.'

Atherton grinned. 'It also means overtime, expenses, petrol money, pub lunches – no wonder the uniformed branch think we have an easy life. And who will you take with you, he asked him innocently?'

'Norma,' Slider said promptly.

'The hell you will!'

'Who's Norma?' Joanna asked, still the obedient feed.

'WDC Swilley,' Atherton said with relish. 'We call her Norma for obvious reasons. She's good fun, drinks like a fish, swears like a matelot – typical CID, in fact. But I don't think it's on, Bill. I can see the Super licensing you to trundle her off in your passion-wagon for a fumble in the aptly named lay-bys. Stopping off for a pub lunch with Becvers or me is one thing, but cock-au-van is going too far.'

The phone rang, and while Atherton was out of the room Joanna turned to lean on Slider's knees and say, 'Do you really think Anne-Marie was involved with some big criminal organisation? It seems so unlikely to me.'

'You prefer Atherton's theory?'

'There must be other explanations. But if it came to it, I'd prefer your theory to his.'

'Why?' he asked, genuinely interested.

'Because you're better looking than him.'

Atherton came back looking triumphant. 'They've found Anne-Marie's car. A forensic team's going over it right now. Also the report on Thompson's car has come in. Nothing of great interest except some long, dark hairs. Very long, dark hairs.'

'You said his girlfriend was dark,' Slider said.

'Short and curly,' Joanna supplied, muted.

'Where was the car found?'

Atherton's triumphant smile widened a millimetre. 'In a back street in Islington, about half a mile from where Thompson lives. Within walking distance, as you might say.'

'But surely,' Joanna protested, 'no-one would be so stupid as to abandon the car of someone they've just murdered so close to their own home?'

'You'd be surprised just how stupid most people really are.'

'Who's on duty – Hunt, isn't it?' said Slider. 'Do you mind if I give him a ring?'

'Use the one in the kitchen,' Atherton said. Left alone, he and Joanna eyed each other cautiously, and then Atherton cleared his throat. Joanna's eyes narrowed in amusement.

'I suppose you're going to warn me off. You're very protective of him, aren't you?'

'You know he's married, don't you?'

'Yes. Yes, I know.'

'Very married. He's never had an affair before – he's just not the type.'

'Is there a type?'

'He's got two kids and a mortgage and a career. He's not going to leave all that for you.'

'Did I expect him to?'

'I'm just warning you for your own good.'

'No you're not,' she said evenly.

He squared up to her. 'Look, any man can get carried away, and if he did leave home in the heat of the moment, it would be disastrous for him. It would ruin him, and I don't just mean materially. He's one of the few really honest men I know, he has a conscience, and the worry and guilt he'd feel about leaving his wife and family would ruin any happiness he might have with you.'

She suppressed a smile. 'You're going very far, very fast. Isn't that what's called jumping to conclusions?'

'The fact that he's done it at all means it's pretty serious. You don't know him like I do. He's not like us – he's from a different generation. He can't take things lightly. And he's very – innocent – about some things.'

'Well,' she said, and looked away, and then back again. 'I think he's old enough to make up his own mind, don't you?'

Atherton rubbed the back of one hand with the fingers of the other, a nervous gesture of which he was unaware. 'I don't want you to put him in a position where he *has* to decide. Don't you see, once that happens he'll be unhappy whichever way he chooses.'

'I don't see that I can help that,' she said seriously.

Atherton felt anger rising, that she took it all so lightly. 'You could break if off, now, before it goes any further.'

'So could he.'

'But he won't. You know that. If you would just leave him alone –'

Now she smiled. 'Ah, but he'd have to leave me alone, too. Have you thought of that?'

Atherton jerked away from her and walked to the fire-place, beat his fist softly on the mantelpiece. 'You could discourage him,' he said at last, his back to her. He was afraid he would lose his temper if he looked at her. 'You could do that.'

'I could,' she conceded. She looked at his tense back thoughtfully. 'I still think, however, that it's his business to decide for himself, not yours or mine.'

He returned. 'It just shows how much you really care for him! You have no scruples about destroying his life, do you?'

She looked at him carefully, as if wondering whether it was worth trying to make him understand. Then she said, 'I don't believe that the status quo is the only workable configuration, or that maintaining it is necessarily the primary purpose of life. Life is rich in possibilities, and on the law of averages alone, some of them are bound to be an improvement.'

Atherton said sharply, 'You'll make a lot of people very unhappy.'

'I don't happen to believe that happiness is the primary purpose of life, either.'

'Crap!' Atherton said explosively. She shrugged and said no more.

In a moment Slider came back. 'I think I'd better take you home,' he said. 'Things are about to hot up.' He glanced from her to Atherton. 'Were you two quarrelling?'

'Discussing,' Atherton said carefully. 'Our views on a number of things are very different.'

'Nonsense,' Joanna smiled. 'We were quarrelling over you – trying to see which of us loves you best.'

Slider grinned, not believing her. 'Who won?'

'I think it was a draw,' she said, and was rewarded by a brief and quirky smile from Atherton.

* * *

In the car he said, 'What were you talking about while I was on the phone?'

'He was trying to persuade me to give you up.'

'Oh!' He sounded dismayed. 'What did you say?'

'That you were old enough to make up your own mind.' It was not entirely what he wanted to hear, as she knew very well.

He sighed. 'Why do things have to be so complicated?' he said helplessly, like so many before him.

'That's how life is. Easy, but not simple.'

'All right for you to say it's easy,' he said resentfully.

'But it is. One always knows what the alternatives are.'

'Perhaps I haven't got your courage.'

'It's not a matter of courage.'

They stopped at the lights. 'Don't be so tough. What is it a matter of?'

'Approach, I suppose. Like pulling off a plaster. There's the inch-by-inch approach. Or you can give one good rip and have done. You always know at the beginning what the end will be, so I always think you might as well – just jump.'

He looked at her, feeling so much and so complicatedly that he couldn't articulate it. The lights went green, and he started off again automatically, without being aware of it.

'All the same,' she said after a moment, 'don't make the mistake of thinking that you can't cope and I can.'

He glanced at her, perplexed. 'But you can cope with anything,' he said.

'Oh yes, I know,' she said wryly. 'That's the trouble. That's what will finish me in the end.'

He wanted to protest that he was not Atherton, that he did not understand riddles; but he found that – and of course – he did. The love he felt for her, knowing its way better than he did, was fierce and tender in such mingled proportions – a cross between ravishing and cherishing – that he felt scoured, shaken, emptied out; and, with that, curiously strong, like a man who had been on a fast. Forty days and forty nights. Stronger than her – and how was that possible?

They arrived at the house. He wanted to make love to her, to sink into her and never surface again. She was the warm precinct of the cheerful day that he never wanted to leave.

'Will you come in?' she asked when he didn't move.

'No, I must go home.'

'And you said you didn't have courage.'

She sat quite still for a moment or two, and then as she began to move he said, 'You know it's Anne-Marie's funeral tomorrow.'

'No, I didn't know. Are you going to it?'

'Privately, not officially. Would you like to come with me?'

'Yes. I'd like to go. In all this it's so easy to forget about her.'

She looked at him seriously to see if he understood what she meant, and of course he did. He touched her face with the tips of his fingers, and then kissed her – on the mouth, but like a benediction.

'I'll pick you up,' he said.

But even forewarned, he hadn't expected the funeral to be so depressing. It turned warm during the night and began to rain, and it went on raining dismally all day, and was so dark that eleven in the morning seemed like four in the afternoon. Added to that there were hardly any mourners, which made everything seem somehow worse. Of course, she had had no relatives apart from the aunt, but Slider had expected there to be friends, people from her past life, though he could not have said who they might be. As it was, Anne-Marie Austen's home life was represented by Mrs Ringwood, attended by her housekeeper and Captain Hildyard, the solicitor, and an old man who seemed to be Mrs Ringwood's gardener; from her working life there was only Joanna, and Martin Cutts.

'I expect others would have come if it hadn't been short notice,' Joanna said without conviction.

'Sue Bernstein phoned Ruth Chisholm in case anyone from up there wanted to come, but it looks as though no-one could make it,' Martin Cutts said.

'I suppose it's too far for them,' Joanna said.

'Nonsense. Birmingham is closer to here than London.'

'Oh. Well, probably they're working today,' Joanna said unconvincingly.

The service was distressingly bald and devoid of spiritual uplift to Slider, who liked his church High or not at all, and could never get over the feeling that the modern translation of the Prayer Book, by being so ugly, was sacrilegious. There was nothing, in fact, to take his mind off the fact that Joanna was seated on the further side of Martin Cutts, and that when she started crying Cutts put his arm round her and she rested her cheek on his shoulder. Slider hated him, with his ready, slippery ease of showing physical affection. Why couldn't I ever have been like that? he wondered resentfully. What Cutts gave and received so easily cost him so much pain and effort.

The committal at the graveside was brief, and as soon as was decently possible everyone hurried away to seek shelter. Slider found himself accosted by Mrs Ringwood, with Captain Hildyard looming supportively at her shoulder.

'I'm surprised to see you here, Inspector,' she said. 'Are you the official police presence?'

'No, ma'am. I'm here in my private capacity.'

She raised an eyebrow. 'Private capacity? What could that be? You weren't a friend of my niece, were you?'

'No, ma'am. But I do feel very much involved in the case – enough so to wish to pay my respects.'

'How refreshing to learn that you chaps have room for human feelings,' Hildyard put in, smiling yellowly behind his moustache to show that it was a joke, though his eyes were as boiled and glassy as ever. They swivelled round to stare at Joanna. 'And you, young lady – were you a friend of our poor, dear Anne-Marie?'

Joanna seemed upset, almost angered by the look and the words. She stared at his tie, avoiding his eyes, and said brusquely, 'I shared a desk with her in the Orchestra. What about you? I never heard her mention you as a friend of hers.'

It sounded rude, challenging, and Hildyard's eyes seemed hostile, though he spoke evenly enough. 'I've known the poor child since she was tiny. Being so much of another generation from her, I hardly like to claim I was a friend, but I know she looked on me with trust and affection. It's the privilege, perhaps, of my profession to win a place in the hearts of our young clients. Many's the time I've popped in to attend to her pony's colic or her puppy's worms, and believe me there's no surer way to win a child's love.'

'Perhaps you'd like to come back to the house for a glass of sherry,' Mrs Ringwood said abruptly to the air in general. Slider was reminded of his Latin lessons at school, when he had learned to construct a sentence that 'expects the answer *no*'. Mrs Ringwood's inflection had just the same effect.

'No thank you, ma'am. I have to be getting back to London,' Slider said, and by a turn of his body managed to place himself alongside Mrs Ringwood on the gravel path, which was only wide enough for two. Hildyard was forced to drop back beside Joanna. 'By the way, Mrs Ringwood,' he went on, lowering his voice and approaching her ear under the umbrella, 'did you ever visit Anne-Marie in Birmingham, after she joined the Orchestra there?'

'Certainly not. Why should I want to visit her?'

'You never went to her flat?'

'I had no reason to.'

'So you've no idea what sort of place it was? Whether she rented it? Whether she shared it with anyone?'

She evinced impatience. 'None at all. I've told you before, Inspector, I knew nothing about her personal life. I suggest you ask some of her musician friends.'

Slider thanked her, and collected Joanna and escaped by a side-path. So it hadn't been the aunt's flat – that disposed of that possibility. But something had been said today – something, sometime, by somebody – that was important, and he just couldn't bring to mind what it was. A bell had been rung in the back of his mind, but it was too far back to be of any help. He left it alone, knowing his subconscious would throw it back to him sooner or later, and returned his attention to Joanna.

Martin Cutts had just asked her if she would go with him to the nearest pub for a pint. She replied with a shake of the head and a single graphic glance towards Slider; at which he grinned, kissed her easily on the lips, said 'See you Wednesday, then,' and left.

'It's half past two closing out here,' she said. Her voice sounded so strange that Slider glanced at her, to find that she was grey with cold and misery and within an inch of tears. He hurried her to the car, wanting to get them away from this place, wanting, absurdly, to take Anne-Marie with them too. She had been a musician as well, and even if no-one had loved her, she had once known the companionship of pubs and the easy kisses of Martin Cutts. The contrast was too harsh – it seemed cruel to leave her behind.

In the car he put on the heater and the blower and drove as fast as the rain would allow back towards the sanity of London. As the car warmed up, Joanna revived.

'Well,' she said first, 'so that's that. Not my idea of a funeral. When I go, I want hundreds of people crying their eyes out, and then going off and getting good and drunk and saying what a great person I was.'

'Yes,' said Slider comprehensively.

'A proper service in the church, too, with candles and hymns and the real words out of the Prayer Book. Not that second-rate, poor man's substitute; that New Revised Non-Denominational Series Four People's Pray-in, or whatever the bloody thing's called.' She glared at him, and suddenly cried out, 'It isn't fair!' and of course she wasn't talking about church services. But he was glad, in a way, that it hadn't been the old-fashioned service, because the familiar words would have reminded him of Mam's funeral. They always did, when he heard them on television or in a film, and still they made him cry. Funerals above all reminded you that there was no going back, that every day something was taken from you that you could never have back.

After a while she said in a small voice, 'When I die, will you promise to see that I'm buried properly, not like that? And I'll promise the same thing for you.'

'Oh Joanna,' he said helplessly, and took her hand into his lap for comfort.

When they reached Turnham Green, however, she revived with the suddenness of youth. 'I'm starving. Do you know what I fancy – a hamburger! A proper one, not a McDonald's. Shall we go to Macarthurs?'

'I can't,' he said relunctantly. 'I've got to go to the station. There's a mass of things to be done, and the meeting to prepare for, I'm sorry.'

'Some love affair this is,' she said, but jokingly, making it easy for him.

'I'll try and call in later, on my way home. If I can't, I'll phone anyway.' She looked so forlorn that he offered his own particular foothold of comfort. 'Don't worry, we can't lose each other now. We can't stop knowing each other.'

She gave him an impish grin, 'Count your chickens! Don't forget once I start working again you'll have two impossible schedules to coordinate!'

'Look at this, guv,' Atherton said, bouncing his Viking length through the open door of Slider's room. 'Anne-Marie's bank statement – and very interesting reading it makes.'

'Midland Bank, Gloucester Road branch?'

'I expect she opened it when she was at the Royal College,' Atherton said wisely. 'Though with her swanky connections, you'd think it would have been Coutts from birth.'

'But she never had any money of her own before, did she?' Slider spread out the pages. 'Well, the totals are pretty modest. No money here for buying Stradivariuses.'

'No, but look here, last August – see? Sundries, three thousand pounds.'

'Is that her pay from the Orchestra?'

'No, that shows up as salary – look, here, and here. But sundries, bloody sundries, is what they call deposits, cash or cheques, made by post or over the counter. And it's gone in no time – four big cheques to cash. Spent it. She must have had expensive habits.'

'No sign of the repayments on the bank loan Joanna mentioned?'

'Oh, that was paid off a long time ago. Look, this is more interesting. Go back a bit further, and what do you find. A big sundry here, five K, one for four here, five again, six and a half here. Roughly every month she pays in a big lump sum and then whips it out in cash. Now what do you make of that?'

'Could she have spent it all? Maybe she had a savings account.'

'Nothing's turned up. Maybe she played the market, or put it on the ponies. But I'm not so interested in where it went as where it came from. Do you know what I think?'

'Tell me,' Slider said indulgently.

'I think she was blackmailing somebody. Or some bodies.'

'And whoever she was blackmailing got fed up and killed her? Have you gone off your Thompson theory, then?'

'Not necessarily. It could be him she was blackmailing.'

'My Uncle Arthur could stick his wooden leg up his arse and do toffee-apple impressions,' Slider said mildly.

Atherton grinned reluctantly. 'Oh well, you're not the only one who can have a hunch, you know. There was something very sinister and unloveable about that young woman. I'm going to keep my eyes open.'

'You do that. Here's something to rest them on – the report on her car.'

'Blimey, the lab really pulled its finger out on that one, didn't it? What did they find?'

'Nothing out of the ordinary, except that on the front passenger seat there were traces of a white powder –'

'*A white powder!*'

'Behave yourself. A white powder which on analysis proved to be pyrethrum and –' he consulted the report – 'piperonyl butoxide.'

'Come again?'

'It's an insecticide with pretty general application. Kills fleas, lice, bedbugs, earwigs, woodlice and so on. Freely available from any garden shop, or Woolworth's – you might find it in any household. Poisonous if you ate enough of it, and can irritate the eyes and nasal tissues if you throw it about or inhale it.'

'It irritates my brain tissues,' Atherton said crossly. 'What's the use of that? She could have bought a tin of it at any time, for any purpose, and spilt some on the seat. Where does that get us?'

'Nowhere. Except that we didn't find a tin of anything like that in her flat. But the other thing was more interesting – also found on the passenger seat, but down the crack between the seat and the back.' He handed over a small square of paper which had originally been folded into four, but had since been crushed and creased and dirtied by its sojourn down the seat cushion. Opening it out Atherton saw that it was a sheet from a note-block, the sort of small pad you keep by the telephone. On it, written at a steep angle, as it might be by someone gripping the telephone receiver between chin and shoulder to leave both hands free, was the word *Saloman,* and a telephone number.

There was an instant of painful blankness, and then Atherton exclaimed, 'Saloman! Saloman of Vincey's!'

'You know who he is?'

'Vincey's of Bond Street, the antiquarian's. Saloman's their expert on violin bows. Andrew Watson, the bloke at Sotheby's, mentioned him when he was looking at the Stradivarius. Is this Anne-Marie's writing, do we know? I suppose we can find out. Did she consult him? It's a lead, anyway, and we've precious few of those.'

Slider smiled at his excitement. 'Leads have a habit of fizzling out on closer inspection. I'll leave this one to you – you're getting to be the violin expert around here. By the way, someone ought to drop in at The Dog and Scrotum and have a chat with Hilda and the regulars. I know they all said they didn't see Anne-Marie that night, but that was the official line. A comfy, private chat ought to get the truth out of them, one way or the other. I suppose,' he added unconvincingly, 'as it's more or less on my way home –'

'Bollards,' Atherton said sweetly. 'You know very well you don't go home that way any more. I'll do it, guv – you shove off to love's young dream.'

'That's awfully good of you, old chap,' Slider said gravely. 'I thought you didn't approve.'

'If you see enough of her, you might get bored. Anyway, you know Hilda fancies me. She's more likely to come across for me than for you. It's my fresh young face and youthful charm – she can't resist 'em.'

Slider shuddered. 'What about the gatekeepers at the TVC?'

'Beevers did 'em. One of them thinks he remembers that she didn't get into the car, just went up to it and then ran back as if she'd forgotten something.'

'A note under the windscreen wiper, perhaps, telling her

to meet the murderer at the pub?'

'Not if the murderer was Thompson.'

'You know what I think about that,' Slider said.

'Maybe she just fancied somewhere different for a change. You can make too much of something, you know.'

Slider met his eyes, and a great number of warnings passed in both directions, which neither was likely to take heed of.

11

Miss World and Montezuma

'Hey,' said Joanna, sitting up and looking down at him in the leaping firelight.

'Hmm?' One side of his body was too hot, the other icy from the draught under the sitting-room door; the floor was hard under his shoulder blades, the rug itchy under his buttocks. All the same, he would have preferred not to have to move for several more hours. Sleep had been in short supply lately.

'You sleep on your own penny,' she said. 'You're supposed to be amusing me.'

'I just did,' he murmured without opening his eyes. He felt the roughness of her hair and a brief pressure on his penis as she bent to kiss it.

'Sex is all very well, but I want you to talk to me as well.'

He groaned and rolled onto his side, and propped his head minimally with hand and elbow. 'What?' he said.

'You look so sweet and ruffled,' she grinned at him. 'Innocent.'

'You look like a dangerous wild animal,' he said. 'Most people look vulnerable when they take their clothes off, but you're just the opposite. You look as though you might eat me.'

'I will if you like,' she offered equably.

'A drink first. All very well for you women – it takes it out of us men.'

149

'You women! Spoken from the depths of your vast experience, I suppose!'

'You don't have to have a baby to be a gynaecologist,' he said with dignity.

She rose fluidly to her feet. 'Can you drink gin and tonic?'

'Does a monkey eat nuts?'

Left alone, he sat up and turned his other side to the fire. He looked around him and wondered at the sense of peace and comfort that this room gave him. He had never, to his memory, sat on the floor in his own house, though he used to in the early days of his marriage when he and Irene had had their little flat. But at home he couldn't in any case have sat on the floor by the fire, since there was neither fireplace nor chimney. This room was neither smart nor elegant, nor even particularly clean, but it was a place where you could do nothing in perfect peace, a room that demanded nothing of you, imposed nothing on you.

A clinking sound heralded Joanna with a large glass in each hand. Ice cubes floated and bumped like miniature icebergs, lemon moons hung suspended, beaded with silver bubbles, and the liquid gleamed with the delicate blue sheen of a bloody large gin. The aromatic scent of it wafted sweetly to his nostrils.

'Lovely,' he said inadequately. She folded down beside him, and held her glass at eye level.

'Aesthetically pleasing,' she acknowledged.

'You're such an animal. It's all pleasure with you – pleasure and comfort.'

'Any fool can be uncomfortable.'

'But what about duty and responsibility?'

She turned her head to rub an itch on her nose against her shoulder, something he couldn't imagine Irene ever doing.

'Those too. One fits them in, you know. But one's first duty is to oneself.'

'All right for you. You don't have a wife and children.'

'Oh, these wives and children!' He looked irritated, and she went on, 'Well, if you can't make yourself happy, you aren't likely to have much success with anyone else, are you? What use would I be to you if I were unhappy?'

'If everyone thought like you –' he began, but she gave convention short shrift.

'Everyone doesn't. The whole point is that the philosophy of irresponsibility is only safe in the hands of the morally trustworthy. So drink your nice drink and don't worry about it. It takes a great deal of practice to become a dedicated hedonist.'

'In other words, you don't want to discuss it.'

'Uh-huh,' she concurred, leaning forward, her glass held clear of their bodies, to kiss him. She slid her tongue into his mouth and he was amazed to feel his instant reaction. Blimey, lad, he addressed his organ inwardly, you're pretty lively for your age. Doing yourself proud, aren't you? He reached behind him blindly for somewhere safe to put his glass so as to free his hands, and the phone started to ring.

Joanna removed her tongue from his mouth. ' "Time watches from the shadow. And coughs when you would kiss".'

'Shall I get it? It's probably for me.'

But she was already up. 'I should have put the answering machine on.'

It was O'Flaherty, starting his week of nights, and fresh from his day off with an assumed and expansive outrage. 'It's gettin' to be a bloody trial trackin' you down, Billy me darlin'. I even rang The Dog an' Bloody Scorpion, till Little Boy Blue said I'd find you in Flagrante Dilecto, and I said to him, I said, that's a pub I never even heard of –'

'I hate to interrupt your Ignorant Man from the Bogs routine, but did you want anything in particular? It's cold away from the fire.'

'I think I got something for you,' O'Flaherty said, dropping abruptly out of role. 'Listen, there's this young feller asking for you. He says he's got something important to tell you, and it's got to be you because he's shit-scared of Atherton. Says Atherton's got it in for him. Wants to see you alone.'

'How d'you rate him?'

'I think he's the goods. Name of Thompson.'

'Christ.'

'Are you deaf, I said Thompson,' O'Flaherty said witheringly.

'Is he there now?'

'No, he wouldn't come to the station in case we locked him up. All this was on the dog an' bone. I got him holdin' fire in The Crown and Sceptic, but only God knows how long he'll stay put. Apart from bein' in mortal terror, he'll be as pissed as a bloody fart unless you get out there soon. Where are you now?'

'Turnham Green. I can be there in ten minutes. Listen, Pat, will you do me a favour? Will you ring a certain person and say what's happened and that I don't know how long I'll be.'

'Ah, Jaysus, Billy –'

'Come on, Pat. Don't start that again.'

'Okay, okay, I'll do it. Now you'd better get for Chrissakes over to dat pub before yer man changes his mind.'

'All right, I'll speak to you later.'

He put the phone down and turned to find Joanna not looking at him. 'A certain person, forsooth,' she said, but quite mildly.

'Simon Thompson wants to see me, alone. Says he's got information for me. I've got to go and see him before he changes his mind.' She nodded acquiescence, turning her face away, sipping her drink and looking into the fire. All sorts of bits of him wanted badly to cleave unto her just then, but he reached for his clothes automatically, however unwillingly. 'I'm sorry.'

She shrugged.

'I'll ring you later, if it's not too late,' he said humbly.

She turned, contrite. 'Ring anyway, even if it is too late. I'll be awake.'

He dressed and kissed her goodbye before he left, but his mind had already left ahead of him.

The pub seemed full for a weekday. Slider stood just inside the door looking around so as to give Thompson a chance to accost him first. Neither, of course, knew what the other looked like, but he pretty soon picked out Thompson from Atherton's description – 'Miss World in trousers' – and from the way he was crouched over an untouched half pint with the preoccupied, inward-looking posture of an animal in pain. The eyes came round to the door, hesitated, went away, and returned to meet Slider's hopefully. Slider nodded slightly and went across and Thompson made room for him on the banquette. As soon as he was near enough, Slider could smell the other man's fear. This was no hoax.

'Mr Thompson?'

Thompson nodded, still hunched wretchedly. 'You're Inspector Slider?'

'How did you know about me?'

'Sue Bernstein said you were in charge of the investigation. She said you seemed like a decent bloke. And she said you're going with Joanna Marshall, is that right?'

Slider coughed slightly, taken aback by the directness of the question.

'Well, I thought you were probably all right. Better than that Sergeant Atherton, anyway. He's got it in for me.' His voice rose a little in panic. 'He thinks I killed Anne-Marie. He's out to prove it, whatever it takes.' He seemed to flinch at the sound of his own words, and crouched lower, looking around him as if he expected Atherton to leap up triumphantly from under the table brandishing a tape recorder.

'I'm sure he doesn't think anything of the kind,' Slider said soothingly. 'We have to ask questions in order to get at the facts, that's all.'

Thompson looked at him hopefully, a film of sweat on his upper lip, his eyes fawning. 'You seem like a reasonable bloke. You don't think I killed her, do you?'

'Well, as a matter of fact I don't,' Slider said, 'but that's neither here nor there, is it?'

'Isn't it?'

'Well, if you really didn't do it, you've got nothing to worry about, have you?'

'It's all very well for you,' Thompson said bitterly, 'but if you were in my position you wouldn't be so cheerful. I had nothing to do with it. You must believe me. I was as horrified as anyone when I heard.'

'Perhaps a bit more horrified?' Slider suggested. 'Well, after all, you had had a relationship with her. You must have been closer to her than anyone else –'

'No-one was close to that girl,' he interrupted with force. 'She was weird and – look, I'm sorry she's dead, but I can't help it. She was mixed up in something and it caught up with her in the end. It was her own fault, that's how I see it.'

'What was she mixed up in?' Slider asked evenly, his heart jumping.

Thompson took the plunge. 'I don't know the details, but I'm pretty sure she was mixed up in some kind of smuggling racket. I got the idea she was beginning to want out, but she'd got in too deep. On the plane coming back from Italy she seemed pretty scared, but she wouldn't tell me what it was about.'

'Ah yes, Italy. Tell me about that. You and she were going around together, weren't you?'

He looked uncomfortable. 'It was just for the tour – that was understood. We'd done it before. We swapped rooms with some other people so that we could sleep together, and everything was all right until the last day, in Florence. We'd been out in the morning, poking around the junk shops in one of those alleys behind the main square – you know.' Slider, who had never been to Florence, nodded. 'Then I said how about getting some lunch and she suddenly said no, she had to go and see somebody. Just sprang it on me like that – never mentioned anything about it before. Well, when you're spending a tour together, you sort of expect to know what the other person's doing, don't you?'

Again Slider nodded.

'So naturally I asked her who she had to see all of a sudden, and she wouldn't tell me. Got quite nasty about it. Eventually she said if I really wanted to know she was going to see her cousin Mario, but it was none of my business, and I never gave her a moment's privacy and – things like that. Suddenly we were quarrelling and I didn't know how I got into it.'

'You think she deliberately engineered the quarrel – so as to get away from you?'

Thompson nodded eagerly. 'Yes, that's it. And she was different, too – jumpy and nervous, looking over her shoulder as if she thought someone might be watching her. Anyway, we argued a bit, and she stormed off, and I – well, I sort of followed her. I didn't really mean to. I was just walking in the same direction at first, because that was the way I wanted to go, and then because I was angry I sort of got the idea that I'd follow her and see where she went and then later I'd face her with this cousin Mario nonsense ...' His voice trailed off.

'You were jealous, perhaps?' Slider suggested. Thompson shrugged. 'Did she see you following her?'

'I don't think so. I had a job to keep up with her, mind you, because she went a hell of a long way, right off the tourist track, and after a while I got scared of losing her, because I'd never have found my way back. I had no idea where I was.'

'Did she seem to know where she was going?'

'Oh yes. She never hesitated. And she took lots of little alleys and back streets and so on. I'd never have remembered the way – it was too complicated.'

Cautious, thought Slider. How the hell did she miss an incompetent bloodhound like Thompson? 'Where did you eventually end up?'

'In an ordinary street, with houses and a few shops on either side. Not a tourist street. Not smart. And then she turned into a doorway.'

'A shop?'

'I didn't see. I was a bit behind her, and when she went in I didn't like to go too close in case she came out again suddenly, and spotted me. So I stood in a doorway further down the street and waited. I kept thinking, suppose there's a back way? Suppose she goes out the back way, I'm really f– in trouble.'

'You didn't notice the name of the street, I suppose,' Slider said without hope.

Thompson looked eager and said, 'Yes, I did. The doorway I was standing in was right opposite the street sign, so I was sort of staring at it for ages. I remembered it because it was so inappropriate – Paradise Alley, only in Italian, you know.'

Blimey, Slider thought, a fact. Someone actually remembers something.

'Go on.'

'Well, she was in there I don't know how long, but it seemed a long time to me, maybe ten minutes, and when she came out she was carrying a bag.'

'What sort of bag? How big?'

'I think you call them carpet bags. You know, like a big sports bag, but soft – canvas I think – and with handles on the top. About this big.' He offered his hands about thirty inches apart.

'Was it heavy?' Thompson looked puzzled. 'How did she walk with it? Did she walk as if it was heavy?'

'Oh,' he said, enlightened. 'No, not really. She just walked normally. Well, I ducked back into the doorway until she'd gone past and then followed her again until we got near the main square and I recognised where I was, and I turned off to the side. But she must have turned off down the next street, because a minute later when I came into the square I bumped into her. She didn't look too pleased to see me, but I put it down to we'd just had a quarrel. So I asked her what was in the bag. Well, it was a natural question, wasn't it?'

'Perfectly. What did she say?'

'I thought for a minute she wasn't going to tell me. I thought she'd tell me to mind my own business. But then she sort of laughed and said olive oil.'

'Olive oil?' Slider was perplexed. Little wheels were whirring and clicking, but the patterns were making no sense.

'Olive oil, two tins, that's what she said. Well, she was nuts on cooking, I knew that. She said it was a special sort you couldn't get in England, and her cousin Mario got it for her to take back.' He shrugged, distancing himself from the whole mess.

'You say she laughed,' Slider said. 'Did she seem happy? Excited?'

'It wasn't that sort of laugh,' Thompson said doubtfully. 'More sort of – as if she was having a secret laugh at me. She wanted to get shot of me, anyway, that was for sure because I said I was going to get some lunch and asked her to come with me, and she said she was going back to the hotel and shot off like a scalded cat.'

'When did you see her next?'

'In the hotel room when I went back to get my fiddle for

the seating rehearsal that evening. She was already there in the room when I arrived.'

'Did you see the bag again?'

'Yes, it was there on the end of her bed. I asked her, actually, if her cousin had given it to her, because it seemed rather a nice sort of thing just to be giving away. She didn't answer right off – looked a bit shifty, you know, as if she was wondering what to say – then she said he'd only lent it to her and that he'd be collecting it from the hall that evening. I'd have followed it up, but she jumped up and said she wasn't waiting for the Orchestra coach, that she wanted some fresh air so she was going to walk to the hall. And she just went. I think she wanted to get away from me, in case I asked her any more questions.'

'She took the bag with her?'

'Yes, and her fiddle case.'

'So you never got to see inside the bag?'

'No. She had it with her in the rehearsal, under her chair, but she must have passed it to this Mario when rehearsal finished, because she didn't have it later. But I've a fair idea what was in it, all the same, and it wasn't olive oil.' He looked at Slider expectantly.

'Not olive oil?' said Slider obediently.

'No. I'm pretty sure it was another fiddle, and a valuable one at that.'

Slider jumped, though he showed nothing more than interest on the outside. 'Why do you think that?'

'Because I was sitting behind her in the seating rehearsal and at the concert, and the fiddle she was playing at the concert wasn't the same one that she was playing during rehearsal.'

'Are you sure?'

'Positive. I knew her usual fiddle, because the varnish was very dark and there was a tiny bit of beading broken off just by the chin-rest which showed up very pale against the dark varnish. But the one she had in the concert was much lighter and when she rested it on her knee I saw it had an unusual sort of grain on the back. But most of all, it sounded different – much, much better. I'd say it was a very valuable one. It might have been a Strad or an Amati or something, in which case it would be worth a fortune.'

'You weren't able to get a closer look at it, I suppose?'

'No, but I'll tell you what – she was very close with it during the interval. She never put it down for a moment – she put it back in the case, and then stood holding the case, even while she had a cup of coffee. Now I've never seen her do that before. I've never seen anyone do that.'

'So you think she collected a valuable violin from this cousin Mario in order to smuggle it to England, swapped it with her own violin, and passed that to him in the carpet bag sometime between the rehearsal and the concert?'

'That's what I think. That night back at the hotel, when she was in the bathroom, I tried to get a look at it, but her fiddle case was locked and obviously I couldn't break it open. That was another thing that convinced me, because she didn't usually lock her case.'

'But surely,' Slider said slowly, 'someone would have noticed that she wasn't playing her usual instrument.'

Thompson looked puzzled. 'Well they did – I did. I noticed.'

'What about her desk partner? Surely she would have noticed straight away?'

Thompson looked disconcerted, and then frowned, evidently upset at having his theory overturned. Then his brow cleared and he looked excited, for a moment almost boyish. 'I remember now – Joanna wasn't at the concert! That's right! She and Anne-Marie went for something to eat after the rehearsal, and Joanna came down with Montezuma's Revenge, and couldn't play the concert. Screaming diarrhoea. Normally we would all just have moved up one, but there was already an odd desk at the back because Pete Norris had broken his finger in Naples, so they just put Hilary Tonks up beside Anne-Marie, and of course she wouldn't know what Anne-Marie normally played.'

But Anne-Marie couldn't have relied on Joanna's being put out of action. Unless she slipped her something during their meal. But was that likely? Slider could hear Atherton's voice saying, *these are deep waters, Watson.*

'How easy would it be to smuggle a violin? What happens to them on the plane?'

'The other instruments go in the baskets, which are loaded in the hold, but usually fiddle players carry their violins with them on the plane, for safety. The instruments get listed on a cartel for the customs, but no-one ever checks them, except to see there's the right number. I mean, if you went out with one and came back with two, someone might notice, but not otherwise.'

'Did Anne-Marie carry hers onto the plane with her on the way home?'

'I can't remember. I think so. I'm not sure.'

'Not sure?'

He looked apologetic. 'It's like an extra arm, you see. You expect a fiddle player to be carrying a fiddle, so you don't really notice. I can't be sure, but I think she did.'

Slider nodded, thinking. 'Did you ever tell Anne-Marie what you suspected?'

'No. I thought it was none of my business. In any case, if she'd managed to smuggle a Strad in, good luck to her. We'd all like one.' He frowned again. 'But actually, I never saw her play it in England. If she did smuggle one in, I suppose she must have sold it.'

'So it wasn't over that that you quarrelled?'

'Quarrelled? Oh –' Surprisingly, he blushed. 'No – that was – but it wasn't my fault. There was never meant to be anything between us after the tour – she knew that. Lots of people did it. And at first it was all right. She behaved just as usual. And then suddenly she seemed to change, started hanging round me, trying to get me to go for drinks with her and that sort of thing. She even tried to get her position changed so she could sit next to me. I told her I was happy with my girlfriend and told her to stop pissing me off. And then she turned nasty, and threatened to tell my girlfriend, and said that I'd led her on and promised to marry her and stuff like that.'

'And had you?'

'No!' His indignation sounded genuine. 'I don't know why she said that. I think she must have been going off her trolley. I never said anything about marrying her. You must believe me.' Slider's face was neutral. 'Helen does,' he added pathetically.

'You told people that she was the person making anonymous phone calls to players' wives, I believe?'

He turned a dull red. 'Well – yes – I suppose so. I was angry – I wanted to get back at her for trying to make trouble. I thought it might stop her.'

'And did it?'

'Well, something did. She left me alone, anyway.'

'Did it make trouble for her in the Orchestra?'

He shrugged. 'If you mean that business with John Brown, he didn't like her anyway. He doesn't like women in orchestras.'

'Tell me about the day she died. You must have seen her at the Television Centre?'

'Of course. But she hadn't given me any trouble since Christmas. I still tried to avoid her, though, just in case.'

'How did she seem to you?'

'Seem to me?'

'Was she happy, sad, frightened, worried?'

'Nothing really. She was quiet. Didn't speak much to anyone. That's how she usually was. I didn't notice anything different.'

'You'd arranged to go for a drink afterwards?'

'With Phil Redcliffe, yes, but during the second session he told me that Joanna and Anne-Marie were coming too. I think he felt sorry for Anne-Marie. I didn't argue with him, but when we finished I went to Joanna and told her that if Anne-Marie was coming, I wasn't going, and she sort of shrugged and said it was up to me – you know the way she is. She's never got any time for people's feelings. So I didn't go.'

'You went where instead?'

'I went home. Well, I went and had a drink first ...' He slowed nervously. 'I had a drink at a pub near home –'

'You may as well tell me the truth,' Slider said kindly. 'We know you didn't go to Steptoes that evening. We know that you did go to St Thomas's. We know that you had someone in your car that night, and that someone wasn't Miss Morris.' Thompson paled sentence by sentence, and Slider added the last one almost tenderly. 'Someone with long, dark hair – hair about the same length and colour as Anne-Marie

Austen's. We found some of her hairs on your car uphol-
stery, you see.'

'Oh Christ,' Thompson whispered. For a moment Slider
thought he was going to be sick, or faint. 'I know what you're
thinking. I know what Sergeant Atherton thinks, but I
swear –'

'Tell me what you did when you left the Television
Centre.'

He swallowed a few times, and then said, 'I did go to the
hospital.'

'Yes, I know. What for?'

'I went to meet someone. One of the nurses. Not Helen.
She's – it's someone I've been seeing a bit recently. Helen
doesn't know, you see. She wouldn't understand.'

I bet she wouldn't, Slider thought. 'All right, give me her
name and address, and we'll check it out. I suppose she'll be
able to confirm that she was with you – until when?'

'After midnight,' Thompson said quickly. Slider wondered
why he picked on that hour. 'We went back to my flat and
had a drink and – and, well, I drove her home in the early
hours. I don't know exactly when, but it was certainly after
midnight.'

'Her name and address.'

He licked his lips. 'I can't. I can't tell you. She's married,
you see. Her husband – she said she was doing overtime
because they were short staffed. If he found out –'

'Mr Thompson, don't you realise that this young lady,
whoever she is, is your alibi? I promise you that we'll be as
discreet as possible when we interview her, but you must give
me her name.' Thompson shook his head unhappily. 'You
realise that if you refuse, we're bound to wonder about your
story? There are certain pieces of evidence which suggest –'

'Oh Christ, you still think I killed her! I swear I didn't!
Why should I? She was nothing to me!' Slider said nothing,
and Thompson dropped his gaze, concentrating on pushing
his beer mug round and round by the handle. 'Look,' he said
at last. 'I'll speak to her. Ask her what she thinks. If she says
it's all right, I'll ring you. Or get her to ring you.' He looked
up desperately. 'It's the best I can do. I can't give her away,
just to save myself.'

Well, there's a turn up, Slider thought. Chivalry from this little shit. Of course, it was possible that he wanted time to speak to the nurse in order to coordinate stories, but Slider didn't think so. Whatever Atherton thought, Slider didn't believe that Thompson was the murderer.

They left the pub together. Outside Slider said, 'Have you got transport, or can I give you a lift somewhere?'

'My car's over there.' He gestured towards the Alfa Spyder parked on the corner. 'How did you find the hairs in it? Or was that a trick?' he asked suddenly.

Slider shook his head. 'That day when you came in to the station to make a statement, we took it round the back and went over it.'

'Are you allowed to do that?' Thompson demanded with a little return of vitality.

'Oh yes,' Slider said gently. Thompson sagged again, and turned away to trail miserably over to his car. Slider watched him go, but his attention was not all for Thompson. Some sixth sense was nagging at him, pulling him towards the alley on the other side of the pub. Something had moved there in the shadows. He walked slowly back, making a bit of business with straightening his raincoat belt, so that he could glance down the alley under his raised arm.

There was nothing. And yet something had disturbed him. It was an animal sense of danger that policemen develop, an instinct about being watched: a sort of subliminal awareness of more incoming stimuli than can be accounted for. He walked back to his car, more certain than ever that the tree up which Atherton was barking contained only a mare's nest full of red herrings.

O'Flaherty looked up. 'Did you get him?'

'Yes. Did you ring Irene?'

'I did. I told her you'd not be home till late.'

'What did she say?'

'She said nothing.' He regarded his friend massively, mournfully. 'I'm askin' you to be careful, darlin'. Now that's all. I'm asking you that, for this isn't a bit like you.'

Slider tried to smile, and found it a surprising effort. 'What a lot of interest you and Atherton are taking in my welfare these days. I can't meet either of you without getting spoonfuls of advice.'

'It's because we love you,' O'Flaherty said with a con man's sincerity.

'It's because you've nothing better to think about.'

'Well, sure, you could be right. And how was your Thompson type?'

'Scared stiff. And look, Pat, there was something else. When I came out of the pub, I had that old, old feeling. Someone was watching us.'

O'Flaherty's face pricked up as visibly as a dog's ears. 'Ah, Jaysus, I knew there was something else! Did you get sight of him?'

'I saw nothing. Why?'

'There was a feller hanging round the station when I came in tonight, and there was something about him that rang a bell, but I just couldn't place him in me memory.'

'What sort of man?'

'Professional lounger. Little runt of a man like a bookie's tout. A real little shit, you know, and Billy, I may be bad at names, but I never forget faeces. I seen him before on the watch, but for the life of me I can't pin him down.'

'I see. Well, I'll be careful. Keep trying to think where you've seen him before, and if you see him again, grab him '

'I will. Sure and he may be nothin' to do with it at all, but –'

'Yes, but,' Slider agreed, and went to his room to write his report. When he had finished he sat for a while with his face in his hands, rubbing and rubbing at his eyes with the heels of his hands in a way which would make an oculist feel faint. His neck ached and he felt tired and depressed, and he wondered if he were sickening for a cold, and knew he wasn't really. It was just his mind trying to escape from things it didn't want to face up to.

Like going home. He tried to think seriously about going home, and found himself instead remembering Joanna sitting up on her knees, naked in the firelight. He wished he could have drawn her as she was just then. He imagined himself a great artist, and Joanna his famous model/mistress. He saw an attic room in Paris, plain white walls bathed in sunshine, Joanna lounging naked on a crimson velvet divan. Then he changed the studio into a self-catering studio flat in a holiday apartment block in Crete. A fortnight's holiday with Joanna after this case was cleared up – to recuperate because he'd had a breakdown through working too hard. And what would Freddie Cameron say about a man who ran away from reality as hard as that?

He smiled at himself and reached for the phone. A man must face reality, deal with his responsibilities, perform his duties, without sparing himself.

He dialled the number, and Joanna answered at the first ring.

'Were you crouched over it?'

'It was beside me. Are you all right? Do you want to come over?'

'It's late. It isn't really fair to put upon you like that.'

'Oh nuts. Who do you think you're talking to?'

'I need you,' he said with difficulty.

'I need you too.' As easy as that. 'Will you stop wasting time?'

He drove by a roundabout route, checking frequently in his rear-view mirror, and when he got to Turnham Green he parked around the corner from Joanna's and walked the rest, eyes and ears stretched, passing her door and pausing beyond the streetlamp to test the air. Nothing. He returned to her house and knocked softly on the door and she let him in at once and said nothing until she had closed the door behind him.

'What was all that about? What were you doing?'

'Making sure I wasn't being followed.'

'That's what I thought. Are you in danger? Or is Irene on to you already?'

He didn't answer. He took her in his arms and buried his face in her hair and then her neck, revelling in the feeling and the smell and the accessible warmth of her. 'That last evening in Florence,' he said, muffled. 'You didn't tell me you went for a meal with Anne-Marie.'

'There was nothing unusual in that. We often ate together.'

'Tell me about it. Where did you go?'

She pulled her face back from him, considering. 'Actually, I'd already eaten before the rehearsal, but she said she was hungry and wanted me to come with her, for the company. I didn't mind – you have to do something. We went to a restaurant nearby –'

'Who chose it? You or her?'

'She did. I wasn't eating – I just watched while she ate.'

'You didn't have anything at all? Nothing to eat or drink?'

'Well, she tried to persuade me to have a glass of wine to keep her company, but I don't like to drink before a concert. So I had a cup of coffee.'

'Was it brought in a cup? Or a pot?'

She looked puzzled. 'Just a cup of espresso, that's all. Why?'

'And when did you start feeling ill?'

'Ill? Oh, it was just a touch of the Montezumas – rather a bad one, though. I couldn't do the concert – just couldn't get off the pan.'

'That was back at the concert hall?'

'I felt a bit queasy as we were walking back. Then just as I was changing it struck. It must have been what I had for supper, I suppose. I had been a bit stupid and eaten some figs.' He didn't reply, and, watching his face she said, 'What are you saying? You don't mean –? Oh no! Come on, that's ridiculous.'

'Is it? I think you were deliberately put out of action for the concert.'

'But she couldn't have put anything in my coffee without my knowing it.'

'She chose the restaurant. That was all she needed to do.'

'Dear God!' She broke away from him and walked a few steps as though trying to distance herself from the unpleasant idea. 'But what was it all in aid of? Why should she want me out of the way?'

'It may be that was the night she swapped violins. She played the Strad in the concert, and you were the one person who would notice.' She only looked at him, still disbelieving. 'Did you notice at any time that she had a large carpet bag with her?'

'Only the one she brought her dress clothes in. It was under her chair during the rehearsal.'

'And what did she do with it after the rehearsal?'

'I don't remember. I suppose she took it back to the dressing-room.'

'Try to remember. It's important.'

'Let me think. Let me think. What did we do? Wait, I remember now! We had to put our fiddles in a lock-up, because the dressing-rooms didn't lock. She asked me to take her fiddle for her while she took her bag to the dressing-room, and then we met again outside at the stage door.'

'So you didn't actually see what she did with the bag? Did she have it with her later?'

Joanna shrugged. 'I didn't notice. Once the Montezumas struck, I wasn't noticing anything.'

'So she might have given it to someone, or left it somewhere for someone to collect, while you were putting her fiddle away.'

She looked carefully at his thoughtful face. 'You really think she was mixed up with some smuggling racket? Some big organisation?'

'I don't know. It's possible.'

'I just can't believe it. Not Anne-Marie.'

'Well, it's only one possible theory. We've really nothing to go on yet.' She still looked unhappy and a little anxious, and so he took her into his arms, and said simply, 'Can I make love to you?'

In the bedroom, she undressed and lay on the bed waiting while he struggled with his own more complicated clothes, and she looked flat and white in the unfiltered streetlight, and when he was ready and she lifted her arms to him, they seemed to rise almost disembodied from a great depth, white arms lifting from a dark sea in supplication, like Helle drowning.

His flesh was cold against hers, starting into warmth where it touched her. He took her face in his hands and kissed her, for once the protector, not the supplicant. Just now she needed him for comfort and reassurance as much as he needed her. It was done between them quickly, not hurriedly but in silence, a thing of great need and great kindness, and no great moment. Afterwards she pulled the covers over him and eased him over onto his side, his head on her shoulder. She kissed him once and folded her arms round him, and feeling at once the blissful heat of her flesh start up all around him, he passed without knowledge into a deep, quiet sleep.

12

Guilt Edged

The shriek of the phone woke him so violently that he could feel his heartbeat pounding all over his body, and a sour, tight ball of panic in his throat. For a moment he didn't know where he was, and then almost immediately the panic resolved into the fear that he had slept the whole night through again, and had been missed at home, and was in trouble.

Cold air trickled down his body as Joanna sat up and reached for the receiver.

'Hullo? Yes. Yes he is. Just a minute.'

Slider sat up too, and sought out the green devil-eyes of the digital clock, and found it was half past two. The air in the bedroom was evilly cold. The weather must be changing. Joanna gave him the receiver and he took it back under the covers with him.

It was O'Flaherty, of course. 'Are you never goin' to go home at all?'

'What's up, Pat?'

'Trouble. You'd better get back here quick – I'll fill you in on the details when you get here. Your little pal Thompson has bought it.'

'Dead?' So soon? Slider felt an undersea confusion working about in his brain. How could it be so soon?

'As mutton. So would you please, sir, very kindly get your for Chrissakes arse over here?'

The Alfa Spyder was parked outside a derelict house in a

168

disagreeably neglected side street about a quarter of a mile from where Thompson lived. A late-night reveller, reeling home, had noticed something odd about the car and taken a closer look. Then, public-spirited despite his terror, he had telephoned the local police before declining to have anything more to do with it and heading rapidly and anonymously into oblivion.

Slider stared down at what had quite recently been Simon Thompson. He was lying across the front seats of his car, his legs doubled up, one arm hanging, and his throat was so deeply and thoroughly cut that only the spinal column was keeping his head on at all. There was blood everywhere. The seat and carpet were soaked with it, as were his left sleeve and the upper part of his clothing. With the tilting of his head, it had even run back into his hair and ears. His eyes were open and staring, his lips were parted, and his cosmetically white teeth had a brown crust around them.

On the floor of the car, under his trailing hand, there was a short-bladed surgical scalpel, presumably the murder weapon, though this was obviously meant to look like a suicide. Slider looked once more at those dark love-locks, dense and sticky with blood, and turned away, sick with anger and remorse.

They hadn't wasted any time. They had got to Thompson before Slider had even begun to be properly worried. He should have been more cautious. He *should* have worried, knowing what he thought they were. He might have prevented this.

The detective constable from 'N' District who had accompanied him, now handed him a small piece of paper. He was very young, one of the new coloured intake, and he looked very sick. Slider was interested to note with the professional part of his mind that a West Indian could be visibly pale, on the verge of greenness.

'We found this, sir, in his right hand. It was what put us on to you.'

Slider opened it out. It had been crushed rather than folded. In horribly uneven writing, speaking eloquently of great fear, it said, *Tell Inspector Slider. I did it. I can't stand it any more.*

The green young detective constable watched him, curiosity restoring some of the blood to his head. 'Do you know what it means, sir? Did you know him?'
'Oh yes,' said Slider. 'I know all about him.'

Slider didn't get home at all. At seven o'clock he had an enormous breakfast in the Highbury station canteen – fried egg, bacon, two sausages, tomatoes, fried bread, and several cups of tea – surprising himself with his own appetite until he remembered he had not eaten the night before. The food warmed him and started his blood running and his brain working, and the period before began to take on a comforting flavour of unreality. He almost stopped remembering that Simon Thompson had blood in his open eyes, that his eyelashes were stiff with it, like some weird punk mascara. At least he stopped minding about it.

Freddie Cameron, grumbling routinely, did the examination.

'What can I tell you?' he said to Slider on the phone. 'Cause of death asphyxiation of course. The windpipe was completely severed. I've sent the internal organs for analysis, but there's no indication of poisoning. Still, you never know. Suicides are notorious for liking a belt as well as braces.'

'Was it suicide?'

Cameron whistled a little phrase. 'You tell me. You're the detective. The wound was equally consistent with suicidal throat-cutting by a left-handed man, or homicidal throat-cutting by ditto standing behind the victim. Was your man left-handed?'

'I don't know.'

'He would also have had to be extremely determined. One never knows how difficult it is to cut a human throat until one tries, and there are usually a number of superficial, preliminary cuts in a case of suicide. It's quite unusual for a suicide to cut so deeply at the first attempt. The edges aren't haggled at all.'

'I suppose the weapon *was* the weapon?'

'No reason to suppose it wasn't.'

'I was surprised at the amount of blood.'

'Who would have thought the old man had so much blood in him? Well, it was a mighty cut, let's say. The heart would have gone on pumping for a moment or two. And alcohol expands the blood vessels.'

'Alcohol?'

'As in Dutch courage. Or Scotch courage in this case. I was nearly gassed when I opened the stomach. There must have been better than a quarter bottle of whisky, only just consumed. You want it not to be suicide, I gather.'

'Do you gather? No, really, I'd sooner it was, but I don't think it was.'

'Nor do I.'

'Opinions, Freddie? That's not like my cautious old medico,' Slider said with a faint smile.

'Firstly, I don't believe in that first-time cut. And secondly there was a fresh chip out of one of his front teeth. The sort of thing that might happen if someone forced you to drink whisky straight out of a bottle, and you struggled.'

Slider was silent, feeling cold at this new image to add to the scenario. 'To render him passive, I suppose,' he muttered.

'Or to add colour to the suicide motif, I don't know. So you'll be looking for your left-handed murderer again, like any Agatha Christie gumshoe?'

'Mixed metaphor,' Slider warned. 'Or at least, mixed media. Anyway, by the evidence of the scalpel, we're looking for a left-handed surgeon.'

'Surgeons can cut with either hand, you ignoramus.'

'Can they?'

'Of course. I can myself. Surely you knew that? Was the note any help, by the way?'

'None at all. Very Agatha Christie, in fact.' Slider was glad to change the subject. 'Though I suppose anyone theatrical enough to commit suicide might easily have the bad taste to leave a melodramatic note. But would a left-handed murderer be clever enough to try a double bluff like that? There wasn't any bruising. I suppose?' he asked wistfully. 'After all, he must have been forced to write that note. You couldn't get up a bruised wrist for me?'

'Unless he was very courageous, the threat of a sharp

blade at his throat would probably have been enough to make him write anything he was told to,' Cameron pointed out.

'He wasn't very courageous,' Slider said, thinking of Thompson bunched over his drink with the pain of his fear. The brave die once, he thought, but the frightened die many times over.

Atherton went with WDC Swilley to interview Helen Morris, and returned a sadder and wiser man.

'She was a little upset,' he told Slider, not meeting his eyes.

'Sit down,' Slider said. 'You look whacked.'

'So do you,' Atherton countered, and opened his mouth to offer his superior comfort, before wisely closing it again. He folded himself down into a chair and laid his long-boned hands on the edge of Slider's desk. 'Well, she identified the writing as Thompson's all right. His left-handed writing, she said.'

Slider's brows went up.

Atherton grimaced. 'Simon Thompson was ambidextrous. Apparently he was left-handed as a child, but playing the violin forced him to become right-handed. You can't play the fiddle back to front because the strings come out in the wrong order and you'd be bowing up when everyone else was bowing down.'

'Is that wrong?'

'Untidy. Anyway, Morris said he could write with either hand, but more usually wrote with his right hand, though for most other purposes he was completely ambidextrous.'

'Is nothing in this damned case ever going to be straightforward?'

'It seems straightforward enough to me, guv. In the emotional stress of his contemplated suicide, he reverted to his ingrained childhood habits, his natural left-handedness.'

'And the chipped tooth?'

'Suppose his hands were shaking? He could easily have done that himself.'

Slider shook his head. 'I wish I could go along with you. But I have an image of that human rabbit threatened by a very inhuman stoat with a sharp blade; so terrified, he writes the note, but in a last desperate attempt to tell the world all is not as it seems, he writes with his left hand, which Helen Morris at least will know is not usual.'

'But he cut his throat left-handed.'

'The murderer, who is very clever, as we know, notices that his victim is left-handed and proceeds to cut his throat for him in a consistent manner.'

Atherton lifted his hands and dropped them. 'That's pure Hans Andersen. The whole cloth. If the murderer was so very clever, why didn't he make the cut look more like suicide?'

'Perhaps he didn't know his own strength. More likely Thompson wouldn't sit still for a nice artistic haggling. One quick, hard slash, and it was all over.'

'Well, I dunno,' Atherton said, sighing. He rubbed the back of his left hand with the fingers of his right. 'It all seems a bit tenuous. If Thompson murdered Anne-Marie Austen, and then committed suicide, it would all make sense, and be so much simpler.

'And we could all go home to tea,' Slider finished for him. He could see that even Atherton had his moments of wanting to run away from reality. 'All the same, life is never that symmetrical.'

'And all the same again, there's actually no evidence that it wasn't suicide,' Atherton pointed out. 'Only your artistic sensibilities.'

There was a silence.

'Any luck at The Dog and Scrotum?'

'Nothing yet. But I'm not finished there, and I'm pretty sure Hilda knows something. I'm going to have another crack at her tonight.'

'Hilda always looks as if she's hiding something,' Slider said. 'Don't fall into that old trap.'

'We've got to have something to show up at the meeting, though. The Super's going to be asking questions about what we do all day.'

'Work our balls off.'

'Yes, but an oeuvre's not an oeuf.'

'Come again?'

'Skip it. Pearls before swine,' Atherton said loftily.

'Eggsactly,' Slider said with a quiet smile.

The young man was quietly spoken, neatly dressed, sensible – every policeman's dream of a witness.

'I noticed the car because it was an MGB roadster. I love MGs. I used to have one myself, but now we've got a kid it isn't practical.'

Married, with child, Atherton noted. Better and better.

'You didn't notice the registration number, I suppose?'

' 'Fraid not. Only that it was a Y registration.'

'Colour?'

'Bright red. I think they call it vermilion.'

He told his story. He had been waiting in the car park of The Dog and Sportsman for his wife, who was working the back shift at United Dairies in Scrubs Lane. They were both working every hour they could, to get together the deposit for a house. Now they had the baby, they wanted to get settled in a place of their own.

Who looked after the baby? – Denise's mum, who lived in the council flats in North Pole Road. That's why they met at The Dog and Sportsman. A bloke from the Dairies dropped Denise off there, Paul picked her up, and they drove round to collect the baby and then home to Latimer Road.

That particular evening he had got there a bit early, so he was just sitting in his car watching the traffic for Denise to turn up, when the roadster had come along. The girl was driving it very fast and flashily, screaming her tyres as she whipped into the car park, breaking hard, and backing into the space opposite him in one movement. When she got out of the car, he'd thought to himself that she was a pretty girl playing tough. She was dressed in a donkey jacket and jeans and short boots, which with a girl as pretty as that made you look twice all right.

What time was that? – About twenty to ten, more or less. He hadn't looked at his watch, but Denise usually got there about a quarter to, and it wasn't more than five minutes before she arrived. Maybe less.

Well, so this girl got out of the car and went towards the

pub, and then this man appeared in front of her. No, he didn't see where he came from – he'd been looking at the car. He just sort of stepped out of the shadows between the parked cars. She stopped at once and they spoke a few words, and then they went back to her car and got in and drove away. That was all.

What did the man look like? – Well, he didn't get a close look at him. He was tall, and wearing an overcoat, a scarf, and one of those brown hats like Lord Oaksey wears on the television. What do you call them, trilbies? Not a young man. How did he know? Well, it was just a sort of impression. Besides, young men didn't wear hats, did they? He didn't see his face, because the hat and scarf sort of overshadowed it. He didn't think he'd recognise him again. Just a well-to-do, middle-aged man in a dark coat and hat.

Did she seem to know the man? What was her reaction to him?

The young man frowned in thought.

Yes, she knew him. She didn't seem to be surprised to see him there. Wait a minute, though – when she first saw him, she turned her head and looked quickly round the car park as if to check if anyone were watching. No, he was sure neither of them saw him. His lights were off and they didn't even glance his way. Just for the first minute he'd thought the man had stopped out to rob her, snatch her handbag or something, and that she'd looked around for help. But that wasn't it. And it was all over in a second. The man said something; she answered; he said something else; and they went back to her car and got in and drove back the way she had come, down Wood Lane towards Shepherd's Bush.

Atherton closed his notebook. 'Thank you very much Mr Ringham. You've been very helpful. Now if you should remember anything else, anything at all, no matter how trivial it seems to you, you will be sure to let me know, won't you. You can reach me on this number.'

'Yes, okay – but look here, I won't be involved in anything, will I? I mean, I can't identify this man or anything, and I've got Denise and the kid to think about.'

Well, all witnesses have their limitations, Atherton thought, and reassured him with some vaguenesses and long words. In his own powder-blue Sierra, driving home to the sanctuary of his civilised little house, cat, real fire and elegant supper, he wondered how far this had got them. Enter Mr X in sinister trilby. He never trusted men who wore hats like that. So they now knew that she met the murderer at The Dog and Scrotum, and though the description was not promising, it might just as well have been Thompson. He was just the kind of jerk who would attempt to disguise himself by wearing a very obvious hat and muffler.

Anyway, at least they knew that she went to the White City in her own car. It would be worth interviewing the residents of Barry House again and asking about a red MGB. Surely someone must have noticed such a speciality car?

The atmosphere in the house was as icy as Slider had expected it to be.

Irene gave him a boiled stare and said, 'There's nothing for supper, except what's in the fridge. I wasn't to know you'd be home, and I'm not endlessly cooking meals to throw them away.'

'It's all right,' said Slider patient under insult. 'I can get myself something.' Even as he said it, he wondered what. Irene was not the sort of person to tolerate leftovers. The fridge would most likely be as innocent of food as an operating-table of germs – and for much the same reason. Atherton had long ago pointed out to him – in a different context of course – the correlation between lack of sexual outlet and an obsession with hygiene.

Both the children were home and had friends in, and Slider was able to use them, as so often before, as a screen. He asked Matthew about his football match, and sat through an interminable verbal action-replay. Matthew's friend, a pinch-nosed, adenoidal boy called Sibod, with such flamingly red hair that it looked like a deliberate insult, repeated everything half a beat behind, so that Slider got it all, or rather failed to get it at all, in an unsynchronised, faulty stereophony.

'So you won, then, did you?' Slider asked at last, groping for comprehension.

'Well, yes, we did win,' Matthew said with an anxious frown, 'and if we win again next Saturday against Beverley's, we win the Shield. Only they're very good, and if we only draw, it goes on goals, and we didn't do very well on goals.' From his worried expression, it was plain that the whole responsibility for their goal-less state rested on his shoulders. Like father, like son.

'Well, even if you don't win, it doesn't matter, as long as you do your best,' Slider said, as parents have said throughout the ages. Simon and Matthew both looked uncomprehending of his stupidity.

'But it's the Shield!' Matthew began, desperate to get this point across to unfeeling parenthood.

Slider forestalled him hastily. 'Matthew, is that bubble gum you're eating? I've told you again and again, I won't have you eating that disgusting stuff. Take it out and throw it away.'

'But you let me eat chewing gum,' Matthew protested. 'Only you can't make decent bubbles with chewing gum.'

'Chewing gum's different,' Slider said. The next question would be why. And since he didn't know, other than that it was personal prejudice, because the smell of bubble gum reminded him of the smell of the rubber mask they used to put over your face to give you gas in the dental hospital back in the dark ages of his childhood, he took refuge in authority.

'Please don't argue with me. Just do as I say. Take it out and throw it away, please – and wrap it in something first,' he added as Matthew, sighing heavily, stumped off towards the kitchen. Simon followed him, and he felt Irene's eye on him, saying as clearly as words, My how you love to play the heavy father, don't you? It's all Action Man, as long as it's only a couple of kids you have to stand up to.

He postponed being alone with her and her eye by going upstairs to see Kate, who was locked into one of her intensely private and uncomfortably ritualised games with Slider's least favourite of her best friends – a fat child called Emma who was so relentlessly sentimental and feminine that it made him squirm with embarrassment. When he pushed open the bedroom door, they were engaged in being school-teachers to a class of six dolls, including a bald and one-legged Barbie of hideous aspect, a toy monkey and a bear. Emma's part at the point of his entry was confined to watching admiringly and breathing heavily through her mouth, but Kate was haranguing her victims in such tones of hectoring sarcasm that Slider wondered afresh if that was the way adults really appeared to children.

'I think I've told you before never, never to do that, haven't I?' Kate was saying to the teddy bear. Slider had long ago named it Gladly, because its eyes were sewn on asymmetrically, and there had been a hymn he had sung in Sunday school when he was a child called 'Gladly my Cross I'd Bear'. Kate had accepted the name unquestioningly as she accepted all the incomprehensibilities of the grown-up world, as if they were nothing to do with her. Slider remembered being as young as that, with a mind gloriously untrammelled by a knowledge of the probabilities. When he was very small, he'd thought God's name was Harold, because of the second line of the Lord's Prayer, and it had not seemed at all surprising. Similarly he had believed for a very long time that there was a senior government official called The Lord Privvy, whose rod of office was an eel.

The thing, he thought, that marked him apart from his own children was that when he learned the truth of these matters it struck him as interesting and memorable. Nothing, he felt, would ever interest Kate beyond her own immediate sensations. She had already created herself in what she considered an acceptable image, and while that image would undergo subtle alterations year by year, the primary purpose of her life would always be the maintenance of whatever was the current version.

He regarded her sadly as she broke off her diatribe and looked at him with disfavour, minute fists on hips, lips narrowed in an uncomfortably familiar way. How was it, he thought, that without ever in the least intending to, we recreate our idiosyncrasies in our children? Already Matthew was exhibiting signs of Slider's overdeveloped sense of responsibility, his indecisiveness and tendency to worry about what he could not change. And Kate was turning day by day into a grotesque caricature of her mother. How could it have happened? For in sad truth, he had spent horribly

little time with either of them since they were babies. Once
they had settled into regular bedtimes, they had been lost to
him. It must be Original Sin, he thought sadly.

He had intended asking his daughter about her fête, but
she said, 'Go away Daddy. We don't want you now,' and
self-respect and a sense of duty obliged him instead to
deliver a lecture on good manners. Kate listened to it with
indifferent eyes and the patience of one who knows that
resistance will only prolong the interruption. She was so
different in that respect from Matthew, who would have
flung himself into the situation with the burning conviction of
a martyr, and ended in tears. Kate, Slider thought, had been
born aged well over forty. Having finished with his bit of
rôle-play, he left the room, and before he had shut the door
behind him he heard Kate's instant resumption of hers: 'Now
I'm sure you don't want me to have to smack you again, do
you?' Even from his limited knowledge of Kate's games, he
didn't think Gladly had much chance of talking himself out
of that one.

And now there was no alternative but to descend to the
realm of snow and ice, and face up to his other responsibility;
his other, he supposed, creation – for Irene had not always
been like this, and what could have shaped her apart from
the interaction of his influence on her basic matter? She was
sitting on the sofa staring at the television, though he knew
she wasn't watching it. It was, however, The News, and one
of the rules Irene had made for herself was that The News
was important and mustn't be disturbed or talked during.

As far as he could see the news was itself and always the
same: on the screen now was a battered street in some hot
part of the world where houses are made of concrete filled
with steel rods, like motorway bridges. An intermittent
brattle of machine-gun fire was punctuating the urgent,
segmented commentary, and interchangeable men in identical drab battledress were running and ducking and, presumably, dying. It struck him as odd how news of war, though
it was repetitive and completely unsurprising, should be
regarded as 'real' news, whereas anything which exemplified
the kindness or inventiveness or compassion of human beings
was included, if at all, only at the end of the bulletin as a sop

to old ladies and housewives – the 'And finally' item.
All the same he was glad for the moment of the flickering
images of death and suffering as a way to avoid talking to his
wife. How many marriages were kept intact that way, he
wondered wearily. His mind felt numb and exhausted with
the effort of guilt and anxiety, and the frustration of being in
the middle of a maze with no idea which was the way out, or
even if there was one. Irene; the children; Anne-Marie;
Thompson; Atherton; the Super: all revolved like Macbeth's
witches, indistinct, dangerous, clamouring for his attention –
all expecting answers from him, who had no idea even of the
questions. O'Flaherty's voice waxed and waned like the sea,
warning him of some danger in a booming, portentous voice;
and far, far away, small and clear like something seen
through crystal, was Joanna – almost out of reach, too far,
and fading, fading . . .

'If you're going to fall asleep, you might as well go to bed,'
Irene said, jerking him back out of a doze. The news had
finished, to be replaced by that witless sitcom about a couple
who had reversed their traditional rôles, she going out to
work while he stayed home and minded the house. The
laughs were presumably generated by the sight of a man
wearing an apron and not knowing how to operate the
dishwasher. It was depressingly 1950s.

'Eh?' he said, trying to look interested in the programme.
The man was holding a nappy and looking at the baby with a
puzzled expression. Any minute now he would say 'Now
which end does this go on?'

'It's useless sitting there pretending you're watching when
you were snoring a minute ago,' Irene went on, and then,
with an excess of vicious irritation, 'I hate it when your head
slips over, and you keep jerking it up every three seconds!'

'I'm sorry,' he said humbly, meaning it, and she just
looked at him with a resentment so chronic, so weary, that he
was filled with a sense of helplessness. It was so vast that for
a moment it seemed to blot out his personality entirely. He
ought to take her hand, ask her what was wrong, try to reach
her and comfort her, this woman whom he daily hurt and
saddened; and yet how could he help her, when it was the
simple fact of his existence which made her unhappy? He

couldn't ask what was wrong, when there was nothing he could do to put it right, and the pity he felt was as useless, as unuseable, as that which he felt for the crumpled bodies on the television news film. That was the intractable, daily dilemma of married life, and it blocked the flow of tenderness, and finally even killed the desire for it.

'I'm sorry,' he said again. It would have been better not to have spoken, to have got up in silence and gone up to bed, leaving the unsayable unsaid. She knew it too. She turned her head away from him, a gesture of adult hurt he had seen her make almost all their lives together.

'For what?' she said.

For what indeed? For the fact that the only way he could live with his crippling sense of responsibility was to be a policeman and do the one thing he could do well to make the world a better place. Fat comfort.

'It isn't nice for me either,' he said at last. 'Never being home. Never seeing my children. Do you know, Kate looked at me just now like a stranger. She just stood there waiting for me to go away again.'

There were many things Irene might have said or done in response to that appeal, but instead, after a short silence, she said in a neutral voice, 'Marilyn Cripps rang earlier on.'

The Cripps were a couple they had met some time ago at a garden party: he was a magistrate, and she was on the PC of Dorney Church and was a voluntary steward for the National Trust at Cliveden. They had a large detached house and a son at Eton, and Irene had been almost humble when after the first meeting Mrs Cripps had proved willing to continue the acquaintance. That was the kind of society she had always longed for; the sort she would have had as of right if Slider had only been promoted as he ought to have been. The wife of a police commissioner might mix on equal terms with the highest in the land.

'She asked us to a dinner party,' she went on unemphatically, 'but I couldn't accept without consulting you. With most husbands, of course, that would be just a formality, but with you I suppose it's hardly even worth asking.'

'Well, when is it, exactly,' Slider began dishonestly, for he knew her indifferent tone of voice was assumed.

'What's the point? Even if you say yes, when the time comes you'll call it off at the last minute, which is so *rude* to the hostess. Or you'll turn up late, which is worse. And even if you do go, you'll complain about having to wear a dinner jacket, and sulk, and sit there staring at the wall and saying nothing, and start like an imbecile if anyone talks to you.'

'Why don't you go without me?' Slider said cautiously.

'Don't be stupid!' She showed a flash of anger. 'We were invited as a couple. You don't go to dinner parties like that on your own. I wouldn't be so inconsiderate as to suggest it.'

There was nothing he could say to that, so he kept silent. After a moment she went on, in a low, grumbling tone, like a volcano building up to its eruption.

'I hate going out without you. Everyone looks at me so pityingly, as if I were a leper. How can I have any kind of decent social life with you? How am I ever going to meet anyone. It's bad enough living on this estate –'

'I thought you liked this estate.'

'You know nothing about what I like!' she flared. 'I liked it all right as a start, but I never thought we'd be staying here permanently. I thought you'd get on, and then we'd move to somewhere better; somewhere like Datchet or Chalfont, where nice people live. Somewhere the children can make the right sort of friends. Somewhere where they give dinner parties!'

Slider managed not to smile at that, for she was deadly serious. 'Well if you're not happy here, we'll move,' he said. 'Why don't you start looking round –'

'How can we move?' she cried, goaded. 'We can't afford anywhere decent on what you earn! God knows you're never here, you work long enough hours – or so you tell me – but where does it get you? Other people are always being promoted ahead of you. And you know why – because they *know* you've got no ambition. You don't care. You won't speak up for yourself. You won't make the effort to be nice to the right people ...'

'There's such a thing as pride –'

'Oh! Pride! Are you proud of being everyone's dogsbody? Are you proud of being left all the rotten jobs? Being left behind by men half your age? They don't respect you for it, you know. I've seen you at those department parties, standing on your own, refusing to talk to anyone in case they think you're sucking up to them. And I've seen the way they look at you. You embarrass them. You're a white elephant.'

She stopped abruptly, hearing the echo of her own words, unforgivable, on the air. He was silent. Policemen should never marry, he thought dully, because they couldn't honour all their obligations and still do their job properly. And yet if they didn't marry, like priests they wouldn't be whole people, and how could they do their job properly if they were in ignorance of the way ninety per cent of people lived?

For a fleeting, guilty moment he thought of Joanna, and how if he were married to someone like her it would be all right. No, not someone like her, but *her*. With her he could be a good policeman, and happy. Happy and good, and understood. His tired mind reeled. He mustn't think about Joanna in the middle of a row with Irene. That was bad.

'I'm sorry,' he said, 'but this is a very bad case I'm in the middle of, and –'

She didn't wait for him to finish. 'You can't even pay me the compliment of being angry, can you. Oh God!' She stared at him, furious and helpless, frozen like an illustration in the *Strand Magazine*. 'Baffled', was the word they would have used.

'Look, I'm sorry,' he began again, 'but this is a particularly horrible case. An old woman and a young man have been killed since the original murder, and I feel partly to blame for that. It's going to take up all my time and energy until I can get further forward, and that simply can't be helped. But I promise you, when it's over, we'll really get down to it and have a long talk, and try to sort things out. Will you try and be patient, please?'

She shrugged.

'And now I think I will go up to bed. I haven't had any sleep for ages, and I'm dead beat.'

Typically, once he had gone upstairs and undressed and cleaned his teeth and got into bed, he found himself wide awake, his mind ready and eager to tramp endlessly over the beaten ground of the case. In self-defence he took up his bedside book, a long-neglected and suitably soporific Jeffrey

Archer, and thus was still sitting up reading when Irene came in.

'I thought you were dead beat,' she said neutrally. The heaviness of her tread spoke of her unhappiness: she had always been a brisk, light mover.

'Getting ready for bed woke me up, so I thought I'd read for a bit,' he said. She turned away to make her own preparations, and he watched her covertly while pretending to be engrossed in the book. In complete contrast to Joanna, she was a woman who looked better dressed than undressed: she had the kind of figure that clothes were designed to look good on, but which was of little interest viewed solely as a body. She was slender without being either rounded or supple; she had straight arms and legs, flat hips, and small, dim breasts which, he thought now, had only ever made him feel sad.

Once, in the few weeks at the very beginning of their marriage, they had both slept naked, but the idea was now so remote that it surprised him to remember it. After those first weeks, Irene had begun to wear her trousseau nightdresses because 'it was a shame to waste them', and he had begun to wear pyjamas because to continue naked while she slept clothed seemed too pointed, like a criticism.

She came back from the bathroom bringing the smell of toothpaste and Imperial Leather with her, neat and almost pretty in her flowered cotton nightgown and with her dark hair composed and shiningly brushed. She was so complete, he thought, but it was not a completeness which satisfied. It was a completeness which suggested that the last word had been said about her, and that nothing about her could be any different: this was Irene, and that was that.

Again, he thought, that was in complete contrast to Joanna, who in his thoughts of her seemed always to be flowing about like an amoeba, constantly in a state of change. Away from her he found it hard accurately to remember her face. Thinking about her at all had to be done cautiously, as if it might push the malleable material of her out of shape.

Irene stopped at the foot of the bed, and was looking at him, her head a little lowered, chewing her bottom lip in a way that made her appear uncharacteristically vulnerable. She had a barrel-at-the-edge-of-Niagara look about her which warned him that she was about to broach a dangerous subject, and he wished he could forestall her; but to do so was to admit that there was no longer any point in caring enough to quarrel, and he couldn't quite do that to her.

'What's the matter?' he asked when it was plain she needed a shove.

For another long moment she hesitated, teetering, and then, all in a rush, she said, 'I know all about her – your girl-friend.'

Strange how the body acknowledged guilt even when the mind felt none. For a moment the hot, peppery fluid of it completely replaced his blood and rushed around his body, making his heart thump unexpectedly in his stomach; yet even while that was happening he had replied calmly and without measurable hesitation, 'I haven't got a girlfriend.'

Irene made a restless, negating movement and went on as if he hadn't spoken. 'Of course, I've known for some time that something was going on, but I didn't know what. I mean, the fact that we haven't made love for fifteen months –'

He was stricken that she knew exactly how long it was. He could only have guessed. But female lives were marked out in periods and pills, and sex for them, he supposed, would always be tied to dates.

'And then, all those times that you're not here – well, some of them are work, I suppose, but not all of them. But I wasn't sure until quite recently what it was.'

'There's nothing going on. You're just imagining things,' he said, but she looked at him, and he saw in the depths of her expression not anger but a terrible hurt; and he saw in one unwelcome moment of insight how for a woman this was a wound which would not heal. A man whose wife was unfaithful would be consumed with anger, outrage, jealousy perhaps; but to a wife, unfaithfulness was a deep sickness that ate away at the bones of self.

'You don't have to lie to me,' she said. 'I could tell from their voices that they knew all about it, Nicholls and O'Flaherty, when they phoned me up with your excuses. And Atherton – I've seen the way he looks at me, pityingly. I suppose they all know – everyone except me. And laugh about it. What a gay dog you are! I bet they slap your back and congratulate you, don't they?'

'You're wrong, completely wrong –'

'I've put up with it so far. But now you've started sleeping the night with her, and using this case as your excuse, and I'm damned if I'll put up with that! It's disgusting! And with a girl young enough to be your daughter! How could you do a thing like that?'

So many things ran through Slider's mind at that moment that he was, mercifully, prevented from speaking. For one thing he was surprised that Irene, even in the grip of oratory, should describe Joanna as being young enough to be his daughter; and another considerable number of brain cells was preoccupied with the problem of how she could possibly have found out. No-one at 'F' District would give him away, he would have staked his life on that, and the notion that she had put a private detective onto him was ludicrous. And underneath these preoccupations was the thought that these were shameful things to be thinking at such a moment, and that he should be feeling bad and guilty and remorseful at having hurt Irene.

And what he did say in the end came out sounding quite calm and natural. 'You're completely mistaken. I haven't got a girlfriend, and I certainly wouldn't be interested in anyone young enough to be my daughter.'

'Oh, you liar!' she cried softly, and with a superbly unstudied movement flung a photograph down on the bed beside him. 'Who's this, then? A perfect stranger? Don't tell me you carry a perfect stranger's picture around in your wallet. You *bastard*! You've never carried a picture of me around with you, never, not even –'

She stopped and turned away abruptly, so that he shouldn't see her crying. Slider picked up the photograph, bemused and amused and relieved and sorry, and most of all just terribly, horribly sad. From the palm of his hand Anne-Marie looked up at him, all sun-dazzle and whipped hair and eternal, unshakeable youth, the little white starfish hand against the dark blue sea frozen for ever in that moment of joyful exuberance.

Loving Joanna had stopped him being haunted by her, but now it all came back to him in a rush; the pointless, pitiful waste of her sordid little death. They had put her down like an old dog, stripped her with the callousness of abattoir workers, and dumped her on the grimy floor of that grim and empty flat. He remembered the childlike tumble of her hair and the pathos of her small, unripe breasts, and a pang of nameless grief settled in his stomach. It was his old grief for a world in which people did such pointlessly horrible things to each other; sorrow for the loss of the world in which he had grown up, where the good people outnumbered the bad, and there was always something to look forward to. It was the reason he had taken this job in the first place, and the thing he had to fight against, because it unmanned him and made him useless to perform it. Oh, but he and his colleagues struggled day after day and could make no jot of difference to the way things were, or the way things would be, and the urge to stop struggling was so strong, so strong, because it was hopeless, wasn't it?

Irene had turned again, and now flinched from the despair in his face. She had always known there was a streak of melancholy in him, which he had tried to hide from her as from himself; but until this moment she had not known how strong it was, or how deep it went. She remembered all at once those stories of policemen who drank themselves insensible the moment they came off duty, who took drugs, or rutted their way to oblivion through countless women's bodies; and of the policemen who committed suicide, unemphatically, like tired children lying down just anywhere to sleep. She wondered what it was that had held Slider together in the face of his own despair, and had little hope that it was her, except in so far as she and the children provided a kind of counter-irritant. She wondered how much longer it would work, and what would happen then; and whether, when the end came, she would have any right to resent her fate as victim of it.

She looked at him with the resignation of a woman who sees that she will never be as important to her husband as his work, and for whom to stop minding is the worst of the possible alternatives. Slider saw the resistance go out of her and was grateful, though he didn't know why it had happened.

He said, 'This is a photograph of the girl who was murdered, Anne-Marie Austen. The case I'm investigating. You can easily check that, if you don't believe me.'

She turned away. 'No,' she said. 'I believe you.' She pretended to be looking in a drawer, to keep her back to him, and her next words sounded curiously muffled. 'I shouldn't have looked in your wallet. I'm sorry.'

'It doesn't matter.'

'It does. I shouldn't have done it.'

He thought she was crying. 'Don't,' he said. 'Come to bed.'

But when she turned she was dry-eyed, only looked very tired. She got into bed beside him and lay down, not touching him, and then turned on her side, facing away from him, her sleep position. Slider put his book down and hesitated, looking down at her. So it was all right again. The danger was over. He had gone up the side turning and the posse had thundered past. It would be all right for a long time now because she would feel guilty about having wrongly accused him.

He wished that he could have made love to her then: it might have comforted them both, and given at least a semblance of resolution to what was otherwise unfinished business between them. But it had been too long since they last did it for habit to achieve the gesture, and he could not do it from the heart of any feelings for her. He switched out the light and lay down. Since there was Joanna, he thought in the dark, he could not do that.

13

A Woman of No Substance

The department meeting was held in the CID room, the other offices being too small to hold everyone simultaneously. The others were all there when Slider went in. WDC Swilley, who hated her real name of Kathleen so much that she actually preferred being called Norma, was sitting on one of the battered desks swinging her long, beautiful legs for the benefit of her colleagues. She was a tall, strong, athletic girl, with the golden skin, large white teeth. streaky-blonde hair, and curiously unmemorable features of a California Beach Beauty. Slider often had the feeling that he was the only member of the department she hadn't seduced, which he felt lent him a certain superiority over the others. Obviously she regarded him as a real person, while the others were only sex objects to her.

She smiled at him now and said, 'Here he comes, crumpled and in a hurry, the perfect example of the Married Middle-Management Man.'

'You missed out some. What about Menopausal?' said Beevers, sitting where he could get the best view of the famous Legs, which often haunted his dreams. He was an almost circular young man, with thick, densely curly light-brown hair, and a rampant and disarming moustache. He was married to a tiny, round brown mouse of a woman called Mary. He adored her, but her serviceable legs only twinkled, never swung.

'How about Manic?' Atherton added.

'Not today,' Slider said, loosening his tie with an auto-

matic gesture. 'Today I am a monument of calm. A man who
has done his homework can't be shaken. Time you youngsters learned that – flair is no substitute for hard work.'

He looked around them as they groaned automatically.
There was DC Anderson, just back from holiday and
probably bulging with photographs he wanted to show
around. He was keen on what he called 'artistic shots', which
nearly all turned out to be various stages of a sunset reflected
on sea and wet sand. The other DCs, wooden-headed, obsessive Hunt and quiet, introverted Mackay, were sitting
solemnly side by side on hard chairs, bracketed by the
sprawling charm of Swilley and Atherton, and counterpoised
by stumpy Beevers, who had a bit missing from his brain and
so could never be made to feel shame or embarrassment.

These, he thought, far more than the three in Ruislip, were
his family; only if it were a family, he was probably the
mother, while the Superintendent was the authoritarian
father. They were one short at the moment, for the DCI,
Colin Raisbrook, had suffered a mild heart attack and was on
extended sick-leave. It was not yet clear whether he would be
returning to the department. If they gave him early retire-
ment, as Slider had long realised with an inward sigh, Irene
would be expecting him to be promoted to DCI in Raisbrook's place; and if he was not, his life would be made
extremely unpleasant.

'It's a filthy day,' Norma said unemphatically, staring out
of the window at the cold and steady rain, 'and due to get
worse. Any moment now Dickson will come breezing
through that door like an advertisement for cosmetic toothpaste, and I shall want to murder him all over again.'

'Hullo Super!' Anderson chirruped, and Hunt obediently
chanted the ritual reply.

'Hullo Gorgeous!'

'If he calls me WDC Snockers once more, I shall murder
him,' Swilley went on undeterred. 'I hate a man in authority
who tries to be funny and then expects you to laugh.'

'I don't think he does,' Atherton said. 'I think he exists
purely for his own gratification.'

This was too far above the head of Hunt, who brought the
tone down to his own level by saying, 'But if you murdered

him, Norm, what would you do with the body?'

'Sell it to the canteen,' Mackay suggested. 'Always roast pork on Wednesdays.'

'I thought they got that from Hammersmith Hospital,' Anderson joined in. 'Wasn't it Wednesday we had that pile-up at Speakers Corner, the Cortina and the artic? Brought the Cortina driver out in pieces?'

'You lot don't get any better. All this fourth-form humour makes me tired,' Atherton said witheringly.

'You're always tired,' Swilley remarked with a sad shake of the head, and Anderson hooted.

'How would you know that, Norma? Let us in on your secret.'

They were interrupted, not before time in Slider's opinion, by the entry of Detective Superintendent Dickson. Dickson was large and broad and weighty, a prize bull of a man – no-one would ever have thought of calling him fat – whose brisk movements, added to the sheer size of him, gave him an unstoppable impetus, like a runaway lorry. He had a wide, ruddy, genial Yorkshire face, held in place by a spreading and bottled nose that spoke of a terrifying blood pressure. He had scanty, sandy hair, and a smile whose front uppers looked too numerous and regular to be his own.

He had survived years of being called Dickson of Shepherd's Bush Green by pretending that he had thought of it first, and had developed, like a compensatory limp, a passion for nicknames of his own. In a service fairly evenly divided between hard men pretending to be soft and soft men pretending to be hard, Dickson was in a category of one: a hard man pretending to be a soft man pretending to be hard. He drank whisky almost as continuously as he breathed, was never seen the worse for it, and one day would be found dead at his desk. Slider could never decide whether he would be glad or sorry at that moment.

'Good morning lads. Good morning Norma,' he breezed, favouring her with the full Royal Doulton. She glowered back. 'Sit down everybody. We've got a lot to get through this morning.'

It was some time before they had cleared away all the other matters and got to the murder of Anne-Marie Austen.

Slider brought them up to date on what they had got so far, and then Dickson gathered their attention.

'I don't mind telling you that the powers that be are not too happy about this case – two more deaths, and nothing concrete to go on. Now either they're very good, or we're very bad, and either way we're going to lose it if we don't get something on the go. As far as the Thompson death goes, "N" District want to know if we think it's part of the same transaction and I take it that we do? All right. They'll do the legwork their end, and liaise with Atherton. Now, what have we got to follow up?'

'The Birmingham end ought to be looked into,' Atherton said with an eye to the main chance. 'We know she was making regular trips there, and there's the question of the flat she rented which she oughtn't to have been able to afford. I could –'

'Right,' Dickson interrupted. 'Bill, you cover that. Take someone with you. Atherton, you're the musical genius around here – follow up this bloody violin. I don't believe no-one's seen the thing since 1940. And get onto this Saloman bloke and find out all about him.'

'Yes, sir,' Atherton said, rolling his eyes at Slider.

'Beevers, I want you to check out the girl's aunt – your face isn't known down there. There's our money motive, strong and nice. Find out who she knows, where she goes, where she was that night. Find out about her trips to London. It's a small village, so you shouldn't have any trouble getting people to talk. Now, what else?'

'I'm convinced it's a large organisation behind it, sir,' Slider said.

'I know you are, and I have to admit it has that smell to me, but there's nothing to prove it isn't just a very ruthless individual.'

'The cuts on her foot, sir – did anything turn up about those?' Dickson didn't immediately answer, and Slider went on, watching him carefully, 'With the Italian connection, I couldn't help wondering if there wasn't some connection with the Family? Those cuts did make it look like a ritual killing.'

There was a short and palpable silence. Dickson's face went

blank, his eyes uncommunicative. 'There's nothing I can tell you about that,' he said evenly. 'Nobody's got anything to say about the letter T.'

'Why shouldn't it be the murderer's initial?' Atherton said smoothly.

'Why indeed,' Dickson agreed, with an air of humouring him.

'Suggestion, sir,' Slider said quickly. Dickson's face became a wary blank again. 'Whether it's an organisation behind it or an individual, my guess would be that the Thompson death was meant to tie up the loose ends: murder, followed by remorse and suicide. I wonder if there might be some mileage in letting them think we bought it? If the villain or villains thought the heat was off –'

'What about Mrs Gostyn?' Atherton interposed.

'Accident. It might even have been one,' Slider said.

'We'd have to get the press to cooperate,' Dickson said, 'but it might just turn something up. I'm in favour. All right, I'll see to it.'

Slider nodded his thanks, but felt curiously unsatisfied. There was something about the way Dickson agreed that made him feel it had been decided beforehand by someone else. Something was going on. Cautiously, he slid a toe into the water. 'What about the Italian end, sir? This Cousin Mario? Can we get any cooperation on him or the house in Paradise Alley?'

Dickson's face grew redder with anger. 'I think you've got quite enough to be going on with already, finding out where she was killed, where the drug came from, what they did with her clothes, just for starters. And who's this bloke O'Flaherty says has been hanging around the station? Has he got anything to do with it?'

'I don't know –' Slider began, and Dickson roared like a bull.

'You don't know bloody much, and that's a fact. I'm telling you, all of you, that there are certain people who are not at all happy about the way this case is going, so let's get to it, and get something concrete down.' He rose to his feet like the Andes, glowered around them for an instant, and then transformed his features grotesquely into a fatherly grin.

'And be careful, all right? You're not in this job to get your bloody heads blown off.'

He power-surged out of the room, leaving Slider feeling more than ever convinced that something was going on that they were not allowed to know about. Dickson had manufactured his rage to prevent the questions being asked that he was not prepared to answer. The others, however, were just shifting in their seats and muttering as if the headmaster had been in a nasty bate and given the whole school a detention.

'The mushroom syndrome,' Beevers said as if he had just thought of it. 'Keep us in the dark and shovel shit over us.'

'Very original, Alec,' Norma said kindly.

He turned his hairy lips upward and smiled graciously at her. 'There's one theory that no-one's thought of, though.'

'Except you, I suppose?'

'Right! Thompson was murdered by a left-handed surgeon, wasn't he? And John Brown, the Orchestra personnel manager, is a raving bender and living with this bloke Trevor Byers, who just happens to be a surgeon at St Mary's. Suppose Austen was blackmailing them, and they got fed up with it and killed her. And Thompson somehow found out about it, and so they did him as well?'

He gazed around his audience triumphantly. Norma clasped her hands to her breast and whispered, 'Brilliant!'

Beevers accepted the tribute. 'This Mafia bullshit!' he went on kindly. 'Now the girl may or may not have smuggled a Stradivarius into the country, but there's no evidence she didn't just do it for herself, or that she ever did it more than once. And, with all due respect to you, guv, it's too clumsy to have been the work of a professional. This is a typical amateur setup, to me.'

'Brains and originality,' Norma remarked. 'You can't do without 'em.'

'Beevers can,' Atherton said.

'We had better leave no stone unturned, I suppose,' Slider said. 'But for God's sake be careful. Don't go blundering about and getting complaints laid against us.'

'Leave it to me, guv,' Beevers said, pleased. 'Softly softly.' He rose and headed for the door. 'Well, I'll love you and leave you. I'm going to –'

'Grin like a dog and run about the city,' Atherton suggested.

Beevers paused. 'Come again?'

'That's a quotation from Psalm 59,' Atherton told him.

Beevers gave him a superior smile. 'We're Chapel,' he said unassailably.

Slider was surprised to have Norma assigned to him for the trip to Birmingham, until she revealed that she knew Birmingham quite well, having lived there for many years. Since he could not take Joanna, both for professional reasons and because she was working, Slider was glad to have Swilley with him. He found her company restful, and he also considered her to be the best policeman in 'F' district, and nicer to look at than an *A to Z*.

'Do you know where this is?' he asked, proffering the address of the flat where Anne-Marie had lived while a member of the Birmingham Orchestra. Martin Cutts had wrenched it out of his memory, and Slider now proposed having a look at it, and if possible a chat with some of the other residents.

'Oh yes. That's part of the new development in the centre. Quite swanky, a bit like the Barbican when it was fashionable. Expensive, but very convenient for the city types.'

It turned out to be a steel-and-glass pillar which reflected the cloudy sky impassively. Slider squinted up at it. 'I should think the views from the top would be magnificent. I wonder where the entrance is?'

'Well hidden,' Norma said as they turned a second corner. 'I wonder if they ever get any mail delivered?'

They found it at last round the third side, a tinted glass door with a security button. When the buzzer sounded they pushed in to find themselves in a foyer which would not have disgraced the headquarters of a multinational consortium. It was four storeys high, fitted out with acres of quiet grey carpet, and the walls which were not sheer glass were panelled in wood. There were glassy displays of rubber plants in chromium tubs, and in the centre of the hall the largest tub of all contained a real, growing, and embarrassed-looking tree.

'Blimey,' Norma breathed in heartfelt tribute. 'Cop this lot!'

They waded their way through the deep pile towards the uniformed security guard who was standing behind an enormous mahogany-veneered desk which was a very irregular trapezoid in shape to prove it was not just functional. The opulence of it all made them feel faintly depressed, as perhaps it was meant to.

'Think of the rents!' Norma whispered.

'And the rates. And the maintenance charges.'

'You'd need a fair amount of naughtiness to pay for that lot,' Norma agreed.

The security guard was looking at them alertly as they completed the long haul to his desk, and before Slider could present his ID, he straightened himself perceptibly and said, 'Police, sir? Thought so. Which one is it you're interested in?'

Slider was amused. 'You have a lot of trouble here?'

'No sir, not a bit. No trouble. A lot of enquiries, though,' His left eyelid flickered.

'We're enquiring about a young lady who lived here about eighteen months ago, a Miss Austen.'

'Miss Austen? Oh yes, sir, she's in 15D, one of the penthouses. Very nice.'

Miss Austen or the flat? Slider thought. So the news of her death hadn't penetrated this far; and also she didn't seem to have given up the flat when she left Birmingham. 'Penthouse, eh?' he said. 'That must cost a bit. Any idea what the rent is?'

With a curious access of discretion, the guard wrote a figure down on his desk-pad and pushed it across with an arms-length gesture. Slider looked, and his eyes watered. Norma, looking over his shoulder, murmured 'Ouch!'

'How long has she lived here?' Slider asked.

'About, oh, four years I suppose. I could look it up for you.'

'Ever any trouble about the rent?'

'Not my department, sir, but I doubt it. The developers would be down on anything like that like a shot. What's she done, then?'

'I'm afraid she's dead.'

'Oh. I thought I hadn't seen her around for a while,' said the guard, and it wasn't even a joke. Such, Slider thought, was her epitaph, this enigmatic girl.

'Do you remember when you last saw her?'

The guard shook his head. 'Must have been a few weeks ago. I never saw much of her anyway, but it's like that in these flats. People don't draw attention to themselves. Besides, there's nothing to notice in a resident coming in or out. Strangers I'd notice – you know how it is.'

'What happens about visitors?'

'Anyone who comes in comes to the desk, and we make a note of it before we ring up to the flat, for security reasons. You can have a look at the books if you like. But of course if a resident brings in a guest themselves, there's no note kept.'

'I see. Well, I'd like to have a look at those books afterwards, but for the moment I'd like to see the flat. You have a key, I suppose?'

'Yes, sir. I'll get the pass key. I'll have to come up with you, though, and let you in. Regulations.'

'Are you allowed to leave your desk?'

'For five minutes, yes, sir. I lock the outer door, then anyone who comes has to ring and I hear them on this.' He patted the portable phone on his hip.

'Very security-conscious, aren't they?'

'Well, sir, there's a lot of influential people in these apartments.'

'Was Miss Austen an influential person?'

'I don't know exactly, sir. She didn't look it. I thought at first she was someone's mistress, but then she didn't seem the type. I suppose she must have been somebody's daughter.'

The sleek, silent lift smelled of wealth, and the door to the penthouse flat was solid wood with brass fittings and an impressive array of locks and bolts and chains.

'We needn't keep you,' Slider said kindly as the guard hesitated. 'You can trust us to leave everything as we find it.'

'Yes sir. When you're ready to leave, if you wouldn't mind ringing down to me, and I'll come up and lock the door again. That's the house phone over there, the white one. And if you need anything else, of course.'

When he had gone, Norma padded further in and let out a soundless whistle. 'Boy oh boy, it's like a set off *Dallas.* Where did she get the money for a setup like this?'

'Thompson thought smuggling. Beevers thinks blackmail.'

'Impossible. It must have been something bigger – and more secure – than that. Dope distribution or something?' Slider shrugged. 'And why did she keep it on once she'd left the Orchestra?'

'Perhaps,' Slider said absently, 'it was her home.'

Home. Something Anne-Marie had never known much about; a word you would find it hard to apply to this place. Norma had got it right when she said *Dallas* – it was like a filmset, not like real life at all. It was furnished with the great expense, but with no individuality, and it was cold, impersonal. He wandered about, looking, touching, feeling faintly sick with distress. Thick pale carpets – skyscraper views over Birmingham through the huge, plate-glass windows – white leather sofas. A giant bed with a slippery quilted satin bedspread – teak and brass furniture – a huge, heavy, smoked glass coffee-table. A cocktail cabinet, for God's sake, and expensive, amorphous modern pictures on the walls.

It was like nothing in real life. It was utterly bogus. It was, he realised in a flash, the sort of thing a person with no experience might imagine they would like if they were very rich – a child's dream of a Hollywood Home. His mouth began to turn down bitterly.

'Sir?' Norma was standing by a bookcase in the corner of the living-room. He went over, and she handed him *A Woman of Substance* by Barbara Taylor Bradford. 'It was on television a while back, d'you remember?'

'Yes,' Slider said. 'Irene used to watch it.'

'It's about a kitchenmaid who rises to be head of a business empire. They used the real Harrods in the film as the department store she ended up owning.'

'Yes, I heard about it.'

'Rags to riches,' Norma went on. 'And look at these others – all the same kind of thing – sagas about wealthy, powerful women. It's the modern escapist fiction for women: luxurious settings, jetsetting heroines who are as ruthless and ambitious as men, and make fortunes and manipulate the lives of their minions.'

'Yes,' Slider said, looking around the room again. 'It fits.'

He saw it now. He stared at the row of crudely coloured, mental boiled sweets on the bookshelf before him and saw Anne-Marie, orphaned as a young child, brought up by an aunt who resented her, sent off to boarding school to get her out of the way, foisted off on a governess during school holidays. He saw her as a child with no friends, horribly lonely, perhaps dogged by a sense of failure because she could not make people love her, turning to books as a refuge, entering a world where things could go the way she wanted them to: a world where the unpopular girl scored the vital goal at hockey and became the school's heroine; where the poor girl saved someone's life and was given a pony of her own. Then in adolescence, perhaps she turned to the stronger meat of romances, where the hero took off the plain girl's glasses and murmured, 'God, but you're lovely!'; and in young womanhood to the candyfloss of the Eighties, the power-woman sagas.

Somehow temptation had come her way, a chance to enter a life of excitement and intrigue and make large sums of money; to be, as she probably saw it, rich, successful and powerful. Why should she refuse? It was illegal, but then who cared about her? Who would be hurt by her failure to be honest? Perhaps she even relished the idea of getting back at the law-abiding people of her childhood who had failed to love her.

He turned from the bookshelves, and imagined her alone here in this shiny, sterile apartment, feeding her vanity of riches and her illusions on pulp fiction, and fighting back the growing conviction that it was all a lie, that her new 'friends' were only using her and cared nothing for her. Was that why she had suddenly tried to marry Thompson, to get hold of her inheritance so that she could escape from the trap she had stepped into so willingly?

Pathetic attempt. The people she was involved with would be ruthless as no fictional characters were. They would not allow her to defect; and at the last moment, he thought, she had realised that. He remembered Martin Cutts's description of the last time he had seen her alone, and of her 'resignation' afterwards. Perhaps, until the very last moment, she had not minded the thought of dying, since life held so little for her.

He had been standing with the book in his hand staring ahead of him at nothing, but now he became aware that something was calling his attention, nagging at the periphery of his mind. He stood still and let it seep in. He was facing the open door into the kitchen, a showroom affair of antiqued pine cupboards and white marble surfaces and overhead units with leaded-light doors, and through the glass of the end cupboard, the one in his line of vision, he could see a vague shape and colour that were naggingly familiar.

'Yes,' he said abruptly, thrust the book into Norma's hand, crossed to the cupboard and snatched open the door. There it was in the corner: the familiar shape of the tin and haunting depiction of the goitrous peasants and the caring, sharing olive trees, and the large and gaudy letters VIRGIN GREEN. He picked up the tin triumphantly and turned with it in his hands.

'That's it,' he said. 'Virgin Green.'

'What is it, sir?' Norma asked, but without much hope of reply. She knew these moods of his, when a lot was going in and nothing much coming out.

'Virgin Green. There's got to be a connection.' And then he saw what he had not noticed before, or at least had not taken in, which was the name and address of the manufacturer, in truly tiny letters at the bottom of the back of the tin: Olio d'Italia, 9 Calle le Paradiso, Firenze.

Slider began to laugh.

Atherton paused outside Vincey's of Bond Street and allowed himself to be impressed. It was either very old, or very well faked, all mahogany and curly gold lettering, and the window display was austere. A heavy, blue velvet curtain hung from a wooden rail half way up at the back of the window, preventing anyone from seeing inside the shop, and its lower end was folded forward in elegant swathes to make a bed for the single article on display – a sixteenth-century lute on a mahogany stand.

Inside the shop was dark, and smelled dusty but expensive. An old Turkish carpet in dim shades of wine-red and brown covered the floor between the door and the old-fashioned high counter which ran the width of the shop. Around the walls were a few heavy, old-fashioned display cases containing a few curiously uninteresting ancient instruments. The atmosphere was arcane, fusty, and eminently respectable. Atherton supposed that ancient instruments must be of interest to somebody, or how could Vincey's continue to function? But the setup seemed precarious in the extreme, considering what rents and rates must be like in Bond Street.

The door had chimed musically when he opened and closed it, and by the time he reached the counter a man had come through the curtained door that led to the nether regions and was regarding him politely. He was small and shrunken and looked about sixty-five, though his face was sharpened by the brightness of his dark eyes behind gold-rimmed half-glasses, and distinguished by an impressive beak of a nose. He had a little straggly grey hair and a great deal of bare pink pate, on the extremity of which he wore an embroidered Jewish skullcap. The rest of his clothes were shabby and shapeless and no-coloured so that, given his surroundings, one might suppose he wore them as a sort of protective colouring. If he kept still, Atherton thought, only his eyes would give away his whereabouts.

'Mr Saloman?' Atherton was not really in any doubt. If ever a man looked like a Mr Saloman, it was he.

'Saloman of Vincey's,' said the man, as if it were a title, like Nelson of Burnham Thorpe. His hands, which had been down at his sides, came up and rested side by side on the edge of the counter on their fingertips. He had the ridged and chalky fingernails of an old man, and his fingers were pointed and the skin shiny and brown, as if they had been rubbed to a patina by years of handling old wood. As they rested there, Atherton had the curious feeling that they had climbed up of their own accord to have a look at him. It unnerved him, and made him draw an extra breath before beginning.

'Good afternoon,' he said as cheerfully as his normally cheerful face could contrive. 'I wonder if you could tell me if you have ever had any dealings with this young lady.'

Saloman did not at once take the proffered photograph. First he subjected Atherton's face to a prolonged examination; and when at last one of his hands relinquished its fingertip grip of the counter and came towards him, Atherton found his own hand shrinking back in reluctance to come into contact with those pointed, brown, animal fingers. Saloman took the photograph and studied it in silence for some moments, while Atherton watched him and formed the opinion that behind the old, hooknosed, impassive façade a very sharp mind was rapidly turning over the possibilities and wondering whether it would be better to know or not to know. Yes, I'm on to something, Atherton thought, with that rapid process of association and deduction which he thought was instinct.

'I have done business with her,' Saloman said at last, returning the picture with an air of finality as if the last word had been said on that subject. It put Atherton on the wrong foot, as it was meant to, and he had to think out the next question.

'Would you mind telling me what the business was and when it took place?'

It was not meant as a question. Saloman smiled the smile of a reasonable man. He almost shrugged. 'Would I mind? Why should I not mind? Who asks me? Young man, you have not told me who *you* are.'

It was a game as they both knew, for Atherton was perfectly well aware that he looked like a policeman. He brought out his ID, and Saloman took it and subjected it to such lengthy scrutiny that he might have been mentally setting it to music. At last he returned it and said, 'So. The young lady.'

'Yes. You did business with her, you said.'

'So, she brought me a violin one day, another day two bows. I valued them for her, and she asked if I would buy them. I bought them, and later I sold them at a profit. That is how my business supports itself – I hope it is not yet a crime? And now will you tell me why you want to know. Has the

young lady got herself into trouble at last?'
'Why should you think so?'
Saloman smiled gently. 'Because she was very pretty and
very young. In the end, life must catch up with the pretty and
young, otherwise how could the old and ugly bear the injus-
tice? What has she done, this one?'
'Nothing illegal, I assure you,' Atherton said, smiling in
spite of himself. 'Can you remember when these transactions
took place?'
Saloman shrugged. 'Remember? No.'
'But perhaps you keep records of purchases and sales?'
'Of course I do. I am a businessman. I pay tax, VAT.
What do you think?'
Atherton, driven, said very precisely, 'Will you please look
up in your records, and tell me when these transactions took
place?'
Saloman smiled the smile of the tiger and brought out a
large ledger and began to go through it from the back
towards the front, slowly. Atherton could only abide in his
breeches. His training, he told himself, must be at least as
good as Saloman's.
It was a long wait. When he had been all through that
ledger Saloman closed it and brought out another, and began
again. Atherton gritted his teeth. At the end of something
near half an hour, Saloman finally shut the book with a slam
that raised an interesting cloud of dust, and said, 'In October
1987 she sold me a Guarnerius. In March 1988 violin bows,
a Peccatte and a gold-mounted Tourte. So, this is what you
want to know?'
'Did she give you her name?'
'It is here in the daybook, Miss A. Austen.'
'When she came in with the fiddle, in October 1987, did
she know what it was, how much it was worth?'
'If she knew these things, why should she ask me to value
it?'
Atherton ground his teeth. 'How did she react when you
told her the value?'
He shrugged. 'Who can remember? Some are glad, some
are not. I don't remember.'
'But you remember her?'

'She was a pretty young woman with a valuable violin.'

'How valuable? What did you give her for it?'

Saloman bent his head to the book again, though he must have known the figure already. 'Three hundred thousand pounds.'

'And the bows?'

'One hundred thousand for the two.'

'And you later sold these items at a profit?'

'Of course. That is my business.'

'Did she ever bring you a Stradivarius?' Atherton looked directly into Saloman's eyes. Was there a flicker? He couldn't be sure.

'No.'

'Are you sure?'

'I am sure.'

'Did you ask her where she got the Guarnerius and the bows?'

'No.'

'You didn't ask? You didn't require any proof of owner-ship from her?'

Now he sighed with faint reproach. 'People own things. Why should they have proof of ownership? They are family heirlooms, perhaps. A violin is not like a Rolex watch, my dear young man. I have from the police a list of stolen instru-ments, and these I look out for, always. What is not on the list I am free to buy and sell. Is it so?'

Saloman inclined his head at a helpful angle, but Atherton could hear the laughter in the air. The eight brown fingers, hooked over the rim of the counter, were grinning trium-phantly at him. You have nothing on us, they said. You can't touch us.

'You've been most helpful,' Atherton said at last.

'I am always happy to help the police.'

'There is one more thing – can you lend me those daybooks for a while?'

'I need them for my daily business,' Saloman protested, but without emphasis.

'I can return them to you tomorrow. I'm sure you can manage for one day.'

Saloman inclined his head in consent and passed the

books across the counter, but the brown fingers gripped them until the last moment before relinquishing them.

'Thank you very much,' Atherton said. He turned away with reluctance, feeling strangely unwilling to have Saloman unseen behind him on the short walk to the door. Outside, Bond Street had never seemed so light and airy and lovely. He had the rest of the day to go through these damned ledgers to find something, but whatever he found, he knew it would at best only suggest, not prove. Saloman was a downy bird, if ever there was one. He had not even made the mistake of denying all knowledge of Anne-Marie, which was what convinced Atherton more than anything that he had been dealing with a very professional criminal.

14

Whom the Gods Wish to Destroy they First Make Rich

The personnel manager of the Birmingham Orchestra – what Slider had come to know was called 'the fixer' – was one Ruth Chisholm, a strong, handsome girl with foxy hair, bright cheeks, and pale, piercing eyes. She gave Slider the answer he was growing to expect about Anne-Marie Austen.

'I didn't know her very well. I don't think anyone did. She kept herself very much to herself. In fact –' she hesitated '– I don't think she was much liked in the Orchestra.'

'Why was that?' Norma asked.

'Well, to begin with, it was said she'd got the job in the first place through influence – someone had had a word with the powers that be and got her in. I don't know if that was true or not, but it's certainly true that she never auditioned for the part, which is unusual for a string player, and that got up people's noses a bit.' She smiled suddenly. 'Musicians are a funny lot. They'd jump at the chance to get their friends in, but if anyone else does it, they snap at them like piranha fish. In theory they like people to get on by ability alone, but it never works that way, and they know it.'

'Was she not good enough for the job?' Norma asked.

'Oh, she was a good player all right – and a good section player, what's more, which is rare. Nowadays they all want to be soloists, and that's no good when there are sixteen of you supposed to sound like one. Anne-Marie fitted in – musically, that is.'

'But not socially?'

'Well – I'll give you an example. She had a flat near the centre of town, which should have made her very popular. People need somewhere close to go, sometimes, between rehearsal and concert. But she never invited anyone back there. That's one of the things people said about her, that she was tight. And standoffish.'

'Was she well off?' Slider asked.

'A musician? You're kidding!'

'I thought she came from a wealthy family?'

She shook her head to signify that she knew nothing about that.

'Do you know who Anne-Marie's special friends were?' Norma asked next. 'Who she went around with?'

Before Ruth Chisholm could answer they were interrupted by an old man in porter's uniform, who sidled up to them and gave a conspiratorial cough into his fist.

''Scuse me sir, but would you be Inspector Slider, sir? Telephone call for you. If you'd like to come this way, sir, I'll put it through to you in the box.' He lowered his voice still further and gave a ghastly wink. 'That way it'd be more private, see.'

Slider gave Norma a glance and a nod, to tell her to get on with it, and followed the old man. A moment later he was easing himself distastefully into the booth in which someone had recently smoked a cigar – one of the things for which he often though the death penalty ought to be brought back. The bell rang, and he picked up the receiver and found Nicholls on the line.

'Hullo, Bill? Ah, I've got a nurrgent message for you from your burrd.' He put so much roll into the last word that Slider couldn't identify it for a moment.

'Oh, you mean Miss Marshall?' he said superbly, and Nicholls chuckled.

'Well if her face is as gorgeous as her voice, you're a lucky man. Anyway, this is it: apparently she's been working today with a guy called Martin Cutts – mean anything to you?' Slider felt the familiar spasm of jealousy and grunted ungraciously. One day, just one day! 'They were talking about the Austen girl, and it seems that he knows where she

used to go to in Birmingham. Is this making sense to you?'
'Yes, yes, go on.'
'Okay. Well, it seems Austen bummed a lift offa this Cutts
guy once, when he was coming up to Birmingham and her
car had broken down, and she asked him to drop her off at
the end of Tutman Street.'
'Tutman,' Slider said, writing.
'Aye. And Cutts says that he was at the kerb a while trying
to get out into the traffic, and he saw her in his rear-view
mirror as she walked away, going down Tutman Street
briskly as if she knew where she was going.'
'Is that all?'
'Aye, that's it. Any use?'
'Could be. It's better than what I've got so far, which is
nothing. Sweet eff ay.'
'You dear old-fashioned thing,' Nicholls chuckled.
'Nobody says that any more. Any message to send back to
your woman?'
'Is she there?' Slider asked eagerly, feeling his heart leap
about in his stomach in a disconcertingly adolescent way.
'No, she's at work. She phoned during the tea-break, as
soon as she could, so that we could relay this to you while
you were still on the scene. Smart woman, eh?'
'She's wonderful. Okay Nutty, thanks. I'll phone her later
myself and thank her properly.'
'I bet you will. I'll tell her that if she rings again.'
'Don't scare her off. How's your mum, by the way?'
'Much better thanks. She's coming out of hospital
tomorrow, thank God. I'm sick of looking after Onan – he
smells.'
'Onan?' Slider asked, but with the feeling he was letting
himself in for it.
'Her budgie. Cheeroh, then, Bill. Happy hunting. Love to
Norma.'
Slider stepped gratefully out into the fresh air of the musty
backstage corridor, and returned to where Norma was
chatting animatedly with Ruth Chisholm. Her technique was
terrific, as he had had occasion to notice before. She raised
an eyebrow as he rejoined them, and relinquished the thread
to him.

'Wasn't Anne-Marie friendly with Martin Cutts for a while?' he asked Ruth Chisholm.

'Friendly?' She grimaced. 'Well, I wouldn't call it that, exactly. They went around together for a while, until Martin left to go to London, but it wasn't anything serious. It never is with Martin. He has a different woman every few weeks.'

From which Slider gathered that she had been taken in herself at some point, and resented it.

'Do you know where Tutman Street is?'

'It's about five minutes' walk from here. One of the old back streets in the centre that hasn't been developed yet.'

'Is there a music shop there, or anything a musician might visit?'

'Not that I know of. There are lots of shops there, groceries and that sort of thing. Anyone might go there, really.'

'I see. Thank you.' He wound up the interview, and a few minutes later he was out in the street with Norma, and telling her about Joanna's message.

'She might not have stopped in Tutman Street,' Norma said. 'She might have gone through it to somewhere else.'

'Yes, I know. It's a slender thread, but it's all we've got.'

Norma looked a little smug. 'Especially since Ruth told me that Anne-Marie hasn't played for that Orchestra since last July.'

'What?'

'Yes – she lied about that. Ruth said why on earth would they book her when they had plenty of good players locally. So whatever she came back to Birmingham for, it wasn't to play in the Orchestra.'

'We'd better hope that it was Tutman Street she was visiting. Oh, by the way,' he remembered suddenly. 'why would anyone call a budgie Onan?'

Norma's face broke into a slow, spreading grin.

'Presumably because he keeps spilling his seed.'

Slider's benevolent deity had seen to it on his behalf that Tutman Street was only a short one. Even so, there would be a period of long and tedious labour involved in making their door-to-door investigation.

'You do that side, and I'll do this,' he said. It was a narrow street of early Victorian shops and houses, very run down and shabby, and the sort of thing that was being renovated and preserved like mad in King's Cross and east of Islington. Here it was simply suffering from the proximity of the new Centre development, and general urban deprivation.

At two he caught Norma between doors and took her round the corner to a greasy spoon for lunch.

'Because we must keep your strength up.'

'Tell me honestly, sir,' she said over hamburger, chips and beans, 'do you think there's any hope?'

'You sound like a Revivalist.'

'No, but really.'

'But really, no, I don't think there's any hope. These people make very few mistakes. But that isn't the point, is it? We just do what we can, and it has to do.'

'Slow and steady wins the race?'

'Only if the hare lies down for a kip, and frankly I've always thought that was a very unlikely story.'

She dabbled a chip in a puddle of tomato sauce. 'I think she was probably just passing through Tutman Street. It's quite close to Marlborough Towers, you know, where she lived. She was probably taking a short cut home.'

'Yes, I know. But we have to go through the motions.'

Late in the afternoon, Norma got a bite. She met with Slider out of sight round the corner, and said breathlessly. 'The owner of that paper shop recognised the mugshot. He said she often used to go to the grocer's shop further down on the other side, and his wife says they sell a special kind of olive oil that's imported in barrels, and you bring your own tin and they fill it up from the tap. They used to see Anne-Marie go past quite often with a tin.'

Slider was silent, his brow drawn with thought.

'I thought you'd be turning cartwheels.' Norma said reproachfully.

'I never know whether to cheer or sob whenever that damned olive oil comes into the picture,' he sighed. 'Come on then, let's go and see.'

The grocery shop was one of those tiny food stores turned into a supermarket by dint of adding a double-sided display down the centre and a cash register by the door. There was nothing unusual about it at first sight: there was the stack of battered wire baskets; the moth-eaten vegetables and brown-spotted apples in cardboard boxes; the freezer cabinet long overdue for defrosting piled high with Lean Cuisine, French-bread pizza and frozen chilli con carne; the cold cabinet sporting sticky, dribbling yoghurt tubs and packets of rubber ham; the chipped lino tiles on the floor and the film of dust over the less popular lines of tins and bottles.

Slider went in alone and wandered along the aisles, pretending to search for something. When he turned the end of the row and looked back towards the cash desk he saw something that alerted his instincts, something that was unusual about this shop. The owner had appeared from somewhere and was standing by the till watching him, and he was not an Asian. He was white and middle-aged, and among the enduring stereotypes of Slider's childhood he would have been put down unerringly as good old Mr Baldergammon who runs the village shop. He was stoutish, pinkish, baldish, and respectable-looking, in a neat brown overall-coat. Had this been a television sitcom he would have been wearing a spotless white grocer's apron, and his eyes would have twinkled benevolently from behind gold-rimmed half-glasses.

Slider moved towards him, his senses alert, and the man said, 'Can I help you, sir?'

He fell a long way short of his stereotype. Unaided by props, his eyes did not twinkle, but glared with muted hostility. He did not smile benevolently, and despite his words, he did not seem at all to want to help Slider, unless it was to help him out of the shop, and pronto.

'I'm looking for olive oil,' Slider said, meeting the eyes at the last moment. The grocer's remained stony.

'You passed it. Top shelf, right-hand side, down the end,' he said curtly.

Slider smiled an amiable smile and cocked an eyebrow at a quizzical angle, expressions he did well and convincingly. 'Oh, well, actually, I'm looking for a special sort. A friend of mine cooked me an Italian meal and she says the olive oil you use makes all the difference. So naturally I asked her what sort she uses and she said it was called Virgin Green. Silly name, isn't it?'

'All we've got is what's on the shelf,' the grocer said coldly.

Slider smiled a little more ingratiatingly. 'But she told me you sell it here, only not in tins, in a barrel, like draught beer, so I thought as I was passing I'd call in and see if I could get some.'

'We don't sell it any more,' he said curtly.

'Oh, but I'm sure it wasn't very long ago she last got some from you. Are you sure you haven't got any, out the back, perhaps?'

The man made an involuntary movement with his eyes towards the door – presumably the door to the storeroom. It was no more than a flicker, quickly controlled, but Slider's scalp was prickling with the briny tension which filled the air. He could almost hear the clicking and whirring.

'I told you, we don't do it any more. Not enough call for it. It was too expensive.'

'Well, could you tell me where you got it from?'

'Italy,' he said impatiently. 'Is there anything else you want?' The question verged on the belligerent, and was obviously meant to be interpreted as Why don't you piss off?

'Oh, no, thanks, that was all,' Slider said, almost Uriah Heeping now, and departed. The grocer slammed the door behind him, and there was a distinctive little click which was the plastic sign hanging from the back of the door being turned to show 'Closed'. Slider went in search of Norma with a sweet singing of success in his ears.

He met her at the appointed rendezvous round the corner, where she was engaged in cat-licking her face clean with the corner of a handkerchief and a pocket mirror. Her hair was ruffled, and her collar slightly askew.

'Anything?' he asked her, eyeing her condition. 'I hope you didn't take any risks.'

'There's an alleyway that runs right along the back to service the back yards. They all had high walls, but to an ex-PT teacher like me –' She shrugged. 'Piece of piss.'

'You were never a PT teacher,' Slider reminded her severely. 'Did you see anything?'

'The door was locked and the window was barred – pretty filthy too – but I hitched myself up and managed to have a look through it. It's just an ordinary storeroom, full of boxes and so on. But on one shelf there are about twenty tins like the one in Anne-Marie's flat.'

Slider sighed with pure pleasure. 'They've made a mistake. At last they've made a mistake – only a small one, but my God!'

'How did you get on?'

'He practically threw me out. Told me they didn't sell olive oil any more – no demand for it. My God, we must really have rattled him!' He stopped and sniffed. 'What have you been treading in?'

'I hate to think,' Norma said, making use of the kerb's edge. 'That yard was the resort of uncleanly creatures. Do you really think we're onto something?'

'I'm sure of it. A shop like that would never deny selling something they had in stock. Come on, my lovely girl, I'm going to buy you a drink. There must be a pub somewhere near here.'

'Anywhere, so long as there's a Ladies where I can clean myself up.'

'Thompson was right,' Atherton said triumphantly as Slider came in. 'She was smuggling!'

Slider simpered. 'Whatever happened to "Good morning, darling, did you sleep well?"'

'I've spent all night going through these daybooks and Anne-Marie's bank statements, and there are some remarkable correlations,' Atherton went on.

'You're not as much fun as you used to be,' Slider complained. 'What daybooks?'

'Saloman of Vincey's. It's an interesting exercise. The turnover of that little shop is astonishing when you've been there and seen how empty it is.'

'In Bond Street you need an astonishing turnover,' Slider pointed out.

'All right, but look at these figures. Saloman admits to buying one fiddle from Anne-Marie, correct name and

address, in October 1987. Now look at the bank statement.'
Slider leaned over his shoulder and followed the line of the
long forefinger. 'He pays her three hundred thousand pounds
– which, by the way, my friend at Sotheby's thinks was on the
high side for those days – and she makes a deposit of four
thousand five hundred. In March '88 he admits to paying her
a hundred thousand for two bows, and she makes a deposit
in her account of fifteen hundred.' He looked up at Slider. 'I
don't have to tell you, do I, that each of those deposits represents exactly one and a half per cent of the purchase price?'

'No, dear. But what happened to the rest of the money?'

'Yes, that's the question. The way I see it, Cousin Mario
gives her the goods, she smuggles them in, sells them to
Saloman, banks her cut, and sends the rest of the money to –
someone.'

'Someone?' Slider said sternly.

Atherton ruffled his hair out of order. 'I haven't worked
that bit out yet,' he admitted.

Slider ruffled the hair back again. 'Only teasing.'

'But look, we can take this further. There are only two
occasions when Anne-Marie's name appears in the daybook,
but every time she made a large deposit in her account,
there's a corresponding sale around the same date at
Vincey's. Sometimes the amounts don't match exactly, but
she may have kept some cash back for immediate expenses –
that's no problem. The other names used on those occasions
are never the same twice. I don't know whether it would be
worth checking them out.'

'I suppose they used her real name twice to make sure she
was implicated and therefore couldn't rat on them,' Slider
mused. 'That's quite feasible. There's no reason why she
shouldn't have had a good fiddle and a couple of bows to
sell, but more than that would look suspicious. But we know
she didn't go on tour as often as once a month.'

Atherton shrugged. 'She needn't necessarily go with an
orchestra. As long as she only took out one fiddle and came
back with one, she was safe enough. And we do know that
she was always taking time off from her Orchestra, ostensibly
to play for outside concerns.'

'True – and we also know that she didn't play for the

Birmingham Orchestra as she said she did.'

'What puzzles me is how they got her own fiddle back to her each time.'

Slider shrugged. 'They may simply have imported it legally, through the normal channels. All they'd have to do would be to pay the duty and VAT, which would be peanuts compared with the value of the fiddle she brought in.'

'But what was the scam, guv? I mean, the fiddles were sold openly at Saloman of Vincey's, and you'd have thought that if there was anything wrong with that setup, it would have been discovered long ago. I mean they knew all about it at Sothebys.'

'We'll have to check up on them, and the olive-oil company and the shop in Tutman Street. But my hunch is that they'll all come out squeaky clean. They'd have to be, to be any use as a laundry service.'

Atherton's eyebrows went up. 'The Italian Connection. So you really think it was The Family after all?'

'I'd bet on it. An elaborate scheme to launder dirty money and pass it back to Italy where it could be used openly and legitimately. Of course, Anne-Marie's part must only have been a tiny one, one little wheel in a huge machine. And when she started to go wrong, she was simply eliminated.'

'Yes, but by whom? We don't seem to be any closer to knowing who actually killed her.'

'When we know how, we'll know who,' Slider said, but without conviction. 'But I'm afraid that aspect may turn out to be the least important of the whole business. I think I'd better go and talk to Dickson. Let me have a copy of those notes about the money, will you?'

When he came back in with the copy, Atherton lounged gracefully against the wall beside Slider's desk in the only patch of sunshine in the room. 'It looks as if you were right all along, guv,' he said. 'I was barking up the wrong tree with that Thompson business. But I wonder if we'll ever be able to prove it wasn't all legit.'

'I doubt it,' Slider said without looking up. 'That's the whole point of laundering.'

'But if a thing is a lie, it ought to be possible to nail it.'

'In an ideal world.'

'We might manage to squeeze them a bit on probability. Look, I did some more working out. We can tell from Anne-Marie's bank statement that she must have been passing around two million pounds to that shop in Tutman Street, and how did they account for that? If olive oil costs, say, thirty pounds a tin –'

'What?'

'Oh yes.' Atherton was pleased at having surprised him. 'Extra virgin oil is very expensive. In Sainsbury's it's about two quid for a little tiny bottle. Now at thirty pounds a tin, they'd have had to record sales of around sixty-seven thousand tins a year to account for the money. And that would be about a hundred and eighty tins of it per day. Can you believe a little shop like that would sell all that much olive oil?'

'Probability isn't proof. And you can bet they've worked out their accounting problems. They needn't have passed all the sales through one shop or one class of goods. And we don't even know that that's where she took the money.'

'No, but she must have gone there for something.'

'And even if you did manage to nail that little shop, you'd only be snipping one tiny blood vessel in the system. You don't imagine that two million pounds was the summit of their ambitions, do you?'

'To quote you on that one, we do what we can, and it has to do. Your trouble is you take everything too seriously. If you can scoop up one little turd, the world is a sweeter place.'

'Thank you, Old Moore,' Slider said, not without bitterness.

She had drawn the heavy, port-coloured curtains against the dreary evening, and lit the fire, and it glinted off things half-hidden in corners and increased the Aladdin's Cave effect of the red Turkish carpet and the cushion-stuffed chairs and sofa.

'You're very late. Was it trouble?'

'I came by a roundabout route, and spent some time driving about watching my rear-view mirror.'

'I hope that's just paranoia.'

'Reasonable precautions, now they've seen my face.' He took her in his arms and kissed her. It seemed to have been a very long time since he had last done that.

After a while she rubbed a fond hand along his groin and remarked, 'At least you always carry a blunt instrument around with you.'

'Not always. Only when I'm with you.'

'You say such lovely things to a girl.' She tilted her head up at him, smiling a long, curved smile. 'Do you want to eat now, or afterwards? Speak now, because things will start to burn soon.'

He laughed. 'You're so basic. It's lovely.'

'It's healthy. Well?'

'Turn the gas off,' he said.

Much later they sat by the fire and ate steak with avocado salad followed by Gorgonzola with a bottle of Rully. Joanna was splendidly, unconcernedly naked – 'Saves on napkins,' she said – while Slider wore only his underpants, because her carpet was so prickly.

'You've changed so much,' she marvelled, 'in such a short time. That first night I met you, you were so reserved. You'd never have done something like this.'

'You've changed me,' he said, stroking her shoulder. 'And you aren't white at all. More butter-coloured.'

'Salted or unsalted?'

'Pure Jersey.'

'It's only the fire light,' she said, turning her head to kiss his hand, and he smiled and shook his head. All his senses seemed sharpened, all sensations heightened. The taste of the food and wine, the blissful heat from the fire on his skin, the shapes of light made by the flames, the small bright sounds of the fire and the ticking clock and the tap of cutlery on plate – everything seemed intensified, more itself, as if he had been transported into a world of paradigms. As perhaps he had, being in love.

They talked of nothing in particular, and gradually Slider fell silent, leaving the chatter to Joanna. She touched on a few subjects, and when they got to the cheese stage she asked him how the case was coming along.

'We're waiting for reports to come in on the shop and Vincey's. But I don't suppose they'll tell us much. If Anne-Marie was mixed up with a big, powerful organisation, it isn't likely we'll be able to pin her murder on them. They'll have covered their tracks.'

'Is that what bothers you?'

'What bothers me most is that if I'm right, my superiors will regard her as an unimportant side issue. People seem to have come to mean a great deal less than money nowadays.'

'Oh Bill!' She smiled, leaning forward to touch his knee. 'That's nothing new. Really, it's just the opposite – that only nowadays have people begun to feel that it's wrong for money to mean more than people. Think of the Victorian times. Think of Roman times. Think of any time in the past.'

He did not look convinced, so she changed the subject and told him about her day and the terrible conductor they were suffering from. She related a few musical anecdotes to him, and saw him trying to be amused and failing, and fell silent. Then, seeing he had allowed her to fail him, he felt guilty, and tried to make it up to both of them by making love to her again.

For the first time in his life he couldn't do it. Long after she had accepted the inevitable he went on trying, until at last she said gently, 'It's no use bullying yourself. If it won't, it won't.'

He rolled over onto one elbow and stared at her. This, then, was the other side of that heightening of awareness – that everything hurt too much.

'I'm sorry,' he said helplessly.

'You shouldn't have tried. It's only made you sad.'

'I didn't want – I wanted us not to be separate.'

'Your feeling like that separates us. For heaven's sake, if you want to be sad in my company, go ahead and feel sad. You don't have to amuse me. You don't have to be on your best behaviour.'

He put out a hand and pulled a lock of her muddled hair. 'I know.'

'No. I don't think you do. Coming here to me is like – oh, I don't know – like going out to tea when you were a child. Best suit, party manners, a break from real life and bread-

and-jam. I'm not real to you at all.'

He was surprised. 'You are! You're the most real thing in my life.'

'Then you should feel that you can be natural with me. Be gloomy, if that's how you feel.'

'But that wouldn't be fair on you.'

She jerked away from him and sat up. 'Oh, fair on me! What's fair on me? What do you think you're doing? When you happen to be here, and you're in a good mood, is that what you think is fair?'

'I don't understand,' he said helplessly.

'I can see that. It's because you don't put yourself to the trouble of thinking. Where will you be sleeping tonight, just answer me that?'

'At home, of course,' he said unhappily.

'Of course!'

'But you know that. What else can I do?'

'Nothing. Nothing. Forget it. Just don't talk about fairness.' She stood up with an abrupt movement of exasperation or hurt, he wasn't sure which, and stood with her back to him leaning on her folded arms on the mantelpiece.

'Joanna, I don't understand. I though you wanted me to be here. I don't want to hurt you. If it hurts you, me being here, I won't come,' he tried.

'Oh, for God's sake! Thank you for the extensive choice.'

He didn't know what else to say, and after a moment she said, 'I think you'd better go. We're only picking at each other.'

But not like this, he thought. He couldn't bear to leave her like this. He hesitated for a long time, and then went and put his hands on her shoulders and turned her. Her eyes were dry and bright and she looked at him searchingly, perhaps to see how much he understood, which was very little.

'When I was a child,' she said suddenly, 'My mother always wound the clock in the sitting-room on a Sunday afternoon, about five o'clock. It was a very evocative sound. And there was a drain in the kitchen under the sink that smelled of very old green soap. And the bricks the house was made of, when the sun warmed them, they smelled like caramel. But no-one will ever say that sort of thing about any house of mine. I build my nest, you see, but nothing grows in it.'

Still he didn't understand, but wisely avoiding words, he kissed her on the forehead and the eyes and the lips, and after a while she responded, and they lay down on the hearth rug again and made love, this time without any trouble.

'You think this will make everything all right again,' she muttered at one point, and he did understand, dimly.

'I love you,' he responded. 'I love you.' He said it again and again, and never used her name because she was not separate from him then, she was part of his substance. Afterwards he lay heavy, like something waterlogged, in her arms, unable to make the terrible effort of moving.

'I'd better go,' he said at last.

'Hardly worth it. You might as well stay here. Move in, and save yourself the journey.'

'I can't,' he said automatically. Did she mean it or was she joking? He dreaded a revival of the argument.

But she only said, 'I know.'

'You don't sound convinced.'

'What do you want, a written guarantee?' she said, but without rancour. 'Go on, you dope. Get thee to thy clonery.'

'Here's the report on that company, Olio d'Italia.' Dickson said, gesturing Slider to a seat. The fragrance of whisky hung on the air all around him like aftershave. 'There was a certain amount of reluctance on the part of our Italian friends to press the enquiry, which in itself tended to confirm what you thought, Bill. There's mud at the bottom of every pool, and some of it's best left unstirred. Still, for what it's worth, they've sent us this profile, and it's pretty much what you'd expect.'

'Oh,' said Slider. Sometimes it wasn't nice to be proved right.

'Olio d'Italia, head office in Calle le Paradiso, however you pronounce that. Run by one Gino Manetti –'

'Cousin Mario,' Slider said. Dickson looked a question and didn't wait for the answer.

'The company itself is a subsidiary of Prodiutto Italiano –

imaginative names these people choose – which is a massive international concern dealing with all sorts of Italian produce – oil, pasta, tomatoes, olives, cheeses, grapes, dried fruit – you name it. The big boy at the head of the parent company is also, surprise surprise, called Manetti – Arturo Manetti. He lives in an enormous villa up in the hills above Florence. Fantastic place, so I'm told, servants, guard dogs, electric fence, armed bodyguards, the lot. Arturo is Gino's uncle, and others of his relations run other subsidiaries. Of course, the reason the Italian security didn't want to run the enquiries too hard is that Arturo is the local Capo.'

'I see.' This business of being proved right got worse and worse.

'Anyway, they've gone into the business, and it's all legit – except that it isn't, of course. They don't sell the oil in Italy at all, as we would have expected. The output of that particular subsidiary is all export, and the two biggest international customers are – want to guess?'

'England and America.'

'Britain and the States – got it in two. Their turnover is pretty big. In this country alone they do two hundred million. That's an awful lot of oil.'

'An awful lot of people like Italian food.'

Dickson looked at him sharply. 'Are you trying to be funny?'

'No sir.'

'I've got a list of their outlets. Some of them are wholesalers, so I doubt if the list is complete as far as retailers go. Obviously they must all sell oil in some form, but I doubt whether more than one or two are actually bent – it wouldn't pay them to run the outfit that way. Your place in Tutman Street is on the list, and everything is backed up by the right paperwork. On paper everything is rose-scented, and that's the way it has to be, of course. No funny business. Nobody with a previous. They'll have people out all the time, agents, looking for likely recruits.

'Who recruited Anne-Marie, I wonder?' Slider said.

Dickson cocked his head. 'From what I gather, she was a cold-blooded unemotional, ambitious little cow. So she was ideal material, wasn't she? I mean, it was either that or the

Foreign Office.' He leaned back and the chair creaked protestingly. 'The other end, the Vincey end, is even more difficult to finger.' He swivelled the chair and knocked a file off the desk with his elbow. Confining him in an office was like keeping a buffalo in the bathroom. 'Vincey's has been in existence as a business for over a hundred years on that same premises in Bond Street. Irreproachable address, first-class clientele and all that. The shop and the goodwill were purchased eleven years ago by an agent acting for an international antiques trading consortium, who had some very big American money behind them. The money traces back to a New York holding company with a Park Avenue address.'

'Swanky.'

'As you say. It's called AM Holdings, and the President of the company is called Walter Fontodi.'

'All impeccably above board?'

Dickson gave a savage smile. 'Squeaky bloody clean. If they could nail this AM Holdings they'd be happy folk over there. But they haven't yet found a way of touching it.'

'So the Vincey end is not a new exercise?'

'That's the way they work. That's the beauty of a family business, isn't it? You can take your time over things. If you don't benefit yourself, your son will, or your grandson. It's all in the bloody Family. That's a joke.'

Slider quirked his lips obediently.

Dickson rocked the chair back and let it fall forward with a thump that shook the floorboards. 'They buy up a place with a first-class record, and run it straight.' And I mean really straight – rates, taxes, VAT, the lot. They do that for a number of years before they ever start using it for their purposes. They want respectable, and they can afford to pay for it. Buying Vincey's and running it at a loss for a couple of years must have cost them a couple of million, but what's that to them? They're handling telephone numbers every year. Probably set it off as a tax loss.'

'And Vincey's really is respectable.'

'Yes, of course. They're simply buying and selling antiques, and if some of their customers are marked cards, so what? They never touch stolen goods. In fact, they're probably more honest than your average dealer. I'm told

Saloman has an excellent relationship with the local police.'

'And who is Saloman?'

'Ah, that's an interesting detail. When they bought the business, it was on the market because the previous owner had died – that was the real, original Saloman. He was in his sixties, and he'd been running Vincey's since 1935. Apparently he was a fantastic old boy, a real expert, knew everything about stringed instruments, and a whale on bows. He'd been a concert violinist in his youth – apparently quite a good one – but for some reason gave it up and went into dealing, and specialised in antiquities.'

Slider raised his brows. 'You mean they took over his name and his reputation? The young man at Sotheby's sent Atherton to Saloman because he was an expert on violin bows.'

'Nice, isn't it? I suppose anyone who was around when the changeover took place would know the old boy had died, but the general public wouldn't, and by now I don't suppose anyone remembers.'

'So who is our Saloman?'

'His name isn't Saloman, of course. He isn't even Jewish, though he wears the hat. He's an Italian, name of Joe Novanto. Came over during the war as a refugee, after the Nazi occupation of Italy. He changed his name to Joseph Neves and got himself a job with Hill's of Hanwell, making violin bows, which apparently was his trade back home. When the war ended he stayed on in this country, and got a job at Vincey's.'

'So he really could do it?'

'Oh yes – that part was genuine all right. He was taken on to repair and renovate bows and instruments they were handling, and he studied the ancient instrument trade under the real Saloman, so he was learning from an expert. And when Saloman died and the business was sold, he took over the name, the reputation, even the character. Of course, the fact that he'd been working there so long would help to confuse the issue – people would recognise him, and in time his identity got fudged over. I don't suppose many people go to a shop like that more than once in their lives.'

'And of course he really did know Saloman's stuff.'

'He's been doing it for twenty-five years.'

'But then, at what stage was he recruited? If it was the organisation that bought Vincey's when the old man died, was Neves already one of them?'

'God knows. I don't suppose we ever shall. But if you want my personal opinion I'd say yes. It's carrying the business of sleepers a hell of a long way, but these people work on a grand scale. You can afford to make plans that take fifty years to mature if it's your own flesh-and-blood that'll benefit. I'd say that Neves, or Novanto, was their man from the beginning, before he ever left Italy, and he was just slipped in when the opportunity came in case he was ever needed. But of course, there's nothing we can pin on him. He not only looks legit, he is, except for using Saloman's name, and that's not a crime.'

'So where do we go from here?'

Dickson looked at him carefully, and placed both his meaty fists on the desk top, making himself larger and squarer than ever. Body language? Slider thought. Dickson wrote the book on it! 'That's the part you're not going to like, Bill. I'm afraid you don't go anywhere: they're taking the case out of our hands.'

'Special Branch?'

'They've got their own operation going on the Family. They know what they're doing. Come on, there's no use looking like that. You must have expected it. I'm only surprised they left it with us as long as they did.'

'And Anne-Marie?' Slider's lips felt numb.

'Well, she's a bit of a side issue really, isn't she? Besides, she was one of their own operators. Obviously they knocked her off when she started being a nuisance, and since they've cleaned up their own mess, you can't expect our boys to get too excited about it. There are bigger fish to fry, and Special don't want us mucking about and treading mud all over their carpet.'

'And Mrs Gostyn? And Thompson?'

Dickson shrugged. 'Look, I know how you feel, but it's more important to nail the blokes at the top than some two-by-four local operator. If we go poking sticks up the network looking for the murderer, we'll scare them into closing it down and a lot of hard work'll have been wasted. In any case, even if you could discover who murdered the Austen girl, it's seven to four on that he's dead by now. They don't tolerate failures, as you know, and anyone who draws attention to himself is a failure. Ipso bloody facto. They'll have topped him, no sweat.'

Slider merely looked at him, and Dickson replaced his fists with his elbows on the desk top and looked beguiling.

'It's not as bad as all that, come on. Instructions are to close the file officially. Thompson killed Austen and then committed suicide, and the old lady was just an accident. That's going on record, and it makes our figures very nice, I can tell you.'

'Our figures?' Slider repeated disbelievingly.

'They're letting us have the credit, officially, and since you did most of the slog, I'm putting it down to you, Bill. It goes on your record. Earns you quite a few more Brownie points. You'll be a Girl Guide in no time.'

Dickson sat back with an expansive smile, inviting Slider to look surprised, grateful, modest and hopeful in that order. The implied promise was in the air: the promise Irene had longed for, for so many years, was dangled, a golden vision, just within reach.

Slider stood up. 'Will that be all, sir?'

Dickson's smile disappeared like the sun going in. The granite showed through the red meat of his face, and his voice was hard and impatient.

'You're off the case. That's official, d'you understand! Forget it.'

As Slider passed the door of the CID room on his way back to his office, Atherton called to him, and he paused and looked in blankly. Beevers was there too, sitting on Atherton's desk reading a newspaper.

'Was it the report on Saloman?' Atherton asked 'Did Dickson have anything?'

'I never thought the old man would go for that schmucky Mafioso angle,' Beevers complained. 'He's always so keen on a good, solid money motive. Now I really think I'm onto something there. I've been breaking my balls over John Brown and his boyfriend, and I think there's something fishy about them.'

'Well we know that,' Atherton said wearily.

'No, something else, I mean. Did you know that Trevor Byers was up before the disciplinary committee of the BMA about eighteen months ago? I can't find out what for, yet – they're as tight as a crab's arse about stuff like that – but it would account for why old Brown's so fidgety. And if Austen had found out about it somehow –'

'The case is closed,' Slider said, stemming the flood. 'Official, from the very top. We're all back on traffic violations.'

'Closed?' they chorused, like Gilbert and Sullivan.

'There are bigger fish to fry. Anything to do with The Family is for Special Branch alone. Hands off, do not touch. And Anne-Marie has become an unimportant side issue.'

In the momentary silence that followed, Atherton noted how Slider always talked about Anne-Marie and never about Thompson, as though the one were an intolerable outrage, and the other no more than he deserved. But he forbore to mention it. Instead he filched the paper out of Beevers' hand and opened it at the entertainments page.

'Oh well, that's that, then,' he said. 'At least we'll have our weekends to ourselves again. I wonder if there are any good shows on.'

'And you can find out if your children still recognise you,' Beevers said to Slider. 'Anyone fancy a cup of tea?'

Slider shook his head without even having understood what he had been asked, and walked away. When he had gone, Beevers turned to Atherton.

'What's up with him, then? Is he cracking up? I hear he took Norma to Birmingham for the day and never even laid a hand on her knee. I mean, that's not normal.'

'Oh shut up, Alec,' Atherton said wearily, turning a page.

Beevers looked complacent. 'Detecting's a young man's job. I've always said so and I always will.'

'Not when you reach forty, you won't.'

'These old guys can't take the pressure, you see. They let things get on top of them. The next thing you know, old Bill will start weeping over suicides and writing poetry. I always say –'

'Oh stuff it!' Atherton said, getting up. He flung the newspaper in the bin and walked away, but Beevers simply raised his voice a little to carry.

'You're not so young any more either, are you, Jim? Time's running out for you too, old lad.'

Left alone, Beevers picked the newspaper out of the bin, smoothed it out, opened it at the sports page, and began to read. He whistled cheerfully and swung his rather short legs, which didn't reach the floor when he was perched on a desk. If they couldn't stand the heat, he thought with his usual originality, they should stay out of the kitchen.

15

A Runt is as Good as a Feast

Slider went back to his office and did a bit of desultory
tidying up, which soon degenerated into sitting at his desk
and staring moodily at the photograph of Anne-Marie. At
the end of any case he usually felt a lassitude, a disinclination
to work, once the momentary excitement of the result wore
off, leaving only deflation and paperwork. But this was much
worse, because he had no answers to the many questions,
nothing to detract from the sense of injustice towards the
victims.

The phone rang and he picked it up reluctantly. It was
O'Flaherty. Even on the phone he sounded massive.

'I've got it, I've got it,' he chortled. 'I've remembered who
the little runt was. It was Ronnie Brenner.'

'Half-inch Brenner? The bloke who used to sell hookey
watches down the Goldhawk Road?'

'No, no, not him. He emigrated – oh, it must be two years
ago.'

'Emigrated?'

'To Norfolk. He's gone straight, got a half-share in a
chicken farm. Plays the trombone in the Sally Army band in
Norwich. He sent me a postcard, the cheeky sod. No, I'm
talking about Ronnie Brenner: little feller, racecourse tout,
bookies' runner, one-time unsuccessful jockey, tipster. You
name it, he's done it, so long as it's to do with harses. He's

always hanging about racecourses – Banbury and Kempton Park mostly, they all have their favourites. We've had him in on sus a few times for hangin' about stables with a pair of binoculars an' a little book, but we've never managed to nail him for anything. No previous, d'you see – that's why I had such a job trackin' him down in me memory. Sure, don't you remember we had a look at him for that doping business at Wembley in '88, but there was nothing on him.'

'Wembley? I don't remember. I think that was when I was away on holiday,' Slider said with an effort. 'I remember you all talking about it when I came back. A bit of excitement in the silly season.' His brain made a determined effort to catch up with him. 'But they don't have horses at Wembley, do they? I thought it was football.'

'The Harse of the Year Show, ya stewpot. Are you awake, son? The local lads pulled him in at Banbury for the same thing, and he laid his hand on his heart and swore he'd never do a thing like that to man's best friend. Touching, it was. There wasn't a dry seat in the house. Anyway, that's who it is. He lives in Cathnor Road. Didn't I tell you I never forget a shit?'

Slider's tired brain was whirling with fragments of conversations, free-associating and making no sense. Atherton's voice said if you scoop up one little turd the world's a sweeter place, and he tried to grab the words as they floated past. 'No previous ... that doping business at Wembley ... so long as it's to do with horses ... Banbury ... Cathnor Road ... never forget a shit   if you scoop '

'Billy, are you there, for Chrissakes? Would you ever speak to me? It's a lonely thing to be a desk sergeant and unloved.'

'A lonely thing ...' Slider took his head in his hands and shook his brain. 'Sorry Pat. I'm a bit tired. Thanks for the information, but it's come too late. The Austen case is closed – official, from the top. It's gone up to Special Branch, so there's nothing more I can do about it. I'm off the case.'

'So long as the case is off you,' O'Flaherty said warningly.

'Ah, don't take it so hard, darlin'. In a long life you'll see worse injustice than that.' Slider didn't answer. 'Brenner may have had nothing to do with it, but if I see him hangin' around I'll pull him in anyway. It doesn't do to let the flies settle.'

'Yeah, okay, thanks Pat,' Slider said vaguely.

'Listen, why don't you go home, insteada roostin' up there. Have an evening off for a change, while you can?'

'Yes, I think I will.'

'And if your wife calls, I'll tell her you're out on a case,' O'Flaherty added drily.

Slider's mind was not with him, and it took a moment before he said, 'Oh, yes, I – yes, thanks. Thanks, Pat.'

'And remind me to tell you some time,' O'Flaherty said very gently, 'what a stupid bastard you are.'

Slider collected his coat, and went out into the grey January afternoon.

The tall, shabby house on Cathnor Road had an air of long neglect and temporary desertion. Slider had been driving about, he hardly knew where, for so long that it was now dark. He had often found before that driving had the effect of releasing his subconscious mind to worry out problems in a way the conscious mind, being too cluttered, could not do; but this time the only conclusion he had come to was that, off the case or not, he wanted to find out what Ronnie Brenner had been up to.

The house was divided into flats, and since it was dark there ought to have been lights in at least some of the windows, but the building gave no sign of life as Slider passed it and parked a little beyond. He walked up the steps to the front door where there was a variety of bells, none of them labelled. He pressed a few at random, and then stood looking about him.

Almost opposite him was the turning that led to the cul-de-sac where The Crown and Sceptre stood. Ah, yes, he thought, that's why Cathnor Road had been ringing bells in his mind. And talking of ringing bells, he pressed a few more, and stepped back to look up at the windows. Almost at once he heard someone hiss from somewhere below him. A small and anxious face was craning up at him from the area door to the basement flat, which was hidden under the steps on which he stood.

'Mr Slider! Down here, quick! Come on, guv, quick as you like!'

The voice was hoarse with urgency, and he obeyed, running down the steps and then down the precipitous, dish-shaped flight into the area. Ronnie Brenner stood half concealed by his door, which he held just enough ajar for Slider to get through.

''Urry up, guv, please. It ain't safe,' he whispered, and Slider went past him into the flat, his senses alert. Brenner took a frightened and comprehensive look around outside, and then closed the door and chained it clumsily.

'Frough here,' he said, inching past Slider in the narrow, dark, malodorous passage and leading the way to the back of the house. 'We can't be seen in here – nothink don't over-look it.'

The room was a surprise to Slider. It was a living-cum-kitchen-cum-dining room, square, and well-lit from a window with a venetian blind over it. One corner was equipped as a kitchen, and the rest was furnished with a square dining-table with barley-sugar legs, a shabby and almost shapeless sofa, two sagging armchairs covered in scratched and scarred leather, and bookshelves along one wall. Though shabby, it was spotlessly clean, and smelled, unlike the passage, not of damp and rotting plaster, but pleasantly of leather and neat's-foot oil.

There were photographs of horses everywhere, framed and hanging on the wall, pinned along the edges of the book-shelves, propped up on the table and the kitchen cabinet, cut out of newspapers and magazines and sellotaped to the fridge door and above the draining-board. At a quick glance Slider could see that all the books on the shelves were to do with horses and racing, ranging from serious turf and stud books to a row of Dick Francis novels in well-thumbed paperback. There was nothing surprising about the room except its existence here, in the basement of a slum house in Shepherd's Bush. Had it been transported, as it stood, to the flat above the stables of a respected stud-groom, Slider would have found it entirely in character.

Turning to face his host, Slider remembered him now, and remembered him as harmless. He was small, undersized, weakly-looking except for the whippy strength of his arms and hands, and the hard lines in his face which told of a lifetime's bitter and losing struggle with weight. He might once have been a handsome man, before the effects of deliberate starvation, exposure to the weather, and a diet of gin and cigarettes designed to stunt him, had browned and wrinkled and monkeyfied him. Under the brown he was at this moment very white, his features drawn and pinched with fear. Ronnie Brenner was plainly a very frightened man.

Slider addressed him kindly. 'Now then, Ronnie – who's been putting the frighteners on you?'

'Christ, Mr Slider, nobody don't need to say nothink. I seen what they do, haven't I? Was you followed, guv?'

'I don't think so. I came a very roundabout way. Is it as bad as that?'

'I wanted to tell you, guv, honest,' he said, fidgeting anxiously with the things on the table. 'I hung about the station for a bit hoping I'd see you, till I see that big Mick sergeant clocking me, then I come away a bit hasty. Him and me have had a brush now and then, see. I fought about phoning you, but I never done it. I never fought you'd come here.'

'Well I did, and here I am. What did you want to tell me?'

'I ain't done nothing, and that's the truth, guv, so help me. You got to believe me. This bloke phoned me up, see, out of the blue –'

'Which bloke?'

'I don't know. He never give me no name. He says, I know you, Ronnie, and I've got a little job for you, what'll pay you nicely.'

'He used your name like that?'

'Yessir. Straight out, Ronnie, he calls me.'

'Did you recognise his voice?'

'No sir. Not to say who he was, but it's a kind of voice I've heard before. What I mean is, it was posh. Posher than yours. Not a Silver-Ring voice, see, but real posh, like the county nobs in the owners' enclosure.'

'Old? Young?'

'Not young. Middle-aged. An' he was ringing me from a coin box, and it must have been long distance because I kept hearing him put money in, every two bleeding seconds nearly. So anyway, he asks me to do this job for him. He says he wants me to find him an empty flat on the White City estate, make it so's he can get in, clean it out, and watch it for a couple of days to see who goes in and out of the block, what times an' that.'

'Did he say why he wanted you to do those things?'

'He says he wants to have a private meeting, and he wants him and his colleagues to be able to get there and go away again without no-one seeing them. Well, it don't sound too bad, so I done it. Well, there's nothink against the law, is there?'

'Breaking and entering is against the law.'

'Yeah, but it was an empty flat, kids break in all the time. He couldn't steal nothink, could he? Just have a meeting there – well, I didn't know what the meeting was about and he never told me, but I said to him, I said, I ain't got no previous, I said, and that's the way I want it to stay. I don't want to get mixed up in nothink heavy, I said, and he said that's why I picked you, Ronnie, he said. I wouldn't want to have to do with no-one what had a record.'

'He said that?'

'Yessir. And he said he'd pay me well and he did, no funny business. Two hundred and fifty a day, he paid me, in five and tens in a jiffy bag frough the letter box.'

'I don't suppose you kept any of the bags?'

'No, I frew 'em away.'

'You didn't notice the postmark?'

Diemmer's face took on a gleam of hope. 'It was Birmingham. I spose that was where he was phoning from, long-distance.'

'And how was he to get the information from you?'

'He phoned me up every day at a certain time and I told him and he paid me. I done it five days, and I can tell you I was glad to get the money. I had a lot of bad luck recently, Mr Slider, and I had some heavy debts.'

'I believe you. Go on.'

'Well, I done it five days, like I said, and then he says all right, that's enough, and I never heard from him again. But then the next week I saw in the papers about the body being found in the flat, and, Christ, I can tell you, I nearly shat myself. I mean, I ain't never 'ad nothink to do with nothink like that! You know me, guv, I'm not in that class – wouldn't hurt a flea, and that's the truth. I didn't know what to do. I just stopped at home and kept the door locked. And then the bloke phoned me up again.'

'The same man?'

'Yessir. He didn't sound so smoove this time though. He sounded as if he was shitting himself an' all.'

'And what day was this?'

'The same day. It was in the papers the noon edition about the body being found, and he bells me the afternoon. I said to him straight off I didn't want nothink to do with him and his bloody money, and he said it wasn't no good me talking like that because I was right in it up to the nostrils.'

'Implicated.'

'That's it, guv, *implicated.* He said I'd got to do what he said or it'd be the worse for me, and he said I hadn't got to get in a panic because what I had to do was easy.'

'What did you have to do?'

'He says I've got to go back to the flats to look for the young lady's handbag.' Slider jumped, and Brenner nodded. 'That's right. He said it might be in all that building stuff lying about, 'cause he fought she might of thrown it out of the car or over the balcony, and if anyone found it we was all for the 'igh jump. Well, I didn't want to go back there, I can tell you, wiv the place crawling wiv plod – no offence, guv – but he says to me, talk bloody sense, he says, I could go round there like I was just sightseeing, but he'd stick out like a sore bloody fumb. Anyway, the long and the short of it is I went round there and I never found nothing. I told him when he belled me, and he said to go back and look again, but I'd had enough, so I hooked it.'

'Where?'

Brenner looked apologetic. 'Isle of Wight. I fought I'd better get where he couldn't find me, and spend the money. But when it came to it, I couldn't spend it. I ain't never 'ad nothink to do with stuff like that, and it scared the shit out of me, guv, I can tell you. So Monday I come back and tried to get in touch with you, waited at the station to see you come out –'

'Why me, Ronnie? I'm flattered and all that, but –'

'Well, I knew Mr Raisbrook was in the cot, and I couldn't talk to none of them kids, all mouf and trousers. They ain't real. They don't know nothink what doesn't come out of a book. But I knew you was straight.' It was a simple and heartfelt tribute.

'Anyway, that night I see you going into The Crown, so I hung about outside in the alley, but you come out with another bloke, so I nipped off.'

'There was someone else there that night, too,' Slider said. 'You know that the man I was with was murdered the next day?'

'Was that 'im? Bloody 'ell, Mr Slider, what's going on? Is it drugs, or what?'

'Worse than that.'

'Something big?'

'Very big, I'm afraid.'

'I wish I'd never touched the bleedin' job,' Ronnie said bitterly, 'but it looked all right at the time. My bloke – is he going to be after me now?'

Slider paused a moment. 'I don't know. It depends on how quickly news travels. You see, we've officially dropped the case, and once they know that, they'll probably pull him out. That means we'll never get the chance to get at him, unless there's anything else you can tell me about him.'

Brenner was a shade whiter even than before. 'Honest, guv, if I knew anything I'd tell you. I ain't holding back.'

'You said he seemed to know you –?'

'A lot of people know me, racing people. That don't mean nothing. His voice did sound a bit familiar, but all the racecourse toffs talk like that.'

'Well if you think of anything, anything at all –'

'I know. You don't need to tell me.'

'By the way, Ronnie, apart from that time outside The Crown, have you been following me, or watching me?'

'No,' he said promptly; and then his jaw sagged as he gathered the implication. 'Gawd 'elp us, he's been following you! He'll know you come here!'

'I don't think so,' Slider said as reassuringly as he could. 'I've been very careful. And as I said, once they know we've dropped it, they won't take any more risks. As long as you keep out of sight for the next few hours, you should be all right. Is there another way out of here?'

'If you climb out the winder, you can get across the garden, frough the fence, across the next garden and over the wall into the alley. I come in that way sometimes. There's a packing case this sider the wall, to give you a leg-up.'

'All right, I'll go out that way, just in case anyone's watching the front. But I don't think they'll bother you after tonight.'

'I hope they know that,' Brenner said woefully.

All the same, Slider parked a distance from Joanna's house and walked the rest, listening with his scalp. He had plenty to think about as he walked, and not much of it added up. Who the hell was the murderer? If he was someone who knew Ronnie Brenner, it was a natural assumption that he must be one of the racing fraternity, but then what was his connection with Anne-Marie? Or was he merely a hired hitman? But there were aspects of the case that made Slider feel restless with that as a conclusion; and he had also the infuriating feeling that there was something on the tip of his brain that he could not quite get to grips with – something he had seen out of the corner of his eye, or something someone had said in passing. If only he could remember what it was, he felt, all the unrelated threads would suddenly weave themselves together into a web strong enough to net the rabbit.

Joanna let him in. 'I haven't got long, you know. I'll have to leave in about an hour.'

He replied only with a preoccupied grunt. She took a close look at his face, and then ushered him without further comment in to the living-room, shoved him into an armchair and brought him a drink. Then she knelt at his feet and rested her arms on his knees and waited for him. Finally he drank a little, stroked her hair absently, and finally looked at her.

'What's happened?' she asked.

'They're closing the case.'

'Why?'

'Apparently they're convinced of the Family connection, and that makes it too big to handle locally. It's going up to the Yard, and they're making it official that Thompson killed Anne-Marie and then committed suicide.'

'To make the villains relax?'

'Partly. And partly because nobody really wants to know who murdered Anne-Marie. She was one of theirs, and they "tidied her up", and who cares?'

'Doesn't Atherton care?'

'Not really. He always said I took this case too personally, and I suppose I did. Atherton's a cool well-balanced personality, and the job is just the job to him.' He knew that wasn't entirely the truth, but it was near enough for the moment. 'But apart from my personal feelings, I hate to leave a job unfinished. There are so many loose threads –'

He lapsed into thought, and she sat quietly drinking her drink and watching him. Even through his preoccupation he felt her presence, just the being near and warming him. After a while he came back and said, 'I'm sorry, this isn't much fun for you.'

'Fun,' she said thoughtfully, 'We only met in the first place, you know, because Anne-Marie was murdered. Sometimes I can't take it in, and when I do, I feel terribly guilty about being so happy with you. She had such an awful life, when you think about it, and for so much loneliness to end like that is dreadful. There wasn't even anyone at her funeral. It's almost –'

Slider sat bolt upright, stopping Joanna in mid-sentence. His expression was so strange that for a moment she thought he was choking or having a heart attack. He grabbed her hand and gripped it so tightly that it hurt her, but he was unaware of it. Suddenly things were slotting into place so fast that he could hardly keep up with them.

'The funeral! At the funeral! I knew at the time someone had said something important, but I couldn't work out what it was, and it's been at the back of my mind ever since. Listen, you told me once that Anne-Marie had said to you that she wasn't allowed to have a pet when she was a child.'

'That's right – her aunt was too houseproud, and didn't want the mess, though I think Anne-Marie thought she forbade it simply out of spite, because of course she has dogs of her own.'

His eyes were very bright, but they were not focused on her. 'There were two things. I have it now. Somebody said – I think you said – that Stourton was nearer to Birmingham than to London. And the bogus vet said that he had known Anne-Marie all her life, and had often taken care of her pony and her puppy.'

'Yes he did. I remember it now. Why would he say that?'

'He made a mistake,' Slider said in a small, deadly voice.

'But what did –'

He gripped her hand even tighter. 'Don't speak!' He was frantic to take hold of the thread of his thoughts as the words tumbled through his brain. They put her down like an old dog. Someone who knew Ronnie Brenner. Piperonyl butoxide. Real posh, like the county nobs. A tall man with a nice voice. Known her since she was a child. A hat like Lord Oaksey wears –

Joanna eased her hand out of his grip and flexed it painfully. 'What is it?' she said very softly.

'We made a mistake at the very beginning. Freddie Cameron made a mistake. He said that only a hospital anaesthetist would have access to Pentathol. But it was he who said they put her down like an old dog. Said it to me as a joke, and I forgot it.'

She was listening, following.

'Vets have to be their own anaesthetists, don't you see? They don't just diagnose, like GPs, they do surgery as well. Pentathol and a surgeon's scalpel. And piperonyl butoxide kills fleas and lice as well as bedbugs and woodlice.'

'Flea powder!' she exclaimed. 'If a vet had traces of it on his clothes, and then sat down in the passenger seat of Anne-Marie's car –'

'He knew her from her childhood – that part was true, at least. He must have known how lonely and alienated she was. He may even have had long talks with her for all we know, got to know the way her mind worked, what her dreams were. It was he who recruited her.' Dickson's voice said in his head, 'It was that or the Foreign Office', and he shook it away as an irrelevance. 'Then she became dangerous and had to be put out of the way.'

'Why?'

'I think, because of the Stradivarius. I have a kind of feeling that playing it at that concert in Florence wasn't part of her orders. I think she took the opportunity of your being taken ill to play it for her own pleasure, and then, having played it, found she couldn't bear to part with it. She kept it instead of passing it on through the system. Then of course she was in trouble. She had to try to get hold of money, went to her solicitor to find out if there was anything coming to her, and discovered she was worth a fortune if only she could get married.'

'That's why she suddenly started pursuing poor old Simon!'

'He was her only hope. She had to move fast, she hadn't time to start from scratch, and the only other man she knew well was already married.'

'Martin Cutts.'

'He was probably more of a friend to her, for all his faults,' Slider said with distaste. 'When she found it was no use, she turned to him for comfort. She was beginning to get very frightened. She said to him, "I'm so afraid".'

'Yes, you told me,' Joanna said quietly.

'She was right to be. Already the order had gone out. The vet – Hildyard – knew Ronnie Brenner. Ronnie hangs out at Banbury racecourse, and that isn't far from Stourton. If we check, I think we'll find Hildyard was a regular there. We may even find he's the official racecourse vet. Ronnie has no previous – they'd never use anyone with a criminal record – but he looks shady enough, the type who'd do a job for cash without asking questions. Ronnie said his contact had a posh voice. And Mrs Gostyn mentioned his voice, too.'

'Who's Ronnie Brenner?'

He hadn't told her that part yet, but he shook the question away – no time now. 'Hildyard must have met Anne-Marie before Christmas – in London, I suppose. That was when he stole her diary, so he knew her movements, and knew she had a free period in January when no-one would miss her. Ronnie found the empty flat for him and watched it to see when there was no-one going in or out on a regular basis. Then Hildyard arranged to meet Anne-Marie at the pub that evening. I don't know how, but I imagine it was a prearranged signal. Something to do with her car – a note under the windscreen or something. She'd been resigned to her fate, but now suddenly she took fright. I suppose she guessed something was up, and now it was upon her she realised she didn't want to die.'

'Yes,' Joanna whispered. She was very pale.

'She ran back to try to get her friends to come with her, thinking that if she turned up at the pub with a group, he'd have to call it off. It would look like something she couldn't have helped, to have a bunch of friends tagging along. But of course, when it came to it, she found she hadn't any friends. She had to go alone.'

Joanna could see that he had forgotten that she was one of the 'friends' in question. She felt a little sick now, and kept her lips tightly closed. He was looking stretched and exhausted, but he went on.

'He met her in the car park, well muffled up, wearing a racing man's brown trilby – a hat like Lord Oaksey wears on the television. They didn't see Paul Ringham sitting in his car with his lights off, waiting for his wife. They left together in her car, with Anne-Marie driving. Perhaps she hoped then that she'd been mistaken. She'd known him all her life – maybe she persuaded herself that he really just wanted to talk.

He finished his drink at a gulp and leaned back in the chair, rubbing his eyes. 'It all fits. But I could never prove it. No proof at all. And anyway, the case is closed – that's official.'

'Wouldn't they reopen it, if you told them what you've just told me?'

'No. I've no evidence. Besides, they aren't interested in Hildyard. They want the men at the top, and they don't want anything to disturb the setup until they're ready. Going after Hildyard would probably lead to them closing down the whole network and starting up again somewhere else. Anne-Marie simply isn't important enough. Oh God, what a world it is. What a bloody awful world.'

He rubbed and rubbed at his face, as if he might rub away his thoughts. There was more here, she could see, than

Anne-Marie. This was the culmination of a long, long story of disappointment and disillusion, frustration and personal conflict. She put up her hands carefully to stop him rubbing, afraid he might hurt himself, and his hands closed like steel traps around hers, making her gasp with fear and pain.

'Hold on to me,' he said, staring at her fiercely. She could feel the unendurable tension through the contact of their hands. 'Hold on to me. I need you. Oh God.'

'You've got me,' she said. But she was afraid. She had never been this close to someone so near the breaking point, and she didn't know what to do. He was so overwound he might snap at any moment.

Instinct took over. He slid forward out of the chair, still holding her hands, and pushed her down onto the carpet. Then he made love to her, not even waiting to take off his clothes, merely undoing and parting them sufficiently for the act. He was not rough with her – he was even kind, but in an impersonal way which came from his character, a kindness which was ingrained in him and nothing to do with her. But she took him, accepted his need, and forgave him for being – as she knew he was – unaware of her as a person just then. She loved him, and knew that it was a kind of love which had made him turn to her to exercise the healing frenzy. All the same it was the beginning of sadness. When it was over he fell against her exhausted, and began to cry, and she held him while he said over and over, 'I'm sorry, I'm sorry.'

'It's all right,' she said. 'I love you.' But she knew it was not to her that he was apologising.

When she had gone to work, leaving him reluctantly, he got into his car and drove slowly around the streets. He couldn't rest. The idea of going home to Ruislip, of talking to ordinary people who didn't know what had happened, nauseated him. He couldn't have endured to explain anything to anyone. His mind threshed at the problem; and somehow the other problem, of Irene and Joanna, had become tangled up in it, so that it was both emotional and intellectual, and he felt he couldn't resolve the one without the other.

Perhaps if he could get Ronnie Brenner definitely to identify Hildyard as the man who had paid him to find the flat, they would let him take up the vet quietly and nail the murder to him without mentioning the organisation at all. It would be easy to impute some other motive to him, without mentioning the Family. If only he could do that, perhaps he would be able to go and live with Joanna, and then everything would be all right.

He must get a statement out of Ronnie straight away. He'd take him in to the station now, and then discuss some way of getting a tape recording of Hildyard's voice. He drove back to Cathnor Road and left the car parked outside The Crown and Sceptre where it was hidden amongst the customers' cars. He walked back to the house, and it was still dark and quiet; the street seemed deserted, too. He went quickly and quietly down the area steps and stood in the shadow under the railings a moment, listening, but everything was still.

And then he saw that the door to Brenner's flat was not completely closed. He stepped closer and saw the dented and splintered wood of the frame where the jemmy had been inserted next to the Yale lock. His scalp began to crawl with a cold dread which worked its way down his body and settled in his feet and legs, weighting them. He pushed the door with a knuckle and it swung inwards into the dark hall, and the abused lock fell off with a thump and clatter that made him jump as though he had touched a live wire. The opening looked like a gaping mouth, and he shivered as he stepped into it. His hair had risen on his scalp so far that he could feel the cold air against the skin. Without realising it, he rose involuntarily on tiptoe as he started down the narrow, black passage.

Half way along his foot struck something that was blocking his way – something large, heavy and soft, a bundle on the passage floor. He drew out his pencil-torch and squatted down and shone it. Brenner's face leapt out of the darkness at him, contused and bulging, the eyes gleaming dully white like hard-boiled eggs stuffed into the sockets. The tip of a tongue, dark blue like a chow's, protruded from between clenched teeth, and there was a smear of blood at the corner of the mouth where he had bitten it. Around

Brenner's neck was a length of plastic-coated wire, the sort you might use in a garden to support climbers. It was drawn so tight that it had disappeared into the concentric rings of swollen flesh to either side of it.

Slider heard himself whimper. He stood up, and his legs were trembling so much that he had to rest his hand against the wall to support himself until he regained control.

After a moment he made himself squat down again and touch Brenner's skin. He felt cold. The murderer must have entered as soon as Slider left, he thought. He must have been watching. Was it Hildyard, or one of the organisation clearing up after him? Well, it hardly mattered now, to him or to Brenner. The only chance of linking Hildyard to the case was now gone. Slider stood up again, felt the blood leaving his head, and had to bend over for a moment until the ringing stopped. Then he walked away quickly, out of the flat, up the area steps, and across the road to his car.

16

Bogus is as Bogus Does

Outside the magic heat-ring of London a cold rain was falling, and in the wet darkness there was nothing to detract from his sense of nightmare. He got lost twice, and another time had to stop and find a phone box with a directory to look up the address. In between whiles, he drove fast. His reasoning mind had shut down, the circuits blown, leaving him in peace. The simple act of driving gave him a spurious sense of achievement, as if he really were getting somewhere at last.

In the village there were only streetlights outside the pub and the post-office stores, and beyond that all was in darkness. Country addresses in any case were always pretty esoteric – you had to be born there to know which was Church Lane, Back Lane, London Road. He drove around, wandering down dark, narrow lanes where unbroken hedges reared at him from the oblivion beyond the headlights, having to backtrack when he snubbed his nose against a dead end, and he found the place in the end completely by chance.

Neats Cottage. Was that a joke? he wondered. It was a pleasant, long, low cottage in the local grey stone with a lichen-gilded roof, typically Cotswold; but it had been horribly quaintified with lattice-paned windows, a front door with a bottle-glass peephole, and olde-worlde ironwork. And one end of the cottage had been bastardised with a hideous redbrick, flat-roofed extension with aluminium-framed windows. Slider presumed this must be the surgery.

The white garden gate gleamed preternaturally, and on it

was a notice painted in black letters on white with the name of the cottage and then simply 'B.HILDYARD, MRCVS'. Surprisingly restrained, he thought, for a man who had given himself away by unnecessary embroidery. The cottage appeared to be completely dark, but as Slider walked down the garden path he saw that in fact one window in the residential end was lit, but glowing only faintly behind thick red curtains. The man was still up. Well, no reason why not. There had been people in the pub, still. It couldn't be so very late.

Slider had no idea what he meant to do. He had come here simply on instinct, a very physical, unthinking instinct; and now, faced with the overwhelming normality of the place, he could think of nothing to do but to go up to the door and knock on it. The elaborate iron knocker did not seem to make much of a noise, and now he was closer he could hear music from within, too muted to identify. Good thick doors and walls, he thought. Then a light went on, a shadow fell across the square glass porthole, and it was flung abruptly wide. And there was the bogus vet, as Slider continued to think of him, towering over him like the Demon King in a pantomime, backed by the light and hard to see.

There was a moment of silence during which Slider had time to appreciate the folly of his being here at all, as well as the remarkable fact that he felt no fear. Indeed, he was aware of an insane desire to say something completely frivolous.

Then Hildyard said, 'You'd better come in.'

He looked past Slider's shoulder into the darkness, and then stepped back and to the side, blocking the way to the left, so that as he stepped over the threshold Slider had no choice but to turn right. Light and music were ahead of him. He obeyed the silent urging and entered a large and comfortable room. It was decorated in the chintz, brass and polished parquet tradition – Irene would have loved it, he thought. Even so, it was warm, pleasantly lit by shaded lamps, and made welcoming by a good log fire in the grate. Music issued from a stereo stack, turned low as for background. It was a classical symphony, Slider recognised, but he didn't know which one.

'Brahms – Symphony Number One,' Hildyard said,

following the direction of his eyes. 'Do you like music? Or shall I turn it off?'

'Please don't,' Slider said. His voice seemed to come out with an effort, as though he hadn't used it for years.

'Won't you sit down?' There was nothing in Hildyard's voice or manner to suggest that this was anything but an ordinary social visit. Slider sat in the chintz-covered wingback by the fire. The dented cushions of its opposite number suggested the vet had been sitting there. Doing what? Slider's roving gaze saw no paper, book, nor even drink to hand. He had just been sitting there, then, listening to the music. Waiting. For what?

Hildyard surveyed his visitor's face for a long moment and then said, as if he had just come to a conclusion, 'What will you have to drink? Whisky? Gin? A beer? I was just going to have one myself.'

'Thank you,' Slider said absently. The warmth, the easy chair, the music were all acting on his aching exhaustion, lulling him, soothing him. He didn't notice that he had made no choice, and his eyes followed Hildyard almost drowsily as he crossed to the table under the window and poured two stiff whiskies from an extremely cut-glass decanter into massive, heavy-bottomed tumblers. There was something about the cut glass that went with the chintz and brass, Slider thought vaguely. It was what Irene though of as Good Taste, and it struck him that it was as bogus as the ideal homes illustrated in the colour supplements – instant decor, everything coordinated, the taste that money could buy. Image without substance, slick, ready-made. Like Anne-Marie's flat in Birmingham. That's what's wrong with me, he thought: I've swallowed the Modern World, and it's made me sick.

He received the glass from the vet in a bemused way, his sense of unreality reaching a peak. He had no idea what he was doing here, what he could possibly achieve, even what he expected to happen. He felt that if he waited long enough he would hear his own voice, but that until he heard it he would not know what he was going to say. Hildyard sat down opposite him with his drink, watching him impassively, and probably assessing pretty accurately the state of his visitor's mind, Slider thought.

'This isn't an official visit,' was what Slider did eventually say.

'So I imagined. You've been taken off the case – grounded, as we used to say.'

'What?' Slider said stupidly.

'During the war. Air force,' Hildyard told him kindly. 'What a picnic that was! Never a dull moment. A lot of us never got over the peace, you know.' He glanced at Slider's hand. 'Drink your drink,' he urged pleasantly. Slider looked at the glass, suddenly wondering, and reading his thoughts, Hildyard said, 'It's just whisky. I've nothing to fear from you. I knew you'd been grounded before you did. Your Commissioner plays golf, you see.'

So he did. Slider remembered. 'And bridge,' he said vaguely. He sipped cautiously. The hot, wheaten ˙taste flooded his mouth, burned pleasantly all the way down and settled in a warm glow in his stomach. The vapours rose instantly inside him, reminding him that he hadn't eaten all day.

'All the same,' Hildyard went on conversationally, 'I was half expecting you. Your presence at the funeral, for one thing. You've been behaving very oddly, you know. There's been talk – there may even be an investigation into your behaviour before very long. "Cracking up", isn't that what you chaps say? Too much pressure, too much work, not enough time off. Trouble at home, too. What are you doing here, at this very moment, for instance? I doubt whether you even really know yourself.'

Slider took a grip on his mind and dragged it away from the fire and the music and the irrelevancies of warmth and comfort.

'I wanted to talk to you. There are some questions I want to ask you, just for my own satisfaction.'

'And what makes you think I will answer any of your questions?' Hildyard leaned back comfortably in his chair and moved one long, bony finger gently to the music. It was the slow movement. 'Lovely piece this, don't you think? Did you know it was through my representatives that Anne-Marie was able to develop her musical talents? Her aunt wanted her to devote herself to something more reliable, especially given the trouble her parents' marriage had caused. But I persuaded her to let Anne-Marie study, and when she came out of the college, I dropped the right words in the right ears to get her into the Orchestra. She never knew that part, of course – but even talent needs a helping hand. Don't you think that was kind of me? But we all wanted Anne-Marie to stay close to home. It was a great blow when she moved to London. That, I think, showed ingratitude.' His smile was unpleasant.

'I should think her aunt would have been pleased,' Slider said with an effort.

'Well, perhaps. She didn't like Anne-Marie. Also she is a musical cretin. I hate to have to say such a harsh thing of my fiancée, but it's the truth. Oh, you didn't know I was going to marry Mrs Ringwood? A lady of mature charms, but none the worse for that; and if she is no friend to the muse, she will at least be very, very rich, especially as you people have had the kindness to wind up the investigation of her late niece. And I can always listen to my music in the privacy of my surgery. One can't have everything.'

'I suppose Mrs Ringwood will live only just long enough to make a new will,' Slider heard himself say. He was appalled, but Hildyard didn't seem to mind. Indeed, he chuckled.

'Come, come, am I so unsubtle? Rest assured, Inspector, that when Mrs Ringwood dies, be it soon or late, there will be nothing suspicious about her death. The doctor will have no hesitation in giving the certificate.'

'Then why did you kill Anne-Marie in that particular way? You could have made it look like a natural death, or even a convincing suicide.'

The vet's face darkened briefly, but he said in a normal-sounding voice, 'One has to award you points for frankness, at all events. Why on earth should you think I killed Anne-Marie?'

It was persuasively natural, and Slider made himself remember Anne-Marie's nakedness, Ronnie Brenner's blue tongue, the fact that Thompson had blood under his eyelids. He felt very tired. He wondered for a moment whether the whisky had been laced with something after all, and then dismissed the idea. Perhaps he really was just cracking up. If so, he had nothing to lose.

'Let's pretend,' he said thickly. 'Just a sort of parlour game. Just for my own satisfaction. I think I've worked it all out, almost everything, but there are one or two points –'

'Do I owe you satisfaction?'

'Not particularly. But all the same, just for argument's sake, I suppose the Pentathol came from your surgery? Your records are all carefully kept, and all drugs fully accounted for, I imagine?'

'Naturally.'

'You arranged to meet her at the pub after her session at the Television Centre. You'd stolen her diary, so you knew she wouldn't be missed for several days. You went in her car. I suppose you'd left yours somewhere so it wouldn't be recognised?'

Hildyard gave a curious little seated bow. 'The trains from Oxford are very good, and frequent,' he said casually, not as if it were an answer to any question.

Slider nodded, accepting the point. 'Yes, Oxford. You had her drive you to the flat Ronnie Brenner had prepared for you. You took her in. You –' He stopped and swallowed. He couldn't say the next bit. 'Afterwards you took her clothes away and drove in her car to Oxford, transferred to your own car and drove home, and disposed of the clothes. I wonder how?' He though for a moment. 'I wonder, do you have a furnace of some kind? What about the bodies of animals you have to put down? I don't suppose everyone wants to bury their own pet.'

'There is a furnace at the back of the surgery,' Hildyard assented. There was an odd gleam in his eye. 'Very similar to the sort used in crematoria. Vaporises everything most efficiently.'

Slider nodded. 'Then you had to go back and clear out her flat, remove all her personal papers so that there could be no possibility she had left anything incriminating. But you forgot the violin – the Stradivarius. So you had to go back a second time. You must have thought, the way things were, that you had plenty of time. It must have been a shock to see in the paper that she'd been identified so soon. You panicked and killed the old lady –'

Suddenly Hildyard looked annoyed. 'My dear sir, do I

look like the sort of man who panics? It was not I who killed the old lady, as you put it. That was a piece of bungled work. There was no necessity for it at all.'

'It may even have been an accident,' Slider said in fairness. 'Even we weren't sure about that. But it was you who dealt with Thompson, wasn't it? He was becoming a threat, getting too close to the truth; and in any case, it was a way to tie up all the loose ends. So you dumped Anne-Marie's car near his house, hijacked him somehow, forced him to write the suicide note, and cut his throat with one of your scalpels. It was clever of you to notice that he wrote left-handed and make the cut left-handed too. A friend of mine says that surgeons have to be able to cut with either hand. Is that true?'

'Oh yes. There are times when the angle of an operation is not accessible to a right-handed cut. Some of the best men operate with both hands simultaneously, holding several instruments in their fingers for quickness' sake.'

Slider was silent, thinking, and after a while Hildyard interrupted with a question of his own.

'I've been wondering how you did manage to identify Anne-Marie's body so quickly. I read in the newspaper report that she was stripped entirely naked and that there were no belongings with her to identify her; nor had she been missed by anyone.'

'The mark on her neck,' Slider said. He was very tired indeed, and closed his eyes for a moment. 'One of my men recognised it as a violinist's mark, so we went round all the orchestras with a photograph.'

'Ah, I see.' He looked thoughtful. 'But there would have been no way to disguise that in any case.'

Slider opened his eyes. 'No. But why the cuts on the foot? Why didn't you make the death look natural, like suicide?'

Something of Hildyard's self-possession left him. His expression wavered, his eyes narrowed with some emotion – anger perhaps? He pressed his lips together as though to prevent himself from speaking unwisely, but after a moment the words escaped him. 'I loved Anne-Marie. You can have no idea! She was my creation. She was my neophyte. I nursed and nurtured what there was in her –' He broke off just as abruptly, and the light in his eyes went cold. He turned his head away and said indifferently, 'Orders from the top must always be obeyed, whatever the individual thinks of them. Unquestioningly. Chaos otherwise. In business as in the services.'

'*Business*,' Slider said, struggling with the warm grip of the armchair, trying to get more upright to express his outrage. 'How can you call it business? If you really did know her all her life, how could you just murder her in cold blood, and feel nothing, and call it business?'

Hildyard rose abruptly and towered over him, but Slider was too far gone to feel any menace. His glass was taken from him by strong fingers and he heard the vet say, 'Damn it, I shouldn't have given you such a big one. I suppose you'd already been drinking before you came here. Come on, pull yourself together, you drunken fool! Can't have you passing out here. You shouldn't have come here anyway. Damn it, I shouldn't have let you in.'

And he still hadn't admitted anything, Slider thought. Not denied, but not admitted. He had no doubt that Hildyard was guilty; but even if the case hadn't been closed, none of this was admissible anyway. No witnesses. No witnesses? The strong hands were on his shoulders now, gripping like steel, and Slider tried to flinch away from them, belatedly alarmed. He loathed the touch which had so recently tightened the wire round Ronnie Brenner's neck.

'You aren't even worried, are you?' he said in bleared outrage. 'You're not human at all, you're a monster. You say you loved Anne-Marie, but you murdered her just because they told you to. And you killed Ronnie Brenner and then just came back here and lit the fire, as if it was all in a day's work.'

The hands were suddenly gone. Hildyard straightened upright and looked at Slider with sudden alertness. 'Killed Ronnie Brenner? What are you talking about?'

'You followed me to his house this afternoon, and when I came out you went in and killed him.'

The vet looked strange. 'No,' he said. 'I haven't been anywhere. I've been here all day.'

Slider struggled. 'Then what –'

'Listen!' Hildyard was suddenly tense, his whole body rigid, his head cocked in a listening attitude. 'Did you hear that?' he whispered. Slider shook his head, meeting the vet's eyes at last, and witnessed a curious phenomenon: the vet's yellowish face seemed to drain completely of blood, turning first white, and then almost greenish, waxy. His eyes seemed to bulge slightly in their sockets, his lips drew back involuntarily off his long teeth. Slider had never seen such terror in a man's face. It was not a pleasant sight.

'They followed you here,' Hildyard whispered. 'Oh Jesus Christ.'

'Who? How?' Slider said, but the vet waved him to silence.

'Wait here. Keep quiet,' he whispered. He put down the glass he was holding and went to the door, opened it a crack and listened a moment, and then slipped out, moving on the balls of his feet, as soundlessly as a cat.

Slider waited. The fire crackled unimportantly. After a while he heaved himself out of the chair and went to the door which Hildyard had left open a crack. The air in the hallway was colder than in the room, and whistled unpleasantly into his ear as he applied it to the gap. He heard the slow, heavy tick of the longcase clock in the hall, and behind that the soft black silence of an empty house.

And then, distantly, a muted thud. It was a tumbling sort of thud, such as might be made by a stack of heavy, soft objects falling over. Slider opened the door wider, and then heard quite clearly from the other end of the house, the surgery end, the loud crash of breaking glass.

His mind was instantly stripped clean of lethargy and fumes. Adrenaline pumped through him as he shot across the hall, flinging open doors, understanding without words what that thud and crash meant. Dickson's voice, 'They don't tolerate failures', was with him as he raced across a dining-room, crashing his shins against a chair that got in his way, through the further door, and into the new part of the house, the extension, which still smelled of plaster. He crossed another small hallway, through a door into the waiting room, which smelled of that disinfectant that vets use, and through the final door into the surgery itself.

Stink of petrol, broken glass, a fierce blaze, dense smoke already building up. On the floor the fallen stack of Hildyard, sprawled face down, the back of his skull smashed by an expert blow to a pink pulp, shards of bone and strands of hair all mashed together. All this Slider gathered in a split second, and already the heat and smoke were too much. His eyes were streaming, he could hear himself coughing and feel the pain in his chest as he dropped to his knees. Must get out.

He took hold of the collar and shoulder of the vet's jacket and tried to drag him backwards towards the door; but the man was an immense weight, and the door seemed an impossible distance away. Slider's mind stepped away from it all, away from the fire and the fear and all the multitude of agonies it had been suffering, and looked down on the scene from a great height, from a cool, dark, impenetrable distance. He was vaguely aware that this was a bad thing to do, but he couldn't now remember why, and he was so tired, and the darkness was too inviting for him to want to try.

17

The Stray Dog Syndrome

'Hullo?'

'Hullo, Joanna.'

'Bill! I didn't think I'd be hearing from you again.'

'Didn't you?' He sounded genuinely surprised.

'It's been a long time,' she said.

'I did phone once or twice before, but I got your answering machine, and I didn't want to talk to that.'

'I wish you had. At least I'd have known –'

'Known what?'

'That you – that you were still around.'

'I'm not really. Around, I mean. I'm away.'

'Oh.' She was determined not to ask questions. For three weeks she had waited with diminishing hope, feeling only that she must not be the one to ask.

After a silence he said, 'You aren't angry with me, are you?'

'No, not angry. Why should I be?'

'Did Atherton phone you?'

'He told me that you were in hospital but that it wasn't serious.'

'Is that all? Nothing else?'

'No. Was he supposed to?'

'I asked him to let you know what was going on. I suppose he forgot. There must have been a hell of a lot to do, especially with me away and Raisbrook not coming back.'

Forgot my arse! Joanna thought. She said, 'Where are you, then?'

'I'm staying with my father in Essex. They gave me long leave.'

'Upper Hawksey,' she remembered.

'That's where I'm calling from now. The thing is – I wondered if you were going to have any time off in the next couple of days? I wondered if you'd like to come out here for the day? It's quite nice – country and all that.'

'Wouldn't your father mind?' She meant, 'what about your wife', and he understood that and answered all parts of the question.

'Irene's not here. She's at home with the children. I didn't want them to miss school. In any case, I'm supposed to be having peace and quiet. I've told Dad about you.'

Joanna's heart gave an unruly, unreasonable leap. 'Oh?'

'He's a good bloke.' He said it like a justification. 'I value his advice. I told him I wanted to ask you to come out, and he said he didn't mind. I think he wants to meet you, though he didn't say so out loud. Well, it's his generation, you know.'

'Yes.'

'Joanna, you're not saying much.'

'I don't know what to say.'

'Are you all right?'

'I'm not sure. I feel as if I've been going through a nightmare.'

'Yes, me too.' Understatement of the decade, she thought. 'Will you come, then? I'd like to have a chance to talk to you. But if you don't feel like coming out I shall quite understand.'

No you won't understand, you diffident bastard, she thought. 'Yes, I'll come, if you want me to. I could come tomorrow.'

'That would be perfect.'

'You'd better give me instructions, then.'

He was waiting for her at the end of the lane, and signalled for her to pull over onto the mud-strip lay-by. She obeyed and got out and stood looking at him, her heart in her mouth. His eyebrows had gone, and his front hair was stubbly, and across the top of his forehead the skin had a shiny, plastic look. His hands were still bandaged. Otherwise, there was no sign of what he had gone through.

But he had a skinned look, as though he had had too close a haircut. His face seemed to have lost flesh, so that his nose and ears were too prominent, and it made him look curiously young. He was wearing a shabby sweater, a pair of baggy cords, and Wellingtons too big for him, and she saw how these suited him much better than town clothes. He was a country boy by birth and blood, and he looked at home here against the bare hedges and the wide, flat, soggy brown fields.

The lack of eyebrows made him look surprised, and his smile was hesitant and shy. She loved him consumingly, and didn't know what to say, how to approach him, even if it were permitted to cross the gap between them.

He said, 'I think it would be best if you were to leave it here. It'll be quite safe, but with mine and Dad's down there already, the lane's getting a bit churned up. Dad's out at the moment. He's usually out all day. We've got the place to ourselves until teatime. Shall we go and have a drink and some lunch? I wasn't sure if you'd be hungry or not.'

He was talking too much, he knew, but he couldn't stop himself, and her silence was unnerving him. He had been thinking about her for so long, and it had made her unreal in his mind. Now seeing her again he didn't know what he was feeling, what he was going to do, whether asking her here had been brave or stupid or right or selfish. They stared at each other awkwardly, out of reach.

'Are you all right?' she asked at last, and nodded towards his bandages. 'Those look a bit fearsome.'

He waved them. 'Oh, they're not as bad as they look. They're nearly healed now, but I wear the bandages to keep them clean. Practically everything I do here seems to involve getting filthy. It's very enjoyable.' He smiled tentatively, but she was still studying him.

'You look thinner. Or is it just the haircut?'

'Both. I had to have the haircut because I'd got singed in a couple of places. You see the old eyebrows are gone. They'll grow back, of course, probably thicker than before. I'll end up looking like Dennis Healey.' She didn't smile at his attempted joke, and he grew serious in his turn. 'Atherton got me out just in time. If it hadn't been for him – and you, raising the alarm ... You saved my life between you.'

She turned her head away. 'Don't,' she said. 'For God's sake, no gratitude. I couldn't stand that.' She was suddenly nervous. 'That isn't what you asked me here for?'

'No. I – No. I wanted to see you. I had to talk to you.' He bit his lip. 'Let's get comfortable first. Come on, there's no sense standing about here.'

She fell in beside him and they walked up the muddy, rutted lane to the house. He led her into the kitchen where they shed their muddied footwear and he sat her at the table – wooden, and scrubbed, like a children's story, she thought – and gave her a gin and tonic.

'I had to send out for supplies for this,' he said, bringing her glass to her between bandaged palms. 'Dad only drinks beer, and homemade wine, and I wouldn't inflict that on you.'

'You didn't have to go to all that trouble. I could have drunk beer,' she said.

'I wanted you to have what you like.' He put the glass down in front of her, and their eyes met. He wanted to touch her, but he didn't know how to cross the space between them. He didn't know what she was thinking. She might not welcome the gesture. But she had come here, hadn't she? Or was that just curiosity?

The silence had gone on too long now. He turned away and fetched his own drink.

'Dad likes to have his tea when he gets in,' he said, 'so I thought we'd just have a light lunch, if that's all right?'

'Anything you like. Yes, that's fine.'

'Can you eat mushrooms on toast? I do them rather nicely.'

'That would be lovely. Can you manage, with your hands?'

'Oh yes. They don't hurt. Don't you do anything – just sit there. I've never had the chance to cook for you yet.'

The words pleased and pained her with their innocence. It was tender, and rather gauche, and she loved him all over again, and was afraid she was going to be asked to pay a second time. She watched him as he moved with assurance around the kitchen where he had grown up. He looked so much younger here, and it wasn't just the effect of the haircut. It was something to do with being back in the parental home. She had noticed before that people shed years when they were once more in the situation of being child to a father or mother.

As the gin eased the tension, he began to talk more naturally, about neutral subjects, and she listened, her eyes following him, her body relaxed. It was when they were sitting opposite each other with food to occupy their hands that he finally turned to the case.

'It seems incredible that I haven't spoken to you since the night Ronnie Brenner was killed. I don't really know how much you know. What made you ring the station, anyway?'

'I don't know,' she said, looking inward, her eyes dark. 'I just had a bad feeling about it: you seemed so strange. So I stopped at the first phone box and rang the station and asked to speak to your friend O'Flaherty, and when he said you weren't there, I told him everything. Of course, you might have gone home, but I couldn't check up on that. I expected him to tell me there was nothing to worry about, but he took it seriously, thank God. He told me he'd find out where you were and ring me straight back.'

She looked to see if he knew all this, but he nodded and said, 'Go on.'

'Well, apparently he sent a radio car round to whatsis-name's house, Brenner, and then of course it was red alert. O'Flaherty and Atherton put their heads together and decided the most likely thing was that you'd gone off to see the bogus vet, and Atherton just got in his car and drove like a mad thing.' She looked at him. 'He does care about you, you know.'

'Yes,' Slider said, looking at his plate. 'And did O'Flaherty phone you back? It must have been hell for you.'

'Not that time, but later. He called back in about ten minutes to tell me what they were doing to find you. But then I had to go on to work, and that was the longest evening of my life. God knows what I played like. It wasn't until I got home that I was able to find out what had happened. That was when Atherton phoned to tell me you were in hospital with shock and minor burns.'

That had been the beginning of the long wait and the slow decline of hope. She could not go and visit, in case Irene was there. She had tried ringing, but the hospital wouldn't give out information except to relatives. And then she had decided that if he wanted her, he would get in contact with her, and that if he didn't, she mustn't make it hard for him. So she had done nothing, and the silence had extended itself, and she had thought that that was her answer.

Now he said, 'They weren't pleased with me, you know. With Hildyard dead, they had to have some sort of investigation into him, and he turned out to be a pretty unsatisfactory customer. He was German by birth – his real name was Hildebrand. He studied veterinary surgery at Nuremburg until the outbreak of the war, and then he joined the Luftwaffe – Intelligence Corps.'

'So that's where he got the "Captain", was it?'

'I suppose so. Anyway, when the German army occupied Italy, he was seconded and given a sort of undercover job liaising with the pro-Nazi Italians, trying to crack the Italian Resistance. And apparently it was at that time that he made contact with the Mafia, and did himself quite a lot of good with under-the-counter deals. At all events, he got very rich, and when the Allies took over he was rich and powerful enough to disappear completely, even though he was a very wanted man.'

'Yes, I should think he was. Everybody would have been after his blood.'

'His only friends were the Mafia, and it looks as though they helped him to escape to England and establish himself. At all events, he disappeared for a while and when he resurfaced, there he was in Stourton-on-Fosse as respectable as you like, following his old trade of veterinary surgeon and digging himself into the local community.'

'And all that time being a sleeper? Or active? Or what?'

'I don't suppose we'll ever know. There's so much we don't know – like who killed Brenner, or Mrs Gostyn. Hildyard more or less admitted killing Thompson, or at least he didn't deny it. And Anne-Marie.' He was silent a moment, and then said, 'Anyway, they aren't going to follow it up. The shop in Tutman Street's closed, and the man I saw there has disappeared. We've evidently disturbed them enough to close down that particular network, and that means I'm not exactly flavour of the month up at the Yard. We'll be watching Saloman from now on, but I don't suppose they'll ever use him again.'

'One thing I've been wondering is how Anne-Marie actually passed the money on.'

'I've been thinking about that, too, and I think it must have been something idiotically simple. I think it was the olive oil tins. I can't account for 'em otherwise. She had two in each of her flats, and Atherton noticed they were quite clean and dry inside, as if they'd never been used. I think maybe she just shoved rolls of bank notes into them and carried them along to the shop, and was given another empty tin in exchange.'

'Surely it can't have been as simple as that?'

'Sometimes the simplest ideas work the best,' he said, and lapsed into silence.

'Well, at least Anne-Marie's murderer got his just deserts,' she said at last, trying to comfort him.

'You sound like Dickson. But it isn't a matter of that. That's just revenge.' He looked at her carefully. 'I want you to understand.' Then he changed his emphasis. 'I want *you* to understand.'

'Go on then. I'm listening.'

It took him a while to begin. 'It's not the way it is in books, you see, where the detective solves the problem and then goes home to tea. In real life, even if you solve the problem, that's only the beginning. You have to assemble all the evidence, construct the case, take it to court, and even then the villain might not go down. He might get off entirely, or he might get a suspended sentence and be straight back out on the street. It's a gamble. And all the time you're constructing the case against him, there's all the other crime going on, and you can't be in two places at once. You never win. You can't win. You never even finish anything. It's like grandmother's steps, only the villains keep just a nose ahead of you, always. And if you get one sent down, there's all the others still in business, you can't stop them all, and in a couple of years the one you got sent down comes out again and picks up where he left off. You never seem to get anywhere, and in the end it drives you crazy. If you let it.'

He looked to see if she was following, and she nodded.

'People have different ways of coping with the frustration. Of course there are some lucky enough or stupid enough not to feel it – like Hunt. And Beevers, too, in a way. Atherton copes by just switching off as soon as he leaves his desk, and concentrating on his social life, food and books and music and so on.'

'Playing the dilettante bachelor.'

'Yes. And it is an act, to an extent. He watches himself doing it, you know, polishes up his performance. Norma's a bit like that, too, only her act is being a tough guy. And there are some who drink, or take drugs, and some who just get brutalised.'

'And then there's you,' she suggested.

'I don't know really how I coped with it. I think, by believing that it was all worthwhile. But somehow from the beginning of this case it didn't work. I minded too much, and I don't know why, unless maybe it was just the last straw. But then I met you.'

She became very still, watching his face.

'You said once that I didn't see you as part of real life, and I think in a way you were right.'

She heard the words with a sense of foreknowledge and despair. He had asked her here to tell her it was over, too much a gentleman to do it other than face to face.

'You were my place to hide,' he went on. 'I see it now. I think I half knew it at the time, and it was very wrong of me to use you like that, but I can only say in my defence that my need was very great. I was right on the edge of a precipice and you were all I was holding on to.'

She nodded again, unable to speak. She couldn't believe that he was going to let her go, now that they had found each other against all the odds; but she knew, and she had always known, that nothing was more likely.

'I've had time to think while I've been here. It's a thing

people hardly ever have, isn't it? Time on their own to think things out properly. Maybe that's why people so often get really basic things wrong. I've never really been on my own since I got married.'

He was coming to it now, she thought. She started to smile, and then realised that was inappropriate. He looked at her very seriously, and it made him look absurdly young, like an earnest sixth-former about to express his conclusion that what was really wanted was world peace and harmony.

'But down here I've had complete peace and quiet, with just Dad. He's very restful, you know – not a great talker. I've thought about everything – most of all about you. And I think that in spite of the way things have happened, you're the only real thing that's happened to me in – well, in the whole of my adult life, really.'

He smiled at her, and reached across for her hand, lifting it to his lips and kissing it – the tenderest gesture a lover can make. She thought it probably wasn't the time to say much more than that yet, so she got up and went around the table to him so that they could get their arms round each other, which was what they both needed most just at that moment.

Mr Slider came into the kitchen just when dusk was beginning to make it worthwhile to pull the curtains and switch on the light, and found Joanna peacefully making tea and boiling eggs while Bill watched the toast. The table was laid and the kitchen was warm and welcoming.

'Hullo, Dad. Get anything?' Bill said over his shoulder.

Mr Slider, who was occupied with pulling off his boots on the mat, only grunted. Joanna looked round and met his unsmiling gaze from under his eyebrows, but he nodded to her gravely and courteously.

'Went up to Hampton Wood in the end,' he said, padding over to the table in stockinged feet and sitting down. 'Got a couple of wood pigeons. Make nice eating by the weekend.' Joanna brought over the teapot, and he offered her the correct, modern courtesy. 'Have a good drive down?'

'Yes, thank you.'

'Ah. That you burning the toast, Bill?'

'Sorry, Dad.'

Father and son sat opposite each other, and Joanna sat between them, and looked from one to the other. They were so alike it made her feel oddly tearful. Mr Slider's grey, close-cropped hair grew in exactly the same way as Bill's honey-brown; his softly aged face and secret mouth must once have looked exactly like those of the man she loved. Most of all, there was in the lines of the older man's face, in the way his mouth curved and in the bright regard of his eyes, the look of a man who has loved another human being completely and successfully, a sweetness that no subsequent loss can eradicate. She liked him, and felt she would have done even if he had not been Bill's father.

Bill and Joanna carried the conversation while Mr Slider made his meal with the economical movements of a man who has earned it. Eventually when they had all finished, Mr Slider pushed back his chair and said, 'Why don't you go and lay the fire, Bill? Joanna and me'll do the washing up.'

Bill gave a comical grimace and went off obediently, and Joanna began to clear the table with a sinking heart. I'm going to be warned off again, she thought; and I shall mind what this lovely old man says to me.

'I'll wash and you dry,' Mr Slider said. 'Don't want you getting dishpan hands.'

He was a slow and methodical washer, and managed to make the little there was go a long way. After the first few plates he looked up and saw her expression and gave her an amused and quirky smile.

'No need to look like that, girl. I'm only his father. I got nothing to do with it.'

'I don't think that's entirely true. Bill values your opinion.'

'Told you that, did he? Ah, well, we're a lot alike, Bill and me, except that I'm handsomer. And I'll tell you something – I like you.'

'I like you too.'

'Well, that's a start.' He went on washing. The next time he looked up it was gravely. 'It's a bad business, this. Bad for everyone. There are no winners when a man's torn between two women, and one of them's his wife. I was lucky. I loved Bill's mother, and I married her, and I never wanted no other. People talk a lot about why marriages break down, but there's only one reason – people stop loving each other, or they never did in the first place. Do you love Bill?'

'Yes. But I would never –' She stopped, embarrassed.

'No, I don't suppose you would.' He fished out an egg spoon and rubbed it minutely. 'Terrible stuff for sticking, egg yolk. No, you'd never try to make up his mind for him. I never would either. I don't think you can make other people's decisions for them, or you shouldn't. The trouble with Bill is he's too sensitive.' He smiled suddenly, and his eyes seemed very blue. 'I know all parents say that. But Bill always was a worrier. Conscientious. He always tried to see both sides of everything, and be fair to everyone, and it gets in his way, see? His conscience runs ahead of his feelings and muddles him up. There, I think that's clean. Haven't got my close-up glasses on, so you'll have to keep an eye on me.'

She took the spoon and dried it without looking at it. 'What do you think he'll do?' It was foolish to ask, but everyone wants reassurance from time to time.

'I don't know. I wish I could tell you, because, to be honest about it, I like you, and I never liked Irene. She was never right for him – too sharp and go-ahead and looking at the prices of things. His mother thought she'd sharpen him up, but I said to her, he's sharp enough in his own way. He sees more than most people, that's all. I'll tell you this much – whatever he does decide, it won't be easy for him. He'll take a long time deciding, and it'll hurt him. It'll hurt you, too,' he said, looking at her appraisingly, 'but I reckon you can take it. And you wouldn't want him, would you, if he was the kind of man that could decide a thing like that easily?'

'No. I suppose I wouldn't.' It wasn't much comfort.

They worked in silence for a while until Mr Slider said, 'There, last spoon, and that's the lot. You're a good little worker. And I tell you what.' She met his eyes and he smiled. 'I reckon Bill's got his head screwed on the right way. It may take a while, but I reckon he'll get it right in the end. And now I'm going to take my bath. Will you still be here when I get back?'

'I don't know,' she said, uncertain how long her visit was meant to last.

'Ah, go on, you don't want to be rushing off to London when you've just got here. Why don't you stay the night? We'll have a bit of supper later, and play a hand of cards. Do you play cribbage?'

'Yes, but –'

'That's all right. I'm past the age of being shocked. You stay and welcome. Fair enough?'

'Fair enough,' said Joanna.

She had to leave the next morning, early. She and Slider walked back down the lane together in silence.

'What's going to happen to us?' she asked at last. 'Have we got a future?'

'I hope so. I want us to have. Is that what you want?'

'I thought you knew that by now.'

He frowned. 'I want to be honest with you. It's going to be hard for me. I've been married a long time – I can hardly imagine not being married, now. And then there's the children – most of all, there's the children. They don't deserve to be made unhappy. Well, Irene doesn't either. It's not her fault.'

She listened to the hackneyed, deadly words, and all the arguments she might have raised passed unuttered through her mind. If he could not see them for himself, there was no point in her saying them.

'But on the other hand, I just don't think I could bear to go on without you now. You're too important to me. And if I want you, I shall have to do something about it, shan't I?'

She nodded, grateful for a man too honest to suggest he might have it both ways.

'What I want to ask you, and I know it will be hard for you, is to give me time. It will take me a while to work my way through this. Can you be patient? I've no right to ask you really, but –'

'I'll be patient. I'm thirty-six years old, and I've never been in love with anyone before. Just be as quick as you can,' she said.

He stopped and faced her and took her hands between his bandaged ones and could find nothing to say.

Looking down at their joined hands she said, 'Tell me something?'

'Anything.'

'What on earth were you doing, trying to rescue a dead bogus vet from the flames?'

He began very slowly to smile. 'I never even thought about it. It was a purely instinctive reaction.'

'You idiot! I love you.'

'I love you too,' he said. They resumed their walk towards her car. 'Did you know they're promoting me?' he said a little further on. 'Now that Raisbrook isn't coming back, they're making me Detective Chief Inspector.'

She looked at him quizzically. 'Why didn't you tell me before? You must be pleased. But I thought you said they weren't very happy with you?'

'They aren't promoting me because they're happy with me. It's a kind of consolation prize, because they aren't going to follow up the Austen case. No, not even that, less than that – it's a kind of booby prize. I've been a bloody nuisance, so they hand me a month's leave and a promotion to keep me quiet.'

She didn't know what to say. 'At least Irene must be glad,' she said at last.

'Irene always said they didn't value me. She was right about that, at least. Even when I get promoted, it's a kind of failure.'

'Don't,' she said, but he stopped her and gripped her hands.

'Oh Joanna, I'm so afraid I'm going to fail you.'

She tried to smile. 'That isn't your fault. It's me. I've been a stray so long, it's hard for anyone to see me as anything else. A stray is no-one's responsibility, you see. You might play with it when it comes up to you in the park, but you don't take it home.'

He looked distressed. 'Don't talk like that. Listen, it's going to be all right. It'll take time, that's all. Be patient with me.'

He took her to the car and watched her get in and fasten the seatbelt, and then he kissed her goodbye through the window, and she drove away. She waved to him before she turned the corner: jaunty and afraid, essentially no-one's dog.